W9-BSH-837

INFORMATION SYSTEMS
FOR MANAGERS

COMPILED BY

MICHAEL J. DAVERN AND
ARUN SUNDARARAJAN

STERN SCHOOL OF BUSINESS
NEW YORK UNIVERSITY

(CUSTOM COMPILED FOR C20.0001 COMPUTER-BASED SYSTEMS
FOR MANAGEMENT SUPPORT)

Pearson
Custom
Publishing

Excerpts taken from:

Information Systems Foundations,
by Leonard M. Jessup and Joseph S. Valacich
Copyright © 1999 by Que ® Education and Training
Published in cooperation with Prentice-Hall, Inc.
A Pearson Education Company
Upper Saddle River, New Jersey 07458

Information Technology in Business: Principles, Practices, and Opportunities
Second Edition, by James A. Senn
Copyright © 1998, 1995 by Prentice-Hall, Inc.

Decision Support Systems and Intelligent Systems, Fifth Edition
by Efraim Turban and Jay E. Aronson
Copyright © 1998, 1995, 1993, 1990, 1988 by Prentice-Hall, Inc.

Business Data Communications and Networking, Third Edition
by Raymond R. Panko
Copyright © 2001, 1999, 1997 by Prentice-Hall, Inc.

This special edition published in cooperation with Pearson Custom Publishing

This publication has been printed using selections as they appeared in their original format. Layout and appearance will vary accordingly.

Printed in the United States of America

10 9 8 7 6 5 4 3 2

Please visit our web site at www.pearsoncustom.com

ISBN 0–536–62022–9

BA 992694

PEARSON CUSTOM PUBLISHING
75 Arlington Street, Suite 300, Boston, MA 02116
A Pearson Education Company

Copyright Acknowledgments

Contents

<u>Full bibliographic details for source materials:</u>

Bell, D.E. (1994) "The Value of Information". *Harvard Teaching Note #9-191-138.*

Evans, P. & T. Wurster. (1997) "Strategy and the New Economics of Information".
Harvard Business Review, vol. 75:5. (Reprint# 97504).

Jessup, L.M. & J.S. Valacich (1999). *Information Systems Foundations.*
Que Education and Training: Indianapolis, Indiana. (ISBN 1-57576-415-6)

Turban, E. & J. E. Aronson (1998). *Decision Support Systems and Intelligent Systems.*
Prentice Hall: Upper Saddle River, New Jersey. (ISBN: 0-13-740937-0)

Panko, R. (2000) *Business Data Networking and Communications.*
Prentice Hall: Upper Saddle River, New Jersey. (ISBN: 0-13-088262-3)

Senn, J.A. (1998). *Information Technology in Business:*
Principles, Practices, and Opportunities.
Second Edition. Prentice Hall: Upper Saddle River, New Jersey. (ISBN 0-13-857715-3)

Tapscott, D., Ticoll, D., & A. Lowy. (2000). "Digital Capital: Harnessing the Power of
Business Webs". Harvard Business School Press. (ISBN: 1-57851-193-3)

Varian, H. & C. Shapiro. (1998) *Information Rules: A Strategic Guide to the Network Economy.*
Harvard Business School Press. (ISBN: 0-87584-863-X)

Introduction

Information Technology has fundamentally altered the operations of organizations and the markets in which they must now compete. Information systems are integral to virtually every domain of business: from financial services to manufacturing; from marketing to corporate strategy and beyond. An understanding of the foundations of information systems and technology is thus an essential component of every successful business person's professional toolkit.

The readings selected for this compilation have been specifically chosen to reflect the integration and balance between managerial and technical subject matter. They cover the diverse range of issues, concepts, principles and methods that are fundamental to understanding the business application of information technology in the Internet age.

The underlying philosophy of the selection of readings that make up each of the seven modules in the text is that information technology is a key source of solutions to business problems and a key creator of business opportunities. Thus, managers must have a solid understanding of the underlying information technology to leverage the solutions and opportunities it offers. Similarly, it is essential technologists need to have a solid understanding of the business problems and opportunities to which information technology innovations may be applied.

While some of the modules appear distinctly technical in nature – to provide basic literacy – the overall focus is on how technology can be applied in business. More specifically, how it can be used to create new markets and products, how it can serve as an agent of change in reorganizing business processes, and how it can radically improve business decision making.

This text has been compiled specifically to introduce students at the Stern School of Business, New York University, to the diverse and ever-changing field of information systems. Befitting the dynamic world it describes, the material should be read in conjunction with assigned on-line readings available from the class web page. We hope the intellectual journey that we have sought to craft for you here is both stimulating and rewarding.

Prof. Michael J. Davern
Course Coordinator – C20.0001
July 2000

Note: Since this text has been compiled from a variety of sources the reader should be aware that any in text references to other chapters or sections are from the original sources and thus the correct corresponding chapter or section may not be present in this custom text.

Module 1: Information Systems Concepts & Technology

Goal: To be able demonstrate literacy in the principles and use of hardware and software components of organizational information systems, and the Internet.

Chapter 1: Information Systems Overview

Scenario: Fleetwood Mac Tickets Online

Imagine that you're sitting at your computer writing a paper on your word processor. You decide to check your email and find a new message from an online ticket service that you've just started doing business with. You open the message and find out that the megaband of the 1970s, Fleetwood Mac, is back on tour again (see Figure 1.1). With your permission, this ticket service tracks your purchases with them, so they know your tastes in music. You recently bought the Beatles Anthology release from them, and they know that you like retro rock groups that pop back onto the music scene. Part of their service is to inform you of upcoming events and album releases that might be of interest to you.

You jump right over to your Internet World Wide Web browser and click on your saved bookmark for the ticket service. After you reach their Web site, you log in with your user ID and password. You are greeted by name and asked whether you enjoyed your recent purchase of the Beatles Anthology. The service then asks whether you're at their site to follow up on the Fleetwood Mac information. This is a very personal service! You click "yes" and are taken into their concert category. (They also deal with sporting events, theater events, and just about everything else for which you can buy a ticket.). For fun, you check out their Top 25 Concerts list, which is tabulated in real time from online information requests. Sure enough, Fleetwood Mac is at the top of the list. You better get your tickets fast.

You click the onscreen map to indicate where you live and are shown the venues near you where Fleetwood Mac will be playing. You choose one of the venues and are shown the onscreen schematic that displays the seating arrangement at that particular venue. You are asked whether you want seats in front, as you have chosen in the past. You say yes and are shown a schematic of the concert hall, with the front seats highlighted. The price and availability of these seats are flashing at the bottom of your screen. The seats are a bit expensive, so you check out the prices and availability of other seats in the hall. While you're checking out other seats, you notice that several of the seats in the front have just been purchased. You immediately click on a block of available seats down in front and click on the order button.

You are asked whether you would like to use the same VISA account again, and your VISA number is posted for you to verify. Everything you do at this Web site is encrypted, or coded, so that it is nearly impossible for anyone to steal your credit card number. In any event, giving your credit card at this Web site is a lot safer than giving it to a stranger over the phone. You choose to pick up the tickets at the "will call" window on the night of the concert. After the

---

FIGURE 1.1

Fleetwood Mac, megaband of the 1970s, on tour in 1997.

ticket purchase is complete, the agency's database is immediately updated so that other people won't be able to buy tickets for your seats.

You are asked whether you would like to buy any Fleetwood Mac goodies for the concert. You say yes so that you can at least browse through their online gift shop. You don't see anything you want to purchase, but you check out the background information on Fleetwood Mac. You follow a link to the home page for a Fleetwood Mac fan club near you and have fun checking out some old pictures of the band. You always got a kick out of the outfits that Stevie Nicks wore. You remember that you recently lost your Fleetwood Mac Rumours compact disc, so you go back to the gift shop and check the price. The price isn't bad, so you make a mental note to come back later and order it.

You click back to the home page of the ticket service and choose to exit. They say thanks and goodbye and ask for your feedback on their service for that day. You type in a line or two of comment about your service with them this time and then return to your word processor. Your purchase of Fleetwood Mac concert tickets online took about 10 minutes, starting from the moment you read the ticket service's email message.

What you did not notice is that while this online ticket service was offering its products and making a sale, it was simultaneously performing several other processes—initiating the printing and distribution of the tickets you ordered, updating its inventory and accounting systems as a result of your transaction, learning about its products and its Web site from the path that you took through the Web, and learning from your written feedback how to improve service to you. This online ticket service is an integrated, enterprise-wide information system, but that doesn't matter much to you. You might even take it for granted that their products are good and their prices are low—they have to be. What matters most to you is that their service is fast and easy. In fact, the online ticket service is the key to the company's success. It provides the company with a critical competitive advantage over their rivals.

Introduction

Many organizations today are using the World Wide Web to conduct business in much the same manner as that described in the preceding scenario. Our scenario is a good example of the many ways that an organization can use leading-edge information systems to conveniently provide high-quality goods and services and, more importantly, gain or sustain a competitive advantage over their rivals.

In this chapter, we provide an overview of information systems. Our objective is to help you gain an understanding of what information systems are and how they have evolved to become an increasingly important part of virtually all modern organizations. After reading this chapter, you will be able to do the following:

1. Understand what the term *information systems* (IS) means.

2. Describe the evolution of computing.

3. Explain the technology, people, and organizational components of an information system.

4. Discuss how information systems can be used to automate, informate, and strategically support business activities.

5. Describe information systems' critical, strategic importance to the success of modern organizations.

To achieve these objectives, we provide an overview of key IS-related terms and issues and explain the importance of understanding how information systems can be used to help organizations be more productive and competitive. In terms of our guiding framework (see Figure 1.2), this chapter *is* The Big Picture—an overview of what information systems are and why it is important for you to know about them. In subsequent chapters, we break down each piece of The Big Picture and provide you with the essential information needed to gain a thorough and comprehensive understanding of information systems.

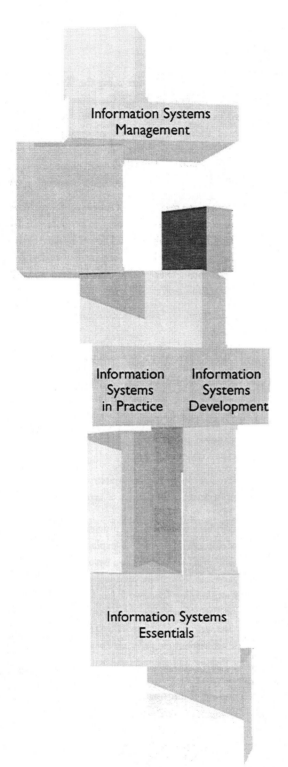

Information Systems
Management

Information
Systems
in Practice

Information
Systems
Development

Information Systems
Essentials

Information Systems Defined

Information systems, such as the online ticket service that we described in the opening scenario, are combinations of hardware, software, and telecommunications networks that people build and use to collect, create, and distribute useful data for organizations. In Figure 1.3, we show these components of information systems and their interrelationships. Information systems are used within organizations to process sales transactions; manage loan applications; and help financial analysts decide where, when, and how to invest. They are also used to help product managers decide where, when, and how to market their products and related services and to help production managers decide when and how to manufacture products. Information systems can also help us in a wide variety of other situations. They enable us to get cash from ATM machines, communicate by live video with people in other parts of the world, buy concert tickets, and much more. So much for standing in line all night to buy concert tickets the following morning!

This book focuses on information systems, the field that encompasses a variety of people involved in the development, use, management, and study of computer-based information systems in organizations. In Figure 1.4, we show the essential ingredients of the definition of IS. Because of the great diversity and rapid changes in the field of IS, several other terms are used to describe the field. These alternative terms include management information systems, data processing management, systems management, business computer systems, computer information systems, and just systems. For better or worse, the term IS seems to be the most commonly used; therefore, we'll stick with the term *information systems* and the acronym *IS*. Next, we describe how the information systems field has evolved to become one of the most important components of modern organizations and one of the most dominant aspects of our economy.

FIGURE 1.2

The big picture: focusing on information sytems overview.

The Rapid Rise in the Development and Use of Technology

Computers are the core component of IS. Perhaps nothing as important has happened to and for businesses over the past decade as the advent of powerful, relatively inexpensive, easy-to-use computing systems. To see this phenomenon, you need only look around your university or place of work. At your university, you may be registering for classes online, using email to communicate with fellow students and your instructors, and completing assignments on networked personal computers. At work, you are probably using a personal computer and email. Your paychecks are probably generated by computer and automatically deposited in your checking account via high-speed networks. Chances are you see a lot more technology now than you did just a few short years ago, and most likely, this technology is a more fundamental and important part of your learning and work than ever before.

One characteristic of this industry is the rapidity with which things change. More than 90 percent of the $25 billion in revenue earned by computer chip manufacturing giant Intel in 1997 came from products that did not even exist in 1996 (McHugh, 1998). Now that is change!

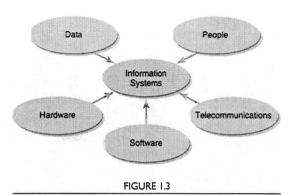

FIGURE 1.3

The components of an information system.

Information systems are combinations of hardware, software, and telecommunications networks
which
people build and use
to
collect, create, and distribute useful data,
typically in
organizational settings.

FIGURE 1.4

The essential ingredients of the definition of IS.

Many of the hot companies in the world today are in the computer industry, and they are experiencing greater than 30 percent sales growth every year. This growth rate is amazing when you consider that the median growth rate for all industries in the U.S. in 1997 was 7.9 percent (McHugh, 1998). Microsoft had a growth rate of more than 36 percent in 1997, with sales at more than $12 billion. Oracle grew around 33 percent, with sales at more than $6 billion. Cisco Systems grew more than 45 percent, with sales of almost $7 billion. These are just a few of the many, many computer-related companies that are growing rapidly and achieving record sales. Not long ago, the computer industry was a relatively minor player in the world's economy; today, it has become the 800-pound gorilla!

The business-computing phenomenon has been chronicled well in the popular business press. We're not necessarily talking about magazines such as *InformationWeek* or *PC Computing*, which naturally always publish stories about computing. Take a look instead at a purely business-oriented publication, such as some recent issues of *BusinessWeek* magazine. In recent years, nearly every issue has included at least one important story about technology in business in addition to the "Technology & You" weekly column.

The cover story in nearly every other weekly issue of *BusinessWeek* in 1997 and 1998 has been about technology or has had a technological component. Figure 1.5 shows some recent *BusinessWeek* covers that concern technological issues. Some of these cover stories have been about the direct use of technology in business, with titles such as "Annual Buying Guide on Computers," "The Software Revolution," "Reinventing the Store,"

FIGURE 1.5

Three BusinessWeek *covers with stories related to technology.*

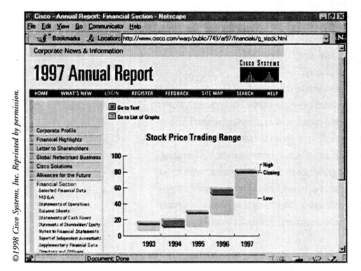

FIGURE 1.6

Graph of Cisco Systems' phenomenal growth in stock value.

"Internet," "Intranets," and so on. In addition, many recent *BusinessWeek* cover stories have featured companies such as Intel, Compaq, Microsoft, IBM, Sun, and Apple. Other cover stories have recommended the best industries and companies to invest in. The companies in the computing and telecommunications industries have continually been one of the bright spots in terms of sustained growth and value in these articles (Smith, Bremner, and Edmondson, 1996). Anyone following the stock market recently has experienced the fever over stocks such as Netscape, Sun, or Cisco Systems (see Figure 1.6 for more information on Cisco's rise). Technology is hot!

If you are in business, going into business in some capacity, or simply interested in some aspect of business, then you should know about technology. As we will discuss throughout this book, technology is being used to radically change how business is conducted—from the way that products and services are produced, distributed and accounted for, to the ways that they are marketed and sold. To be the best you can be in business today—even if your area is finance, accounting, or marketing—technology is critical.

IS Past and Present

You just read about how information systems technology has evolved to become a big part of modern organizations and our economy. Next, we provide a quick summary of how all this occurred and review additional details on the components of a modern information system.

The Evolution in Computing

The information systems field has rapidly evolved over the past 50 years (see Figure 1.7). This evolution is highlighted by several key developments that begin or end particular eras of computing. Although the date when one era begins or ends could be debated, at least five clearly distinct eras of computing can be defined:

- Mainframe
- Interpersonal computing
- Minicomputer
- Internetworking
- Personal computer

Each era has been marked by major events. Naturally, some of these eras of computing overlap. Nonetheless, we define each era as the time when specific types of technologies and applications dominated the information systems field.

The mainframe era of computing had its beginnings with the introduction of ENIAC (Electronic Numerical Integrator and Calculator), the first electronic digital computer, in 1946, and UNIVAC (Universal Automatic Computer), the first general-purpose computer, in 1951 (see Figure 1.7). The introduction of these rather large, complex, expensive computers influenced the early years of IS. Throughout the 1950s and 1960s, organizations relied primarily on mainframe computers sold by IBM and other firms— large, general-purpose computers capable of performing many tasks simultaneously while hundreds, even thousands, of people use them at the same time. Mainframe computers were used for transaction processing and related business applications. Given their size and cost, mainframe computers were nearly always kept locked away in safe, separate computer facilities.

The minicomputer era began in the late 1960s and continued throughout the 1970s and 1980s (see Figure 1.7). During this time, the world witnessed the development and tremendous sales growth of minicomputers made by Digital Equipment Corporation, Data General Corporation, and others. A minicomputer is a medium-sized computer that was meant to be a smaller, less expensive alternative to the mainframe. Compared to mainframes, minicomputers were much less expensive to buy and operate, making computing accessible to more than just the largest organizations.

The industry then shifted from these early computing eras to the personal computer era (see Figure 1.7). A personal computer fits on a desktop, is most often used by a single user, and is far less expensive than either mainframes or minicomputers. Early precursors to modern personal computers, such as the MITS Altair, were available as early as 1975, and the Apple I was introduced in 1976. However, many argue that the real beginning of the personal computer industry came in 1981, with the highly successful introduction of the IBM PC. Much of the success of the personal computer has been fueled by Microsoft pioneer Bill Gates' goal to put a computer on every desk and in every home.

In the late 1980s computing once again shifted, this time from the personal computing era to what Steve Jobs, cofounder of Apple Computers, called the interpersonal computing era (see Figure 1.7). Suddenly, organizations were using computer networks to connect their personal computers together and to the company's mainframe and minicomputers. Companies such as Banyan, Novell, and Artisoft flourished.

In the 1990s, we've seen another shift in computing in organizations. We have now moved from the interpersonal computing to the internetworking era (see Figure 1.7). In this new era of computing, people in organizations are integrating their disparate computers and networks into seamless, responsive enterprise-wide information systems. This integration is enabling customers' direct access into an organization's systems, connecting one organization's enterprise-wide systems to the systems of other organizations, and connecting everything to the Internet—the global network of networks. The objective is to put valuable data at everyone's fingertips and to enable electronic commerce in a variety of forms.

FIGURE 1.7

The evolution of computing.

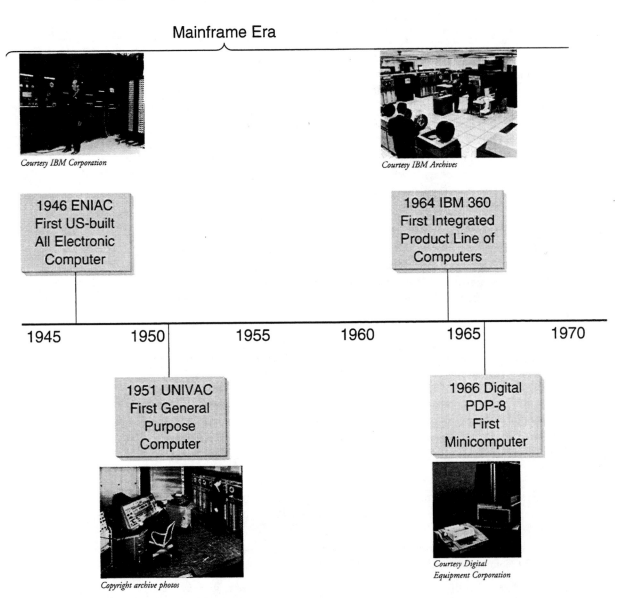

Mainframe Era

Courtesy IBM Corporation

Courtesy IBM Archives

1946 ENIAC
First US-built
All Electronic
Computer

1964 IBM 360
First Integrated
Product Line of
Computers

1945　　1950　　1955　　1960　　1965　　1970

1951 UNIVAC
First General
Purpose
Computer

1966 Digital
PDP-8
First
Minicomputer

Copyright archive photos

*Courtesy Digital
Equipment Corporation*

In this internetworking era, software companies such as Netscape and hardware companies such as Sun Microsystems have flourished. Netscape produces software to enable users to easily and quickly browse and access content on the Internet. Sun produces workstation computers, which are versatile, multi-user computers (typically using a version of the UNIX operating system) that have quickly become the servers forming the backbone of the Internet. Workstations come in a variety of sizes and prices, but they are generally somewhere in between personal computers and minicomputers in terms of their power and price.

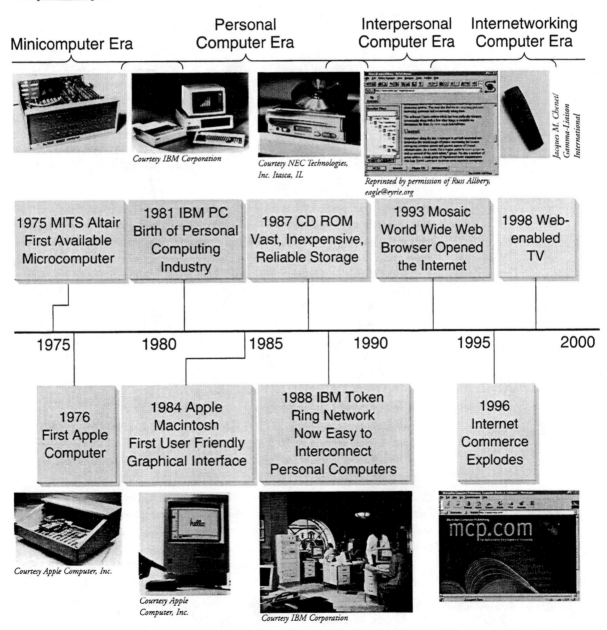

Minicomputer Era

Personal
Computer Era

Interpersonal
Computer Era

Internetworking
Computer Era

Courtesy IBM Corporation

Courtesy NEC Technologies, Inc. Itasca, IL

Reprinted by permission of Russ Allbery, eagle@eyrie.org

Jacques M. Chenet/ Gamma-Liaison International

1975 MITS Altair
First Available
Microcomputer

1981 IBM PC
Birth of Personal
Computing
Industry

1987 CD ROM
Vast, Inexpensive,
Reliable Storage

1993 Mosaic
World Wide Web
Browser Opened
the Internet

1998 Web-
enabled
TV

1975   1980   1985   1990   1995   2000

1976
First Apple
Computer

1984 Apple
Macintosh
First User Friendly
Graphical Interface

1988 IBM Token
Ring Network
Now Easy to
Interconnect
Personal Computers

1996
Internet
Commerce
Explodes

Courtesy Apple Computer, Inc.

Courtesy Apple Computer, Inc.

Courtesy IBM Corporation

mcp.com

IS Today

As you can see, times have changed in IS since the early mainframe days. Today, when you talk about the technology side of IS, you're not just talking about mainframes anymore—although mainframe computers still play a vital role in IS planning and implementation for some large organizations. In most organizations today, the field of IS encompasses a diverse range of computing and networking technologies, from supercomputers, mainframes, and minicomputers to workstations, personal computers, and personal digital assistants (as illustrated in Figure 1.8). The IS field also ranges from local area networks to wide area networks and wireless data communication. It includes a wide variety of useful peripheral devices as well, such as scanners and laser printers. The task of connecting all these computers and devices together has become almost more important than the computers themselves. What's interesting about this technology side of IS is not necessarily that so many more, better technologies are available, but that in many cases, the technology rests in the hands of the users and not the IS personnel.

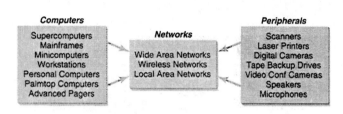

FIGURE 1.8

The technologies of IS come in a variety of flavors.

In addition to the changes to the technology side of IS, the people of IS are changing as well. Many more women are in IS positions than there were just a few short years ago. Also, it is now more common for an IS professional to be a polished, professional systems analyst, dressed in a sharp business suit—someone who can talk fluently about both business and technology. Similarly, today's systems programmers are well-trained, highly skilled, valuable professionals who garner high wages and play a pivotal role in helping firms be successful. For example, today good programmers with skills in SAP R/3 (Systems, Applications, and Products in Data Processing, Release 3) are so valuable that some organizations are willing to pay $150,000 a year to get them. In short, times have changed for IS. The people have changed, and the technology has changed. IS is an important field and a growing profession. For an example, read how the career of one IS professional evolved.

The Technology Side of IS

Let's break down the definition of IS we discussed earlier in the chapter and think about each part of that definition. We'll begin by discussing the core of IS—the computer-based information system. In Part 2, we'll talk more about the nuts and bolts of computer-based systems.

Computer-based information systems are a type of technology. **Technology** is any mechanical and/or electrical means to either supplement or replace manual operations or devices. In this basic sense, some sample machine technologies include the heating and cooling system for a building, the braking system for an automobile, and a laser used for surgery. In Figure 1.9, we show the relationship between technologies and computer-based information systems.

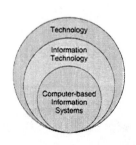

FIGURE 1.9

Venn diagram depicting the relationship between technologies and computer-based information systems.

We use the term **information technology** to refer to any use of machine technology that is controlled by or uses information in some important way. For example, one type of information technology is a programmable robot on the shop floor of a manufacturing firm that receives component specifications and operational instructions from a computer-based database.

On one level, we could argue that any technology makes use of information in some fundamental way, as does each of the three examples of basic technology listed earlier. However, information technologies, such as programmable manufacturing robots, use relatively more information and in a relatively more sophisticated way. You might think that we are splitting hairs with the difference between technologies and information technologies. While the difference is subtle, it is important. Information technologies use machine technologies as building blocks and then combine them and integrate them with computing and networking technologies. A technology such as a mechanical drill press is nice, but it's even better when combined with a computer database that instructs that drill press when and how to act.

Information technologies and information systems are similar. Remember that we defined an information system as a combination of hardware, software, and telecommunications networks that people build and use to collect, create, and distribute data. Information systems are computer-based information systems that contain current data. Their ultimate goal is to provide information to users in a way that helps them to do things. An example of an information system would be the computer-controlled drill press that we described earlier, combined with other shop floor equipment in such a way that a person could monitor and control each piece of equipment from a separate, possibly remote, computer.

Other examples of information systems include a series of integrated electronic spreadsheets used for a budget, an order-fulfillment system for managing customers' purchases, or a set of linked pages on the World Wide Web. You may be asking,"Does my PC at work or school count as part of the company's or university's IS?" Our answer is, yes—exactly! IS includes personal, group, organizational, interorganizational, and even global computing systems.

The People Side of IS

The information systems field includes a vast collection of people who develop, maintain, manage, and study information systems. The career opportunities for a person with IS training have never been better, and they will continue to improve over the next ten years (King, 1998). *Money Magazine* calls being a systems analyst—a common IS career—one of the best jobs in the world today (Marable, 1995).

The U.S. Department of Commerce is predicting huge labor shortages for people with skills in using, designing, developing, and managing information systems. A recent edition of *CIO magazine*—a leading journal for IS executives—dedicated an entire issue to the IS staffing crisis. *Computerworld* reported that more than 350,000 technology-related jobs were unfilled in 1998 (King, 1998). Furthermore, the Commerce Department predicts that this labor shortage for IS workers is only going to increase over the next decade. Even if you don't plan to pursue an IS-related career, you should be interested in this shortage. For example, because virtually all industries heavily rely on IS professionals, not just computer hardware and software companies, the shortage in skilled workers may have a big impact on the economy. The U.S. Bureau of Labor Statistics has reported that high demand for technology-related workers and escalating salaries could lead to inflation in the economy and lower corporate profits over the next decade (Hoffman, 1998).

The field of IS includes those in organizations who design and build systems, those who use those systems, and those responsible for managing those systems. In Table 1.1, we list some of these types of careers and the salaries you might earn in various IS positions. The people who help develop and manage systems in organizations include systems analysts, systems programmers, systems operators, network administrators, database administrators, systems designers, systems managers, and chief information officers. Throughout this book, we'll talk more about these various people and what they do.

Table 1.1 Some of the types of people in IS.

Some IS Activities	Typical Careers	Salary Ranges
Develop	Systems analyst	$40,000–$80,000+
	Systems programmer	$50,000–$80,000+
	Systems consultant	$50,000–$100,000+
Maintain	Database administrator	$75,000–$100,000+
	Webmaster	$40,000–$75,000+
Manage	IS director	$75,000–$100,000+
	Chief information officer	$100,000–$200,000+
Study	University professor	$50,000–$100,000+
	Government scientist	$50,000–$100,000+

Another significant part of the IS field comprises the people who work in IS consulting firms such as IBM, Electronic Data Systems (EDS), and Andersen Consulting. These consultants advise organizations on how to build and manage their systems and, more recently, sometimes actually build and run systems for those organizations. The systems consulting and systems integration areas are red hot. Companies such as IBM, which have traditionally been hardware/software companies, are now doing a lot of systems consulting and related work. Similarly, companies such as Andersen, which specializes in offering systems consulting and/or systems integration (such as EDS), are doing very well.

Another very large group of people in the IS field is made up of university professors throughout the world who conduct research on the development, use, and management of information systems. These IS academic researchers typically work in a school or college within a university, such as a School of Business.

Non-academic researchers who conduct research for agencies such as the Department of Defense or for large corporations such as IBM, Xerox, Hewlett-Packard, and AT&T face almost unlimited opportunities. These professionals generally conduct more applied research and development in the information systems field. For example, a researcher for a major computer manufacturer might be developing a new computer product or examining ways to extend the life of a current product by integrating leading-edge components with the older architecture. Other groups involved in the IS field include "head-hunter" agencies that help IS professionals find jobs and publishers who bring you IS books (such as this one!) and magazines. You get the picture—the field is big and diverse!

The Organizational Side of IS

The last part of our IS definition is the term organization. Information systems are used in all types of organizations—professional, social, religious, educational, and governmental. In fact, the U.S. Internal Revenue Service launched its own site on the World Wide Web (shown in Figure 1.10). The IRS Web site was so popular that approximately 220,000 users visited it during the first 24 hours and more than a million in its first week—even before the Web address for the site was officially announced!

We've now covered each part of our definition of IS, shown again in Figure 1.11. We've talked about the great diversity of people in the IS field and the wide variety of functions they perform. In the next section, we focus on how information systems can be applied within organizations.

The Dual Nature of Information Systems

Now that we have a working definition of IS, let's talk more about why information systems are so important and interesting. Technology is often like a sword—you can use it effectively as a competitive weapon to win, but as the old saying goes, those who live by the sword sometimes die by the sword.

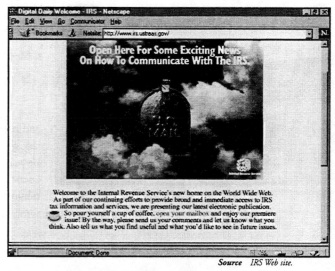

Source IRS Web site.

FIGURE 1.10

The Web site of the U.S. Internal Revenue Service.

Information systems are combinations of hardware, software, and telecommunications networks which people build and use to collect, create, and distribute useful data, typically in organizational settings.

FIGURE 1.11

A representation of the definition of IS, as shown in Figure 1.3.

An Information System Gone Awry: The Denver International Airport

A BRIEF CASE

What happens when an information system is implemented poorly? Perhaps the most notable example of an information system gone wrong in recent years is the automated baggage-handling system for the new, $4.2-billion Denver International Airport (DIA), which is shown in Figure 1.12.

Like the newly constructed DIA, the new underground, automated baggage-handling system for the airport was intended to be amazing. This information system would not only coordinate the automated check in and routing of all luggage for all customers throughout the airport, but it would also enable airport employees to monitor the flow of baggage and literally locate bags anywhere in the airport. The system, which cost $200 million, included the following features:

- 21 miles of steel track

- 4,000 independent "telecars" that would route and deliver luggage among the counters, gates, and claim areas of 20 different airlines

14

Ron Coppock/Gamma-Liaison

FIGURE 1.12

The $4.2-billion Denver International airport.

■ 100 networked computers

■ 5,000 electric eyes

■ 400 radio receivers

■ 56 bar-code scanners

Due to software glitches, the system opened, damaged, and misrouted cargo, forcing airport authorities to leave the system sitting idle for nearly a year (Gibbs, 1994). Because of this and other delays, the airport was not opened and was literally wasting away, at a cost of $1.1 million a day in interest and operating costs, for quite some time.

The DIA story has a happy ending, or beginning, as it were. The automated baggage system is now operational for United Airlines, while other carriers at DIA still use standard baggage-handling methods. The airport is now operational, making money and winning awards. Indeed, the baggage-handling system is one of many ways that this organization is attempting to be innovative and to outdo the competition. However, the airport is still useful as an example of how a problematic information system can adversely affect the performance of an organization.

⬭ A BRIEF CASE ⬭ ── **An Information System That Works: Federal Express** –

Just as there are examples of information systems gone wrong, there are many examples of information systems gone right. For example, take Federal Express's innovative use of information systems (see Figure 1.13).

FedEx, the world's largest express transportation company, delivers more than 2 million items to over 200 countries each business day. FedEx uses extensive, interconnected information systems to coordinate more than 110,000 people, 500 aircrafts, and more than 35,000 vehicles worldwide.

To improve its services and sustain a competitive advantage, FedEx now offers services on the World Wide Web. Customers can now visit the FedEx Web site and track a FedEx package anywhere in the world, find out about FedEx's delivery options and costs, and download FedEx's popular FedExShip PC-based software to prepare packages, verify them online, and print bar-coded shipping documents. FedEx plans

FIGURE 1.13

The Web site for Federal Express.

to soon offer as part of their Web site a digitized map of the world linked to their underlying tracking system, which will show customers the exact location of their packages at any point in time and at any part of the world. These and other information systems assure FedEx a position of dominance in the shipping business for many years to come.

Information Systems for Competitive Advantage

The DIA and Federal Express systems are both good examples of information systems' use for a couple of reasons. First, these two examples are typical of large, complex, new information systems for large organizations—systems that are so large in scale and scope that they are difficult to build and can make or break an organization. It is important to handle the development of such systems the right way the first time around.

Second, each of the choices made in developing these new systems was **strategic** in its intent. These systems weren't developed solely because managers in these organizations wanted to do things faster or because they wanted to have the latest, greatest technology. These systems were developed strategically to help organizations gain or sustain some **competitive advantage** (Porter, 1980), or an edge over rivals. Let's not let this notion slip by us—technology is an enabler of strategic, competitive advantage.

Although we described information systems' uses at two relatively large organizations, using information systems for competitive advantage also occurs in small firms. In fact, information systems can be used to enable firms of all types and sizes to gain or sustain a competitive advantage over their rivals.

IS for Automating: The First Step

You can view and use information systems in many ways, as summarized in Figure 1.14, but we believe that the strategic perspective is the most important. Let's first talk about some other points of view and see how they can and should build up to the strategic perspective.

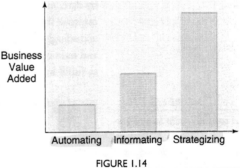

FIGURE 1.14

The business value added from automating, informating, and strategizing mentalities toward IS.

One simple way to view information systems is in terms of **automating**. Someone with this perspective thinks of technology as a way to continue doing the same things he has been doing in an organization, but to do them faster and, perhaps, more cheaply with the help of technology. Let's look at a typical example.

A person with an **automating mentality** would take an existing loan application screening process and automate it with technology. The individual might have someone input information about the loan applications (or perhaps the entire loan application) into a computer database so that those involved in decision making for the loans could process the applications faster, easier, and with fewer errors. The use of this technology would probably save some time, paper, and, subsequently, money. Better yet, the individual could even have customers complete the loan application online, saving even more time and money. In Figure 1.15, we show how long the automated process takes. On a larger scale, such a transition from a manual to an automated process might enable the organization to remove or better deploy employees, leading to further cost savings.

① Applicant Completes Loan Application and Submits It	1.5 Days
② Employee Checks Application for Errors	2.5 Days
③ Employee Inputs Application Data into System	2.5 Hours
④ Computer Performs Initial Screening Process	2.3 Seconds
⑤ Committee Decides on Any Loans for Over $100,000	30 Days
⑥ Applicant Notified	1 Hour

Switch to online loan application for both in-store and remote customers

2 hours

FIGURE 1.15

Information technology helps managers improve the loan approval process.

Many of the significant early gains from computing in organizations came from automating previously manual processes. While nothing is actually wrong with this view and this use of information systems, it is a bit shortsighted. Much more can be done with technology than is being exploited in this instance. In the next section, we'll explain what else can be done.

IS for Informating: The Second Step

Another way to view and use information systems was described cleverly by Shoshana Zuboff (1984) as **informating**. Zuboff explained that a technology informates when it provides information about its operation and the underlying work process that it supports. In other words, the system not only helps us to automate but also to learn to improve its day-to-day operation.

The **informating mentality** builds on the automating mentality because it recognizes that information systems can be used as a vehicle for organizational learning and change as well as for automation. In a useful 1993 article in *Harvard Business Review*, David Garvin described a **learning organization** as one that is "skilled at creating, acquiring, and transferring knowledge, and at modifying its behavior to reflect new knowledge and insights." Figure 1.16 shows how a computer-based loan processing system can help a manager plan more effectively. The processing system tracks types of loan applications by date, month, and season and notifies the manager of trends so that the manager can improve the efficiency and effectiveness of the application process. The manager plans accordingly for the timely ordering of blank application forms, "just-in-time" staffing and training of personnel in the Loan department, and better management of funds used to fulfill loans.

FIGURE 1.16

A computer-based loan processing system enables the manager to improve the efficiency and effectiveness of the application process.

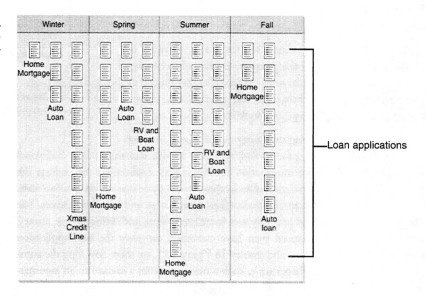

For example, let's return to our automating example with the computer-based loan application processing system. In addition to using the automated system to process loans faster and easier and save costs, the organization could use it to learn a great deal about the business process involved. Using an informating approach might allow those working on the system to track and learn about the types of applications filed by certain types of people at certain times of the year, the patterns of the loan decisions made, or the loan applications and the subsequent performance of those loans. In short, this new system creates data about the underlying business process that can be used to better monitor, control, and change that process.

A combined automating and informating approach, in the long run, is more effective than an automating approach alone. If the underlying business process supported by technology is inherently flawed, an informating use of the technology might help you detect the problems with the process and change it. For example, in our loan processing example, an informating use of technology may help us to uncover a pattern among the loans accepted that enables us to distinguish between low- and high-performing loans over their lives and, subsequently, change the criteria for loan acceptance.

If, however, the underlying business process is bad, and you are using technology only for automating, you are more likely to continue with a flawed or less-than-optimal business process. In fact, such an automating use of the technology may mask the process problems. With a computer-based loan application processing system, you cannot readily "see" the process or the data unless informating aspects are built into the system. You might eventually take the process for granted and conclude that the system works. You might find yourself saying that it's faster and easier this way, things are fine, or tell others to just let the system do its thing.

If the technology acts as a magnifier, it may cause the process to become exponentially bad. For example, with a bad underlying set of loan acceptance criteria, a person might manually review four applications in a day and, because of the problematic criteria used, inadvertently accept two "bad" applications per week on average. If you automated the same faulty process, with no informating aspects built in, the system might help to review twelve applications per day, with six "bad" applications accepted per week on average. The technology would serve only to magnify the existing business problems. Without informating, it is more difficult to uncover bad business processes underlying the IS application. Worse, you might subsequently choose to automate (that is, spend even more time and money) additional bad-business processes.

IS as Strategic Enabler: The Final Step

We've described the automating and the informating approaches toward using information systems. Now, let's talk about using information systems strategically.

Using information systems strategically occurs when a person thinks of ways to use the technology as an enabler of **organizational strategy** and competitive advantage. Fundamental to this approach is the assumption that the use of information systems ought to fundamentally support the mission and strategy of the organization. Let's talk about these concepts of organizational strategy and planning and then see how they fit with information systems.

18

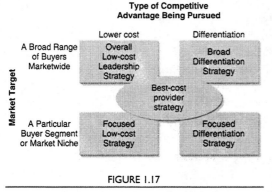

Type of Competitive
Advantage Being Pursued

FIGURE 1.17

Five generic organizational strategies.

Courtesy Thompson, A.A. and Strickland, A.J. III, 1995. Strategic
Management: Concepts and Cases, *8th Edition*, Homewood: Richard D.
Irwin, Inc.

When senior managers conduct **strategic planning**, they form a vision of where the organization needs to be headed, convert that vision into measurable objectives and performance targets, and craft a strategy to achieve the desired results. In Figure 1.17, we show some common organizational strategies. An organization might decide to pursue a low-cost leadership strategy, as does K-Mart or Packard-Bell. Alternatively, an organization might decide to pursue a differentiation strategy, whereby it tries to provide better products or services than its competitors, as does Porsche, Nordstrom, or IBM. It also might target a particular segment of consumers, as did Apple for many years with its focus on home and educational computing. Still other organizations might pursue a middle-of-the-road strategy of being the best-cost provider, offering good quality products and services at reasonable prices, as does Wal-Mart.

A person with a strategic approach tries to find ways information systems can be used to achieve the organization's chosen strategy. This individual undoubtedly wants to take advantage of any benefits that come from automating and informating, but he/she also looks for strategic benefits and ways to help the organization gain or sustain a competitive advantage. An organization has a competitive advantage whenever it has an edge over rivals in attracting customers and defending against competitive forces (see Porter, 1985, for a useful discussion on the concept of competitive advantage). For most businesses, it is not enough to simply aim to make money. Each business must have a clear vision, one that focuses their investments in resources such as information systems and technologies to help achieve competitive advantage.

Sources of Competitive Advantage

Some sources of competitive advantage include the following:

- Having the best-made product on the market
- Delivering superior customer service
- Achieving lower costs than rivals
- Having a proprietary technology
- Having shorter lead times in developing and testing new products
- Having a well-known brand name and reputation
- Providing customers more value for their money

Each of these sources of competitive advantage can be gained or sustained through the effective use of information systems. For example, rental car agencies compete fiercely with each other to provide the best cars, the best service, and the best rates. It's a constant competitive battle. Companies find it difficult to differentiate themselves, so they discover clever ways to use information systems to improve customer service.

──────── Avis-Rent-A-Car ──────── ⟨ A BRIEF CASE ⟩

In order to sustain a competitive advantage over rivals in the area of customer service, Avis-Rent-A-Car customer service representatives wait for the customer out in the lot, armed with specially designed, hand-held computers and printers either strapped around their waists or over their shoulders. With this "Avis Roving Rapid Return" service (shown in Figure 1.18), the representative inputs the license number of the car on the portable computer when he sees the customer driving in to return a car. Inputting this information brings up the customer's rental contract. As the customer gets out of the car, the representative inputs the mileage and the fuel level, while a second attendant retrieves the customer's luggage and places it on the curb. By the time the customer has exited the car and stood next to her luggage, the representative has already printed the customer's receipt (if she had previously paid by credit card). The representative hands it to the

© *Michael Newman/Photoedit*

FIGURE 1.18

Avis Roving Rapid Return.

customer immediately with a smile and a "Thank you!" The service encounter for the customer is fast and pleasant. That's using technology for competitive advantage! In Table 1.2, we show how Avis's computer-supported process compares with the traditional rental car service encounter.

Table 1.2 The Avis airport computer-supported service encounter versus the traditional airport rental car service encounter.

	Traditional Rental Car Return Service Encounter	Avis's Computer-Based Service Encounter
	Return car to lot attendant, get bags from another attendant, walk inside and wait in line to settle contract with another attendant, walk out, and board a shuttle.	Return car to lot attendant, grab receipt and bags, and board shuttle.
Elapsed time	5–10 minutes	2–3 seconds
Number of people to interact with	2–3 people	1–2 people
Average number of steps customer takes	60–75 steps	5–10 steps
Relative efficiency	Low	High

Not all uses of information systems for competitive advantage are necessarily as exotic as Avis's use of hand-held computers. An organization might simply be using a more common technology, such as a shared computer database, but in a strategic way. Let's look again at our computer-based loan application processing example.

A person with a strategic approach would like a loan processing application for its automating and informing benefits, as discussed earlier. In addition, however, this person would have chosen this application in the first place because people in his organization have agreed that three achievements are absolutely critical to the strategy and success of the organization—processing loan applications faster and better, proactively re-engineering this particular business process, and better integrating this process with other business processes. This person likes the loan processing system because it adds value to the organization in the short term AND matches the organization's strategy. In short, this system has been deemed essential to the long-term survival of the firm.

Alternatively, a person with a strategic approach might have determined that the loan application processing system might not be a good fit with the organizational strategy, even though the system is likely to add value to the organization in other ways. For example, the managers of this organization may have determined that in order to succeed, they must grow and generate new products and services. They should deploy their assets and invest in technologies in ways that achieve these objectives. In this situation, the loan application processing system might still provide automating and informating benefits, but it would provide little or no direct strategic value. Indeed, spending money, time, and other resources on such a system would be foolish if growing and generating new business were paramount. An elaborate loan system would do this organization little good if, overall, they lost out to rivals and ultimately went out of business.

The online ticket service in the chapter opening scenario is another good example of how an organization can use an information system to achieve a competitive advantage over rivals. The online ticket system enables customers to buy tickets quickly and easily, which is critical in the ticket industry. In addition, the system enables the organization to market, sell, and manage the ticket-selling process efficiently (automating), as well as to learn from customers' behaviors at their Web site, their purchase patterns, and their written online feedback (informating). This system does everything that it should: automating, informating, and enabling strategy.

IS and Value Chain Analysis

One popular way organizations can determine how information systems are strategically important to their long-term survival is through **value chain analysis** (Porter, 1985; Shank and Govindarajan, 1993). Think about an organization as a big input/output process. At one end, supplies are purchased and brought into the organization (see Figure 1.19). Those supplies and resources are then integrated in some way to create products and services, which are marketed, sold, and then distributed in many ways to customers. Finally, some future service is provided after the initial sale of these goods and services. Throughout this process, there are opportunities for people and groups in the organization to add value to the organization—by bringing in supplies in a more effective manner, improving products, selling more products, and so on. This process is known as the value chain within an organization.

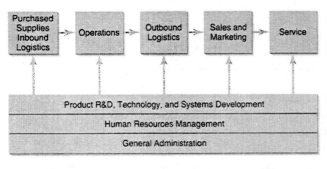

FIGURE 1.19

A sample generic organizational value chain.

Value chain analysis is the process of analyzing an organization's activities to determine where value is added to products and/or services and the costs that are incurred for doing so. Because IS can automate many activities along the value chain, value chain analysis has become a very popular tool for applying IS for competitive advantage. In value chain analysis, you first think about and then draw the value chain for your organization by fleshing out each of the activities, functions, and processes where value is or should be added. Next, determine the costs—and the factors that drive costs or cause them to fluctuate—within each of the areas in your value chain diagram. You then **benchmark** (compare) your value chain and associated costs with those of other organizations, preferably your competitors. You can then make changes and improvements in your value chain to either gain or sustain a competitive advantage.

The Role of Information Systems in Value Chain Analysis

The use of information systems has become one of the primary ways that organizations are making changes and improvements in their value chains. In Figure 1.20, we show a sample value chain and some ways that information systems can be used to improve productivity. For example, many organizations now use Electronic Data Interchange (EDI), a set of standards and methods for connecting businesses together electronically (for example, connecting a business with its suppliers) so that they can exchange orders, invoices, and receipts online in real time. Using EDI is one proven way to use information systems to improve the front end of the organizational value chain.

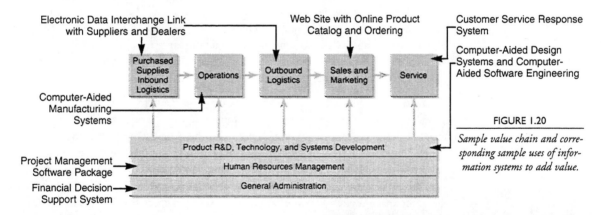

FIGURE 1.20

Sample value chain and corresponding sample uses of information systems to add value.

One of the more innovative ways to use information systems to improve the back end of the value chain, the service after the sale, is to provide service to customers online in real time. For example, owners of McLaren's $850,000 F1 Supercar plug into the car an accompanying modem kit that enables McLaren engineers to diagnose the car and make adjustments to it over the phone lines in real time (see Figure 1.21). That may sound exotic and restricted to those few individuals who can afford an $850,000 automobile, but this method is also being used by computer companies and others to diagnose and maintain their customers' products remotely and, in some cases, to download new software products.

Gamma-Liaison

FIGURE 1.21

The McLaren F1 supercar.

The Technology/Strategy Fit

You might be asking, if any information system helps to do things faster and better and helps save money, who cares whether or not it matches the company's strategy? Good question. One answer is that most organizations are typically faced with many different, valuable systems that could be built, but due to constraints on time, money, and other resources, they cannot all be built simultaneously. When you manage an organization, you can't afford to do everything, so you must prioritize the list of alternative, proposed systems and choose to build those that add the most value—those that give the biggest bang for the buck. In other words, you should choose systems that help automate and informate, as well as have strategic value. In most cases, you don't want systems that don't match the strategy, even if they offer automating and informating benefits.

For example, you probably don't want a system that helps differentiate your products based on high quality when the organizational strategy is to be the overall industry low-cost leader. For example, creating an expensive computer-aided design system would probably add exorbitant costs to the process and would likely defeat the strategy of spending less in the production of products and, subsequently, selling products at the lowest possible prices.

In any event, it simply makes good business sense to have a clear organizational strategy and to have systems that fit well with the strategy. Building systems solely because they help you to do things faster and improve business processes—without having a clear sense of their strategic value—is not a sensible practice. It's like being out on the ocean in a powerfully motored boat without knowing your destination or why you want to reach it. Your competitors know where they should be going and will, undoubtedly, beat you to the finish line. Furthermore, if you are unknowingly headed for trouble, your powerful, fast motor will only hasten your trip.

Organizations that have a combined automating, informating, and strategic approach first get a clear sense of the overall mission and strategy of the organization. Next, they lay out a clear plan for using information systems that support the overall organization plan. These two plans—one for the organization and the other for the information systems—are tightly coupled. All decisions about, and actions on, information systems are driven by these dual plans. Essentially, we want you to start thinking strategically about information systems. As you can see, there is a lot more to the field of IS than bits, bytes, and hackers.

Everyone Must Think Strategically for Every Technology Decision

Managing technology well has become a strategic necessity, and managing technology for competitive advantage is the way to do it. Thinking this way requires systems personnel to see the big picture and to be long-term, critical thinkers. They must also know the business side and the technology side of the organization. Furthermore, systems personnel must see technology as a means to serve the business's ends, rather than seeing technology as an end in itself. This kind of strategic thinking isn't just for the chief information officer and other high-ranking information systems managers. This kind of thinking is absolutely essential for everyone in the organization, including personnel from marketing, operations, finance, human resources, or accounting—not just the systems analysts and programmers.

In order to be successful, everyone who participates in business decisions that involve technology must have a strategic mindset. Even if we're only talking about the purchase of a new PC in an organization, we shouldn't be concerned only with what microprocessor it has or how large the hard disk is. Instead, we should think first about how this technology is used to help add value, and second about what technical specifications will be needed to accomplish the task effectively.

Talking with...

Robert R. Ridout, CIO and Vice-President of Information Systems at DuPont

Educational Background

B.S. in Mathematics (computer science concentration), College of William and Mary

Job Description

Mr. Ridout is responsible for the stewardship of information systems and information technology globally for DuPont. DuPont's worldwide IS organization consists of 23 strategic business units and 7 functional units, all networked to a small, centralized component at headquarters. Mr. Ridout is also responsible for leading and managing the newly formed DuPont IT Alliance (a 10-year, $4-billion deal with Computer Sciences Corporation and Andersen Consulting, providing DuPont's businesses with access to the "best of the best" in information technology). He also oversees a distributed organization of 1,200 DuPont IT professionals.

Critical Success Factors

An intimate understanding of the businesses within DuPont and their strategic directions and key business drivers. A keen ability to articulate the competitive advantage of IT services and solutions in order to achieve competitive advantage in the marketplace. Open, honest, and frequent communications with executive and senior management in the company. The ability to sense the external technology and business environments and to create and communicate vision and direction for the corporation. The ability to motivate and lead a network of people from around the world.

Advice to Students

Make the most of your college experience—study hard, look for opportunities to broaden yourself, and always be receptive to new opportunities and ideas. Whatever your profession, take the time to learn the larger business perspective and how your job relates to the strategy and goals of your firm. Be self-reliant and chart your own path for success. Plan your own career paths and development areas. Always strive for excellence. Hone your communication skills, both verbal and written. These are critical for your success, and you should always work towards perfecting your ability to communicate with people at all levels, internal and external to your company. Stay abreast of the latest technology trends and keep focused on how these technologies can add business value. Always be respectful toward others. Your success will be dependent on your ability to provide leadership and vision to an increasingly diverse and global workforce.

ETHICAL PERSPECTIVE: THE NEED FOR A UNIFIED INFORMATION SYSTEMS CODE OF ETHICS

Given that computers and information systems are now a fundamental part of doing business, opportunities for misusing and abusing information, computers, and systems now abound. For example, an organization that manages your credit card transactions might sell data on your purchasing behavior to another organization that has information from a survey you filled out about your lifestyle. This new information might then be sold to a third organization, which uses the information to market to you via the mail some specialty products or services they believe you are likely to be interested in. Alternatively, purchasing data about someone with a name similar to your own may appear in your credit report, causing you to wrongly be denied a loan.

This new wired world we live in causes us to ask some important new ethical questions. Who owns information, particularly information about us? Which information should be private, and who should be given access to which information? Who is responsible for the accuracy of information? Should guidelines be set for how business organizations and business professionals use information, computers, and information systems, and if so, what should these guidelines be? Academic and business leaders have suggested and supported the idea of an information systems code of ethics to be adhered to by all.

Currently, computer-related professional organizations throughout the world have written codes of ethics for their members, including the Association for Computing Machinery, the Australian Computer Society, the Canadian Information Processing Society, the Institute for Electrical and Electronics Engineers, and the International Programmers Guild. The codes differ in minor ways. Some are more general, while others are more specific. Some emphasize different ethical issues than do others. Furthermore, there is no unified code of ethics for all computer-related professionals, and there is no code of ethics for the information systems profession in particular.

Information systems professionals "meet frequently in professional conferences, read and contribute to professional publications, and share a professional jargon," so they should also have a uniform and coherent code of ethics. Such a uniform code could provide guidance to professionals on acceptable conduct and could help raise awareness and consciousness of important ethical issues. Some people also believe that a code would go a long way toward promoting a positive public image of information systems professionals worldwide. The public would be assured that the profession is concerned about the welfare of society, employers, clients, and sister organizations. Perhaps more importantly, the new unified code would be without regard to national borders, a must in this age of borderless networking.

ISWorld Net, the Web site for information systems academics, has a Professional Ethics page, which is intended to provide a forum for discussing issues concerning the practice of the information systems profession (http://csrc.lse.ac.uk/iswnet/profact/ethics.htm). The philosophy of a code of ethics is summarized on that Web page as follows: "The real challenge is not to indulge in a never-ending debate on the feasibility or necessity of having a code of ethics, but rather, to be able to capture the essence of our profession to be shared and provide as a guiding light to the many more people who are already or who would one day be part of this profession."

Some governmental policy makers believe that a formal unified code of ethics for the information systems profession is paramount. "Many [European Union] member states perceive the need now for some discipline, some kind of regulatory framework or code of ethics," says the Italian telecommunications minister at a meeting of the EU's culture and telecommunications ministers. It remains to be seen whether or not a unified code is developed and ratified. One thing is certain: As technology continues to advance rapidly, new information systems ethical issues arise every day.

Questions for Discussion

1. Do you believe that there is a need for a unified information systems code of ethics? Why or why not?

2. What are some other advantages of having a unified code? What are some of the disadvantages, limits, and barriers to a unified code?

3. How could such a unified code be made to cope with the fast pace of technological development around the globe?

Sources Oz, Effy. 1992. Ethical standards for information systems professionals: A case for a unified code. MIS Quarterly, December, 16:4:423–433. Wall Street Journal, May 3, 1996, B5B

INTERNATIONAL PERSPECTIVE: GLOBAL COMPETITIVENESS

The U.S. isn't the only player in the IS game; the competition to produce and use computer-based knowledge and the means of transferring it is fierce from Thailand to Israel and from France to Chile. Companies around the globe plan to use IS as part of their strategy to obtain a competitive edge over rivals, and governments are pushing technology use as a means of bringing their countries into competition on the world market. Newspapers and journals abound with evidence of these trends, as countries in Europe open their markets and relax rules and as competition in corporate networks and mobile phone services multiplies at a furious pace. Business alliances in Italy, Germany, and France have made investments in the billions in an effort to introduce competition to the formerly monopolized communications markets. Even developing nations, among them Chile and the Philippines, have opened previously state-owned communications enterprises to competition in order to secure critical investment and to help push them into the global information economy.

Use of technology also increases the possibilities for expansive growth. The days of privileged information may be waning—no longer will connections and human networks be the sole source of a business's success in Japan or Hong Kong. In addition, the explosion of electronic commerce via the Internet is causing a rush to enter the global market. The savings and the opportunities available through the electronic exchange of goods and services have the potential to support the creation of thousands of new businesses and to encourage the expansion of local businesses around the world.

The globalization of IS and the need to stay competitive are changing not only the way companies worldwide do business, but also the ways in which companies are run. Tasks are being simplified, the Internet is giving companies access to international regulatory information at the touch of a key, and Japanese companies and their American subsidiaries around the world can meet without plane tickets being purchased. To conduct business successfully with videoconferencing, electronic mail, and other forms of electronic (and often instantaneous) communication, businesses in both the East and West must learn to adapt to a variety of management styles and learn a new language of communication.

In fact, as companies join global networks and do business with those in other countries, new employment opportunities abound. The successful employee in the age of instant global communication may be the one who can function well in a variety of cultural and linguistic spheres. Lack of multicultural representatives in an era of global contact could cause businesses to lose their competitive edge. Having women lead a videoconference with Saudi businessmen or making a cultural gaffe while communicating with a Japanese customer could have major financial repercussions.

Technology is also changing people's lives as governments strive to help their economies compete. In India, for example, only a very small percentage of the village population has access to a telephone or a phone line. With government support aimed at economic development on a monumental scale, over 15 million additional telephones throughout the country are expected to be connected by the year 2000.

Embassies and foreign ministries are joining the information revolution, allowing governments to obtain critical policy-making information instantaneously. This quick access results in changes in diplomatic strategies, giving governments less time and less secrecy in which to act; however, it also provides needed economic data in areas such as import and export and changes in trade law. As technology is employed to assist in economic development, it also encourages individuals to seek and share information. Communist countries, such as China, have found that they now have less control over their populations because the Internet allows access to formerly inaccessible information and enables people to broadcast to the world in ways that were not possible before. With the Internet, it's far easier for Taiwanese political activists to compete for the world's attention than ever!

Questions for Discussion

1. Can companies from different countries really compete with each other in terms of information technology, given that the basic telephone wiring infrastructures within countries are vastly different from one another—with some countries far ahead of others?

2. What role should information technology play in the growth and expansion of a company internationally?

3. How can you best prepare yourself to use information technology to enable your future employer's strategy and competitive advantage?

26

Summary

1. **Understand what the term information systems (IS) means.** Information systems are combinations of hardware, software, and telecommunications networks, which people build and use to collect, create, and distribute useful data typically in organizational settings. Information systems also used to represent the field in which people develop, use, manage, and study computer-based information systems in organizations. IS is a huge, diverse, growing field that encompasses many different people, purposes, systems, and technologies.

2. **Describe the evolution of computing.** Computing technology has evolved over the past fifty years. Over this time, five distinct computing eras have occurred. During the mainframe computer era, which spanned from the 1940s to the 1970s, the dominant technology was the large, general-purpose computer that supported hundreds of users. The minicomputer era extended from the late 1960s to the 1980s. Like mainframes, minicomputers could support a large number of users, but they were much less expensive to buy and operate and much easier to program than mainframes. Minicomputers helped to bring computer technology into smaller organizations. The personal computer era began in the early 1980s. The introduction of the IBM PC was the era's most significant event. The hallmark of the era was the low-cost computer that made its way onto the desktops of many homes and offices. The interpersonal computing era began in the late 1980s, as networking technology interconnected large and small computers. Human-to-human communication through electronic mail, bulletin boards, and chat rooms became a dominate computing application. The internetworking computing era began in the mid- to late-1990s with the development of the Internet's World Wide Web browsing tool, Mosaic. The dominant application in this current era of computing is interconnecting enterprise-wide networks and information systems into a seamless, worldwide network to support communication and commerce.

3. **Explain the technology, people, and organizational components of an information system.** Information systems combine hardware, software, and telecommunications networks that people build and use to collect, create, and distribute useful data in organizations. The technology part of information systems is the hardware, software, and telecommunications networks. The people who build, manage, and use information systems make up the people component. Finally, information systems reside within organizations, so they are said to have an organizational component. Together, these three aspects form an information system.

4. **Discuss how information systems can be used to automate, informate, and strategically support business activities.** Automating business activities occurs when information systems are used to do a business activity faster or more cheaply. IS can be used to help automate. It can also be used to improve aspects of an operation in order to gain dramatic improvements in the operation as a whole. When this occurs, technology is said to informate because it provides information about its operation and the underlying work process that it supports. Using information systems strategically occurs when the technology is used to enable organizational strategy and competitive advantage.

5. **Describe information systems' critical, strategic importance to the success of modern organizations.** Using information systems to automate and informate business processes is a good start. However, information systems can add even more value to an organization if they are conceived, designed, used, and managed with a strategic approach. To apply information systems strategically, you must understand the organization's value chain and be able to identify opportunities in which you can use information systems to make changes or improvements in the value chain to gain or sustain a competitive advantage.

Key Terms

Information systems	Automating	Strategic mentality
Technology	Automating mentality	Organizational strategy
Information technology	Informating	Strategic planning
Strategic	Informating mentality	Value Chain analysis
Competitive advantage	Learning organization	Benchmark

Review Questions

1. What is "Information Systems"?

2. Describe the types of people in the field of IS.

3. How is "information technology" different than generic "technology"? Provide examples of each.

4. List some sources of competitive advantage.

5. What is "automating," and what does it mean to have an automating mentality?

6. What is "informating," and how is it different than automating?

7. What is a "learning" organization? Describe how an organization can learn.

8. What is a "strategic mentality," and why is it important?

9. List the five generic organizational strategies.

10. Describe the role that information systems can play in value chain analysis. *increases productivity*

11. Explain the phrase "technology/strategy fit." What can happen if there is not a good technology/strategy fit?

Problems and Exercises

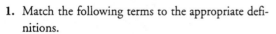 **Individual**   **Group**   **Field**   **Web/Internet**

1. Match the following terms to the appropriate definitions.

   _____ Information systems

   _____ Strategic

   _____ Competitive advantage

   _____ Informating

   _____ Strategic mentality

   _____ Organizational strategy

   _____ Strategic planning

   _____ Value chain analysis

   a. Using technology in such a way that it provides information about its operation and the underlying work process that it supports

   b. Analyzing an organization's activities to determine where value is added to products and/or services and the costs that are incurred for doing so, as well as comparing the activities, added value, and costs of the organization to those of other organizations in order to make improvements in the organization's operations and performance

   c. Important in or essential to a planned series of activities for obtaining a goal or desired result

   d. Combinations of hardware, software, and telecommunications networks that people build and use to

28

collect and create useful data and then disseminate that data to those who need it

e. When an organization has an edge over rivals in attracting customers and defending against competitive forces

f. A person with this mentality recognizes the importance of technology for automating and informating but believes that technology is primarily an enabler of organizational strategy and competitive advantage

g. The process whereby members of an organization form a vision of where the organization needs to be headed (that is, the organization's mission), develop measurable objectives and performance targets for that vision, and craft a strategy for achieving the vision, objectives, and targets

h. An overall game plan for how an organization will achieve its primary mission

2. Imagine that you had to explain to a five-year-old child what the field of information systems is. Write down your explanation in terms that the five-year-old child would best understand. Chances are, you will form an explanation that will be effective for adults as well.

3. Is the recent growth in information systems' development and use in organizations just a fad, or will information systems' use in organizations continue to be important and pervasive? Why? How do your fellow classmates feel about this? Do they agree with you?

4. Some people argue that the benefits provided by using information systems for competitive advantage are fleeting because rival firms can easily copy these same uses of information systems. Discuss this with a small group of classmates. Do you agree? Why or why not? Present some counterarguments.

5. Some people argue that simply automating with information systems is enough. They claim that trying to informate with technology is not necessary. What arguments and examples can you offer to persuade them that informating with information systems has value beyond merely automating?

6. To stop thinking about technology as a tool for automating and to develop an informating and strategic mentality toward information systems can be a difficult, radical change in perspective for some people. How difficult do you think it is to get people to make these paradigm shifts in the real world? Why? Do your classmates agree with you? What can be done to help them see the world differently?

7. Is it truly possible for organizations to learn? Why or why not?

8. Imagine an organization that deploys information systems with no rhyme or reason, for which the technology/strategy fit is nonexistent. Form a group of classmates and determine what this organization might look like. How is this organization using information systems? Is this organization likely to be successful? Why or why not?

9. Is the process of benchmarking an ethical activity? Why or why not?

10. Consider an organization that you are familiar with, perhaps one that you have worked for or have done business with. Describe the types of information systems

that this organization uses and whether or not they are useful. If there are ways that this organization should be using information systems but is not, describe how this organization might make better use of information systems.

11. Identify someone who works within the field of information systems, as an information systems instructor, professor, or practitioner (for example, as a systems analyst or systems manager). Find out why this individual got into this field and what he or she likes and dislikes about working within the field of MIS. What advice can he or she offer to someone entering the field?

12. Choose an organization and identify its strategy. You can determine this information by looking for clues in the organization's annual report, advertisements, and/or its site on the World Wide Web. Can you identify anything about this organization's information systems that suggest to you that their information systems are aligned well with their strategy? If so, describe the technology/strategy fit for this organization. If not, describe some ways that information systems could be used to best enable the organization's strategy.

13. Consider an organization you are familiar with that does not appear to use information systems strategically. List at least four reasons why information systems are not used strategically within this organization. Are these reasons justifiable? Why or why not? What are the implications for this organization if its members continue to deploy information systems in this way?

14. Interview a manager within an organization with which you are familiar. Perhaps this individual works where you work or at your university or college. Ask this person a series of questions to help you understand his or her perspective on information systems and their value. For example, ask what value information systems provide in his or her organization. When finished with the interview, review your interview notes and determine whether this person has an automating mentality, an informating mentality, a strategic mentality, or some combination of these perspectives toward information systems. Does this person appear to have a healthy, useful perspective toward information systems? Why or why not? If not, how could this person be helped to better understand the potential of information systems?

15. Form a small group of classmates. Choose an idea for a valuable new product or service that you could offer as part of a start-up firm. What will be your basic organizational strategy (for example, differentiation based on high quality, low cost leadership, and so on)? Describe four ways that you can use information systems to enable your strategy. Prepare a 10-minute class presentation on your organizational strategy and how you will use information systems in your firm.

16. Consider the scenario from the previous question and imagine that a new competitor has entered the market and is doing exactly what you are doing. How can you use information systems to gain or sustain a competitive advantage over this rival firm? How easily can this rival firm copy your use of information systems for competitive advantage? What other steps can you take to sustain your competitive advantage?

17. Search the World Wide Web for several organizations that you like or are interested in. Using only their home pages and related links, determine each company's organizational strategy and their information systems strategy. Can these be determined from the documentation available through the World Wide Web? Do you have a clear understanding of these organizations' approaches to information systems? Were your fellow classmates able to find any better information from their searches?

18. Consider the scenario that opened this chapter regarding the purchase of concert tickets from an online system. This system provided a competitive advantage over the ticket company's rivals. Identify additional systems that you as a customer can interact with that also provide some competitive advantage for the organization running the system. What are these competitive advantages? How many of these systems are Web-based?

Real World Case Problems

1. IT Spending in '98: Full Speed Ahead

After eight years of record economic expansion in the United States, economists still expect 1998 to repeat 1997. Even with the massive Asian currency collapse, IT investors are still spending high dollars. It is the complexity of business that is causing IT to make the investment to assist their customers in dealing with these issues.

A recent survey by *InformationWeek* and *VARBusiness* of 250 senior IT managers reports that IT spending will increase by 18 percent and that more than 70 percent of those managers will spend it through IT resellers. The Web will be used for purchasing PCs in 1998 by 25 percent of IT managers. Other expenditures on the agenda are as follows: training, with its direct correlation between application productivity and training; network storage for intranets and electronic business applications; Windows NT 5.0; Novell NetWare 5.0 upgrades; and network computer purchasing. However, the most important project looming ahead is the year 2000 conversion. This project is driving the cost of IT spending higher than ever. DHL Worldwide Express, the multinational package courier, plans to spend $25 million on the year 2000 problem during the next two years to fix their 20 million lines of programming code.

Approximately 29 percent of the year 2000 budgets will go toward testing the revitalized applications. "The biggest time-consumer is in the testing—testing end-to-end systems around the world to make sure everything works right," states Joseph Riera, CIO and senior VP of DHL Airways, Inc. In the future, managers are planning to decrease costs and make it easier to do business with DHL by creating better customer access through the company's Web site.

Other current issues include globalization and mergers, such as at Smith Barney, a domestic firm, and at Salomon Brothers, an international firm. Now Peter Remch, Vice President of Smith Barney, is faced with the issues of trading systems to support Europe's Euro currency. In the end, no matter what applications are completed, managers will still have key applications moved to the backburner because IT money always runs out before all projects are completed.

a. What does it mean when so many companies continue to increase their spending on IT, even in the face of stock market drops and foreign currency collapses?

b. Is it a bad idea for DHL and other firms to be diverting so many IT resources to solve their Year 2000 problems? Why or why not? Remember, for systems in which years have been coded as two-digit numbers (for example, 85) rather than four-digit numbers (for example, 1985), in the year 2000 (a k a Y2K), the two digits "00" will be interpreted as the year 1900, causing miscalculations and potential systems crashes.

c. How important is it to firms such as Smith Barney to spend IT resources on systems to support the internationalization of the business, such as tweaking trading system software to support Europe's Euro currency? Why?

Source Weston, Rusty. 1998. "IT Spending in '98: Full Speed Ahead." InformationWeek, January 5, 16–17.

2. Social Security Gets It Right

The Social Security Administration's (SSA) sound management has led the way toward modernizing its vast data center and deploying a nationwide network of desktop work stations. The agency, which currently has more than 3.5 million lines of code and 25 million transactions per day, serves a large number of demanding clients.

The key to the SSA's success, states Greenwalt, a staffer for the Senate Governmental Affairs Committee, is that "they got out from under Health and Human Services and started approaching things like a company." SSA uses automation as a manufacturing function.

In 1996, a law was enacted that required federal agencies to have a CIO. In reality, it didn't change much at the SSA. The SSA already saw IT as critical to getting a major part of the work done. In many agencies, communication is near to impossible because the IT group is down several layers in the organization. However, at the SSA, the agency's deputies provide a business perspective and assist in IT acquisitions.

The SSA has adopted a conservative approach to modernization by not reinventing the wheel or making unnecessary changes. They have reduced their dependence on mainframes, converted 80-some applications to Windows NT servers, and decreased access time from several minutes to 30 seconds. The SSA's rollout of 60,000 workstations to 1,400 offices is about half done. They are also upgrading the communications network and are on target to meet their $280 million budget. All of this success is due to having a strategic plan.

a. Why have other U.S. federal agencies had such disastrous results in building, acquiring, and managing IT projects?

b. Why has the U.S. Social Security Administration been so successful in using IT?

c. How important is the successful use of IT to the Social Security Administration? What would happen—and with what repercussions—if their systems failed?

Source Cone, Edward. 1998. "Social Security Gets It Right." InformationWeek, January 12, 48.

References

Applegate, L.M., and R. Montealegre. 1995. Eastman Kodak Co.: Managing information systems through strategic alliances. Harvard Business School, 9-192-030.

Brady. 1998. Information from: http://www.whbrady.com/. Verified: Feb. 2, 1998.

Garvin, D. A. 1993. Building a learning organization. *Harvard Business Review* (July–August): 78–91.

Gibbs, W. W. 1994. Software's chronic crisis. *Scientific American,* September, 86–95.

Hoffman, T. 1998. Group targets software labor shortage. *Computerworld,* January 12, 96.

King. J. 1998. Nerdy image feeds labor crisis. *Computerworld,* January 12, 1; 96.

Marable, L.M. 1995. The fifty hottest jobs in America. *Money,* March, 114–116.

McHugh, J. 1998. Computers and software. *Forbes,* January 12, 122–128.

Porter, M. E. 1985. *Competitive strategy.* New York: Free Press.

Shank, J. K., and V. Govindarajan. 1993. *Strategic cost management.* New York: Free Press.

Smith, Bremner, and Edmondson. 1996. Be it ever so pricey, high tech is still hot. *BusinessWeek,* June 17, 100–101.

Zuboff, S. 1984. *In the age of the smart machine: The future of work and power.* New York: Basic Books, Inc.

32

Related Readings

Attewell, P. 1992. Technology diffusion and organizational learning: The case of business computing. *Organization Science*. 3(1): 1–19.

Boland, Tenkasi, and Te'eni. 1994. Designing information technology to support distributed cognition. *Organization Science* 5(3): 456–475.

Cohen, W.M. and D.A. Levinthal. 1990. Absorptive capacity: A new perspective on learning and innovation. *Administrative Science Quarterly* 35(1): 128–152.

Dowling, M.J. and J.E. McGee. 1994. Business and technology strategies and new venture performance: A study of the telecommunications equipment industry. *Management Science* 40(12): 1663-1677.

Huber, G.P. 1991. Organizational learning: The contributing processes and the literatures. *Organization Science* 2(1): 88–115.

Jarvenpaa, S.L. and B. Ives. 1993. Organizing for global competition: The fit of information technology. *Decision Sciences* 24(3): 547–580.

Macdonald, S. 1995. Learning to change: An information perspective on learning in the organization. *Organization Science* 6(5): 557–568.

Mata, Fuerst, and Barney. 1995. Information technology and sustained competitive advantage: A resource-based analysis. *Management Information Systems Quarterly* 19(4): 487–505.

Reich, B.H. and I Benbasat. 1996. Measuring the linkage between business and information technology objectives. *Management Information Systems Quarterly* 20(1): 55–81.

Sethi, V. and W.R. King. 1994. Development of measures to assess the extent to which an information technology application provides competitive advantage. *Management Science* 40(12): 1601–1627.

Stein, E.W. and V. Zwass. 1995. Actualizing organizational memory with information systems. *Information Systems Research* 6(2): 85–117.

Swanson, E.B. 1994. Information systems innovation among organizations. *Management Science* 40(9): 1069-1092.

Zhu, Priehula, and Hsu. 1997. When processes learn: Steps toward crafting an intelligent organization. *Information Systems Research* 8(3): 302-317.

Chapter 2: Information Systems Hardware

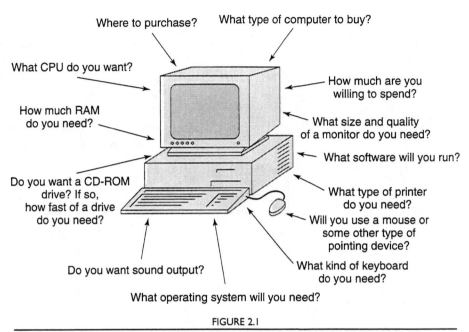

Where to purchase?

What type of computer to buy?

What CPU do you want?

How much are you willing to spend?

How much RAM do you need?

What size and quality of a monitor do you need?

What software will you run?

Do you want a CD-ROM drive? If so, how fast of a drive do you need?

What type of printer do you need?

Will you use a mouse or some other type of pointing device?

What kind of keyboard do you need?

Do you want sound output?

What operating system will you need?

FIGURE 2.1

The questions you face when purchasing a PC.

Windows-based computer with an Intel microprocessor, manufactured by one of the more dominant computer makers—such as IBM, HP, Compaq, Packard Bell, Dell, or Gateway 2000—and loaded with the fastest CD-ROM player and microprocessor, the best monitor and printer, and as much RAM and hard drive space as you can afford. This way, you are more likely to bet on a winner that will remain current for a longer period of time.

Our goal in this scenario is to illustrate how complex, difficult, and important something as simple as selecting a personal computer can be. In the rest of this chapter, we remove some of the mystery surrounding information system hardware. After you understand what all the pieces are and how they work together to make a computer system, you will be better able to make informed purchasing decisions for you and your organization.

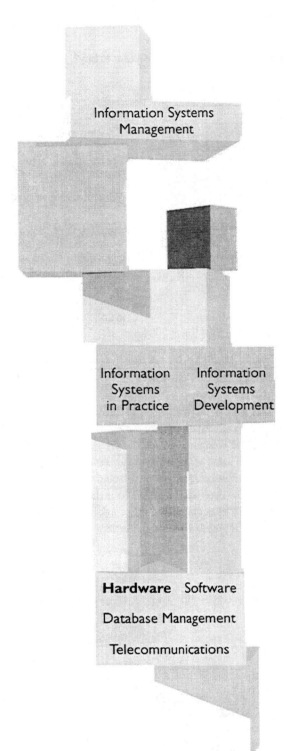

Information Systems
Management

Information
Systems
in Practice

Information
Systems
Development

Hardware Software

Database Management

Telecommunications

Introduction

As pointed out in the opening scenario, a broad range of options are available to you when you purchase a computer-based information system, and hardware is a central ingredient. Over the years, the price of hardware has become less expensive, making it possible for individuals and organizations of all sizes to take advantage of computer-based technologies. However, large computer systems can still easily cost more than a million dollars. Facing days of ever-shrinking budgets and a more competitive marketplace, organizations must take care to select the right hardware for the job or risk making a costly mistake. In order to make more informed decisions about IS hardware, you must have an understanding of what IS hardware is and how it works.

After reading this chapter, you will be able to do the following:

1. Understand the important role of information systems hardware in the success of modern organizations.

2. Describe key elements of information systems hardware.

3. List and describe the types of computers that are being used in organizations today.

4. Explain how hardware has evolved and where it is headed.

Given the importance technology plays in our lives, it is useful to understand the key underlying elements of IS hardware. Our approach in this chapter is not to bog you down with facts and jargon but to provide you with an overview. In terms of our guiding framework—The Big Picture—this is the first of four chapters focusing on the essential elements of information systems (see Figure 2.2).

FIGURE 2.2

The big picture: focusing on information systems hardware.

The Importance of Information Systems Hardware

As we discussed in Chapter 1, "Information Systems Overview," computer-based information systems are a key enabler for the competitive strategy and many day-to-day activities of nearly every modern organization. As a result, organizations have a strong motivation for acquiring the right equipment. As we showed in the opening scenario, making hardware choices is complicated. If an organization buys too little, its people may be idle while waiting for these under-powered systems to finish processing. If an organization buys too much, hardware may sit idle because it is unneeded or seldom used, while the firm incurs a large expense.

Organizations need information systems hardware in today's rapidly changing and highly competitive global economy for numerous reasons. There is an increasing need for real-time information. For example, global financial markets change by the second. If your organization relies on this data, you must have the capability to capture, store, and route this information to the appropriate decision makers instantaneously (see Figure 2.3). Alternatively, let's suppose that you own a manufacturing company that manages their inventories using a Just-In-Time (JIT) approach. At this company, the levels of manufacturing supplies and finished goods, as well as the costs associated with managing these inventories, are kept to a minimum. Computer monitoring of inventories must instantly notify suppliers when additional raw materials are needed so that your manufacturing processes do not go idle. The exchange of real-time information is needed in countless other situations as well. Remote offices must be connected with home offices. Remote sales personnel must be able to process orders, check product availability, communicate with their supervisor, and so on. In all instances, computer hardware facilitates the exchange of real-time information. This is strong motivation for investing in IS hardware.

Phil Cantor/Superstock

FIGURE 2.3

Wall Street trader analyzing rapidly changing data.

Key Elements of Information Systems Hardware

Information systems hardware is classified into three types: input, process, and output technologies (see Figure 2.4). Input-related hardware includes devices used to enter information into a computer. Process-related hardware transforms inputs into outputs. The central processing unit (CPU) is the device that performs this transformation, with the help of several other closely related devices that store and recall information. Finally, output-related hardware delivers information in a usable format to users. The focus of this section is to describe each of these three key elements of information systems hardware.

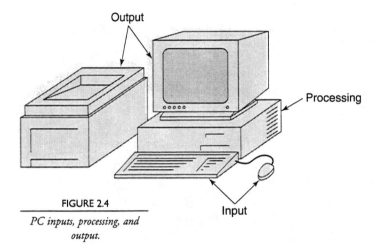

FIGURE 2.4

PC inputs, processing, and output.

Input: How Information Is Entered into an Information System

In order for information systems hardware to perform a task, data must be input into the system. As you will see, this can be done in many ways because different types of information can be entered more easily using one type of input device versus another. For example, keyboards are currently the primary means to enter text and numbers. Alternatively, architects and engineers often want to enter their designs and drawings into computers. Many special types of pointing devices have been developed to simulate the process of drawing or sketching on a sheet of paper. A great deal of research and development has been conducted to identify optimal ways to input various types of information and to build and sell new input devices. In this section, we describe some of the most commonly used input devices. To organize this discussion, we classify input methods into four general categories by the type of information being entered: entering original text/numbers, selecting and pointing, entering batch data, and entering audio and video. Table 2.1 summarizes the fundamental characteristics of each category.

Table 2.1 Methods of providing input to an information system.

Information Category	Representative Device(s)
Entering original text/numbers	Keyboard
Selecting and pointing	Mouse Trackball and joysticks Touch screen Light pen
Entering batch data	Scanners Bar code/optical character readers
Entering audio and video	Microphones and speakers Video and digital cameras MIDI

Entering Original Text/Numbers

One of the primary computer-based applications is the entry of text and numbers. The primary device used to support this type of input is the **keyboard**. Used first as the input method on typewriters, keyboard data entry is a mainstay of the computer industry. A recent advance in keyboard technology is the development of ergonomically correct keyboards, which are designed to reduce the stress placed on the wrists, hands, and arms when typing. Figure 2.5 shows a normal keyboard and the Microsoft Natural keyboard. When typing for long periods, some users develop aching, numbing, and tingling in their arms, wrists, or hands. These injuries are generally referred to as **repetitive stress injuries**. The broadened use of computers in the workplace and the associated injuries to workers, resulting in more sick days and insurance claims, has made the ergonomics of keyboards and employees' workstations much more important to organizations. In the bulleted list that follows Figure 2.5, we describe ways to reduce repetitive stress injuries.

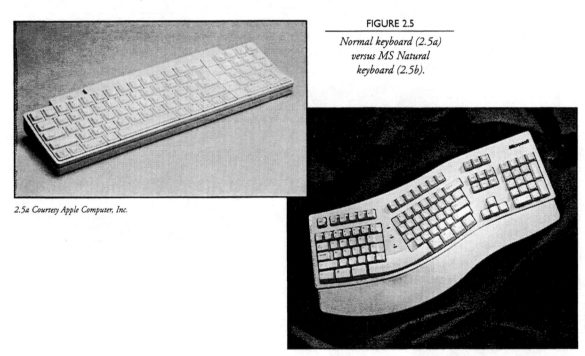

FIGURE 2.5

Normal keyboard (2.5a) versus MS Natural keyboard (2.5b).

2.5a Courtesy Apple Computer, Inc.

2.5b Courtesy Microsoft Corporation

- Have an ergonomically designed workplace—desk, chair, monitor size and angle, keyboard height and position.

- Take frequent breaks from typing. When your wrists and fingers start to ache, take a break.

- Maintain a straight wrist position when typing. Don't let wrist bend up/down or left/right.

- Avoid resting on your wrists while typing. Keep your wrists elevated off the desk.

■ Use a light touch on the keys. Don't press harder on the keyboard to enter information than you need to press.

■ Maintain good health habits and exercise your arms, wrists, and hands.

Selecting and Pointing

In addition to entering text and numbers, **pointing devices** are used to select items from menus, to point, and to sketch or draw (see Figure 2.6). As with keyboards, you probably have used a pointing device, such as a mouse, when using a graphical operating environment (such as Microsoft Windows) or when playing a video game. Several of the most popular types of pointing devices are listed in Table 2.2.

Table 2.2 Selecting and pointing devices.

Device	Description
Mouse	Pointing device that works by sliding a small box-like device on a flat surface; selections are made by pressing buttons on the mouse.
Trackball	Pointing device that works by rolling a ball that sits in a holder; selections are made by pressing buttons located near or on the holder.
Joystick	Pointing device that works by moving a small stick that sits in a holder; selections are made by pressing buttons located near or on the holder.
Touch screen	A method of input for which you use your finger; selections are made by touching the computer display.
Light pen	Pointing device that works by placing a pen-like device near a computer screen; selections are made by pressing the pen to the screen.

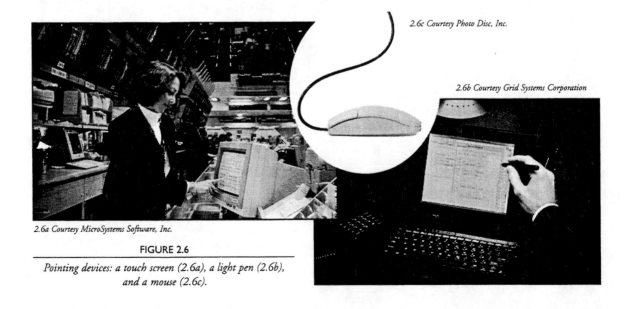

2.6c Courtesy Photo Disc, Inc.

2.6b Courtesy Grid Systems Corporation

2.6a Courtesy MicroSystems Software, Inc.

FIGURE 2.6

Pointing devices: a touch screen (2.6a), a light pen (2.6b), and a mouse (2.6c).

The Birth of the Mouse

Speaking of mice, although it is true that Apple Computer made the mouse popular in the 1980s, the real inventor of the mouse was Doug Engelbart. He invented it in the early 1960s while working for the Stanford Research Institute (SRI). It was not until the mid-1980s that Apple Computer contacted SRI to purchase the rights to the mouse—reportedly for only about $40,000! Dr. Engelbart is also credited as the original developer of hypertext and videoconferencing—all in the 1960s. Many of these discoveries were not widely known or diffused into mainstream computing for almost 30 years. (For more information on the birth of the mouse and Dr. Engelbart, visit http://www.superkids.com/aweb/pages/features/mouse/mouse.html or use a search engine and search for "Doug Engelbart." You are likely to come up with a lot of hits!)

Entering Batch Data

Along with keyboards and pointing devices, a third category of computer-based input is referred to as **batch input**. Batch input is most often used when a great deal of routine information needs to be entered into the computer. Two widely used batch data input devices are scanners and bar code/optical character readers. **Scanners** convert printed text and images into digital data. They range from a small handheld device that looks like a mouse to a large desktop box that resembles a personal photocopier, both of which are shown in Figure 2.7. Rather than duplicating the image on another piece of paper, the computer translates the image into digital information that can be stored or manipulated by the computer. Special **text recognition software** can convert handwritten text into the computer-based characters that form the original letters and words. Insurance companies, universities, and other organizations that routinely process large batches of forms and documents have applied scanner technology to increase employee productivity.

FIGURE 2.7

Handheld (2.7a) and flat-bed (2.7b) scanners.

2.7a Courtesy Intermec Technologies Corp.

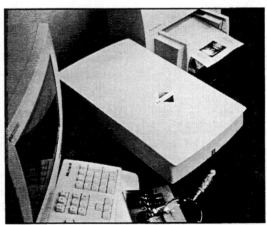

2.7b Courtesy Hewlett-Packard Company

An extension of the general purpose scanner is the **bar code/optical character reader**. Like scanners, these devices use light to scan magnetic information on a package or document and then input this information into a computer. Figure 2.8 shows a sample bar code reader. For example, grocery stores use bar code readers as clerks pass the UPC (Universal Product Code) over a bar code reader implanted in the checkout stand. Banks use optical character readers to process batches of checks through their systems. The U.S. military uses bar codes to assist in inventorying bombs, ammunition, and other precious equipment. Needless to say, a broad range of organizations has gained significant benefits from applying scanner-related technologies to their day-to-day operations.

FIGURE 2.8

UPC bar code and check.

```
John Doe                                          0101
123 Main Street                                   12-345
Anywhere, USA 00000              _____ 19 ___   00

Pay to the
order of _____ $ [      ]
_____ DOLLARS

First National Bank
Downtown Branch
P.O. Box 456
Anywhere, USA 00000
Memo _____
⑆121000358⑆0101⑈01234⑈56789⑈        ⑈000000276 5⑈
```

Audio and Video

An emerging method for entering information is through **audio input** devices. Audio-based input, which can be done in several ways, is helpful when a user's hands need to be free to do other tasks. A special form of controlling and manipulating audio input is through the Musical Instrument Digital Interface (MIDI). MIDI is a specification for using the computer to record, sample, mix, and play music. Musical instruments, amplifiers, and other equipment can be connected to a computer through a MIDI.

A final way in which information can be entered into a computer is through **video input**. For example, televisions and videocassette recorders can be connected to computers as input devices. Digital cameras have also been developed to quickly capture still images. Video input is widely used to assist in security-related applications, such as room monitoring and employee verification. Also, teleconferences can be held on your personal computer using simple video cameras, which cost less than $100 (see Figure 2.9).

FIGURE 2.9

Connectix QuickCam video camera.

QuickCam is a registered trademark of Connectix Corporation.

In manufacturing applications, high-resolution video cameras are used to evaluate the quality of products by taking a picture of a new product or part and comparing this image with one stored in a database. If the images match, the part passes a quality control inspection. If the images do not match, the part can be rejected without human intervention. Both audio and video input are expected to increase in popularity in the near future.

In this section, we have described numerous options for providing input to a computer. After information is entered into a computer, it can be processed, stored, and manipulated. In the next section, we describe the processing aspects of information systems hardware.

Processing: Transforming Inputs into Outputs

Computer input and output are easy for us to understand, yet the language computers use to process information is not easy for us to understand. The computer converts inputs into a language it understands, a language made up of special computer codes. This means that all text, numbers, sounds, and video must be converted into a common format that the computer can store and manipulate. The language of internal computer processing is in binary notation. Binary information is simply a series of 0s and 1s. Each 0 or 1 is referred to as a **bit** or binary digit. A combination of eight bits is typically referred to as a **byte**. For example, one keyboard character, such as the letter "A," is stored as a single byte of information.

To translate a word, number, or sound into a series of binary digits, the computer industry has developed internal computer language codes that represent and translate information. For example, the most widely used code for representing text and numbers is called **ASCII** (American Standard Code of Information Interchange, pronounced "askey"). Table 2.3 shows the ASCII codes for representing the alphabet and the numbers 0–9. Standard codes for representing graphics, sounds, and video have also been developed. When you enter information into a computer, it automatically translates the information into binary.

Table 2.3 ASCII codes for alphabet and numbers.

Character	ASCII-8 Binary Code	Character	ASCII-8 Binary Code
A	1010 0001	S	1011 0011
B	1010 0010	T	1011 0100
C	1010 0011	U	1011 0101
D	1010 0100	V	1011 0110
E	1010 0101	W	1011 0111
F	1010 0110	X	1011 1000
G	1010 0111	Y	1011 1001
H	1010 1000	Z	1011 1010
I	1010 1001	0	0101 0000
J	1010 1010	1	0101 0001
K	1010 1011	2	0101 0010

continues

Table 2.3 Continued.

Character	ASCII-8 Binary Code	Character	ASCII-8 Binary Code
L	1010 1100	3	0101 0011
M	1010 1101	4	0101 0100
N	1010 1110	5	0101 0101
O	1010 1111	6	0101 0110
P	1011 0000	7	0101 0111
Q	1011 0001	8	0101 1000
R	1011 0010	9	0101 1001

Within the processing component of the computer, there are three key internal elements: primary storage, secondary storage, and the central processing unit (CPU), as depicted in Figure 2.10. When information is input to a computer, it is temporarily stored in primary storage before being permanently stored in secondary storage or being manipulated by the CPU. Likewise, when information is output from a computer, it is stored in primary storage before being sent to some output device, such as a video display or printer. For example, if you type a term paper on your PC, the characters you type are moved from the keyboard to the primary storage area (see Figure 2.10). This movement of characters is controlled by the CPU (and the operating system—see Chapter 3, "Information Systems Software," for a discussion of operating systems). When you save your work, these characters are copied from the primary storage to a secondary storage device, such as a floppy disk (see Figure 2.10). The CPU controls this movement of characters to the secondary storage. At some later date, when you decide to print a copy of your paper, you make this request by inputting commands to the processor. After they are input, these commands are stored in primary storage and interpreted by the CPU. After they are interpreted, the CPU instructs the secondary storage to recall your term paper and load it into primary storage. The CPU can send your term paper to the printer after it is loaded into primary storage (see Figure 2.10).

FIGURE 2.10

Computer components showing the path through primary storage, secondary storage, and the central processing unit.

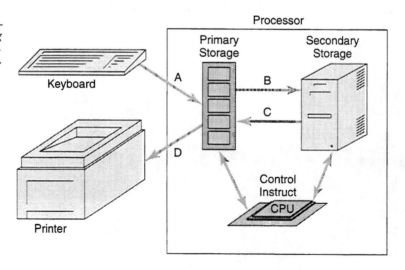

In sum, all input and output passes through primary storage. All information stored in secondary storage is moved to primary storage before being output or manipulated. The CPU is the "traffic cop" in the process. It interprets the meaning of commands. It translates input into binary information and binary information into information that can be understood by humans. CPU controls both input and output processes. Now that you have a general understanding of what happens during processing, we describe in detail each of these three processing components.

Primary Storage: Storage for Current Information

When a computer makes calculations or manipulates data in some way, it needs a place to store the information it is currently working on. This storage location is called **primary storage**, or simply memory. Memory is measured in bytes. Each byte is about one keyboard character (see Table 2.4). For example, a paper that you write for class may contain 30 thousand bytes (in computer lingo, 30 kilobytes or 30KB). A large software program may contain several million bytes (megabytes or MB). Databases containing billions of bytes of information (gigabytes or GB) make up IRS taxpayer records. Memory is very important to a computer's performance. Without enough memory, some programs may not run, and if they do run, they may run very slowly. Computers have different types of memory—each type having somewhat different characteristics and roles in information processing. We describe each in more detail in the sections that follow.

Table 2.4 Elements of computer storage.

Name	Number of Bytes	Description	Abbreviation
Kilobyte*	1,000*	One thousand bytes	KB
Megabyte	1,000,000	One million bytes	MB
Gigabyte	1,000,000,000	One billion bytes	GB
Terabyte	1,000,000,000,000	One trillion bytes	TB

* A kilobyte is actually 1,024 bytes.

ROM (Read-Only Memory)

ROM is memory that cannot be changed by the processor or user of the computer, hence the name read-only. ROM is nonvolatile, meaning that it does not lose its instructions when the computer is powered off. Because of this characteristic, computer manufacturers typically use ROM to hold the instructions for starting the computer and for running predefined maintenance processes.

not expandable

RAM (Random-Access Memory)

RAM is what we most commonly think of as memory. Unlike ROM, RAM is volatile and can be changed as you work on your computer. For example, when you load an application such as Microsoft Word to type a paper for class, both the application program and your paper are stored in RAM. If you turn the computer off without saving, you will lose your work. In essence, when the computer is turned off, RAM loses all its stored values and instructions. Therefore, anything in RAM that the user wants to reuse should be written to secondary storage. Many personal computers sold today are

expandable

equipped with 16 megabytes (MB) of RAM, an amount needed to run popular operating systems such as Windows 95 and Windows NT. RAM is typically configured as a SIMM (single in-line memory module), which is simply a small circuit board that contains one or more RAM chips. A sample SIMM chip is shown in Figure 2.11.

FIGURE 2.11

A SIMM chip.

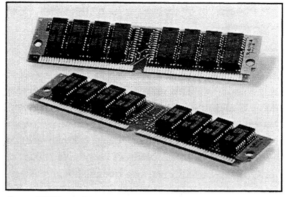

Courtesy IBM Corporation

Cache Memory

Cache memory is a special type of RAM that is extremely fast and expensive. Cache memory is used to store information that is used a lot by the CPU. Cache memory can dramatically boost the speed of a computer by storing commonly used instructions that would normally be stored on RAM or on a secondary storage device, such as a fixed disk. When these instructions are needed, the CPU can quickly retrieve them from the cache, rather than from some other, slower storage area. To compare the relative amounts of RAM and cache, a typical PC with 16MB of RAM may have only 256 or 512KB of cache memory.

Secondary Storage: Keeping Information for Later Use

Secondary storage archives data and programs so that they can be accessed as needed. Computer processing does us little good unless we can store the information for later use. Several technologies have evolved in the last 50 years for storing computerized data. Table 2.5 describes many storage methods and provides a comparison of their speed, method of access, and relative cost. We describe each of these secondary storage methods in the following sections.

Table 2.5 Comparing methods of secondary storage.

Type	Speed	Method of Data Access	Relative Cost/MB
Magnetic tape	Slow	Sequential	Low
Floppy disks	Slow	Direct	Low
Fixed disks	Fast	Direct	High
Compact discs	Medium	Direct	Medium
Optical disks	Fast	Direct	Medium

FIGURE 2.12

*Sequential access of
information.*

Magnetic Tape

Magnetic tape was one of
the earliest methods of
storing and retrieving
computer-generated data.
Just as with audio cassette
tapes, data is written by
magnetically rearranging
the atoms on the tape.
Tape uses **sequential data**

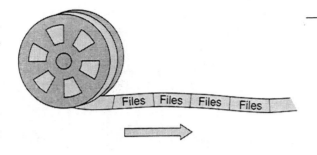

access, meaning that if you want to access a particular piece of information, you must
wind through the tape to get to the location of that information, as depicted in Figure
2.12. After that information is located, it can be read into the computer. Similarly, you
must be very careful when writing to tape. If any information is stored where you are
writing, you will overwrite that information—much like taping over a song on an audio
tape. Magnetic tape is primarily used today for backing up large amounts of data, such
as payroll records. It is rarely used as a primary means of secondary storage. While it is
very cheap, it is also very slow because you have to move sequentially through the tape
to write and retrieve information.

Floppy Disks

Floppy disks were the next widely used technique for providing secondary computer
storage. A floppy disk is a small magnetic disk protected from dirt and dust by
a plastic coating. A *read/write head*, which is positioned very close to the disk surface,
reads or writes information to and from the disk while the disk is spinning, as depicted
in Figure 2.13. Because the read/write head can move back and forth across the disk surface, information on the disk can be accessed directly. You don't need to read other data
that was recorded before. This type of access—going directly to the spot on the disk
where the desired information is stored—is called **direct data access** (or random access).
Direct data access was a major breakthrough in secondary storage technology because it
significantly enhanced the speed of storing and retrieving computer-based information.
The first floppy disks available in the 1970s were eight inches across and stored less than
a few hundred thousand bytes.

Today's floppy disks are typically 2.5 inches and can be formatted to hold 1.44MB or
2.88MB of information. Very high-capacity floppy drives, such as Iomega's ZIP Drive,
store more than 100MB on a single disk! Until recently, floppy disks were the primary
means to transfer information from one computer to another and to distribute retail
software. As newer applications become more sophisticated and therefore larger, more
applications are distributed using CD-ROMs, which are discussed in the next section.

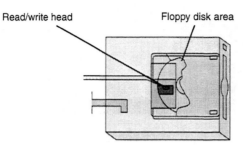

FIGURE 2.13

Floppy disk area and read/write head.

Fixed Disks

Fixed disks, also referred to as hard disks or hard drives, are an extension of the floppy disk technology, but they have much greater capacities and data transfer speeds. Therefore, fixed disks have become the most commonly used method for providing secondary storage. A typical fixed disk has several magnetic layers, called platters, that are located in a sealed, clean environment, as shown in Figure 2.14. Fixed disks have several read/write heads, one for reading and writing to each separate surface. Fixed disks also spin at very high speeds, and the read/write heads are positioned to be very close to (but not touching) the magnetic surface. Because fixed disks spin at a much higher rate and the sealed environment allows special high-storage capacity materials to be used, each platter has a huge storage capacity and a much faster data transfer rate than a floppy disk. A single fixed disk, for example, can hold hundreds or thousands of megabytes of information.

FIGURE 2.14

Multiple fixed platters and read/write heads.

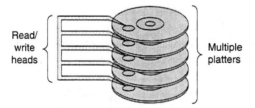

CD-ROM (Compact Disc-Read-Only Memory)

CD-ROM is an increasingly popular method for distributing software and backing up information. Using the same technology as audio CD players, lasers burn information onto a compact disc by creating pits in the disc, as shown in Figure 2.15. Information is retrieved from the disk by having a special type of laser interpret the sequence of pits as data. CD-ROMs are typically a WORM (write-once, read-many) technology; after data is written to the disc, it cannot be changed.

FIGURE 2.15

CD-ROM picture magnified to show pits on the surface.

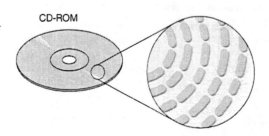

CD-ROMs are popular with software developers for distributing systems and data. The average CD-ROM holds 650MB of information—*the same amount it takes over 450 individual floppy disks to hold!* Like floppy and fixed disks, CD-ROMs provide direct access to information. The data transfer rates for CD-ROM technology are not as high as they are for a fixed disk, but they are still much faster than for a floppy. When CD-ROM disks are copied from a master disk with the same data pattern, they can cost manufacturers less than $1 each to produce. CD-R (CD-Recordable) drives have been available to the public in the last few years. These drives enable you to create CD-ROMs on your personal computer. CD-R drives are becoming increasingly inexpensive and can be found for less than $750. Blank recordable discs cost less than $10 each. Given that the cost of this storage is about one cent per megabyte, many companies are turning to CD-Rs for backup and archiving of data.

Optical Disks

Optical disks are an emerging technology born from research and development related to CD-ROMs. Like CD-ROM technology, optical disks provide direct access to data, with the added benefit of being able to be rewritten many times. Optical disks also have tremendous capacities. They often have more than one gigabyte (GB) on a single disk. The disks themselves are relatively inexpensive, often around $100 for a one-GB disk. Optical disk players, however, still cost over $1,000, making optical disks too costly to be widely used by individuals and organizations.

The Central Processing Unit: The Brain of the Computer

The final process component is the **central processing unit (CPU)**, where the computer calculates and manipulates data. The CPU, also referred to as the computer's main microprocessor, processor, or chip, is composed of millions of tiny transistors. These transistors arranged in complex patterns that allow the CPU to interpret and manipulate data. The inner workings of a CPU are very complex. For most of us, it is easiest to think of a CPU as being a "black box" where all the processing occurs. The CPU is a small device made of silicon. For example, the Intel Pentium II® CPU is about 2 square inches in surface area and less than .5 inch thick, as shown in Figure 2.16. Within these two square inches are more than 5 million transistors!

The number of transistors that can be packed into a modern CPU and the speed at which processing and other activities occur are remarkable. For example, the Intel Pentium II® can complete hundreds of mil-

Courtesy Intel

FIGURE 2.16

The Intel Pentium II.

lions of operations every second. To achieve these incredible speeds, things must occur very rapidly within the computer, and the things that occur the fastest are inside the CPU (see Table 2.6). For example, it takes a fixed disk about 10 milliseconds to access information. Within a CPU, however, a single transistor can be changed from one state to another in about 10 picoseconds (one trillionth of a second). This means that activities occur inside the CPU about one billion times faster than they do in a fixed disk. The primary reason for this huge speed difference is that CPUs only operate on electronic impulses. Fixed disks have both electronic and mechanical activities occurring, such as the spinning disk and moving read/write head. Mechanical activities are extremely slow relative to electronic activities, which move at close to the speed of light!

Table 2.6 Elements of computer time.

Name	Fraction of a Second	Description	Example
Millisecond	1/1000	One thousandth of a second	Fixed disks access information in about 10–20 milliseconds.
Microsecond	1/1,000,000	One millionth of a second	A 200MHz CPU executes approximately 200 million operations in a second—or about 200 operations every microsecond.
Nanosecond	1/1,000,000,000	One billionth of a second	Most types of RAM used in PCs have access times (the time needed to read information from the RAM to the CPU) from 60–100 nanoseconds (lower is better). Most cache memory has access times of less than 20 nanoseconds.
Picosecond	1/1,000,000,000,000	One trillionth of a second	Inside a CPU, the time it takes to switch a circuit from one state to another is in the range of 5–20 picoseconds.

When you decide which computer to purchase, one of your primary considerations is its overall speed. Over the years, CPU manufacturers, such as Intel, Motorola, and Digital Equipment Corporation (DEC), have spent a considerable amount of effort defining how best to measure the performance of a computer. The easiest way to compare the performance of one computer to another is to contrast the number of instructions each can perform in a given period of time. Because CPUs operate at such high speeds, the unit of time for this comparison is typically only one second. Most modern computers can perform more than a million instructions in a second. This is quite a shift from the original "big iron" mainframe computers of the 1950s, 60s, and 70s, which took up many large rooms and processed fewer than one million instructions in a second.

Now that you understand more about how information is input into a computer and how it is processed, we can turn our attention to the third category of hardware—output technologies.

Output: How Information Is Displayed and Printed

After information is input and processed, it must be presented to the user. Although information can be entered into the computer in several different ways, our output choices are relatively simple. Computers can display information on a screen, print it, or emit sound. Details on how each of these types of devices operate are discussed in the sections that follow.

Video Output

Monitors are typically used to display information from a computer. They usually consist of a cathode ray tube (CRT), which is similar to a television, but with much higher resolution. Monitors can be color, black and white, or monochrome (meaning all one color, usually green or amber). Notebooks and other portable computers use liquid crystal display (LCD) or plasma screens because a CRT is too bulky for a portable device. The research and development of monitor technologies is focusing on creating lightweight, low-cost, high-resolution devices. Because display monitors are being embedded into a broad range of products and devices, such as automobiles, to display global positioning, route maps, and other relevant information, they must be sturdy, reliable, lightweight, and low in cost. Someday, all televisions and computers will use lightweight display panels that are similar to those used on notebook and laptop computers.

Paper-based Displays

Information can be printed in several different ways, as shown in Figure 2.17. A **plotter** is normally used for transferring engineering designs from the computer to drafting paper, which is often as big as 34"×44". Several pens are used by the plotter as it draws each of the lines individually. **Dot-matrix printers** are older, electric-typewriter-based technology for printing information to paper. Letters are formed using a series of small dots. Once the most commonly used type of printer, dot-matrix printers are now mostly found printing voluminous batch information, such as periodic reports and forms. **Inkjet printers** use a small cartridge to transfer ink onto paper. This process creates a typewriter-like image that can initially smear because the ink is wet when it is sprayed onto the paper. Inkjet printers can be designed to print both black and white and color. **Laser printers** are the most commonly used printers today. They use an electrostatic process to force ink onto the paper, literally "burning" the image onto the paper. The result is a high-quality image considered necessary for almost all business letters and documents. Laser printers can also produce color images, but high-end color laser printers can cost in excess of $10,000.

ETHICAL PERSPECTIVE: DESKTOP PUBLISHING AND COMPUTER CRIME

Personal computers. Desktop publishing software. Scanners. Color printers. These have become the tools of trade for a new form of computer crime involving the alteration of images and the creation of bogus documentation. Rapid advancements, decreased prices, and increased availability of hardware and software for desktop publishing and artwork have made it much easier for people to falsify images and documents or to simply create them out of thin air. Without much more than a PC, a scanner, and a good desktop publishing package or photo/video editing package, anyone can take an original image and modify it in nearly any way. The image created will be of professional quality.

Using this technology to manipulate the signature on a copy of a check, once thought to be a complex task, is now relatively easy. Sophisticated computer criminals can now use the technology to manipulate more complex images. It is now relatively easy to take a snapshot of a person and change the skin tones, eye color, hair color, and facial expressions. Even placing an image of one person's head on another person's body is a fairly easy task. Some useful purposes do exist for this technology. For example, department stores increasingly rely on this technology to show their customers the look of new clothes, hairstyles, or contact lenses. In addition, plastic surgeons are now using similar technology to show their patients the results of multiple potential surgeries inexpensively. The problems arise when this technology is used to make people look different than they really look without their knowledge and consent. How many times have you wondered whether or not the photograph on the cover of the tabloid sitting on the supermarket shelf was modified? Chances are that it was.

Similarly, the same technology allows the computer user to not only change simple colors on a photograph or an image, but to completely overhaul the image itself. Backgrounds can be exchanged and people can be deleted or added—creating an entirely new picture or image. These capabilities can be used toward positive, creative ends. For example, the last feature film you saw probably used computer-generated or computer-modified filming.

Unfortunately, these capabilities are often used illegally and unethically. A *New York Newsday* cover photograph in February of 1994 after the now infamous attack on Nancy Kerrigan showed figure skaters Kerrigan and Tonya Harding practicing together on the ice. However, they were not on the ice together, as they were in the digitally doctored image. This image caused much debate in journalistic corners about the "ultimate journalistic sin."

A similar form of this type of computer crime involves the use of high-resolution scanners and laser printers to create fake documentation, IDs, tickets, and even counterfeit money. Criminals can take the original image, scan it, modify it, and print electronically "forged" copies. Given its monetary implications and close ties to more traditional forms of forgery, this form of computer crime is much more closely watched by the police and the government than the doctoring of images.

The U.S. government has been constantly fighting the counterfeiters by producing increasingly complex currency and by making people aware of what to look for in counterfeit money. You may, for example, have recently used the new $100 bill, designed to be more difficult to counterfeit.

One of the difficulties with computer crimes of this nature is that the criminal only needs to purchase several components of completely legal technology and be able to use them. There is no crime in owning a computer, a scanner, a color printer, or desktop publishing software, and each is fairly easy to set up and use. Furthermore, in the technology realm, what is unethical isn't always illegal. The fight to stop computer crime is not easy or well-defined.

Questions for Discussion

1. The United States government recently began circulation of new $100 bills that are more difficult to scan and copy. However, this circulation came at a significant cost. The price for the technology and research was well over $750,000. Is the government's costly effort to keep our money tamper-resistant the best solution to money counterfeiting? Why or why not?

2. What should be done to either punish or stop people from committing these types of computer crimes? Why?

3. Do you believe that it is wrong to alter someone's personal photographic image without her consent? What if the person were famous?

Sources *February 17, 1994*. New York Times, A12. *Figures are from communication with Dale Servetnick, Staff Assistant at the Office of Public Correspondence of the U.S. Treasury Department. For specific information on the $100 bill, see the U.S. Treasury Department's home page at http://www.us.treas.gov.*

INTERNATIONAL PERSPECTIVE: THE EVOLUTION OF THE ASIAN GIANTS

Indonesia, Legend, Mitac, Creative Technology—not familiar with the names of these high-tech companies? You don't have long to wait! These Asian businesses—located in Asian countries as disparate as Japan, the Philippines, Singapore, Korea, and Taiwan—are developing global strategies that are quickly providing them with a competitive advantage in the world marketplace. These companies are taking on new managerial styles, dividing into smaller units, and spreading throughout the globe as they strive to lead the world in the production of PCs and computer parts, telecommunications equipment, integrated circuits, and digital services. In partnership with the U.S. and other companies, Asian high-tech firms are quickly becoming technology powerhouses around the world.

A case in point is Texas Instruments' Thai partner, the Alphatec Group, packagers and testers of microchips. The group is undertaking massive expansion and expects to reach $4 billion in sales by the year 2000—making this achievement in an area of the world that is expected to be the second biggest market (after the U.S.) within the next several years. What is driving the success of Alphatec? Clifford (1996) attributes much of its success to the fact that its chair, Charn Uswachoke, received a good education and training in the U.S. and has many years of experience dealing with Western organizations and people. In addition, the ethnic Chinese community in Thailand, of which Uswachoke is a member, provides financial support to the group.

Developing high-tech industries in countries that do not yet have them is not that easy, however; many companies experience a scarcity of qualified employees, a lack of knowledge about the design and construction of physical plants, and inadequate IT infrastructures. Workers brought in from partner companies or hired as consultants from outside of the region risk area-specific diseases, culture-bound problems, and management style clashes, in addition to any number of other uncertainties.

Asian companies are being helped by the boom in technology use in Asia. Brull, Hof, Flynn, and Gross (1996) note projections that the Japanese alone will spend over $600 billion on telecommunications products and services by the year 2000, a 53 percent increase from 1993. In addition to the increase in chip exports to overseas buyers, this boom has had a major impact on Japan's Fujitsu, Ltd. Now the top computer manufacturer in Japan and second in the world after IBM, Fujitsu is branching out into Internet and multimedia and is putting the weight of its financial and technical capabilities behind this new venture. However, to break into markets overseas, where it has not been successful in the past, Fujitsu has had to change the way the business is run and the kind of products it markets. Changes include relaxing the strict Japanese standards of dress and conduct, allowing employees to make their own hours and work on their own projects, and hiring younger, Western-educated employees with cutting-edge views of what the future can be.

Many factors could stop the advance of these Asian companies in IT markets. If the chip market, for example, were to bottom out, many of the companies that have staked their fortunes in this area would be in trouble. For the time being, however, the IT companies would do well to keep an eye on their competitors in the East.

Questions for Discussion

1. What other factors have precipitated the rise of the Asian companies?

2. What factors could inhibit the continued success of these Asian companies?

3. What should U.S. companies do to maintain a strategic advantage?

Sources Brull, Hof, Flynn, and Gross. 1996. *Fujitsu gets wired*. Business Week, March 18, 110–112.

Clifford, M. 1996. *The magical moneyman of Thailand*. Business Week, Dec 25./Jan. 1, 52.

FIGURE 2.17

A plotter (2.17a), a dot matrix (2.17b), an inkjet (2.17c), and a laser printer (2.17d).

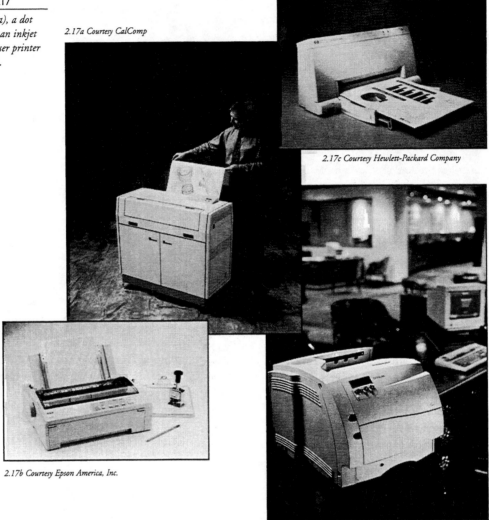

2.17a Courtesy CalComp

2.17c Courtesy Hewlett-Packard Company

2.17b Courtesy Epson America, Inc.

2.17d Courtesy Lexmark International

Audio Output

A computer can now also transmit audio as output. With the use of small specialized speakers and a *sound card*, stereo-quality sound can come from a computer. The computer translates digits into sound by sending data to a sound card that interprets this data into tones. The tones are then sent to the speakers for output. Musicians and composers often use this output to simulate a full orchestra when working on new or unfamiliar pieces of music.

Now that you have a fundamental understanding of how computer hardware works, we can discuss the types of computers that people and organizations typically use.

Types of Computers

We talked about the three basic hardware building blocks—input, process, and output technologies—that you would find in nearly every computer, large or small. In this section, we describe the many different types of computers that are made up of these three basic building blocks. Table 2.7 gives you a sneak preview of the types of computers we will discuss. Computers come in all shapes, sizes, degrees of power, and costs. We will present these computer types to you, beginning first with the fastest, biggest, and most costly computers, and ending with the slower, smaller, and cheaper computers.

Table 2.7 Relative comparison of types of computers.

Type of Computer	Performance	Memory (RAM)	Physical Size	Typical Cost Range
Supercomputer	1 to 100 GigaFLOPS*	100 to 2000GB	Like an automobile	$1,000,000 to over $20,000,000
Mainframe	Up to 1000 MIPS	Up to 2GB	Like a refrigerator	$1,000,000 to over $10,000,000
Minicomputer	250 to more than 500 MIPS	Up to 2GB	Like a file cabinet	$10,000 to over $100,000
Workstation	100 to 500 MIPS	32 to 64MB	Fits on a desktop	$5,000 to over $50,000
Microcomputer	100 to 300 MIPS	16 to 32MB	Fits on a desktop	$1,000 to over $5,000

* GigaFLOPS, billions of floating point operations per second, and MIPS, millions of instructions per second, are both common metrics for computer speed ratings.

Supercomputers

The most powerful and expensive computers that exist today are called **supercomputers**. Figure 2.18 shows a Cray supercomputer, one of the more popular computers in this class. Supercomputers usually cost many millions of dollars. They are equipped with numerous very fast processors that work in parallel to execute several instructions simultaneously. These special-purpose computers are used by researchers and scientists to solve very complex problems that were literally unsolvable until these computational giants were created (Cray Research, 1998). For example, Sandia National Laboratories uses a supercomputer to model fallout from

Courtesy SiliconGraphics Computer Systems

FIGURE 2.18

The Cray supercomputer.

nuclear explosions and other nuclear phenomena. This particular machine has several gigabytes of RAM and the computational horsepower of more than 9,000 Pentium processors. Pharmaceutical companies, such as Eli Lilly and Dow Chemical, use supercomputers to design and evaluate new combinations of chemical elements in order to quickly identify promising prescription drugs and treatments. An extensive staff is usually required to operate and maintain supercomputers and to support the researchers and scientists using them.

Mainframes

The backbone of large corporate computing has historically been large, high-powered computers called **mainframes**. Figure 2.19 shows an IBM mainframe, one of the more popular computers in this class. These machines can be the size of a large refrigerator (and even larger), and they often cost several million dollars to purchase. In spite of their size and cost, however, a few companies even own more than one. While mainframe computers typically don't have the power and speed of supercomputers, mainframe computers are still very fast and are normally used for enterprise-wide computing. Many federal and state governments use mainframe computers to manage the massive amount of data generated by day-to-day governmental activities. Federal agencies, such as the Internal Revenue Service (IRS), have several mainframe computers to handle the massive databases related to individual and corporate payroll and tax information. Large corporations, such as Alamo Rent-A-Car, American Airlines, and Holiday Inn, use mainframes to perform repetitive tasks, such as processing reservations.

FIGURE 2.19

IBM mainframe.

Courtesy IBM Corporation

IBM at the Olympics

The company synonymous with mainframe computing is IBM, which has long dominated the mainframe market. Today, IBM provides many organizations with some of the most powerful mainframes ever created (see Table 2.8). For the 1996 Summer Olympics in Atlanta, IBM provided the Olympic Committee with the free use of an IBM System/390. This machine served as the heart of a networked computing environment used by 150,000 athletes, coaches, officials, media, and other members of the Olympic family during the 1996 Olympic Games. One key component of this system was the "Results System," which delivered real-time information to the broadcasters reporting on the games worldwide.

Table 2.8 Applications of IBM mainframe computers in organizations (IBM, 1998).

Organization	Application
Alamo Rent-A-Car	Customer reservation and car tracking system
American Airlines	Global customer reservation system (Saber)
Holiday Inn	Global reservation system
State governments	Payroll, individual and company taxes, motor vehicle licensing, division and offices of government, and so on
Universities	Student grades, course registrations, payroll, financial management, and so on

See IBM's World Wide Web home page (http://www.ibm.com) for more on how mainframe computers are being used.

Minicomputers

Minicomputers are scaled-down versions of mainframes. They were created when companies had needs for fast enterprise computers but did not need all the power of a mainframe or could not afford one. For example, a mid-sized business might use a minicomputer to process its payroll, to conduct online order entry, and to perform other tasks, but it might not have the funds or the workload to justify buying a mainframe computer. In this way, minicomputers have become integral to many smaller and mid-sized organizations. These computers usually cost tens to hundreds of thousands of dollars. As with mainframes, IBM is a leader in the minicomputer market, with its AS/400 model. Manufacturers such as Hewlett-Packard have done quite well in this portion of the market as well, however. The midrange market as a whole has been declining as workstations and microcomputers have become faster and have absorbed some of the functionality once required of minicomputers and mainframe computers.

Allstate Insurance

Allstate Insurance has had great success using minicomputers (IBM, 1998). Allstate has approximately 15,000 employees—and another 13,000 agents who link into their systems for support. On a typical day, their information systems must handle more than 30 million transactions. In the aftermath of a natural disaster, however, Allstate may see its already heavy workload increase by 50 percent. For example, in the first 12 days following Hurricane Andrew in 1992, Allstate received more than 7,000 claims per day from southern Florida alone.

In the face of disaster, most people expect from their insurance company exactly what they expect from the police or fire departments—an instant response, without excuses. To achieve this, Allstate uses several IBM minicomputers. These minicomputers, located in one of three data centers in different parts of the country, are linked together through high-speed data networks. Linking these smaller machines together allows Allstate to dynamically shift work between sites as workloads change. This strategy also allows Allstate to quickly add capacity to their system as needed. The design of using multiple, independent processors has allowed Allstate to take many of the peaks and valleys out of their systems response, leading to better customer service.

Courtesy Sun Microsystems, Inc.

Workstations

Workstations are a relatively new class of computers. They have the power and operating systems of some minicomputers, but they typically fit on a desktop and can be placed nearly anywhere (rather than requiring their own closet or room). Many relatively new computer hardware companies, such as Silicon Graphics, Sun Microsystems, and DEC, are leaders in this market. Workstations are a special class of microcomputer (as is your PC). They have an extremely fast CPU (or multiple CPUs), large capacities of RAM and secondary storage, and video displays that are of a very high quality. Workstations generally cost between $5,000 and $50,000. Figure 2.20 shows a Sun Sparcstation, one of the more popular computers in this class. Workstations are often used by engineers to design new products with processing-intensive applications, such as computer-aided design (CAD); by financial analysts modeling stock market fluctuations; and by researchers working with large, complex, computational-intensive applications. For example, researchers at NASA are using workstations to study the effects of global warming on ocean surface temperatures. Workstations' sales have also seen a boost in recent years because they are often used as Web servers.

Microcomputers

Microcomputers, also referred to as personal computers, fit nicely on desktops, generally cost between $1,000 and $5,000, and are most commonly seen in homes and offices. Figure 2.21 shows Compaq personal computer, one of the popular computers in this class. Microcomputers can be relatively stationary desktop models or portable, notebook-sized computers that weigh about five pounds or less. High-end microcomputers can cost more than $10,000 and rival the power and speed of low-end workstations. These types of microcomputers are often used as network and Web servers. In the last few years, the popularity of microcomputers has exploded. Within organizations, microcomputers are the most commonly used computing technology for knowledge workers and are becoming almost as commonplace as the telephone. For individuals and families, more microcomputers than televisions are now sold in the United States each year. Clearly, the computer revolution was motivated by the microcomputer. Given the huge impact microcomputers have had on business and society, let's delve a bit deeper into the development and types of microcomputers for a moment.

FIGURE 2.21

The Compaq Presario 4240ES.

©1998 Compaq Computer Corporation

Apple Macintosh
A BRIEF CASE

From a computer hardware perspective, the microcomputer revolution was led by two firms: Apple and IBM. In 1984, Apple Computer developed the Macintosh (The "Mac," shown in Figure 2.22), which pioneered the idea of making computers easy to use through the use of a graphical user interface (GUI). Users no longer had to remember special words and commands to use the computer. GUI allowed them to see pictures and text and to choose their options with a mouse rather than typing those options with a keyboard. The GUI made the Macintosh very popular with K–12 schools and educators, among other users.

2.22b Courtesy Apple Computer, Inc.
Photo by John Greenleigh.

2.22a Courtesy Apple Computer, Inc.

FIGURE 2.22

An original Apple Macintosh (2.22a) and a recent PowerMac (2.22b).

Apple used a proprietary hardware architecture (based on the Motorola 68000 family of microprocessors) and a proprietary software operating system in the Mac. Therefore, you could purchase hardware and operating system software only from Apple. Similarly, your Mac could only be opened up and worked on by certified repair persons. Although this strategy allowed Apple to control the price and development of its hardware and software, it was not widely supported by the microcomputer marketplace. Many people wanted lots of choices of places and vendors from whom to buy computers and software, and they wanted competition among multiple vendors to breed low prices. Consequently, Apple decided in early 1996 to license the operating system and hardware architecture to other companies. Many computer experts feel that Apple retains only a relatively small (3 percent) share in the business marketplace as a direct result of its business strategies. Only time will tell if Apple can turn around its performance.

(A BRIEF CASE) ─────────────────── **─IBM Personal Computer─**

The most dominant microcomputer architecture is based on the original IBM personal computer (or just PC), which was developed in 1981. (See Figure 2.23). The road taken by the IBM PC is quite different than that taken by the Macintosh. Unlike Apple, IBM licensed its architecture to other companies in the mid-1980s. Many companies licensed the technology and produced "IBM-compatible" products. This resulted in a great deal of competition and rapid changes in the PC marketplace, leading to a general trend of lower prices and higher performance. Consequently, the PC-based architecture dominates the microcomputer marketplace today. The two most dominant players in this market are Intel and Microsoft; Intel is a dominant player because the architecture is based on the Intel family of microprocessors. Microsoft is a dominant player because most PCs run the Microsoft Windows operating system.

FIGURE 2.23

An original IBM PC (2.23a) with a recent IBM PC (2.23b).

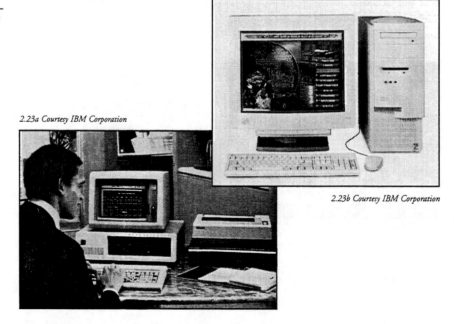

2.23a Courtesy IBM Corporation

2.23b Courtesy IBM Corporation

Apple Responds: The PowerPC

In an effort to combat the near monopoly of Intel and Microsoft in the microcomputer marketplace, old rivals Apple, IBM, and Motorola have introduced the PowerPC. The PowerPC is designed to run either the Macintosh operating system or PC-based operating systems (Apple, 1998). The Power Macintosh came to market in 1995, using the PowerPC processor and the Mac operating system. Since then, several other software vendors have made versions of their operating systems available on the PowerPC (for example, Windows NT and IBM AIX). Only time will tell if the PowerPC will have a significant impact on the microcomputer marketplace.

Portable and Handheld Computing

Two areas of the microcomputer marketplace that are rapidly taking off are portable and handheld computing. Portable computing devices, such as laptop and notebook computers, are becoming very common in business today, as shown in Figure 2.24. Many manufacturers have designed lightweight, rugged computers

©Allen McInnis/Gamma-Liaison International

FIGURE 2.24

A businesswoman using a notebook computer in the airport.

designed to travel with the businessperson either across town or around the world. These computers are equipped with flat display, and the entire system weighs in at between 5 and 10 pounds! Portable computers normally use a trackball or alternative pointing device integrated into the system rather than an external mouse. As the portability and expandability of these computers increases, many executives are choosing single, high-performance portable computers as their only PC rather than having both a desktop and a portable computer (see Table 2.9).

Table 2.9 Desktop versus portable computer tradeoffs.

Desktop Computer	Portable Computer
One location for use	Mobile—any location for use
Lower price	Higher price
Expandable	Very limited expandability
Better ergonomics—full size/high resolution color screen, large keyboard, and so on	Cramped ergonomics—small screen, limited color quality, small keyboard, awkward pointing device, and so on
Relatively easy to service/repair	Hard to service/repair

Handheld computers are very lightweight, ranging from about the size of a small calculator to the size of large billfold-style wallet. They function as electronic organizers, electronic mail readers, and monitors for remote systems. The Apple Newton, shown in Figure 2.25, is an example of a handheld computer. As the circuitry of microprocessors continues to shrink and their performance increases, more extremely lightweight and compact computers will be developed.

FIGURE 2.25

Apple Newton.

Courtesy Apple Computer, Inc. Photo by Frank Pryor.

Portable and handheld technologies are becoming very broadly used by organizational "road warriors," who spend days on the road, and by telecommuters, who work remotely from home. For example, portable computers can be equipped with a high-speed fax/modem linked via cellular phone to a central information bank. Such a configuration allows re-mote personnel to easily share information with the organization, customers, suppliers, and other relevant parties. These technologies have allowed organizations to distribute personnel around the world more easily and for less expense. In fact, many believe that mobile technologies are prompting a radical change in our conception of an office or of going to work. We now have the *virtual office*. It is likely that microcomputer technology will continue to influence what we do and how we do it for a long, long time.

Evolution of Information Systems Hardware

Over the last 50 years, information systems hardware has gone through many radical changes. In the World War II era, almost all business and government information systems consisted of file folders, filing cabinets, and document repositories. Huge rooms were dedicated to the storage of these records. After it was stored, information was often difficult to find, and corporate knowledge and history were difficult to maintain. Most information was known only by certain employees. If or when these employees left the firm, so did all the corporate knowledge. Needless to say, management and organizations needed a better way to keep track of information.

The solution to the information storage and retrieval problems facing organizations of the 1940s has been the modern digital computer. As briefly discussed in Chapter 1, computers have gone through many changes over the past 50 years. We described the evolution of computing eras and the dominant technology of each era. Shifts in computing eras were facilitated by fundamental changes in the way computing technologies worked. Each of these fundamental changes is referred to as a distinct generation of computing (see Table 2.10). In the sections that follow, we describe each of these generations.

Table 2.10 Generations of computing (Freed, 1995).

Generation	Defining Event	Computing Era	Major Characteristics/Events
1 (1946–1958)	Vacuum tubes	Mainframe era begins	ENIAC and UNIVAC were developed
2 (1958–1964)	Transistors	Mainframe era continues	UNIVAC was updated to use transistors
3 (1964–1990s)	Integrated circuits	Mainframe era ends; Minicomputer era begins and ends; Personal computer era begins	IBM 360—integrated circuits and general-purpose operating system; Microprocessor revolution: Intel, Apple Macintosh, IBM PC, MS-DOS
4 (1990s–present)	Multimedia	Personal computer era ends; Interpersonal computing era begins; Internetworking era begins	High-speed microprocessor and networks; High-capacity secondary storage; Low cost/high performance integrating video, audio, and data

Source Freed, L. 1995. The history of computing. Emeryville, CA: Ziff-Davis Press.

The First Generation: Vacuum Tubes

Developed in 1946, the ENIAC was one of the first computers. It was the size of a room, and it had more than 18,000 vacuum tubes, as shown in Figure 2.26. ENIAC could perform approximately 5,000 additions or 500 multiplications in a minute, which was a huge accomplishment for the time. However, it was replaced by the UNIVAC from Sperry Corporation in 1950. UNIVAC also used vacuum tubes, and it, too, filled a large room. In order to operate, these computers needed to be kept in cool, air-conditioned rooms. If they got too hot, they would break. Some computers during this era were even water-cooled, as is a radiator in an automobile engine, in an attempt to help solve this overheating problem. In 1956, IBM invented the first magnetic disk storage to help replace tape storage devices.

FIGURE 2.26

ENIAC and a vacuum tube.

Courtesy Corbis-Bettman

Courtesy Corbis-Bettman

The Second Generation: Transistors

By 1958, the UNIVAC was being produced with transistors instead of vacuum tubes. Transistors generated less heat, were much smaller, worked faster, and were much more reliable than vacuum tubes. These first transistors were each slightly smaller than a dime. Today's computers also use transistor technology, but now there are several million transistors in a single microprocessor—which is itself just larger than a dime. The performance of UNIVAC by 1958 was significantly greater than that of first-generation machines, performing thousands of operations in a second.

The Third Generation: Integrated Circuits

In 1964, the IBM 360 (shown in Figure 2.27) used integrated circuits (IC) for the first time, as well as the first general-purpose operating system. These circuits were called integrated circuits because each IC, or chip, had multiple transistors on it. The development of ICs was a major breakthrough in speed and reliability. A general-purpose operating system allowed computers to be more easily programmed and to therefore more easily shift from one application to another. Prior to this point, computers were configured to run one application at a time. When a new application was desired, the computer had to be significantly reconfigured, often taking many hours, if not days. In short, operating systems transformed computers from *special-purpose* to *general-purpose* machines. During this period of time (1963, to be exact), DEC produced the PDP-5 line of minicomputers, which would be a staple in business computing for the next 20 years.

FIGURE 2.27

An IBM 360.

Courtesy IBM Archives

The next major IS hardware event occurred in 1971, when Intel developed the Intel 4004, the world's first microprocessor. Desktop computing could now be a reality. In 1975, the Altair 8800 was introduced as the first microcomputer. Two Harvard students, William Gates and Paul Allen, founded Microsoft when they wrote a version of the BASIC computing language for the Altair 8800. In 1976, Steve Jobs and Steve Wozniak built the first Apple computer in their garage. Together, they founded Apple Computers. Just five years later, in 1981, two events occurred that have profoundly influenced the development of computing ever since. First, IBM introduced the PC. Second, Microsoft acquired the rights to an operating system called Q-DOS from a small computer manufacturer, Seattle Computer Products. Within a short period of time, Q-DOS became PC-DOS. And the rest is history. In 1987, Microsoft wrote Windows 1.0 for the PC, and in 1989 Intel created the 486 processor. By the time Intel announced the Pentium processor in 1993, the "Wintel" (Windows/Intel) dynasty was off and running.

The third generation has evolved rapidly, as summarized in Table 2.11. The processors of 1995 are approximately 5,000 times faster than their 1971 counterparts. An analogy of the rapid evolution of computer performance as it relates to automobiles has been widely circulated on Internet bulletin boards and discussion groups. This analogy states that "if automotive technology had kept pace with computer technology over the past few decades, you would now be driving a car with a top speed of 10,000 miles per hour, that would weigh about 30 pounds, and would travel a thousand miles on a gallon of gas. Additionally, the sticker price of this car would be less than $50" (Anonymous). In response to all this goading, Detroit grumbles: "Yes, but would you really want to drive a car that crashes twice a day?" (Anonymous). Nonetheless, the evolution in computing is remarkable.

Table 2.11 Comparison of Intel CPU microprocessors (Intel, 1998).

Processor	Initial Year	Data Width	Number of Transistors	Clock Speed	Addressable Memory	MIPS
4004	1971	4bits	2,300	108KHz	640bytes	0.06
8088	1979	8bits	29,000	5–8MHz	1MB	0.33–.075
80286	1982	16bits	134,000	6–12MHz	16MB	0.9–2.66
80386	1985	32bits	275,000–855,000	20–33MHz	4GB	5–11.4
80486	1989	32bits	1.2–1.6 million	16–100MHz	4GB	13–70.7
Pentium	1993	64bits	2.1 million	60–166MHz	4GB	70.4–250
Pentium Pro	1995	64bits	5.5 million	150–300MHz	64GB	250–500
Pentium II	1997	64bits	7.5 million	233–400MHz	64GB	400

The data width roughly reflects the number of bits that can be manipulated by the CPU at one time (more is better). The clock speed of a computer is measured in hertz (Hz), which is similar to the revolutions per minute (RPM) within automobile engines. One cycle per second is therefore 1Hz; KHz=kilohertz (thousands of cycles); MHz= Megahertz (millions of cycles). Again, more is better. Addressable memory refers to how much RAM the CPU can effectively read and write to. As is often the case with computers, more is better.

The Fourth Generation and Beyond

Experts disagree over whether we are now in the third or fourth generation of computing hardware because integrated circuits are still the primary component of today's computers. Some experts feel that the microcomputer revolution that is currently occurring marks the beginning of the fourth generation of computing. In the fourth generation, radically new applications are being developed. One important development is multimedia, which is the integration of voice, video, and data in a standard microcomputer. Apple's HyperCard, introduced in 1987, was the first application to integrate voice, video, and data. Over the past few years, the use of CD-ROMs and faster CPUs has allowed developers to create and distribute multimedia applications. Doing so was not possible before, due to the large storage and processing requirements of video and sound data. Another multimedia application that is gaining popularity is interactive, desktop videoconferencing, as shown in Figure 2.28. Videoconferencing is becoming widely available through the use of the Internet. Software such as Cornell's CuSeeMe, low-cost video cameras, high-speed modems, and other network connections are freely available on the Internet. Currently, less than 5 percent of large businesses use desktop videoconferencing as a standard communication option for their employees. It is predicted, however, that this figure will increase to 15 percent by the year 2000 (Intel, 1998).

FIGURE 2.28

People using a desktop video-conferencing system.

©*Jon Feingersh/The Stock Market*

Computing technology is getting much faster, much smaller, much easier to use with a broader range of applications, and, most importantly, much less expensive. This evolution has had several implications for organizational computing. First, the end users of information are now empowered to do their own computing, called *end-user computing*. Individuals in organizations no longer have to wait for someone else to provide a report or to analyze some data. People are empowered to solve their own informational problems. Due to this empowerment, the IS department in many organizations no longer has to attend to the day-to-day computing needs of knowledge workers. This empowerment has thus freed up the IS staff in many organizations, enabling them to focus on broader, more strategic applications of technology. Individuals and families have also been empowered to buy their own computers. You can use your PC to write letters, analyze finances, surf the Web, and communicate with your friends and loved ones around the world. The concept of owning your own high-performance computer was unthinkable less than 30 years ago.

The evolution of computer-based technology has progressed from large, slow, unreliable machines—known as the "big iron"—to small, fast machines that can sit on every desktop. The most interesting aspect of this evolution of smaller, faster, cheaper technology is that most experts feel that it will continue. Given how much the computer hardware has evolved over the past 50 years, it is hard to imagine what will occur over the next 50 years. Hang on for the ride!

The Future of Information System Hardware

In this final section, we briefly look ahead at the future of information systems hardware. This discussion of future technology issues could be a book in itself, but we will limit our comments to just a few key issues. We can make one easy prediction about the future of information systems hardware: Computer technologies will continue to become smaller, faster, cheaper, and more pervasive.

—— Moore's Law: Smaller, Faster, Cheaper for How —— Much Longer?

A BRIEF CASE

The general trend in computing is for smaller, faster, and cheaper devices. But for how long can this trend continue? In the 1970s, Dr. Gordon Moore, then a researcher at Intel, hypothesized that computer-processing performance would double every 18 months. When Moore made this prediction, he did not limit it to any specified period of time. This bold prediction became known as "Moore's Law." Interestingly, Dr. Moore has been basically correct so far. Feature size—the size of lines on the chip through which signals pass—has been reduced from about the width of a human hair in the 1960s (20 microns—a micron is equal to one millionth of a meter), to the size of a bacterium in the 1970s (5 microns), to smaller than a virus today (.35 micron—the size of the feature width on an Intel Pentium Pro). Figure 2.29 shows this trend.

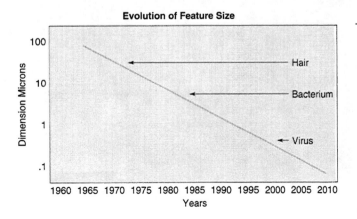

FIGURE 2.29

Shrinking feature size.

Reductions in feature size are the key determinant of processing performance, and each reduction in feature size leads to an equivalent increase in performance. At some point, however, the physical limits of miniaturization on silicon will be reached. In fact, until recently, many felt that Moore's prediction was in some jeopardy. Recent advances by researchers at IBM and Texas Instruments have resulted in the development of a feature width of .18 micron, however (*Scientific American*, August 1996). Experts believe this breakthrough will power the continued evolution of smaller, faster, and cheaper technology well into the 21st century.

With the continued improvements in computer chip technology, all kinds of innovative computers and computer uses are made possible and feasible. Read on to learn more about three specific applications—virtual reality, wearable computing, and smart cards—that are now available and are likely to become more pervasive in the near future.

Virtual Reality

Virtual reality (VR) uses computer programs, along with specialized viewing devices, to give users the impression that they are in an alternative world that is created by the computer. In this world, three-dimensional graphics, sound, and touch are being simulated. The goal of VR research is to develop computer-based environments that simulate **all** human senses—touch, smell, and hearing, and so on (see Figure 2.30). VR is applied in many ways other than the obvious applications for games and entertainment. The military uses VR to simulate combat conditions for troops and pilots—without risk to people or machines. In fact, the U.S. Marine Corps has modified the popular interactive game DOOM and adapted it to their own weapons, locations, and tactics for training. Doctors are using VR to simulate new procedures before trying them on humans. The U.S. Department of Energy in Richland/Hanford, Washington, uses VR to train workers who will be working in radioactive areas. Through VR technology, workers can be trained to maintain equipment in a realistic setting without being exposed to radioactivity. Many feel that the application of VR technologies is limitless and will be one of the hottest technology areas in the 21st century and beyond.

FIGURE 2.30

VR headgear.

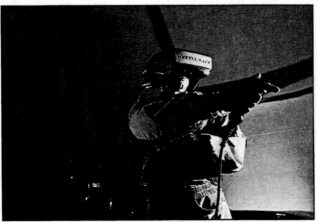

©*Seth Resnick/Gamma-Liaison International*

Wearable Computing

Related to VR is wearable computing. Researchers at the Massachusetts Institute of Technology (MIT) are experimenting with computers that are strapped to people, like a tool belt, and used for processing information remotely. For example, it is envisioned that cellular telephones will soon be the size of wristwatches—in fact, the ability to make cellular calls will be a feature of your wristwatch! Voice commands for dialing will replace keypads. Others believe that special computers can be embedded on clothing to act as sensors and monitors, which would potentially be very useful for the elderly and individuals with physical or mental limitations. Business executives could have a computer in their pocket monitoring day-to-day events, keeping a calendar, and providing automatic and dynamic reminders of upcoming events and meetings. One researcher at MIT, Steve Mann, attaches a camera to his head and a computer to his side. He transmits images in real-time over a wireless network to his World Wide Web page to better understand how wearable computing might work and be used. (Curious? Visit Steve at http://www.mit.edu.)

Smart Cards

A more down-to-earth application of technology that is quickly coming down the track is the use of smart cards. Used already in many European countries, smart cards are a special type of credit card that has a small microprocessor and memory embedded into it. One smart card could serve as personal identification, credit card, automated teller machine (ATM) card, telephone credit card, transit pass, carrier of crucial medical information and insurance, and so on. The beauty of a smart card is that you would need only one card. This one card could substitute for all the credit and ID cards that currently fill your wallet or purse. Additionally, because of the technology embedded in the card, smart cards are much more resistant to tampering than current credit cards with magnetic strips. Most importantly, smart cards have large storage capacities, so they can engage in a sequence of questions with the holder to verify the validity of information and the identity of the card holder.

Talking with...

Marilyn McCoy Franklin, Senior Systems Engineer at Advanced Hardware Architecture, Inc.

Educational Background

B.S. in Zoology and B.S. in Computer Science, University of Idaho

Job Description

Ms. Franklin's main job is to design behavioral system environments for the integrated circuits (ICs) and to simulate and verify the IC design in this system. This involves modeling peripheral interface chips that talk to the IC, such as SCSI chips, DRAMs, microprocessors, and so on. After designing the IC and the chips interfacing it, she simulates the customer's environment

Bill Watts. Hot Shots Photography © 1998.

to verify that the chip functions as specified. This is all done in the software before the chip is fabricated. By thoroughly testing chips in this manner, she ensures that a high percentage of the chips work as specified straight from the fabricator, preventing costly returns.

Critical Success Factors

To be successful, you need to enjoy what you do. If you enjoy what you do, you'll have the drive to do your job well. It's also important that you can work well with others in a team environment. How others perceive you can greatly affect your career success. You also need to be flexible. Job requirements and needs can change drastically in engineering in order to keep up with the current technology.

Advice to Students

Be practical rather than idealistic in choosing a career. Can the career you've chosen support you? How hard is it to find a job in that field now and in the future? Any practical knowledge you can gain prior to graduating will ensure you a better chance of getting a job. Be aggressive in trying to find relevant jobs for your career prior to graduating because it can make a big difference in how employers perceive you. Especially good are the summer intern jobs.

Summary

1. **Understand the important role of information systems hardware in the success of modern organizations.** Nearly every modern organization uses computer-based information systems as a key enabler for their competitive strategy and many day-to-day activities. Computer-based information systems allow for the high-speed capturing, processing, storage, and routing of information to the appropriate decision maker. These capabilities allow organizations to more easily and more rapidly do business in our increasingly global economy.

2. **Describe key elements of information systems hardware.** Information systems hardware is classified into three types: input, process, and output technologies. Input-related hardware consists of devices used to enter information into a computer. Process-related hardware focuses on transforming inputs into outputs. The central processing unit (CPU) is the device that performs this transformation with the help of several other closely related devices that store and recall information. Finally, output-related hardware focuses on delivering information in a usable format to users.

3. **List and describe the types of computers that are being used in organizations today.** Computers come in all shapes, sizes, degrees of power, and costs. The five general classes of computers are supercomputer, mainframe, minicomputer, workstation, and microcomputer. A supercomputer is the most expensive and most powerful category of computers; it is primarily used to assist in solving massive research and scientific problems. A mainframe is a very large computer that is the main, central computing system for major corporations and governmental agencies. A minicomputer is a computer with a lower performance than mainframes but a higher performance than microcomputers. Minicomputers are typically used for engineering and mid-sized business applications. A workstation is a very high-performance microcomputer, typically used to support individual engineers and analysts in solving highly computational problems. A microcomputer is used for personal computing, small business computing, and as a workstation attached to large computers or to other small computers on a network.

4. **Explain how hardware has evolved and where it is headed.** Over the last 50 years, information systems hardware has gone through four distinct generations. The first generation of computing used vacuum tubes; during this period, computers were very slow and unreliable. The second generation of computing used transistors; during this period, computers became faster and significantly more reliable. The third generation of computing used integrated circuits or chips; during this period, computers became very powerful, much smaller, and much less expensive. The defining event for the current generation of computing, the fourth generation, is multimedia—the integration of video, audio, and data.

Key Terms

Keyboard
Repetitive stress injuries
Pointing devices
Mouse
Trackball
Joystick
Touch screen
Light pen
Batch input
Scanners
Text recognition software
Bar code/optical character reader
Audio input

Video input
Bit
Byte
ASCII
Primary storage
ROM—read-only memory
RAM—random-access memory
Cache memory
Secondary storage
Magnetic tape
Sequential data access
Floppy disks
Direct data access

Fixed disks
CD-ROM
Optical disks
CPU
Monitors
Plotter
Dot-matrix printers
Inkjet printers
Laser printers
Supercomputers
Mainframes
Minicomputers
Workstations
Microcomputers

Review Questions

1. Describe the four different categories of information that can be input into a computer. (36)

2. What causes repetitive stress injuries? (37)

3. How are bits and bytes related? (41) 8 bits = 1 byte

4. How do a computer's primary storage, secondary storage, ROM, and RAM interact? 43-44

5. Describe the differences between sequential data access and direct data access. 45

6. Compare and contrast the five different methods of secondary data storage. 44+

7. What are the common measurements of a computer's processing speed? Hertz 63

8. Compare and contrast the five computer types presented in this chapter. How do they differ in size, memory, speed, cost, target users, and so on? 53

9. Summarize the history of the microcomputer from the perspective of Apple and IBM. 57 + 58

10. What role has Microsoft played in the evolution of information systems hardware?

11. Describe some of the emerging areas of information systems hardware for the 21st century.

Problems and Exercises

◈ **Individual**   ◈ **Group**   ☞ **Field**   ◖ **Web/Internet**

◈ 1. Match the following terms to the appropriate definitions:

_____ Trackball

_____ Batch input

_____ Bit

_____ ROM

_____ Cache memory

_____ Sequential data access

_____ Plotter

_____ Workstation

a. The smallest unit of information in a computer—a single 0 or 1

b. A category of computer, based on a very high-performance microcomputer, that is typically used to support individual engineers and analysts in solving highly computational problems

c. A data access method in which information is accessed and stored in a sequence

d. A type of pointing device that works by rolling a ball that sits in a holder; selections are made by pressing buttons located near or on the holder

e. A type of primary memory that you cannot erase or add to—you can only read information from it

f. A paper-based output device that uses pens to draw information onto paper

g. A type of data input in which you enter a "batch" of information at one time

h. A type of primary memory that the CPU uses to store information it uses a lot

◈ 2. Imagine that you have decided it is time to purchase a new computer. Analyze your purchase options with regard to using this computer for personal productivity versus business productivity. What differences might your potential usage make on your hardware choices? Why?

◈ 3. Imagine that you have just informed your supervisor that you will need to purchase new computers for yourself and three fellow employees. Your supervisor states that she has heard in the news that computer prices are dropping constantly, and she feels that you should wait a bit before making this purchase. She adds that you can still be 100 percent effective with your current computer and software. Develop a counterargument explaining why you should make the purchase now instead of waiting. Will this be a hard sell? Why or why not?

4. In a small group of fellow classmates, explain why employers need to be concerned about repetitive stress injuries. How do these injuries affect productivity? How do they affect morale? Have any of the group members suffered from repetitive stress injuries?

 5. Many people have a mental image of a joystick being good only for game playing. Provide reasons and examples to convince them that joysticks are a legitimate input device for modern computers. How are joysticks different from a mouse or a trackball?

 6. What happens when a computer runs out of RAM? Can more RAM be added? Is there a limit? How does cache memory relate to RAM? Why is RAM so important in today's modern information systems world? Search the World Wide Web for RAM retailers. Compare their prices and options.

 7. Do you feel that floppy disks will go the way of the dodo bird or the 8-track player sometime in the near future? Why or why not? How do your classmates feel? Support your reasoning with examples or scenarios and provide a summary for the rest of the class.

 8. Back in the 1970s, today's microcomputer would have had enough computing power to send a rocket to the moon. Now, these microcomputers seem to be outdating themselves every two years. Will this era of continuous improvement end? When will it end, if it does? Why or why not?

 9. Within a small group of classmates, discuss the implications of having more than one type of hardware platform within an organization. What might be the advantages? What are some of the disadvantages? Would your group recommend such a situation?

 10. Interview an IS Manager within an organization that you are familiar with. Determine what issues played a role in the latest information systems hardware purchase this person made. How is the real world different, if at all, from the descriptions in the chapter?

 11. Based on your experiences with different input devices, which do you like the best? Why? Which do you like the least? Why? How do your fellow classmates rate these and other input devices? Are their preferences due to the devices' design or usability, or are they based on the integration of the device with the entire information system?

 12. The end of the chapter provides information on three possible products for the future. Of the three, which one(s) has had the most coverage in the popular press? Why do you think this is so? Which do you feel will have the broadest implementation the soonest? Why?

 13. Choose an organization with which you are familiar that utilizes several different types of computers. Which types do they use? Which of the five categories of computers are being used at this company? Are there any plans to expand their computer usage to another category? Why or why not?

14. In simple language, explain what happens with the keystrokes that you type into a computer using a keyboard. Be sure to discuss memory, processing, and inputs. Draw any diagrams that may help you with this explanation.

15. In a small group, describe your experiences with IBM-compatible and Macintosh computers. Which did you use first? What about the others in the group? Which do you use now? If you have changed, why? What influences your computer-purchasing decisions?

16. As a group, choose a few of the computer hardware vendors—as illustrated in the scenario at the beginning of the chapter—that sell computers to the general public. These include Dell, Compaq, IBM, Gateway, Apple, and Packard Bell. Using their home pages, determine what options these vendors provide for input devices, processing devices, and output devices. Does it seem that this company has a broad range of choices for their customers? Is there something that you did not find available from this company? Present your findings in a 10-minute presentation to the rest of the class.

Real World Case Problems

1. Power Play: How the Compaq-Digital Deal Will Reshape the Entire World of Computers

Since coming to Compaq six years ago, CEO Eckhard Pfeiffer has regularly sent shockwaves through the PC business. In 1992, he forced competitors to react quickly or lose business by slashing PC prices by 32 percent. Last year, he again slashed prices, announcing a line of home computers priced below $1,000. On January 26, 1998, Pfeiffer created another shakeup—reaching every corner of the $700-billion computer world—by announcing that he and Digital CEO Robert Palmer had concluded four days of negotiations, with the outcome being a record-breaking $8.7-billion acquisition. The deal was the largest in computer industry history, creating a computer giant of $37.5 billion in revenues, second only to IBM in computer sales.

This acquisition has propelled Compaq from the upstart, wild, woolly PC generation into the high-tech big-league companies that supply the world's most complex and critical information systems. Compaq now has the ability to sell everything, from $649 handheld computers to super-powerful $2-million fail-safe computer servers. In addition, Compaq has the use of Digital's 22,000-strong service and consulting staff.

Compaq's timing was strategic. Customers are now changing from mainframes to powerful servers that are tied to banks of PCs and buying new equipment to help fend off problems caused by the year 2000. Compaq now has the ability to offer solutions to low-cost, powerful, computing systems and has the staff to install and maintain the systems. They have the ability to deliver low-cost PC economics into the high-end computing markets that were previously dominated by IBM, Hewlett-Packard, and Sun Microsystems. Compaq spends $.15 for every $1 in sales, compared to $.24 and $.27 for Hewlett-Packard and IBM, respectively. Even Dell Computer Corporation and Gateway 2000 can no longer assume business as usual. Compaq increased the stakes by adding service and support.

Compaq, the largest seller of Windows software and Intel chips, may now be on a par with Microsoft Corporation and Intel Corporation in setting the agenda. Eighty-seven percent of PCs run Windows and 89 percent use Intel's processor, called Wintel. These three companies now have the ability to handle complex computing jobs, from financial databases to inventory management. In the past, customers were attracted to Compaq's low pricing but would often use a service provider such as Digital. They now have the best of both worlds.

a. Was it a good idea for Compaq to acquire Digital? Why or why not?

b. If you were at the helm of IBM, what would your next move be? What if you were at the helm of Microsoft?

c. To rephrase the title of the article, "How will the Compaq-Digital deal reshape the entire world of computers?" What's your forecast?

Source 1998. *Power Play: How the Compaq-Digital deal will reshape the entire world of computers,* BusinessWeek, *February 9, 91–97.*

2. Let's Talk! Speech Technology Is the Next Big Thing in Computing

At IBM's T. J. Watson Research Center, excitement abounds. Scientists have been trying since the 1960s to develop a software program that can recognize what people say, and they have done so—with 95 percent accuracy. However, last summer IBM beat most of its competitors to the market with a snazzy, affordable, speech program called ViaVoice Gold. The program translates spoken sentences into text on a computer screen and lets users open Windows programs by voice command.

Already at Watson Research Center, scientists have begun to work on the next generation of voice technology, which will have a dramatic impact on how we live and work. At the center, a researcher may be testing an automated airline ticket reservation system by asking the computer for flight information. In a speech lab, a researcher may be accessing a database full of digitized CNN news clips using nothing but spoken words. Others may be accessing 3D images of molecules, cylinders, and topographic maps on a wall-sized display by motioning or speaking to images.

With these models, IBM is moving toward the dream of scientists the world over: machines that understand "natural language"—sentences as people actually speak them, unconstrained by special vocabulary or context. Previously, start-up companies have sold specialized speech-recognition programs, but these programs had small vocabularies, required speaker training, and demanded unnatural pauses between words. MIT, Carnegie Mellon, SRI, and Lucent Technologies are also racing to get their products out to industry.

Speech may very well be the bridge between humans and technology. Few people enjoy mouse-clicking through Internet sites, memorizing commands, or searching files that are hardly ever used. In addition to being tedious, these kinds of processes are not open to those who lack digital skills or education. "Speech is not just the future of Windows, but the future of computing itself," states Microsoft CEO, Bill Gates.

a. What are some of the useful applications of systems employing natural language capabilities?

b. Will people be willing to use these systems, or will they prefer traditional methods of inputting data into computers?

c. What are some tasks and/or situations in which systems using natural languages just don't make sense?

Source 1998. *Let's talk! Speech technology is the next big thing in computing,* BusinessWeek, *February 23, 61–72.*

References

Apple, 1998. Information from: www.apple.com. Verified: January 28, 1998.

Cray Research, 1998. Information from: www.cray.com. Verified: January 8, 1998.

Datamation, 1996. Videoconferencing to take off, May 1. Information from: www.datamation.com. Verified: January 29, 1998.

Freed, L. 1995. *The history of computing.* Emeryville, CA: Ziff-Davis Press.

IBM, 1998. Information from: www.ibm.com. Verified: January 29, 1998.

Intel, 1998. Information from: www.intel.com. Verified: January 29, 1998.

Related Readings

Amini, M.M., and R.E. Schooley. 1993. Supercomputing in corporate America. *Information and Management* 24(6): 291–303.

Bailey, D.H. 1997. Onward to Petaflops computing. *Communications of the ACM* 40(6): 90–92.

Briggs, Dennis, Beck, and Nunamaker. 1993. Whither the pen-based interface? *Journal of Management Information Systems* 9(3): 71–90.

Burgess, Ullah, Van Overen, and Ogden. 1994. The PowerPC 603 microprocessor. *Communications of the ACM* 37(6): 34–42.

Coll, Zia, and Coll. 1994. A comparison of three computer cursor control devices: Pen on horizontal tablet, mouse and keyboard. *Information and Management* 27(6): 329–339.

Harris, A.L., and D.S. Dave. 1994. Effects of computer system components on the price of notebook computers. *Information and Management* 27(3): 151–160.

Hillis, W.D., and L.W. Tucker. 1993. The CM-5 connection machine: A scalable supercomputer. *Communications of the ACM* 36(11): 30–40.

Kennedy, Bender, Connolly, Hennessy, Vernon, and Smarr. 1997. A nationwide parallel computing environment. *Communications of the ACM* 40(11): 62–72.

Khanna, T., and M. Iansiti. 1997. Firm asymmetries and sequential R&D: Theory and evidence from the mainframe computer industry. *Management Science* 43(4): 405–421.

Moore, G.E. 1997. The microprocessor: Engine of the technology revolution. *Communications of the ACM* 40(2): 112–114.

Peak, D.A., and M.H. Azadmanesh. 1997. Centralization/decentralization cycles in computing: Market evidence. *Information and Management* 31(6): 303–317.

Peleg, Wilkie, and Weiser. 1997. Intel MMX for multimedia PCs. *Communications of the ACM* 40(1): 24–38.

Sites, R.L. 1993. Alpha AXP architecture. *Communications of the ACM* 36(2): 33–44.

Chapter 3: Information Systems Software

Scenario: Fast Cash at an ATM

Think about how you use an Automated Teller Machine (ATM). Typically, you place your ATM card into the slot, enter your Personal Identification Number (PIN), and press the Enter button (or some other button that confirms that the number you entered is correct). You then press a button to choose to *withdraw* money and another button to choose to withdraw from your *checking* account. You then enter the amount you want to withdraw and press the Enter (or "correct") button. The ATM you are using might have a Fast Cash button, which you can press to be issued $40 or $50 immediately. You then take your cash, card, and receipt. If you were transferring money from your savings account to your checking account, the process would be just as easy, perhaps even faster. You would choose a button to *transfer* money from savings to checking, enter the amount, and confirm it. That's it!

Now think about what is happening behind the scenes when you use an ATM to get cash. Is there a teller back there shuttling your money back and forth and keeping records as you push buttons on the ATM? Hardly. Your ATM transaction generates data to tell the bank to do something with your account. For example, the machine tells the bank to check whether you have enough money in your account for it to give you cash or to transfer $100 from your savings account to your checking account. Your PIN, your request, and the balances in your checking and savings accounts are all pieces of information that serve as the raw material for your bank. As in traditional manufacturing, the raw material must be processed. The processing done in a financial institution for an ATM transaction is all

information oriented. When you transfer $100 from savings to checking, the bank subtracts the $100 from your savings account and adds it to your checking account by manipulating a series of numbers associated with your bank accounts. No physical currency has been moved from one vault in the bank to another. Rather, the bank has used and manipulated information to accomplish your transaction, as shown in Figure 3.1. The bank's outputs are also information oriented. The ATM machine prints out a slip of paper showing you the date and time of your request and showing that $100 was, in fact, transferred from your savings account to your checking account. At the end of the month, your bank statement shows the ATM transaction processed earlier that month and gives you current balances on both your checking and savings accounts.

The bank services that we have just discussed—an ATM transaction and a bank statement—are forms of information. Therefore, it should not be surprising that small banks spend over double the U.S. company average of 4 percent of their budgets on information technology, and large banks may spend up to 16 percent, a total that adds up to tens of billions of dollars across the whole industry each year. Overall, about $150 billion each year is spent in the U.S. on information technology (Fishauf, 1994). At the heart of all of this information technology is software—sets of instructions that control the operations of computer hardware. In our ATM example, software instructs the ATM to ask you for your PIN number, verifies that your PIN number is correct, checks whether there is enough

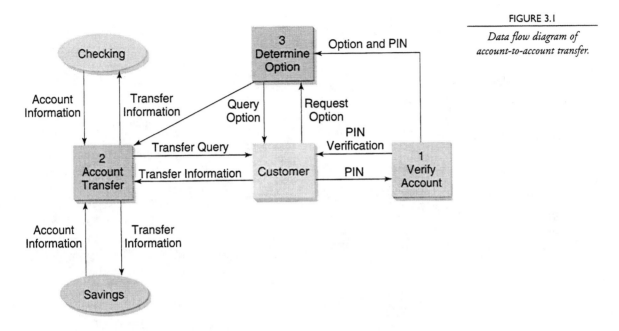

FIGURE 3.1

*Data flow diagram of
account-to-account transfer.*

money in your account, and so on. Software drives the entire ATM process, as it does all other information technology uses.

Companies such as your bank remain successful by providing innovative services. Increasingly, a key component in providing innovative services such as ATM machines is the use of information technologies. These advanced information technologies are always useless unless software guides the hardware to perform the desired service. In this chapter, we talk more about this essential component of information systems.

Introduction

A key component of all information systems is software. Hardware and software form a tightly coupled system; that is, hardware and software operate together to perform operations or tasks desired by users. Without software, the biggest, fastest, most powerful computer in the world is nothing more than a fancy paperweight. It relies on software to run programs, solve problems, and presentinformation to its user(s).

After reading this chapter, you will be able to do the following:

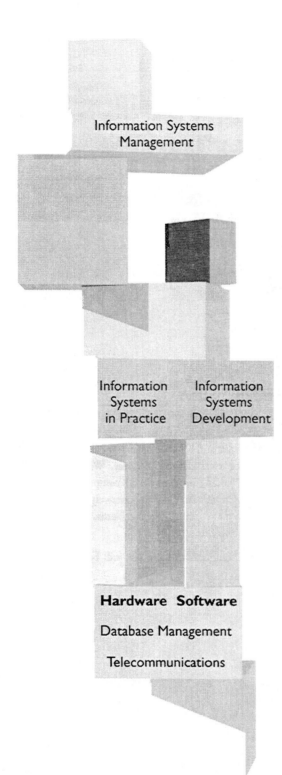

1. Understand the importance of information systems software for today's organizations.

2. Describe the common functions of systems software.

3. Explain the various types of application software.

4. Describe the characteristics of various types of programming languages.

5. Discuss the evolution of computer software.

Information technologies such as the ATM in the opening scenario are playing an increasingly larger role in our lives. Given this increasing role, it is useful to better understand information systems (IS) software. In terms of our guiding framework—The Big Picture—this is the second of four chapters focusing on the essential elements of information systems (see Figure 3.2). We begin by discussing the importance of information systems software to the success of modern organizations.

The Increasing Importance of Software to Organizations

Today's organizations rely on information systems more than ever before. This reliance is due in large part to the rapidly expanding capabilities of modern hardware and software systems, which enable organizations to process increasing amounts of information quickly, cheaply, and efficiently. For today's organizations, information systems are no longer a luxury that helps them perform their job; they are a necessity. Virtually every major company in the U.S. today has a World Wide Web site for selling products and supporting customers. Just a few short years ago, no company had a Web site. Needless to say, a lot has

FIGURE 3.2

The big picture: focusing on information systems software.

changed over the past few years. This growth and importance of information systems has been evident throughout the 1990s and is likely to increase in the 21st century.

An increasingly large percentage of the money spent on information technology is spent on software, as shown in Figure 3.3. In the 1960s, for example, computer hardware was relatively rare and therefore expensive. Software costs were only a small percentage of the costs associated with using information technology. This situation has reversed itself today. In today's business environment, it is not uncommon for software costs to exceed 75 percent of the cost of information systems. Software has become a very large investment for any organization, with most companies spending from 5 to more than 20 percent of their annual revenues on information systems.

Several trends explain this shift in technology spending. First, as outlined in the previous chapter, advances in hardware technology have allowed hardware manufacturers to produce even more capable machines at lower costs. Therefore, organizations are able to buy more computers without a large increase in their investments. In today's businesses, it is not unusual for almost every employee to have a computer (or sometimes, more than one) on his desk. Second, today's software is increasingly complex and takes more time to develop. Because of this development time, which includes updating software so that it can run efficiently on new hardware, software costs are more expensive. Finally, because of the demand for skilled programmers, salaries for those employees have increased, resulting in higher software costs. Needless to say, information systems in general, and software in particular, are big business.

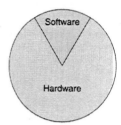

1960s–1970s

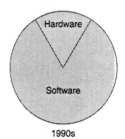

1990s

FIGURE 3.3

Shift from hardware costs exceeding software costs in the 1960s to the opposite in the 1990s.

The History of Microsoft

A BRIEF CASE

Microsoft Corporation, founded in 1975 by William H. Gates and Paul G. Allen, is today the largest software company in the world, with sales of more than $12 billion and 22,000 employees (see Figure 3.4). Table 3.1 provides a brief summary of some of the major events that have shaped Microsoft's history (Microsoft, 1998). Over the past two decades, Microsoft has outgrown five separate headquarters. The current corporate headquarters is located in Redmond, Washington—the Microsoft Corporate Campus—which has numerous interconected buildings, giving it a university look and feel. Because of Microsoft's growth, several additional buildings seem to always be under construction. Today, Microsoft markets a broad range of products for personal computing: personal productivity tools, development tools and languages, systems software, hardware peripherals, books, and multimedia applications.

Microsoft's latest slogan is "Where do you want to go today?" This question can easily be turned back to Microsoft. In fact, they have answered their own question. Microsoft has developed their own version of a World Wide Web browser to compete with Netscape Navigator (we discuss this competition in more detail later in the chapter). In addition to Internet Explorer, Microsoft has numerous software applications for creating and manipulating Web pages. The company has forged alliances with banks and other financial institutions in order to set standards for managing digital cash. The Microsoft

FIGURE 3.4

Microsoft employee and sales growth (Microsoft, 1998).

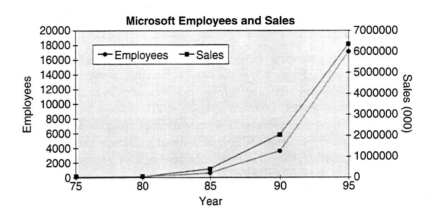

Wallet, which is now available, can be used to make purchases via the Internet without the user having to give credit card numbers or other sensitive information. It acts as a virtual credit card linked to real money. Microsoft is obviously continuing to develop and explore new applications and new technologies in their never-ending desire to place a computer on every desk. As Microsoft continues to grow and help evolve the computer industry, they will continue to turn today's important discoveries into tomorrow's practical standards.

Table 3.1 Key events in the history of Microsoft (Microsoft, 1998).

Year	Event
1975	BASIC language interpreter developed for Altair
1981	MS-DOS and IBM PC are wed
1982	MS-DOS licenses to 50 computer hardware companies
1985	Windows 1.0 released
1990	Windows 3.0 released
1993	Windows NT released
1994	MS Office becomes number one in product category
1995	Windows 95 and Internet Explorer released
1996	MS-NBC 24-hour news, talk, and information network is established
1998	Windows 98 released

Even though software costs continue to grow, organizations should not be deterred from this investment. Today's software is extremely capable, allowing organizations to operate in an environment that is increasingly fast-paced and complex. In fact, software remains one of the best investments a business can make. Software can help businesses plan and execute their strategy. As we described in Chapter 1, "Information Systems Overview," companies that are able to use information systems to improve their competitive position may thrive where others fail in today's information age.

The SABRE GROUP

In an attempt to improve its position in the airline industry, American Airlines led the travel industry into the computer technology age in the late 1950s with the first true computer reservations system, the Magnetronic Reservisor. That seed grew into the Semi-Automated Business Research Environment—SABRE—in 1963. This mainframe system was able to process 84,000 telephone calls per day. Today, the system can handle over 20 million equivalent calls, which are now processed electronically. That reservation system has grown into a network of over 30,000 travel agencies, 3 million online consumers, and numerous corporations, which are all accessing real-time travel information over the Internet, 24 hours a day, 7 days a week, 52 weeks a year (see Figure 3.5).

Courtesy of The Sabre Group

To run this massive reservation system, American Airlines built the world's largest privately owned computer system in Tulsa, Oklahoma. SABRE gave American Airlines a big competitive advantage; in fact, the airline industry argued that SABRE gave American Airlines an "unfair" competitive advantage because many travel agents used SABRE for booking flights and AA flights were often the first on the list of available flights. As a result, AA was forced to change the way the software worked and to operate SABRE as an independent corporation, The SABRE Group, under the AA parent company, AMR Corporation. This reorganization was completed in 1996. Today, The SABRE Group owns and manages this system, as well as the next generation of systems used throughout AMR. An estimated $40 billion in travel products and services is purchased through the SABRE system each year. In October 1996, 18 percent of the equity of The SABRE Group was sold in an initial public offering that raised nearly $500 million; the remaining 82 percent of the company is under AMR control. Although no longer a part of American Airlines, SABRE is a key reason AA grew into one of the world's most successful airlines and why AMR corporation is so profitable (for more information, see SABRE, 1998).

FIGURE 3.5

Screen from online travel system.

Companies can also take advantage of systems and software *internally*. That is, they can use software to help them re-engineer or rightsize the organization. For example, consulting companies often use one type of software, groupware, to draw on common expertise in the firm. By sharing information through groupware, managers are able to access the status of projects instantly and consultants are able to be more responsive to client needs. This kind of efficiency may enable the firm to hire fewer consultants each year. Hiring fewer consultants results in fewer costs for relocating and training new personnel. Rightsizing does not have to mean that people lose their jobs. In this example, rightsizing simply means hiring fewer new people each year, while pooling expertise. This expertise is distributed throughout the company, to everyone's benefit.

New software and systems are often used to help standardize procedures and share expertise. For example, General Motors recently selected SAP R/3 (Systems, Applications, and Products in Data Processing) financial software to help manage their worldwide financial resources (SAP, 1998). Until recently, GM's four major regions of business—North America, South America, Europe, and Asia Pacific—used different financial methods and systems. Standardizing on SAP will allow information integration never before possible. Training employees to use the new software effectively is fundamental to GM's success. An added benefit of providing new skills to employees is that many find these new skills stimulating, giving them an added sense of their importance to the organization. Thus, this training leads to increased productivity.

As you can see, software can help provide innovative services and new ways to do business. However, the term "software" can often be confusing because it is used in many different ways. The next section describes different types of software and details their place in today's organizations.

Key Information Systems Software Components and Issues

Before you can understand how information systems software operates to manipulate data and instruct hardware, it is important to distinguish between "data," "information," "knowledge," and "wisdom," terms that are often erroneously used interchangeably. **Data** is raw material, recorded, unformatted information—such as words and numbers. Data has no meaning in and of itself. For example, if I asked you what 465889724 meant or stood for, you could not tell me. However, if I presented the same data as 465-88-9724 and told you it was located in a certain database, in John Doe's file, in a field labeled "SSN," you might rightly surmise that the number was actually someone named John Doe's social security number.

Data formatted with dashes or labels is more useful. It is transformed into **information**, which can be defined as a representation of reality. In the previous example, 465-88-9724 was used to represent and identify an individual person, John Doe. Information relies on context cues, such as a particular question or label (as in the previous example) that is familiar to the recipient. Let's draw on the ATM scenario earlier in the chapter. A raw list of all the transactions at a bank's ATM machines over the course of a month would be fairly useless *data*. However, a table that divided ATM machine users into two categories—bank customers and non–bank customers—and compared the two groups' use of the machine—such as, their purpose for using the ATM machines and the times and days on which they use them—would be incredibly useful *information*. A bank manager could use this information to recruit new customers.

Knowledge is needed to understand relationships between different pieces of information. For example, you must have knowledge to be aware that each individual only has one social security number and can be uniquely identified by that social security number. Knowledge represents some form of accumulated information. It is a body of governing procedures, such as guidelines or rules, that are used to organize or manipulate data in order to make it suitable for a given task.

Finally, **wisdom** can be thought of as accumulated knowledge. Wisdom goes beyond knowledge in that it represents broader, more generalized rules and schemas for understanding a specific domain or domains. Wisdom allows you to apply concepts across different types of problems or understand how to apply concepts from one domain to new situations. Understanding that a unique individual identifier, such as a social security number, can be applied in certain programming situations to single out an individual record in a database is the result of accumulated knowledge. Wisdom can be gained though academic study, personal experience, or, ideally, both.

Understanding the distinctions between data, information, knowledge, and wisdom is important because all are used in the study, development, and use of information systems—information systems software in particular. Information systems **software** can be defined as a program or set of programs that controls the operation of computer hardware, along with any documentation that accompanies that program. A program is simply a set of coded instructions that are read and executed by a computer. **Computer programs**, which are written in programming languages, direct the hardware circuitry to operate in a predefined way. **Documentation**, the set of books and/or instructions that accompanies the computer program, is designed to assist the user in successfully operating the computer program. Documentation often includes instructions for how to install and operate the program, as well as troubleshooting tips for common problems. Traditionally, documentation has been provided in the form of books and manuals. However, software companies are increasingly including online documentation— electronic documentation embedded within the program itself—in addition to or sometimes as an alternative to more traditional, external forms.

The two basic types of information systems software are systems software and application software. In the next section, we discuss systems software and how it supports the overall operation of the computer hardware.

Systems Software

Systems software is the collection of programs that forms the foundation for the basic operations of the computer hardware. Systems software, or the **operating system**, as it is sometimes called, performs and coordinates the interaction between hardware devices (for example, the CPU and the monitor), peripherals (for example, printers), and application software (for example, a word processing program), as shown in Figure 3.6.

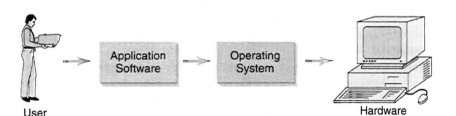

User   Application Software   Operating System   Hardware

FIGURE 3.6

Operating systems coordinate the interaction between users, application software, and hardware.

Operating systems are generally written in assembly language, a very low-level computer programming language that allows the computer to operate as quickly and efficiently as possible. The operating system is designed to insulate you from this low-level language and make computer operations as unobtrusive as possible. Essentially, the operating system performs all of the day-to-day (and nanosecond to nanosecond!) operations that we often take for granted when operating a computer. Just as our brain and nervous system control our bodies' breathing, heartbeat, and senses without our conscious realization, the systems software controls the computer's basic operations transparently.

Common Systems Software Functions

Many tasks are common to almost all computers. These include getting input from a keyboard or mouse, reading and/or writing data from a storage device (such as a hard disk drive), and presenting information to you via a monitor. Each of these tasks is performed by the operating system, just as a manager of a firm oversees people and processes (as depicted in Figure 3.7).

FIGURE 3.7

A manager (OS) overseeing the operations of many different departments: file management, disk management, and peripherals.

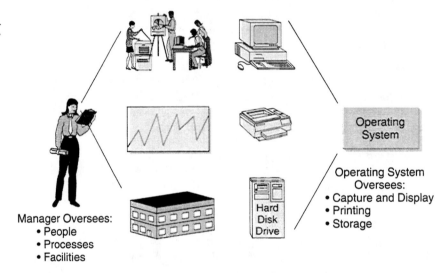

Manager Oversees:
- People
- Processes
- Facilities

Operating System

Operating System Oversees:
- Capture and Display
- Printing
- Storage

For example, let's say you want to copy a word processing file from a floppy disk onto your computer. Many of today's operating systems make this very easy for you. Using an operating system with a graphical user interface (GUI), such as Microsoft Windows, you simply drag an icon of the word processing file you want to copy onto an icon of your hard disk. With a few clicks of your mouse, the file on the floppy disk has been copied to your hard drive. Seems easy, right? Thanks to the operating system, copying the file *is* relatively easy. However, underlying the icons and simple dragging operations is a complex set of coded instructions that tells the electronic components of the computer that you are transferring a set of bits and bytes located on the floppy disk to a location on your internal hard disk. Imagine if you had to program those sets of instructions every time you wanted to copy a file from one place to another. Productivity would grind to a halt! Therefore, the operating system manages and executes these types of system operations so that you can spend your time on more important tasks.

The operating system performs many different tasks, including the following:

- Booting (or starting) your computer
- Reading programs into memory
- Managing memory allocation to those programs
- Managing where programs and files are located in secondary storage
- Maintaining the structure of directories and subdirectories
- Formatting disks
- Controlling the computer monitor
- Sending objects to the printer

The operating system is typically stored on disk, and a portion of it is transferred into temporary memory when the computer starts up. After the operating system is in memory, it can go about its task of managing the computer and providing an **interface** for you. It is through this interface that you interact with the computer. Many people refer to the interface as the "dialogue" between the user and the computer. One type of interface is a **command-based interface**. This type of interface requires you to type text commands into the computer to perform some basic operation. You could type the command "DELETE File1" to erase the file with the name "File1." Many mainframe computers use a command-based user interface. For example, a specific job control language (JCL) is used to control how jobs are run on large mainframe computers. MS-DOS (Microsoft–Disk Operating System) is also an example of an operating system using a command-based user interface.

Today, the most common type of interface for the PC is called a **graphical user interface** (GUI). The GUI uses pictures and icons as well as menus to send instructions back and forth from the user to the computer system. Because GUIs enable users to avoid inputting sometimes arcane commands into the computer, most people consider them easier to use and learn than other user interfaces. As a result, they are popular. Some of the benefits of GUIs are listed in the bulleted list that follows. Examples of systems software using a GUI are Windows 95 and 98, Windows NT, and the Macintosh OS. Figure 3.8, a modification of Figure 3.6, shows how the GUI links the application and systems software by presenting information to the users in a common way.

- Intuitive
- Consistency
- Flexibility
- Ease of use
- Ease of learning
- Undo
- Linking
- Embedding

FIGURE 3.8

*GUI links software applica-
tions and systems software.*

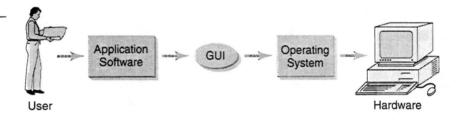

User · Application Software · GUI · Operating System · Hardware

Types of Operating Systems

Just as there are many kinds of computers, there are many different kinds of operating systems. In general, these operating systems—whether for large mainframe computers or for small notebook computers—perform similar operations. Obviously, large multi-user supercomputers are more complex than small desktop systems; therefore, the operating system must account for and manage that complexity. However, the basic purpose of all operating systems is the same.

A BRIEF CASE ——————————— **The Roots of MS-DOS** ——————

Interestingly, some confusion has surrounded the origins of Microsoft's MS-DOS, the most widely used operating system in the history of computers. MS-DOS is arguably the product that catapulted Microsoft into the software giant it is today. When IBM decided to enter the microcomputer market with the IBM PC in the early 1980s, they needed an operating system. Because IBM's focus was on hardware, they contracted with Microsoft to deliver the operating system and some programming language compilers. Microsoft did not have an operating system, but they were aware that a small hardware company, Seattle Computer Products, had developed an operating system called Q-DOS (Quick and Dirty Operating System) that could be relatively easily modified to run on the IBM PC. This operating system was not written to run on the Intel 8088, the CPU used in the IBM PC, but for a close cousin, the Intel 8086. On July 27, 1981, Microsoft purchased Q-DOS and turned it into MS-DOS with the help of the original author of the software, former Seattle Computer engineer, Tim Patterson. The purchase price for Q-DOS, including sole ownership rights for it, was around $50,000! That purchase was a key reason why Microsoft has emerged as the leading producer of microcomputer software and, as a result, Bill Gates has become the richest person in the world. Sadly, Seattle Computer Products no longer exists. Tim Patterson is still an employee at Microsoft. To show that it really is a small world, Joe Valacich, one of the authors of this book, took his first job after finishing his undergraduate degree in computer science with Seattle Computer Products in 1983. At that time, Seattle Computer focused on designing and manufacturing add-on boards for the IBM PC and designing a high-performance computer system called the Gazelle. In the remainder of this section, we describe some popular operating systems.

MVS/ESA (Multiple Virtual Storage/Enterprise Systems Architecture). This is a proprietary operating system used on large IBM mainframe computers. MVS/ESA has high reliability and multilevel security for enterprise-wide systems management. It has the capability to effectively support massive transactions.

Daniel Sheehan/Gamma Liaison International

UNIX. This is a multi-user, multitasking operating system that is available for a wide variety of computer platforms. UNIX was developed in 1969 at Bell Labs. It is an open operating system, which means that people and organizations are free to copy, modify, adapt, or write application software for it. It is most commonly found on workstation-class computers made by vendors such as Sun Microsystems, Digital Equipment Corporation, Hewlett-Packard, and Silicon Graphics, although versions of UNIX run on other hardware platforms, such as personal computers and supercomputers. Many vendors have developed their own versions of UNIX—for example, IBM's AIX and HP's HP-UX.

MS-DOS. (Microsoft–Disk Operating System). This is a command-based operating system used on IBM-compatible PCs. The first version of MS-DOS was introduced in 1981, and the operating system is still being used today. However, newer GUI-based operating systems have been developed, which have replaced MS-DOS as the most common operating system found on today's PCs.

OS/2. An operating system developed by IBM for powerful PCs that was introduced in 1988. OS/2, which features a graphical shell, has many powerful functions. OS/2 can run applications written for MS-DOS, Windows, or OS/2.

FIGURE 3.9

Bill Gates and the Windows 98 introduction.

Windows. Developed by Microsoft, Windows was originally simply an operating system shell designed to present a graphical interface to MS-DOS. However, newer versions of Windows, such as Windows 95 and 98, are independent, fully functional operating systems that do not require MS-DOS to operate (see Figure 3.9). Windows NT is a more industrial-strength version of Windows that is typically used for high-end computer servers and workstations in organizational networks.

Macintosh OS. The Macintosh OS was the first commercially popular graphics-based operating system, making its debut in 1984. The Macintosh OS is used in Apple Macintosh personal computers. The graphical user interface used in the Macintosh OS was developed based on research conducted by XEROX PARC (Palo Alto Research Center) that was designed to improve the usability of computers. The Macintosh OS refined and made popular some truly unique technical breakthroughs that had been developed earlier at XEROX PARC, such as icons, menus, and the mouse. Today, the principles embodied in the Macintosh OS have been incorporated into all major GUI-based operating systems, such as Windows 95 and 98. Figure 3.10 shows how you would copy a file within three different operating systems environments: MS DOS, MS Windows, and the Macintosh.

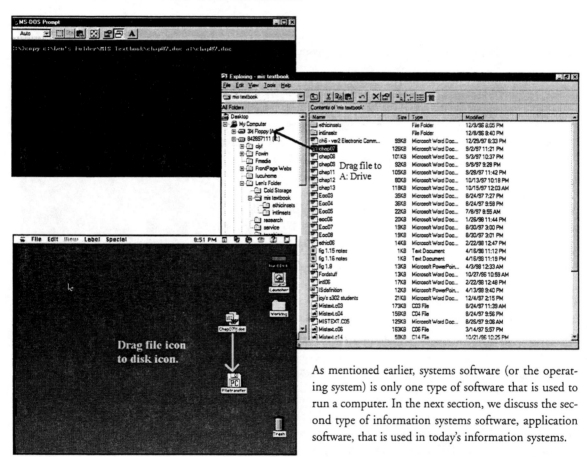

As mentioned earlier, systems software (or the operating system) is only one type of software that is used to run a computer. In the next section, we discuss the second type of information systems software, application software, that is used in today's information systems.

FIGURE 3.10

Copying a file using different operating systems, MS-DOS, Windows, and Macintosh.

Application Software

Unlike systems software, which manages the operation of the computer, **application software** performs a specific task, such as writing a business letter or manipulating a series of forecasts to come up with the most efficient allocation of resources for a project. The application program interacts with the systems software (which, in turn, interacts with the computer hardware) to accomplish the job.

- Accounts receivable
- Accounts payable
- Cash-flow analysis
- Desktop publishing
- General ledger
- Inventory control
- Order entry

- Payroll
- Purchasing
- Receiving
- Resource planning
- Shipping
- Stock and bond management
- Tax planning and preparation

The two basic types of application software are those 1) developed specifically by or for a particular organization (called customized or proprietary software) and 2) those purchased off-the-shelf, which can be used by a variety of people and/or organizations to meet their specific needs (called commercial software). These two types of software will be discussed next.

Customized Application Software

Customized application software is developed based on specifications provided by a particular organization. This software may be developed in-house by the company's own IS staff or it may be contracted, or outsourced, to a specialized vendor charged with developing the software to the company's contractual specifications. Customized application software has two primary advantages:

1. *Customizability*—Because the software is customized, it can be specifically tailored to meet unique user requirements. For example, suppose a retailer needs a kiosk in its store to help shoppers locate specific products. Many shoppers may not be familiar with computers and may be intimidated by operating a keyboard or a mouse. With customized software, the company could develop a touch screen input interface, with which users could simply point at objects in a catalog. The computer could then process this information and tell the user that, for example, women's shoes are located on the first floor in the southeast corner and provide a map of the store. The retailer-specific touch screen is one example of how customized software might be used to meet user (shopper) needs.

2. *Problem specificity*—With customized software, the company pays only for the things specifically required for its users or tasks. For example, company- or industry-specific terms or acronyms can be included in the program, as can unique types of required reports. Such specificity is not possible in off-the-shelf programs that are targeted to a general audience. This is important because customized application software can provide a good value; the user gets exactly what she needs and nothing else.

Off-the-Shelf Application Software

After reading our previous discussion, you might assume that customized application software is automatically the best way to go. This is not the case. Off-the-shelf software programs are very common in organizations today. **Off-the-shelf application software** is typically used to support common business processes that do not require any specific tailoring. Advantages of the off-the-shelf application software include the following:

1. *Lower cost*—Because off-the-shelf applications are developed for more general markets, the development company is able to distribute its development costs across a larger customer base and therefore reduce the cost for individual customers.

2. *Faster procurement*—Customized software takes a notoriously long time to develop. Because it is designed to meet specific requirements, a lengthy process of understanding specific user and task needs, programming, testing, and maintenance is required for customized applications. Off-the-shelf programming, on the other hand, can simply be purchased and installed by users.

3. *High quality*—Many off-the-shelf programs are of high quality. Software development has become a highly competitive industry; therefore, companies that produce shoddy products are often forced out of the marketplace by higher-quality competitors. In addition, developers have access to a large customer base and can ensure that their product continues to meet customer needs through continual research and testing. As customers identify flaws in the software, the company can upgrade their product to ensure that any problems are rectified for future users.

4. *Lower risk*—Developing customized software in house requires a large amount of resources (personnel, time, and financial), and this may be the first time the software application has ever been used. Therefore, you can always depend on a number of unknowns in the software's performance and in the time of its delivery. Existing off-the-shelf application software is relatively easy to evaluate through in-house testing, talking with other customers, or from software reviews in the popular and trade press.

Combining Customized and Off-the-Shelf Applications Software

It is possible in some cases to combine the advantages of customized and off-the-shelf software. In these cases, companies may be able to purchase off-the-shelf software and then modify it for their own use. For example, a retailer may want to purchase an off-the-shelf inventory management program and then modify it to account for the specific products, outlets, and reports it needs to conduct its day-to-day business. In some cases, the company selling the off-the-shelf software makes these customized changes for a fee. Other vendors, however, do not allow their software to be modified. Oracle Applications and SAP are two very popular off-the-shelf application software suites that provide a set of customizable, wide-ranging business modules.

Examples of Information Systems Application Software

Application software is often categorized according to its design. Another useful way to categorize application software is by the type of application or task it supports. The two task-oriented categories for application software are large, business-oriented systems and office automation or personal productivity tools. Applications in the former category are purchased or developed by the organization to support the central, organization-wide operations of the company. Those in the latter category are tools primarily used to support the daily work activities of individuals and small groups. We'll describe each type of application software in the following sections and give some examples.

Business Information Systems

Business information systems are applications developed to perform the organization-wide operations of the firm. For example, most organizations have payroll applications to process their payrolls. A payroll application may take as inputs the individual time sheets completed by managers each week. These time sheets can be in the form of computerized sheets that can be read by optical scanners. Time sheets can be fed through the optical scanner to create a file of time sheet data, organized by employee (probably by using social security numbers, as mentioned earlier in the chapter). After the time sheet data is sorted by employee, it can be processed. That is, the application software can look at the pay rate for each employee, as well as the number of regular and overtime hours worked by each employee, to come up with a gross pay figure. Next, the application can consider the federal, state, and local taxes that must be deducted from the employee's gross pay. After all deductions are calculated, the application arrives at a net pay figure. This amount is what is actually paid to the employee.

At this point, the application has taken all time sheets, organized and sorted them by employee, and calculated gross pay, deductions, and net pay for each employee. These figures form a payroll master file. The payroll master file is created and backed up, perhaps on a tape drive on a mainframe computer. Next, the application must process checks so that they can be distributed to employees. To do this, the payroll application may create a check and register file. The check file might include the date, the employee's name, the social security number, and the net pay for the employee. The register file contains all of the previous elements, along with the time period, gross pay, and deductions for that time period for the employee's records. The check file is sorted by department, and checks are printed. Registers (a record of the checks printed) are also sorted and printed for distribution to employees.

This may not seem to be a complex process to conduct for only two or three employees. However, consider a large governmental organization, such as the Department of Defense, which must process and account for millions of employees' checks. Suddenly, a relatively simple process becomes a potential information-processing nightmare. Fortunately, very sophisticated application software exists, which can easily handle these very large data-intensive operations.

The same holds true for virtually any business operation you can think of. The "Mom and Pop" general store of the early 1900s may have been able to manage its inventory in the back of a notebook or on a handwritten ledger, but the "Mom and Pop" general store of the 21st century cannot afford to forego the benefits of computerizing operations. In particular, the mega-retailers of today, such as JC Penney, Sears Roebuck and Company, and Lands' End, must manage millions of pieces of merchandise and millions of transactions on a daily basis. These businesses rely on inventory management, order processing, billing, and shipping applications to conduct their operations. Without sophisticated, large-scale business application software, these businesses could not survive.

Office Automation/Personal Productivity Application Software

The second major type of application software is often grouped into a category called **office automation** or **personal productivity software**. Individuals or groups who want to accomplish a wide range of tasks typically use this type of software. Many of the large, well-known software companies, including Microsoft, Netscape, and Lotus, produce office automation software. Table 3.2 outlines some of the more popular personal productivity tools.

Table 3.2 Some examples of popular personal productivity tools.

Tool	Examples
Word Processor	Microsoft Word, Corel WordPerfect, Lotus AmiPro
Spreadsheet	Microsoft Excel, Lotus 1-2-3
Database management system	Borland Paradox, Microsoft Access, Borland dbase, Microsoft FoxPro
Presentation software	Microsoft PowerPoint, Software Publishing Corporation Harvard Graphics
PC-based email	Lotus cc:Mail, Microsoft Mail, Novell Groupwise
Web browser	Netscape Navigator, Spyglass Mosaic, Microsoft Internet Explorer

A BRIEF CASE ⟩——————————— **Microsoft Office** —————————

Microsoft Office 97's success should give you an idea of just how popular personal productivity software tools are becoming. It is the fastest selling business application ever. During 1997, Office 97 sold more than 20 million licenses, at an average rate of more than 60,000 per day (Microsoft, 1998). Microsoft Office provides the user with a suite of personal productivity software tools (see Table 3.3). In the past, many organizations purchased one tool from software vendor A and a second from software vendor B. Microsoft's strategy has been to bundle several popular tools into a single integrated suite of tools. This integration makes installation and ongoing maintenance much easier.

For example, suppose a company chooses to purchase a word processor from software vendor A, a spreadsheet from software vendor B, and an electronic mail system from vendor C. To install this software would require three separate installation activities. Software tends to evolve and change, so vendors often release new versions of their software on at least a yearly basis. In this scenario, each upgrade to the software requires the installation of the new version. Imagine that users have more than three types of software, but five or ten different packages from five or ten different vendors. Imagine also that an organization has thousands of PCs to upgrade and maintain. Note that many organizations keep commonly used software tools such as word processors on a common server that all users can access to ease installation and maintenance. Microsoft's strategy of having a suite of commonly used tools bundled on a single CD-ROM makes things much easier to install and maintain, no matter how and where the software is stored by the organization. As a result, other software companies are finding themselves at a big disadvantage. None have as broad a suite of tools as Microsoft. The result of this competitive advantage is that Microsoft Office has become the standard personal productivity software at increasing numbers of organizations, such as the World Bank, Chrysler Corporation, Dell Computer Corporation, and countless others. In the following sections, we describe several categories and examples of these tools and take a closer look at six types of personal productivity software.

Table 3.3 Personal productivity tools in Microsoft Office 97 Professional.

Tool Name	Primary Function
Word	Word processing for document preparation and desktop publishing
Excel	Spreadsheet for analyzing and organizing data
Outlook	Electronic mail and calendar for communication and personal schedules
PowerPoint	Presentation software to create graphics and presentation slides
Access	Database management system to store and report data

Word Processing. Word processing software is probably the most widely known and used type of personal productivity software. Although the purpose of word processing software has always been to produce a wide range of documents—from business letters to reports—today's word processors bear little resemblance to their predecessors of five or ten years ago. Today's word processors have incorporated powerful desktop publishing features that allow you to produce sophisticated layouts of your documents (see Figure 3.11). Today's word processors also enable you to import or create graphics, charts, or tables. Some even enable you to link charts or tables embedded in their word processing document to spreadsheets or graphics programs so that when a table is updated in a spreadsheet, that same table is automatically updated in the word processing document.

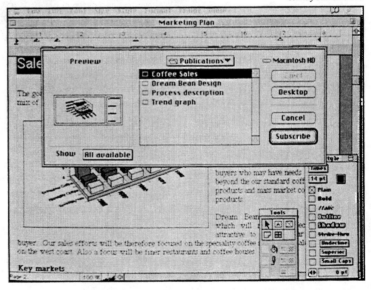

Courtesy FileMaker Inc.

FIGURE 3.11

A document created with a word processor.

Spreadsheets. Spreadsheets are important personal productivity tools for today's managers. Just as word processors allow you to work with and manipulate text, spreadsheets allow you to do the same with numbers. Spreadsheets are wonderfully adept at automatically calculating standard math operations. For example, finding the average of a series of numbers in a column, such as the average sales for a given period of time or region, is very simple to do with a spreadsheet. Spreadsheets can also be used to generate a wide variety of graphs to help present and summarize data. This capability makes them powerful forecasting tools that are invaluable for spotting and analyzing trends. Like word processors, today's spreadsheets offer many powerful features, including sophisticated statistical analysis, the capability to write macros (a type of programming that allows you to customize spreadsheets to automate routine tasks), and optimization routines, which walk you through a series of questions in order to arrive at a problem solution. Figure 3.12 shows a spreadsheet document.

FIGURE 3.12

A document created with a spreadsheet.

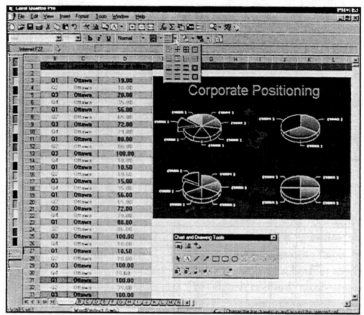

Courtesy Corel Corporation

Database Management Systems (DBMS). A database management system is designed to help us store and manipulate data in all formats—text, numerical data, or, in some cases, whole documents, graphics, or photos. Database systems are used on virtually all types of computers, from mainframes to PCs. They run some of the most powerful business-oriented applications that are used in organizations today. However, some PC-based database management systems fall into the personal productivity category. Database management systems enable you to view, manipulate, and summarize vast volumes of rich data in meaningful ways. Today's database systems offer graphical user interfaces and facilities for helping you formulate queries (see Figure 3.13) Powerful form generation features allow users to customize input forms that are used to enter data into the database and output forms (for example, preformatting a standard company report). We'll talk more about this important type of software in the next chapter.

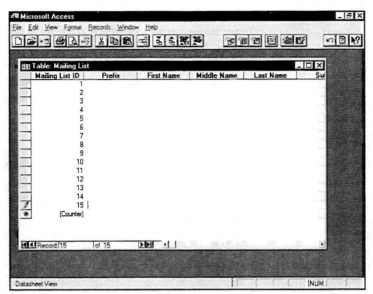

Courtesy Microsoft Corporation

FIGURE 3.13

Database screen shot.

Presentation Software. Presentation software is used for creating graphics and presentations. For example, sales teams can create presentations that help sell the company's products to prospective clients. The presentation might be presented using 35mm slides or overheads. An audio-visual tool that simply projects the screen images from a notebook computer onto a large 6-foot wide screen could also be used. Presentation software offers sophisticated layout options that enable you to create professional-looking presentations. Presentation software allows you to enter text or bulleted statements into an outline. It then takes that outline and generates titles, headings, and subheadings on eye-pleasing backgrounds. You can also import or link slides with spreadsheet or word processing documents so that any updates in one automatically update the other. Today's presentation software also offers you the option of specifying unique transitions between slides (for example, having one slide fade out and then be replaced by another or having the slide appear to drop off the bottom of the screen while the next slide appears to slides down from the top). Presentation software makes these operations relatively simple for you to create, so you can generate impressive, attention-grabbing displays (see Figure 3.14).

© *Bob Schatz/Gamma-Liaison*
International

FIGURE 3.14

A salesperson giving a presentation.

Electronic Mail. An innovation for many offices is electronic mail, or email (see Figure 3.15). These packages allow you to send electronic mail messages and files to others via a computer network. When attached to a network, all users have their own electronic mailboxes, in which they can send and receive messages. Electronic mail offers advantages over traditional (postal) mail, phone calls, or memos because it is often cheaper and faster to use. Newer electronic mail software features graphical user interfaces. With this software, you can compose messages offline, which the computer sends at a designated time.

FIGURE 3.15

Diagram of an email message being sent between two users over a network.

Internet and World Wide Web Browser Software. An even newer innovation for most offices is the use of the international Internet network and the World Wide Web (see Chapter 6, "Electronic Commerce and the Internet," for more information). Growth in the use of the Internet and World Wide Web has skyrocketed over the last few years. The Internet links people and networks from all over the world, allowing those at one location to send messages and access computers thousands of miles away, perhaps even on another continent. The World Wide Web is a graphical portion of the Internet that allows you to navigate through linked pages to other sites (called home pages). A relatively new type of office automation software is becoming a standard tool in many organizations—World Wide Web browsing software, or browsers. These browsers allow you to easily navigate a series of linked pages on the Web. Browser software also lets you view and download files, bookmark some of your favorite or commonly used Web pages for easy and immediate access later on, and connect to various Web search engines that allow you to look for information about a topic you are interested in.

A BRIEF CASE ——————————— **Browser War** ———

Web browsers have become an increasingly important tool for organizations. One of the most interesting ongoing developments in the software industry relates to the antitrust allegations by the U.S. Department of Justice (DOJ) against Microsoft for their Web browser, Internet Explorer (IE). At the root of this controversy is whether Microsoft's inclusion of IE with Windows 95 violated a 1995 consent decree in which the company agreed not to "tie" products to the operating system. In these proceedings, the DOJ has argued that bundling IE with Windows 95 is a violation of the decree (Ziff-Davis, 1998). Microsoft has argued that the browser is a part of the operating system and is therefore allowed under the consent decree. The issue gets even messier with the release of Windows 98, the recently released version of Microsoft's popular operating system, which was released in 1998. Windows 98 completely integrates the Web browser into the operating system. This issue will likely be a long-fought battle because it involves much more than Web browsers. It hits at the root of the multibillion dollar software market. Some in the software industry are arguing that because Microsoft controls a substantial part of the microcomputer operating system market, any bundling of nonoperating system applications with the operating system gives Microsoft an unfair competitive

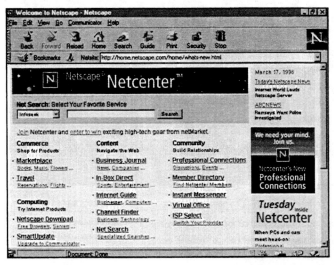

FIGURE 3.16

A Netscape screen showing a home page.

advantage over other software companies. Opponents of Microsoft fear that while today it is browsers, tomorrow it will be application programs and development tools. Such expansion would shut many companies out of the software business. Figure 3.16 shows a Netscape screen shot.

Programming Languages

All of the application software previously discussed is based on some programming language. A programming language is the computer language used by the software vendor to write application programs. For application software such as spreadsheets or database management systems, the underlying programming language is invisible to the user. However, programmers in an organization's information systems group and, in some instances, end users, can use programming languages to develop their own specialized applications. Many different types of programming languages exist, each with its own strengths and weaknesses. Some of the popular languages used in businesses today are included in Table 3.4.

Table 3.4 Some common programming languages.

Language	Application	Description
Ada	General purpose	Named after Ada, the Countess of Lovelace, who long ago envisioned computing machines. Ada is the Department of Defense's standard system development language for a broad range of applications.
BASIC	General purpose	Beginner's All-Purpose Symbolic Interaction Code. BASIC is a relatively simple language that has evolved into a very powerful language for developing systems with graphical user interfaces.
C/C++	General purpose	Third in a series (that is, Version C) of programming languages developed at AT&T Bell Labs. C is a very complex and powerful language that is used for a broad range of system- and application-level programming. C++ is an object-oriented extension of C.
COBOL	Business	Common Business Oriented Language. COBOL is the most widely used language for developing large data processing applications. Despite being challenged by newer languages, COBOL remains a popular alternative for many businesses.
FORTRAN	Scientific	Formula Translator. FORTRAN is used primarily for developing scientific and engineering applications. Like COBOL, it remains a popular language.
Java	World Wide Web	Java is an object-oriented programming language developed at Sun Microsystems. It is quickly becoming the programming language for the Internet.

98

Compilers and Interpreters

Programs created using programming languages must be translated into code—called assembly or **machine language**—that the hardware can understand. Most programming languages are translated into machine languages through a type of systems program called a **compiler**, as depicted in Figure 3.17. The compiler takes an entire program written in a programming language, such as C, and converts it into a completely new program in machine language that can be read and executed directly by the computer. Use of a compiler is a two-stage process. First, the compiler translates the computer program into machine language, and then the machine language program is executed.

FIGURE 3.17

How a compiler does its job.

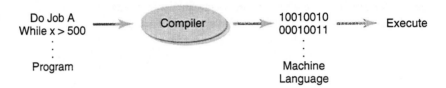

Some programming environments don't compile the entire program into machine language. Instead, each statement of the programming code is converted into machine language and executed one statement at a time, as depicted in Figure 3.18. The type of program that does the conversion and execution is called an **interpreter**. In sum, programming languages can be implemented by using either a compiled or an interpretive method.

FIGURE 3.18

How an interpreter does its job.

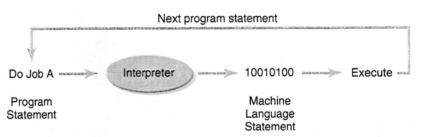

The Evolution of Information Systems Software

Information systems software continues to evolve. To understand where software may be headed in the future, it is useful to first understand where it came from.

Generations of Programming Languages

Like the evolution of IS hardware (see Chapter 2, "Information Systems Hardware"), the evolution of software can be described in terms of generations. In the following sections, we describe five generations of software.

First Generation: Machine Language

As you can imagine, the first generation of programming languages was quite crude by today's standards. Initially used in the 1940s, the first generation of programming languages was called machine languages. This is because programmers wrote their code in binary code, telling the computer exactly which circuits to turn on and which to turn off. As described in the previous chapter, binary code is written as a series of 1s and 0s, called bits. These bits are combined in order to turn the electronic circuits on and off and to perform operations on the computer. For example, a program statement in machine language that is used to simply add two numbers together might take several lines of code. More complex operations required thousands or hundreds of thousands of lines of code. Hobbyists who in 1975 bought the widely available first "personal" computer, the MITS Altair 8800 (which had to be assembled piece by piece, with some soldering required!), were forced to interact with their new computer by flipping toggle switches up and down on the front panel to program commands bit by bit. Now that's hacking!

Machine language is considered a low-level language. It is very unsophisticated and therefore very difficult to write. Because it is so difficult, very few programs are actually written in machine language. Programmers rely on higher-level languages instead. Still, all higher-level programs must eventually be translated into machine language by the computer before being executed.

Second Generation: Assembly Language

Assembly language, which is one step up from machine language, was first developed in the early 1950s. In assembly language, the binary code of 1s and 0s was replaced by symbols that are easier to understand. Letters were used to stand for a series of binary statements. For example, the letter "A" could be used to "Add" two numbers instead of relying on several lines of code. Because second-generation languages and those that followed relied on symbols instead of binary code, they are often called **symbolic languages**.

As mentioned previously, programs written in assembly language still must be converted into machine language by an **assembler** in order to run.

Third Generation: High-level Languages

Take a look again at Table 3.4. The languages listed in this table are all high-level languages, or third-generation languages. FORTRAN, the first third-generation language, was developed in the mid-1950s by IBM. These types of programs use symbols in their code, which are then translated into machine language. The difference between these high-level languages and second-generation languages is that the high-level languages use English-like words and commands. Continuing with our example, a third-generation programming language might use the English word "add" or the instruction "VARIABLE 3 = VARIABLE 1 + VARIABLE 2" to specify an addition operation. This is much easier to understand than its alternatives, using 1s and 0s in machine language or using the letter "A" in assembly language. A statement written in a high-level language usually translates into several machine language instructions. High-level languages are much easier to program than lower-level languages because they require fewer steps to achieve the same operation.

Different high-level languages are more appropriate for different types of tasks. Looking at Table 3.4, you can see that some high-level languages are better for scientific, or math-oriented applications. Other languages, such as COBOL, may be better for handling the large numbers of files that are common in business applications. Programmers must fully understand the tasks that are to be accomplished with the new application in order to choose the best programming language for those tasks.

Fourth Generation: Outcome-oriented Languages

As you might expect, fourth-generation languages are an even higher-level breed of language than third-generation languages. First developed in the 1970s, fourth-generation languages are even more like English, and they tend to focus on the desired output instead of the procedures required to get that output (as is the case for third-generation languages). Fourth-generation languages (4GLs) are often used to write and execute queries of a database. For example, the widely used database query language called Structured Query Language (SQL) is considered a fourth-generation language (see Figure 3.19).

```
SELECT LAST FIRST
FROM CUSTOMER
WHERE CREDIT_LIMIT = 100

DIEHR GEORGE
JANKOWSKI DAVID
HAGGARTY JOSEPH
JESSUP JAMIE
VALACICH JAMES
VALACICH JORDAN
```

FIGURE 3.19

Several lines of SQL, a 4GL language.

4GLs enable users to ask computers to provide certain information using sentence-like statements in English. For example, Figure 3.19 shows a 4GL statement that can be used to print a certain variable if that variable is greater than $100.00. If it is not greater than $100.00, then the computer prints another variable, Y.

Fifth Generation: Natural Languages

Fifth-generation languages (5GLs), although they are still not widespread, are being used in some expert system or artificial intelligence applications. 5GLs are called natural languages because they allow the user to communicate with the computer using true English sentences. For example, Hewlett-Packard and other software vendors have developed tools for document search and retrieval and database queries that let the user query the documents or database with English-like sentences. These sentences are then automatically converted into the appropriate commands (in some cases Structured Query Language) needed to query the documents or database and produce the result for the user. In some cases, if the system doesn't understand exactly what the user wants, it can ask for clarification. The same code shown in Figure 3.19 might appear as shown in Figure 3.20 if a natural language were used.

```
BEGINNING WITH THE LAST NAME ON THE FOL-
LOWING LIST OF CUSTOMERS, FIND CUSTOMERS
WHO HAVE A CREDIT LIMIT OF $100.

DIEHR GEORGE
JANKOWSKI DAVID
HAGGARTY JOSEPH
JESSUP JAMIE
VALACICH JAMES
VALACICH JORDAN
```

FIGURE 3.20

The same code used in Figure 3.19 as it would appear in a natural language.

Although 5GL languages are not common and are still being further developed, they have been used to forecast the performance of financial portfolios, help diagnose medical problems, and estimate weather patterns.

What's next after 5GL? Will the 6GL be a computer system that we simply talk to and instruct what to do, as we would another human? We might simply ask it if the accounts payable ledger exceeds $100.00. Even better, we might ask it to pay any existing bills under $100.00 and notify us whenever a bill for over $100.00 comes in. Perhaps the system could, over time, grow to know us and infer meaning from what we say or don't say. We might someday simply say, "Take care of the payables," and the system would automatically know what we meant from past experience, handle the payables accordingly, and then say, "Next time, say please."

While we haven't quite perfected the type of 6GL that we describe, programming languages continue to evolve. One new characteristic for describing programming languages is whether or not they are object-oriented. Next, we introduce object-oriented and visual programming languages.

Object-oriented Languages

Object-oriented programming languages are among the newest types of programming languages (see Satzinger and Orvik, 1996). Instead of separating variables, procedures, and data, as in traditional programming languages, object-oriented programs group all pieces together into "objects." An example of an object might be employee identification and payroll information and a set of corresponding rules for calculating monthly payroll for a variety of job classifications and tax rules. This process of grouping the data and instructions together into a single object is called **encapsulation**. By encapsulating the instructions and data together, programs are easier to maintain because the things that are grouped together are protected or isolated from other parts of the program. A programmer can go in and make major changes to object B without having any of those changes ripple throughout the program and affect object A.

A second characteristic of object-oriented languages is **inheritance**, which means that all lower-level, or children, nodes in an inheritance hierarchy inherit the characteristics of the parent node. For example, if engineers within a firm are determined to be part of the parent class called employees, they would automatically inherit any of the properties defined for the employee class, such as the property that all employees have a unique, nine-digit identification number. In traditional programming languages, data and processing steps are not coupled together, and lower-level procedures don't always inherit properties of a higher level one. As a result, reusing code is possible but much more complex, time-consuming, and error-prone than it is for object-oriented languages. In other words, after an object is created, it can be much more easily plugged into a number of different applications. Just as a radio made by Pioneer can be plugged into several different cars, an object can be plugged into several different applications.

Object-oriented languages are currently among the most popular languages, and their use continues to grow. C++ is an object-oriented enhancement of the original C programming language. Smalltalk, developed by Xerox, is also gaining strength in the business market. You can also see elements of object-oriented programming in Visual Basic and in multimedia authoring tools, such as Asymetrix Toolbook.

In addition to being object-oriented, programs and programming languages can also be **event-driven**. Unlike programs written in procedural programming languages, programs written with the event-driven approach do not follow a sequential logic. The programmer does not determine the sequence of execution for the program. The user can press certain keys and click on various buttons and boxes presented to her. Each of these user actions can cause an *event* to occur, which triggers a program procedure that the programmer has written. Programming languages, which are object-oriented, tend to also be useful for event-driven programming, as is Microsoft's Visual Basic. In addition to being object-oriented and event-oriented, programming languages are also visual.

Visual Programming Languages

As mentioned earlier in this chapter, today's system and application software often makes use of graphics through graphical user interfaces. Although the heavy use of graphics makes GUI applications easy to use (hopefully, anyway), it also makes them very difficult to program. In order to help programmers develop these graphical environments for their applications, visual programming languages have been created.

Visual programming languages make programming easier and more intuitive. They allow the programmer to create the graphics-intensive applications that today's business users demand. For example, to make a button appear for the user on a particular screen at a particular point in time, a programmer using a visual programming language only needs to bring up the screen where the button is to appear, choose the button from a palette of choices, drag and drop the button to the proper location, size and style the button with a few mouse clicks, and click on the button's pop-up menu to set the properties that will control its behavior (see Figure 3.21). To accomplish the same tasks with a traditional programming language was much more difficult and time-consuming, and it required far more expertise. We would have had to describe in many, many painstaking lines of programming code exactly which pixels on the screen were to be colored in to make the button appear, what colors were to be used, and exactly how the button was to behave when clicked. Programs such as Visual Basic or Visual C++ (a visual derivative of the object-oriented C++) are popular examples of visual programming languages.

As you can see, the development of programming languages is an ongoing process of change and innovation. These changes often result in more capable and complex systems for the user. The final section of this chapter explores trends that can be seen in the software developed by today's programmers.

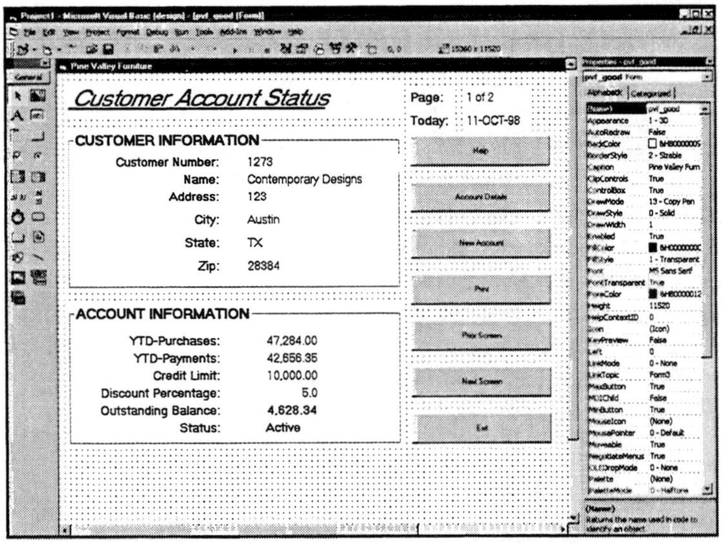

Screen shot reprinted by permission of Microsoft Corporation.

FIGURE 3.21

Visual Basic development environment.

Emerging Trends in Software

Writing a trends section in any information systems book is dangerous because today's trend can quickly become tomorrow's history. However, it is worth mentioning a couple of recent developments that may significantly change how we think about software and, ultimately, computing.

Merging of Hardware and Software

Although it has been useful to think of hardware and software as separate, independent, distinct components of information systems, the line between the two is becoming more and more blurred.

For example, many small computers have been developed that contain software directly programmed into the computer itself (usually coded into a microchip). These computers are designed to perform a single task or set of tasks easily and efficiently. Have you ever signed for a package from Federal Express? Today, when you sign for a package, your signature is recorded electronically on a computer tablet and is communicated to a central set of computers that track each and every package in the Federal Express system. This clipboard makes it possible for you to call a carrier (or even better, to access their World Wide Web site), enter a package tracking number, and find out the location of that package. Federal Express's automated clipboard is a good example of an application where the software is embedded with the hardware (the computer tablet and stylus).

Also, some of today's automobiles contain sophisticated on-board computer hardware/software that manages, corrects, and diagnoses all systems in the automobile, from oxygen flow to whether the taillights are operating properly. Computer chips monitor all of these operations. Are these chips hardware? Yes. Are they software? Yes. You can see that the distinction between hardware and software is becoming a little murkier than it once was. Computer chips with complex on-board software are finding their way into more and more devices throughout our homes and offices—for example, home appliances, credit cards, and door locks.

Integrated Telecommunications

In information systems today, a system's hardware and software are almost always tied to some form of telecommunications. In fact, as in the preceding section, a system's telecommunications capabilities are almost inseparable from the hardware/software itself.

Returning to our Federal Express example, once you sign for a package, that information is communicated (probably via satellite) to the company's central computers. As mentioned earlier, automobiles also make heavy use of hardware/software systems, including an integrated telecommunications system. Have you ever seen an automobile that had a built-in map system that could plot and track your route to a given destination? While this system currently exists mainly in today's very expensive luxury cars, such systems will probably be commonplace within the decade. These systems make use of a Global Positioning System (or GPS) to track where your car is in relation to your intended destination, as shown in Figure 3.22. In GPS systems, a chip in your car communicates with a GPS satellite to plot your position anywhere on the earth and can compare the information about your current location with your desired destination. On-board systems

104

then figure out how to reconcile those differences and plot that information on a map. GPS systems are standard equipment on today's aircraft and ships and will likely become common in tomorrow's automobiles, bicycles, or golf carts!

FIGURE 3.22

A GPS system in a car.

Another example of an integrated software and telecommunications system is the simple voice mail systems offered by many vendors today. Callers can leave voice mail messages that can be stored on a computer and then retrieved later by the intended recipient. Like email, this integrated software/telecommunications system enables people to avoid the hassle of playing telephone tag all day just to deliver a short message to someone.

Similarly, touch-tone routing systems can be used to enable users calling into a company to get information automatically or can be routed to someone who can help them. For example, many financial institutions allow a user to get existing balances on accounts over the phone by simply entering her account number and a personal identification number (PIN). The user may then be presented with a number of choices (for example, hitting "1" to get a checking balance, "2" to get a savings balance, "3" to get current loan rates, or "4" to speak with a customer service representative). The goal of these systems is to permit greater access to the customer (customers can access information 24 hours a day), while relieving personnel strains for the financial institution.

The World Wide Web promises to revolutionize the intermingling of telecommunications and software. Software physically located in one place might be linked to other locations around the globe. For example, it is possible to conduct a teleconference over the Internet (see Figure 3.23). The teleconferencing software controls who gets to talk and controls the views that each user has. At the same time, it interfaces with sophisticated telecommunications systems in order to compress and decompress audio and visual images being sent from several locations. The user does not have to see or manage this process himself. If he did, no work could ever get done, because his attention would be focused on *how to communicate* rather than *the task at hand.* Today's software systems that integrate telecommunications allow the user to focus on business-related tasks, rather than on how to make the computer and/or telecom-

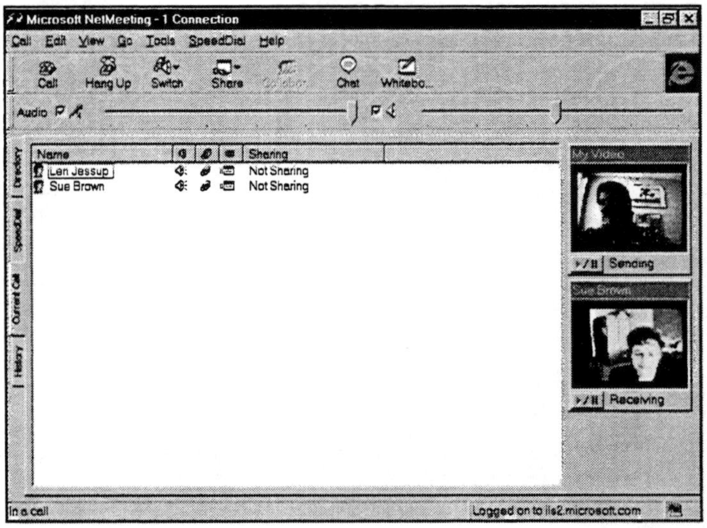

FIGURE 3.23

Screen shot from NetMeeting.

munications systems work. If these systems become widely used, and early evidence suggests that they will (Arnaut, 1998), companies will greatly reduce travel expenses.

One other interesting way that the Web is changing our notions of telecommunications and software is through the rising popularity of the Java programming language. Java is an object-oriented programming language that runs across multiple hardware platforms and operating systems. Java can be used to create small programming applications, called applets, that appear on Web pages in much the same way images do, except that, unlike images, applets can be dynamic and interactive. For example, applets could be used to create animations, figures, or even areas on the user's screen where she can respond by clicking a mouse or by inputting text. An applet might contain a game that the user can play on her computer (Lemay and Perkins, 1996).

You use Java to write and compile the applet and then link the applet to your Web page. When a Web user views your page with the embedded applet, his Web browser downloads the applet to his local system and executes it (see Figure 3.24). In a sense, Java allows you to write and dynamically ship little programs back and forth across the Internet that other people can use quite easily and quickly without knowing they have downloaded and are running a special piece of software. Let's apply this to the banking scenario from the beginning of the chapter. The bank we described might choose to enable customers to do some of their banking via the Web. The bank could easily write a Java application that, when a customer visited the bank's Web site and clicked on the right button, would automatically download itself on the customer's computer, launch itself, and enable the customer to quickly and easily set the parameters for a loan—such as the loan amount, number of months until payoff, and the interest rate. The same Java program could then automatically calculate and present the payment amount for the customer on her Web browser.

These are just some of the emerging trends in software. As you read this chapter, more trends are developing that will replace those mentioned here. Software remains an exciting and innovative area where capabilities continue to grow at unprecedented rates. Stay tuned!

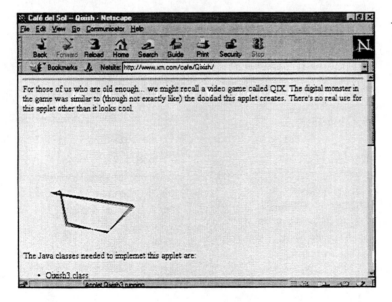

FIGURE 3.24

An applet on a browser screen.

ETHICAL PERSPECTIVE: VENI, VIDI, VICI—I CAME, I SAW, I HACKED

When you hear the term "computer hacker," you might imagine a techno-geek, someone who sits in front of her computer all day and night attempting to break the ultra-super secret security code of one of the most sophisticated computer systems in the world, perhaps a computer for the U.S. Military, a Swiss bank, or the CIA. While this fits the more traditional profile for a computer hacker, there is no clear profile today. More and more people have the skills, tools, and the motive to hack into a computer system. A modern-day hacker could be a disgruntled, middle-aged, white-collar worker sitting at a nice desk on the fourteenth floor of the headquarters building of a billion-dollar software manufacturer.

Computer hackers, also known as crackers, have been around for decades. For the most part, we associate hackers with their pranks and crimes involving security systems and viruses. Hackers have caused the loss of billions of dollars' worth of stolen goods, repair bills, and lost goodwill with customers. The premise for the movie *War Games* is based on this more traditional notion of the "typical" young hacker whose prank goes awry. However, many companies are beginning to take advantage of this highly technical and computer-literate community in their own research and development, as exemplified in the movie *The Net*.

In an attempt to create the perfect software program, companies are hiring hackers to find the bugs in the software prior to its release to the public. These companies may be manufacturing anything—from a new release of a software game, to a serious business application, to security software for banks. In some cases, the hackers have been formerly convicted and are now using their programming expertise to help the firms battle against other hackers. These firms essentially contract with the hackers to attempt to break into their systems, steal data, copy files, and otherwise cause havoc. These firms reason that they would rather have a contracted hacker attempting to break in, modify, or steal their software than another, unknown hacker. If there are weaknesses in the software, the contracted hacker can help the firm identify and address them before the product is released for general use. As you can imagine, using hackers in this way requires a lot of trust from the firms. However, such a relationship between firm and hacker can be quite beneficial.

A similar successful practice has been the use of the general public to find bugs and loopholes in early versions of software. These beta versions of software are made available to the public, who are asked to report any bugs, loopholes, errors, and so on while using the software. The manufacturer uses the information from these pseudoconsultants to fix the software before final release. This process is far cheaper than using in-house or contracted experts, yet it is not as efficient or as extensive. Software producers, such as Microsoft and Netscape, have made very good use of this practice. In addition to being a vehicle for improving the software, this practice also has the strategic marketing value of prebuilding market share before the final release of a software package.

Still, hackers with negative intentions do exist, and they continue to cause problems for companies and government organizations. Efforts to thwart hackers have increased. New hardware solutions, such as passkey microchips, work for only one user at a time. There are new software solutions, such as better encryption algorithms. Finally, there are new organizational solutions, such as the use of internal emergency response teams. Like the Computer Emergency Response Team at Carnegie Mellon, many businesses and government agencies are now staffing their own teams. The government has also announced plans for a "hacker SWAT team" that would remain on alert for large-scale national emergencies. As long as there are smart people with the capabilities to hack into systems and the motivation to do harm, other smart people will continue to devise technological and organizational solutions to thwart them.

Questions for Discussion

1. Can former criminals really be trusted to put forth their best efforts for these software manufacturers?

2. Do you feel the media generates too much hype regarding hacking and hackers? Or is the danger legitimate?

3. Are you concerned about hackers cracking the security codes on the computer programs at your bank and accessing your account and other sensitive information?

Source Kerr, Deborah. 1998. Hacker stoppers? Companies bought $65 million worth of network-intrusion tools last year but capabilities still lag what's promised. InformationWeek. April 20, 140-144.

INTERNATIONAL PERSPECTIVE: SOFTWARE PIRACY ACROSS INTERNATIONAL BORDERS

A major international issue businesses deal with is the willingness (or unwillingness) of governments and individuals to recognize and enforce the ownership of intellectual property—in particular, software copyright. Piracy of software and other technologies is widespread internationally. The Business Software Alliance (BSA) points to countries such as China, Thailand, Turkey, Indonesia, Iran, Saudi Arabia, and Kuwait as those with the highest percentages of illegal software.

In the United States, $2,876,922,400 worth of illegal software was pirated in 1994. Roughly 35 percent of all of the software in use in the country is running from illegal copies, which is only the tip of the iceberg. The BSA estimates that in 1994, U.S. companies lost $101,000,000 from pirated software in Saudi Arabia alone. Around 90 percent of all of the software in the kingdom is illegal. China is another country notorious for software piracy, with a rate of 90 percent of all software in the country pirated. It is said that Chinese companies can take one legitimate software purchase and churn out enough copies to satisfy the entire country's needs.

An ethical problem? Perhaps in part, but there are other perspectives that business people must acknowledge and deal with as well. In part, the problem stems from countries' differing concepts of ownership. Many of the ideas about intellectual property ownership stem from long-standing cultural traditions. For example, the concept of individual ownership of knowledge is traditionally a strange one in countries such as Saudi Arabia, where knowledge is meant to be shared. Plagiarism doesn't exist in a country where words belong to everyone. By the same token, piracy does not exist either. This view is gradually changing, and the Saudi Patent Office recently granted its first patents.

In other cases, there are political, social, and economic reasons for piracy. In many other countries, software publishers are simply not catering to the needs of consumers, who often simply do not have the funds to purchase software legitimately. This is true in many areas of South America and other regions with low per capita income. It is particularly true of students and other members of university communities, whose needs are critical in some areas.

In China, these and other forces come into play. Although the Chinese government claims to enforce treaties, only a handful of intellectual property cases in China have ever been decided in favor of foreign companies. One of the few was brought by the Walt Disney Company, which won a $77,000 judgment against Chinese companies that were producing books based on Disney films. In an era of high growth and little internal policy, treaties, although given lip service, are difficult to enforce.

The Chinese might be resistant to following copyright laws for several reasons. Kenneth Ho (1995) notes that historically, the Chinese (along with many other cultures) have had a strong emphasis on learning by copying. Ho notes that copying well is regarded as a compliment to the originator of the work. In addition, for many Chinese individuals, the concept of ownership of intellectual property is not only foreign, but something that goes against the notion of the value of the society over the individual.

Other factors leading to piracy or infringement of intellectual property agreements throughout the world include lack of public awareness about the issue, lack of an industrial infrastructure that can produce legitimate software, and the increasingly high demand for computer and other technology products. The U.S. has repeatedly pressured and threatened other countries accused of pirating. It is interesting to note, however, that few of these cultural and economic explanations are valid in the U.S. but that we lead the world in the sheer volume of illegal software in use. Businesses that operate in glass offices should surely not throw stones.

Questions for Discussion

1. How can businesses accommodate the cultural perspectives of other groups while remaining competitive?

2. Should American businesses address the needs of the economically and technologically poor around the world? If so, in what ways?

3. How can the high volume of pirated software in the U.S. be explained?

Sources   Ho, Kenneth. 1995. *A study into the problem of software piracy in Hong Kong and China.* London School of Economics and Political Science. See http://pluto.houston.com.hk/hkgrpd/piracy.html

Talking with...

Patrick Casey, Senior Systems Analyst at Interart Distribution, Inc.

Education

B.A., Indiana University; M.B.A., Indiana University

Job Description

Mr. Casey is responsible for the analysis and design of new and/or existing data systems. He coordinates resources, schedules, and communication for the implementation of new systems or major enhancements to existing systems. Mr. Casey is also responsible for applications development of critical modules for large systems.

Critical Success Factors

Technical competence is, of course, a must. On that foundation, seek to see things through the eyes of your customers. Avoid speaking of IT issues in techno-babble, but phrase them—and see them—as much as possible through the lens of business objectives and user deliverables. Make your objectives concrete and measurable (in God we trust; everyone else is required to provide facts).

Advice to Students

Be objective, not ego-protective. Understand your role—and the role of your projects—in the "big picture." Regularly reassess the usefulness of operations. Don't accept criticism; welcome it!

Summary

1. **Understand the importance of information systems software for today's organizations.** As the use of computer-based systems has continued to rise, software has become a larger percentage of an organization's total technology costs. Because software gives life to the information system hardware, it has become the key enabler for today's business strategies, allowing businesses to compete in today's dynamic environment and facilitating re-engineering, or rightsizing, business operations in order to become as efficient as possible.

2. **Describe the common functions of systems software.** Systems software is the collection of programs that form the foundation for the basic operations of the computer hardware. Systems software, or the operating system, performs many different tasks. Some of these tasks include booting your computer, reading programs into memory, managing memory allocation to those programs, managing where programs and files are located in secondary storage, maintaining the structure of directories and subdirectories, formatting disks, controlling the computer monitor, and sending objects to the printer. The systems software manages the dialogue you can have with a computer using either a command-based or graphical interface. A command-based interface requires that text commands be typed into the computer, while a graphical user interface (GUI) uses pictures and icons as well as menus to send instructions back and forth from the user to the computer system.

3. **Explain the various types of application software.** You can find a large number of computer software applications. Some, which are called customized application software, are developed specifically for a single organization. This kind of software is tailored to an organization's unique requirements. Off-the-shelf application software is not customized to the unique needs of one organization but is written to operate within many organizations. In

general, off-the-shelf software is less costly, faster to procure, of higher quality, and less risky than customized software. Business information systems are applications developed to perform the firm's organization-wide operations, such as payroll or inventory management. Office automation or personal productivity software is designed to support activities such as word processing and electronic mail.

4. **Describe the characteristics of various types of programming languages.** A programming language is the computer language used by programmers to write application programs. In order to run on a computer, programs must be translated into binary machine language. Programming languages are translated into machine languages through special types of programs, which are called compilers and interpreters.

5. **Discuss the evolution of computer software.** There have been five generations of programming software. The first generation used machine language, which told the computer exactly which circuits to turn on and which to turn off. The second generation used assembly language, which used symbols to represent a series of binary statements. Assembly language made it much easier to write programs. The third generation used high-level languages, such as FORTRAN, COBOL, C, and Java. The difference between these high-level languages and second-generation languages is that the

high-level languages use English-like words and commands, making it even easier to write programs than it was with the assembly language. Fourth-generation languages are called outcome-oriented languages because they contain even more English-like commands and tend to focus on what output is desired instead of the procedures required to get that output. Again, these languages made it even easier to program. Fifth-generation languages are called natural languages because they allow the user to communicate with the computer using true English sentences.

Although not part of this generational evolution, object-oriented programming and visual programming are relatively new enhancements to programming languages. Object-oriented languages group together data and their corresponding instructions into manipulatable objects. Visual programming languages use a graphical interface that allows programs to be visual objects for the applications that need a graphical interface. Both object-oriented and visual programming languages are making it easier for programmers to develop today's complex software systems. While it has been useful to think of hardware and software as separate, independent, distinct components of information systems, the line between the two is becoming increasingly blurred. In the future, the distinction between hardware and software will continue to blur.

Key Terms

Data	Command-based interface	Compiler
Information	Graphical user interface	Interpreter
Knowledge	Application software	Symbolic languages
Wisdom	Customized application software	Assembler
Software	Off-the-shelf application software	Object-oriented programming languages
Computer programs	Business information systems	Encapsulation
Documentation	Office automation or personal productivity software	Inheritance
Systems software	Machine language	Event-driven
Operating system		Visual programming languages
Interface		

Review Questions

1. Compare and contrast the terms "data," "information," and "knowledge."

2. Describe the two basic types of information systems software.

3. Describe at least four different tasks performed by an operating system.

4. What is the difference between a command-based interface and a graphical user interface?

5. Describe the similarities and differences among at least three major operating systems in use today.

6. List some of the advantages of using off-the-shelf application software.

7. Describe how office automation software differs from business information systems.

8. Describe the six major types of office automation software outlined in this chapter.

9. Explain the differences between a compiler and an interpreter.

10. What does the term "4GL" mean and how does it differ from "3GL" and "5GL"?

11. Describe several examples of technology that have incorporated the trend of merging hardware and software.

Problems and Exercises

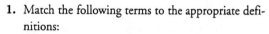 Individual   Group   Field   Web/Internet

1. Match the following terms to the appropriate definitions:

____ Information

____ Computer program

____ Systems software

____ Graphical user interface

____ Customized application software

____ Business information systems

____ Compiler

____ Object-oriented programming languages

a. Translates the computer program into machine language, which is then executed by the computer

b. An interface that enables the user to select pictures, icons, and menus in order to send instructions to the computer

c. Data formatted in such a way that it has additional value

d. Applications developed to perform the organization-wide operations of the firm

e. The collection of programs that performs and coordinates the interaction among hardware devices, peripherals, and application software

f. A set of coded instructions written in a programming language that directs the hardware circuitry to operate in a predefined way

g. Programming languages that group together data and their corresponding instructions into manipulatable objects

h. Software developed based on specifications provided by a particular organization

2. Imagine that your boss has just told you that "this piece of software is useless because all it does is store numbers and text." How would you explain the usefulness of this software application to your boss so that he would understand its importance to the company? Be sure to use terms such as "data," "information," "software," and so on.

3. Discuss the following in a small group of classmates. Many long-time computer users have grown up with command-based interfaces to the computer's operating system. Based on what you know about resistance to change from Chapter 2, outline a detailed explanation of the advantages of moving to a graphical user interface (GUI) so that these long-time users will be convinced to make the switch.

4. As a group, discuss the implications for an organization of having more than one operating system. What might be the advantages? What are some of the disadvantages? Would you recommend such a situation? Can you find organizations using the World Wide Web that specifically mention their utilization of multiple operating systems in their information system architecture? Do these organizations comment on this arrangement or simply mention its existence? Prepare a 10-minute presentation to the rest of the class of your findings.

5. Imagine that you are in charge of procuring software applications for your division of a company. You are in need of a powerful business information systems software application that will control most of the accounting and bookkeeping functions. Based on your current knowledge of the intricacies of the accounting profession and its practices, would you be more likely to purchase this application as a customized software application or an off-the-shelf software application? Why did you select this choice? What would make you choose the other option?

6. Do you feel that 5GL programming languages will lead to the 6GL "proposals" mentioned in this chapter? Why or why not? Discuss this idea with some of your classmates. What would you like to see as a part of the next generation of programming languages?

7. Based on the information within this chapter and others within this textbook, discuss the importance of a single decision to purchase one software application over another—for example, purchasing Microsoft Excel instead of Lotus 1-2-3. Who will be affected? How will they be affected? What changes might occur because of the purchase?

8. Interview an IS manager within an organization with which you are familiar. Determine the extent to which this person gets the data, information, knowledge, and wisdom needed to get the job done effectively. Does she obtain this information from IS sources? If not, how could IS be used to help?

9. In a small group of classmates, discuss the following. Based on your own experiences with computers and computer systems, what do you like and dislike about different operating systems that you have used? Were these uses on a professional or a personal level, or both? Who made the decision to purchase that particular operating system? Did you have any say in the purchase decision?

10. Choose an organization with which you are familiar that utilizes a variety of different software applications. Are these software applications customized applications, off-the-shelf applications, or a combination of the two? Talk with some of the employees to determine how they feel about using customized versus off-the-shelf software applications.

11. Search the World Wide Web for organizations that specialize in creating customized software applications for their clients. What specific product categories do these organizations specialize in, if any? Were you able to find any pricing information directly from their home pages?

12. Have the off-the-shelf software applications you've experienced met your requirements? Were you able to perform the functions and routines that you needed? Did the software meet your expectations? Would you have bought this type of software if you knew then what you know today?

13. Form a small group and describe your experiences with programming languages. Have you utilized them professionally? Based on the definitions in this chapter, with what generation of languages were you working? Were you aware of this designation prior to reading this chapter?

14. Choose an organization with which you are familiar that does a lot of in-house programming and utilizes a variety of different programming languages. Determine the generation level of these languages. Are the same personnel programming most (or all) of the languages, or are different personnel programming for each of the languages? Is this assignment of programmers intentional or unintentional?

15. Choose an organization with which you are familiar that utilizes a variety of different software applications. As a group of classmates, determine whether these software applications are from the same vendor or different vendors. Does this organization have compatibility problems between applications? Are there any plans underway to solve these compatibility problems? Who is trying to solve the problems, the programmers and end users or management?

16. Imagine that you and a friend are at a local ATM machine getting some cash from your account to pay for a movie. The ATM machine doesn't seem to be working. It is giving you an error message every time you press any button. Is this most likely a software-related problem or a hardware-related problem? Why? Use the information in this chapter and in the previous chapter to help you make your decision.

Real World Case Problems

1. ZAP! How the Year 2000 Bug Will Hurt the Economy

Robert Cowie, CIO of Genzyme Corporation, the biotech giant, realized early in 1996 that nearly every major system in the company would be unable to handle dates in the next century—the Year 2000 problem. If left uncorrected, the production equipment, the research and development computers, and the computers handling order taking and billing would all fail on or before January 1, 2000. Cowie is fortunate; thanks to an early start, the systems in his firm will all be repaired well ahead of the deadline.

Organizations that are not ready for the year 2000 are in for a serious awakening. Already the Securities &

Exchange Commission has been strongly encouraging companies to report the effect of the Year 2000 problem on their earnings. Although many believe the issue has generated too much hype, the Year 2000 problem is starting to have a significantly negative impact on the U.S. economy. A recent analysis by Standard & Poor's DRI shows the growth rate in 1999 to be 0.3 percentage points lower as companies divert resources to solve the problem. The Year 2000 problem could also cut one half a percentage point off growth in 2000 and in 2001. This growth reduction is the same size as the economic damage from the turmoil in East Asia. The total cost of the Year 2000 problem could be as high as $119 billion in lost economic output between now and 2001. Inflation will increase and productivity growth will be lower than it otherwise would have been. Instead of creating or installing new productivity-enhancing systems, every company is diverting money and staff toward fixing the Year 2000 problem.

Management consulting firms have added approximately 200,000 new workers over the past two years. Additionally, programmers' wages are dramatically increasing due to the need to correct this problem. Some businesses are doomed to have computer failures in 2000. A December 1997 survey by Howard Rubin at Hunter College found that two out of three companies did not have detailed plans to address the Year 2000 problem. Even the Federal Reserve is under pressure to raise interest rates, which would further run the risk of increasing the post–2000 slowdown.

a. Is this just a bunch of hype promoted by consulting companies, or is the Year 2000 problem real? Why?

b. What are some of the types of firms and systems that are likely to be adversely affected by this problem?

c. Robert Cowie, CIO of Genzyme Corporation, fixed his firm's Year 2000 problems early. What are the implications of NOT fixing the problem on time?

Source 1998. *Zap!: How the Year 2000 bug will hurt the economy.* BusinessWeek, *March 2, 93–97*

2. Java for the Enterprise: Faster, Easier to Manage, More Scalable

In 1997, Sun Microsystems announced its eagerly awaited Enterprise JavaBeans specification—the industry's first server-specialized component model. Oracle also announced another Java milestone—the vendor's entire suite of client/server applications, Oracle Applications 10.7 NCA, was delivered as an all-Java package. These all-Java products and technologies were designed to push Java further into the mainstream.

Mike Anderson, director of application services at Home Depot, a $20-million home improvement chain center, says that they have been building mission-critical applications that he plans to implement throughout their 700 locations nationwide. These applications include inventory replenishment, human resource systems for training, job applicant requirements and benefits, and a virtual office for remote store managers.

Sabre Technologies and the Ralston Purina Company will both be using Java for cross-platform benefits. Sabre's Qik-Access product, which includes easy-to-use airline reservations, airport departure control, and travel agency systems, was written in C++ and is on more than 100,000 PCs using OS/2, Windows, and DOS. Rewriting the program in Java allows customers to use network computers and other thin clients to gain Sabre access to the smaller customers in the marketplace.

Ralston Purina will follow similarly with Packview, a Java-based manufacturing application for managing managers' schedules and equipment for packing rooms. Packview, as with Qik-Access, will run on multiple platforms. Applications that were once written in C or C++ can now be handled by JavaBeans. Companies can use JavaBeans to increase their flexibility in creating applications on the Internet; however, JavaBeans is still in the first draft—not in the final stage.

a. How important is Sun's unveiling of its Enterprise JavaBeans specification and Oracle's delivery of its products as all-Java packages? Why?

b. Why are firms such as Home Depot and Ralston Purina so attracted to Java?

c. Should firms and universities still spend resources on training people to program in languages such as C, C++, Visual Basic, and COBOL?

Source Levin, Rich. 1997. *Java for the enterprise.* InformationWeek, *December 8, 18–20.*

References

Arnaut, G. 1998. No frills, just service with a screen. *New York Times*, January 26, C5.

Fishauf, L. 1994. The Information Age in charts. *Fortune*, April 4, 75.

Fitzgerald, M. 1990. 'When' is now at Sears. *Computerworld*, October 8, 67.

Lemay, L., and C. L. Perkins. 1996. *Sams Teach Yourself Java in 21 Days*. Indianapolis, Indiana: Sams Publishing.

Microsoft, 1998. Information from: www.microsoft.com. Verified: February 7, 1998.

SABRE, 1998. Information from: www.amr.com. Verified: February 7, 1998.

SAP, 1998. Information from: www.sap.com. Verified: February 7, 1998.

Satzinger, J. W., and T. U. Orvik. 1996. The object-oriented approach: Concepts, modeling, and system development. Danvers, Massachusetts: boyd & fraser publishing company.

Ziff-Davis, 1998. Information from: www.sap.com. Verified: February 7, 1998.

Related Readings

Druschel, P. 1996. Operating system support for high-speed communication. *Communications of the ACM* 39(9): 41–51.

Dumas, J., and P. Parsons. 1995. Discovering the way programmers think about new programming environments. *Communications of the ACM* 38(6): 45–56.

Gentner, D., and J. Nielson. 1996. The anti-Mac interface. *Communications of the ACM* 39(8): 70–82.

Glass, R.L. 1997. The next date crisis and the ones after that. *Communications of the ACM* 40(1): 15–17.

Glass, R.L. 1997. The ups and downs of programmer stress. *Communications of the ACM* 40(4): 17–19.

Glass, R.L. 1997. Cobol—A contradiction and an enigma. *Communications of the ACM* 40(9): 11–13.

Kekre, Krishnan, and Srinivasan. 1995. Drivers of customer satisfaction for software products: Implications for design and service support. *Management Science* 41(9): 1456–1470.

Kim, J., and F.J. Lerch. 1997. Why is programming (sometimes) so difficult?: Programming as scientific discovery in multiple problem spaces. *Information Systems Research* 8(1): 25–50.

Klepper, R., and D. Bock. 1995. Third and fourth generation language productivity differences. *Communications of the ACM* 38(9): 69–79.

Nachenberg, C. 1997. Computer virus–antivirus coevolution. *Communications of the ACM* 40(1): 46–51.

Rudnicky, Hauptmann, and Lee. 1994. Survey of current speech technology. *Communications of the ACM* 37(3): 52–57.

Wiebe, Hirst, and Horton. 1996. Language use in context. *Communications of the ACM* 39(1): 102–111.

Chapter 4: Organizational Information Systems

Scenario: Making Better Loan Decisions

The Big Loan Bank (BLB) specializes in making loans in excess of $20,000,000 to municipalities for major construction projects. After having completed a third "Detailed Loan Study" in a year that failed to result in a loan, the president of the Big Loan Bank (BLB), George Hubman, called his chief information officer, Michelle Williams, to his office for a brainstorming session.

"Michelle, before issuing a loan, we conduct a lengthy and expensive study called a 'Detailed Loan Study.' In this study, detailed environmental and economic impact studies are performed. On average, these studies can take up to 6 months, yield a report in excess of 1000 pages, and can exceed $250,000 in costs.

"Additionally, we do not recover the costs of conducting these studies unless we actually issue the loan. In other words, the investment in the study is lost if the loan is not issued! Recently, we have conducted three studies that failed to result in a loan. Over the past year, we have had significantly fewer loans issued relative to the number of projects studied (see Figure 7.1). We must discover a better way of conducting and paying for these studies or we are going to have to get out of the big loan business.

"I wanted to come by and see whether you had any ideas on how we could use information technology to help with this problem."

"Well, George, it sounds as if you need a system to help you pick which projects to study and which projects to reject."

"Exactly!" replied George. "I need a system to help me make better choices *before* we conduct the study and spend $250,000. Is that possible?"

Michelle replied, "BLB has some of the best information systems technology in the banking industry, so options are open to us to help with this problem. For example, if we could identify some easy-to-gather factors that would help us determine which projects are good and which are bad, we could build a model that would help you make a rough prediction of good and bad projects. Such a system would at least enable you to identify the clear winners and losers. Over time we could refine our model so that eventually we could be making very reliable predictions. Are there some easy-to-identify factors that seem to distinguish good and bad projects?"

"Oh yes, there are a few factors that really make a difference," replied George. "Currently, we look at these factors only after agreeing to do the study. I guess there is no reason why we couldn't change the way we do things. It would require that we conduct a 'mini-study' to get this data, which wouldn't be free, but it would be a lot cheaper than $250,000! If we can get you this data, do you think you can build a system to help us with our decision-making?"

Introduction

The focus of this chapter is to describe several types of information systems that are widely used in organizations. Some of the systems described are relatively new, while others have been mainstays in organizations since the 1960s. Information systems have evolved with the changes in organizations and technology. To help you to better understand the various types of information systems, this chapter describes where and how each is commonly used in organizations.

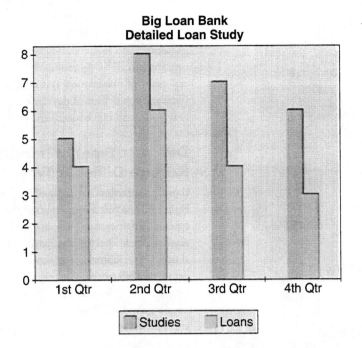

Big Loan Bank
Detailed Loan Study

FIGURE 7.1

Detailed Loan Study
summary report.

□ Studies □ Loans

After reading this chapter you will be able to do the following:

1. Describe the characteristics that differentiate the operational, managerial, and executive levels of an organization.

2. Explain the characteristics of the three information systems designed to support each unique level of an organization: transaction processing systems, man-agement information systems, and executive information systems.

3. Describe the characteristics of three information systems that span the organizational, managerial, and executive levels: decision support systems, expert systems, and office automation systems.

4. Explain the general information system needs of various organizational functional areas.

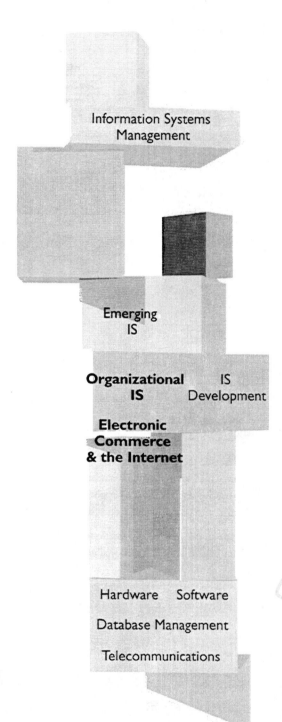

Information Systems
Management

Emerging
IS

Organizational   IS
   IS   Development

**Electronic
Commerce
& the Internet**

Hardware   Software

Database Management

Telecommunications

Like Chapter 6, "Electronic Commerce and the Internet," this chapter focuses on describing how organizations are using and applying information systems (see Figure 7.2). The next section begins by describing the different types of information required throughout the various levels of organizations. This is followed by a discussion of the general types of information systems used in organizations. Finally, you will learn about the information systems that span organizational boundaries.

Different Types of Information Require Different Types of Systems

Every organization is composed of levels, as illustrated in Figure 7.3. As you might expect, given the vastly different types of activities that occur at different levels of an organization, each level can have vastly different informational needs. The following sections describe some of the fundamental differences between organizational levels and their informational needs. This discussion provides you with a general foundation for understanding why there are various types of information systems, each with unique characteristics.

Operational Level

At the **operational level** of the firm, the routine day-to-day business processes and interaction with customers occur. At this level, information systems are designed to automate repetitive activities, such as sales transaction processing. In short, operational-level systems are primarily designed to improve the efficiency of business

FIGURE 7.2

The big picture: focusing on organizational information systems.

processes and the customer interface. Managers at the operational level, such as foremen or supervisors, make day-to-day decisions that are highly structured and recurring. For example, a supervisor may decide when to reorder supplies or how to best allocate personnel for the completion of a project. Given these characteristics, models can be created to help operational managers make these relatively straightforward decisions. In fact, the decisions are often so straightforward that "decisions" can be programmed directly into operational information systems so that they can be made with little or no human intervention. An inventory management system, for example, could keep track of inventory and issue an order for additional inventory when levels dropped below a specified level. Operational managers would simply need to confirm that an order was desired. Figure 7.4 summarizes the general characteristics of the operational level.

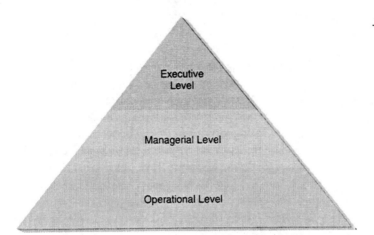

FIGURE 7.3

Levels of an organization.

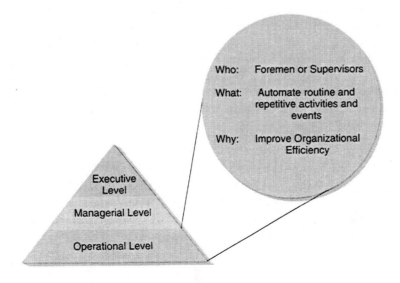

FIGURE 7.4

Operational level of an organization.

─────── **Transaction Processing at Eddie Bauer** ───

The advent of the Internet and electronic commerce has caused Eddie Bauer, a leading retailer of casual clothing and products, to extend its transaction processing system to include Web-based sales (IBM, 1998). Based in Seattle, Washington, Eddie Bauer has more than 500 retail outlets and a very successful catalog business. In the catalog business, telemarketers enter customer orders into the company's *transaction processing system*. Unfortunately, transactions coming from their electronic commerce Web site were not integrated into their existing systems. To solve this problem, they now use a single IBM database that integrates order processing from both sources. By integrating these transactions into a single system, Eddie Bauer can more rapidly process orders and more easily manage inventory. A single transaction processing system is making operations at Eddie Bauer much more efficient.

Managerial Level

At the **managerial level** of the organization, functional managers focus on monitoring and controlling operational-level activities and providing information to higher levels of the organization. Managers at this level, often referred to as mid-level managers or functional managers (for example, marketing manager, finance manager), focus on effectively utilizing and deploying organizational resources to reach the strategic objectives of the organization. Mid-level managers typically focus on problems within a specific business function, such as marketing or finance. Here, the scope of the decision is usually contained within the business function, is moderately complex, and has a time horizon of a few days to a few months. For example, a marketing manager may decide how to allocate the advertising budget for the next business quarter or some fixed time period. Managerial-level decision making is not nearly as structured or routine as operational-level decision making. In fact, managerial-level decision making is generally referred to as *semi-structured* decision making because solutions and problems are not clear-cut and often require judgment and expertise. For example, an information system could provide a production manager with summary information about sales forecasts for multiple product lines, inventory levels, and overall production capacity. This manager could use this information to create multiple production schedules. With these schedules, the manager could examine inventory levels and potential sales profitability, depending upon the order in which manufacturing resources were used to produce each type of product. Figure 7.5 summarizes the general characteristics of the managerial level.

─────── **Decision Making at Sara Lee** ────

Managers within the meat division of Sara Lee—whose brands include Jimmy Dean, Hillshire Farms, Ballpark Franks, Kahn's, and West Virginia Hams—were having a tough time analyzing their retail sales data (HP, 1998). Because each brand had its own separate computing infrastructure, managers were having difficulty integrating information to make decisions related to planning and forecasting demand. To solve this problem, Sara Lee began to use the Decision Support Suite from Information Advantage, running on a Hewlett-Packard 9000 server. This system integrates information from these separate systems and provides managers with the capability to view the data in many different ways. Before, the IS department would spend three to four days each month loading and formatting the data from the prior month to create a series of management reports. Today, up-to-the-minute information is available to managers, and monthly system maintenance takes less than three hours. Using this system, Sara Lee is making much more effective decisions.

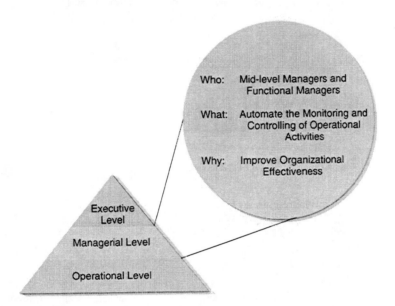

FIGURE 7.5

Managerial level of an organization.

Executive Level

At the **executive level** of the organization, managers focus on longer-term strategic issues facing the organization. Managers at this level include the president and chief executive officer (CEO), vice presidents, and possibly the board of directors. Collectively, we will refer to these managers as "executives." Executive-level decisions are often very complex problems with broad and long-term ramifications for the organization. Executive-level decision making is often referred to as being *messy* or *ill-structured* because executives must consider the ramifications of their decisions on the overall organization; understanding how a given decision impacts the overall organization makes executive decision making extremely complex. For example, top managers may decide to develop a new product or discontinue an existing one. Such a decision may have vast, long-term effects on the organization. Information systems are used to obtain aggregate summaries of trends and projections of the future to assist executive-level decision making. Figure 7.6 summarizes the general characteristics of the executive level.

FIGURE 7.6

*Executive level of an
organization.*

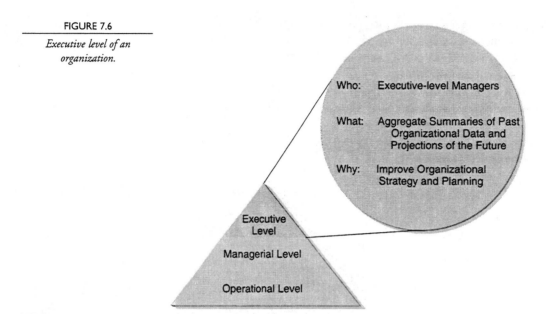

FIGURE 7.6

*Executive level of an
organization.*

A BRIEF CASE

Executive Information at Blue Cross Blue Shield of Florida

The health insurance industry has grown to be highly complex and highly competitive. To be successful, companies must be able to change their product offerings and services rapidly based on changing market needs. Depending on the question of the moment, executives must be able to make sense of a vast amount of changing information. Information related to market segments, such as adults versus children, geographical region, aliments, and funding arrangements, must be compared and contrasted as part of the decision making process. To help manage this type of information at Blue Cross Blue Shield of Florida, executives use a special type of information system called an *executive information system* (EIS) from SAS (SAS, 1998). This EIS enables executives to examine extremely complex data easily in textual and graphical summaries. This system is helping the executives of Blue Cross Blue Shield of Florida to more easily deal with the complexities of their rapidly changing environment and achieve a strategic advantage.

In summary, most organizations have three general levels: operational, managerial, and executive. Each level has unique activities, and each requires different types of information. The next section examines various types of information systems designed to support each organizational level.

General Types of Information Systems

An easy way to understand how all information systems work is to use an input, process, and output model—the basic systems model (see Checkland, 1981 for a thorough discussion). Figure 7.7 shows the basic systems model that can be used to describe virtually all types of systems. For example, a taxi service is a "physical" system that has customers as an input, transportation provision as a process, and payment for service as an output. All types of information systems can be decomposed into the basic input, process, and output elements. For example, Figure 7.8 shows elements of a payroll system decomposed into input, process, and output elements. The inputs to a payroll system include time cards and employee lists, as well as wage and salary information. Processing transforms the inputs into outputs that include paychecks, management reports, and updated account balances. The remainder of this section uses the basic systems model to describe various types of contemporary information systems. The next section describes one fundamental type of organizational information system: the transaction processing system.

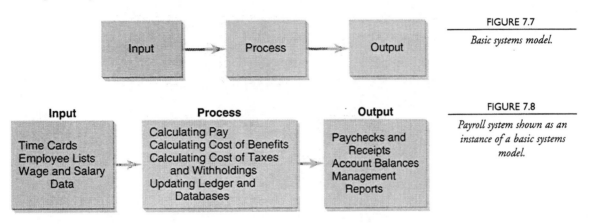

FIGURE 7.7

Basic systems model.

FIGURE 7.8

Payroll system shown as an instance of a basic systems model.

Transaction Processing Systems

Many organizations deal with repetitive types of activities. Grocery stores repeatedly scan groceries at the checkout counter. Banks repeatedly process checks drawn on customer accounts. Fast food restaurants repeatedly process customer orders. All these examples represent events in the business world, events referred to as **transactions**. In short, transactions are events that occur as a regular part of a business's day-to-day operations. **Transaction processing systems** (TPSs) are a special class of information systems designed to process business events and transactions. Consequently, TPSs often reside close to customers at the operational level of the organization, as illustrated in Figure 7.9.

The goals of transaction processing systems are to automate repetitive information processing activities within organizations to increase speed and accuracy and to lower the cost of processing each transaction—that is, to make the organization more *efficient*. Because TPSs are typically used to process large volumes of information, organizations have spent considerable resources designing TPSs to maximize the processing speed and accuracy while lowering the cost of processing each transaction. One of the easiest ways to do so is to reduce or eliminate people from the process. Reducing or eliminating people from the process not only reduces transaction costs, but it also reduces the likelihood of data entry errors. Consequently, much of the evolution of TPSs has focused on reducing the role people play in the processing of organizational transactions. The types of activities supported by TPS include:

- Payroll processing
- Sales and order processing
- Inventory management
- Product purchasing, receiving, and shipping
- Accounts payable and receivable

FIGURE 7.9

Transaction processing system resides at the operational level.

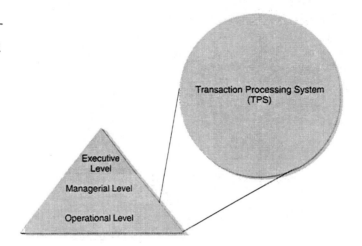

Architecture of a Transaction Processing System

The basic model of a TPS is shown in Figure 7.10. When a business event or transaction occurs, **source documents** describing the transaction are created. Source documents, paper or electronic, serve as a stimulus to a TPS from some external source. Source documents can be processed as they are created (known as "online processing") or they can be processed in batches (known as "batch processing"). **Online processing** of transactions provides immediate results to the system operator or customer. For example, an interactive class registration system that immediately notifies you of your success or failure in attempting to register for a class is an example of an online TPS. **Batch processing** of transactions occurs when transactions are collected and then processed together as a "batch" at some later time. Banks often use batch processing when reconciling checks drawn on customer accounts. Likewise, your university uses batch processing to process end-of-term grade reports—all inputs must be periodically processed in batches to calculate your grade point average. In general, when customers need immediate notification of the success or failure of a transaction, system designers use online processing. When immediate notification is not needed or is not practical, batch processing is the chosen system design approach. Table 7.1 lists several examples of online and batch transaction processing systems.

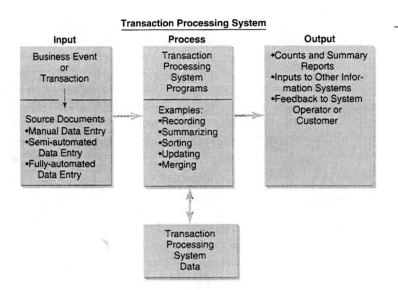

FIGURE 7.10

Architecture of a transaction processing system.

Table 7.1 Examples of online and batch transaction processing systems.

Online TPS	Batch TPS
University class registration processing	Student final grade processing
Airline reservation processing	Payroll processing
Concert/sporting event ticket reservation processing	Customer order processing (for example, insurance forms)
Grocery store checkout processing	Bank check processing

Information entry with a TPS can be manual, semi-automated, or fully automated. *Manual data entry* refers to having a person *manually* enter the source document information into the TPS. For example, when you apply for a new driver's license, a clerk enters information about you into a Driver's License Recording System, often copying the information from a form that you filled out.

A second method for system input in a TPS is *semi-automated data entry*. In a semi-automated data entry system, some type of data capture device speeds the entry and processing of the transaction. For example, a checkout scanner in the grocery store is an example of a semi-automated entry device. The checkout scanner speeds the checkout for the customer and also provides accurate and detailed data directly to many types of information systems. Another example of a semi-automated TPS would be an electronic mall on the World Wide Web. In this mall, customers enter their purchase requests, which go directly to an order fulfillment system without any additional human intervention.

Fully automated data entry requires no human intervention. In essence, two computers "talk" to each other via a communications link. For example, for automobiles built at Ford Motor Company, each part used in the manufacturing process represents a transaction in the inventory management systems. At some point in the process, the inventory management system automatically contacts a supplier's computer system to request additional raw materials. An electronic linkage between computers to share data related to business operations is referred to as electronic data interchange (EDI). Many organizations spend considerable effort with their suppliers and customers working on EDI standards so that more and more information can be exchanged without human intervention.

The characteristics of a TPS are summarized in Table 7.2. In general, inputs to a TPS are business events or transactions. The processing activities of a TPS typically focus on recording, summarizing, sorting, updating, and merging transaction information with existing organizational databases. Outputs from a TPS typically reflect summary reports, inputs to other systems, and operator notification of processing completion. People that are very close to day-to-day operations most often use TPS. For example, a checkout clerk at the grocery store uses a TPS to record your purchases. Supervisors may review transaction summary reports to better control inventory, to manage operations personnel, or to provide better customer service. Additionally, inventory management systems may monitor transaction activity and use this information to manage inventory reordering activity. This is an example of the output from the TPS as being the input to another system.

Table 7.2 Characteristics of a transaction processing system.

Inputs	Business events and transactions
Processing	Recording, summarizing, sorting, updating, merging
Outputs	Counts and summary reports of activity inputs to other information systems feedback to system operators or customers
Typical User	Operational personnel and supervisors

A BRIEF CASE ───── **Transaction Processing System at Ford Motor Company**

The World Wide Web enables customers to use TPS to order products or obtain information. For example, Ford Motor Company uses the WWW to enable customers to easily obtain information about products and dealers. Figure 7.11 shows a screen from Ford's WWW site in which customers can locate their nearest dealer (Ford, 1998). The inputs to this system are zip codes entered by customers. Processing occurs back at Ford in Dearborn, Michigan, where a TPS matches the customer's zip code to one in a database containing all dealers. When a match is made, the output of the system is a report back to the customer giving the name, address, and phone of the closest dealer. In creating this online TPS, Ford has provided a valuable customer service with no human intervention. The cost for processing this transaction for Ford is virtually nil. Alternatively, if a customer calls Ford on an 800 number requesting the same information, Ford pays for the phone call and for the personnel answering the customer's question—a much higher transaction cost. Remember that the goal of TPS is to increase the speed and accuracy and lower the cost of processing for each transaction. Ford achieved all three goals with the creation of the "Dealer Locator" feature on their Web site.

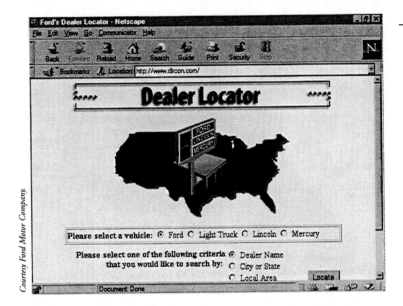

Courtesy Ford Motor Company.

FIGURE 7.11

Ford's Dealer Locator system on the World Wide Web.

Management Information Systems

Management Information System (MIS) is a term with two meanings. It is often used to describe the field of study that encompasses a variety of people involved in the development, use, management, and study of computer-based information systems in organizations. It is also used to refer to a specific type of organizational information system. These MISs are typically used to produce regular and ad hoc reports to support the ongoing, recurring decision making activities associated with managing an entire business or a functional area within a business. Consequently, an MIS often resides at the managerial level of the organization, as shown in Figure 7.12.

Remember that transaction processing systems automate repetitive information processing activities to increase *efficiency*. The basic goal of a management information system is to help mid-level managers make more *effective* decisions. In other words, MISs are designed to get the right information to the right person in the right format at the right time to help her make better decisions. MISs can often be found throughout the organization. For example, a marketing manager may have an MIS that contrasts sales revenue and marketing expenses by geographic region so that she can better understand how regional marketing promotions are performing. Examples of the types of activities supported by MISs include:

- Sales forecasting

- Financial management and forecasting

- Manufacturing planning and scheduling

- Inventory management and planning

- Advertising and product pricing

FIGURE 7.12

Management information systems reside at the managerial level.

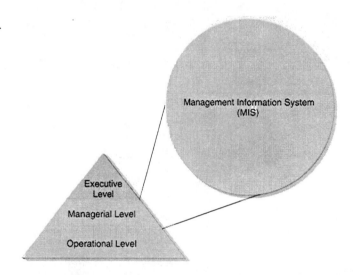

Architecture of a Management Information System

The basic architecture of an MIS is shown in Figure 7.13. At regular intervals, managers in most organizations need to review summary information of some organizational activity. For example, a sales manager may review the weekly performance of all his sales staff. To conduct this review, an MIS summarizes the total sales volume of each salesperson in a report. This report may provide a plethora of information about each person, including the following:

- What are this salesperson's year-to-date sales totals?

- How do this year's sales figures compare to last?

- What is the average amount per sale?

- How do sales change by the day of the week?

As you can see, a manager can review much about each salesperson. Imagine the difficulty of producing these weekly reports manually if the organization has 50 salespeople, 500 salespeople, or even 5000 salespeople! It would be very difficult, if not impossible, to create these detailed reports on each sales person without an MIS. Ironically, as you can see by our example, the processing of an MIS is typically not all that complicated. In most cases, the processing amounts to combining the information from multiple data sources into a structured report.

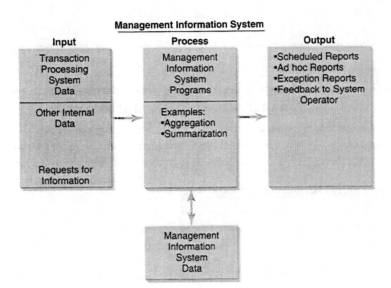

FIGURE 7.13

Architecture of a management information system.

Managers can also use an MIS to make *ad hoc* requests for information. For example, if a particular product is not selling as well as forecasts predicted, the manager can request a report showing which salespeople are selling the product effectively and which aren't. MIS can also be used to produce *exception reports* that highlight situations that are out of the normal range. For example, a manager with a large number of sales personnel can produce an exception report highlighting those not achieving minimum sales goals. Remember that the goal of the MIS is to help the organization be more effective. By focusing the manager's attention on the correct information, the MIS helps the organization take a first step in becoming more effective.

The characteristics of an MIS are summarized in Table 7.3. In general, inputs to an MIS are transaction processing data produced by a TPS; other internal data, such as sales promotion expenses; and ad hoc requests for special reports or summaries. The processing activities in an MIS are relatively simple. In most cases, the processing aspect of the system focuses on data aggregation and summary. Outputs are formatted reports that provide scheduled and routine information to a mid-level manager. For example, a store manager can use an MIS to review sales information to identify products that aren't selling and are in need of special promotion. The following university enrollment system example illustrates the architecture of an MIS.

Table 7.3 Characteristics of a Management Information System.

Inputs	Transaction processing data and other internal data scheduled and ad hoc requests for information
Processing	Aggregation and summary of data
Outputs	Scheduled and exception reports feedback to system operator
Typical User	Mid-level managers

A BRIEF CASE

Tracking University Enrollment with a Management Information System

All universities track class enrollments during student registration periods. An example of one such system—the course enrollment system shown in Figure 7.14—is being used by the faculty and administrators at Indiana University. With the course enrollment system, administrators can track which classes are filling up and which aren't. During a week-long registration period, more sections of a particularly popular class can be added, while courses failing to attract students can be removed. This enables administrators to move faculty resources to where the demand is and, in essence, more effectively manage university resources.

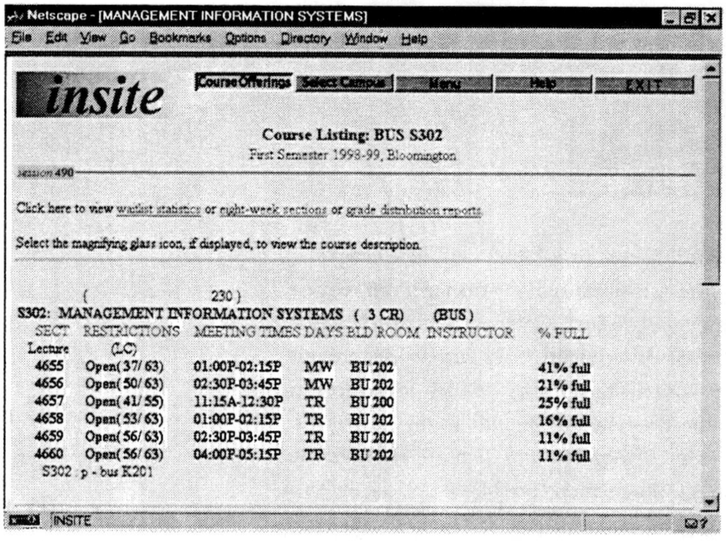

FIGURE 7.14

University course enrollment system MIS report.

Executive Information Systems

In addition to operational personnel and mid-level managers, top-level managers or executives can use information technology to support their day-to-day activities. Information systems designed to support the highest organizational managers are called **executive information systems** (EISs). As you might expect, an EIS resides at the top of the organization at the executive level, as shown in Figure 7.15. The basic goals of an EIS are to provide information to the executive in a very aggregate form so that she can scan information quickly for trends and anomalies. Although EISs are not as widely used as other types of information systems, this trend is rapidly changing because more and more executives are becoming comfortable with information technology and because an EIS can provide substantial benefits to the executive. In essence, the EIS provides a one-stop shop for a lot of the informational needs of the executive. Activities supported by an EIS include:

- ■ Executive-level decision making
- ■ Long-range and strategic planning
- ■ Monitoring of internal and external events and resources
- ■ Crisis management
- ■ Staffing and labor relations

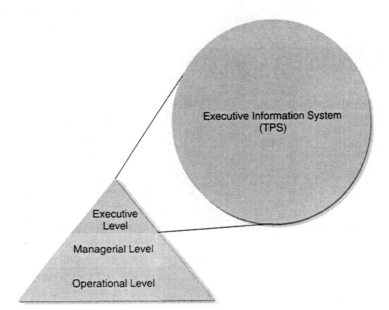

FIGURE 7.15

Executive information systems reside at the executive level.

One key element of an EIS is its capability to deliver both "soft" and "hard" data to the executive decision maker. Soft data includes textual news stories or other non-analytical information. Alternatively, hard data includes facts and numbers. Lower-level TPSs and MISs generate much of the hard data provided by an EIS. Providing timely soft information to executive decision makers has been much more of a challenge. For example, deciding how to get the late-breaking news stories and information to the system in a format consistent with the EIS philosophy was a significant challenge to organizations. Some organizations subscribe to online services such as Dow Jones as a source for their soft data; however, Dow Jones provides a relatively narrow band of information and its information is not formatted in a user-friendly manner that suits everyone's needs. People are often needed to monitor the online service to select appropriate information and to translate the information into a user-friendly format. This is clearly a time-consuming and inexact process.

A product on the World Wide Web called Point Cast Network (PCN) has radically changed how many executives can gain soft information by offering a customized and user-friendly format. PCN provides information on almost any subject or industry, virtually as it hits the news wires. Figure 7.16 shows a typical screen from PCN. Topics, arranged as separate "Channels," range from headline news, sports, and weather to the tracking of news and financial information about a specific industry or company (see Table 7.4). One of the most powerful features of PCN is that it can be customized to filter information so that only the information deemed relevant to the executive is delivered by the system. For example, if an executive is interested in the software, Internet/online, and telecommunications industries, a dialog box can be used to select these industries. Stories related to these industries will be tracked; all others will be ignored. Special versions of PCN are also created for specific industries, such as aerospace, automotive, banking, consumer markets, government, health care, legal, IT management, real estate, and telecommunications. PCN information can be updated once a day or every few minutes depending upon your Internet connection. PCN is supported by "billboard" advertisements much like television commercials, which means that one of the most exciting things about PCN is that it is free to the user!

Courtesy of PointCast, Inc.

FIGURE 7.16

Screen from Point Cast Network.

Table 7.4 Point Cast Network channels and description.

PCN Channel	Description
News	Track national, international, political, and business news.
Sports	Track news stories, team standings, schedules, and scores for professional and college sports.
Companies	Track news and stock reports for a particular company that is traded on the AMEX, NASDAQ, and NYSE exchanges.
Industries	Track news and market valuations for particular industries or for major stock markets.
Weather	Track weather information for most national and international cities as well as graphic weather maps for the continental United States, Europe, and Asia.
Lifestyles	Track horoscopes and state lottery results.
Pathfinder	Track news from Time-Warner's online daily versions of *Time, Money,* and *People* magazines.
LA Times	Display news from several sections of the *Los Angeles Times* newspaper.
TechWeb	Display articles on current topics in high technology.

Source   PCN. 1998. Information from:

Architecture of an Executive Information System

The basic architecture of an EIS is shown in Figure 7.17. Inputs to an EIS are all internal databases and systems as well as *external* databases that contain information on competitors, financial markets, news (local, national, and international), and any other information deemed important by the executive in making day-to-day decisions. This suggests that an EIS could potentially "overload" the executive with too much information from too many sources. Systems designers spend considerable effort customizing the EIS so that only the most important information is provided in its most effective form. To do this, they use information filters to select information that is deemed relevant by the ex-ecutive. Also, output information is provided to executives by systems designers in a highly aggregated form, often using graphical icons to make selections and bar and line charts to summarize data, trends, and simulations. Finally, large monitors that make things easy to see are typically used. The characteristics of an EIS are summarized in Table 7.5.

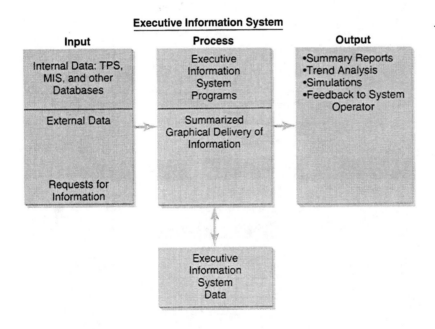

FIGURE 7.17

Architecture of an executive information system.

Table 7.5   Characteristics of an executive information system.

Inputs	Aggregate internal and external data
Processing	Summarized graphical delivery
Outputs	Summary reports, trends, and simulations feedback to system operator
Typical User	Executive-level managers

Although data is provided in a very highly aggregated form, the executive also has the capability to *drill down* and see the details if necessary. For example, suppose an EIS summarizes employee absenteeism and the system shows that today's numbers are significantly higher than normal. This can be shown to the executive in a running line chart (see Figure 7.18). If the executive wants to understand the details as to why absenteeism is so high, a selection on the screen can provide the details behind the aggregate numbers (see Figure 7.19). An EIS also can connect the data in the system to the absentee employees responsible for the data in the organization through the use of the organization's internal communication network (for example, electronic or voice mail). In other words, after reviewing the detailed absenteeism figures, the executive can quickly send a message to the manager in charge of manufacturing personnel to discuss the problem she discovered in the drill-down.

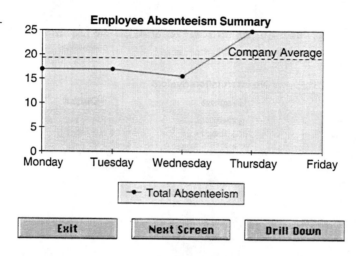

FIGURE 7.18

Total employee absenteeism line chart.

FIGURE 7.19

Drill-down numbers for employee absenteeism.

Absenteeism Drill Down

	Monday	Tuesday	Wednesday	Thursday
Manufacturing	10	11	6	19
Professional	2	2	0	1
Clerical	3	1	3	2
Sales	0	0	1	2
Support	2	3	5	1

Exit	Prior Screen	E-mail

A BRIEF CASE

Using an Executive Information System at Texaco Brazil

Texaco Brazil needed a way to easily monitor the activities of its units throughout the country. Management knew that with this capability, they could become one of Brazil's leading petroleum distributors. To support them in finding a solution, Texaco turned to

Commander EIS, produced by Comshare (Comshare, 1998). Using Commander, Texaco executives analyze company results daily. They track activity in each business unit down to the factory, branch, and service station level. Sales, purchases, cash flow, expenses, stocks, and deadlines can be monitored minute by minute. Because the information is continuously updated, management can react to even small market fluctuations, making flexible and proactive decision making possible. Since the EIS installation, Texaco Brazil attributes a lot of its success to the EIS. In fact, since installing the EIS, Texaco Brazil has become Texaco's leading operating unit in its Latin American business units.

Information Systems that Span Organizational Boundaries

The preceding section examined three general classes of information systems within s pecific hierarchical levels in the organization. Organizations also use other information systems that cannot be neatly associated with a particular level. On the contrary, these systems span all levels of the organization (see Figure 7.20). Four types of boundary-spanning systems are:

- Decision support systems

- Expert systems

- Office automation systems

- Functional area information systems

This section describes each of these in more detail.

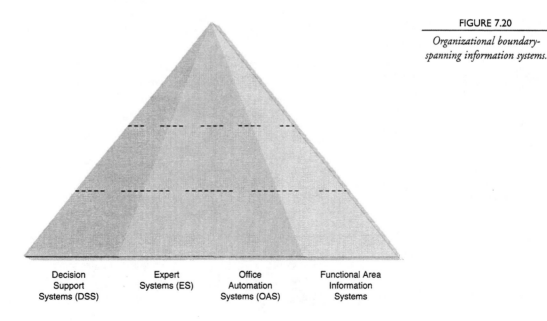

FIGURE 7.20

Organizational boundary-spanning information systems.

Decision Support Systems (DSS)   Expert Systems (ES)   Office Automation Systems (OAS)   Functional Area Information Systems

Decision Support Systems

Decision support systems (DSSs) are special-purpose information systems designed to support organizational decision making. A DSS is typically designed to solve a particular recurring problem in the organization. This problem may occur at the shop floor level or in the executive suite. Most often, DSSs are used by managerial-level employees to help them solve the semi-structured problems they typically address, much like the problem described in the chapter-opening scenario. That scenario described a situation in which bank managers were trying to successfully predict good and bad loans. The key distinction between a DSS and other types of previously described information systems is that with a DSS, the user actively uses decision analysis tools to either analyze or create meaningful data to address non-routine problems. In other words, a DSS is designed to be an "interactive" decision aid, whereas the systems described previously—TPS, MIS, and EIS—are much more passive.

The goal of a DSS is to augment human decision making performance and problem solving ability by enabling users to examine alternative solutions to a problem. A powerful feature of a DSS is its capability to enable you to play "what if" analyses with a problem, which means you can examine alternative problem scenarios and results. For example, a cash manager for a company could examine "what if" scenarios of the effect of various interest rates on cash availability. Results are displayed in both textual and graphical formats. The most commonly used DSS is an electronic spreadsheet, such as Microsoft Excel.

Architecture of a Decision Support System

Given that the most commonly used DSS is an electronic spreadsheet, the architecture of a DSS is relatively simple. A DSS has three main components: models, data, and a user interface (see Figure 7.21) (Sprague, 1980). **Models** are simply the ways in which the DSS allows data to be manipulated. For example, if you have some historic sales data, you can use many different types of "models" to create a forecast of future sales. One technique would be to take an average of the past sales. The formula you would use to calculate the average is the model—a relatively unsophisticated model, but a model nonetheless! A more complicated forecasting model might use time-series analysis or linear regression. Virtually countless models are used in organizations to support ad hoc decision making (see Table 7.6).

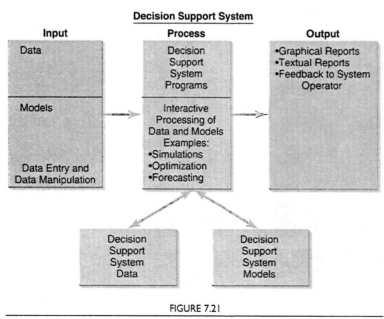

FIGURE 7.21

Architecture of a decision support system.

Data for the DSS can come from many sources, including TPS, MIS, and other information sources. The user interface is simply the way in which the DSS takes information from you and how it formats the DSS results.

Table 7.6 Common DSS models for specific organizational areas.

Area	Common DSS Models
Accounting	Cost analysis, discriminant analysis, break-even analysis, auditing, tax computation and analysis, depreciation methods, budgeting.
Corporate Level	Corporate planning, venture analysis, mergers and acquisitions.
Finance	Discounted cash flow analysis, return on investment, buy or lease, capital budgeting, bond refinancing, stock portfolio management, compound interest, after-tax yield, foreign exchange values.
Marketing	Product demand forecast, advertising strategy analysis, pricing strategies, market share analysis, sales growth evaluation, sales performance.
Personnel	Labor negotiations, labor market analysis, personnel skills assessment, employee business expense, fringe benefit computations, payroll and deductions.
Production	Product design, production scheduling, transportation analysis, product-mix inventory level, quality control, learning curve, plant location, material allocation, maintenance analysis, machine replacement, job assignment, material requirement planning.
Management Science	Linear programming, decision trees, simulation, project evaluation and planning, queuing, dynamic programming, network analysis.
Statistics	Regression and correlation analysis, exponential smoothing, sampling, time-series analysis, hypothesis testing.

The characteristics of a DSS are summarized in Table 7.7. Inputs are data and models. Processing supports interactive merging of data with models to examine alternative solution scenarios. Outputs are graphs and textual reports. DSS users are typically mid-level managers, but DSS tools can be used by virtually anyone in the organization at any level. The next section discusses an example of a DSS that you might use at home.

Table 7.7 Characteristics of a decision support system.

Inputs	Data and models data entry and data manipulation commands (via user interface)
Processing	Interactive processing of data and models simulations, optimization, forecasts
Outputs	Graphs and textual reports feedback to system operator (via user interface)
Typical User	Mid-level manager (although a DSS could be used at any level of the organization)

Using a Decision Support System to Buy a Car

When you buy a new car, one of your biggest concerns after deciding what you want to purchase is deciding how you will pay for your new vehicle. Will you pay cash? Or, if you are like most of us, will you finance most or part of the purchase price? Organizations face the same decisions every day when purchasing supplies, raw materials, and capital equipment: Should they pay cash or finance these purchases? What information do they need to know to make this decision? What tools do companies use to help in making these decisions? Interestingly, the tools that they use are relatively simple

ETHICAL PERSPECTIVE: SOFTWARE PIRACY AND INTELLECTUAL PROPERTY RIGHTS?

Have you ever gone to a friend's house with a blank disk and copied a program or a game that you wanted? Did you know that this is called software piracy? You have just "stolen" from the software producer their due profits from the sale of one unit of merchandise and you have broken U.S. copyright laws. People do it all the time, you say. The reason people do it is because it is easy and they don't get caught—not because it is the right thing to do.

When you purchase software, you are typically allowed to copy the software onto your personal computer's hard drive and make one copy of the software onto a second disk or set of disks for backup.

You're probably asking yourself how making one more extra copy of this piece of software is going to hurt the software vendor. Vendors say that it hurts plenty. Imagine that you developed a small software program and you sold 50,000 copies of it at $20.00 each, for a total of $1,000,000. Pretty good, huh? You then find out that several people who legitimately purchased the product turned right around and allowed their friends and work associates to illegally copy the program. It later turns out that you lost over 5,000 potential "sales" to these illegal copies, an additional 10% in sales volume and an additional $100,000 in revenue. Ouch! You probably could have used that additional money. To put this on a more personal level, imagine having to take a pay cut right now of between ten and fifteen percent and not being able to do anything about it. Not so simple an issue anymore, is it?

Business organizations and software vendors have expended lots of time and resources to produce the software that we now use at home and at work, and they believe that in addition to recouping their costs, they have a right to enjoy a bit of a profit for their labors. In general, software vendors and businesses have gotten tougher about illegal copying of their software. As a result, most business organizations have cracked down on illegal copying and usage of personal computer software (after some rather embarrassing public software inspections turned up many infractions). In addition, software companies such as Microsoft, IBM, and AT&T have joined forces to establish the Electronic Licensing and Security Initiative to develop software tracking "tokens" that will enable a company to track its licensed software.

Although businesses have cracked down on illegal copying of software, illegal copying in university settings in the U.S. is still fairly widespread. Most universities now have public computing sites where students and faculty have free access to many software applications. In some cases, students are able to legally download software to be used at home while they are enrolled as students. Unfortunately, many of these students continue to use the software upon graduation without ever purchasing it from the manufacturer as intended. In addition, students often freely exchange software with each other. Some people believe that software vendors are not as concerned with the illegal proliferation of software on university campuses because they see this as a potentially useful way to pre-build the market share for their software tools. Indeed, it is probably not a bad idea to have university students train on your software tools, given that they are likely to then choose to use these same tools when then enter the work world, where copies of the same software are likely to be legal purchases. In any event, this puts universities and faculty in a precarious situation (Im, J.H. & Van Epps, P.D. 1992).

The rise of the Internet has brought copying to a new level. Material on the Internet, especially the World Wide Web, is very easy to copy. This includes programming code, text, graphic images, corporate logos, pictures, and even ideas. Little protection is available to those who publish copyrighted information via the Internet. However, legislation is pending in Congress that would make it a crime to electronically copy any copyrighted material from the Internet. This bill has received support from software manufacturers and criticism from educational institutions and libraries. The criticism stems from the fact that the bill has no provision to allow such institutions fair use of the material for educational purposes. Such provisions do exist for analog material, and according to the Digital Future Coalition, this bill goes too far and fails to find a reasonable middle ground.

Questions for Discussion

1. Should people in educational institutions be allowed to copy software freely (with some restrictions, of course)?

2. How does software piracy affect the selling price of software?

3. Should software piracy be stopped? Why or why not? How could it be stopped?

Sources 1996. *Alliance seeks ways to secure software distributed on the Internet*. The Wall Street Journal. May 8, B6.
Jacobson, Robert L. 1996. *Educators tell Congress to consider their needs in copyright law.* Chronicle of Higher Education 42 (May 17): A27.
1992. Im, J.H., and P.D. Van Epps. *Software piracy and software security measures in business schools.* Information and Management 23: 199–203.

INTERNATIONAL PERSPECTIVE: BUSINESS INTELLIGENCE SYSTEMS IN SOUTH AFRICA

With the changing political and economic climate brought about by the recent social upheavals in South Africa, organizations are scrambling to keep up with transformations in all sectors of business and government. Managers have turned to using Business Intelligence Systems (BIS) in the attempt to "improve the flow and quality of management information" (Robertson, 1996). Software such as Impromptu and Powerplay (Cognos) and Lightship (Pilot Software) are some of the tools being chosen to help people use the flow of information more accurately and efficiently, enabling organizations to predict, for example, the potential success of specific marketing decisions.

BIS, also known as executive information systems, are used to gather key corporate and external data on factors that are critical to the success of the firm. These data are then ported to the business decision maker's desktop computer so that he can quickly see the performance of the firm on a number of key indicators. Many systems also enable the decision maker to drill down to deeper and deeper levels of data if need be.

Although BIS have been widely used in the U.S. and other countries, the use of these systems in South Africa is relatively new. One problem with this new implementation of BIS is the low availability and reliability of current data in South Africa. In the past, many businesses and government organizations employed their own isolated systems; these now must be integrated, and problems such as data overlap, incompatible data structures, and missing data must be remedied.

Robertson (1996) reports that the Department of Defense (DoD) in South Africa is one major organization that is working toward integration; the task is to bring together into a cohesive whole the seven pieces that formerly made up the armed forces of the government, the homelands, and other regions of the country. The DoD is using Pilot Software's Lightship as part of its process of gathering key performance indicators from the variety of systems involved in its shift from a typical military function-based system to a more corporate-like information structure. Robertson notes that, by employing BIS, the DoD has saved time and money and has been able to make wiser choices as it alters to fit the changing needs of South Africa.

Other South African organizations, such as Eskom Distribution (electricity) and Norwich Life (insurance), are also using BIS to "help meet the challenges of an increasingly complex South African" marketplace (Robertson, 1996). BIS are enabling these organizations to project the impacts of specific business choices, charting trends and changes, and identifying critical bits of information. For example, BIS are being used to forecast population increases and sales trends in specific regions to determine whether and when expansion into these regions is warranted.

The move toward using information systems to support business decision making in South African organizations has been difficult. Managers in business and governmental organizations have found that to deploy these systems well, they must find sources of good information, procure them, consolidate them from often incompatible systems and formats, and then present them in usable, useful ways to decision makers. Although these are formidable problems, South African organizations must solve them if they are to compete with each other and with the rest of the world.

Questions for Discussion

1. As a consultant newly appointed to assist a South African organization with the deployment of BIS, where would you start? How would you proceed in developing successful BIS in this context?

2. What does the future hold for South African organizations if they are not successful in developing their use of business intelligence? in developing their use of BIS?

3. What other ways can information technology be used to gather and manage business intelligence?

Source Robertson, I. 1996. Briefing Book. *Available at* http://www.briefingbook.co.za/cases.

and readily available to you. To illustrate how a DSS can be used to assist organizational decision making, we will continue with your purchasing of a new car. After going through this example, you will have a better understanding of how organizations use decision support technology to help their employees make day-to-day decisions.

Assume that you have decided to purchase a new car and have selected the year, make, model, and options for this new vehicle. Further suppose that the selling price of the car is $20,000 and that you plan to make a $2,500 down payment. You feel that you can "comfortably" make a payment of about $400 per month. Now, given these factors, you are curious about how different financing options might influence your monthly payments and cash flow. To get an idea of what is possible, you decide to contact your local credit union. As you can see from Table 7.8, interest rates vary depending upon the duration of your loan—lower rates with a shorter duration, higher rates with a longer duration. At this point, you now have all the information you need to analyze your financing options.

Table 7.8 Interest rates and loan duration.

Interest Rate	Loan Duration
7% per year	3 years
10% per year	4 years
12% per year	5 years

You decide to use Microsoft Excel to help you make your financing decision. Excel has a loan analysis template (Excel uses the term "template" to refer to models) bundled with current releases. In this template, you enter the loan amount, annual interest rate, and length of the loan (see Figure 7.22). With this information, the loan analysis DSS automatically calculates your payment, total amount paid, and the amount of interest paid over the life of the loan. With this tool, you can easily change any of the input amounts to examine "what if" scenarios—"What if I finance the loan over four years rather than five?" This is exactly how organizations examine their financing options when they make purchases. Using this tool, you decide to purchase your new vehicle over five years (see Table 7.9). Of course, you don't like the fact that your total interest payment will be almost $6,000, but you have really fallen in love with this new car and don't want to spend more than $400 per month. Happy motoring!

Table 7.9 Loan analysis summary.

Interest Rate	Loan Duration	Monthly Payment	Total Paid	Total Interest	Feasible Payment
7% per year	3 years	$540.35	$19,452.57	$1,952.57	No
10% per year	4 years	$443.85	$21,304.57	$3,804.57	No
12% per year	5 years	$389.28	$23,356.67	$5,856.67	Yes

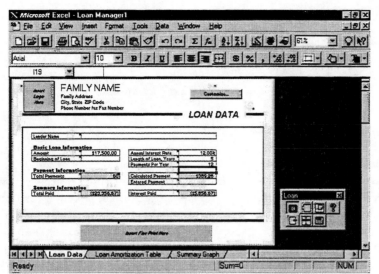

FIGURE 7.22

Loan analysis template in Microsoft Excel.

Screen shot reprinted by permission from Microsoft Corporation.

The next section discusses expert systems, a type of organizational information system that is closely related to decision support systems.

Expert Systems

An **expert system** (ES) is a special type of information system that uses knowledge within some topic area to solve problems or provide advice. Expert systems are used to mimic human expertise by manipulating knowledge (understanding acquired through experience and extensive learning) rather than simply information (see Turban, 1995, for more information). Human knowledge can be represented in an ES by facts and rules about a problem coded in a form that can be manipulated by a computer. When you use an ES, the system asks you a series of questions, much as a human expert would. It continues to ask questions, and each new question is determined by your response to the preceding question, matching the responses to the defined facts and rules, until the responses point the system to a solution. The most difficult part of building an ES is acquiring the knowledge from the expert and getting this knowledge into a consistent and complete form capable of making recommendations. ESs are used when expertise for a particular problem is rare or expensive. In this way, organizations hope to more easily and inexpensively replicate the human expertise. ESs are also used when the knowledge about a problem will be incomplete—in other words, when judgment will be used to make a decision with incomplete information. Examples of the types of activities that can be supported by expert systems include the following:

- Medical diagnosis

- Machine configuration

- Automobile diagnosis

- Financial planning
- Train and container loading
- Computer user help desk
- Software application assistance (for example, Microsoft Help "Wizards")

Architecture of an Expert System

As with other information systems described previously, the architecture of an expert system can be described using the general systems model (see Figure 7.23). Inputs to the system are questions and answers from the user. Processing is the matching of user questions and answers to information in the knowledge base. The processing in an expert system is called *inferencing*, which simply refers to the matching of facts and rules as well as determining the sequence in which questions are addressed to the user. The output from an expert system is a recommendation and possibly an explanation as to why the system made the recommendation that it did. The general characteristics of an expert system are summarized in Table 7.10.

FIGURE 7.23

Architecture of an expert system.

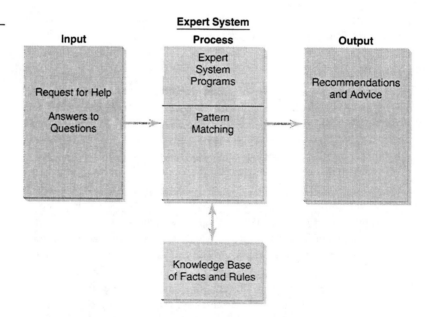

Table 7.10 Characteristics of an expert system.

Inputs	Request for help, answers to questions
Processing	Pattern matching
Outputs	Recommendation or advice
Typical User	Mid-level manager (although an expert system could be used at any level of the organization)

An Expert System on the Web

Expert systems can be designed to assist in solving a wide range of problems. Historically, expert systems have been standalone applications that ran on personal computers. Recently, MultiLogic, Incorporated, a leading producer of expert system technology, has developed a system that enables expert systems to be delivered via the World Wide Web (MultiLogic, 1998). At the MultiLogic Web site, you can test several demonstration ESs (http://www.multilogic.com). One system, for example, is designed to guide holders of restricted stock on their investment options. Restricted stock is acquired privately through corporate mergers or stock options. It is not registered with the SEC and is subject to legal restrictions on its distribution and sale. The system analyzes the investor's responses to several questions and presents personalized investment advice, much as a professional broker would do (see Figure 7.24).

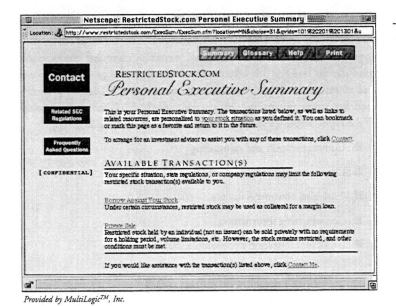

Provided by MultiLogic™, Inc.

FIGURE 7.24

MultiLogic Web-based expert system.

The second interesting feature displayed by this system is its explanation of why the system came to the conclusion that it did or why certain questions are being asked. This is a very powerful feature for training personnel and for helping users believe the system's recommendation.

Picking Better Loan Projects

A BRIEF CASE

Micro Support, Inc., a developer of expert system solutions, developed an expert system to help a bank make better loan predictions before a detailed study was performed. The system divides loans into three categories: likely to be issued, unlikely to be issued, and gray area. The bank can drop the loans that are unlikely to be issued prior to investing resources in the full study, resulting in great savings. It can pursue the loans likely to be issued with confidence that the costs will be recovered. Human experts determine whether the bank should proceed with a full study on the gray area loans. The expert system was built for a bank that specializes in very large loans, similar to the one in the opening scenario. In addition to predicting the loan study outcome, the expert system also recommends the best source of funding for the potential loan—either Ginnie Mae, Fannie Mae, Freddie Mac, or private funds—by evaluating the many requirements associated with each loan. The knowledge base created to assist in making this prediction contained 380 rules and required approximately three months to develop.

Office Automation Systems

The **office automation system** (OAS) is the third type of contemporary information system that spans organizational levels. As described in Chapter 3, OASs are technologies for developing documents, scheduling resources, and communicating. Document development tools include word processing and desktop publishing. Scheduling tools include electronic calendars that help manage human and other resources, such as equipment and rooms. For example, "smart" electronic calendars can examine the multiple schedules to find the first opportunity when all resources (people, rooms, equipment, and so on) are available. Communication technologies include electronic mail, voice mail, fax, videoconferencing, groupware, and other collaborative technologies. Examples of the types of activities supported by an OAS include the following:

- Communication and scheduling
- Document preparation
- Analyzing and merging data
- Consolidating information
- Group collaboration and decision making

Architecture of an Office Automation System

The general architecture of an OAS is shown in Figure 7.25. The inputs to an OAS are documents, schedules, and data. The processing of this information is relatively simple, focusing on storing, merging, calculating, and transporting this data. Outputs include messages, reports, and schedules. The general characteristics of an OAS are summarized in Table 7.11.

Table 7.11 Characteristics of an office automation system.

Inputs	Documents, schedules, data
Processing	Storing, merging, calculating, transporting
Outputs	Messages, reports, schedules
Typical User	All organizational personnel

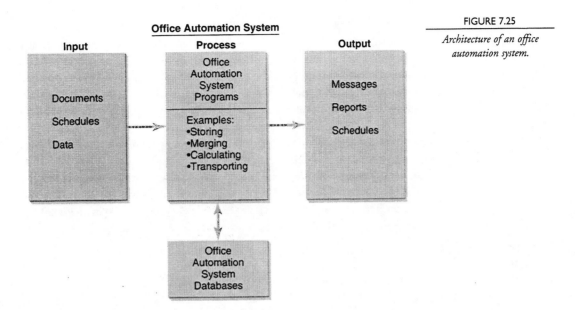

FIGURE 7.25

Architecture of an office automation system.

Automating Your Daily Calendar

A powerful tool for helping you get to class on time is Microsoft Outlook's Calendar. For example, at the beginning of the semester, you can enter your class meeting times into the system. After they are entered, you can make this appointment automatically recur as long as you like (see Figure 7.26).

Additionally, you can set an alarm to notify you a few minutes before class. The alarm is a great feature to use to remind you of meetings with friends and colleagues or to notify you when your favorite TV show is on. If you live in a dorm or house with a local area network, you can enable your friends to see your schedule on their PCs. This feature enables others to quickly identify good times for meetings or to find you if you are not in your room. In short, this calendar program can truly automate your home or office.

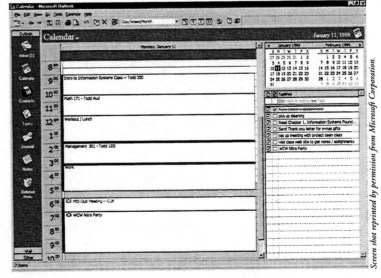

Screen shot reprinted by permission from Microsoft Corporation.

FIGURE 7.26

Coordinating a schedule in the Microsoft Outlook Calendar.

Functional Area Information Systems

A final group of cross-organizational-level information systems are those designed to support a specific **functional area information system**. These systems may be any of the types described previously—TPS, MIS, EIS, DSS, ES, and OAS—and are designed to support the needs of a specific business function (see Figure 7.27). A functional area represents a discrete area of an organization that focuses on a specific set of activities. For example, people in the marketing function focus on the activities that promote the organization and its products in a way that attracts and retains customers. People in accounting and finance focus on managing and controlling capital assets and financial resources of the organization. Table 7.12 lists various organizational functions, describes the focus of each one, and lists examples of the types of information systems used in each functional area. The systems listed in the Table are representative of the types of systems used by various organizational functions; of course, different organizations have a differing mix of systems.

Table 7.12 Organizational functions and representative information systems.

Functional Area	Information System	Examples of Typical Systems
Accounting and Finance	Systems used for managing, controlling, and auditing the financial resources of the organization.	■ Inventory management ■ Accounts payable ■ Expense accounts ■ Cash management ■ Payroll processing
Human Resource	Systems used for managing, controlling, and auditing the human resources of the organization.	■ Recruiting and hiring ■ Education and training ■ Benefits management ■ Employee termination ■ Workforce planning
Marketing	Systems used for managing new product development, distribution, pricing, promotional effectiveness, and sales forecasting of the products and services offered by the organization.	■ Market research and analysis ■ New product development ■ Promotion and advertising ■ Pricing and sales ■ Analysis ■ Product location analysis
Production and Operations	Systems used for managing, controlling, and auditing the production and operations resources of the organization.	■ Inventory management ■ Cost and quality tracking ■ Materials and resource planning ■ Customer service tracking ■ Customer problem tracking ■ Job costing ■ Resource utilization

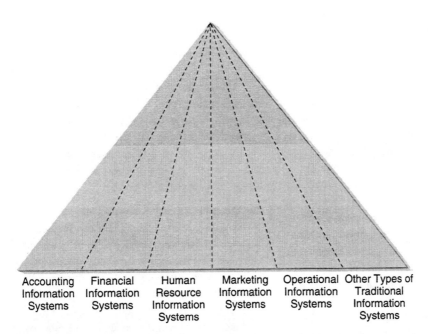

FIGURE 7.27

Functional area information systems.

Accounting Information Systems | Financial Information Systems | Human Resource Information Systems | Marketing Information Systems | Operational Information Systems | Other Types of Traditional Information Systems

Talking with...

William "Butch" Winters, Division President, EDS Corporation, Internet and New Media Business Unit

Educational Background

B.B.A. in Marketing, Southern Methodist University; B.F.A., Southern Methodist University

Job Description

Mr. Winters developed the Internet and New Media business unit for EDS. He is responsible for the Sales, Marketing, Technical, Financial, and Operations aspects of the division. He is responsible for directing this 500-person unit that targets electronic commerce opportunities within, and long-term consulting opportunities with, Fortune 100 organizations. Mr. Winters ensures that the core competencies of business strategy, technological strategy, and creativity are fully deployed among the unit's clients.

Critical Success Factors

People resources must exist to enable the three competencies of business strategy, technological strategy, and creativity. Without people, there is nothing. A strong vendor relationship is important to both understand the available technology and to gain insights into future technologies. Access to capital is vital in the information technology and electronic commerce areas.

Advice to Students

Understand the business goals and issues facing you and your organization. Know how to use technology to meet these goals successfully. Be pro-active in your use of technology; don't wait for a need to arise.

Summary

1. **Describe the characteristics that differentiate the operational, managerial, and executive levels of an organization.** At the operational level of the firm, the routine day-to-day business processes and interaction with customers occur, and information systems are designed to automate repetitive activities, such as sales transaction processing. Operational-level managers such as foremen or supervisors make day-to-day decisions that are highly structured and recurring. At the managerial level of the organization, functional managers focus on monitoring and controlling operational-level activities and providing information to higher levels of the organization. Mid-level or functional managers focus on effectively utilizing and deploying organizational resources to reach the strategic objectives of the organization. At this level, the scope of the decision is usually contained within the business function, is moderately complex, and has a time horizon of a few days to a few months. At the executive level of the organization, decisions are often very complex problems with broad and long-term ramifications for the organization. Executive-level decisions are often referred to as being *messy* or *ill-structured* because they must consider the ramifications of the overall organization.

2. **Explain the characteristics of the three information systems designed to support each of the unique levels of an organization: transaction processing systems, management information systems, and executive information systems.** Transaction processing systems (TPSs) are designed to process business events and transactions and reside close to customers at the operational level of the organization. These systems are used to automate repetitive information processing activities to increase speed and accuracy and to lower the cost of processing each transaction—that is, to make the organization more *efficient*. Management Information Systems (MISs) reside at the managerial level and are designed to produce regular and ad hoc reports to support the ongoing, recurring decision making activities associated with managing an entire business or a functional area within a business. These systems are used to help mid-level managers make more *effective* decisions. Executive information systems (EISs) are used to provide information to an executive in a very aggregate form so that information can be quickly scanned for trends and anomalies. These systems are used to provide a one-stop shop for a lot of the informational needs of the executive.

3. **Describe the characteristics of the three information systems that span the organizational, managerial, and executive levels: decision support systems, expert systems, and office automation systems.** Decision support systems (DSSs) support organizational decision making and are typically designed to solve a particular recurring problem in the organization. DSSs are most commonly used to support semi-structured problems that are addressed by managerial-level employees. A DSS is designed to be an "interactive" decision aid. An expert system (ES) is a special type of information system that uses knowledge within some topic area to solve problems or provide advice. Expert systems are used to mimic human expertise by manipulating knowledge (understanding acquired through experience and extensive learning) rather than simply information. ESs are used when expertise for a particular problem is rare or expensive. In this way, organizations hope to more easily and inexpensively replicate the human expertise. Office automation systems (OASs) are technologies for developing documents, scheduling resources, and communicating.

4. **Explain the general information system needs of various organizational functional areas.** Functional areas represent discrete areas of organizations and typically include: accounting and finance, human resource management, marketing, and production and operations management. Functional area information systems are designed to support the unique requirements of specific business functions.

Key Terms

Operational level	Online processing	Decision support system (DSS)
Managerial level	Batch processing	Models
Executive level	Management information system (MIS)	Expert system (ES)
Transactions		Office automation system (OAS)
Transaction processing system (TPS)	Executive information system (EIS)	Functional area information system

Review Questions

1. Compare and contrast the characteristics of the operational, managerial, and executive levels of an organization.

2. What is meant by "semi-structured" decision making? How does it relate to this chapter?

3. Describe the differences between online processing and batch processing. Give examples of each.

4. What are the three methods used for inputting data into a transaction processing system? Provide examples of each.

5. Differentiate the two meanings of Management Information Systems, one from Chapter 1 and one from this chapter.

6. How does a Management Information System differ from a Transaction Processing System in terms of purpose, target users, capabilities, and so forth?

7. What is an "exception report," who uses it, and how is it used?

8. How does an executive information system "drill down" into the data?

9. What are the four types of information systems that traditionally span the boundaries of organizational levels?

10. Explain the purpose of a model within a decision support system.

11. Provide some examples of functionally specific information systems and needs within an organization.

Problems and Exercises

 Individual   **Group**   **Field**   ○ **Web/Internet**

 1. Match the following terms to the appropriate definitions:

Operational level

Transactions

Transaction processing system

Source document

Online processing

Management information system

Decision support system

Expert system

a. An information system designed to process day-to-day business event data at the operational level of an organization

b. A special-purpose information system designed to mimic human expertise by manipulating knowledge (understanding acquired through experience and extensive learning) rather than simply information

c. The bottom level of an organization, where the routine day-to-day interaction with customers occurs

d. A special-purpose information system designed to support organizational decision making primarily at the managerial level of the organization

e. Processing of information immediately as it occurs

f. Repetitive events in organizations that occur as a regular part of conducting day-to-day operations

g. An information system designed to support the management of organizational functions at the managerial level of the organization

h. Documents created when a business event or transaction occurs

 2. In an expert system, who is really the expert: the computer or the programmer? Why?

 3. Do you feel that, as much as possible, transaction processing systems should replace human roles and activities within organizations? Why or why not? What do some of your fellow classmates think? How much cost savings will there be if these humans are still needed to run the systems? What if you were the person being replaced? Will all errors necessarily be eliminated? Why or why not?

 4. Imagine that your boss has asked you to build an inventory transaction system that would enable the receiving and shipping clerks to enter inventory amounts for purchases and sales, respectively. Discuss the pros and cons of building this system as an online processing system versus a batch processing system. Which would you recommend to your boss?

5. The National Sales Manager for ABC Corp. is interested in purchasing a software package that will be capable of providing "accurate" sales forecasts for the short term and long term. She has asked you to recommend the type of system for this purpose. In a small group, determine the system that you would recommend. In what categories would this system fall, according to the chapter? Would you have any reservations about such a system? Why or why not?

6. Discuss the importance of the user interface of an executive information system. What issues are unique to this type of system over the others discussed in the chapter? What about the users of such systems necessitates a carefully constructed user interface? Do a search on the World Wide Web for executive information systems. What interface issues are discussed? Are these the same issues you came up with?

7. Discuss with some of your classmates the advantages and disadvantages of executives using products such as PointCast to gain information. Why might this be a bad idea? Who is ultimately controlling the information being sent through the system?

8. Explain why sometimes models do not always predict the future. Why is this important for users of decision support systems? Can these anomalies be avoided?

9. In simple terminology, explain the differences between a transaction processing system and a functional area information system? Are they necessarily different? Why?

10. Interview a top-level executive within an organization with which you are familiar. Determine the extent to which the organization utilizes executive information systems. Does this individual utilize an EIS in any way? Why or why not? Which executives do utilize an EIS?

11. Discuss the following in a small group of classmates: Based on your experiences with transaction processing systems (in everyday life and/or in the workplace), which ones used online processing and which used batch processing? Did these choices fit the system, the information, and the environment? Would you make any adjustments? Why?

12. Using any program you desire, create a template that you could use in the future to determine monthly payments on car loans. Use the situation within the chapter as an example of the kind of information that can change. Compare your template with those of several classmates. How are they different? Also, compare your group's templates with the one at http://carpoint.msn.com/LoanCalc. Would you have categorized the program you used to create this template as a decision support system before doing this exercise? Do you now?

13. Describe your experiences with expert systems to some of your classmates. In what situations were they encountered? Did you actually use the system or was it used by another individual on your behalf? Why would it be more beneficial for someone else to manipulate the expert system over yourself? What experiences have your classmates had with expert systems? (Hint: think about an automotive repair shop.)

14. Choose an organization with which you are familiar that utilizes office automation systems. Which systems do they use? Which functions have been automated and which have not been? Why have some functions not been automated? Who makes the decision of which office automation system to implement?

15. Conduct a search on the World Wide Web for "personnel management systems" using any browser you choose. Assuming that all these products perform basically the same tasks and provide the same basic functionality, what will make the difference in the purchasing decision? Personnel management is just one area in which management information systems are utilized. Do other areas have the same abundance of product choices as well?

16. Have each member of a small group interview an IS manager within an organization with which she is familiar. Of the three categories of information systems—transaction processing, management, and executive—which is utilized most in this organization? Why? Have any of these areas experienced an increase or decrease in the last few years? What predictions for the future does this manager have regarding traditional information systems? Do you agree? Prepare a 10-minute presentation to the class of your findings.

17. Imagine that you are Michelle Williams, the CIO of Big Loan Bank, as described in the scenario at the beginning of the chapter. The President of Big Loan Bank, George Hubman, wants to know whether you can help him. What do you tell him? If you are able to help, what type of information system would be appropriate for this situation? Why?

Real World Case Problems

1. Software for the Hard Sell: By Adding Functionality, Sales-force Automation Systems Are Overcoming a Bad Reputation.

The need for efficiency and increased productivity in sales has made automation a high priority with sales forces. Following years of unsuccessful implementations and lack of product acceptance, sales force automation software may be coming into use. Both Oracle and market leader Siebel Systems, Inc., are introducing major upgrades that will address traditional limitations by easing implements, improving usability, and connecting better with back-office applications, such as accounting and manufacturing systems. The SFA applications will significantly reduce selling cycles and create closer relations with customers. Applications include modules for tracking and prospecting sales, for analyzing customer data and for predicting future sales, and a sales-configuration system for helping users determine products and pricing arrangements.

When the Ritz-Carlton Hotel Co. in Atlanta started thinking about sales force automation in 1994, there was no appropriate software for them to use. Now the Ritz-Carlton plans to implement software from Sales Vision, Inc., for 700 of its sales reps by this summer. This will be the first attempt to coordinate all the hotels and salespeople on a single system. In the past, corporate customers such as meeting planners might receive phone calls from numerous Ritz-Carlton sales reps because information was not shared in the organization. This new system will help solve this coordination problem and enable the employees of the Ritz-Carlton to understand the needs of their customers.

Traditionally, this SFA software has underperformed because it had no vertical focus and because the original SFA software was more tailored to the sales manager than to the sales person. Sales people refused to use it because it didn't help them and they felt as if they were being micromanaged. Now the software has been redesigned and it focuses on different industries, such as insurance, banking, telecommunications, consumer packaged goods, and pharmaceuticals. This refocusing should dramatically decrease the implementation time.

Oracle and Onyx Software Corp. are joining the list of companies producing sales force automation software. They will also be unveiling new software designed for sales force applications and smaller companies. In late 1997, SAP bought a 50 percent stake in European Kiefer and Veittinger at the same time as they were developing their own product.

a. Should sales-force automation tools be categorized as decision support systems, office automation systems, transaction processing systems, or executive information systems? Why?

b. To which level within the organization (operational, managerial, or executive), and to which functional area of the firm are sales-force automation tools most useful?

c. Why is the use of sales-force automation tools so important to an organization such as the Ritz-Carlton Hotel?

Source Stein, Tom. 1998. *Software for the hard sell.* Information Week. March 2, 18–19.

2. Is It All a Project? Project Management Software Is Running across the Business.

Project management software, once the domain of small technical groups and highly technical industries, including aerospace, engineering, and defense, is now Web-based and easy to use, making the tools available for general business operations.

This software now runs applications such as financial and resource allocation projects. A.C. Nielson, an international marketing research company, now uses Project Planner (P3) software to plan and manage its budget. They use it to manage people working on multiple projects. With the tremendous change in organizational business, the capacity to estimate project completion is no longer enough.

The $850 million project management software market is expected to increase as much as 20 percent this year. Of this, desktop products make up almost $300 million of the market with Web-based, client-server, and mainframe products and services accounting for the rest. Of these software packages, Microsoft Project accounts for two-thirds of sales. Project 98, the newest version of MS Project, is simpler to use, has better control of project schedules, and includes Web features that allow for project member collaboration.

Web-enabled tools are enabling users who work from different computer platforms (for example, Windows-PCs, Macintosh PCs, UNIX Workstations) to access to project information. Charles Schwab & Company in San Francisco needed a Web-based project management system with cross-platform capabilities and real-time delivery and interactivity. They selected PlanView, Inc.'s Web-based software to implement consistency in how they manage their products.

Managers will have templates to guide them through the steps of the project, and to compare projects and have common expectations. With project management tools, there is a business process change that must take place. You must change the way people work, which is exactly the kind of cultural change that is the hardest to do.

a. To which level within the organization (operational, managerial, or executive) and which functional area of the firm is project management software most useful?

b. What is the pay-off to using project management software at a company like Charles Schwab & Co.? How can they justify spending up to $100,000 on project management software?

c. Why has it become so important to firms that project management software become Web-enabled?

Source Carillo, Karen M. 1998. *Is it all a project?* Information Week, February 23, 100–106.

Traditionally, this SFA software has underperformed because it had no vertical focus and because the original SFA software was more tailored to the sales manager than to the sales person. Sales people refused to use it because it didn't help them and they felt as if they were being micromanaged. Now the software has been redesigned and it focuses on different industries, such as insurance, banking, telecommunications, consumer packaged goods, and pharmaceuticals. This refocusing should dramatically decrease the implementation time.

Oracle and Onyx Software Corp. are joining the list of companies producing sales force automation software. They will also be unveiling new software designed for sales force applications and smaller companies. In late 1997, SAP bought a 50 percent stake in European Kiefer and Veittinger at the same time as they were developing their own product.

a. Should sales-force automation tools be categorized as decision support systems, office automation systems, transaction processing systems, or executive information systems? Why?

b. To which level within the organization (operational, managerial, or executive), and to which functional area of the firm are sales-force automation tools most useful?

c. Why is the use of sales-force automation tools so important to an organization such as the Ritz-Carlton Hotel?

Source *Stein, Tom. 1998. Software for the hard sell.* InformationWeek. *March 2, 18–19.*

2. Is It All a Project? Project Management Software Is Running across the Business.

Project management software, once the domain of small technical groups and highly technical industries, including aerospace, engineering, and defense, is now Web-based and easy to use, making the tools available for general business operations.

This software now runs applications such as financial and resource allocation projects. A.C. Nielson, an international marketing research company, now uses Project Planner (P3) software to plan and manage its budget. They use it to manage people working on multiple projects. With the tremendous change in organizational business, the capacity to estimate project completion is no longer enough.

The $850 million project management software market is expected to increase as much as 20 percent this year. Of this, desktop products make up almost $300 million of the market with Web-based, client-server, and mainframe products and services accounting for the rest. Of these software packages, Microsoft Project accounts for two-thirds of sales. Project 98, the newest version of MS Project, is simpler to use, has better control of project schedules, and includes Web features that allow for project member collaboration.

Web-enabled tools are enabling users who work from different computer platforms (for example, Windows-PCs, Macintosh PCs, UNIX Workstations) to access to project information. Charles Schwab & Company in San Francisco needed a Web-based project management system with cross-platform capabilities and real-time delivery and interactivity. They selected PlanView, Inc.'s Web-based software to implement consistency in how they manage their products.

Managers will have templates to guide them through the steps of the project, and to compare projects and have common expectations. With project management tools, there is a business process change that must take place. You must change the way people work, which is exactly the kind of cultural change that is the hardest to do.

a. To which level within the organization (operational, managerial, or executive) and which functional area of the firm is project management software most useful?

b. What is the pay-off to using project management software at a company like Charles Schwab & Co.? How can they justify spending up to $100,000 on project management software?

c. Why has it become so important to firms that project management software become Web-enabled?

Source *Carillo, Karen M. 1998. Is it all a project?* InformationWeek, *February 23, 100–106.*

Vandenbosch, B., and S.L. Huff. 1997. Searching and scanning: How executives obtain information from executive information systems. *Management Information Systems Quarterly* 21(1): 81–107.

Watson, H.J., and M.N. Frolick. 1993. Determining information requirements for an EIS. *Management Information Systems Quarterly* 17(3): 255–269.

Ye, L.R., and P.E. Johnson. 1995. The impact of explanation facilities on user acceptance of expert systems advice. *Management Information Systems Quarterly* 19(2): 157–172.

Yoon, Guimaraes, and O'Neal. 1995. Exploring the factors associated with expert systems success. *Management Information Systems Quarterly* 19(1): 83–106.

Chapter 5: A Tour of the Internet and the World Wide Web

CHAPTER OUTLINE

LEARNING OBJECTIVES

When you have completed this chapter, you should be able to

1. Explain how individual computers and server computers interact on the Internet.

2. Describe the two types of capabilities of the Internet.

3. Identify the 11 principal communication and retrieval capabilities of the Internet.

4. Summarize how the Internet knows the location of a particular user on the Net.

5. Describe the use of pages on the World Wide Web.

6. Explain the purpose of hyperlinks and their role on the World Wide Web.

7. Describe the characteristics of browser software and relate them to the different types of information that can be included in a home page.

A Mosaic for the Future

A young, restless innovator, fueled by pizza, Oreo cookies, Bach, shredded newspapers, and algorithms, looked inside the computer organization he was with in 1990. He looked at the leading computer manufacturers of the day. He was not seeing the future!

The Internet had emerged out of the academic and scientific communities. Some said it was loaded with opportunity. Others said it was loaded with problems. To Marc, the Internet was "a giant hole in the middle of the world." The software to access it was at least 10 years behind what was running on the desktops of offices all over America. To tease out any useful information, you had to enter detailed commands by hand. This was the past, not the future.

One night late in 1992, Marc and a colleague at Illinois' National Center for Supercomputing Applications (NCSA) sat at a table at the Espresso Royale café in Champaign-Urbana discussing the capabilities and limits of the Internet and the World Wide Web. They wrestled with the idea of making the Web easily accessible. "Let's go for it," they decided.

Between December 1992 and March 1993, Marc and Eric, complementing each other in marathon code-writing sessions, completed a mere 9,000 lines of program instructions (for comparison, Microsoft needed 11 million lines to create Windows 95!). But that was all they needed to produce the most rapidly propagated software program in computer history. In writing Mosaic, the first graphical interface for the Internet's World Wide Web, Marc Andreessen and Eric Bina changed forever the world of information technology, for Mosaic made the World Wide Web widely accessible to ordinary people.

As time passed, the pair brought in other young programmers to work on additional features that would extend Mosaic's reach. By the time Andreessen graduated from the University of Illinois in December 1993 and left NCSA, some 40 programmers were plugging away at Mosaic software.

Andreessen attracted the attention of Jim Clark, founder of the innovative computer company Silicon Graphics, located in California's Silicon Valley, south of San Francisco. Fascinated by the possibilities of Mosaic's graphical browser program, Clark signed up Andreessen and formed a new company, Mosaic Communications, to produce the next generation of graphic software to access the World Wide Web. Eric Bina also became part of the new company, as did others who had worked at NCSA.

After hearing rumors of a possible legal challenge from NCSA over intellectual property rights to Mosaic, Andreessen and Clark dropped the notion of using ideas from their first software program. Instead, they started from scratch, rethinking and redesigning the software capabilities needed to utilize the World Wide Web even more effectively than Mosaic had.

Their new program was Netscape, which became the name of their company. It included many more features than Mosaic and had richer graphic layouts, as well as all-important security safeguards. To ensure that the greatest number of people would use Netscape, the company gave the software away on the Net. Within a few months, Netscape had captured 70 percent of the market for browser software on the Internet. When the company went public in 1995, investors fought to acquire its shares. The opening price was $24. By the end of the first day of public trading, Netscape was going for $87 a share.

Only a few years ago, the Internet interested few people. Today, it's hard to read a newspaper, watch a television program, or even get into a business discussion without hearing about the Internet or its most popular graphical component, the World Wide Web. If you're still unfamiliar with the Internet and wonder whether you're missing out on something . . . you are!

Internet/Net
A communication network that is itself a connection of many other networks.

The **Internet**—commonly called the **Net**—is a communication network that is itself a connection of many other networks. Hence the name: **inter**connection of **net**works.

The Internet is used on a frequent basis by some 30 million people today, and more and more gain access to it every day. It is radically changing people's daily lives. In fact, enthusiasts believe the Internet is the most profound invention since the printing press—or at least since the computer itself was invented. It has given birth to a good many IT applications. For example, electronic mail—written messages sent electronically over communication links—was born on the Internet. Knowledgeable people are convinced that the Internet will be the foundation of the future U.S. Information Superhighway. In this chapter, we will examine the origin and evolution of the Internet, see what it can do today, and consider its future.

Origin of the Internet

The value of a network lies as much in *whom* it connects as in *how* it connects. The Internet, a network of networks, originated back in the 1960s, when the U.S. Department of Defense established the network to provide researchers and government officials with access to such IT resources as radio telescopes, weather analysis programs, supercomputers, and specialized databases. From this origin as a vehicle for the exclusive use of government and educational institutions, the Internet has expanded prodigiously. Today, over half of all U.S. Internet addresses belong to people who got them through a private employer or a commercial access provider.

More than 150,000 new users join the Internet each day. Host computers are added daily, and the number of networks interconnected on the Internet doubles

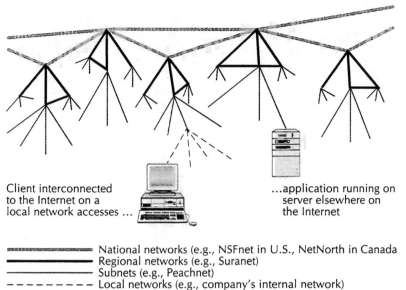

FIGURE 3.1
Structure of the Internet

Client interconnected
to the Internet on a
local network accesses ...

...application running on
server elsewhere on
the Internet

━━━━━━ National networks (e.g., NSFnet in U.S., NetNorth in Canada)
━━━━━━ Regional networks (e.g., Suranet)
─────── Subnets (e.g., Peachnet)
─ ─ ─ ─ ─ Local networks (e.g., company's internal network)

every year. The rate of growth will likely peak in the not-too-distant future because at current growth rates, everyone on planet Earth would be connected to the network by the year 2002!

The U.S. government, through the National Science Foundation, paid a decreasing share of the operating cost of the Internet through 1995, when all government funding was phased out. The bulk of the cost to operate the Internet is paid by the users. For example, universities and other institutions pay for operating their host computers and interconnecting them to the network. There is, however, no charge for sending a message from one computer to another.

The *Information Technology in Practice* feature entitled "Vinton Cerf: Father of the Internet" introduces the man who has done more than anyone else to democratize the Net.

Computers on the Internet

The software an individual uses to access the Internet is running on his or her **client computer.** The client computer communicates with a **server computer** to access data and information. **Client-server computing** (Figure 3.1) is a characteristic of the Internet: Through the Internet, client computers interact with server computers, transmitting and receiving data and information. Data and information transmitted by the server computer are processed by the software running on the client computer (Figure 3.2).

client computer
The computer that accesses the information stored on a server computer.

server computer
The computer that contains data and information that can be accessed by a client computer.

client-server computing
A type of computing in which all data and information retrieval requests and responses pass over a network. Much of the processing is performed on the server computer, and the results of that processing are transmitted to the client computer.

Client Computer
(Individual User)

Server Computer
(on the Internet)

Request for Data and Information

Response from Server

FIGURE 3.2
Client/Server Computing

INFORMATION TECHNOLOGY IN PRACTICE

Vinton Cerf: Father of the Internet

Vinton Cerf is known as the "Father of the Internet" for his pioneering work in developing information technology to support the network and for his unending efforts to help the Internet grow. Cerf started with the principle that anyone should be able to talk to anyone else. Then he developed the TCP/IP protocol on which the Internet is built. This protocol greatly facilitated the Internet's growth by making networks open and thus permitting interconnection among them. Today, the ability to "surf on the Internet"—to ride freely from network to network the way a surfer rides from wave to wave—gives Internet users an endless wave of connectivity.

Cerf, who is part of the executive management team at MCI, headquartered in Washington, D.C., remains very active in the field of information technology. In a recent interview, he shared his thoughts on the surprises, capabilities, and possibilities of the Internet:

I guess the surprises come because the spread of the system has been so rapid in unexpected quarters. And so when I get e-mail from people who are in obscure places around the world saying, "Hi, I'm on the Net," I'm always surprised. When I get e-mail from somebody in China and somebody in Africa, I'm always stunned. . . . Those are the kinds of surprises that are happening now, and of course the new applications that have come along, like Internet Multimedia and World chat, are surprises just because I almost invariably underestimate the amount of human creativity there is out there, especially with millions of people trying things.

The Internet makes it far easier for the individual voice to be heard than any other communication medium ever has. The most interesting question now is: How will we take advantage of the opportunities provided by the Net?

SOURCE: "Poet-Philosopher of the Net," *Educom Review*, Vol. 31 (May–June 1996), p. 38.

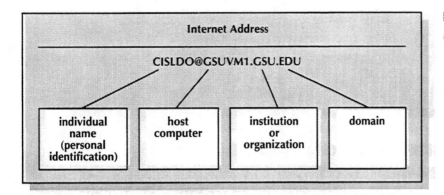

FIGURE 3.3
Internet Addresses

The *Rethinking Business Practices* feature entitled "Visa's Intranet Revolutionizes Internal Communication" describes how this worldwide credit card company has capitalized on the Internet's powerful capabilities for internal communication.

Internet Addresses

Everyone on the Internet has an address from which to send and receive messages. An Internet address has four parts: (1) the user's personal identification, (2) the name of the host computer, (3) the name of the institution or organization, and (4) the domain name (Figure 3.3).

The university or business that provides your access to the Net will assign you a personal identification name. This personal ID is often some combination of your name and the name of the network serving your location or work group within the organization. The university or business also connects one or more of its computers—called a *host computer*—to the Internet. Each host computer is given a unique identification code, which is included in your address.

The Network Information Center is the central authority responsible for assigning a range of addresses to an organization. The organization itself is responsible for assigning a specific host computer to one of the addresses within its range. Each organization also belongs to a domain that identifies the nature of its networks. Domain codes typically identify the type of organization—commercial (com), educational (edu), or government (gov)—or its country location—Australia (au) (Figure 3.4).

Domain	
Name	**Explanation**
.AU	Country code for Australia
.COM	Commercial organization
.EDU	Educational institution
.GOV	Government organization

FIGURE 3.4
Internet Domains

RETHINKING BUSINESS PRACTICES

Visa's Intranet Revolutionizes Internal Communication

The Internet's universal reach makes it possible to establish communications instantly with a server anywhere in the world. It's not surprising, then, that Net enthusiasts tend to focus on linking up with distant locations.

Yet, another advantage of the Internet is capturing the attention of business, and that is its ability to break down the communications walls *inside* companies. Companies are creating *intranets,* or networks that run inside the company, using the Internet's capabilities to do so.

Visa International, Inc., the worldwide credit card company, was having trouble keeping its customer contact directory (two four-inch-thick volumes) up-to-date. With 19,000 member banks, Visa found that its directory was out of date as soon as it was published because of the normal volume of personnel and telephone changes at the banks. Visa International executives Cathy Basch and Deborah McWhinney saw the Internet as an opportunity to solve this problem. They established an internal intranet Web site to house the directory so that quick changes could be made to the listings anytime. Now, whenever any of Visa's 1,200 employees access the directory from their desktop computers, they know they are getting the most up-to-date information. Visa is looking into setting up other intranets to help service its member banks.

Visa's intranet is shielded from outside access by "firewall" security software—a program that establishes a barrier that Internet users outside the company cannot penetrate. Thus, many types of information can be posted on Visa's internal Web sites that would never be published on the Internet.

Other international companies, such as the auto manufacturer Ford, the information technology service group EDS, and France's Cap Gemini Sogeti, are using intranets to link project teams scattered across the globe so they can share information, including drawings and design information. Hypertext links within Web pages can bring together scattered information for easy access. At the same time, an intranet can be used to disseminate knowledge within the organization. Thus, a project team member can post a report on the project, linking it to his or her home page, and others in the company can add their knowledge or experience to the report.

Because intranets draw on the power of the Web, they are much more sophisticated than e-mail. Entire documents can be posted on an intranet. The document's pages may contain colorful graphics and high-resolution photographs, and if the need arises, audio and video segments can be linked to the document—all available for viewing with a click of the mouse.

Because intranets use the infrastructure of the Internet, multiple communication paths from one site to another are available, making access reliable. Furthermore, since intranets can interconnect many different types of computers, the problem of isolated islands of information is overcome.

How widespread are intranets? Software builder Netscape claims that most of its Web server software is bought for use *inside* companies.

Capabilities of the Internet

There are two main things you can do on the Internet:

- **Communicate.** You can contact and exchange information with friends and organizations anywhere in the world. The Internet's special features allow you to participate in conversations, sharing ideas, opinions, and news with other users.
- **Retrieve.** You can access a broad range of data and information from other computers, or simply *sites,* on the network. You can also retrieve copies of information—including narratives, photographs, sound, and video—and bring them right into your own computer. The Internet's retrieval capability includes software. That is, computer software can be located and delivered immediately from commercial software manufacturers or from individuals who create and share software. Not too long ago, overnight delivery of software was considered immediate. Now *immediately* means *instantly:* you get copies of software, documents, and messages as soon as you ask for them.

A variety of capabilities (sometimes referred to as *Internet tools*) support communication and retrieval on the Internet (see Table 3.1).

Communications Capabilities

The principal communications features of the Internet are e-mail, user groups. chat sessions, mailing lists, and Telnet.

e-mail/electronic mail
A service that transports text messages from a sender to one or more receivers via computer.

E-MAIL. E-mail—short for **electronic mail**—is the most widely used function of the Internet. Anyone can transmit a message to anyone else on the Internet

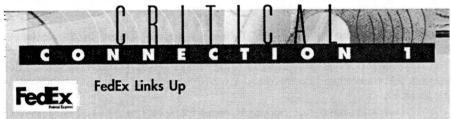

FedEx Links Up

For Federal Express Corporation, keeping track of the more than 2 million packages it carries on an average day is no small feat. As a status tracking aid, the company includes an identification number on the label that accompanies every package. When customers want to know whether a package has been delivered, all they need to do is call FedEx and provide the package tracking number. Within moments, information on the package is displayed on the customer service representative's computer display screen and the customer's question can be answered.

In order to provide even better service, FedEx has established a site on the Internet's World Wide Web. Now customers can contact the company on the Web, enter the package tracking number themselves, and see the tracking and delivery information displayed on their workstation screen. More than 30,000 customers use the Internet to track their packages every day.

TABLE 3.1 *Internet Capabilities*

INTERNET CAPABILITY	TOOL	DESCRIPTION
Communication	Electronic mail (e-mail)	Sends and receives messages between locations on the Internet.
	Usenet	Worldwide discussion format where notices can be posted for anyone to view.
	Chat sessions	Interactive discussions in which parties on the network exchange ideas and observations electronically.
	Mailing lists	Each mailing list has subscribers who receive messages as part of an ongoing discussion of the list's topic.
	Telnet	A means of communicating with the user's own system at a home location by way of the Internet.
Retrieval	FTP (file transfer protocol)	Used for transferring files containing documents or software between computers on the Internet.
	Archie	A search database of documents and software at FTP sites suitable for transfer to the user's computer.
	Gopher	Searches the Internet for textual information using a hierarchy of menus.
	Veronica	Searches the Internet using a user-supplied keyword and connects to the appropriate Gopher computer.
	WAIS	Locates files in databases using keywords.
	World Wide Web (WWW)	Searches and retrieves information in a variety of forms (including audio and video) using hyperlinks.

simply by including the intended recipient's e-mail address in the message. Anyone who sends you a message over the Internet must supply your address. The network processes your address to determine where you are located on the Internet and then routes the message to your computer. (More on electronic mail in Chapter 10.)

Your computer need not be on in order for someone to send mail to you because the network to which you are attached will retain any messages directed to you in storage. Thus, the network acts as your "electronic mailbox." When your computer is on and interacting with the network, you can ask it to display the messages currently in your mailbox.

An e-mail message can be directed to a group of recipients, large or small, so that each member of the group receives the same message at virtually the same time.

An e-mail message may be a sentence or two intended to communicate an idea or trigger an action. Or it may be an entire document of several pages containing graphical illustrations.

Usenet/User's Network
A system of worldwide discussion groups, not an actual physical network.

USENET. Usenet—short for **User's Network**—is a system of worldwide discussion groups. It is not an actual physical network. Rather, it is like a bulletin board—an electronic bulletin board—where notices can be posted for anyone to view. For example, there are Usenet discussion groups on physical fitness, computer technology, job listings, personal résumés, diabetes, *Star Trek* shows and movies, the Beatles . . . almost any topic you can imagine. If no discussion group exists for the topic you're interested in, you can start your own.

Usenet discussion groups are regularly added and removed from the Internet. The system administrator at a particular host site determines whether to carry a Usenet discussion group originating at that site.

CHAT SESSIONS. A live, interactive discussion—meaning all parties to the discussion are actually on the network, interacting through their computers—is known as a **chat session.** For example, members of a consulting project team who cannot be at a single location at the same time might use the Internet's chat capability to exchange ideas through their PCs linked to the Internet. Each will see the others' comments simultaneously and be able to respond immediately, keying comments into the computer (Figure 3.5). The comments will appear simultaneously on the other members' computer display screens.

chat session
A live interactive discussion where all parties are actually on the network, interacting through their computers.

MAILING LISTS. Mailing lists interconnect people who choose to participate in an ongoing discussion on a particular topic. The messages might be comments and opinions; announcements; discussions of new products, tools, or services; book, article, theater, movie, or music reviews; or just about any other information of interest to a group of persons.

You join a mailing list by subscribing electronically. Information submitted by any group member is automatically sent to you and stored by the host computer to which you are attached. You are then electronically notified that you have received information.

There are thousands of mailing lists on the Internet. You can join as many as you want—and have time to read.

You may be confused about the Internet's communication services at this point, thinking they all sound rather similar. But there are important differences for the user.

E-mail is delivered to your electronic mailbox automatically and the messages wait there until you are ready to read them. With e-mail, you have very little control over what you receive. Anyone who has your e-mail address can send you whatever he or she wishes.

A mail list will also deliver messages that appear automatically in your electronic mailbox, but this service is selective. You have to subscribe to a mailing list to get the messages.

Usenet groups and chat sessions are services that do *not* deliver messages to your mailbox. Instead, you must sign on to Usenet groups and chat sessions each time, and then receive and send messages on the display screen of your computer while you're using it. Usenet is a bulletin board you access and contribute to, while chat sessions are live, interactive discussion sessions that feel like conversations.

TELNET. The essence of the "network of networks" concept, **Telnet** is the network capability that permits remote sign-on from whatever computer you are currently using. Any computer in the Internet can be accessed from any other computer in the Internet. If you are away from your college or organization, you can use Telnet to communicate with your own system back at your main location.

Telnet
The means users employ to communicate with their own systems through the Internet when they are away from their home location.

166

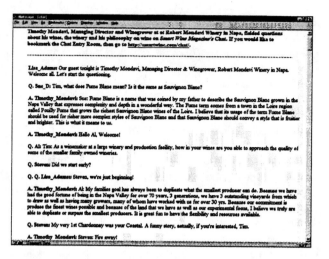

FIGURE 3.5

A Chat Session

All you need do is use the Telnet capability and provide it with your Internet address. Telnet takes care of finding the system and connecting you to it.

Retrieval Capabilities

Communication is the first reason for using the Internet. The other reason is to retrieve information. Enormous amounts of data and information are stored throughout the vast networks that make up the Internet. However, since the Internet is huge, continually evolving, and operating without any central governing body, how can you know what information is out there? There is no master directory listing all the information that can be retrieved by users. So how do you know where to go to get what you want?

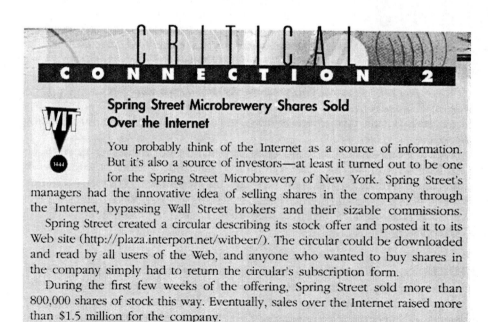

CRITICAL CONNECTION 2

Spring Street Microbrewery Shares Sold Over the Internet

You probably think of the Internet as a source of information. But it's also a source of investors—at least it turned out to be one for the Spring Street Microbrewery of New York. Spring Street's managers had the innovative idea of selling shares in the company through the Internet, bypassing Wall Street brokers and their sizable commissions.

Spring Street created a circular describing its stock offer and posted it to its Web site (http://plaza.interport.net/witbeer/). The circular could be downloaded and read by all users of the Web, and anyone who wanted to buy shares in the company simply had to return the circular's subscription form.

During the first few weeks of the offering, Spring Street sold more than 800,000 shares of stock this way. Eventually, sales over the Internet raised more than $1.5 million for the company.

There are four ways to retrieve information on the Internet: anonymous FTP and Archie, Gopher and Veronica, WAIS, and the World Wide Web.

ANONYMOUS FTP AND ARCHIE. You can transfer data and information from other computers connected to the Internet to your computer. For example, IBM, like many computer vendors, uses the file transfer protocol information retrieval capability to make notes and tips, as well as new versions of software, available to its personal computer customers by way of the Internet. **File transfer protocol (FTP)** is an Internet method that allows you to connect to another computer on the Net and transfer its files to your computer (Figure 3.6). The electronic files can contain anything that it is possible to store in a computer: data, pages of text (including entire books and newspapers), graphical images, photographs, music, recorded speeches, and software—including freeware and shareware (programs that the authors give away or allow users to try without a charge, while retaining ownership).

Other computers besides IBM's permit transfer of files on the Internet. The first step is to connect to the FTP site by entering its address into your computer so the Net can process it and make the connection. If the site is private, meaning the owner controls who can retrieve files, you must transmit a password. Many

file transfer protocol (FTP)

An Internet method that allows you to use a password to connect to another computer on the Net and transfer its files to your computer.

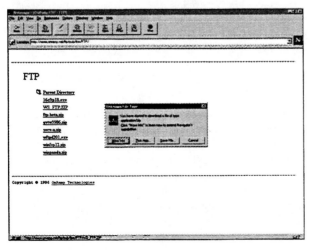

FIGURE 3.6
Internet Retrieval Tools

anonymous FTP site
A public FTP site that does not require you to use a special password to gain access.

Archie
A server that lists the contents of anonymous FTP sites.

keywords
A string of letters or words that indicates the subject to be searched.

Gopher
A server that organizes descriptions of information located on the Internet in the form of easy-to-use hierarchical menus.

Veronica
An internet program that uses keywords to search Gopher menus.

Wide Area Information Servers (WAIS)
A retrieval method that searches databases on the Internet and creates a menu of articles and manuscripts containing the keywords provided.

FTP sites, in fact, are public, so anyone can retrieve their files. To use these public or **anonymous FTP sites,** you simply enter the password *anonymous* and retrieve the files from the site.

If you don't know the address of an FTP site, you use Archie to find what you need. An **Archie** server contains a list of the contents of all anonymous FTP sites. There are many Archie servers on the Internet. Archie software, on your client computer, will search an Archie server using a string of letters or words, called **keywords,** that you enter to describe the subject you are interested in. Archie's response is a set of addresses for FTP sites containing information matching the keywords—addresses that you can use to connect to the FTP site to retrieve the information.

GOPHER AND VERONICA. **Gophers** are servers that organize descriptions of information located on the Internet in the form of easy-to-use hierarchical menus. Through Gopher, you locate and connect with an Internet computer by choosing from a series of menu descriptions that progressively narrow your search until you locate the Internet computer you are seeking. Once you have it, you can read, print, transfer, or transmit the file's text information.

Gopher computers have a search capability, called **Veronica,** which is similar to the FTP's Archie. Veronica is an Internet program that uses keywords to search Gopher menus. Once you tell Veronica the keywords, it will search all Gopher server menus, and when it has completed the search, it will provide you with a menu of items it has found. Selecting any items from the menu will automatically connect you to the Gopher site containing that information.

WAIS. The third way to search the Internet uses **Wide Area Information Servers (WAIS),** a retrieval method that will search the contents of databases on the Net for you. WAIS servers keep track of the location and contents of hundreds of databases on the Internet, and every document in a WAIS database is fully indexed on every word and phrase. (In contrast, Gopher servers only index by menu title.)

To conduct a search using WAIS, you enter the name of the database you wish to search and a set of keywords. Using your information, the WAIS server will search every work in every article in the specified database, producing a menu of articles and manuscripts containing the keywords you provided. Entries are listed in order of occurrence of the keywords, with articles containing the most occurrences listed first. You can select which articles and manuscripts you want shown on your display screen.

The essential difference between WAIS and the other search methods is that, unlike Archie and Veronica, which search file or menu *names,* WAIS searches the *contents* of the files.

Gophers? Archie? Veronica? You may be amused by the strange names for these Internet search capabilities. Here's how they came about.

The Gopher search capability, invented at the University of Minnesota, is named after the mascot of the university's athletic teams—the Golden Gophers. Because gophers burrow underground, the portion of the Net searched by Gopher servers soon became known as *Gopherspace.*

Archie is named after the comic book character of the same name. Soon after this search mechanism was created, the developers of a search mechanism for Gopherspace extended the fun by creating Veronica, an acronym for Very Easy Rodent-Oriented Net-wide Index to Computerized Archives, named for Archie's girlfriend in the comic book.

There's also a lesser-known search tool called *Jughead,* named for yet another character in the same comic book. Jughead, which stands for Jonzy's Universal Gopher Hierarchy Excavation And Display, was developed at the University of Utah by Rhett "Jonzy" Jones. This tool is used to search a single Gopher server. You might say Veronica searches across Gopherspace, while Jughead burrows deeper into Gopherspace! ▓

WORLD WIDE WEB. The **World Wide Web (WWW)**—known to most users as simply **the Web**—is a set of interconnected electronic documents, called **Web pages,** that are linked together over the Internet. Web software searches the Web to find pages containing keywords you enter. Special keywords in the pages of Web documents, called **hyperlinks,** connect, or link, documents to one another. Recognized on your computer display screen as words and symbols highlighted by color, underline, or blinking words and symbols, hyperlinks are your connection to other documents on the Web (Figure 3.7). By using Web software to follow the links in a document, you can jump to related information in any file on the Web. When you click on a hyperlink, the Web software processes the address contained in the hyperlink, connects to the location, and displays information from the linked location. Clicking on successive hyperlinks enables you to jump from location to location to obtain the information you want.

The Web is the fastest-growing part of the Internet. For many people, the Web *is* the Internet, for that is the only part of the Net they use.

The *Information Technology in Practice* feature entitled "Internet Accessibility: Opportunities for Everyone" illustrates the many ways the Internet's World Wide Web can be used by people from all walks of life. The next section of this chapter tells you how to browse the Web to get the most from its capabilities.

Table 3.2 summarizes the retrieval methods we have just discussed.

World Wide Web (WWW)/the Web
A set of interconnected electronic documents linked together over the Internet.

Web pages
Interconnected electronic documents.

hyperlinks
Words and/or symbols highlighted by blinking, color, or underline that connect one document to another related document on the Web.

WWW pages............

Hyperlinks between
pages...........

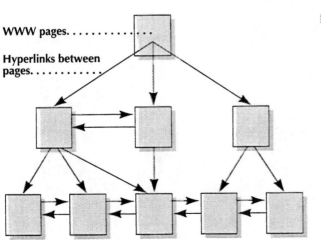

FIGURE 3.7
Hyperlink Structure

INFORMATION TECHNOLOGY IN PRACTICE

Internet Accessibility: Opportunities for Everyone

Eighteen coffee houses in San Francisco have gone on the Internet, installing terminals to allow their customers to interact with the network. Like jukeboxes, these Internet terminals accept quarters. Each quarter pays for four minutes of use, during which customers can send messages across the world or down the street to another coffee house, enter an electronic discussion on their favorite topic, or read through an electronic newsletter. Wayne Gregori, founder of SF Net, the firm that builds and programs café terminals, says, "We specifically target cafés in low-income areas. We're trying to get the have-nots on the computer."

Electronic entrepreneurs are taking to the Internet the way settlers once took to the offer of free land in the West after the Civil War. One such entrepreneur, Carl Malamud, created Internet Multicasting service, a weekly radio program distributed over Internet Talk Radio since 1993. Network users whose comput-

ers are equipped with speakers can download the program to their computers and listen to all or a portion of it whenever they have time.

As the Internet has grown, business users have become accustomed to its capabilities and have learned how to capitalize on them commercially. The Commercial Internet Exchange is a public data internetwork that offers unrestricted commercial connectivity without violating the restrictions against commercial traffic that prevail on some portions of the Internet.

Software Tool and Die (ST&D), a Brookline, Massachusetts, consulting firm that specializes in software development, has linked up to the Internet to provide consulting and programming services. It is not necessary for ST&D's people to ever meet customers face-to-face because they can converse with them easily through e-mail and can transfer files quickly over the other Internet communications services. ST&D also runs a public access bulletin board that makes software and services available.

Electronic entrepreneur Carl Malamud.

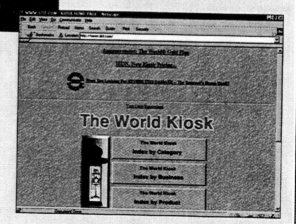

An Internet coffee house in San Francisco.

TABLE 3.2 *Internet Retrieval Methods*

RETRIEVAL METHOD	WHAT IT DOES	HOW IT DOES IT	WHAT IT GETS
FTP (file transfer protocol)	Transfers files between computers on the Internet.	User enters address of FTP site along with password for private site or "anonymous" for anonymous FTP site.	Copy of file is transferred over the Internet to user's computer.
Archie	Searches for documents and software at FTP sites.	Searches index of anonymous FTP sites for files (indexed by title and keyword). User types in keyword describing the files wanted.	Displays a list of FTP addresses showing where the files are available. User can enter addresses to transfer file from FTP site.
Gopher	Searches for textual information.	Searches menus of contents of interconnected Gopher servers. User types in keyword describing information wanted.	Displays menus listing contents of server located through the search. User chooses from successive menus until the desired file is found. Located files can be transferred, read, printed, or transmitted to another user.
Veronica	Searches for text information residing on Gopher computers.	Searches for text that appears in Gopher menus. User types in keywords relating to the document to be found.	Displays a menu containing the results of the search. User selects a choice from the menu to connect to the desired Gopher site.
WAIS	Searches for documents in specified databases.	Searches index to large text and document databases. User types in name of database and keywords relating to information to be found.	Results are listed in order by the number of keyword occurrences. User clicks on entry to display the desired document.
World Wide Web (WWW)	Searches for electronic pages.	Searches Web pages on the Internet. User types in keyword identifying information to be found.	Results are listed in order by number of keyword occurrences. User clicks on hyperlink to jump from location to location.

Browsing the World Wide Web

Graphical browser software, introduced in the early 1990s, triggered widespread use of the Web by individuals, universities, companies, and government. With interest in the Web skyrocketing, it was inevitable that there would be a tremendous growth in Web pages. This section of the chapter describes how to browse WWW pages, the HTML language, browser software, URL addresses identifying Web sites, and Net search tools.

Browsing the Web's Many Pages

Electronic pages are the most distinguishing characteristic of the Web. Here we discuss the characteristics of Web pages and tell you how to access these pages using browser software.

WEB PAGES. Pages in a Web document are specially formatted files that can display text, graphical, and image information. They can also include clips of audio and video information, which readers can play if their computers are equipped with the necessary hardware and software.

home page
The first page of a Web site, which identifies the site and provides information about the contents of electronic documents that are part of the site.

The **home page** is the first page you see when you access a Web site. It identifies the site and provides information about the contents of electronic documents that are part of the site (i.e., a table of contents or map). Often the home page uses graphical symbols, or icons, to supplement text in describing other information that is part of the Web site. The home page contains links to other pages.

Figure 3.8 shows the home page for the City of Paris, France. Notice how quickly you can identify the subject of this page—Paris. The city's name stands out because of its size, attractive color, and bracketing images of prominent statues in central Paris. Text information in the middle of the page further identifies the Web site and offers helpful information on accessing other information at the Paris Web site.

The City of Paris home page also contains links to other information. Eight of these links are visible, each a word or phrase underlined to signify that it is a hyperlink. For example, if you wanted to view this home page in the French language, you could click on the hyperlink *Vr.Française*. Or if you wanted a table of contents for the City of Paris document, you would click on *Contents*. Each of the page's hyperlinks works in the same way.

Images, or icons, are also used to signify hyperlinks on Web pages. Clicking on the image activates the hyperlink. The four images at the bottom of the City of Paris home page are hyperlinks that serve the same purpose as the text hyperlinks for *The City, Its Culture, Tourist Information,* and *Paris Kiosque*. These icons are also activated by a click of the user's mouse.

CREATING WEB PAGES USING HTML. A Web page's features take shape when the user specifies the location and appearance of the information. A set of commands—**hypertext markup language (HTML)**—specifies the position, size, and color of text, the location of graphic information, and the incorporation of sound and video (Figure 3.9). HTML commands also identify the words or images that will serve as hyperlinks to other documents. When the computer processes files containing HTML commands, it creates and displays the page and prepares the hyperlinks.

hypertext markup language (HTML)
A set of commands that specifies the position, size, and color of text, the location of graphic information, and the incorporation of sound and video. HTML commands also identify the words or images that will serve as hyperlinks to other documents.

HTML consists of a series of *tags* that set off sections of text that will appear on a Web page. Used in pairs, the tags mark the beginning and end of an HTML section (such as the head, title, or body areas of a page). Tags are recognized by their angle brackets (<>). An initial tag identifies the beginning of a section

FIGURE 3.8
Home Page for the City of Paris, France

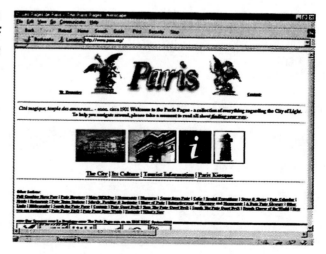

TAG	DESCRIPTION
Structure	
<HTML> ... </HTML>	Identifies the document as an HTML document and its beginning and end.
<HEAD> ... </HEAD>	Identifies the head, one of two parts of an HTML document.
<BODY> ... </BODY>	Identifies the body of the document, the other part of an HTML document.
<TITLE> ... </TITLE>	Identifies the document's title.
<!- ... ->	Sets off a comment within a document. (Browser software does not display comments on a Web page.)
Block Elements	
<H1> ... </H1>	Identifies a first-level heading (the highest level) within the document. It is customary to use a level 1 heading as the first element in the body of an HTML document.
<H2> ... </H2>	Identifies a second-level heading within the document.
<H3> ... </H3>	Identifies a third-level heading within the document.
<H4> ... </H4>	Identifies a fourth-level heading within the document.
<H5> ... </H5>	Identifies a fifth-level heading within the document.
<P> ... </P>	Sets off paragraphs within the document.
<CENTER> ... </CENTER>	Centers the block (the content between the tags) on the page when it is displayed.
<TAB>	Describes the number of spaces to indent: e.g., <TAG INDENT = 5> will indent the text 5 characters until the end of the paragraph (no closing tag is required).
Hypertext Links	
<A> ... </A>	Marks the start (HREF) or end (NAME) of a link: e.g., <A HREF=url>text to be highlighted as hyperlink</A>.
In-line Images	
<IMG>	Used to place an in-line image into the page at the designated location: e.g., <IMG SCR=../image.gif"> where SCR indicates the file name, image.gif, containing the image to be embedded (there is no closing tag).
Formatting	
<P>	Start a new paragraph; insert a blank line.
 	Start a new line.
<HR>	Insert a ruler line.
<B> </B>	Boldface type.
<I> </I>	Italic type.
<U> </U>	Underline.
<PRE> </PRE>	Maintains formatted space. (HTML will remove extra spaces, tabs, and blank lines except when instructed to retain preformatted spacing by the <PRE> tag.)
&	Inserts special character.

FIGURE 3.9 *Common HTML Tags*

(<HEAD>), and a second tag, which includes a slash (/), signifies the end of the section (</HEAD>).

The basic structure of a page will conform to this standard sequence:

```
<HTML>
 <HEAD>
    This is the section of the document where the purpose of the page is
    described. The comments here are not intended to be displayed by the
    browser; they are for informational purposes only.
 </HEAD>
 <BODY>
    This is the section of the document that contains the information and graph-
    ical images the browser will display. It also contains hyperlinks to other
    Web pages.
 </BODY>
</HTML>
```

Creating a Web page consists of preparing a document that includes the tags and a combination of text, hyperlink references, and graphics. Figure 3.9 lists the most common HTML commands used in creating Web pages.

The HTML commands describing a page are stored on a Web server. When retrieved by browser software, they are processed to create the page and its links, which are shown on the user's display screen (Figure 3.10).

Software developers have created tools to assist people in preparing Web pages (Figure 3.11). Some of these tools provide example HTML segments that users can modify to create the page they want without writing the HTML from scratch.

Plenty of books are available that will familiarize you with HTML and help you create your own pages on the Web (see *Suggested Readings* at the end of the chapter). Alternatively, you can use the Web itself to retrieve information on HTML and page construction. For example, you may want to visit the following Web locations:

http://nearnet.gnn.com/gnn/netizens/fieldguide.html
(provides a field guide to home pages)
http://nearnet.gnn.com/gnn/netizens/construction/html
(includes a home page construction kit) ▨

Browser Software

Web browser
Client computer program designed to locate and display information on the World Wide Web.

To take advantage of the graphical nature of the Web, you need a browser program.[1] **Web browsers** are client computer programs designed to locate and display information on the World Wide Web. With a Web browser you can display Web pages, jump between Web pages, using hyperlinks, and search the Web for pages of topical interest. It was when graphical Web browser programs were introduced in the early 1990s, making the creating and viewing of electronic pages possible, that interest in the Web shot up. Individuals, universities, companies, and governments began to use Web pages to display information and invite communication with people on the Internet.

---

[1]A variety of browser programs are available. Many can be downloaded from the Internet and loaded on a PC or workstation. Some are available without charge.

HTML for Web Page

Web Server

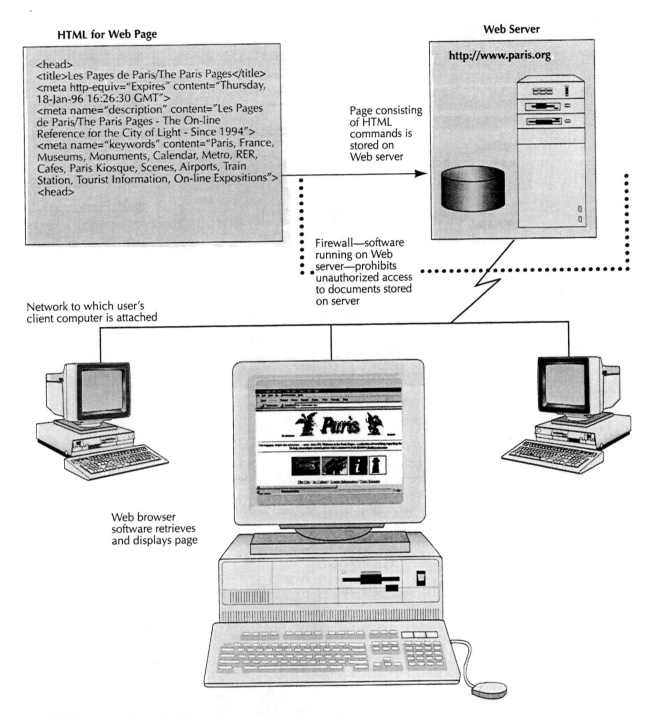

http://www.paris.org

```
<head>
<title>Les Pages de Paris/The Paris Pages</title>
<meta http-equiv="Expires" content="Thursday,
18-Jan-96 16:26:30 GMT">
<meta name="description" content="Les Pages
de Paris/The Paris Pages - The On-line
Reference for the City of Light - Since 1994">
<meta name="keywords" content="Paris, France,
Museums, Monuments, Calendar, Metro, RER,
Cafes, Paris Kiosque, Scenes, Airports, Train
Station, Tourist Information, On-line Expositions">
<head>
```

Page consisting
of HTML
commands is
stored on
Web server

Firewall—software
running on Web
server—prohibits
unauthorized access
to documents stored
on server

Network to which user's
client computer is attached

Web browser
software retrieves
and displays page

FIGURE 3.10 *World Wide Web Page Structure*

A page displayed on a PC connected to the Web is the result of a creation using HTML that is stored on a Web server, retrieved and transmitted over interconnecting networks, and viewed on a PC using a Web browser.

176

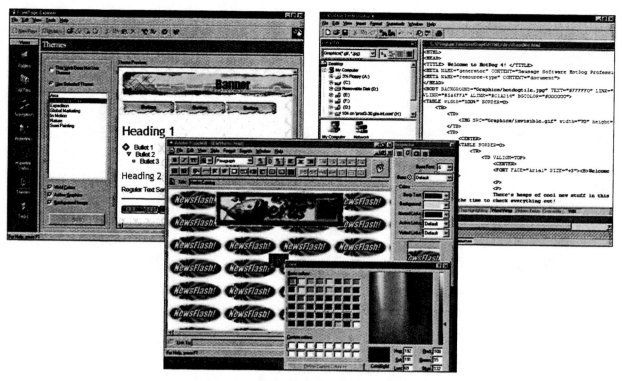

FIGURE 3.11 *WWW Development Tools*

Web browsers are typically activated by clicking on an icon that is associated with the program (Figure 3.12).

Two types of browsers are used with the Web: text-based and graphical. **Text-based browsers** display only text information, either a line at a time or a full screen at once (Figure 3.13). *Line browsers,* the simplest type of text-based browser, display information by writing one line after another on the display screen. As the screen fills, all lines scroll up and the new line is added at the bottom of the screen.

text-based browser
A type of browser used with the Web that displays only text information, either a line at a time or a full screen at once.

FIGURE 3.12
Browsers Client Program

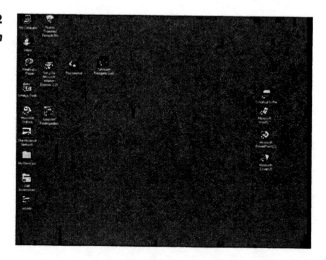

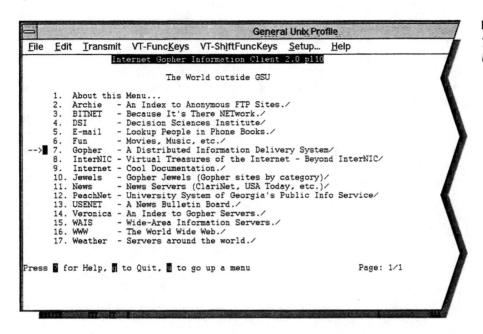

FIGURE 3.13
Text-based Line Browser Used to Access the Internet

A *screen browser,* as its name suggests, uses the entire display screen and can write information anywhere on the screen. Although the software for a screen browser is more complicated than that for a line browser, since it must know the characteristics of a specific display device and how to determine positions on the screen, users of the Web find information displayed by screen browsers easier to use because they see a full screen of information at once rather than individual lines appearing one after the other.

Today, regular users of the Web typically rely on a graphical screen browser. The distinguishing characteristic of a **graphical browser** is its capability for displaying both text and images (called *in-line images*) within a page. The image may be an icon, a photograph, or a drawing. Some pages also include animated images.

Graphical browsers display a window consisting of the display and nine principal components (Figure 3.14):

graphical browser
A type of browser used with the Web that displays both text and images within a page.

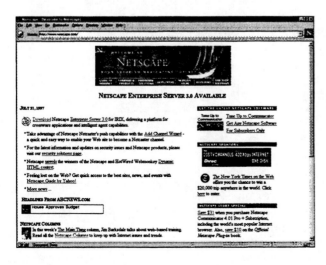

FIGURE 3.14
Netscape Graphical Browser

1. **Title bar**—displays the name of the browser and the page currently displayed.
2. **Menu bar**—contains the browser commands for creating, editing, navigating, and invoking special actions involving the page currently displayed.
3. **Net site**—displays the address of the Web site providing the page currently displayed.
4. **Toolbar**—contains icons that represent frequently used commands included in the menu bar, such as

   Forward—moves ahead to pages in the history list.
   Backward—moves back to pages in the history list.
   Open file—makes a file ready to use.
   File store—writes a copy of the current file to storage.
   History list—keeps track of all WWW pages visited in a particular session, thus providing the capability for a user to jump directly to any of those pages.
   Print—prints a copy of the page currently displayed.
   Home page—returns to the home page of the site at which the user is connected to the WWW.
5. **In-line image**—graphics embedded (at the page creator's option) in the page to enhance its appearance and visually convey information about the nature of the page.
6. **Hyperlinks**—icon or text links (usually signified by an underline or different color) that can be selected to jump to another page.
7. **Status bar**—displays the address of the highlighted link.
8. **Activity indicator**—an icon that signals the user that an activity, such as locating a WWW site or transmitting information from another location, is in process.
9. **Scroll bars**—allow the user to move the window up or down for viewing information.

WWW's URL Addresses

Uniform Resource Locator (URL)
A document's address on the WWW.

As with all Internet locations, each Web page location has its own address. The **Uniform Resource Locator (URL)** is the document's address on the WWW, so named because it is a consistent system for identifying Web sites that all page developers use. In Figure 3.8, http://www/paris.org is the address for the home page of the Paris Pages.

The URL is determined on the basis of the Internet address of the site. Its general format is:

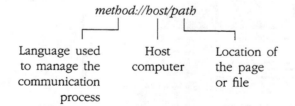

Hence, a browser pointed at the page identified by URL http://www.paris.org uses the hypertext transfer protocol (HTTP), the communication language employed by WWW clients and servers. When the browser connects to this page, it retrieves a file called *paris* in a directory named *org* (the abbreviation for organization).

American Airlines	American Airlines' Internet Ticket Auction

American Airlines had been offering last-minute ticket specials to customers of a local cable station in the vicinity of its Dallas, Texas, home base. When it learned that people were watching the announcements on TV and then using e-mail to tell their friends about the specials, American decided it had stumbled upon a new marketing channel.

In 1996, the airline began auctioning tickets over the Internet. Announcements of available tickets are posted on the Internet for 24- and 40-hour periods, during which Net users can bid on the tickets. American periodically posts the high bid during the auction period. At the end of the period, the highest bidders get the right to purchase the available tickets.

Navigating the WWW

To take advantage of what the WWW has to offer, you must know how to navigate from page to page. This is actually quite easy. You merely point the browser to a specific URL location, or, if you do not know the URL, you ask the Web to search for information or scan a directory.

SEARCHING WITH SEARCH ENGINES. To find information on the Web when you do not know its location—that is, its URL—you start a search by invoking a program, called a **search engine,** from within the browser to scan the network. The search is guided by a keyword or phrase that you enter (Figure 3.15). For instance, if you want to search for information on World Cup Soccer, you simply enter the phrase "world cup soccer" (in any combination of upper- and lower-case letters) when prompted to do so by the search engine.

search engine
A program invoked from within the browser that scans the network by using a keyword or phrase.

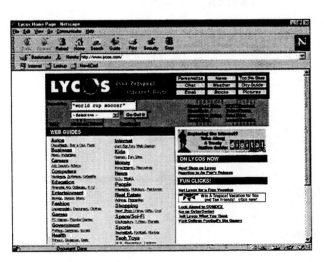

FIGURE 3.15

Home Page for the Lycos Search Engine

Many different search engines are available on the Web, most without a fee. These search engines go by such names as *WebCrawler* (which can be found at http://www.webcrawler.com), *Lycos* (http://www.lycos.com), and *Infoseek* (http://www.infoseek.com).

directory
A listing of information by category.

DIRECTORIES. A Web **directory** is a listing of information by category. To find information in the directory, you choose the most important category by clicking on the category name, and continue through successive choices, each with more specific options, until you find what you're looking for.

Yahoo! is one of the most widely used directories. When you reach *Yahoo!* (http://www.yahoo.com), you see a subject list, including Arts, Business and Economy, Computers and Internet, Education, Entertainment, Health, and so forth (Figure 3.16a). If you're interested in a topic related to Business and Economy, you click on this *Yahoo!* area and a more detailed subject list will appear (Figure 3.16b).

The key to using both search engines and directories effectively is to plan in advance. Know what subject list is likely to contain what you're looking for and the keywords that will most accurately describe the topic.

surfing
Moving among a number of networks that are linked together, or internetworked.

internetworked
The linking of several networks.

To say that you are **surfing** the Web or the Net is a common way of expressing that you are moving among a number of separate networks that are linked together—that is, **internetworked.** In the ocean, when you ride a surfboard from wave to wave, you are moving across the water's surface. In surfing the Web or Internet, you are moving across networks, skipping from page to page or site to site.

a) Home Page for the Yahoo! Directory

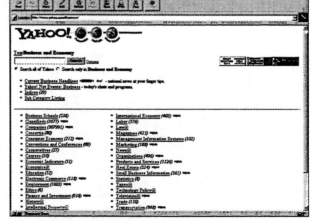

b) A Yahoo! Directory Listing

FIGURE 3.16 *Web directories help locate information on the Internet by topic and keywords.*

USING THE INTERNET'S OTHER CAPABILITIES. Search engines can also scan for Gopher, FTP, newsgroups, and other sites to locate information, and the browser can retrieve, transmit, or view the files as they are located. Files at these locations have addresses that use the URL conventions outlined in this section. For example, the address of an FTP file will be ftp://(name of FTP file or site), while that of Gopher will be gopher://(name of Gopher site or file).

Internet Information

If you want more information on the Internet, check out your local bookstore and you will be sure to find a variety of books on its features and capabilities. The *Internet Yellow Pages,* for instance, lists available services and databases. Directories describing the thousands of mailing lists on the network are also available. The Internet's popularity has also spawned numerous newsletters and periodicals, including *The Internet Business Journal, The Internet Letter,* and *Internet World* (Figure 3.17). Each provides tips on network capabilities and pointers to interesting sites.

A Final Word

The World Wide Web and the Internet are still in their infancy, so you can be sure that many innovative uses for them will emerge in the next few years. People will certainly find clever new ways to capitalize on their capabilities for incorporating sound, video, animation, and high-resolution graphics. We can only guess at what will result.

FIGURE 3.17
Internet and World Wide Web Books and Magazines

SUMMARY OF LEARNING OBJECTIVES

1 Explain how individual computers and server computers interact on the Internet. A client computer—the computer on an individual's desktop—requests data and information from a server computer on the network. The requested data and information are transmitted to the client computer, where the recipient uses them as he or she wishes.

2 Describe the two types of capabilities of the Internet. The Internet supports communications and retrieval capabilities. Its communications capabilities allow the exchange of information between senders and receivers virtually anywhere in the world. Through the Internet's retrieval capabilities, individuals have access to data and information from other networks connected to the Internet.

3 Identify the 11 principal communication and retrieval capabilities of the Internet. The Net's communications capabilities are e-mail, Usenet, chat sessions, mailing lists, and Telnet. Its retrieval capabilities are FTP, Archie, Gopher, Veronica, WAIS, and the World Wide Web (WWW).

4 Summarize how the Internet knows the location of a particular user on the Net. Everyone on the Internet has a unique address. That address consists of four components: a personal identification, a host computer identification, the name of the institution or organization, and the domain name. All Internet messages are routed to a location according to these address components.

5 Describe the use of pages on the World Wide Web. Each WWW location consists of a series of pages or documents that contain text, graphics, images, and audio or video information. They may also contain links (called *hyperlinks*) to other pages. The home page is the main page at a specific location. All other pages are linked to the home page.

6 Explain the purpose of hyperlinks and their role on the World Wide Web. Hyperlinks (or hypertext) are keywords that connect WWW locations. When a hyperlink is activated by clicking on the linked word, a jump to the connected location occurs without any need to use menus or other means to access the location. Pages containing hyperlinks are the most visible characteristic of the World Wide Web.

7 Describe the characteristics of browser software and relate them to the different types of information that can be included in a home page. Browsers are client software programs that connect with servers on the Internet. Most WWW browsers are graphical, meaning they can display icons, graphics, and images. Individuals use the browser by clicking on hyperlinks or icons or by entering addresses (URLs) on the Internet. The browser, in turn, makes the interconnection, transferring information from the network to the display screen of the client computer.

KEY TERMS

CRITICAL CONNECTIONS

1   FedEx Links Up

When FedEx executives saw how successful the company's package tracking site on the Internet was with customers, they wondered if they could use these same capabilities to enhance communication within the company. They quickly set up some internal intranet sites, and their fast success let to the establishment of others. Soon there were more than 60 intranet sites within FedEx. Today, the thousands of desktop computers on employees' desks are all being equipped with Web browser software to enable internal communication.

Questions for Discussion

1. What possible uses for the intranet can you think of for FedEx?

2. How would you determine whether Federal Express is benefiting from its intranet sites?

3. If customers can access Federal Express's tracking system on the Internet, do you think they can also access the company's intranet sites? Why or why not?

2   Spring Street Microbrewery Shares Sold Over the Internet

When the Securities and Exchange Commission (SEC), which oversees the trading of stocks in the United States, got wind of the Spring Street offering over the Internet, the company voluntarily stopped trading to give the SEC time to investigate this novel practice.

After completing its review, the SEC made only a minor adjustment to Spring Street's stock offering: investors would now have to send their payment to a third party—an escrow agent—rather than directly to Spring Street. Spring Street's managers also agreed to make financial information on the company and its stock's trading history available to the SEC and others. In effect, the SEC, through its review of Spring Street, has endorsed trading on the Internet.

Questions for Discussion

1. Are the risks of purchasing stocks over the Internet different from those assumed when buying through

a broker? What does a broker do for a buyer in return for collecting a commission?

2. Do you think stock trades over the Internet are a potential threat to traditional trading centers like the New York Stock Exchange? Explain the reasoning behind your answer

3   American Airlines' Internet Ticket Auction

American Airlines American Airlines has also started sending out e-mail messages about last-minute fare specials. To receive these messages, you must register at American's Web site (http://www2.amrcorp.com/cgi-bin/aans).

The airline's Internet auction has sold tickets ranging in price from one-tenth to one-half their original value. All types of tickets are available through this auction:

first- and business-class tickets, as well as tickets to resorts and exotic locations. American has found the Internet auction an effective way to lower ticket costs since it permits the airline to deal directly with customers, cutting out the travel agent's commission. It has also proved an effective way to sell tickets that would otherwise go unused.

Questions for Discussion

1. Do you think the Internet is a good vehicle for selling surplus tickets at the last minute?

2. How can the Internet help reduce the airline industry's costs of selling and distributing tickets?

3. Do you think other airlines will follow American into the Internet auction arena?.

URLs Find Home

In this exercise, you'll journey onto the Internet's World Wide Web, using the browser's rich capabilities. As you visit different Web sites, you'll see dramatic differences between the way each site's designer has chosen to display information.

To get started, sign on to the Internet. Click on the appropriate icon to activate the browser software. If you're using either the Netscape Navigator or Microsoft Explorer browsers, you'll see one of these icons on your computer:

As soon as the browser is loaded and the Internet connection made, you'll see a home page

display. The address for the home page shown on the screen can be found on the browser's location line, near the top of the screen.

Netsite:	http://www.lycos.com/	▾

Compare the address shown on the location line with the home page address—the URL—for your institution or service provider.

1. If your institution's home page URL is different, enter that URL in the location line (check your notes from the Net_Work application in Chapter 1, where you recorded the URL). Do this by clicking on the location line and keying the URL over the original URL. A new home page will appear on the screen. Move the vertical scroll bar on the right side of the page up or down to view the information clearly.

2. To see a different home page, enter the URL for Netscape Navigator: http://www.netscape.com.

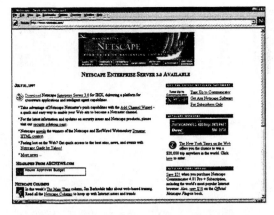

3. You can jump back and forth between the two home pages by clicking on the browser's Back or Forward button near the top of the display.

4. What are the differences between the home pages? Consider the size and style of the text information and note the use of color. What does the graphic image on Netscape's home page convey? Does the home page of your institution or service provider include graphics (perhaps a mascot, seal, or logo)?

5. What hyperlinks are embedded in each page? Hyperlinks are usually identifiable as text that is underlined or set off in a different color or as an icon.

6. Try the hyperlinks to see where they take you. Click on a hyperlink and you'll jump to a new page. You may see hyperlinks on the new page as well. Click on another hyperlink to see where that takes you.

7. Now go back to your starting point, in one of two ways:
   a. Click and the previous display will appear. Do this several times and you'll see each of the preceding screens, until you come to your starting point.
   b. Click on and the browser will jump directly to the home page.

8. Visit some other interesting Web sites, checking their contents and their design. Which ones stand out in your mind and why? Which are the easiest to navigate? The most difficult? Which appear to have useful information?

You might want to visit these sites:[2]

The U.S. Library of Congress: http://lcweb.loc.gov

The Smithsonian: http://www.si.edu

The White House: http://whitehouse.gov

The U.S. Bureau of the Census: http://www.census.gov

The Government of Canada: http://debra.dgbt.doc.ca:80/opengov/

The Government of Mexico: http://www.presidencia.gob.mx

9. For each site you visit, explore the hyperlinks. Behind each link you'll find some interesting features. For example, you can send an e-mail message to the White House, view one of the Smithsonian's collections via its on-line images, test your knowledge of French as you explore information on Canada's legislative bodies, or get a glimpse of Mexico's rich heritage.

10. When you're done, don't forget to sign off. Click on File on the menu bar. Then on the File menu, click Exit.

The wide world of the Internet awaits your next sign-on!

[2]Web sites can be "busy" because of high use, in which case you might see an informative message displayed on your screen. Also, Web site operators may move their home page to a different URL, sometimes linking the old page to the new (when they do not, a message may state that the URL is no longer used).

GROUP PROJECTS AND APPLICATIONS

Project 1

At one time, there were only a few Net search engines. In recent years, however, many new engines have been created. Most regular Net users have a favorite search engine. Which one do you like best? To find out, perform the following group activity with three or four members of your class.

Your goal is to answer *one* of the following questions:

- Which three companies in the United States spend the most each year on advertising? The most on public relations?
- In what year was the novel *Tom Jones* published? Who wrote it? Name two other English literary works also published that year.
- Which New Jersey counties use the 201 area code? Which three New Jersey towns have the highest per capita income?
- In which museum is Edvard Munch's "The Scream" displayed? Which museum owns the largest collection of paintings by Grandma Moses?

Each member of your group should use a different search engine to find the answer to the question you've chosen. Some search engines to try:

- *Alta Vista*   http://www.altavista.com
- *Excite!*   http://www.excite.com
- *Infoseek*   http://www.infoseek.com
- *Lycos*   http://www.lycos.com
- *WebCrawler*   http://www.webcrawler.com
- *Yahoo!*   http://www.yahoo.com

How long did each member of your group take to find the answer? Compare your answers with those of other groups. How do the various engines and directories differ? Are some more appropriate for particular types of research than for others? Report on the results of your searches to the class.

Project 2

Subscribers to Usenet groups often become members of a "virtual community" in which they exchange ideas and sometimes develop friendships. Groups of four or five students should subscribe to and monitor the activities of a Usenet group for a period of two weeks. Choose any topic in which the group is interested, from the standard to the unexpected.

At the end of two weeks, report to the class on the activities of your Usenet group. Is the group popular? What topics is it discussing? Have you begun to correspond with anyone?

Project 3

Very few companies have been able to make money through the Internet. Setting up and maintaining a Net site can be expensive. Free sites, such as search directories, are presently supported by advertising, but advertisers may not be willing to advertise on the Net in the future unless they see a return on their investment.

Form a team and visit a local company that has a home page on the Internet. Interview someone in the information technology or advertising department about the company's Internet philosophy. Some questions you might ask:

- Who designed the company's site—a company employee or an outside expert?
- Who maintains the site? Who is in charge of answering any e-mail that comes through the site?
- Does the company advertise on the Net? If so, where? Who designed the advertisements? How much do the ads cost?
- How many "hits" does the company get on its ads? In other words, how many people see the ad each week or month? Has the company been able to make a direct connection between its sales revenue and its Internet ads?
- What are the company's plans for using the Internet in the future?

Prepare a two- to five-page written summary of the interview.

REVIEW QUESTIONS

1. Was the Internet developed by public or private organizations? Who pays for the cost of operating the Internet today?
2. What is the significance of the name *Internet?*
3. Describe the characteristics of client and server computers. What is the relationship between client-server computing and the Internet?
4. What are host computers? How are host computers involved in the Internet?
5. How is an Internet address determined? Who assigns Internet addresses?
6. Describe the two types of activities possible on the Internet.
7. What are the characteristics of each of the five communications capabilities of the Internet?
8. Describe the similarities and differences among Gopher, Veronica, and Archie retrieval tools.
9. What is an FTP site? A WAIS server?
10. What is the most distinguishing characteristic of the World Wide Web?
11. How do text-based and graphical browsers differ? Do they have the same purpose?
12. When is HTML needed for use of the WWW? Who uses HTML?
13. How does a URL enable a WWW user to find and retrieve information?
14. Describe the importance of pages for the World Wide Web. What contents are included in a page?
15. What is a home page? How is a home page created?
16. Describe the purpose of a search engine. Who uses a search engine? What information must be provided before a search engine can work?
17. What is the difference between a search engine and a directory?
18. Why is using the Internet sometimes called *surfing?*

DISCUSSION QUESTIONS

1. The Internet is in its infancy; it exploded onto the business scene relatively recently. Hence, companies are still learning how to capitalize on its features. What characteristics of the Internet do you feel are most important to business and why? Do you think *every business,* from the largest corporations to the smallest "mom-and-pop" stores, will soon be Internet users? Why or why not?
2. What features of intranets do you believe underlie their rapidly growing use in business? What advantages does an intracompany intranet offer that cannot be obtained through use of ordinary e-mail?
3. Businesses have developed another use of the intranet to link selective business partners over the Internet. Access to these *extranets* is controlled in the same way as intranets so that only authorized companies can view company information. Develop three examples illustrating when a company might want to establish extranets to interconnect with outside companies.
4. The Net's FTP capabilities make it possible to transfer files containing digital information between virtually any locations. What are examples of ways in which businesses could use this capability to service their customers? Do you think companies can deliver their products by means of FTP? Why or why not?

SUGGESTED READINGS

Berghel, Hal. "Cyperspace 2000: Dealing With Information Overload," *Communications of the ACM 40* (February 1997). The author, a respected research scientist, examines the technology revolution brought about by the Internet, with implications for the way it will change daily living into the next century. The credibility of the Internet is examined from different dimensions in order to compare its impact to such other historical inventions as the printing press and the compass.

Martin, Michael H. "The Next Big Thing: A Bookstore?" *Fortune 134* (December 6, 1996): 68–170. This article, part of a special information technology issue covering the Internet, describes how business is using the Net to do more than exchange information. Companies, including amazon.com, who have come into existence to serve customers over the Net are discussed in this and the accompanying articles.

Nelson, Stephen L. *Microsoft FrontPage*. Microsoft, 1997. Describes the creation of Web pages using Microsoft's popular FrontPage construction software. The guide includes do's and don'ts as well as helpful hints that lead to functional and attractive Web pages.

Udell, Jon. "Net Applications: Will Netscape Set the Standard?" *Byte 22* (March 1997): 66–72,ff. This forward-looking article describes the manner in which Netscape will change its browser software in the future, promising to further change the world of computing. The evolution of Netscape software to link groups of individuals is discussed. Examples from business demonstrate the expected benefits of these advances.

Yourdon, Edward. "Java, the Web, and Software Development," *Computer 29* (August 1996): 25–30. What's the big deal about the Web? According to this distinguished computer pioneer, it marks the birth of dynamic computing on rented components. Seven key issues for developers of full-scale Internet applications are discussed.

Zimmerman, Paul H. *Web Page (Essentials)*. Que Books, 1997. A practical and comprehensive book describing the creation of Web pages. Projects in the book guide readers through creation of pages, adding hyperlinks, and effective use of color and graphics.

Module 2: The Business Value of Information and Technology

Goal: To be able to critically discuss and evaluate the business value impacts of information systems.

Chapter 6: The Value of Information

Collecting information is a valuable tool for decision makers. Information is sometimes collected to aid general understanding, and often purely out of curiosity, but on occasion information is collected to aid in making a particular decision. For example, a consumer products company might survey customers about the design of a new product that is still not finalized for production. A purchasing manager might learn about the costs other industries face before putting pressure on her suppliers to lower their prices.

Information is usually obtained only at some cost. Marketing research costs money and time: test markets are expensive to conduct and (often more important) they can delay introduction even of successful products. The decision to collect information can be analyzed to see if the *expected value* of the information exceeds its cost of collection.

Information is seldom perfect. *Sample* information may be inaccurate for several reasons: pure sampling error; measurement bias (what respondents say is not necessarily what they will do); and selection bias (the sample is not representative of the population). The results of a test market, for example, may not be a perfect indicator of the outcome of a new-product introduction for any or all of the above reasons.

Michelle's Movers

Michelle's Movers (MM) rents out trucks with a crew of two on a daily basis, usually to homeowners who are moving house, or to companies with delivery problems. On one particular day Michelle is a truck short and intends hiring one from a local truck rental firm. The question she faces is, how big a truck should she hire? A large truck costs $200 per day (including insurance, fuel, etc.), a small truck $130/day. The advantage of hiring the small truck may be offset if the load is too big, necessitating that the crew make two trips. The additional cost of making two trips (overtime, truck mileage) she assesses at $150. She assesses the probability that two trips will be necessary as 0.40.

Question 1   Assuming there are no other ramifications to her decision, should she rent a large truck or a small truck?

Professor David E. Bell prepared this note as a basis for class discussion.

Question 2   What would it be worth to Michelle to know for sure whether a small truck would be adequate for the job? [For example, she might send someone a day in advance to examine the job at first hand.]

To answer question 1 we may draw the following tree:

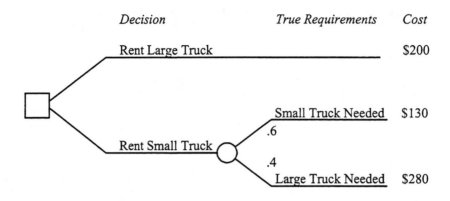

The expected cost of renting a small truck is 0.6 * 130 + 0.4 * 280 = $190. Thus she should rent a small truck.

To answer question 2, let's first assume that the information Michelle gets suffers from none of the possible inaccuracies discussed above: it is "perfect" information. To analyze Michelle's problem, we must draw a more complex tree:

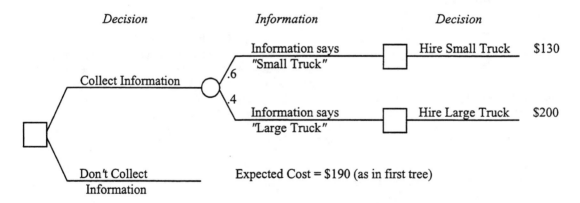

The expected value of the "Collect Information" decision is 0.6 * 130 + 0.4 * 200 = $158. This is $32 cheaper than the expected cost without the information. Thus the expected value of information is $32. Michelle would be better off first getting the information and then deciding what to do if the cost of getting it were less than $32; if it exceeded $32, however, she would be better off just going ahead and renting a small truck.

A way to see this directly is to recognize that we save $80 by collecting the information if a large truck is needed, and this occurs with probability 0.4 (and 0.4 x $80 = $32). In more complicated settings it may not be possible to deduce the answer so easily.

The Value of Imperfect Information

We assumed in our example that the information, once obtained, would be perfectly accurate. This is not always the case.

Suppose that the person sent in advance to inspect the job is known to make mistakes. Michelle believes that even if this person reports "Large Truck Needed" then the probability that a large truck is indeed needed is 0.80. Similarly if the person reports "Small Truck Needed" then there is only an 80% chance that a small truck is needed.

How much is advance information of this nature worth?

Before proceeding with the analysis, note that it will certainly be true that this information is worth less than $32. We may solve this problem with the following tree:

Exhibit 1

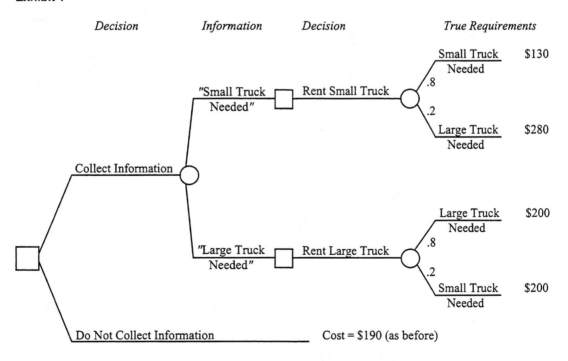

Decision	Information	Decision		True Requirements

This tree is almost complete. It lacks, however, one piece of probabilistic information: how likely is our informant to say "Small Truck" versus "Large Truck"? You may think that the appropriate probabilities ought to be .6 and .4 respectively because these are the probabilities of a small and large truck being needed. But this is not entirely consistent. Consider the following tree:

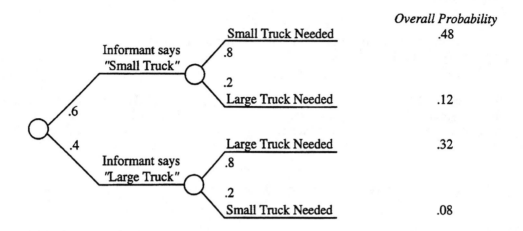

According to this tree there is a 0.56 probability that a small truck will in fact be needed (0.48 + 0.08) and a 0.44 probability that a large truck will be needed (.12 + .32). These aren't quite the same as 0.6 and 0.4 respectively. To see this problem more clearly, suppose our informant is right half the time and wrong half the time, then even if we almost certainly needed a large truck, our informant is just as likely to *say* "Large" or "Small".

To find the correct probability p that our informant will *say* "Large Truck Needed" we need to solve the following equation

$$p * 0.8 + (1-p) * 0.2 = 0.4$$

or in words:

*Probability Informant says "Large Truck" * Probability this is correct*
*+ Probability Informant says "Small Truck" * Probability this is wrong*
= Overall Probability of Large Truck.

The solution to this equation is $p = \frac{1}{3}$.

Placing this information in *Exhibit 1* we may fold back the tree to find the expected value of the "Collect Information" branch:

$$\frac{2}{3}[0.8 * 130 + 0.2 * 280] + 1/3 * 200 = \underline{\$173\frac{1}{3}}$$

This means we would be prepared to pay up to $16.67 (the $190 expected cost of acting without further information less the $173.33 cost of acting with imperfect information) for this "imperfect" information.

Bayes' Rule

Information is not always provided in just the format you need for a decision tree. For example, you might know the probability that a successful entrepreneur has an MBA, when what you'd really like to know is the probability that a person with an MBA will be a successful entrepreneur.

The thinking process by which one converts probabilities of one type into the other is known as Bayes' Rule (Bayes invented the rule!).

Let's suppose that 60% of all successful entrepreneurs have MBAs (and 40% don't). Let's suppose further that 20% of *unsuccessful* entrepreneurs have MBAs and 80% don't. To find the answer we want, we still need to know what proportion of entrepreneurs are successful. Let's say 5%. Now we draw the following tree:

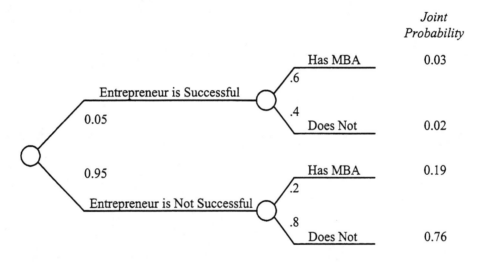

Joint Probability

Has MBA	0.03
Does Not	0.02
Has MBA	0.19
Does Not	0.76

Instead of payoffs we write down the joint probabilities, for example the probability that an entrepreneur is successful *and* has an MBA is 0.03.

The question we want to answer is "what proportion of MBAs who are entrepreneurs are successful?" From the tree we see that a proportion 0.22 of entrepreneurs have MBAs (= .19 + .03). Of this 0.22, 0.03 are successful, so $\frac{0.03}{0.22}$ is the answer we seek, or 13.6%. [These numbers also suggest that entrepreneurs without an MBA have only a $\frac{0.02}{0.78}$ = 2.6% chance of success.]

There is a substantial discrepancy between the number 60% (proportion of successful entrepreneurs who have MBAs) and 13.6% (proportion of entrepreneurs with MBAs that are successful) yet the two statements are often viewed as interchangeable by a lay audience!

Module 3: Business Modeling

Goal: To be able to apply the basic concepts and principles for modeling business
problems with information systems.

Chapter 7: Modeling and Analysis

In Chapter 4 we introduced the first major component of DSS: the database and its management. In this chapter, the second major component—the model base and its management—is presented. *Caution* is in order because modeling can be a very difficult topic; it is as much an art as a science.

The purpose of this chapter is not for the reader to master the topics of modeling and analysis. Rather, the material is geared toward gaining familiarity with the major ideas. We walk through some basic concepts and definitions of modeling before introducing the influence diagram, which can aid a decision maker in sketching out a model of a situation. We next introduce the idea of modeling directly in spreadsheets. Only then do we describe the structure of some successful, time-proven models and methodologies: decision analysis, decision trees, optimization, heuristic programming, and simulation. We next touch on some new developments in modeling tools and techniques and conclude with some important issues in model base management.

The outline of this chapter is

5.1 OPENING VIGNETTE: SIEMENS SOLAR INDUSTRIES
SAVES MILLIONS BY SIMULATION[1]

Siemens Solar Industries (SSI) is the world's largest-volume maker of solar electric products. SSI operates in an extremely competitive market. Before 1994, the company suffered continuous problems in photocell fabrication, including poor material flow, unbalanced resource use, bottlenecks in throughput, and schedule delays. To overcome the problems, the company decided to build a *cleanroom* contamination-control technology. Cleanrooms are standard practice in semiconductor businesses, but they had never been used in the solar industry. The new technology in which there is perfect control of temperature, pressure, humidity, and air cleanliness, was shown in research to improve quality considerably. In addition, productivity is improved because of fewer defects, better material flow, and reduced cycle times.

Because no one in the solar industry had ever used a cleanroom, the company decided to use a simulation, which provided a virtual laboratory where the engineers could experiment with various configurations of layouts and processes before the physical systems were constructed. Changes can be made quickly and inexpensively in a simulated world because physical changes need not be made. The simulation model enabled the prediction of the effects of changes and what-if analyses. A major benefit of the simulation-modeling process was the knowledge and insight the company gained in understanding the interactions of the systems being designed.

Computer simulation allowed SSI to compare numerous alternatives quickly. The company attempted to find the best design for the cleanroom and evaluate alternative scheduling, delivery rules, and material flow with respect to queue (waiting line) levels, throughput, cycle time, machine utilization, and work-in-progress levels.

The simulation was constructed with a tool called ProModel (from ProModel Corp., Orem, UT, http://www.promodel.com). The tool allowed the company to construct simulation models easily and quickly and to conduct what-if analyses. It also included extensive graphics and animation capabilities.

The simulation involved the entire business process, the machines, equipment, workstations, storage and handling devices, operators, and material and information flows necessary to support the process. Many scenarios were developed and experiments run. Using brainstorming, the builders came up with many innovative suggestions that were checked by the simulation. Incidentally, the company involved a group of students from California Polytechnic University in San Louis Obispo in the design and implementation of the system.

The solution identified the best configurations for the cleanroom, designed a schedule with minimum interruptions and bottlenecks, and improved material flow, while reducing work-in-progress inventory levels to a minimum.

All in all, the simulation enabled the company to improve the manufacturing process of different solar products significantly. The cleanroom facility has saved SSI over $75 million each year. The simulation showed how to integrate the cleanroom with manufacturing processes in the most efficient manner.

---

[1]Condensed from J. R. Vacca, "Faking It, Then Making it," *Byte,* Nov. 1995.

The opening vignette illustrates a complex decision for which prior experience was not available. By modeling a hypothetical cleanroom, the engineers were able to experiment with different configurations and alternatives quickly and inexpensively. The modeling approach used is called *simulation*. At SSI, the simulation was implemented using commercially available software; however, sometimes it is necessary to build a simulation application directly in a programming language.

The simulation approach saved the company a great deal of money. Instead of building an expensive facility and then experimenting with how best to use it, the engineers did it all on the computer. If you were to review the events leading up to the first flight to the moon, you would discover that it was simulated many times before its actual liftoff. It is very easy to make changes in a model of a physical system and its operation with computer modeling.

Modeling is a key element in most DSS and a *necessity* in a model-based DSS. Examples of how to model (and how not to model) decision problems may be found in Evans [1991]. Modeling can be performed in different ways. Simulation is a very popular modeling approach, but there are several other approaches. As an example, let us look at the case of the Frazee Paint Company (see Appendix A at the end of this book). Frazee's DSS includes three types of models:

- A statistical model (regression analysis), used for finding relationships among variables. This model is preprogrammed in a DSS development software tool.

- A financial model for developing income statements and projecting financial data for several years. This model is semistructured and is written with a special DSS financial planning language called the Interactive Financial Planning System (IFPS).

- A linear programming optimization model to determine the best media selection. It is solved using commercially available management science software. To use this model, the DSS must interface with commercially available software.

The Frazee case demonstrates that a DSS can be composed of several models, some standard and some custom made, used collectively to support the advertisement decisions in that company. It also demonstrates that some models are built directly in the DSS software development package, some need to be constructed, and others can be accessed by the DSS when needed. Modeling is not a simple task. The model builder must balance the simplification and representation requirements of the models.

Some of the major issues involved in modeling are problem identification and environmental analysis, variable identification, forecasting, the use of multiple models, model categories (or appropriate selection), model management, and knowledge-based modeling.

Identification of the Problem and Environmental Analysis

This issue was discussed in Chapter 2. One aspect that was skipped is **environmental scanning and analysis,** which is the monitoring, scanning, and interpretation of the collected information. It is often advisable to analyze the scope of the domain and the forces and dynamics of the *environment*. It is necessary to identify the organizational culture and the corporate decision-making process (who makes decisions, degree of centralization, and so on). For further discussion see Costa [1995] and Xu and Kaye [1995].

Identification of the Variables

The identification of the model's variables (decision and other) is of utmost importance, and so are their relationships. Influence diagrams, described in Section 5.5, can be helpful in this process.

Forecasting

Forecasting is essential for the construction and manipulation of the models because the results of a decision based on a model will usually occur in the future. See the book's Web site (http://www.prenhall.com/turban) for some details about forecasting methods.

Multiple Models

DSS may include several models (sometimes dozens, each of which represents different parts of the decision-making problem). For example, Myint and Tabucanon [1994] constructed a DSS that aids decision makers in selecting the most appropriate machines for flexible manufacturing systems. The following models were used: A **multicriteria model** prioritized alternatives so only high-priority machine configurations would be considered an optimization model, called goal programming, identified an optimal configuration, and a multicriteria model was used again to conduct a sensitivity analysis. Some of these models are standard and built into DSS development generators and tools. Others are standard but are not available as built-in functions. Instead, they are available as free-standing software that can interface with a DSS. The nonstandard models must be constructed from scratch.

Categories of Models

Table 5.1 classifies DSS models into seven groups. It also lists several representative techniques in each category and indicates where we discuss each one. Each technique may be applied to either a static or a dynamic model (Section 5.3), which

TABLE 5.1 Categories of Models.

Category	Process and Objective	Representative Techniques
Optimization of problems with few alternatives (Section 5.7)	Find the best solution from a small number of alternatives	Decision tables, decision trees
Optimization via algorithm (Section 5.8)	Find the best solution from a large or an infinite number of alternatives using a step-by-step improvement process	Linear and other mathematical programming models, network models
Optimization via analytical formula (Sections 5.8, 5.12)	Find the best solution, in one step, using a formula	Some inventory models
Simulation (Sections 5.10, 5.15)	Finding a good enough solution, or the best among the alternatives checked, using experimentation	Several types of simulation
Heuristics (Section 5.9)	Find a good enough solution using rules	Heuristic programming, expert systems
Other models	Finding what-if using a formula	Financial modeling, waiting lines
Predictive models (Web site)	Predict future for a given scenario	Forecasting models, Markov analysis

may be constructed under assumed environments of certainty, uncertainty, or risk (Section 5.4). To expedite model construction, one can use modeling languages (see Sections 5.6, 5.12–5.14).

Model Management

To maintain their integrity and thus their applicability, models, like data, must be managed. Such management is done with the aid of model base management software (Section 5.16).

Knowledge-based Modeling

DSS uses mostly quantitative models, whereas expert systems use qualitative, knowledge-based models in their application. Some knowledge is necessary to construct solvable (and thus usable) models. We defer the description of knowledge-based models until Chapter 6.

5.3 STATIC AND DYNAMIC MODELS

DSS models can be classified as static or dynamic.

Static Analysis

Static models take a single snapshot of a situation. During this snapshot everything occurs in a single interval. For example, a decision on whether to make or buy a product is static in nature. A quarterly or annual income statement is static, and so is the investment decision example in Section 5.7.

During a static analysis, stability of the relevant data is assumed.

Dynamic Analysis

Dynamic models are used to evaluate scenarios that change over time. A simple example would be a 5-year profit and loss projection in which the input data, such as costs, prices, and quantities, change from year to year.

Dynamic models are *time dependent*. For example, in determining how many checkout points should be open in a supermarket, it is necessary to consider the time of day because there are changes in the number of people that arrive at different hours.

Dynamic models are important because they show *trends* and patterns over time. They also show averages per period, moving averages, and comparative analysis (such as profit this quarter against profit in the same quarter of last year). Furthermore, once a static model is constructed to describe a given situation, say product distribution, it can be extended to represent the dynamic nature of the problem. For example, the transportation model (a type of network flow model) describes a static model of product distribution. The model can be extended to a dynamic network flow model to accommodate inventory and backordering (see Aronson [1989]).

5.4 TREATING CERTAINTY, UNCERTAINTY, AND RISK[2]

The concepts of **certainty, uncertainty,** and **risk** were introduced in Chapter 2. When we build models, any of these conditions may occur. Here are some important modeling issues for each condition

Certainty Models

Everyone likes certainty models because they are easy to work with and can yield optimal solutions. Many financial models are constructed under assumed certainty. Of special interest are problems that have an infinite (or a very large) number of feasible solutions. They are discussed in Sections 5.8 and 5.9.

Uncertainty

Managers attempt to avoid uncertainty as much as possible. Instead, they attempt to acquire more information so that the problem can be treated under certainty or under calculated risk. If you cannot acquire more information, you must treat the problem as an uncertain problem (see Bell and Schleifer [1995] and Matthews and Scott [1995]).

Risk

Most major business decisions are made under assumed risk. Several techniques can be used to deal with risk analysis. They are discussed in Sections 5.7 and 5.10 and in Fabrycky et al. [1996].

5.5 INFLUENCE DIAGRAMS

After a decision-making problem is analyzed, understood, and defined, it is time to construct a model. Just as a flowchart can be used as a graphic representation of computer program flow for design purposes, an influence diagram can be used to map a model's design. An **influence diagram** is a graphic representation of a model used to assist in model design, development, and understanding. An influence diagram provides visual communication to the model builder or development team. It also serves as a framework for expressing the exact nature of the relationships of the MSS model, thus assisting a modeler in focusing on the model's major aspects. The term *influence* refers to the dependency of a variable on the level of another variable. Influence diagrams appear in several formats. We use the following convention, suggested by Bodily [1985].

Rectangle = a decision variable

Circle = uncontrollable or intermediate variable

Oval = result (outcome) variable: intermediate or final

---

[2] Sections 5.4, 5.5, 5.7–5.10, and 5.15 are adapted from Turban and Meredith [1994].

The variables are connected with arrows, which indicate the direction of the influence (relationship). The shape of the arrow also indicates the type of relationship. The following are typical relationships:

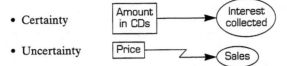

- Certainty

- Uncertainty

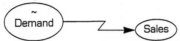

- Random (risk) variable: place a tilde (~) above the variable's name.

- Preference (usually between outcome variables): a double-line arrow $\Rightarrow$.
  Arrows can be one-way or two-way (bidirectional), depending on the direction of influence of a pair of variables.

Influence diagrams can be constructed at any degree of detail and sophistication. It enables the model builder to map all the variables and show *all* the relationships in the model, as well as the direction of the influence. An application with complex variability is proposed by Smith [1995].

Example. Consider the following profit model:

Profit = Income − Expenses
Income = Units sold × Unit price
Units sold = 0.5 × Amount used in advertisement
Expenses = Unit cost × Units sold + Fixed cost

An influence diagram of this simple model is shown in Figure 5.1.

FIGURE 5.1 An Influence Diagram for the Profit Model.

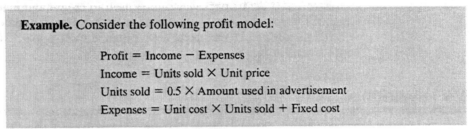

Software

There are several software products available for the creation and maintenance of influence diagrams. The solution process of these products transforms the original problem into graphic form. Representative products are

- *Analytica* (Lumina Decision Systems, Los Altos, CA, http://www.lumina.com). Analytica supports hierarchical diagrams, multidimensional arrays, integrated documentation, and parameter analysis.
- *DPL* (from Applied Decision Analysis, Menlo Park, CA, dplept@adaino.com). This product provides a synthesis of influence diagrams and decision trees.
- *DS Lab* (from DS Group Inc., Greenwich, CT). See Section 5.12.
- *INDIA* (from Decision Focus Inc., Palo Alto, CA, http://www.dfi.com). The solution process of this product transforms the original problem into a new, reduced form in an attempt to determine optimal policy.
- *PrecisionTree* (from Palisade Corp., Newfield, NY, http://www.palisade.com). PrecisionTree creates influence diagrams and decision trees directly in the Excel spreadsheet.

For a comparative analysis of these and other packages, see Buede [1996]. Also, standard computer graphics software packages and computer-aided software engineering (CASE) packages can be used to create and maintain influence diagrams. Influence diagrams can be used to focus on the important variables and their interactions. We next turn to an implementation vehicle for models: the electronic spreadsheet.

5.6 MSS MODELING IN SPREADSHEETS

Models can be developed and implemented in a variety of programming languages and systems. They range from third-, fourth- and fifth-generation programming languages to CASE systems and others that automatically generate much of the code. In this book, we focus primarily on electronic spreadsheets (with their supplements) and financial and planning languages (fourth-generation programming languages and systems) (discussed in Section 5.13).

As personal computers diffused throughout modern organizations (and were purchased by individuals), the strength and flexibility of electronic spreadsheets were quickly recognized as easy-to-use implementation software for the development of a wide range of applications in business, engineering, mathematics, and science. As PCs evolved and their capabilities expanded, so did those of spreadsheet packages. Furthermore, extensions known as **spreadsheet add-ins** were developed for structuring and solving specific model classes in the spreadsheet framework. These include Solver (Frontline Systems Inc., Incline Village, NV) and What'sBest! (a version of Lindo for spreadsheets, Lindo Systems Inc., Chicago, IL) for performing linear and nonlinear optimization, and @Risk (Winston [1996]) for performing simulation studies. Because of fierce competition in the market, the better add-ins were incorporated directly into the spreadsheets in later releases (for example, Solver in Excel is the well-known GRG-2 nonlinear optimization software).

Now, the **electronic spreadsheet** (or, more simply, *spreadsheet*) is the most popular *end-user modeling tool* (see Figure 5.2). What makes the spreadsheet a useful tool is the incorporation of a large number of powerful financial, statistical, mathematical, logical, date and time, and string functions. Combined with the easy

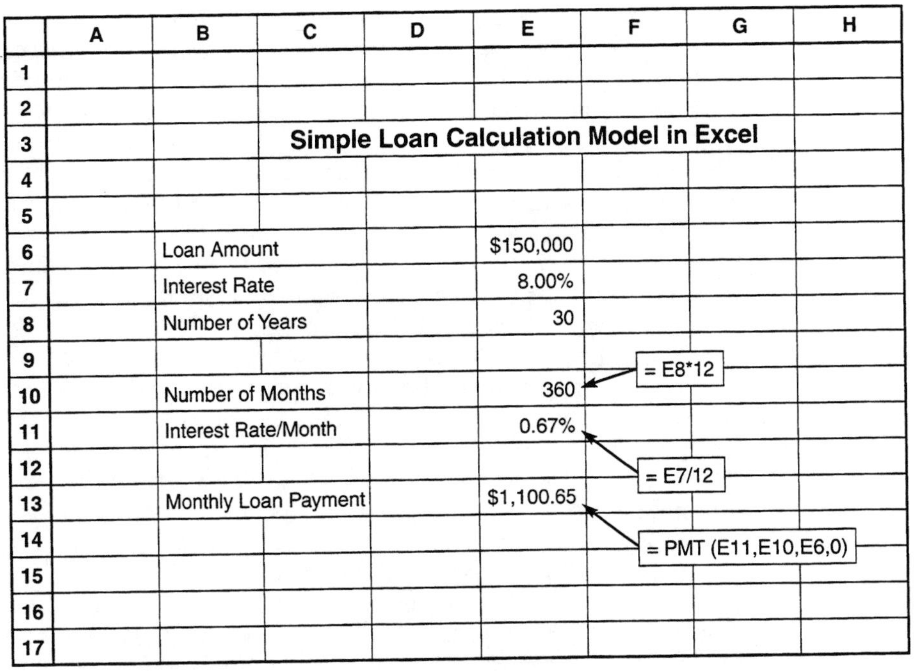

FIGURE 5.2 Excel Spreadsheet Static Model Example of a Simple Loan Calculation of Monthly Payments.

use of external add-in functions and solver tools, they can perform model solution tasks such as linear programming and regression analysis. The spreadsheet has evolved into an important tool for analysis, planning, and modeling. See Ragsdale [1995] and Winston and Albright [1996] for details.

Additional important spreadsheet features include those of programmability of command sequences into *macros,* what-if analysis, and goal seeking. It is a simple matter to change a cell's value and immediately obtain the result of the change. Goal seeking is accomplished by indicating a set or target cell, its desired value, and a changing or adjustable cell. Rudimentary database management is included in most spreadsheets. These include special functions and commands for data selection, querying, and sorting. The programming productivity of building DSS can be enhanced with the use of templates, macros, and other tools.

Interaction with other tools and database software may be needed in a specific MSS application. Most spreadsheet packages provide fairly seamless integration by reading and writing common file structures. Furthermore, many other packages (database, word-processing, for example) can read and write files in the most popular spreadsheet formats. Specific related worksheets may also be linked together (for example, if the results of one depend on those of another) either actively (live) or passively (the output of one becomes the input of another).

The two most popular PC spreadsheet packages are Microsoft Excel and Lotus 1-2-3. Either may be purchased as a standalone spreadsheet or as a component of an integrated *suite* (Microsoft Office contains Excel, Lotus SmartSuite contains Lotus 1-2-3). These suites generally contain, in addition to the spreadsheet, a word processor (Word for Office, Word Pro for Lotus 1-2-3), a database management system (Access, Approach), a graphic presentation package (PowerPoint,

Freelance Graphics), and possibly organization and communications software. Newer releases have Web browser and Web page generation capabilities. Although the operation of each application package within a suite is independent of the others, each one can easily access files created in the other ones.

In Figure 5.2 we show a simple loan calculation model (the boxes on the spreadsheet describe the contents of the cells containing formulas). A change in the interest rate (performed by typing in a new number in cell E7) is immediately reflected in the monthly payment (in cell E13). The results can be observed and analyzed immediately. If we required a specific monthly payment, goal seeking may be used to determine an appropriate interest rate or loan amount.

A spreadsheet can be used to build static or dynamic models. For example, the monthly loan calculation spreadsheet shown in Figure 5.2 is static. Although the problem affects the borrower over time, it indicates a single month's performance that is replicated. A dynamic model, on the other hand, represents behavior over time. The loan calculations in the spreadsheet shown in Figure 5.3 indicate the effect of prepayment on the principle over time. Risk analysis may be incorporated into spreadsheets by using its built-in random number generators to develop simulation models (see Section 5.10 and Appendix W5-A on the book's Web site: http://www.prenhall.com/turban).

Spreadsheets were developed for personal computers, but they are also available for larger computers with increased capabilities. The spreadsheet framework is the basis for more powerful modeling tools, as described in Section 5.14.

In Appendix W5-A, on the book's Web site, we describe an economic order quantity simulation model (under assumed risk) constructed in a spreadsheet (Excel). Also on the book's Web site, we show how a spreadsheet can be used for the simulation of cash flows. See Grauer and Barber [1996] for details about and tutorials for Excel and Microsoft Office.

5.7 DECISION ANALYSIS OF A FEW ALTERNATIVES (DECISION TABLES AND TREES)

Decision situations that involve a finite and usually not too large number of alternatives are modeled by an approach called **decision analysis,** in which the alternatives are listed with their forecasted contributions to the goal(s), and the probability of realizing such a contribution, in a table or a graph. They can be evaluated to select the best alternative.

There are two distinct cases: a single goal and multiple goals. Single-goal situations can be approached by using **decision tables** or **decision trees.** Multiple goals (criteria) can be approached by several other techniques (described later).

Decision Tables

Decision tables are a convenient way to organize information in a systematic manner. For example, an investment company is considering investing in one of three alternatives: bonds, stocks, or certificates of deposit (CDs).

The company is interested in one goal: maximizing the yield on the investment after 1 year. If it were interested in other goals such as safety or liquidity, then the problem would be classified as one of *multicriteria decision analysis.*

The yield depends on the status of the economy (often called the *state of nature*), which can be in solid growth, stagnation, or inflation. The following estimates of annual yield were solicited from experts:

- If there is solid growth in the economy, bonds will yield 12 percent, stocks 15 percent, and time deposits 6.5 percent.
- If stagnation prevails, bonds will yield 6 percent, stocks 3 percent, and time deposits 6.5 percent.
- If inflation prevails, bonds will yield 3 percent, stocks will bring a loss of 2 percent, and time deposits will yield 6.5 percent.

The problem is to select the one best investment alternative. Note: Investing 50 percent in bonds and 50 percent in stocks, or other combinations, must be treated as new alternatives.

FIGURE 5.3 Excel Spreadsheet Dynamic Model Example of a Simple Loan Calculation of Monthly Payments and the Effects of Prepayment.

	A	B	C	D	E	F	G	H
1								
2								
3		Dynamic Loan Calculation Model with Prepayment in Excel						
4								
5								
6		Loan Amount			$150,000			
7		Interest Rate			8.00%			
8		Number of Years			30			
9						= E8*12		
10		Number of Months			360			
11		Interest Rate/Month			0.67%			
12						= E7/12		
13		Monthly Loan Payment			$1,100.65			
14						= PMT (E11,E10,E6,0)		
15								
16								
17		Figure 5.3 Dynamic Loan Calculation Model with Prepayment in Excel						
18								
19		= C20			= B24+C24		A $100 Prepayment every Month Loan is Paid off in Month 270	
20	= E13		$100.00					
21		Normal	Prepay	Total	Principle			
22	Month	Payment	Amount	Payment	Owed			
23	0				$150,000	= E23*(1+E11)–D24		
24	1	$1,100.65	$100.00	$1,200.65	$149,799			
25	2	$1,100.65	$100.00	$1,200.65	$149,597			
26	3	$1,100.65	$100.00	$1,200.65	$149,394			
27	4	$1,100.65	$100.00	$1,200.65	$149,189	Copy the Cells in Row 24 into Rows 24 through Row 383 to get 360 Months of Results	
28	5	$1,100.65	$100.00	$1,200.65	$148,983			
29	6	$1,100.65	$100.00	$1,200.65	$148,776			
30	7	$1,100.65	$100.00	$1,200.65	$148,567			
31	8	$1,100.65	$100.00	$1,200.65	$148,357	Ext. through Row 383		

The investment decision-making problem may be viewed as a two-person game. The investor makes a choice (a move) and then nature happens (makes a move). The payoff is shown in a table representation (see Table 5.2) that represents a mathematical model. According to our definition in Chapter 2, the table includes *decision variables* (the alternatives), *uncontrollable variables* (the states of the economy), and *result variables* (the projected yield). Note that all of the models in this section are structured in a spreadsheet framework.

There are two specific cases to consider: uncertainty and risk. For uncertainty, we do not know the probabilities of each state of nature. For risk, we assume we know the probabilities with which each state of nature will occur.

Treating Uncertainty

One can use one of several approaches to handle uncertainty. For example, the *optimistic approach* involves considering the best possible outcome of each alternative and selecting the best of the bests (stocks). The *pessimistic approach* involves considering the worst possible outcome for each alternative and selecting the best one (CDs). For details on these and other approaches, see Turban and Meredith [1994]. All approaches for handling uncertainty have serious deficiencies. Therefore, any modeler should attempt to collect sufficient information so that the problem can be treated under assumed certainty or risk.

Treating Risk

Let us assume that the chance of solid growth is estimated to be 50 percent, that of stagnation 30 percent, and that of inflation 20 percent. Then the decision table is rewritten with the known probabilities (see Table 5.3). The most common method for solving this **risk analysis** problem is to select the alternative with the largest *expected value*. An expected value is computed by multiplying the results (outcomes) by their respective probabilities and adding them. For example, for bonds we get $12(0.5) + 6(0.3) + 3(0.2) = 8.4$ (invest in bonds, for an average return of 8.4 percent).

However, this approach can be a dangerous strategy. Even if there is an infinitesimal chance of a catastrophic loss, the expected value may seem reasonable, but the investor may not be able to handle the loss. One must remember that the investor makes the decision only *once*. For example, suppose a financial advisor presents you with an "almost sure" investment of $1,000 that will double your money in one day. Then he says, "Well, there is a 0.9999 probability that you will double your money, but unfortunately there is a 0.0001 probability that you would be liable for a $500,000 out-of-pocket loss." The expected value of this "investment" is

$$0.9999(\$2,000 - \$1,000) + 0.0001(-\$500,000 - \$1,000)$$
$$= \$999.90 - \$50.10 = \$949.80$$

However the effect of such a loss could be catastrophic for the investor.

TABLE 5.2 Investment Problem Decision Table Model.

Alternative	States of Nature (Uncontrollable Variables)		
	Solid Growth	Stagnation	Inflation
Bonds	12.0%	6.0%	3.0%
Stocks	15.0	3.0	−2.0
CDs	6.5	6.5	6.5

	Solid Growth 0.50	Stagnation 0.30	Inflation 0.20	Expected Value
Alternative				
Bonds	12.0%	6.0%	3.0%	8.4% (maximum)
Stocks	15.0	3.0	−2.0	8.0
CDs	6.5	6.5	6.5	6.5

TABLE 5.3 Decision Under Risk and Its Solution.

Decision Trees

An alternative presentation of the decision table is a decision tree. A decision tree has two advantages: First, it shows the relationships of the problem graphically, and second, it can deal with complex situations in a compact form (such as multiperiod investment problems). However, it can be cumbersome if many alternatives or states of nature are involved. TreeAge Software Inc. (Williamstown, MA, http://www.treeage.com) produces powerful, intuitive, and sophisticated decision tree analysis software called DATA.

Other Methods of Treating Risk

Several other methods of treating risk are discussed later in this book. Specifically, they are simulation, certainty factors, and fuzzy logic.

Multiple Goals

A simplified case of **multiple goals** in investment is shown in Table 5.4. Three goals (or criteria) are considered: yield, safety, and liquidity.

Notice that this situation is under assumed certainty; that is, only one possible consequence is projected for each alternative (in the more complicated cases, a risk or uncertainty can be considered). Notice also that some of the results are not numerical but qualitative (such as Low and High).

An example of a multicriteria DSS for strategic planning is given by Tavana and Banerjee [1995]. The authors develop a method to capture the decision maker's beliefs through a series of sequential, rational, and analytical processes. The Analytic Hierarchy Process (AHP) was used (see Saaty [1995, 1996]). Many software packages are available for dealing with decision analysis and multicriteria decision making. These include DecisionPro (Vanguard Software Corp.), Expert Choice (Expert Choice Inc.), Logical Decisions (Logical Decisions Group), and Visual IFPS/Plus (Comshare Inc.). See DSS in Action 5.1, the book's Web site (http://www.prenhall.com/turban), and Greenfield [1996].

TABLE 5.4 Multiple Goals.

Alternatives	Yield	Safety	Liquidity
Bonds	8.4%	High	High
Stocks	8.0	Low	High
CDs	6.5	Very high	High

SOLVING MULTICRITERIA PROBLEMS

The issue of multicriteria (goal) decision making was presented in Chapter 2. One of the most effective approaches to the problem is the use of weights based on the decision-making priorities. However, soliciting weights (or priorities) from managers is a complex task, as is the calculation of the weighted averages needed for choosing the best alternative. The process is complicated further by the presence of qualitative variables. One method of multicriteria decision making is called the Analytical Hierarchy Process developed by Saaty [1996] (also see http://www.expertchoice.com and the book's Web site at http://www.prenhall.com/turban). Here are representative examples.

The replacement of several milling machines at Deutsche Aerospace Airbus, Germany, required the development of a strategic plan to address both automation in manufacturing systems and machinery replacement. It was necessary to develop and explore different planning alternatives ranging from extending the life of existing machinery to total replacement with a new manufacturing system and to evaluate these alternatives through economical and technological criteria. Quantitative (finance and technological) and qualitative

(intangible) benefits of investments in new manufacturing systems were to be considered. The company used commercial packages (AutoMan and Expert Choice) to conduct the planning.[†]

Expert Choice is used by a leading bank to evaluate lending risks and opportunities in foreign countries. This bank had previously used research reports to weigh economic, financial, and political considerations. Although the bank was satisfied with the quality of the reports, both the bank and the consultant preparing the reports felt that the information was not being put to best use. The complex data and decision-making process often resulted in too much or too little weight being placed on various aspects of the decision process. The bank's credit committee also had difficulty integrating the expert information into the deliberation process. Consequently, the bank's consultant prepared an Expert Choice model, enabling the credit committee to use the most recent information in making comparisons among factors. Without any prior exposure to personal computers or Expert Choice, the bankers began using the software and evaluating the subject country within a matter of minutes.[‡]

[†](*Source:* Based on Oeltjenbruns et al., "Strategic Planning in Manufacturing Systems," *International Journal of Production Economics,* March 1995.)

[‡](*Source:* Condensed from material provided by Expert Choice Inc., Pittsburgh, PA.)

5.8 OPTIMIZATION VIA MATHEMATICAL PROGRAMMING

The concept of optimization was introduced in Chapter 2, where an example of linear programming was developed. **Linear programming (LP)** is the best-known technique in a family of optimization tools called **mathematical programming.** It is used extensively in DSS (see DSS in Action 5.2). Linear programming models have many important applications in practice. An assignment problem (a type of linear programming problem) was used to determine the best way to dispose of snow in the City of Montreal (see DSS in Action 5.3).

Mathematical Programming

Mathematical programming is a family of tools designed to help solve managerial problems in which the decision maker must allocate scarce resources among various activities to optimize a measurable goal. For example, the distribution of machine

DSS IN ACTION 5.2

OPTIMIZATION AT TEXACO FOR PLANNING AND SCHEDULING

Gasoline blending is a critical refinery operation. In the 1980s Texaco developed OMEGA, an optimization-based decision support system, to assist in planning and scheduling its blending operations. OMEGA ran primarily on minicomputers and on a mainframe computer system. In 1990 Texaco began replacing OMEGA with StarBlend, a Microsoft Windows application, running on personal computers and client/server networks. Star-Blend uses a multiperiod extension of OMEGA's blending model written in the GAMS modeling language and extracts model data from relational databases. Its improved features make it easier to use and it enables blenders and blend planners to more readily incorporate future requirements into current blending decisions. By 1996 Star-Blend was operational in all Texaco refineries. As federal and state regulations on auto emissions become more complex, StarBlend's importance will continue to increase.

(*Source:* Condensed from B. Rigby et al., "The Evaluation of Texaco's Blending System," *Interfaces,* Sept./Oct. 1995.)

DSS IN ACTION 5.3

MATHEMATICAL PROGRAMMING MODEL HELPS DISPOSE OF MONTREAL'S HEAVY SNOW

Snow removal and disposal are expensive winter activities that affect the quality of life and the environment in cities throughout the world. To facilitate traffic flow in urban regions that receive heavy snowfall, snow is first plowed from streets and sidewalks and then hauled to disposal sites. A city is typically divided into many sectors that are cleared of snow concurrently. An assignment problem that assigns snow removal sectors to snow disposal sites can be formulated as a multi-resource, generalized assignment problem, a kind of mathematical programming problem, or more specifically, a large-scale combinatorial (integer programming) problem.

There are 60 sectors and 20 disposal sites in the City of Montreal, and an average of 300,000 truckloads (7 million cubic meters) of snow hauled each year by 660 trucks. Transporting snow is expensive: the average cost is $0.24 (Canadian) per cubic meter of snow. This is an important strategic problem.

Using the straight-line distance from the center of each sector to each disposal site, the goal is to find an assignment that minimizes the sum of the distances from the center of the sectors to the disposal sites, given the hourly capacity of each disposal site and the capacity of the trucks.

Solution of the integer model to optimality took 4.5 hours with CPLEX, a fast commercial code, on a Sun Sparcstation 10. A fast heuristic method was developed to convert a more easily found linear programming solution into an integer solution. The average execution time of the heuristic was about 6 seconds, and the system found objective values that were within a few percent of the optimum, along with sensitivity results. Satisfied with these results, the decision makers performed many what-if analyses to determine whether a heavy winter would necessitate the opening of new snow disposal sites. The consequences of closing a site were also evaluated; the objective degraded a mere 0.15% in cost, with each truck traveling, on average, only an additional 14 meters.

Various scenarios were tested to minimize snow removal and disposal costs and to improve the quality of life for the citizens of Montreal.

(*Source:* Condensed from J. F. Campbell and A. Langevin, "The Snow Disposal Assignment Problem," *Journal of the Operational Research Society,* Vol. 46, 1995, 919–929.)

time (the resource) among various products (the activities) is a typical allocation problem. LP allocation problems usually display the following characteristics:

Characteristics

- A limited quantity of economic resources is available for allocation.
- The resources are used in the production of products or services.
- There are two or more ways in which the resources can be used. Each is called a solution or a program.
- Each activity (product or service) in which the resources are used yields a return in terms of the stated goal.
- The allocation is usually restricted by several limitations and requirements called constraints.

The LP allocation model is based on the following rational economic assumptions:

Assumptions

- Returns from different allocations can be compared; that is, they can be measured by a common unit (such as dollars or utility).
- The return from any allocation is independent of other allocations.
- The total return is the sum of the returns yielded by the different activities.
- All data are known with certainty.
- The resources are to be used in the most economical manner.

Allocation problems typically have a large number of possible alternative solutions. Depending on the underlying assumptions, the number of solutions can be either infinite or finite. Usually, different solutions yield different rewards. Of the available solutions, one (sometimes more than one) is the *best,* in the sense that the degree of goal attainment associated with it is the highest (that is, total reward is maximized). This is called an optimal solution, which can be found by using a special algorithm.

Linear Programming

In Chapter 2, we presented a simple product-mix problem and formulated it as an LP problem. In the book's Web site, we provide more details on linear programming, a description of another classic LP problem called the blending problem, and an Excel spreadsheet formulation and solution.

Every LP problem is composed of *decision variables* (whose values are unknown and are searched for), an *objective function* (a linear mathematical function that relates the decision variables to the goal and measures goal attainment and is to be optimized), *objective function coefficients* (unit profit or cost coefficients indicating the contribution to the objective of one unit of a decision variable), *constraints* (expressed in the form of linear inequalities or equalities that limit resources, and/or requirements; these relate the variables through linear relationships), *capacities* (which describe the upper and sometimes lower limits on the constraints and variables), and *input–output (technology) coefficients* (which indicate resource utilization for a decision variable).

The uses of mathematical programming, especially of linear programming, are fairly common in that there are standard computer programs available. Thus, optimization functions are available in many DSS tools such as Excel or IFPS/Plus. Also, it is easy to interface other optimization software with Excel, database management systems, and similar tools. Optimization models are often included in decision support implementations, as shown in DSS in Action 5.2 and 5.3.

5.9 HEURISTIC PROGRAMMING

The determination of **optimal solutions** to some complex decision problems could involve a prohibitive amount of time and cost, or may even be impossible. Alternatively, the simulation approach (Section 5.10) may be lengthy, complex, and even inaccurate. In such situations, it is sometimes possible to arrive at *satisfactory* solutions more quickly and less expensively by using **heuristics.**

The heuristic procedure can also be described as finding rules that help to solve complex problems (or intermediate subproblems to discover how to set up these subproblems for final solution by finding the most promising paths in the search for solutions), finding ways to retrieve and interpret information on each experience, and then finding the methods that lead to a computational algorithm or general solution.

Although heuristics are used primarily for solving ill-structured problems, they can also be used to provide satisfactory solutions to certain complex, well-structured problems (such as large-scale combinatorial problems that have many potential solutions to explore; see Sun et al. [1997]) much more quickly and cheaply than optimization algorithms. The main difficulty in using heuristics is that they are not as general as algorithms. Therefore, they can normally be used only for the specific situation for which they were intended. Another problem with heuristics is that they may obtain a poor solution.

Heuristic programming is the approach of using heuristics to arrive at feasible and "good enough" solutions to some complex problems. "Good enough" is usually in the range of 90–99.9 percent of the objective value of an optimal solution.

Heuristics can be quantitative, so they play a major role in the DSS model base (see DSS in Action 5.4). They can also be qualitative, and then they play a major role in providing knowledge to expert systems.

Methodology

Heuristic thinking does not necessarily proceed in a direct manner. It involves searching, learning, evaluating, judging, and then again searching, relearning, and reappraisal as exploring and probing take place. The knowledge gained from success or failure at some point is fed back and modifies the search process. More often than not, it is necessary to redefine either the objectives or the problem, or to solve related or simplified problems before the primary one can be solved.

Tabu search heuristics (Glover and Laguna [1993] and Sun et al. [1997]) are based on intelligent search strategies to reduce the search for high-quality solutions in computer problem solving. Essentially, the method "remembers" what high-quality and low-quality solutions it has found, and tries to move toward other high-quality solutions and away from the low-quality ones. The tabu search methodology has proved successful in efficiently solving many large-scale combinatorial problems (such as the fixed-charge transportation problem; see Sun et al. [1997]). Another class of heuristic methods is that of **genetic algorithms,** which in the simplest case start with a set of randomly generated solutions and recombine pairs of them at random to produce offspring (the recombination into a new generation is modeled after the process of evolution). Only the best offspring and parents

HEURISTICS ROUTE MILK TANKERS IN INDIA

Lipton India Ltd. is an Indian subsidiary of Unilever and a maker and distributor of Lipton Tiger Tea and dozens of other products, including dairy products. About 70 milk collection centers are spread within a radius of 150 kilometers from Etahtown (300 km from New Delhi). Farmers deliver milk every morning to the collection centers, but not all of them are open every day. The collected milk is then delivered to the dairy by tankers. Pickups must be done early in the day because of refrigeration difficulties at the collection centers. The amount of milk at each center varies greatly, so scheduling of the pickups and routing of the tankers (which come in five sizes) is difficult. The tankers are leased from a transportation vendor.

The problem is to find the best routing plan for the tankers. Lipton wanted to minimize its collection cost and to collect the milk early, possibly with one visit per center per day. To ensure quality, tankers should not travel more than 5 hours per trip and must also meet other constraints (summer temperatures go up to 120° F in that region). Attempts to use optimization failed, so the company developed a set of heuristics based on rules used in vehicle routing problems. For example, a rule might be to go from each center to the nearest one until the tanker is full, or a constraint is violated. Another rule is that the first pickup must be the farthest from the dairy. The schedule is generated daily on a PC. The company knows which centers are open every day, and approximately how much milk will be picked up at each station. Because the tankers differ in capacity and cost/ton/mile, it is necessary to best match routes and tankers, so the computer model includes complex cost calculations and what-if capability.

The DSS has five menus that deal with the supply of milk, the availability of vehicles, the computed routes, and the costs. In addition to saving $35,000 per year, the company improved the quality of its products through faster collection. Additional Lipton DSS applications include determining how many collection centers to open or close and how many vehicles of each size to include in the fleet.

(*Source:* Condensed from J. K. Shankaran and R. R. Ubgade, "Routing Tankers for Daily Milk Pickup," *Interfaces,* Sept./ Oct. 1994.)

are kept to produce the next generation. Random mutations may also be introduced. These methods are described in depth in Chapter 18.

When to Use Heuristics

The following are some scenarios where the use of heuristics is appropriate:

- The input data are inexact or limited.
- Reality is so complex that optimization models cannot be used.
- A reliable, exact algorithm is not available.
- The computation time of simulation is excessive.
- It is possible to improve the efficiency of the optimization process (for example, by producing good starting solutions using heuristics). Then we combine heuristics and optimization.
- Complex problems are not economical for optimization or simulation, or take an inappropriate amount of time.
- Symbolic rather than numerical processing is involved (as in expert systems).
- Quick decisions are to be made and computerization is not feasible (some heuristics do not require computers).

Advantages and Limitations of Heuristics

The major advantages of heuristics are as follows:

- They are simple to understand and therefore are easier to implement and explain.
- They help in training people to be creative and come up with heuristics for other problems.
- They save formulation time.
- They save computer programming and storage requirements.
- They save computer running time and thus real time in decision making.
- They often produce multiple acceptable solutions.
- Usually it is possible to develop a theoretical or empirical measure of the solution quality (for example, how close the solution's objective value is to an optimal one).
- They can incorporate intelligence to guide the search. Such expertise may be problem specific or based on expert's opinions embedded in an expert system or search mechanism.
- It is possible to apply efficient heuristics to models that could be solved with mathematical programming. Sometimes heuristics are the preferred method, and other times the heuristic's solutions are used as initial solutions for the mathematical programming search methods.

The primary limitations of heuristics are as follows:

- An optimal solution cannot be guaranteed. Sometimes the bound on the objective value is very bad.
- There may be too many exceptions to the rules.
- Sequential decision choices can fail to anticipate future consequences of each choice.
- Interdependencies of one part of a system can sometimes have a profound influence on the whole system.

One major decision-making area that has benefited from the development and use of efficient heuristics is vehicle routing. See Basnet et al. [1996] and DSS in Action 5.4. Heuristic methods have been described in Reeves [1993]. For a categorized survey with several hundred references, see Zanakis et al. [1989]. For information about recent developments in heuristic methods (tabu search, genetic algorithms, and simulated annealing), see Rayward-Smith [1995].

5.10 SIMULATION

Simulation has many meanings. In general, to *simulate* means to assume the appearance of the characteristics of reality. In MSS, it generally refers to a *technique for conducting experiments (such as what-if analyses) with a digital computer on a model of a management system.*

Because DSS deals with semistructured or unstructured situations, it involves complex reality, which may not be easily represented by optimization or other models, but can often be handled by simulation. Therefore, simulation is one of the most commonly used tools of DSS. See Fishwick [1995] and Winston [1996].

Major Characteristics

To begin, simulation is not strictly a type of model; models in general *represent* reality, whereas simulation usually *imitates* it. In practical terms, this means that there are fewer simplifications of reality in simulation models than in other models.

Second, simulation is a technique for *conducting experiments*. Therefore, simulation involves the testing of specific values of the decision or uncontrollable variables in the model and observing the impact on the output variables.

Simulation is a *descriptive* rather than a normative tool; that is, there is no automatic search for an optimal solution. Instead, a simulation describes or predicts the characteristics of a given system under different circumstances. Once the characteristics' values are computed, the best among several alternatives can be selected. The simulation process often consists of the repetition of an experiment many, many times to obtain an estimate of the overall effect of certain actions. It can be performed manually in some cases, but a computer is usually needed.

Finally, simulation is usually called for only when a problem is too complex to be treated by numerical optimization techniques (such as linear programming). **Complexity** here means that the problem either cannot be formulated for optimization (for example, because the assumptions do not hold) or the formulation is too complex or the problem is stochastic in nature (exhibits risk or uncertainty).

Advantages of Simulation

Simulation is used in MSS because

- Simulation theory is fairly straightforward.
- A great amount of *time compression* can be attained, giving the manager some feel as to the long-term (1 to 10 years) effects of various policies in a matter of minutes.
- Simulation is descriptive rather than normative. This allows the manager to ask what-if questions. Thus, managers who use a trial-and-error approach to problem solving can do it faster and cheaper, with less risk, using simulation and computers (as opposed to using trial and error with a real system—see the opening vignette).
- An accurate simulation model requires an intimate knowledge of the problem, thus forcing the MSS builder to constantly interface with the manager.
- The model is built from the manager's perspective and in his or her decision structure.
- The simulation model is built for one particular problem and typically will not solve any other problem. Thus, no generalized understanding is required of the manager; every component in the model corresponds to a part of the real-life model.
- Simulation can handle an extremely wide variety of problem types, such as inventory and staffing, as well as higher managerial level functions such as long-range planning. Thus, it is always available when the manager needs it.
- The manager can experiment with different variables to determine which are important, and with different alternatives to determine which is best.
- Simulation generally allows for inclusion of the real-life complexities of problems; simplifications are not necessary. For example, simulation may use real probability distributions rather than approximate, theoretical distributions.
- It is very easy to obtain a wide variety of performance measures directly from the simulation.
- Simulation is often the only modeling tool for DSS where problems can be nonstructured.
- There are simulation (Monte Carlo) add-in packages for spreadsheets (such as @Risk; see Winston [1996]).

Limitations of Simulation

The primary disadvantages of simulation are as follows:

- An optimal solution cannot be guaranteed.
- Constructing a simulation model can often be a slow and costly process.

- Solutions and inferences from a simulation study are usually not transferable to other problems. This is because the model incorporates unique factors of the problem.
- Simulation is sometimes so easy to sell to managers that analytical solutions that can yield optimal results are often overlooked.
- Simulation software is not so user-friendly, so special skills are often required.

The Methodology of Simulation

Simulation involves setting up a model of a real system and conducting repetitive experiments on it. The methodology consists of a number of steps (Figure 5.4). The following is a brief discussion of the process.

Problem Definition

The real-world problem is examined and classified. Here we specify why simulation is necessary. The system's boundaries and other such aspects of problem clarification are handled here.

Construction of the Simulation Model

This step involves the determination of the variables and their relationships and the gathering of necessary data. Often, a flowchart is used to describe the process. Then a computer program is written.

Testing and Validating the Model

The simulation model must properly represent the system under study. This is ensured by testing and validation.

Design of the Experiments

Once the model has been proven valid, an experiment is designed. Determining how long to run the simulation is included in this step. There are two important and conflicting objectives: accuracy and cost. It is also prudent to identify typical (mean and median cases for random variables), best-case (for example, low-cost, high-revenue), and worst-case (for example, high-cost, low-revenue) scenarios. These help establish the ranges (of the decision variables) in which to work and also assist in debugging the simulation model.

FIGURE 5.4 The Process of Simulation.

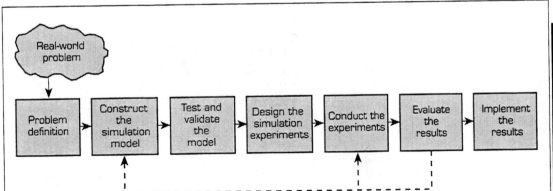

Conducting the Experiments

Conducting the experiment involves issues ranging from random number generation to presentation of the results.

Evaluating the Results

Here, we determine the meaning of the results. In addition to statistical tools, we may use sensitivity analyses.

Implementation

The implementation of simulation results involves the same issues as any other implementation. However, the chances of implementation are better because the manager is usually more involved in the simulation process than with other models.

Types of Simulation

There are several types of simulation. The major ones described in this book are as follows.

Probabilistic Simulation

In this type of simulation one or more of the independent variables (such as the demand in an inventory problem) are probabilistic. That is, they follow certain probability distributions. The two subcategories are discrete distributions and continuous distributions.

- *Discrete distributions* involve a situation with a limited number of events (or variables) that can take on only a finite number of values.
- *Continuous distributions* are situations with unlimited numbers of possible events that follow density functions such as the normal distribution.

The two types of distributions are shown in Table 5.5.

Probabilistic simulation is conducted with the aid of a technique called Monte Carlo.

Time-dependent Versus Time-independent Simulation

Time-independent refers to a situation in which it is not important to know exactly when the event occurred. For example, we may know that the demand for a certain product is three units per day, but we do not care *when* during the day the item was demanded. Or, in some situations, time may not be a factor in the simulation at all.

TABLE 5.5 Discrete Versus Continuous Probability Distributions.		
Daily Demand	*Discrete*	*Continuous*
	Probability	
5	0.10	Daily demand is
6	0.15	normally distributed
7	0.30	with a mean of 7
8	0.25	and a standard
9	0.20	deviation of 1.2.

On the other hand, in waiting line problems, it is important to know the precise time of arrival (to know whether the customer will have to wait). In this case, we are dealing with a *time-dependent* situation.

Simulation Software

Hundreds of packages of simulation building tools for a variety of decision-making situations are available (see Section 5.15). These include spreadsheet add-ins.

Visual Simulation

The graphic display of computerized results, which may include animation, is one of the more successful new developments in computer–human interaction and problem solving. It is described in Section 5.14.

Object-oriented Simulation

Some recent advances in the area of developing simulation models using the object-oriented approach. (See Appendix W4-A on the book's Web site, Briccarello, Bruno, and Ronco [1995], and Ninios, Vlahos, and Bunn [1995]).

We show an example of a spreadsheet-based economic order quantity simulation model (under assumed risk) in Appendix W5-A on the book's Web site. We also show on the book's Web site both spreadsheet and Visual IFPS/Plus simulation models for evaluating a simple cash-flow problem under assumed risk. DSS in Action 5.5 describes a front-end modeling tool to simplify the development and reduce the development time of building simulation models.

5.11 MULTIDIMENSIONAL MODELING

The concept of multidimensionality was introduced in Chapter 4, from a data point of view. Here we discuss multidimensionality from a spreadsheet and analysis perspective.

The original spreadsheets were two-dimensional. Later, with the introduction of Windows, spreadsheet packages introduced what they called a 3-D approach. This allows the user to keep three different sets of data on the screen simultaneously, but not really work with three dimensions. Often, however, managers do need to work with three or more dimensions. For example, sales data may be needed by region, by product, by month, and by salesperson all on the same screen. And such data need to be manipulated (for example, by what-if analyses). The solution is provided by *multidimensional modeling tools*. Some of these tools can handle 16 or more dimensions. Many data warehouses allow multidimensional access of the data for analysis with multidimensional modeling systems.

To describe **multidimensional modeling,** we will briefly look at four views of the same data (Figure 5.5). Each view is organized differently (for different users). A typical multidimensional tool such as CA-Masterpiece/2000 (from Computer Associates) enables a nonprogrammer to move from one presentation to another by giving one or two short commands. The tool can compare, rotate, and "slice and dice" corporate data across different management viewpoints. It has data manipulation and drag-and-drop capabilities through which users can quickly change the shape of the spreadsheets. For example, one can shift rows and columns. Although it is possible to do this with a regular spreadsheet, it can be done in CA-Masterpiece much faster and without the errors that are common when a similar task is done

DSS IN ACTION 5.5

SIMULATION IS EASIER BECAUSE OF A FRONT-END SYSTEM MODEL GENERATOR

The apparel industry in the United States is undergoing significant changes, particularly in the methods used to manufacture garments. This change is caused by market pressures for rapid style changes and quick response to customer orders. Many firms are beginning to experiment with new system designs such as modular manufacturing to improve the process, minimize system variability, improve quality, and reduce cost.

A front-end system was developed to provide nonexperts in simulation a tool for quickly and easily conducting a more complete analysis of system performance in the apparel industry than has been possible in the past. In a similar way, financial planning languages have revolutionized computer programming so that managers can implement their own models. This front-end system is provided through a user-friendly interface, and generates WITNESS (a simulation package) input. The front-end system can capture WITNESS output and display it in an easy to read format. What-if analyses can be done quickly, without the expertise of a master model builder. The entire

system runs on a personal computer. The front-end system has been successfully used by three apparel firms to design and evaluate modular manufacturing systems. The three real-world models indicate that the front-end system is very effective. In case 1, a manufacturing simulation model that originally took some 6 weeks to develop was implemented in less than 10 minutes. Model modifications were done in less than 5 minutes. The second case, that of the Lee plant in Bayou LaBatre, AL, managers developed an operational model of their jean manufacturing facility involving 20 stations and 14 operators in less than 4 hours. Case 3 was a plant of the children's clothing manufacturer Andover Togs in Pisgah, AL. An 8-station and 8-operator model was developed in less than 1 hour.

The rapid prototyping ability of the front-end system allowed manufacturing engineers with minimal or no simulation experience to build, run, and test complicated WITNESS simulation models in very short time frames. Error-free code is typically developed.

(*Source:* P. A. Farrington, B. J. Schroer, and J. Wang, "Front-End System for Modeling Modern Apparel Manufacturing Systems," *Computers in Industrial Engineering,* Vol. 28, No. 2, 1995, 267–277.)

with a standard spreadsheet. However, recent releases of Excel and similar products allow simple spinning of columns and rows. They also have limited "slice and dice" capabilities.

Example: Four Dimensions of One Report (Figure 5.5)

In Figure 5.5a, original data are entered for the first year and a formula automatically computes the data for the next year (20 percent increase). The table shows hours spent in traveling by country and by mode of transportation.

In Figure 5.5b, by clicking on "Travel" and "Hours," the data are rearranged so comparison by hours by mode of transportation are made.

In Figure 5.5c, another rearrangement is made by a double click.

In Figure 5.5d, a subsummary creates a new category (Europe) with a total computed.

Charts for any of the above can be created by selecting the appropriate presentation from a menu, usually by clicking on the desired graphics template and the presentation to be displayed. In this view, the formulas used by the multidimensional tools are shown. Notice that the formulas are not tied to a specific cell

		This Year	Next Year
Canada	Planes	740	888
	Trains	140	168
	Automobiles	640	768
Japan	Planes	**430**	516
	Trains	**290**	348
	Automobiles	**150**	180
France	Planes	**320**	384
	Trains	**460**	552
	Automobiles	**210**	252
Germany	Planes	**425**	510
	Trains	**430**	516
	Automobiles	**325**	390

The formula calculates as soon as you enter the new data

(a)

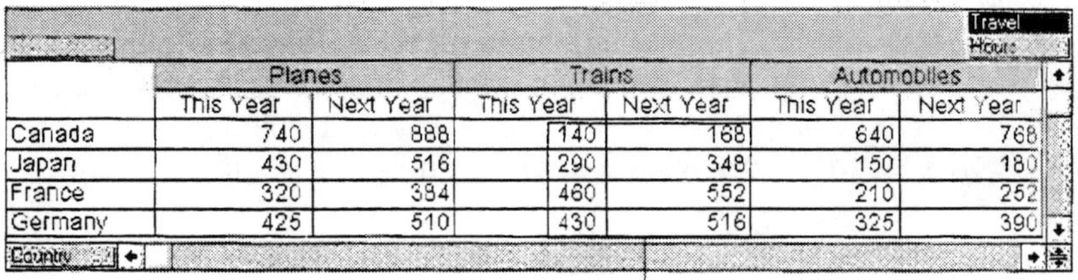

Now the hours spent traveling on trains each year are easy to compare

(b)

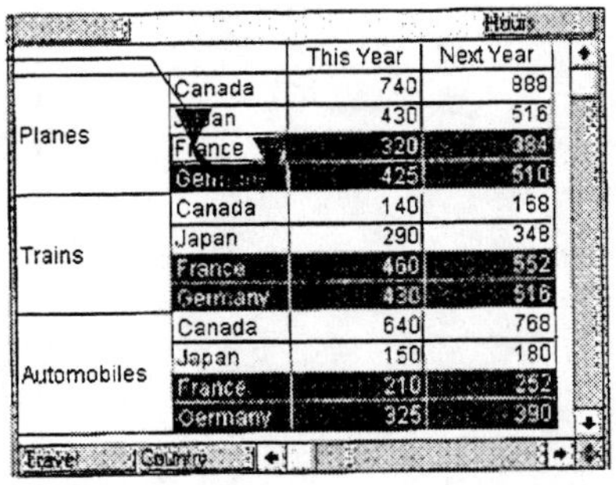

(c)

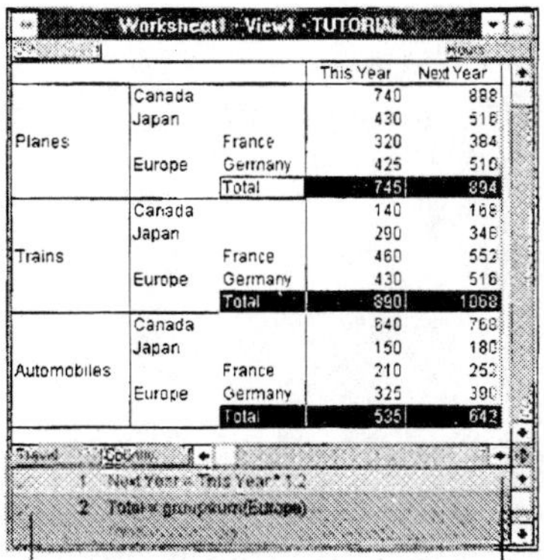

- The software adds a *Total* item
- The software adds formula 2 and calculates *Total*
- Auto-making shades the formulas using two shades of gray

Shows that formula 2, as the formula with the higher number in the list, calculates all Total cells

Shows that formula 1 potentially calculates cells (in this case, the cells *Total:Next Year*)

(d)

FIGURE 5.5 Four Views That Demonstrate Multidimensionality.

address, so they can be applied to many cells simultaneously. Multidimensional modeling and viewing tools are available from database, EIS, data warehouse, and OLAP vendors (for example, InfoSuite from Platinum Technology, Oakbrook Terrace, IL; and BrioQuery's Enterprise Multidimensional Analysis Tool and Desktop OLAP).

5.12 VISUAL SPREADSHEETS

Users encounter two major difficulties with spreadsheets: Formulas are often hard to decipher, and time sequences are too difficult to handle. **Visual spreadsheets** attempt to overcome these shortcomings. These tools allow the user to make calculations, as with an ordinary spreadsheet, but without cells, columns, and rows. Instead, the user can visualize the models and formulas using influence diagrams. A program that implements visual spreadsheets is called DS Lab (from DS Group Inc., Greenwich, CT).

Instead of cells, DS Lab uses symbolic elements, as in an influence diagram. An example is shown in Figure 5.6. For example, variables are shown as circles, and constants as squares.

The software enables the user to conduct English-like modeling. In addition, over 200 built-in mathematical, financial, time, goal-seeking, and logical functions are available with a click of the mouse. When selected, a function is inserted into a script, including its argument syntax, in plain English. Also, there are predefined

FIGURE 5.6 A Loan Analysis Model Constructed with DS Lab.

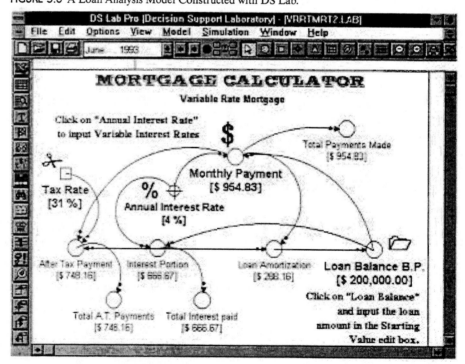

(*Source:* Courtesy of DS Group Inc.)

connecting elements. They are used with the functions to build a model. Thus, the construction requires mainly using the mouse for pointing and clicking.

Time is one parameter defined in the model's steps; the program has a built-in calendar to define hours, days, weeks, months, or years. The model can also define other dimensions, such as location or product type. The program then automatically generates the values for each step. Results can be printed in graphic form. For example, Figure 5.6 shows a home mortgage calculator with the first payment to be made in June 1996, for a $200,000 loan, at an interest rate of 4 percent for 30 years. It shows data that can be presented in a table: monthly payment, loan amortization, loan balance, and so on. Because the interest rate varies, the user can perform what-if calculations with the interest rate and get a different payment schedule printed for all payments. The table also shows the tax benefit (reducing the actual payment to $748.16 from $954.83). Outputs can be exported to any Windows program for further manipulation, printing, or graphing. Integration with Excel is automated, allowing exporting with a single mouse click. What-if analysis and goal seeking are executed easily, and so are simple simulations.

5.13 FINANCIAL AND PLANNING MODELING

Many DSS applications deal with financial analysis and planning. Therefore, it makes sense to develop DSS building tools to rapidly build such applications. Spreadsheet software can do the job, but special tools can do it more efficiently or effectively. Such tools are being developed around **financial planning modeling software.**

A major property of financial modeling is that their models are algebraically oriented. That is, the formulas are written in the manner in which one would write equations. Spreadsheets, on the other hand, write their models with a computation or calculation orientation.

Definition and Background of Planning Modeling

The definition of a planning model varies somewhat with the scope of its application (see DSS in Focus 5.6). For instance, financial planning models may have a very short planning horizon and entail no more than a collection of accounting formulas

DSS IN FOCUS 5.6

TYPICAL APPLICATIONS OF PLANNING MODELS

Financial forecasting	Workforce planning
Pro forma financial statements	Profit planning
Capital budgeting	Sales forecasting
Market decision making	Investment analysis
Merger and acquisition analysis	Construction scheduling
Lease versus purchase decisions	Tax planning
Production scheduling	Energy requirements
New venture evaluation	Labor contract negotiation fees
Foreign currency analysis	

for producing pro forma statements (that is, a static model). On the other hand, corporate planning models often include complex quantitative and logical relationships among a corporation's financial, marketing, and production activities. In this sense, the model has great utility because any of the coordinated subroutines composing the comprehensive model may be isolated for narrower applications. Furthermore, most financial models are dynamic (multiyear) models.

In addition to generic DSS-based planning models, there are several industry-specific ones, such as for hospitals, banks, and universities. For example, Educom's Financial Planning Model (EFPM) is used by several hundred universities as a DSS construction tool for financial, long-range planning, and other university administration decisions.

Financial and planning modeling systems are fourth-generation programming languages. The models are written in an English-like syntax (as a result, they are self-documenting) and the model steps are nonprocedural. Today, there are about 100 planning and modeling software development packages[3] on the market. They are available for all types of hardware. Popular examples include Visual IFPS/Plus (Comshare Inc., Ann Arbor, MI, http://www.comshare.com) (see Gray [1996] and Appendix W5-B on the book's Web site, where we introduce the basic concepts of IFPS), ENCORE Plus! (Ferox MicroSystems Inc., Alexandria, VA, http://www.ferox.com), and SORITEC (Sorites Group, Springfield, VA, http://www.cray.com/PUBLIC/APPS/DAS/CODES/SORITEC.html). Other financial and planning modeling systems are embedded in EIS and OLAP tools.

The major differences between financial modeling-based tools and DBMS-based tools are provided in Table 5.6 and discussed in Chapter 4. In Figure 5.7, we show the Visual IFPS/Plus model described in the influence diagram model in

TABLE 5.6 Comparison of Financial Modeling Generators with Those Based Around DBMS.

	Major Advantages (Strong Points)	Major Disadvantages (Weak Points)
Financial modeling-based tools	Financial reporting (and consolidations with some systems) Forecasting Sensitivity analysis Usually easier to learn for financial people Many built-in financial and statistical routines	Limited sorting with older two-dimensional packages Limited data entry Limited handling of text with data Some systems are two-dimensional and require DBMS for consolidation
DBMS-based tools	Data (record)-oriented Best text handling Best sort/merge Data integrity Strong in ad hoc, unstructured queries, and analysis	Cumbersome with time-series problems Cumbersome with multidimensional applications (multiple passes of the data required) Cumbersome in sensitivity analysis applications

Source: Developed by Neil Dorf, Xerox Corporation, Los Angeles.

---

[3]Software development packages will be called DSS tools or DSS generators.

```
COLUMNS 2000..2010
\Model to show relationships among variables
\
\Annual Result Variable:
PROFIT = INCOME – EXPENSE
\
\Decision Variable:
AMOUNT USED IN ADVERTISEMENT = 10000, PREVIOUS * 1.1
\
\Intermediate Result Variables:
INCOME = UNITS SOLD * UNIT PRICE
EXPENSE = UNITS COST * UNIT PRICE + FIXED COST


\
UNITS SOLD = .5 * AMOUNT USED IN ADVERTISEMENT
\
\Initial Data:
UNIT COST = 10, PREVIOUS * 1.05
UNIT PRICE = 20, PREVIOUS * 1.07
FIXED COST = 50000, PREVIOUS * .5, PREVIOUS * .9
\
\To Complete the Model, we normally would take a Net Present Value Calculation:
DISCOUNT RATE = 8%
NET PRESENT VALUE PROFIT = NPVC (INCOME, DISCOUNT RATE,
EXPENSE)
```

FIGURE 5.7 IFPS Model and Solution of the Profit Model Shown in the Influence Diagram in Figure 5.1. The model has been expanded to include expressions for the unknown initial data and for the decision variable.

Figure 5.1 (see Section 5.5). We provide a list of typical applications of planning models in DSS in Focus 5.6. See DSS in Action 5.7 for a sample of financial planning language applications.

5.14 VISUAL MODELING AND SIMULATION

One of the most exciting developments in computer graphics is **visual interactive modeling (VIM)** (see DSS in Action 5.8). The technique has been used for DSS in the area of operations management with unusual success (see Bell [1991]). The technique appears under several names and variations, such as *visual interactive problem solving, visual interactive modeling,* and *visual interactive simulation.*

Visual interactive modeling (VIM) uses computer graphic displays to present the impact of different management decisions. It differs from regular graphics in that the user can intervene in the decision-making process and can see the results of the intervention. A visual model is a graphic used as an integral part of decision making or problem solving, not just as a communication device. The VIM displays the effect of different decisions in graphic form on a computer screen. See Au and Paul [1996] and Belton and Elder [1994].

VIM can represent a static or a dynamic system. Static models display a visual image of the result of one decision alternative at a time. (With computer windows, several results can be compared on one screen.) Dynamic models display systems that evolve over time. The evolution is represented by **animation.** A snapshot example of a generated, animated display of traffic at an intersection from the

FINANCIAL PLANNING APPLICATIONS

Although many financial planning languages have disappeared, and many of their capabilities are embodied in spreadsheets and databases, IFPS/Plus (Comshare Inc.) and Encore! (Ferox Microsystems Inc.) have demonstrated marketplace longevity. The attractive modeling system features for managers include the following:

- The models are easy to write, maintain, and modify.
- The models are compact.
- They handle large models.
- The command syntax is also easy to use.
- The overall system is user-friendly.
- The models are written in a nonprocedural, English-like manner.
- Queries are easy to write.
- Database interfaces are easy to develop.
- They have many financial, statistical, and mathematical functions.
- **What-if analyses** and goal seeking are easy to execute.
- Models can embody risk via Monte Carlo simulation.
- The language structure is general for a variety of applications.

Applications that appear in the literature include

- Military personnel housing determination
- Equipment replacement optimization model
- Merger and acquisition targeting in the pharmaceutical industry
- Employee benefits package evaluations
- Financial modeling for oil well service firms
- Bridging the gap between marketing and manufacturing via simulation
- Pro forma balance sheets and income statements
- Managerial planning for a toy company
- Freestanding modeling and forecasting workstations
- Budget planning for a major national pizza chain
- Consolidation of sales, budgeting, and reporting for an auto parts manufacturer
- Tracking progress toward goals for a bank
- Income statement consolidation for projected cash flow for loan packaging
- Model consolidation for a public utility
- Financial analysis for controlling costs for a clothing manufacturer
- Forecasting cash flows to automate a treasury management system
- Debt and service analysis for a major building project
- Aggregate production planning models
- Asset liability (funds) management for a U.S. national bank
- Credit review in commercial lending for a loan administration department
- General forecasting
- Staff productivity evaluation
- Financial statement review for commercial bank loans

Orca Visual Simulation Environment (Orca Computer Inc., Blacksburg, VA, http://www.orcacomputer.com) is shown in Figure 5.8.

One of the most developed areas in dynamic VIM is **visual simulation.** It is a very important technique for DSS because simulation is considered a major approach in DSS. Visual Interactive Simulation (VIS) is a decision simulation in which the end-user watches the progress of the simulation model in an animated form using graphics displays. The user may interact with the simulation and try different decision strategies. Belton and Elder [1994] suggest that VIM is an approach that has, at its core, the ability to allow decision makers to learn about their own subjective values. This learning can be very beneficial in designing DSS. Animation systems that produce realistic graphics make this methodology possible. Such sys-

VISUAL INTERACTIVE DSS MAKES RAILROAD COMPANIES COMPETITIVE

To compete with road and air modes of transportation, railroad companies must reengineer themselves. A critical area is the maintenance of the cars, tracks, and other infrastructure, which cost more than 20 percent of the revenue. Using VIM, Canadian Pacific Co. and Santa Fe Corp. are reducing their maintenance costs and increasing their reliability and service levels. Railroads are continuously monitoring the condition of their infrastructure, collecting vast amounts of information. This information can be used to predict track conditions based on future loadings. The stored data formulas used to be accessed manually. Using VIM, the railroads can combine map information with additional dimensions such as age of the rail, speed restrictions, signals, bridges, and crossings, and access data electronically. The user can interrogate the maps for required information. Santa Fe uses the VIM to help monitor and prioritize track maintenance work, link planning, and scheduling and graphically provide the location of track maintenance. It is a kind of interactive geographic information system (GIS). The computerized maintenance planning system assists in the scheduling of gangs for track maintenance in a cost-effective manner with minimal disruption to commercial traffic. A DSS model that includes dozens of factors and variables configures the best solutions. The system generates schedules, lists of work to be done, and even Gantt charts that visually support scheduling. Once the information is visible to the planner, he or she can perform what-if analysis, changing resource levels, job content, and schedules. Financial results are also measured. In addition, actual performance is compared to the planning, and revisions can be executed quickly. The program is basically a track maintenance simulation. The simulation is supported by visual animation of equipment, which is moved along the tracks. Productivity is constantly monitored as well. Several related decisions are also supported by the system.

(*Source:* Based on K. Concannon and S. Tudor, "Visual Interactive DSS Streamline Maintenance Operations," *OR/MS Today*, Dec. 1992.)

tems include RealiMation (RealiView), Dynamic Animation Systems (Immersive Environments), and Synthetic Engineering Inc. (Extreme Simulators). The latest visual simulation technology is coupled with the concept of virtual reality, where an artificial world is created for a number of purposes, from training to entertainment to viewing data in an artificial landscape. For more on virtual reality, see Chapter 7.

Conventional Simulation

Simulation has long been established as a useful method of giving insight into complex MSS problem situations. However, the technique of simulation does not usually allow decision makers to see how a solution to a complex problem is developing through time, nor does it give them the ability to interact with it. The simulation technique gives only statistical answers at the end of a set of particular experiments. As a result, decision makers are not an integral part of the simulation development, and their experience and judgment cannot be used to directly assist the study. Thus, any conclusions obtained by the model must be taken on trust. If the conclusions do not agree with the intuition or practical judgment of the decision maker, a confidence gap will appear regarding the use of the model. See Fishwick [1995] for more on simulation.

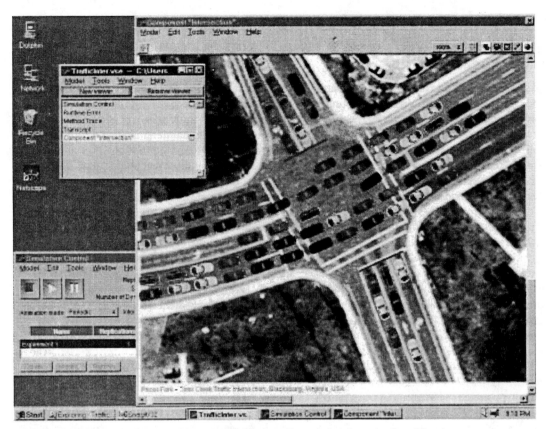

FIGURE 5.8 Example of a Generated Image of Traffic at an Intersection from the Orca Visual Simulation Environment.

(*Source:* Courtesy of Orca Computer, Inc., Blacksburg, VA.)

Visual Interactive Simulation

The basic philosophy of VIS is that decision makers can interact with the simulated model and watch the results develop over time. (Download a MODSIM III demo from CACI Products Company at http://www.caciasl.com/modsim.html.) This is achieved by using a visual display unit. Decision makers can also contribute to the validation of that model. They will have more confidence in its use because of their own participation. They are also in a position to use their knowledge and experience to interact with the model to explore alternative strategies.

Simulation can be interactive at the design stage, at the model running stage, or both. To gain insight into how systems operate under different conditions, it is important to be able to interact with the model while it is running so that alternative suggestions or directives can be tested (see DSS in Action 5.9). The (production) A.G.I. Line Simulators from the Abraham Goldratt Institute (New Haven, CT) visually simulate factory production lines of up to 30 stations. The user sets the buffer stock level (work-in-process inventory) in front of each station (a decision variable); each station has stochastic completion times and breakdowns, and job arrivals are also stochastic. The simulation is viewed on the screen, so the user can immediately see the impact of the decisions (the inventory piling up in front of each station). Other policies can be attempted in developing an effective scheduling

VISUAL INTERACTIVE SIMULATION: AIR TRAFFIC CONTROL IN THE ORCA VISUAL SIMULATION ENVIRONMENT (VSE)

The focus of the Orca Visual Simulation Environment (VSE) is on creating and maintaining a simulation model graphically, hierarchically, and under the object-oriented paradigm to let the VSE automatically generate an executable model. A photograph or other image of the system can be scanned, edited, and used in the virtual interactive simulation. Then, the VSE's state-of-the-art automation-based software engineering paradigm is used in building complex visual simulation models. Complex statistical experimental designs are created under the object-oriented paradigm. Even simulation debugging is handled graphically.

For an air traffic control simulation model, an input data file is created from the FAA Official Airline Guide (OAG) data file to contain longitudes and latitudes of 200 cities and 1,000 flight schedules worldwide. At the startup of simulation, the input data file is read in and the 200 cities are created and placed on the map. Based on the flight information, dynamic objects representing the aircraft are instantiated. Double-clicking on an aircraft image during animation displays its inside top-level view. Double-clicking on a city image similarly displays its inside top-level view. The animation is viewed on two 17" color monitors of a Pentium 133 PC.

(*Source:* Condensed from Visual Simulation Environment (VSE) brochure, Orca Computer, Inc., Blacksburg, VA, http://www.OrcaComputer.com, Oct. 1996.)

strategy. See Robinson [1994] for an overview of VIS in business, and Hansen [1996] on how it can be used in business process reengineering. Rohrer [1996] and Thav [1996] also describe the importance of VIS in manufacturing. For example, animated VIS is provided by AIM (Pritsker Corp.), GPSS/PC (Minuteman Software), and VisSim (Visual Solutions). See the book's Web site (http://www.prenhall.com/turban) for a representative list of VIS software with animation.

Visual Interactive Models and DSS

VIM was used with DSS in several operations management decisions (see Case Application W5.1 on the book's Web site and Chau and Bell [1996]). The method consists of priming a visual interactive model of a plant (or company) with its current status. The model then rapidly runs on a computer, allowing management to observe how a plant is likely to operate in the future. A similar approach was used to assist in the consensus negotiations among senior managers for the development of their budget plans.

An example of VIM is waiting line management (queuing). A DSS in such a case usually computes several measures of performance (such as waiting time in the system) for the various decision alternatives. Complex waiting line problems require simulation. The VIM can display the size of the waiting line as it changes during the simulation runs. The VIM can also graphically present the answers to what-if questions regarding changes in input variables.

The VIM approach can also be used in conjunction with artificial intelligence. The integration of the two techniques adds several capabilities that range, from the ability to build systems graphically, to learning about the dynamics of the system.

High-speed parallel computers such as those made by Silicon Graphics Inc. (CA) make large-scale, complex animated simulations feasible in real time.

General-purpose dynamic VIM software is commercially available for both mainframe and personal computers. For example, the Orca Visual Simulation Environment (Orca Computer Inc., Blacksburg, VA) and CyberVision, ExoDIS, and DISplay (Computer Explorations Inc.) provide VIM capabilities. For a representative list of packages with animation, see the book's Web site. For a complete list, see Sim.TECH [1996].

5.15 READY-MADE QUANTITATIVE SOFTWARE PACKAGES

Some DSS tools offer several built-in subroutines for constructing quantitative models in areas such as statistics, financial analysis, accounting, and management science. These models can be called up by one command, such as

- SQRT: This function calculates the square root of a number that may be a part of an inventory model.
- NPV: This function calculates the net present value of a collection of future cash flows for a given interest rate. It also may be a part of a make-versus-buy model.

In addition, many DSS tools can easily interface with powerful standard quantitative standalone software packages. Another organization of preprogrammed quantitative models is via templates. **Ready-made quantitative models** (preprogrammed models) can be used to expedite the programming time of the DSS builder. Some of these models are building blocks of other quantitative models. For example, a regression model can be a part of a forecasting model that supports a financial planning model. For example, Visual IFPS/Plus can have template models with variables initially at 0. When activated with a Datafile, the model replaces the variables at 0 with model lines from the Datafile. Thus, a complicated model may be easily used with many sets of data. Spreadsheets have the same capability, but data must carefully be inserted.

Statistical Packages

Several statistical functions are built into various DSS tools; for example typical functions are mean, median, variance, standard deviation, kurtosis, t-test, chi-square, various types of regression (linear, polynomial, and stepwise) correlations, and analysis of variance.

Regression analysis executed in SPSS (an example is shown on the book's Web site) exhibits the following three features:

- A one-word command triggered the analysis.
- The equation for best fit for the model is clearly identified.
- The report is automatically formatted.

More power can be obtained from standalone statistical packages, some of which can be interfaced easily with Excel and other popular spreadsheets. Typical packages are SPSS, Minitab, SAS, Systat, and TSP. Stat Pac Inc. (Edina, MN) provides a survey analysis package called StatPac Gold. Most spreadsheets, such as Excel, also contain fairly sophisticated statistical functions and routines.

Management Science Packages

There are several hundred management science packages on the market for models ranging from inventory control to project management. Several DSS generators include optimization and simulation capabilities. For example, see Figure 5.9. Lists of

FIGURE 5.9 Monte Carlo Analysis Performed with Stratagem.

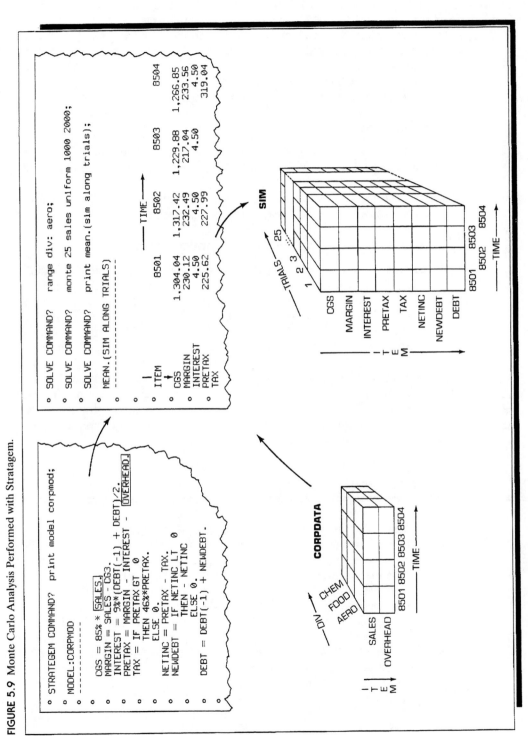

(*Source:* Courtesy of Computer Associates.)

representative management science packages can be found in management science journals (such as *OR/MS Today* and INFORMS OnLine on the Web at http://www.informs.org). QSB+ (see Chang and Sullivan [1996]) is an example of a fairly comprehensive and robust academic management science package. IBM's Optimization System Library (OSL) and CPLEX (CPLEX Optimization Inc.) are commercial ones. Simulation packages include GPSS (and GPSS/PC), ProModel, SLAM, SIMAN, and SIMSCRIPT (see Sim.TECH [1996]). Many academic packages are available directly from their authors and via the Web (see ucsu.colorado. edu/~xu/software.html).

Financial Modeling

Financial functions (such as net present value and internal rate of return) are built into most spreadsheet and DSS tools. Most free-standing financial modeling systems are now embedded in EIS development systems, OLAP systems, **multidimensional spreadsheets,** and visual spreadsheets. Such packages are available from Comshare Inc., Pilot Software Inc. and Computer Associates.

Other Ready-made Specific DSS (Applications)

In addition to ready-made tools, there is an increasing number of ready-made DSS application software products. A number of these are spreadsheet add-ins such as What'sBest! (Lindo Systems Inc., Chicago), Solver (Frontline Systems Inc., Incline Village, NV), @Risk (simulation Add-in for Excel, Palisade Corp.), @Brain (neural network add in for Lotus 1-2-3, Talon Development Co., Milwaukee), and Evolver (genetic algorithm add-in for Excel, Palisade Corp.). Sometimes it is necessary to modify the source code of the package to fit the decision maker's needs. Some actually produce source code from the development language. For example, many neural network packages can produce a deployable version of their internal models in the language C. The price of these products is declining and their availability is increasing. Examples are listed in Table 5.7 and on the book's Web site (http://www.prenhall.com/turban).

5.16 MODEL BASE MANAGEMENT

The concept of a **model base management system (MBMS)** calls for a software package with capabilities similar to those of the DBMS. Unfortunately, although there are dozens of commercial DBMS packages, there are no comprehensive model base management packages currently on the market. Limited capabilities, which a model management package should exhibit, are provided by some spreadsheet programs and financial planning–based DSS tools.

One reason for this situation is that each organization uses models somewhat differently. Furthermore, there is not a small set of model classes as there are for database structures (like relational, hierarchical, network, object-oriented). As we have seen earlier in this chapter, another reason is that some MBMS capabilities (such as selecting which model to use and deciding what values to insert) require expertise and reasoning capabilities. Thus, MBMS could be an interesting area for the application of expert systems and other artificial intelligence approaches (see Chapter 18, Chang et al. [1993] and Klein and Aronson [1995]).

An effective model base management system will make the structural and algorithmic aspects of model organization and associated data processing invisible

TABLE 5.7 Representative Ready-made Specific DSS.

Name of Package	Vendor	Description
AutoMod, AutoSched	AutoSimulations Bountiful, UT http://www.autosim.com	3-D walk-through animations for manufacturing and material handling; manufacturing scheduling
Budgeting & Reporting	Helmsman Group Inc. Plainsboro, NJ http://www.helmsmangroup.com	Financial data warehousing
FACTOR/AIM PACKAGING	Pritsker Corp. Indianapolis, IN http://www.pritsker.com	Manufacturing simulator with costing capabilities, high-speed/high-volume food and beverage industry simulator
MedModel, ServiceModel	ProModel Corp. Orem, UT http://www.promodel.com	Healthcare simulation, service industry simulation
OIS	Olsen & Associates Ltd. Zürich, Switzerland http://www.olsen.ch	Directional forecasts, trading models, risk management
OptiPlan Professional, OptiCaps, OptiCalc	Advanced Planning Systems Inc. Alpharetta, GA	Supply chain planning
PLANNING WORKBENCH	Proasis Ltd. Chislehurst, Kent, England http://www.proasis.co.uk	Graphically based planning system for the process industry
StatPac Gold	Stat Pac Inc. Edina, MN	Survey analysis package
TRAPEZE	Trapeze Software Group Mississauga, ON http://www.trapsoft.com	Planning, scheduling, and operations
TruckStops, OptiSite, BUSTOPS	MicroAnalytics Inc. Arlington, VA	Distribution management and transportation

to users of the MBMS. Such tasks as specifying explicit relationships between models to indicate formats for models and which model outputs are input to other models are not placed directly on the user of an MBMS but handled directly by the system (see Dhar and Matthias [1993]).

The following are desirable capabilities of MBMS:

- *Control.* The DSS user should be provided with a spectrum of control. The system should support both fully automated and manual selection of models that seem most useful to the user for an intended application. This will enable the user to proceed at the problem-solving pace that is most comfortable for his or her experiential familiarity with the task at hand. It should also be possible for the user to introduce subjective information.

- *Flexibility.* The DSS user should be able to develop part of the solution using one approach and then be able to switch to another modeling approach, if this is preferable.

- *Feedback.* The MBMS of the DSS should provide sufficient feedback to enable the user to be aware of the state of the problem-solving process at any time.

- *Interface.* The DSS user should feel comfortable with the specific model from the MBMS that is in use at any given time. The user should not have to laboriously supply inputs when he or she does not wish to do so.

- *Redundancy reduction.* This can be accomplished by use of shared models and associated elimination of redundant storage.
- *Increased consistency.* This can be achieved through the ability of multiple decision makers to use the same model and the associated reduction of inconsistency that may result from use of different data or different versions of a model.

To provide these capabilities, it appears that an MBMS design must allow the DSS user to

- *Access and retrieve existing models*
- *Exercise and manipulate existing models,* including model instantiation, model selection, and model synthesis, and the provision of suitable model outputs
- *Store existing models,* including model representation, model abstraction, and physical and logical model storage
- *Maintain existing models* as appropriate for changing conditions
- *Construct new models* with reasonable effort when they are needed, usually by building new models, using existing models as building blocks

A number of auxiliary requirements must be achieved to provide these five capabilities. For example, there must be appropriate communication and data changes among models that have been combined. In addition, it must be possible to analyze and interpret the results obtained from using a model. This can be accomplished in a number of ways (for example, by the use of expert systems; see Chapter 18.)

Modeling Languages

There are a number of specialized modeling languages that act as front ends to the software that actually performs the optimization or simulation. They function in many ways like the model-building part of financial planning languages. These essentially front end the working or algorithmic code and assist the manager in developing and managing models. Some popular mathematical programming modeling languages include LINGO (Lindo Systems Inc.), AMPL (Fourer et al. [1993]), and GAMS (Brooke et al. [1992]). For an example of a modeling language developed for simulation, see DSS in Action 5.5.

Relational Model Base Management System (MBMS)

As is the case with a relational view of data, a model is viewed as a virtual file or virtual relation. Three operations are needed for relational completeness in model management: execution, optimization, and sensitivity analysis.

Object-oriented Model Base and Its Management

Using an object-oriented DBMS construct it is possible to build an **object-oriented model base management system (OOMBS)** that maintains logical independence between the model base and the other DSS components, facilitating intelligent and stabilized integration of the components. Huh [1993] developed such a system, which could greatly enhance the capabilities of MBMS. For additional discussion, see Muhanna [1993] and Muhanna and Pick [1994]. Also see Briccarello et al. [1995] and Ninios et al. [1995].

Models for Database and MIS Design and Their Management

Models describing efficient database and MIS design are useful in that the deployed systems will function in the best way. This is much like the situation described in the chapter's opening vignette. A model is developed to describe and evaluate a nonexistent aspect of the business. Then, when the system is deployed, it functions as if the decision makers have had many years of experience in running the new system. Thus, the model building and evaluation are training tools for the DSS team members. Models for database and MIS design include those of Cerpa [1995] and Kilov and Cuthbert [1995]. Also see Cook [1996].

Enterprise and Business Process Reengineering Modeling and Model Management Systems

Models for describing the enterprise involving business process reengineering are described by Buzacott [1996], Jarzabek and Ling [1996] and van der Aalst [1996].

For details on recent developments and issues in model management systems, see Chang, Holsapple, and Whinston [1993], Klein and Aronson [1995], and Suh et al. [1995].

Chapter Highlights

- Models play a major role in DSS. They can be of several types.
- Models can be either static (single snapshot of a situation) or dynamic.
- Analysis is conducted either under assumed certainty (most desirable), risk, or uncertainty (least desirable).
- Influence diagrams show graphically the interrelationships of a model. They can be used to enhance the presentation of spreadsheet technology.
- Electronic spreadsheets have many extended capabilities, including what-if analysis, goal seeking, optimization, and simulation.
- Electronic spreadsheets provide a programming language for modeling and computations.
- Decision tables and decision trees are useful for modeling and solving simple decision-making problems.
- The major tool of optimization is mathematical programming.
- Linear programming is the simplest tool of mathematical programming. It attempts to find an optimal allocation of limited resources under organizational constraints.
- The major parts of a linear programming model are the objective function, the decision variables, and the constraints.
- Heuristic programming involves problem solving using general rules or intelligent search.
- Simulation is a widely used DSS approach that involves experimentation with a model that assumes the appearance of reality.
- Simulation can deal with more complex situations than optimization, but it does not guarantee an optimal solution.
- Expert Choice is a leading software tool for solving multicriteria decision-making problems.
- Forecasting methods are critical in predicting the outcome of decisions to be made today.
- Multidimensional modeling allows users to easily create models, display the results in different ways, and then conduct sensitivity analysis.
- Many DSS development tools include built-in quantitative models (financial, statistical) or they can easily interface with such.

- There are special languages available for financial modeling.
- Visual interactive modeling is an implementation of a graphical user interface (GUI). It is usually combined with simulation and animation.
- Visual interactive simulation (VIS) is increasingly being used to show simulation results in an easily understood manner.
- Spreadsheet modeling and results can be presented in an influence diagram format (visual spreadsheets).
- Model base management systems perform tasks analogous to DBMS.
- Artificial intelligence techniques are being increasingly used in MBMS.

Key Words

animation
certainty
complexity
decision analysis
decision table
decision tree
dynamic models
electronic spreadsheet
environmental scanning and analysis
financial planning modeling software
forecasting
genetic algorithms
heuristic programming
heuristics
influence diagram
linear programming (LP)
mathematical programming
model base management system (MBMS)
multicriteria modeling
multidimensional modeling

multidimensional spreadsheets
multiple goals
object-oriented model base management system (OOMBMS)
optimal solution
ready-made quantitative models
regression analysis
relational model base management system (RMBMS)
risk
risk analysis
simulation
spreadsheet (electronic)
spreadsheet add-in
static models
tabu search
uncertainty
visual interactive modeling (VIM)
visual simulation
visual spreadsheet
what-if analysis

Questions for Review

1. What are the major types of models used in DSS?
2. Distinguish between built-in models and models that need to be built.
3. Distinguish between a static model and a dynamic model. Give an example of each.
4. What is an influence diagram? What is it used for?
5. What is an electronic spreadsheet?
6. What makes an electronic spreadsheet so conducive to the development of DSS?
7. What is an expected value?
8. What is a decision table?
9. What is a decision tree?
10. What is an allocation problem?

11. List and briefly discuss the three major components of linear programming.
12. What is the role of heuristics in modeling?
13. Define visual simulation and compare it to conventional simulation.
14. Define multidimensional modeling.
15. Describe visual spreadsheets.
16. Define visual interactive modeling (VIM).
17. Define a planning model and compare it with a financial planning model.
18. What is a model base management system?
19. Why is the development of generic model base management systems so difficult?

Questions for Discussion

1. What is the relationship between environmental analysis and problem identification?
2. Even though many of the examples described in Evans [1991] do not directly relate to DSS, the concepts often apply to the DSS building effort. Using the Evans book, identify three misapplications, fallacies in modeling, disastrous applications, or modeling misconceptions. Describe what went wrong, as well as what it takes to build successful decision models in these cases.
3. What is the difference between an optimistic approach and a pessimistic approach to decision making under assumed uncertainty?
4. Explain the differences between static and dynamic models. How can one evolve into the other?
5. Explain why solving problems under uncertainty sometimes involves assuming that the problem is to be solved under conditions of risk.
6. Explain why an influence diagram can be viewed as a model of a model.
7. What type of language is a spreadsheet?
8. Spreadsheet software is now appearing as multidimensional. Explain how this is possible. Explain the benefits of multidimensionality.
9. Excel is probably the most popular software for the PC. Why? What can you do with this package that makes it so attractive?
10. Review the latest capabilities of Excel. Compare them with the capabilities of an ideal DSS generator as discussed in Chapters 3 and 8. How wide is the gap? Be specific.
11. What is the difference between decision analysis with a single goal and decision analysis with multiple goals (criteria)?
12. Why are allocation problems so difficult to solve?
13. Explain how linear programming can solve allocation problems.
14. What are the advantages of using a spreadsheet package to create and solve linear programming models? What are the disadvantages?
15. Give examples of three heuristics with which you are familiar.
16. Describe the general process of simulation.
17. List some of the major advantages of simulation over optimization.
18. What are the advantages of using a spreadsheet package to perform simulation studies? What are the disadvantages?
19. List some advantages of optimization over simulation.
20. Compare the methodology of simulation to Simon's four-phase model of decision making. Does the methodology of simulation map directly into Simon's model? Explain.
21. What is the role of a planning and modeling language? How does it differ from a general programming language? How does it relate to DSS?

22. Compare a multidimensional spreadsheet software to a regular one. What are the major advantages of the former? Are there any disadvantages?

23. Explain the relationship between influence diagrams and visual spreadsheets.

24. What features make financial and planning models useful for decision makers?

25. Several computer games, such as Flight Simulator II, DOOM, and GATO, can be considered visual simulation. Explain why.

26. Explain why VIM is particularly helpful in implementing recommendations derived by computers.

27. Compare the linear programming features available in spreadsheets to those in ready-made quantitative software packages.

28. There are hundreds of DBMS packages on the market for personal computers and several dozen for mainframes. Why don't we have such packages for model base management systems (MBMS)?

29. Does Simon's four-phase decision making model fit into most of the modeling methodologies described? How or how not?

Questions for the Opening Vignette

1. Explain how simulation was used to evaluate a nonexistent system.

2. What was learned about running the cleanroom from using the simulation model?

3. How could the time compression capability of simulation help in this situation?

4. How did the simulation results help the SSI engineers learn about their decision-making problem? Were they able to focus better on the structure of the real system? How did this save development and operating costs of the real cleanroom?

Exercises

1. Create the spreadsheet models shown in Figures 5.2 and 5.3.
   a. What is the effect of a change in the interest rate from 8 percent to 10 percent in the spreadsheet model shown in Figure 5.2?
   b. For the original model in Figure 5.2, what interest rate is required to decrease the monthly payments by 20 percent? What change in the loan amount would have the same effect?
   c. In the spreadsheet shown in Figure 5.3, what is the effect of a prepayment of $200 per month? What prepayment would be necessary to pay off the loan in 25 years instead of 30 years?

2. Create a Visual IFPS/Plus model to implement the worksheet in Figure 5.3. (Note that the Student Version of Visual IFPS/Plus has limits on model size, so you may not be able to create the entire model for all 360 months.) Compare the complexity of the models. Solve a problem with a 3-year loan of $10,000 at 10 percent.

3. *Class exercise.* Everyone in the class should write their weight, height, and gender on a piece of paper (no names please!). If the sample is too small (you will need about 20–30 students), add more students from another class. Create a regression (causal) model for height versus weight for the whole class, and one for each gender. If possible, use a statistical package and a spreadsheet and compare their ease of use. Also, produce a scatterplot of the three sets of data (the data points). Do the relationships appear linear? How accurate were the models (how close to 1 is the value of R^2)? Does weight *cause* height, does height *cause* weight, or does neither really *cause* the other? Explain. How can a regression model like this be used in building design? diet/nutrition selection? a longitudinal study (say over 50 years) in determining whether students are getting heavier and not taller, or vice versa?

4. It has been argued in a number of different venues that a higher education level indicates a greater average income. The real question for a college student might be, "Should I stay in school?" Using U.S. Census data (.WK1 and.WK3 files available on the Web) from Census Tables P8 and P9 (USSTXP8.XLS and USSTXP9.XLS; see the Internet Exercises in Chapter 4), for the 50 states and Washington, DC, develop a linear regression model (causal forecasting) to see whether this is true. (Note that some data massaging might be necessary.) How high was the R^2 value (a measure of quality of fit)? Do not forget to scatterplot the data. Does the relationship appear to be linear? If not, check a statistics book and try a nonlinear function. How well did the nonlinear function perform? For these variables, do you believe that higher average education level tends to "cause" higher average income? Explain.

   When you get to Chapter 18, build a neural network model and compare it to the other two. Which five states have the highest incomes, and which five states have the highest average education levels?

5. Set up spreadsheet models for the decision table models of Section 5.7 and solve them.

6. It has been suggested that DSS generators are English-like and have a variety of analysis capabilities.

   a. Even though you may not have formal training in IFPS, see whether you can identify the purpose and the analysis capabilities of the following IFPS program:

   MODEL FIRST[4]

   ```
    1 COLUMNS 1–5
    2 INVESTMENT = LAND + BUILDING
    3 RETURN = SALES – COSTS
    4 PRESENT VALUE = NPVC(RETURN, DISCOUNT RATE, INVESTMENT)
    5 INTERNAL RATE OF RETURN = IRR(RETURN, INVESTMENT)
    6 \ INPUT DATA
    7 LAND = 200, 0
    8 BUILDING = 100, 150, 0
    9 SALES = 500, PREVIOUS + 100
   10 COSTS = SUM(MATERIALS THRU LABOR)
   11 MATERIALS = 10 + 0.20 * SALES
   12 OVERHEAD = .10 * SALES
   13 LABOR = 20 + 0.40 * SALES
   14 DISCOUNT RATE = 0.20, PREVIOUS
   ```

   b. Suppose we change the sales to be under assumed risk, that is, replace the SALES line and insert a line following it:

   ```
   9   SALES = NORRANDR(EXPECTED SALES, EXPECTED SALES/10)
       EXPECTED SALES = 500, PREVIOUS + 100
   ```

   and use

   ```
   MONTE CARLO 200
   COLUMNS 5
   HIST PRESENT VALUE, INTERNAL RATE OF RETURN
   FREQ PRESENT VALUE, INTERNAL RATE OF RETURN
   NONE
   ```

   What do these statements do to this new model?

7. Your client is considering an investment of $1,000 in a new product venture that will cause an immediate increase of $400 in the client's annual gross sales. It is assumed the usefulness of this new product will end after 5 years, that its sales will increase by 15 percent per

[4]Model FIRST is adapted from P. Gray, *Visual IFPS for Business,* Prentice Hall, Upper Saddle River, NJ, 1996.

year for years 2 and 4, and that sales in the final or fifth year will be half those of the fourth year. Although this illustrative exercise involves only a few trivial calculations, please use formulas throughout your model that could easily be extended over more time, with more complex relationships, thus showing the power of spreadsheets.

The incremental variable costs for this new product are estimated at 40 percent of sales. The estimated incremental annual fixed costs begin at $30 for year 1, increase by $5 during each of the remaining 4 years of the new product's useful life, and then end. The initial investment, all during year 1, includes $400 of expenses that are immediately deductible from the firm's taxable profits. The remaining $600 of the investment is capitalized and charged out as depreciation expense over several years, starting during year 1. The income tax rate applicable to the incremental net profit contribution of this new product is 45 percent for all years and all amounts. Because a reported accounting loss on this new product reduces other taxable profits, a cash savings of taxes payable of this same percentage will occur for years that show an accounting loss.

Part 1. Develop a spreadsheet model for these proposed expenses, taxes, and net profit for each of the 5 years. Assume the $600 capitalized part of the investment is depreciated in equal amounts ($150 per year) over years 1 through 4.

Part 2. Now extend the spreadsheet model of Part 1 to include the incremental cash flow for each of the 5 years and the cumulative cash flow for each year. Cash flow includes all investments, expenses, and taxes as outflows, and revenues as inflows.

Part 3. Extend Part 2 to show the net present value, at a 20 percent annual discount factor, of the incremental cash flow for this proposed 5-year investment venture. If possible, also show the internal rate of return, or yield, of this investment.

Part 4. The time period and calculation method for charging the depreciation expense of an investment against incremental taxable income can influence the cash-flow pattern, and hence the attractiveness, of an investment. Extend the spreadsheet of Part 3 to examine the impact on periodic net cash flow, and the total net present value and the internal rate of return, of the following different depreciation options:

a. Current option of equal allocation of the $600 total over 4 years, that is, a straight-line depreciation schedule over 4 years.

b. Then show straight-line over 5 years.

c. And, straight-line over 3 years.

d. Finally, use the sum-of-year's-digits method over 4 years. Notice that the digits 1, 2, 3, and 4 sum to 10; hence first-year depreciation is 4/10 of the total capitalized investment, and the following years are 3/10, 2/10, and 1/10, respectively.

8. Many managers know that a small percentage of the customers contribute to most of the sales. Similarly, much of the wealth in the world is concentrated in the hands of a few. This phenomenon is called the 80–20 rule, the A-B-C, and the value-volume, and it is attributed to the famous economist Pareto. How can this phenomenon be used in modeling? What kind of approach is this: optimization, simulation, or heuristic?

9. Assume that you know that there is one irregular coin (either lighter or heavier) among 12. Using a two-pan scale you must find that coin (is it lighter or heavier?) in no more than three tests. Solve this problem and explain the weighing strategy that you use. What approach to problem solving is used in this case?

10. Use a map of the United States (or your own country). Starting from where you are now, identify a location on the other side and plot out a route to go from here to there. What (heuristic) rules did you use in selecting your route? How does your route compare to published distances (if available) between the locations?

11. Use the Expert Choice software to select your next car. Evaluate cars on ride (from poor to great), looks (from attractive to ugly), and acceleration (seconds to 60 mph).
Consider three final cars on your list. Develop

a. A problem hierarchy

b. A comparison of the importance of the criteria against the goal

c. A comparison of the alternative cars for each criterion

d. An overall ranking (synthesis of leaf nodes with respect to the goal)

e. A sensitivity analysis.

Maintain the inconsistency index lower than 0.1. If you initially had an inconsistency index greater than 0.1, what caused it to be that high? Would you really buy the car you selected? Why or why not?

Also develop a spreadsheet model using estimated preference weights and estimates for the intangible items, each on a scale from 1 to 10 for each car. Compare the conclusions reached with this method to those found in using the Expert Choice model. Which one more accurately captures your judgments and why?

12. Build an Expert Choice model to select the next president of the United States (if it is not an election year, or you do not live in the United States, select a relevant election). Whom did you choose? Did your solution match your expectations?

Extra Credit. On the Web, find the *Which & Why* software and their demo on Presidential Selection. Run it, examine the results, and compare it to what you did first.

13. *Job selection using Expert Choice.* You are on the job market (use your imagination, if necessary). List the names of four or five different companies that have offered you a job (or from which you expect to get an offer). (As an alternative, your instructor may assign Graduate or Undergraduate Program Selection.) Write down all the factors that may influence your decision as to which job offer you will accept. Such factors may include geographic location, salary, benefits, taxes, school system (if you have children), and potential for career advancement. Some of these factors (criteria, attributes) may have subcriteria. For instance, location may be subdivided further into climate, urban concentration, cost of living, and so on.

If you do not yet have a salary figure associated with a job offer, you should guess a reasonable figure. Perhaps your classmates can help you determine realistic figures.

a. Model this problem in a spreadsheet (Excel) using some kind of weighted average methodology (you set the criteria weights first) (see the current Rand-McNally *Places Rated Almanac* for an example).

b. Construct an Expert Choice model for your decision problem, and use the pairwise comparisons to arrive at the best job opportunity.

c. Compare the two approaches. Did they yield the same results? Why or why not?

d. Write a short report (one or two typed pages) explaining the results, including those of the weighted average methodology, and for Expert Choice, explain each criterion, subcriterion (if any), and alternative. Describe briefly which options and capabilities of Expert Choice you used in your analysis, and show the numerical results of your analysis. To this purpose, you may want to include printouts of your AHP tree, but make sure you circle and explain the parts of interest on these printouts. Discuss the nature of the tradeoffs you encountered during the evaluation process. You may want to include a meaningful sensitivity analysis of the results (optional).

To think about: Was the Expert Choice analysis helpful in structuring your preferences? Do you think it will be a helpful aid in your actual decision-making process? Comment on all these issues in your report.

14. Solve the blending problem described on the book's Web site at http://www.prenhall.com/turban (use either Excel's Solver Tool or a student version of a linear programming solver such as Lindo or QSB+. If you do not have one, search the Web to identify one [see the Internet Exercises] and download the demo version). In a spreadsheet model, use trial-and-error to obtain an answer. Record your best effort. Solve it with the optimizer. Did you get the same results as are reported in the Web site? Examine the solution (output) reports for the answers and sensitivity report. Lower the right-hand side of the first constraint by 1 unit. What happened to the solution when you solved this modified problem? Using the original formulation, try modifying the objective function coefficients (try lowering the first one by 0.32 and then by 0.34) and examine what happens. What item in the solution reports indicates the change in the solution?

15. *Small DSS development.*[5] The senior management of Francesca's Elite, an international women's clothing retailing chain, has decided that a World Wide Web presence is necessary to maintain a competitive position in the market. Their plan is to make all of their merchandise, both in-store and catalog items, available for purchase over the Web with either credit card or e-money payments. They also feel that the Web project will have a 3-year life span, after which some new technology will be used. The following options are currently available:

- A major computer hardware and software firm (MCHSF Inc.), with experience in this area, has developed a plan for Francesca's with a one-time startup fee of $30,000, a $2,500 monthly maintenance contract, and 5 percent commission on sales. There is no fee per hit (potential customer access).
- Francesca's IS department is considering starting their own internal Web site. Their best estimates are that there would be an $80,000 initial startup fee (for initial training, equipment, and software purchases), a $1,000 monthly maintenance fee, $1,200 in additional monthly expenses (additional marketing and IS personnel to maintain the site), plus a $300 monthly communication fee (to link to the Internet). The cost per hit is zero.
- A local company, WEBCO, with some experience, will contract to provide a shadow Web server; that is, potential customers will think that they are accessing Francesca's server, even though it will be running on one of WEBCO's Web servers. The cost for this option is a one-time $75 initialization fee, $100 per month maintenance fee, and $3.00 per hit. Francesca's must still provide their own Web pages, but WEBCO has online catalogs into which they can insert their own product lines.

The advantages of the first option are that the firm has experience and will provide support and consulting. The disadvantages are that Francesca's Elite will not develop any in-house expertise and have no direct control over the implementation. The advantages of the second option are that there is more flexibility, but the firm must hire or dedicate existing IS and marketing staff to the project (which is partly true for the other two options). However, some of the IS programmers are excited about the possibility of working with the latest communication and access tools and have indicated that an intranet could be developed in conjunction with this project. This could be used for internal e-mail, video conferencing, voice mail, data warehousing, data mining, and employee access to needed data. The third option is the low-cost alternative. Francesca's will get some flexibility, but will still need some in-house expertise (probably at a minimal additional cost). The Web provider will help somewhat by providing samples of pages.

There is an expectation that, on average, 5 percent of the hits result in sales, averaging $200 apiece, so the expected sale is $10/hit. This also takes into consideration the advertising value of the Web site; that is, potential customers may view merchandise on the Web and then purchase it later at a store.

Assume that Francesca's pays 50 percent of its gross sales for goods, distribution, and other (nonWeb-related) overhead, that all three options are available and can be up and running at the start of year 1, that you can ignore the time value of money (cost of capital is 0 percent), and that all financial parameters are valid for the duration of the project (3 years).

a. Design and implement a decision support system in a spreadsheet (Excel) to determine which option is the most cost effective (forgetting about the intangibles) for various numbers of hits per month (initially try 500, 1,000, 1,500, . . . , 5,000).
b. Francesca's management wants a break-even chart embedded in the worksheet. This chart should show the ranges over which each option is cost effective. Clearly identify these values numerically and on the chart.
c. How sensitive is the third option to the cost per hit? How does this option's range of cost-effectiveness change as the cost per hit ranges from $.50 to $5.00?

[5]Problem inspired by E. Messmer, "Clothing Outfit Goes Worldwide on the Web," *Network World,* Aug. 26, 1996, p. 37.

    d. What if the cost of capital is 8 percent? All things being unchanged, re-solve Parts a and b.

    e. How can you take the intangible aspects of this decision-making situation into consideration? Do so and report your findings.

16. At the Ma-Pa Grocery (mentioned in Chapter 2), Bob and Jan have set up a meeting with you to discuss the possibilities of applying simulation, optimization (linear programming), and heuristics to solving their daily bread stocking problem. Until now, they have been using trial-and-error fairly unsuccessfully. But by doing so, they have gathered some data and would like you to build and solve some prototype models to help them in their decision making. Parts a and b are from Jan's data gathering and Part c is from Bob's.

    a. *Simulation.* A loaf of fresh bread sells for $1.95, day-old bread sells for $.40 and costs $.75, and lost customer goodwill is worth $.60 per loaf. Daily demand for bread is normally distributed with a mean of 350 and a standard deviation of 40. Set up and run a 100-day simulation model in a spreadsheet. (*Hint:* Excel is recommended.) Use the =ROUND(NORMINV(RAND(),Mean,Std),0) functions to generate the daily demand. (Is it necessary to use integer loaves? Is it necessary to use only positive demand?) Turn off the spreadsheet's Automatic Recalculation. Clearly identify the decision variable and the results. What stock quantity yields the best resulting net profit? Create a histogram of the resulting net profits. If available, use a simulation add-in (such as @Risk) or a version of Visual IFPS/Plus (or other fourth-generation language) that supports Monte Carlo simulation. Compare the ease of implementation and the amount of information provided by each approach.

    b. *Heuristic.* Modify the simulation models developed in Part a to test the following heuristic policies: Stock the same number of loaves of bread as the demand was 7 days earlier, or stock the average of the previous 7 days of demand (rounded to a whole number) for 100 days.

    c. *Optimization.* Ignore the above problem data. The maximum shelf space for bread is 400 loaves, and it must all be placed on the shelf first thing in the morning. Bob pays a stockperson $3.60 per hour and this person can stock 1 loaf per second. This person has 5 minutes available to stock bread in the morning. Develop a linear programming model of this problem and solve it (using the solver tool in Excel or another LP optimization package). Is this realistic? What about the demand for bread being probabilistic? How is that being handled (or is it)?

Group Projects

1. *Software demonstration.* Each group is assigned a different state-of-the-art DSS software product to review, examine, and demonstrate in class. The specific packages available will depend on what is available from your instructor and what the interests of each group are. You may need to download the demo from a vendor's Web site, depending on your instructor's directions. Do a half-hour presentation, which should include a hands-on demonstration of selected capabilities of the software and your critical evaluation of the software. Try to make your presentation interesting and instructive to the whole class. The main purpose of the presentation is to expose everyone to as much state-of-the-art software as possible, both in-breadth (through the presentations by other groups) and in-depth (through the experience you have in exploring the ins and outs of one particular software product). Also write a report (up to 10 pages) with your findings and comments regarding this software.

2. *Expert choice software familiarity.* Have a group meeting and discuss how you chose a place to live when you moved to start your college program (or where you are now). What factors were important then for each individual, and how long ago was it? Have these criteria changed? As a group, identify the five to seven most important criteria used in making the decision. Using the current group members' living arrangements as choices, develop an Expert Choice model describing this decision-making problem. Do not put your

judgments in yet. You should each solve the EC model independently. How many of you selected your current home using the software? If so, was it a close decision, or was there a clear winner? If some group members did not choose their current homes, what criteria made the result different? Or did the availability of better choices that meets their needs become known? How consistent were your judgments? Do you think that you really prefer to live in the winning choice? Why or why not? Finally, take an average of the results for all group members (take an average by adding up the synthesized weights for each choice and dividing by the number of group members). Was there a clear winner? Whose home was it and why did it win? Were there any close second choices? Turn in your results in a summary report (up to two typed pages), with copies of the individual Expert Choice runs.

Major Group Term Project 1

Identify a decision-making problem in a real-world environment and apply the Analytic Hierarchy Method via the Expert Choice software to it. Find a business or organization, preferably one where you (or someone in your group) are working, used to work, or know an employee or owner. Otherwise, you might consider campus organizations or departments with which you are affiliated. Essentially, you need a contact willing to spend a little time with your group. The problem should involve clear choices (you may need to identify these) and some intangible aspects (not all factors should be strictly costs and benefits in currency). You will have to spend some time learning about the problem at hand. Interview the decision maker, identify important criteria and choices, and build an Expert Choice model. Try your judgments in solving the problem with the prototype (record the results). Then, use the expert's (the decision maker's) judgments and get his or her opinion of how the software helped or hindered the decision-making process.

The four deliverables are

1. *One-page proposal.* Turn in a one-page proposal describing the Expert Choice project you intend to do. Indicate the project title, the client, and the expected results. This proposal should be due about 5 weeks before the final due date.

2. *Intermediate progress report (maximum two pages typed).* In this short report, describe the nature of your application and indicate how far along you are. Experience shows that you may be in trouble if you wait too long to work on this group project, so start seriously working on it as soon as you can. This should be due 3 weeks before the final due date.

3. and 4. *Final project presentation and report (maximum of 10 typed pages, excluding appendices).* The report must include a letter (on letterhead) from the client indicating his or her opinion of the project and interaction with your group (two sentences are sufficient). Will they use the method or the software? Does the client believe the choice? Why or why not? Can they save money by implementing the suggestion? How closely does the suggestion match what the client is doing? What, if any, were the limitations imposed by the software? How did they affect your ability to do the project? What was the most difficult part of doing the project? The group presentations (20 minutes per group) should be scheduled during the last week of the course, with the report due at the same time.

Major Group Term Project 2

Use the outline described for the first project, but use a methodology and a software package that your instructor provides or recommends. This could involve developing an optimization-based DSS, a database-based DSS, a document-based DSS, or a Web-based DSS.

Major Group Term Project 3

Develop a real-world DSS that links a database to a transportation (a type of linear programming) model through a user interface. The database should contain the raw data about the potential transportation routes along with supply and demand points. The database should also handle the user interface and provide managerially meaningful descriptions of the routes, after the optimization system is called.

Internet Exercises

1. Search the Internet and identify software packages for linear programming, simulation, inventory control, project management, statistics, and financial modeling. What types of organizations are providing these packages? Are any free?

2. Search the Web for the newest software packages and books on DSS modeling. What seems to be the major focus of each? Prepare a short report.

3. Do a Web search to identify companies and products for decision analysis. Find at least one demo package, download it (or try it online if possible), and write up a report on your experience.

4. Use the Internet to obtain demo software from management science or statistics vendors (try the SAS Institute Inc., SPSS Inc., CACI Inc., and Lindo Systems Inc.). Also, be sure to look for shareware (fully functional packages that can be tried for a limited time for free). Try some of the packages and write up a report on your findings.

5. Access the Microsoft Web site (http://www.microsoft.com/) and find information about Excel. Also, access Comshare's Web site (http://www.comshare.com/) to explore Visual IFPS/Plus for the PC and Expert Choice Inc.'s Web site (http://www.expertchoice.com/) to explore Expert Choice.

6. Identify a company involved in animation or visual interactive simulation over the Web. Are any of the products Web-ready? Do any of them provide virtual reality capabilities (covered in Chapter 7) or real-time, online simulations? Try one if you can and write up a brief report on your experiences.

Debate

Some people believe that managers do not need to know the internal structure of the model and the technical aspects of modeling. "It is like the telephone or the elevator; you just use it." Others claim that this is not the case and the opposite is true. Debate the issue.

Term Paper

Select a current DSS technology or methodology. Get your Instructor's approval. Write a five-page report detailing the origins of the technology, what need prompted the development of the technology, and what the future holds for it over the next 2, 5, and 10 years. Use electronic sources, if possible, to identify companies providing the technology. If demo software is available, acquire it and include a sample run in your paper.

References

Aronson, J. E. (1989). "A Survey of Dynamic Network Flows." *Annals of Operations Research,* Vol. 20.

Au, G., and R. J. Paul. (1996, May 24). "Visual Interactive Modelling: A Pictorial Simulation Specification System." *European Journal of Operational Research,* Vol. 91, No. 1.

Basnet, C., L. Foulds, and M. Igbaria. (1996, March). "FleetManager: A Microcomputer-based Decision Support System for Vehicle Routing." *Decision Support Systems,* Vol. 16, No. 3.

Bell, D. E., and A. Schleifer, Jr. (1995). *Decision Making Under Uncertainty.* Cambridge, MA: Course Technologies Inc.

Bell, P. C. (1991). "Visual Interactive Modeling: the Past, the Present and the Prospects." *European Journal of Operational Research,* Vol. 54, No. 3.

Belton, V., and M. D. Elder. (1994, Nov.). "Decision Support Systems: Learning from Visual Interactive Modeling." *Decision Support Systems.*

Bodily, S. E. (1985). *Modern Decision Making.* New York: McGraw-Hill.

Briccarello, P., G. Bruno, and E. Ronco. (1995). "REBUS: An Object-oriented Simulator for Business Processes." *Proceedings of the IEEE Annual Simulation Symposium, Los Alamitos, CA.*

Brooke, A., D. Kendrick, and A. Meeraus. (1992). *GAMS Release 2.25: A User's Guide.* South San Francisco: The Scientific Press.

Buede, D. (1996, Aug.)."Decision Analysis Software Survey: Aiding Insight III." *OR/MS Today.*

Buzacott, J. A. (1996, May). "Commonalities in Reengineered Business Processes: Models and Issues." *Management Science,* Vol. 42, No. 5.

Cerpa, N. (1995). "Pre-physical Data Base Design Heuristics." *Information Management,* Vol. 28, No. 6.

Chang, A. M., C. W. Holsapple, and A. B. Whinston. (1993, Jan.). "Model Management Issues and Directions." *Decision Support Systems,* Vol. 9.

Chang, Y. L., and R. S. Sullivan. (1996). *QSB+ 2.1.* Upper Saddle River, NJ: Prentice Hall.

Chau, P. Y. K., and P. C. Bell. (1996, May). "A Visual Interactive Decision Support System to Assist the Design of a New Production Unit." *INFOR,* Vol. 34, No. 2.

Cook, M. A. (1996). *Building Enterprise Information Architectures: Reengineering Information Systems.* Upper Saddle River, NJ: Prentice Hall.

Costa, J. (1995). "An Empirically Based Review of the Concept of Environmental Scanning." *International Journal of Contemporary Hospitality Management,* Vol. 7, No. 7.

Dhar, V., and J. Matthias. (1993, Jan.). "On Modeling Process." *Decision Support Systems.*

Evans, J. R. (1991). *Creative Thinking in the Decision and Management Sciences.* Cincinnati: South-Western.

Fabrycky, W. J., G. J. Thuessen, and D. Verma. (1996). *Economic Decision Analysis,* 3rd ed. Upper Saddle River, NJ: Prentice Hall.

Fishwick, P. (1995). *Simulation Model Design and Execution: Building Digital Worlds.* Englewood Cliffs, NJ: Prentice Hall.

Fourer, R., D. M. Gay, and B. W. Kernighan. (1993). *AMPL A Modeling Language for Mathematical Programming.* South San Francisco: The Scientific Press.

Glover, F., and M. Laguna. (1993). "Tabu Search." In C. R. Reeves, ed. *Modern Heuristic Techniques for Combinatorial Problems.* Oxford, England: Blackwell Scientific Publications.

Grauer, R. T., and M. Barber. (1996). *Exploring Microsoft Office Professional for Windows 95, Volumes I and II, Version 7.0.* Upper Saddle River, NJ: Prentice Hall.

Gray, P. (1996). *Visual IFPS/PLUS for Business.* Upper Saddle River, NJ: Prentice Hall.

Greenfield, L. (1996, Nov. 17). "Decision Analysis Tools." *The Data Warehousing Information Center* (Web page: pwp.starnetinc.com/larryg/decision.html).

Hansen, G. (1996). *Automating Business Process Re-engineering: Using the Power of Visual Simulation Strategies to Improve Performance and Profit,* 2nd ed. Upper Saddle River, NJ: Prentice Hall.

Hillier, F. S., and G. J. Lieberman. (1995). *Introduction to Operations Research,* 6th ed. New York: Irwin.

Huh, S. Y. (1993, March/April). "Model Base Construction with Object-oriented Constructs." *Decision Sciences.*

Jarzabek, S., and T. W. Ling. (1996, May). "Model-based Support for Business Reengineering." *Information & Software Technology,* Vol. 38, No. 5.

Kilov, H., and L. Cuthbert. (1995). "Model for Document Management." *Computer Communications,* Vol. 18, No. 6.

Klein, G., and J. E. Aronson. (1995, Aug.). "Model Management Using Fuzzy Belief Functions." *Proceedings of the Inaugural Meeting of the Association for Information Systems,* Pittsburgh.

Matthews, C. H., and S. G. Scott. (1995, Oct.). "Uncertainty and Planning in Small and Entrepreneurial Firms: An Empirical Assessment." *Journal of Small Business Management.* Vol. 33, No. 4.

Muhanna, W. E. (1993, Feb.). "An Object-Oriented Framework for Model Management and DSS Development." *Decision Support Systems.*

Muhanna, W., and R. A. Pick. (1994, Sept.). "Meta-modeling Concepts and Tools for Model Management: A Systems Approach." *Management Science.*

Myint, S., and M. T. Tabucanon. (1994, Jan.). "A Multiple-criteria Approach to Machine Selection for Flexible Manufacturing Systems." *International Journal of Production Economics.*

Ninios, P., K. Vlahos, and D. W. Bunn. (1995). "Industrial Simulation: System Modelling with an Object Oriented/DEVS Technology." *European Journal of Operational Research,* Vol. 81.

Ragsdale, C. (1995). *Spreadsheet Modeling and Decision Analysis.* Cambridge, MA: Course Technologies Inc.

Rayward-Smith, V. J., ed. (1995). *Application of Modern Heuristic Methods.* Henley-on-Thames, UK: Alfred Waller in association with UNICOM.

Reeves, C. R., ed. (1993). *Modern Heuristic Techniques for Combinatorial Problems.* Oxford, England: Blackwell Scientific Publications.

Robinson, S. L. (1994, Feb.). "An Introduction to Visual Interactive Simulation in Business." *International Journal of Information Management,* Vol. 14, No. 1.

Rohrer, M. (1996, May/June). "Visualization and its Importance in Manufacturing Simulation." *Industrial Management,* Vol. 38, No. 3.

Saaty, T. L. (1995). *Decision Making for Leaders: The Analytic Hierarchy Process for Decisions in a Complex World,* Revised ed. Pittsburgh: RWS Publishers.

Saaty, T. L. (1996). *Decision Making for Leaders,* Vol. II. Pittsburgh: RWS Publishers.

Sim.TECH. (1996). *Sim.TECH Member Directory and Buyers' Guide.* Pittsburgh: Sim.TECH (Simulation Software Vendors Association).

Smith, J. Q. (1995, Oct.). "Handling Multiple Sources of Variation Using Influence Diagrams." *European Journal of Operational Research.*

Suh, C. K., E. H. Suh, and D. M. Lee. (1995, April). "Artificial Intelligence Approaches in Model Management Systems: A Survey." *Computers & Industrial Engineering,* Vol. 28, No. 2.

Sun, M., J. E. Aronson, P. G. McKeown, and D. Drinka. (1997). "A Tabu Search Heuristic Procedure for the Fixed Charge Transportation Problem." *European Journal of Operational Research,* in press.

Tavana, M., and S. Banerjee. (1995). "Strategic Assessment Model (SAM): A Multiple Criteria Decision Support System for Evaluation of Strategic Alternatives." *Decision Sciences,* Vol. 26, No. 1.

Thav, O. (1996, June). "Insights via Interactivity: The Right Simulation Package Furthers Corporate Goals." *Manufacturing Systems,* Vol. 14, No. 6.

Turban, E., and J. Meredith. (1994). *Fundamentals of Management Science,* 6th ed. Homewood, IL: Irwin.

van der Aalst, W. M. P. (1996, July). "Business Process Redesign: A Petri-net-based Approach." *Computers in Industry,* Vol. 29, Nos. 1,2.

Winston, W. L. (1996). *Simulation Modeling Using @Risk.* Belmont, CA: Wadsworth.

Winston, W. L., and S. C. Albright. (1996). *Practical Management Science: Spreadsheet Modeling and Applications.* Belmont, CA: Wadsworth.

Xu, X. Z., and G. R. Kaye. (1995). "Building Market Intelligence Systems for Environment Scanning." *Logistics Information Management,* Vol. 8, No. 2.

Zanakis, S. H., et al. (1989, June). "Heuristic Methods and Applications: A Categorized Survey." *European Journal of Operational Research.*

Module 4: Management of Data and Systems Development

Goal: To be able to appreciate the interrelationships between technical and managerial issues in the development of information systems in general, and database systems in particular.

Chapter 8: Database Management

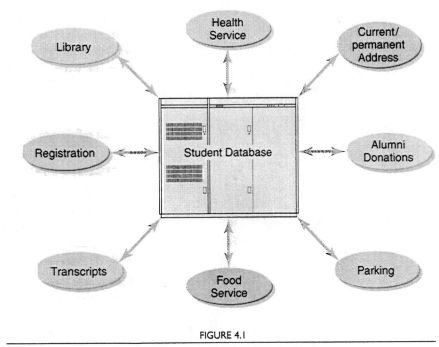

FIGURE 4.1

Types of information gathered in the student database.

Introduction

In the first three chapters of this book, we have learned about computers and their role in the workplace. In Chapters 2, "Information Systems Hardware," and 3, "Information Systems Software," we discussed computer hardware and software, but we did not discuss in detail how the computer stores and processes the information that is vital to the success of the firm. Databases and database management systems store this key information.

You may hear people in organizations refer to their information as mission-critical corporate data. They use and rely on their information every day. Whether this information is about customers, products, invoices, suppliers, markets, transactions, or competitors, an organization would be in dire straits without it. In large organizations, this information is stored in databases that can be billions (giga-) or trillions

(tera-) of bytes in size. If an organization lost this data, it would have difficulty pricing and selling its products or services, cutting payroll checks for its employees, and even sending out mail. To say that an organization's data is mission critical is not an overstatement.

After reading this chapter, you will be able to do the following:

1. Describe why databases have become so important to modern organizations.

2. Describe what database and database management systems are and how they work.

3. Explain four emerging database trends: client/server computing, object-oriented databases, data mining, and integrating Web applications.

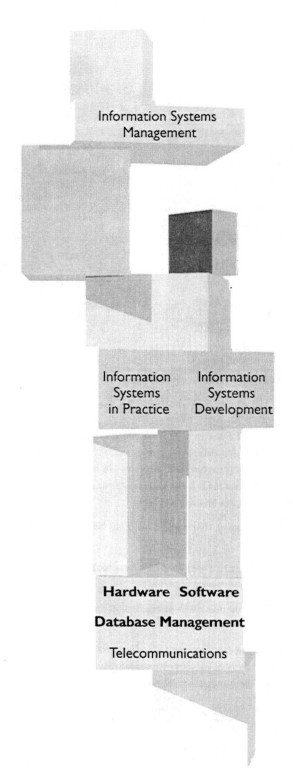

Information Systems
Management

Information
Systems
in Practice

Information
Systems
Development

Hardware Software

Database Management

Telecommunications

Information technologies, such as the ATM in the opening scenario of the last chapter, are playing an increasingly larger role in your lives. Given this increasing role, it will be useful to further your understanding of IS software. In terms of our guiding framework—The Big Picture—this is the third of four chapters focusing on the essential elements of information systems (see Figure 4.2). We begin by discussing the importance of information systems software to the success of modern organizations.

Database Management for Strategic Advantage

As we discussed in the introduction, an organization's **databases** are often their lifeblood. Let's think about why these databases, technology unknown to the business world 50 years ago, are so vital to organizations today.

Increasingly, we are living in an information age. Information once taken for granted or never collected at all is now used to make organizations more productive and competitive. Stock prices in the market, potential customers who meet our criteria for our products' target audience, and the credit rating of wholesalers and customers are all types of information—data that is organized and presented in a manner that makes it useful for us. Think about this book you are reading, which is in itself information. Also think about the other information sources used in its creation. The publishers had to know available authors capable of writing this book. The publishers also had to have information on you, the target audience, in order to determine that it was valuable to write this book and to suggest a writing style and collection of topics. Market information had to be used to set a price for the book, and information on reliable wholesalers and distribution partners had to be used to get the books from the publisher to you, the consumer.

FIGURE 4.2

The big picture: focusing on database management.

In addition to using databases to create this book, the publisher also uses databases to keep track of the book's sales, to determine royalties for the authors, to set salaries and wages for employees, to pay employees, to prospect for new book opportunities, to pay bills, and to perform nearly every other function in the business. For example, to determine royalties for authors on books sold, information must be collected from hundreds of bookstores and consolidated into a single report. Large publishers, such as Macmillan Computer Publishing, must regularly do this for thousands of books! Needless to say, the publisher could not effectively function without the use of computer databases.

Other types of organizations use databases to support their operations as well. Indeed, the process of using databases to create and sell this book are quite similar to the way other types of organizations use databases to create and sell their products. For example, the process of producing the Lands' End clothing catalog and marketing and selling their products to us is heavily database dependent. Companies such as Lands' End not only use databases to design and create their catalogs, but they also heavily depend on those databases containing information about us and our purchasing behavior. Some of these companies even produce tailor-made catalogs and other mailings for specific individuals based on the purchasing information stored in corporate databases.

NOVUS Financial

For a more specific example of the value of database systems, consider NOVUS Financial Corporation, a part of Dean Witter, Discover & Co. NOVUS offers a variety of consumer loans—everything from auto and boat loans to home mortgages. To stay ahead in today's competitive world of money lending, NOVUS realized it needed to make some changes in its information management systems. To be successful, NOVUS has to work fast, be flexible, and deliver the best customer service it can. The company's inflexible, outdated mainframe-based system made these goals impossible to achieve. To realign its information management systems for a better competitive advantage, NOVUS chose database products from Oracle Corporation.

In creating their new system, NOVUS wanted an environment that would satisfy customer service requests with one phone call. All of NOVUS's customer service functions are centralized in Sioux Falls, South Dakota, where more than 100 customer service professionals handle address changes and payment tracking. In the past, customer data was so spread out and inaccessible that follow-up calls to customers were inevitable. Users are delighted with the new database system's power and ease of use. Customer service representatives can access and share account information on a single screen without having to re-key the account number. NOVUS has also integrated all of their loan-related modules—customer, asset, vendor, and sales producer—so that all data is completely accessible across modules. This new database system has enabled NOVUS to improve customer service, improve the productivity of the customer service and developer staffs, reduce technology expenses, enable faster product time-to-market, and reduce paper flow. In other words, this database system is giving NOVUS a competitive advantage (see Oracle, 1998 for more on the success of NOVUS).

In a similar way, the fifth largest airline in America, U.S. Airways—with 2500 jet flights per day—is using an IBM database system to better manage its in-flight meal and video services. By analyzing upgrade, no-show, and cancellation patterns, U.S. Airways can more accurately predict how many meals are needed on each flight. Unused meals are a significant cost for airlines. Additionally, the database allows managers to understand which beverages are being carried but not being ordered. Like the food and beverages data, the number of headsets ordered for in-flight movies is also being analyzed and compared with the demographics of the passengers. Through this analysis, U.S. Airways is better able to provide movies that the majority of their customers really want to watch. When more passengers enjoy the in-flight movie, headset sales and customer satisfaction increase. Using this approach to managing their in-flight services, U.S. Airways paid for their investment in their database system within two months of use. Their long-term goal is to someday have a system that allows all customers to enjoy their favorite meal or drink and to be able to watch their favorite movie when flying U.S. Airways (for more information, see IBM, 1998).

As illustrated in these examples, database management systems have become an integral part of the total information systems solution for many organizations. Database management systems allow organizations to easily retrieve, store, and analyze information. Yet, it was not always this easy. Next, we describe how information was managed prior to computer-based database management systems.

Databases Before the Use of Computers

Think about what it would mean to have volumes of important information but to not have computers. All of the information mentioned in the previous examples needs to be collected, stored, analyzed, and updated, and it is easiest to do so using computers. If this book were priced using old manufacturing cost data written down several years ago, you would probably be very happy with the low price of your book, but the publisher would probably soon go out of business. If the list of wholesalers were stored on a blackboard that could be smudged or erased easily, you would find that it wouldn't be a very effective method over the long term. In order to manage data in the past, many people, lots of storage space, and painstaking care were needed. Data was kept in books, ledgers, card files, folders, and file cabinets—or sometimes simply in people's heads! Response times were long, and the process was labor intensive. Reported data was often incomplete or incorrect as a result.

Computers are used to automate much of the data processing done today. You can use computers to receive data electronically, store it, update it with new data feeds, and analyze numerical data using complex algorithms. Many uses for and analysis of data required in business today would have been impossible just a few years ago, particularly for large organizations with terabyte databases. Databases store the data, procedures are run against the database to analyze the data, and the data from them can be displayed as information. All of these tasks can be done relatively quickly and easily with the help of computers. Figure 4.3 highlights how computers help us store data efficiently.

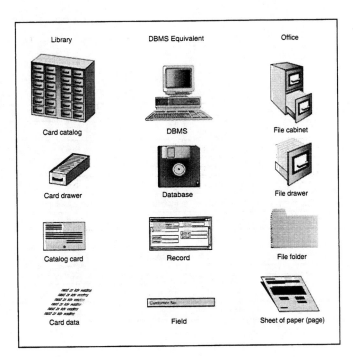

FIGURE 4.3

Computers make the process of storing and managing data much easier.

The Database Approach

To understand databases, we must familiarize ourselves with the terminology. In Figure 4.3, we compare some of the terminology with their equivalents in a library or a business office. Today, we use **database management systems** (DBMS) to interact with the data in databases. A DBMS is a software application with which you create, store, organize, and retrieve data from a single database or several databases. Microsoft Access is an example of a popular DBMS for personal computers. In the DBMS, such as Access, the individual database is a collection of related records and other files about entities. An **entity** is something you collect data about, such as people or classes (see Figure 4.4). We often think of entities as **tables**, where each row is a record and each column is a field. Each record consists of many **fields,** which are individual pieces of information. For example, a person's last name or social security number might be a field. A **record** is a collection of related fields within a single entity.

Before there were DBMSes, organizations used the file processing approach or another comparative approach to electronically store and manipulate data. Data was usually kept in a long, sequential computer file, which was often stored on tape. In addition, information about entities often appeared in several different places throughout the information system, and the data was often stored along with, and sometimes embedded within, the programming code that used the data. The concept of separately storing information about entities in nonredundant databases had not yet been envisioned, so files often had repetitive data about a customer, supplier, or another entity. When someone's address changed, it had to be changed in every file where that information occurred, an often tedious process. Similarly, if the programming code were changed, the corresponding data typically had to be changed along with it. This was often no better than the pen-and-paper approach to storing data.

Field Types

ID Number	Last Name	First Name	Street Address	City	State	Zip code	Major
209345	Vance	James	1242 N. Maple	Bloomington	Indiana	47401	Recreation
213009	Haggarty	Joe	3400 E. Longvi	Bloomington	Indiana	47405	Business Management
345987	Borden	Chris	367 Ridge Roa	Bloomington	Indiana	47405	Aeronautical Engineering
457838	Jessup	Mike	12 Long Lake	Bloomington	Indiana	47401	Computer Science
459987	Chan	Virginia	8009 Walnut	Bloomington	Indiana	47405	Sociology
466711	Monroe	Lisa	234 Jamie Lan	Bloomington	Indiana	47401	Pre-Medicine
512678	Austin	John	3837 Wood's E	Bloomington	Indiana	47401	Law
691112	Sherwin	Jordan	988 Woodbridg	Bloomington	Indiana	47404	Political Science
910234	Moore	Larry	1234 S. Grant	Bloomington	Indiana	47403	Civil Engineering
979776	Dunn	Pat	109 Hoosier Av	Bloomington	Indiana	47404	Psychology
983445	Pickett	Steve	989 College	Bloomington	Indiana	47401	Sports Science

Field

Record
(One Row)

FIGURE 4.4

This sample data table for the entity student includes eight fields and eleven records.

It is possible for a database to only consist of a single file or table. However, most non-trivial databases managed under a DBMS consist of several files, tables, or entities. The power and sophistication of the DBMS allow the tables to be joined, or linked, where there are similarities and to operate as a single database. A DBMS can manage hundreds, or even thousands, of tables simultaneously. These tables are linked as part of a single system. The value of the database approach is best evidenced with these large, complex sets of interrelated databases. The DBMS helps us manage the tremendous volume and complexity of interrelated data so that we can be sure that the change is automatically carried for every instance of that data if, for example, a student or customer address is changed. Such a change literally ripples out through all parts of the system where that data might occur. Using the DBMS prevents unnecessary and problematic redundancies of the data, and the data is kept separate from the programming code in applications. The database need not be changed if a change is made to the code in any of the applications. It is easy to see why the database approach now dominates nearly all of computer-based information systems used today.

Key Database Issues and Activities

In this section, we describe the database approach in more detail. We discuss the key issues and activities involved in the design, creation, use, and management of databases. We start by describing how people use databases, beginning with the entry of data.

Entering and Querying Data

Several tasks are performed using a database. Some of these tasks can be done by data entry clerks or managers; others require skilled database administrators and programmers. The general trend has been toward using DBMS software that is easy to use, enabling end users to create and manage their own database applications. At some point for all database applications, data must somehow be entered into the database.

Data gets into the database through data entry. A clerk or other data entry professional creates records in the database by entering data. This data may come from telephone conversations, preprinted forms that must be filled out, historical records, electronic files, or other means of getting data (see Figure 4.5A). Data entry is usually not performed by entering data into the database files as the computer sees them. Today, most applications enable us to use a *graphical user interface* (GUI) to create a **form**, which typically has blanks where the user can enter the information or make choices, each of which represents a field within a database record (see Figure 4.5B). This form presents the information to the user in an intuitive way so that the user can easily see and enter the data. The form might be online or printed, and the data could even be entered directly by the customer rather than by a data entry clerk. Forms can be used to add, modify, and delete data from the database.

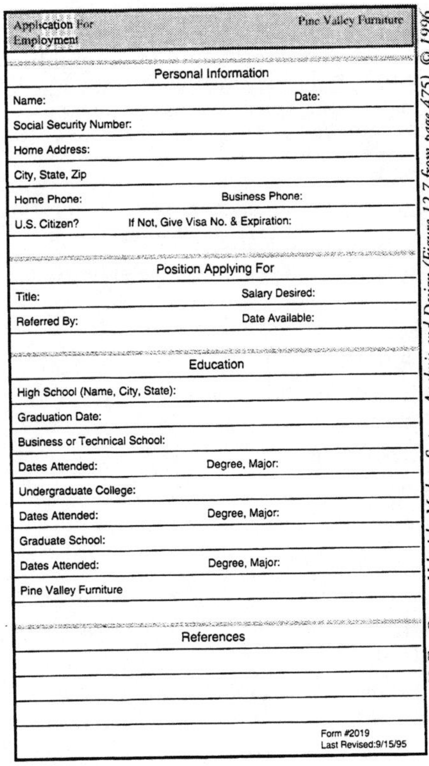

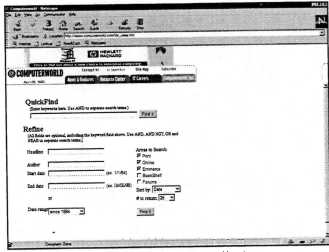

FIGURE 4.5A

Preprinted form.

Source Hoffer, George, Valacich, *Modern Systems Analysis and Design* (Figure 12.7 from page 475). © 1996 Benjamin/Cummings Publishing Company. Reprinted by permission of Addison Wesley Longman.

4.5B *Used by permission of* Computerworld *(www.computerworld.com)*

FIGURE 4.5B

Form A is an example of a preprinted form, while form B is an example of a computer-based entry form.

QBE easier than SQL

Querying the database is how we get information from it. To complete this task, we must have a way of interfacing with the database, usually through a form of query language. **Structured Query Language** (SQL) is the most common language used to interface with databases. Figure 4.6 is an example of a SQL statement used to find students who made an "A" in a particular course. These grades are sorted by student ID number.

```
SELECT DISTINCTROW STUDENT_ID, GRADE
FROM GRADES
WHERE GRADE = "A"
ORDER BY STUDENT_ID;
```

FIGURE 4.6

This sample SQL statement would be used to find students who earned an "A" in a particular course and to sort that information by student ID number.

Writing SQL statements requires a lot of time and practice, especially when dealing with complex databases with many entities or when writing complex queries with multiple integrated criteria—such as adding numbers while sorting on two different fields. Many DBMS packages have a simpler way of interfacing with the databases—using a concept called **query by example** (QBE). QBE capabilities in a database enable us to fill out a grid, or template, in order to construct a sample or description of the data we would like to see. Modern DBMS packages let us take advantage of the drag-and-drop features of a GUI to quickly and easily create a query. Conducting queries in this manner is much easier than typing the corresponding SQL commands. In Figure 4.7, we provide an example of the QBE grid from Microsoft's Access desktop DBMS package.

Screen shot reprinted by permission from Microsoft Corporation.

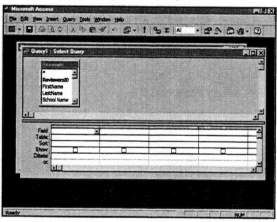

FIGURE 4.7

This screen capture from Microsoft Access shows the QBE grid that a user would fill out to describe the data he wants to see.

Creating Database Reports

In addition to ways to interactively query a database, most DBMS packages include a report writer feature. A **report** is a compilation of data from the database that is organized and produced in printed format. Reports are typically produced on paper, but they can be presented to users onscreen as well. Report writers, a special component accessed with the DBMS, are used to take data from the database to be manipulated (aggregated, transformed, or grouped) and displayed for the users in a useful format.

An example of a report is a quarterly sales report for a restaurant, as shown in Figure 4.8. Adding the daily sales totals, grouping them into quarterly totals, and displaying the results in a table of totals creates such a report. However, reports are not limited to text and numbers. Report writers enable us to create reports using any data in the databases at whatever level we choose. For example, we could add breakdowns of the data that show the average daily sales totals by days of the week to the restaurant report. Furthermore, this report could easily be improved by adding graphics. Perhaps we could show the quarterly sales totals in a bar chart. Each of these reports could be presented to the user either on paper or online. We could even create automatic links between the underlying sales data located in the database and the fields on the report in which the underlying data is used. In this way, the reports could be automatically updated every time they are produced.

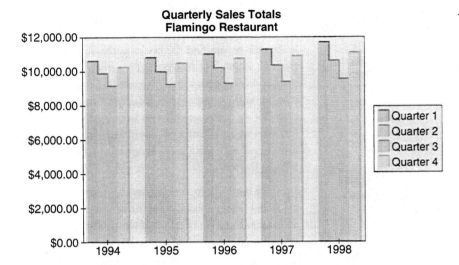

FIGURE 4.8

The quarterly sales report could either show text and numbers or a bar chart and could include the level of detail captured by the database data.

Book-of-the-Month Club

A BRIEF CASE

Database reports are making a big impact at the Book-of-the-Month Club (BOMC), the oldest and largest mail-order book club in the U.S., with more than 3.5 million members. Since its inception in 1926, the BOMC has shipped over 570 million books! Recently, the BOMC switched from a proprietary mainframe system to an Oracle database system. Using the new system, customer service representatives can be trained to use the system in about three days—versus 20 with the old system. Because the new system uses a database that can produce reports easily, the BOMC can analyze their data in ways never before possible. Reports are generated on the kinds of books being bought and the type of people ordering them. As a result, the BOMC has been able to fine-tune their acquisition strategy and marketing efforts. In addition to sophisticated analysis, the system provides customers who contact service representatives with very rapid response times. A customer's record can be recalled from the database in less than two seconds. Online reports provide complete information for the service representative, which helps to provide the best possible customer service. The Oracle database reporting environment is helping the company achieve its goal of becoming an unrivaled customer service organization—providing the books customers want with rapid response to questions. (For more information on BOMC, see Oracle, 1998).

Data Structure

The best database in the world is no better than the data it holds. Conversely, all the data in the world does you no good if it is not organized in a manner in which there are few or no redundancies and in which you can retrieve, analyze, and understand it. Therefore, the organizational database really has two parts, the data and the structure of that data.

two parts of database make it what it is → actual data + structure

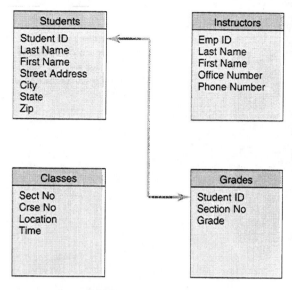

Students
- Student ID
- Last Name
- First Name
- Street Address
- City
- State
- Zip

Instructors
- Emp ID
- Last Name
- First Name
- Office Number
- Phone Number

Classes
- Sect No
- Crse No
- Location
- Time

Grades
- Student ID
- Section No
- Grade

Students

Student ID	Last Name	First Name
555-39-3232	Jones	Joe
289-42-8776	Carter	Billy

Grades

Student ID	Sect No	Grade
555-39-3232	3596	A
289-42-8776	5287	B
483-69-2294	5287	C+
862-21-9765	9876	A-

FIGURE 4.9

The attributes for and links among the four entities—students, instructors, classes, and grades.

entity → one particular piece or preview of info → for many diff. things (ex → instructors for all diff people)

Let's refer back to the library example in Figure 4.3 to better understand what the structure of data means. We know that we can find the books in the library based on the card catalog. The card catalog is a structure for finding the books. Each book has three cards, one each for the title, the author, and the subject. These classifications are a model, or representation, for the data in this system. Likewise, we must have a data model for databases. A **data model** is a representation of entities and their relationships in the real world.

Much of the work in creating an effective organizational database is in the modeling. If the model is no good, the database will not be effective. If the database is relatively small, the effects might not be so bad. However, in a corporate database, there are many entities, perhaps hundreds or thousands. In this case, the implications of a poor data model can be catastrophic. A poorly organized database is difficult to maintain and process—thus defeating the purpose of having a database management system in the first place. For example, think back to the scenario we used to open this chapter. We talked about the use of data at a school and mentioned several types of entities—students, instructors, classes, and grades. Each of these entities has attributes, which appear as fields in the database. Attributes of students might be their last names, first names, middle initials, and student ID numbers. Each of the other entities has attributes as well. Figure 4.9 shows attributes and links among four entities.

For the entity students, each student is represented as a record (or row) in the student table, and the attributes that describe each student appear as fields in each student record. The DBMS can sort an entity based on the information in a field. To do so, the field must be labeled as a *key*. The DBMS can sort that data in an ascending or descending order.

For the DBMS to distinguish between entities correctly, each instance of an entity must have one unique attribute. In our example, each student must be uniquely identified. A name alone will not work because students may have the exact same name. We must create and use a unique identifier in the database, which is called the **primary key**. For example, the student ID number is the primary key in the student table because no two students can have the same student ID number. The primary key can also be a combination of two or more attributes, called a combination primary key. An example of this might be the grades entity shown in Figure 4.9. The combination of student ID number and section number uniquely refers to an individual student and the semester she took the particular class because she may have taken the class more than once.

Data Type

Each field, or attribute, in the database needs to be of a certain type. For example, a field may contain text, numbers, or dates. This **data type** helps the DBMS organize and sort the data, complete calculations, and allocate storage space.

After the data model has been created, there needs to be a format for entering the data in the database. A **data dictionary** is a document—sometimes published as an online, interactive application—prepared by the designers of the database to aid individuals in data entry. The data dictionary explains several pieces of information for each attribute, such as the name of the field, whether or not it is a key or part of a key, the type of data expected in the field (dates, alphanumeric, numbers, and so on), and valid values for a field. Some data dictionaries include information such as why the data item is needed, how often it should be updated, and on which forms and reports the data appears.

One powerful use of data dictionaries is to enforce business rules. Business rules, such as who has authority to update a piece of data, are captured by the designers of the database and included in the data dictionary to prevent illegal or illogical entries from entering the database. For example, a validation check for a warehouse might be that the date the order was shipped could not be before the date the order was placed. The designers of the database for this business process would capture this rule in the data dictionary and prevent invalid ship dates from being entered into the database.

Database Management Systems Approaches

Now that we have discussed data, data models, and the storage of data, we need a mechanism for joining entities that have natural relationships with one another. For example, there are several relationships among the four entities we described previously—students, instructors, classes, and grades. Students are enrolled in classes. Likewise, instructors teach multiple classes and have many students in their classes in a semester. It is important to keep track of these relationships. We might, for example, want to know which courses a student is enrolled in so that we can notify her instructors that she will miss courses because of an illness. The three main DBMS approaches, or models, for keeping track of these relationships among data entities are hierarchical, network, and relational.

The Hierarchical Model

The **hierarchical database model** was the first model designed to join entities. DBMS packages that have followed this model refer to entities in a parent-child relationship. Records in parent entities can have many child records, but each child can have only one parent. Referring to our school example, a department (parent) can offer many courses (children), but each course belongs to only one department. This relationship, also called a *one-to-many relationship*, is very common in databases for organizations. However, forcing this parent-child relationship on data may be too restrictive and demanding for many databases. We sometimes also find pieces of data that have different relationships to each other, in which it is not always clear which is the parent and which is the child.

To better understand this problem, think back to our student example (see Figure 4.10). A student can be enrolled in many different courses at one time, and a course can have

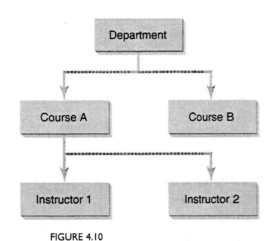

FIGURE 4.10

This hierarchical model depicts departments as parents of courses and courses as parents of instructors.

many different students enrolled at any one time. We do not necessarily have a one-to-many relationship here, and it is not clear which entity should be the parent and which should be the child. These types of problems can make the hierarchical model inadequate for many applications.

The Network Model

The network database model is much more flexible than the hierarchical model. With this model, there can be multiple children and parents. An example of this is a course with many sections (see Figure 4.11). Several different instructors could teach the sections of that course. One section of a course could even be team-taught by multiple instructors. Furthermore, the same instructor could teach multiple sections of a course and even more than one type of course. This relationship, also called a *many-to-many relationship*, is easier to represent with the network model than with the hierarchical model.

hierarchil →
one to many

network →
many to many

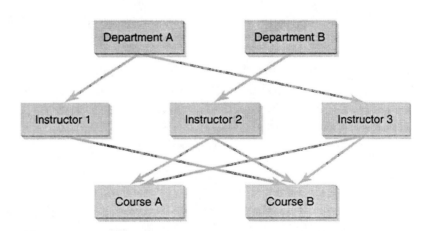

FIGURE 4.11

This network model depicts multiple parent-child relationships among entities.

The network model's flexibility is also its weakness. As the size and complexity of the databases in the organization become greater, so do the complexity and confusion in the model. In organizations with hundreds or thousands of entities, many of which have complex one-to-many and many-to-many relationships with one another, the network model quickly becomes too cumbersome for the database management system to manage effectively.

The Relational Model

The most common DBMS approach in use today is the relational database model. A DBMS package using this approach is often referred to as a relational DBMS, or RDBMS. With this approach, the DBMS views and presents entities as two-dimensional tables, with records as rows and fields as columns. Like a mathematical union operation, tables can be joined when there are common columns in the tables. The uniqueness of the primary key, as mentioned earlier, tells the DBMS which records should be joined with others in the corresponding tables. This structure supports very powerful data manipulation capabilities and linking of inter-related data. Database files in the relational model can be thought of as being three-dimensional in that a database has rows (one dimension), columns (a second dimension), and can contain a row of data in common with another file (a third dimension). This three-dimensional database is potentially much more powerful and useful than traditional, two-dimensional, "flat file" databases (see Figure 4.12).

A good relational database design eliminates unnecessary data duplications and is easier to maintain than a poor design, in which most of

Department Records

Department No	Dept Name	Location	Dean
Dept A			
Dept B			
Dept C			

Instructor Records

Instructor No	Inst Name	Title	Salary	Dept No
Inst 1				
Inst 2				
Inst 3				
Inst 4				

FIGURE 4.12

With the relational model, we represent these two entities, department and instructor, as two separate tables and capture the relationship between then with a common column in each table.

the effort is expended in correctly identifying the entities, their attributes, and the relationships between those entities. The relational DBMS supports one-to-many relationships, many-to-many relationships, and one-to-one relationships between entities. To design a database with clear, nonredundant relationships, you perform a process called normalization.

Normalization

To be effective, databases usually must be efficient. Developed in the 1970s, **normalization** is a technique to make complex databases more efficient and more easily handled by the DBMS (Date, 1990). To better understand the normalization process, let's return to the scenario in the beginning of this chapter. Think about your report card. It looks like nearly any other form or invoice. Your personal information is usually at the top, and each of your classes is listed, along with an instructor, a class day and time, the number of credit hours, and a location. Now think about how this data is stored in a database back at the school. Imagine that this database is organized so that in each row of the database, the student's identification number is listed on the far left. To the right of the student ID are the student's name, local address, major, and phone number. In addition, the row contains course and instructor information, as well as a final course grade (see Figure 4.13). Notice that there is redundant data for students, courses, and instructors in each row of this database. This redundancy means that this database is not well organized. If, for example, we want to change the phone number of an instructor who has hundreds of students, we have to change this number hundreds of times.

Student ID#	Student Name	Campus Address	Major	Phone	Course ID	Course Title	Instructor Name	Instructor Location	Instructor Phone	Term	Grade
A121	Joy Egbert	100 N. State Street	MIS	555-7771	MIS 350	Intro. MIS	Van Deventer	T240C	555-2222	F'98	A
A121	Joy Egbert	100 N. State Street	MIS	555-7771	MIS 372	Database	Hann	T240F	555-2224	F'98	B
A121	Joy Egbert	100 N. State Street	MIS	555-7771	MIS 375	Elec. Comm.	Chatterjee	T240D	555-2228	F'98	B+
A121	Joy Egbert	100 N. State Street	MIS	555-7771	MIS 448	Strategic MIS	Chatterjee	T240D	555-2228	F'98	A–
A121	Joy Egbert	100 N. State Street	MIS	555-7771	MIS 474	Telecomm	Gilson	T240E	555-2226	F'98	C+
A123	Larry Mueller	123 S. State Street	MIS	555-1235	MIS 350	Intro. MIS	Van Deventer	T240C	555-2222	F'98	A
A123	Larry Mueller	123 S. State Street	MIS	555-1235	MIS 372	Database	Hann	T240F	555-2224	F'98	B–
A123	Larry Mueller	123 S. State Street	MIS	555-1235	MIS 375	Elec. Comm.	Chatterjee	T240D	555-2228	F'98	A–
A123	Larry Mueller	123 S. State Street	MIS	555-1235	MIS 448	Strategic MIS	Chatterjee	T240D	555-2228	F'98	C+
A124	Mike Guon	125 S. Elm	MGT	555-2214	MIS 350	Intro. MIS	Van Deventer	T240C	555-2222	F'98	A–
A124	Mike Guon	125 S. Elm	MGT	555-2214	MIS 372	Database	Hann	T240F	555-2224	F'98	A–
A124	Mike Guon	125 S. Elm	MGT	555-2214	MIS 375	Elec. Comm.	Chatterjee	T240D	555-2228	F'98	B+
A124	Mike Guon	125 S. Elm	MGT	555-2214	MIS 474	Telecomm	Gilson	T240E	555-2226	F'98	B
A126	Jackie Judson	224 S. Sixth Street	MKT	555-1245	MIS 350	Intro. MIS	Van Deventer	T240C	555-2222	F'98	A
A126	Jackie Judson	224 S. Sixth Street	MKT	555-1245	MIS 372	Database	Hann	T240F	555-2224	F'98	B+
A126	Jackie Judson	224 S. Sixth Street	MKT	555-1245	MIS 375	Elec. Comm.	Chatterjee	T240D	555-2228	F'98	B+
A126	Jackie Judson	224 S. Sixth Street	MKT	555-1245	MIS 474	Telecomm	Gilson	T240E	555-2226	F'98	A–
...	...	...	...	...	...	...	...	...	...	...	...

FIGURE 4.13

Database of students, courses, instructors, and grades with redundant data.

Elimination of data redundancy is a major goal and benefit of using data normalization techniques. After the normalization process, the student data is organized into five separate tables (see Figure 4.14). This reorganization helps simplify the ongoing use and maintenance of the database and any associated analysis programs.

Student Table

Student ID#	Student Name	Campus Address	Major	Phone
A121	Joy Egbert	100 N. State Street	MIS	555-7771
A123	Larry Mueller	123 S. State Street	MIS	555-1235
A124	Mike Guon	125 S. Elm	MGT	555-2214
A126	Jackie Judson	224 S. Sixth Street	MKT	555-1245
...	...	...	...	...

Class Table

Course ID	Course Title
MIS 350	Intro. MIS
MIS 372	Database
MIS 375	Elec. Comm.
MIS 448	Strategic MIS
MIS 474	Telecomm
...	...

Teaching Assignment

Course ID	Term	Instructor Name
MIS 350	F'98	Van Deventer
MIS 372	F'98	Hann
MIS 375	F'98	Chatterjee
MIS 448	F'98	Chatterjee
MIS 474	F'98	Gilson
...	...	...

Instructor Table

Instructor Name	Instructor Location	Instructor Phone
Chatterjee	T240D	555-2228
Gilson	T240E	555-2226
Hann	T240F	555-2224
Valacich	T240D	555-2223
Van Deventer	T240C	555-2222

Enrolled Table

Student ID#	Course ID	Term	Grade
A121	MIS 350	F'98	A
A121	MIS 372	F'98	B
A121	MIS 375	F'98	B+
A121	MIS 448	F'98	A–
A121	MIS 474	F'98	C+
A123	MIS 350	F'98	A
A123	MIS 372	F'98	B–
A123	MIS 375	F'98	A–
A123	MIS 448	F'98	C+
A124	MIS 350	F'98	A–
A124	MIS 372	F'98	A–
A124	MIS 375	F'98	B+
A124	MIS 474	F'98	B
A126	MIS 350	F'98	A
A126	MIS 372	F'98	B+
A126	MIS 375	F'98	B+
A126	MIS 474	F'98	A–
...	...	...	...

FIGURE 4.14

Organization of information on students, courses, instructors, and grades after normalization.

Normalization →
elimination of
data redundency →
faster, more
efficient +
therefore more
effective

Associations

The associations, or relationships, among entities in our data structures help determine whether a database is well designed. The three types of associations among entities are one-to-one, one-to-many, and many-to-many. Table 4.1 summarizes each of these three associations and how they should be handled in database design.

Table 4.1 Rules for expressing associations among entities and their corresponding data structures.

Relationship	Example	Instructions
One-to-One	Each team has only one home stadium, and each home stadium has only one team.	Place the primary key from each table in the table for the other entity as a foreign key.
One-to-Many	Each player is on only one team, but each team has many players.	Place the primary key from the entity on the one side of the relationship as a foreign key in the table for the entity on the many side of the relationship.
Many-to-Many	Each player participates in games, and each game has many players.	Create a third entity/table and place the primary keys from each of the original entities together in the third table as a combination primary key.

To better understand how associations work, consider Figure 4.15, which shows four tables—Home Stadium, Team, Player, and Games—for keeping track of the information for a basketball league.

To obtain meaningful information from these tables, we must be able to create relationships between them. For example, the Home Stadium table lists the stadium name and capacity but not the city in which the stadium is located. Only through making an association with the Team table can we obtain this information. For example, if each team has only one home stadium, and each home stadium has only one team, we have a one-to-one relationship between the team and the home stadium entities. In situations in which we have one-to-one relationships between entities, we place the primary key from one table in the table for the other entity as a foreign key (see section A. in Figure 4.16). We can choose in which of these tables to place the foreign key of the other. After doing this to the team entity, we can identify which stadium is the home for a particular team.

Home Stadium

Stadium ID	Stadium Name	Capacity	...

Team

Team ID	Team Name	Location

Player

Player ID	Player Name	Position

Games

Team ID (1)	Team ID (2)	Date	Final Score

FIGURE 4.15

Associations keep track of the information for a basketball league.

When we find a one-to-many relationship—for example, each player plays for only one team, but each team has many players—we place the primary key from the entity on the one side of the relationship, the team entity, as a foreign key in the table for the entity on the many side of the relationship, the player entity (see section B. in Figure 4.16). In essence, we take from the one and give to the many, kind of a Robin Hood strategy. When we find a many-to-many relationship (for example, each player plays in many games, and each game has many players), we create a third, new entity—in this case, the Player Statistics entity and corresponding table. We then place the primary keys from each of the original entities together into the third, new table as a new, combination primary key (see section C. in Figure 4.16).

A. One-to-one relationship: Each team has only one home stadium, and each home stadium has only one team.

Team

Team ID	Team Name	Location	Stadium ID

B. One-to-many relationship: Each player is on only one team, but each team has many players.

Player

Player ID	Player Name	Position	Team ID

C. Many-to-many relationship: Each player participates in many games, and each game has many players.

Player Statistics

Team 1	Team 2	Date	Player ID	Points	Minutes	Fouls

FIGURE 4.16

Tables used for storing information about several basketball teams, with fields added in order to make associations.

You may have noticed that by placing the primary key from one entity in the table of another entity, we are creating a bit of redundancy. We are repeating the data in different places. We're willing to live with this bit of redundancy, however, because it enables us to keep track of the inter-relationships among the many pieces of important organizational data that are stored in different databases. By keeping track of these relationships, we can quickly answer questions such as, "Which players on the SuperSonics played in the game on February 16 and scored more than 10 points?" In a business setting, the question might be, "Which customers purchased the 1998 forest green Ford Explorer XLTs with four-wheel-drives from Thom Roberts at the Roberts' Ford dealership in Bloomington, Indiana during the first quarter of 1998, and how much did each of them pay?" This kind of question would be useful in calculating the bonus money Thom should receive for that quarter or in recalling those specific vehicles in the event of a recall by the manufacturer.

You now have an understanding of the importance of creating simple, clear data structures for your database. If you decide to take more information systems courses, you will likely have opportunities to learn more about these concepts and techniques. For now, you know the basics that will help you understand the databases you will use in your career.

Recent Developments Affecting Database Design and Use

As is true for all computing and information systems, there are constantly new developments that have important implications for how we design, create, use, and manage databases in organizations. For example, the move to relational DBMS packages and the development of powerful personal computer-based DMBS packages fundamentally changed the way databases are used and enabled many more people to build them. In the next section, we discuss four more recent developments: client/server computing, object-oriented databases, data mining, and Web links to organizational databases.

Databases and Client/Server Computing

Database applications in organizations have become so large and complex and serve so many different purposes and people that they sometimes do not run efficiently on any one computer. **Client/server architecture** was designed to help solve this problem. In a client/server architecture, the application is divided into two parts (see Figure 4.17). The database itself resides on a powerful computer, called a **database server**. The programs used to manipulate the database reside on a user's desktop computer, called a client. In other words, you can retrieve data from the server by running an application at your desktop computer. This client application usually consists of forms, reports, and other visual tools to aid you in modifying data in the database and in displaying it onscreen or in a printout. Table 4.3 highlights popular DBMS packages.

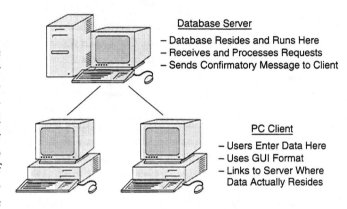

Database Server
- Database Resides and Runs Here
- Receives and Processes Requests
- Sends Confirmatory Message to Client

PC Client
- Users Enter Data Here
- Uses GUI Format
- Links to Server Where Data Actually Resides

FIGURE 4.17

With the client/server approach to databases, the data actually resides on a server, while users enter data and perform other database functions from their own client computers.

Table 4.2 Some popular DBMS packages.

Desktop	Midrange	Mainframe
Access	SQL Server	Informix
Paradox	Rdb	Oracle
Approach	RMS	Sybase
dBASE	CA-Ingres	DB2

Object-Oriented Databases

Some databases have begun to embrace the object-oriented design techniques used in programming. For many of the same reasons that object-oriented programming is popular, **object-oriented databases** (OODBs) are becoming popular. OODBs treat tables, queries, and other components as generic, reusable objects that can be mixed and matched and used in many different applications (Norman, 1996). Modularity and the opportunity for relatively quick and easy reuse of objects is appealing to organizations investing a great deal of time and money into their databases. Fortunately, for the most part, the OO languages, such as C++ or Smalltalk, carry over easily to OODBs.

OODBs are not meant to replace the relational data model; the paradigm used in OODBs supports the relational model. Objects can relate to objects much as entities relate to entities. Using OODBs is better than using the relational model, however, because OODBs can handle complex, user-defined data types. Recall the data types supported by the relational model; they are limited to text, floating-point numbers, integers, and dates. OODBs also support the encapsulation of both data and the methods used to manipulate the data, whereas the models we discussed earlier separate the data from the procedures used to act upon them. Objects can also inherit data and methods from other objects, something not possible in traditional database designs.

While many popular database management systems have object-oriented characteristics, full-fledged OODBs are still somewhat experimental. OODB vendors are primarily small start-up companies that have yet to gain a large amount of market share. Examples of OODBMs on the market today include Illustra, MATISSE, and Total ORDB. For any OODB to be successful, it must be compatible with SQL. SQL has been the standard for data manipulation since the 1970s. Any technology that requires programmers to learn a completely different way of interacting with it will have difficulty gaining acceptance. As it is, object-orientation is so different from traditional ways of writing software that it is difficult to get developers to embrace the technology. Although there are many perceived advantages of OODBs, there are also still very few success stories related to them. The theoretical foundation is exciting, but not yet widely accepted, unlike the relational model.

Data Mining

To support more effective information management, many large organizations are using **data mining**. This is a method used by large firms to sort and analyze information to better understand their customers, products, markets, or any other phase of their business for which data has been captured. With data mining tools, you can graphically drill down from summary data to more detailed data, sort or extract data based on certain conditions, and perform a variety of statistical analyses, such as trend analysis, correlation analysis, forecasting, and analysis of variance. Data mining is also referred to as online analytical processing (OLAP). It is very closely related to the IS academic research area, decision support systems (see Chapter 7, "Organizational Information Systems"). Some of the software tools for data mining include ProBit and Pilot Software's Decision Support Suite. Sales of software, hardware, and services for data mining are expected to grow from $2 billion in 1995 to $8 billion in 1998 (Foley, 1996). In order to effectively mine data, special types of databases, called data warehouses and data marts, are created.

Data Warehouses

Many large organizations are building **data warehouses**, which integrate multiple, large databases and other information sources into a single repository. This repository is suitable for direct querying, analysis, or processing. Much like a physical warehouse for products and components, the data warehouse involves the physical storage and distribution of data on computer-based information systems. The data warehouse appears to the user as a virtual storehouse of valuable data from the organization's disparate information systems and, perhaps, from other external sources. It supports the online analysis of sales, inventory, and other vital business data that has been culled from operational systems. The purpose is to put key business information into the hands of more decision makers, and the driving force is the need for data access. Table 4.3 lists some sample industry uses of data warehouses. Data warehouses can involve hundreds of gigabytes, even terabytes, of data. They usually run on fairly powerful mainframe computers, and can cost millions of dollars.

Data warehouses represent more than just big databases. An organization that successfully deploys a data warehouse has committed to pulling together, integrating, and sharing critical corporate data throughout the firm.

Table 4.3 Sample industry uses of data warehousing (adapted from: Boar, 1998).

Uses of Data Warehousing	Representative Companies
Retail	
Analysis of scanner check-out data	Wal-Mart
Tracking, analysis, and tuning of	Kmart
sales promotions and coupons	Sears
Inventory analysis and redeployment	Osco/Savon Drugs
Price reduction modeling to "move"	Casino Supermarkets
the product	W. H. Smith Books
Negotiating leverage with suppliers	Otto Versand Mail Order
Frequent buyer program management	
Profitability analysis	
Product selections for granular	
market segmentation	
Telecommunications	
Analysis of the following:	AT&T
Call volumes	Ameritech
Equipment sales	Belgacom
Customer profitability	British Telecom
Costs	Telestra Australia
Inventory	Telecom Ireland
Purchasing leverage with suppliers	Telecom Italia
Frequent buyer program management	
Banking and Finance	
Relationship banking	Bank of America
Cross-segment marketing	Bank One
Risk and credit analysis	Merrill Lynch
Merger and acquisition analysis	CBOE
Customer profiles	CNA
Branch performance	

Source Copyright © 1998, NCR Corporation. Used with permission.

Data Marts

Rather than storing all enterprise data in one monolithic database, many organizations have created multiple **data marts,** each containing a subset of the data for a single aspect of a company's business—for example, finance, inventory, or personnel. Data marts have been popular among small and medium-sized businesses and among departments

272

within larger organizations, all of which were previously prohibited from developing their own data warehouses due to the high costs involved.

Data marts typically contain tens of gigabytes of data, as opposed to the hundreds of gigabytes in data warehouses. Therefore, they can be deployed on less powerful hardware with smaller disks. The differences in costs between different types of data marts and data warehouses can be significant. The cost to develop a data mart is typically less than $1 million, while the cost for a distributed data mart can approach $10 million. The cost for an enterprise-wide data warehouse can exceed $10 million (Foley & DePompa, 1996). With this amount of money on the table, the data mart business is heating up. For example, Informatica, which bills itself as "the enterprise data mart company," estimates that data mart software sales will grow 351 percent between 1995 and 1998, from $153 million to $690 million. Companies such as Computer Associates, NCR Corp., Sybase, Software AG, Red Brick Systems, and others are coming out with new products and services that make it easier and cheaper to deploy these scaled-down data warehouses.

Many organizations that cannot afford a data warehouse first built themselves a data mart. This may not be an optimal decision. Some experts believe that users should create enterprise data warehouses first and then build data marts as highly summarized subsets of the warehouse. These experts believe that doing so helps keep the data clean and nonredundant, which helps maintain its integrity. In any event, large organizations often deploy a data warehouse and multiple data marts. For example, Merck-Medco Managed Care Inc., a subsidiary of Merck & Co. in Montvale, New Jersey, runs both a 500-GB data warehouse and six smaller data marts.

Linking Web Site Applications to Organizational Databases

A recent database development is the use of databases to create links between sites on the Web to organizational databases. For example, many companies are enabling users of their Web site to view product catalogs, check inventory, and place orders—all actions that ultimately read and write to the organizations' databases.

The applications on the Web site are created using Hypertext Markup Language (HTML) editors and other Web development tools, such as SoftQuad HotMeTaL, Netscape LiveWire Pro, and Microsoft FrontPage. They are managed with Web server software, such as NCSA HTTPd, Netscape Commerce Server, and Microsoft Internet Information Server. Using these tools, it is easy to create interactive forms that users can access on the Web. These forms pass data from the form to the database, and vice versa. To shuttle data, queries, and other information back and forth between Web applications and databases, developers create common gateway interface (CGI) scripts in PERL, Microsoft VBScript, or programming languages, such as C (Hermann, 1996). The databases are created using standard DBMS packages, such as Microsoft Access or Oracle, and they can be housed on nearly any hardware platform.

This evolution in computing provides users with easy, fast access to an organization's processes and data. Many companies are using Web-based interfaces to databases in order to greatly improve customer service. We will talk more in Chapter 8, "Emerging Information Systems," about the implications of using such technologies to improve customer contact. As you might expect, security is critical with applications like this. Any time you let people or data into critical organizational databases, you must ensure the safety and integrity of those databases. Organizations that link Web sites to back-end databases are careful to use _firewall_ applications, which act much like physical firewalls in monitoring the kinds of data traffic that are passed back and forth and in blocking unwanted data traffic.

CNN Interactive

An example of successfully linking a large corporate database with a Web interface can be found at CNN Interactive. CNN Interactive provides a free, online custom news service to hundreds of thousands of subscribers around the world. Using the World Wide Web, the site delivers up-to-the-minute news from over 100 sources and offers more than 2,000 categories of customized news options, ranging from sports and health to recreation, pop culture, crime, and consumer issues. On a typical week, 20,000 new articles are stored. CNN Interactive uses an Oracle database to dynamically build personalized news pages for hundreds of thousands of daily users. These pages are updated every 15 minutes to deliver the most current information. This application is only made possible by the sophisticated database system, which manages the vast amount of changing information and automatically builds the customized Web pages (for more information, see Oracle, 1998).

Effective Management of Databases

We've come full circle in this chapter. We first explained why databases are so important to organizations and then described how databases are developed and used. We can now talk more about how organizational databases can be managed effectively. Of the many roles taken in managing organizational databases, none is more important than that of the **database administrator** (DBA). The DBA is responsible for the development and management of the organization's databases. The DBA works with the _systems analysts_ (described in great detail in later chapters), programmers, and data modelers to design and implement the database.

Along with these technical tasks, the DBA must also work with users and managers of the firm on more managerial and organizational issues relating to the database. For example, the DBA must properly implement the relevant business rules and validity checks on the database data, as set forth by managers. The DBA is also responsible for implementing some security features, such as designating who can look at the database and who is authorized to make changes. The DBA should not make these decisions unilaterally; rather, these are business decisions made by organizational managers that the DBA merely implements.

In a later chapter, you learn more about the systems analysis and design process. For now, you should know that the process of database development for an organization can be very complex. It usually involves a team of systems personnel, users of the database, and managers. Together, they determine the form and function of the database. In some organizations, the DBA is a specific job, while in others, people with other job titles perform DBA functions. Although you may not find someone with the DBA title, you can be sure that someone is fulfilling the DBA functions—either formally or informally—if the organization is using computer databases well.

ETHICAL PERSPECTIVE: DATABASE PROPRIETORSHIP AND INFORMATION OWNERSHIP

It happens to all of us. Nearly every day in the mail, we receive unwanted solicitations from credit card companies, department stores, magazines, or charitable organizations. Many of these envelopes are never opened. We ask the same question over and over again: "How did I get on another mailing list?" Your name, address, and other personal information were most likely sold from one company to another for use in mass mailings. You probably did not give anyone permission to buy or sell information about you, but that is not a legal issue, or a matter of concern, for some firms.

Who owns the computerized information about people—the information that is stored in thousands of databases by retailers, credit card companies, and marketing research companies? The answer is that the company that maintains the database of customers/subscribers legally owns the information and is free to sell it. Your name, address, and other information are all legally kept in a company database to be used for the company's future mailings and solicitations. However, the company can sell its customer list or parts of it to other companies who want to do similar mailings. This is where the problems begin. For instance, LL Bean, the outdoor and apparel retailer, can sell names and addresses from its customer database to companies looking for a similar customer base or buying pattern. Of course, LL Bean would not sell parts of their list to competitors. The list is to be used only once and can be used again only with repayment of the initial fee. Still, many people are concerned that these companies have full ownership of this purchasing and demographic data.

There are limits, however, to what a company can do with such data. For example, if a company stated at one time that its collection of marketing data, including demographic (who am I and where do I live) and psychographic (what are my tastes and preferences) data, was to be used strictly internally as a gauge of its own customer base and then sold that data to a second company years later, would be unethically and illegally breaking their original promise.

Companies collect data from credit card purchases (by using a credit card, you indirectly allow this) or from surveys and questionnaires, which obtain demographic and psychographic data. By filling in a survey at a bar, restaurant, supermarket, or mall, you are implicitly agreeing that this data can be used as the company wishes (within legal limits, of course).

What is even more problematic is the combination of this survey data with transaction data from your credit card purchases. How do you know who is accessing these databases? This is an issue that each company must address at both a strategic/ethical level (is this something that we should be doing?) and at a tactical level (if we do this, what can we do to ensure the security and integrity of the data?). The company needs to ensure proper hiring, training, and supervision of employees who have access to the data, as well as to implement the necessary software and hardware security safeguards.

Do you want to stop receiving junk mail? To have your name added to the Direct Marketing Association (DMA) Pander File—the list of names that are never to be included in junk mailings or database selling—write to the Direct Marketing Association, Mail Preference Service, PO Box 9008, Farmingdale, New York, 11735-9008. Provide your name and address, and you should notice a reduction after about 90 days. For more information, you may call the DMA at 1-212-768-7277 during regular business hours.

Questions for Discussion

1. Is having your name included on the Pander File enough? Should other legal measures be taken to ensure the confidentiality of information about us? Why or why not?

2. What other ethical issues concerning property and information ownership have you heard about or encountered?

3. Right now, there are no laws or FTC regulations concerning the use of names on company databases. The DMA is a self-regulated group with its own policies. Does this make you feel any less comfortable about the use of your name and information?

INTERNATIONAL PERSPECTIVE: INFORMATION AND ECONOMIC POVERTY—GLOBAL HAVES AND HAVE NOTS

Today, the Internet enables us to tap into vast and varied stores of information around the globe. Unfortunately, not everyone around the world has equal access to these global data stores. Just as there have been economic haves and have nots, in this wired world, there are those who now live in information poverty.

In mid-1995, about 70 percent of all computers (single and multi-user) connected to the Internet worldwide were located in the U.S. (Holderness, 1995). Holderness contrasts that statistic with a statistic from this past April, when Vietnamese academics announced the first dozen text-only connections in the country. In many countries, the possibility of Internet access does not mean that there are users who are able and technology that is capable of taking the opportunity. While the Internet reaches into well over 100 countries now, nearly half the world's population is without telephones and, thus, has no Internet access.

Internet users in some developing countries spend up to 25 times what those in the U.S. spend to make connections that are not only slower and more precarious, but also do not have advanced capabilities, such as graphics and sound. This trend seems to be leading not only to information poverty in some parts of the world, but to increasing economic poverty, as the developing countries—rich in natural resources—are excluded de facto from world trade and world information.

Holderness implies that access to and the instant transfer of data will change commerce and the way that humans communicate. It seems that it is already doing so. Kaljee (online) notes that "Clearly the technological revolution that took place once the benefits of access to the Internet became clear to the general public has been limited to the developed countries only." (See http://www.sas.upenn.edu/African_Studies/ASA/Marcel_Kaljee.html) He claims that the move away from using the Internet for mostly personal email and research to major advertising campaigns and other focused marketing is creating new markets, from which the developing countries are excluded. The factors that excluded developing countries from global trade in the past—trade restrictions and lack of physical infrastructure, such as roads—are not major hindrances on the information superhighway. Now that the Internet is attracting such a large number of consumers and businesses worldwide, people in these developing countries need to get connected.

Kaljee notes that the Internet systems that do exist in these developing countries are antiquated by U.S. standards. Mobile telecommunications exist in some developing countries. Packet radio networks, which can be used to broadcast packets of data via radio waves, reach into some areas that are without phone lines (and where phones will not be feasible for quite some time). Satellite telecommunications are employed in some areas, but mostly for broadcast—and then not to the rural areas. ISDN (Integrated Services Digital Network) phone lines have been introduced in only a few areas.

Developed countries should assist developing countries in gaining greater access to the Internet for many reasons. Holderness (1995) suggests that the poorer countries are not receiving such help for the same reasons that they should. He claims that access in developing countries could help the problem of "brain drain" there; outstanding academics could be recognized as part of a borderless Internet-based academe without having to travel to the U.S. or the U.K. He also notes that the lack of information access makes countries in the Southern Hemisphere even more dependent on those in the North and increases the distance between information haves and have nots, not only on a global scale, but within countries as well. In times when information is money, access to information seems closely guarded by those who have it.

An economic system seems to be developing in accessing global information sources, such as the Internet. How this system will shape the future of the global economy is purely speculative, but perhaps some balance can eventually be reached by the time that the currency is solely informational and the infrastructure is purely technology based.

Questions for Discussion

1. Who should be initiating and funding the development of IS in developing countries? Why?

2. Predict what the world will look like in 50 years if the information gap continues to increase.

3. In your opinion, what is likely to happen with respect to developing countries going online? In what kind of time frame?

Sources Holderness, M. 1995. *Falling through the net. New Statesman and Society* 8 (Oct. 13): 24. Kaljee, M. Feeder. *Roads close the information gap: low cost public e-mail systems for access to the information highway.* Available online at http://www.sas.upenn.edu/African_Studies/ASA/Marcel_Kaljee.html.

Talking with...

Marty Schick, Senior Database Analyst at Indiana University

Educational Background

B.A. in History, Rollins College; M.B.A., Butler University

Job Description

Marty Schick is primarily responsible for the maintenance and support of all DB2 databases that are used to support Indiana University's administrative needs. She also has the primary responsibility for data modeling activities performed by the Database Administration Team. She has secondary responsibility for Sybase Databases, which exist on a variety of UNIX platforms. Sybase Databases are used in support of the university's administrative systems.

Critical Success Factors

A key factor to success in the information systems world today is to develop a good customer service orientation. Customers can be clients from an external department that you support, co-workers, or fellow team members. Time management is also a crucial factor in succeeding in the information systems world. Identifying and prioritizing tasks ensures that the most value is received for time invested. Another critical success factor is to be flexible. The information systems world is changing on a daily basis. You must be willing to learn new technologies to keep pace with the environment.

Advice to Students

Pursue a well-rounded education. By being exposed to many different aspects of the business and technical world, you can learn how businesses function, as well as how to be a provider of information technology services. Understanding the functionality of businesses is critical to providing quality information services.

Summary

1. **Describe why databases have become so important to modern organizations.** Databases often house mission-critical organizational data, so proper design and management of the databases is critical. If designed and managed well, the databases can be used to transform raw data into information that helps people do their jobs faster, cheaper, and better, which ultimately helps customers and makes the firm more competitive.

2. **Describe what database and database management systems are and how they work.** A database is a collection of related data organized in a way that facilitates data searches. A database contains entities, fields, records, and tables. Entities are things about which we collect data, such as people, courses, customers, or products. Fields are the individual pieces of information about an entity, such as a person's last name or social security number, that are stored in a database cell. A record is the collection of related fields about an entity; usually, a record is displayed as a database row. A table is a collection of related records about an entity type; each row in the table is a record and each column is a field. A database management system is a software application with which you create, store, organize, and retrieve data from a single database or several databases. Data is typically entered into a database through the use of a specially formatted form. Data is retrieved from a database through the use of queries and reports. The data within a database must be

adequately organized so that it is possible to effectively store and retrieve information. The three main approaches to structuring the relationships among data entities are the hierarchical database model, the networked database model, and the relational database model. The most widely used approach today is the relational database model.

3. **Explain four emerging database trends: client/server computing, object-oriented databases, data mining, and integrating Web applications with organizational databases.** Client/server database environments allow large and complex database systems to be divided into two parts. The database itself resides on a powerful computer, called a database server. The programs used to manipulate the database reside on a user's desktop computer, called a client. Object-oriented databases (OODBs) treat tables, queries, and other components as generic, reusable objects that can be mixed and matched and used in many different applications. OODBs are not meant to replace the relational data model, but to support and extend the relational model by allowing the storage of more complex, user-defined data types, such as sound and video. Objects within an OODB can also inherit data and methods from other objects, something not possible in traditional database designs. Data mining is a popular application of database technologies in which information stored in organizational databases, data warehouses, or data marts is sorted and analyzed to improve organizational decision making and performance. A data warehouse is the integration of multiple, large databases and other information sources into a single repository or access point that is suitable for direct querying, analysis, or processing. A data mart is a small-scale data warehouse that contains a subset of the data for a single aspect of a company's business—for example, finance, inventory, or personnel.

Many organizations are allowing employees and customers to access corporate databases management systems via the World Wide Web. These capabilities are allowing greater flexibility and innovative products and services.

Key Terms

Databases	Query by example	Normalization
Database management systems	Report	Client/server architecture
Entity	Data model	Database server
Tables	Primary key	Object-oriented databases
Fields	Data type	Data mining
Record	Data dictionary	Data warehouses
Form	Hierarchical database model	Data marts
Querying	Network database model	Database administrator
Structured Query Language (SQL)	Relational database model	

Review Questions

1. Explain the difference between a database and a database management system.

2. List some reasons why record keeping with physical filing systems is less efficient than using a database on a computer.

3. Describe the relationship among the following terms: entity, field, record, and table.

4. Describe the key, combination key, and primary key within an entity.

5. How do SQL and query by example relate to each other?

6. Describe the differences in the use of parent and child designations in the hierarchical and network DBMS models.

7. What is the purpose of normalization?

8. In a client/server architecture, what aspect of the database has been separated from the data itself (that is, what aspects of the database are on the client and what aspects are on the server)?

9. Describe from a business standpoint some of the potential opportunities for combining database applications with the World Wide Web.

Problems and Exercises

◆ **Individual**   ◆ **Group**   ☞ **Field**   ◐ **Web/Internet**

◆ 1. Match the following terms to the appropriate definitions:

____ Database

____ Database management system

____ Field

____ Query by example

____ Network model

____ Relational model

____ Client/server architecture

____ Database server

a. Individual pieces of information about an entity, such as a person's last name or social security number, which are stored in a database cell

b. The part of a client/server database system running on a server that provides database storage and access to client workstations

c. A collection of related data organized in a way that facilitates data searches

d. A DBMS approach in which entities can have multiple parent-child relationships

e. A software application with which you can create, store, organize, and retrieve data for one or many databases

f. A distributed processing system in which a client application that needs data or software gets it from a server that is a source for some or all of the needed data or software

g. The capability of a DBMS to enable us to request data by simply providing a sample or a description of the types of data we would like to see

h. A DBMS approach in which entities are presented as two-dimensional tables that can be joined together with common columns

2. Imagine that a fellow student has seen an announcement for a job as a database administrator for a large corporation, but is unclear about what this title means. Please explain to your friend in very clear wording the role of a database administrator.

3. How and why are organizations without extensive databases falling behind in competitiveness and growth? Is this simply a database problem that can be fixed easily with some software purchases? In a small group, search the World Wide Web for stories or news articles that deal with the issue of staying competitive by successfully managing data. How are these stories similar to each other? How are they different? Prepare a 10-minute presentation to the class on your findings.

4. In a group of classmates, discuss the implications that the current downsizing, reorganizing, and redefining of organizations and their functions may have for the employees previously responsible for managing the extensive filing systems within their organizations. Would their computer literacy make a difference? Does everyone in the group agree? Why or why not?

5. Why would it matter what data type is used for the fields within a database? How does this relate to programming? How does this relate to queries and calculations? Does the size of the database matter?

6. Discuss the issue of data accuracy, based on what you have learned from the chapter. Does a relational model handle accuracy issues any better than a hierarchical or network model? Does a computer database handle accuracy issues better than a filing system? Who (or what) is ultimately responsible for data accuracy?

7. As a group, argue for and against the following statement: Using a database is faster than manually searching for information. Provide clear reasons and/or examples for your arguments. What conclusions can you draw from this discussion?

8. Have several classmates interview a database administrator within an organization with which they are familiar. To whom does this person report? How many employees report to this person? Is there a big variance in the responsibilities across organizations? Why or why not?

9. Consider an organization with which you are familiar. Describe the organization's approach to database management. What job positions exist to handle these responsibilities? Is there a database administrator? How long has the current database (or set of databases) been in effect?

10. Interview an IS Manager within an organization with which you are familiar. Determine what types of databases are currently in use (hierarchical, network, or relational). What are these databases used for (that is, what type of data do they store)? Who uses the databases and how do they use them (for queries, reports, and so on)?

11. Based on your understanding of a primary key and the following sample grades table, determine the primary key field(s) that would best satisfy all the necessary requirements.

STUDENT ID	COURSE	GRADE
100013	Visual Programming	A-
000117	Telesystems	A
000117	Introduction to MIS	A

12. Based on your previous work and/or professional experiences, describe your experiences with database systems. Were they relational databases or another type? Discuss your experiences with other classmates. What role did you play in utilizing the database and the data within it? How are the experiences of your classmates different?

13. Search the World Wide Web for an organization's home page that utilizes a link between the home page and their own database. Describe the data that the browser enters and the possible uses for this data within the organization. Can you retrieve company information, or can you only send information to the company? How is the data displayed on the home page?

14. Select an organization with which you are familiar that utilizes "flat file" databases for their database management. Determine whether they should move to a relational database. Why would you make this recommendation? Is it feasible to do so? Why or why not?

15. Discuss the following in a small group. Using the scenario outlined at the beginning of this chapter, consider how you have dealt with the database(s) at your educational institution. Have you filled out a lot of paperwork that was then entered by someone else? Did you actually do some of the data entry for your account? What kind of information were you able to retrieve about your account? From where was the database administered? Were you able to access it online?

Real World Case Problems

1. Anatomy of a Failure: The Inside Story of a Fatally Flawed Data Warehouse Project

In 1995 the CEO of a company we'll name Close Call Corporation was playing golf with a software vendor. Close Call's CEO knew he needed to make drastic technology changes to transform his business and that these changes needed to be made quickly. Beginning with $200 in the 1970s, his teleservices company was now worth over $100 million. He was intent on selecting the most direct path to get the double-digit growth he wanted when the vendor offered advice.

Close Call's telemarketing and catalog sales business units had been operating totally independently. The company had gone public, and the rapid growth was putting pressure on its old proprietary system. The vendor convinced the CEO that a data warehouse could be up and running in four months and would provide a unified solution for the business units.

With 1996 reporting to be a pennant year, the timing couldn't have been more disastrous. Not only did the company expand from 6 to 116 call centers, but it also implemented new, open switching systems in new centers for automatic dialing and call routing and needed to update the internal management system for human resources and internal audit. The CEO assured everyone 1996 would be memorable—but unfortunately, it was not memorable for the reasons he had hoped.

The positive culture was a thing of the past. The CEO believed all he had to do was hire the right consultant. This time he faced an IS staff already stretched to the limit. The CEO set deadlines and a budget before the project team was on board. Then five consultants with experience were hired. Inside the organization, the users didn't understand the analytical environment, and therefore, didn't know what they were missing that could have helped them with their job. They saw no value in the new system. The lack of demand for this system foretold the outcome of the users' effort and commitment. The scope of the project became scaled down to a pilot, and the time frame was pushed back. The CEO stuck to his guns, but he never did understand the enormity of the project. From the onset, the data warehouse lacked a clearly defined business objective. The users had certainly never asked for any system with greater analytical abilities. Finally, things started to fall apart. The MIS director never reached out to the business users, and each user group wanted the other group to spend time on it.

   a. Why are data warehouses and other large-scale systems that cut across the organization so difficult to implement?

   b. Does Close Call Corporation really need a data warehouse? Why or why not?

   c. What would you recommend that Close Call Corporation do next? Why?

Source Paul, Lauren Gibbons. 1997. The anatomy of a failure: The inside story of a fatally flawed data warehouse project. *CIO Enterprise* (November 15): 55–60.

2. Survival of the Fastest: Facing a Competitive Threat from Upstart Rivals, State Street Global Advisors Had to Build a New Customer Service System for Retirement Plan Transactions—and Do It Quickly

State Street Global Advisors (SSGA), a caretaker of corporate retirement plans, was responsible for managing retirement plans for about 2 million employees of 120 corporations. The biggest challenge that SSGA faced in managing these plans was to reallocate assets from stock funds to bonds or vice versa, based on the market performance. The availability of the technology had reduced the transaction time from 6 weeks to 24 hours. Aggressive mutual fund companies focused on capturing the retirement plan business were driving the customer service standards even higher. SSGA realized the increasing importance of improving the efficiency of its transaction process if it was to remain a major player in the marketplace. SSGA's business strategy hinged on its ability to act as an extension of its clients' benefits department. The company decided to build a client/server workflow customer service system because the customer service center played a key role in attracting and retaining customers. The company spent $15 million over five years on building this workflow customer service system.

Prior to automating the process, the customer service reps were involved with a lot of paperwork and spent time answering phone calls. This process was prone to mistakes, and the company had spent a considerable amount of time correcting the mistakes. Moreover, when investors wanted to reallocate the assets, SSGA would have to wait until the first of a new month to perform the transaction. The reps had to memorize the rules of each retirement plan because they varied from company to company.

At present, the use of database technology has simplified and increased the efficiency of the customer service department's activities. SSGA's customer service center system revalues assets every day and allows representatives to compile transactions in less than 24 hours. Almost all of the necessary information, including the rules for each plan, is available online, which helps the reps answer customer inquiries promptly without having to put callers on hold. The system also has a sophisticated help function tailored for each individual plan. This function informs the representative whether or not the participant is eligible to enroll in a plan. The representatives no longer have to memorize the nuances of every plan and hence can provide service to more companies. Previously, reps serviced employees of half a dozen companies. Now, each rep handles 14 to 15 plans on average.

The use of the system has enabled the representatives to perform transactions accurately 99.8 percent of the time. It has also increased the efficiency of the workers and helped them to better serve the customers. As a result, customer satisfaction has increased and has contributed to the company moving from tenth in its industry to third.

The project challenged SSGA's IT department with an ambitious time frame and unfamiliar technology. To ensure the success of the system, SSGA involved its customer service reps in the design of the prototype and listened to users' suggestions. Companies that underestimated the impact that faster customer service would have on the industry and failed to take action are out of business now. SSGA, by accurately sensing the movement of the market and responding quickly to it, grew to be an industry leader.

a. How was database technology used for this new system? How important is the database in this case?

b. Summarize the benefits gained from the customer service system. Is this enough to convince even the most skeptical CFO that a project like this is worth the money?

c. What can other firms learn from State Street's use of database technology?

Source Fabris, Peter. 1998. Survival of the fastest. CIO Enterprise (February 1): 56–58.

References

Boar, B. 1998. Understanding data warehousing strategically. NCR white paper at http://www.3ncr.com/product/whitepapers/bboar1.htm. Information verified: April 7, 1998.

Date, C. J. 1990. *An introduction to database systems.* New York: Addison-Wesley Publishing Company, Inc.

Foley, J. 1996. Data dilemma. *Information Week*, June 10, 14–16.

Foley, J. and B. DePompa. 1996. Data marts: Low cost, high appeal. *Information Week,* March 18, 20–21.

Hermann, E. 1996. *Sams Teach Yourself CGI Programming with PERL in a Week.* Indianapolis, Indiana: Sams.net Publishing.

IBM, 1998. Information from: www.ibm.com. Verified: February 7, 1998.

Norman, R. 1996. Object-oriented systems analysis and design. Upper Saddle River, New Jersey: Prentice Hall, Inc.

Oracle, 1998. Information from: www.oracle.com. Verified: February 7, 1998.

Related Readings

Brachman, Khabaza, Kloesgen, Piatetsky-Shapiro, and Simoudis. 1996. Mining business databases. *Communications of the ACM* 39(11): 42–48.

Cerpa, N. 1995. Pre-physical database design heuristics. *Information and Management* 28(6): 351–359.

Chan, Wei, and Siau. 1993. User-database interface: The effect of abstraction levels on query performance. *Management Information Systems Quarterly* 17(4): 441–464.

Clark, G.J. and C.T. Wu. 1994. DFQL: Dataflow query language for relational databases. *Information and Management* 27(1): 1–15.

Clifford, Croker, and Tuzhilin. 1996. On data representation and use in a temporal relational DBMS. *Information Systems Research* 7(3): 308–327.

Kulkarni, V.R. and H.K. Jain. 1993. Interaction between concurrent transactions in the design of distributed databases. *Decision Sciences* 24(2): 253–277.

Leitheiser, R.L. and S.T. March. 1996. The influence of database structure representation on database system learning and use. *Journal of Management Information Systems* 12(4): 187–213.

Premerlani, W.J. and M.R. Blaha. 1994. An approach for reverse engineering of relational databases. *Communications of the ACM* 37(5): 42–49.

Ram, S. and S. Narasimhan. 1994. Database allocation in a distributed environment: Incorporating a concurrency control mechanism and queuing costs. *Management Science* 40(8): 969–983.

Ram, S. 1995. Deriving functional dependencies from the entity-relationship model. *Communications of the ACM* 38(9): 95–107.

Segev, A. and J.L. Zhao. 1994. Rule management in expert database systems. *Management Science* 40(6): 685–707.

Storey, V.C. and R.C. Goldstein. 1993. Knowledge-based approaches to database design. *Management Information Systems Quarterly* 17(1): 25–46.

Weber, R. 1996. Are attributes entities?: A study of database designers' memory structures. *Information Systems Research* 7(2): 137–162.

Chapter 9: The Information Systems Development Process

Scenario: Changes to the University Transcript Reporting System

Second Millennia Real Estate (SMR) is your state's largest residential and commercial real estate sales company. SMR has had a long history of providing summer internships to university business students. Internships with SMR are highly coveted due to SMR's statewide presence, offering students flexibility with location during the summer months. Most students are assigned to work within SMR's residential sales group. Interns within the residential sales group focus primarily on supporting local sales agents with day-to-day sales support activities such as staffing open houses, placing and collecting signs, and drafting advertisements and property descriptions. Within the commercial sales group, interns engage in activities similar to those of the residential group, but also focus on providing property management and investment management services to commercial customers.

Imagine that you have just applied for an internship with SMR, hoping to be selected by the commercial sales group. During the application process, you are asked to provide a copy of your academic transcripts and are told that these must be mailed to SMR within the next week. You have an older copy of your transcript that you could provide but would rather provide one that contained your most recently completed courses, given that you have made some substantial improvements in your GPA the past few terms.

To obtain a copy of your most recent transcript, you contact your school's registrar, Jackie Wang. Unfortunately, she informs you that it will take at least two weeks for you to get a copy with your most recently completed courses. Ms. Wang can, however, provide you with a copy of your transcript without the most recently completed term's grades today. You ask why transcripts with the most recently completed term's grades take an extra two weeks. She explains that student grade transcripts with the most recently completed classes are being produced by hand and are caught in a two-week backlog. Alternatively, transcripts without the most recently completed grades can be produced by the school's Transcript Reporting System immediately. You press further and ask why the Transcript Reporting System can't include the most recently completed classes. Ms. Wang explains that when the school changed from a quarter-based to a semester-based academic calendar in the prior term, the Transcript Reporting System was not capable of supporting transcripts that had classes from both the quarter system and the semester system. "Quarter-based credit hours are two-thirds of semester-based credit hours," she explains. "Our current system just cannot handle this difference when computing grade point averages. We are having the system completely changed to support transcripts with both quarter and semester grades, but it won't be available for at least another month or so."

Frustrated at this point, you ask, "Why does it take so long to make a few changes to a system?" The registrar explains that the school has been working on this change to the Transcript Reporting System for several months and that many steps had to be performed, as outlined in Figure 9.1. She explains that she and her staff began the process by meeting with several systems analysts from the University Computing Service—a group that develops and supports computer systems at your univer-sity. "During the meeting, we described what changes were occurring in the academic calendar and how these changes were problematic to the Transcript Reporting System. After several meetings over the past few months, the analysts were able to clearly understand what was needed in the new system and were now able to design changes to the existing system. We spent most of our time discussing what we wanted and designing how it would work. Only a small part of the time will be spent on actual programming. Full implementation where they install and train us to use the new system is still at least a month away. I cannot tell you how much time and energy has gone into making the few changes to this system—much more than I have ever imagined!"

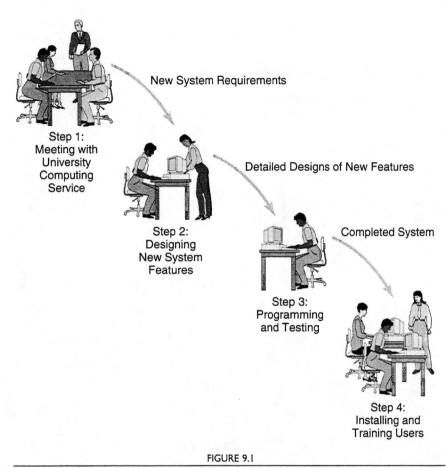

New System Requirements

Step 1:
Meeting with
University
Computing
Service

Detailed Designs of New Features

Step 2:
Designing
New System
Features

Completed System

Step 3:
Programming
and Testing

Step 4:
Installing and
Training Users

FIGURE 9.1

The steps in the changes to the system.

You explain to the registrar that you need a full transcript as soon as possible to complete your application to SMR. You also explained why you feel that a transcript containing the grades from the most recently completed semester would likely enhance your chances within SMR because of their reputation of using academic achievement as an important criteria in the selection process. Ms. Wang is sympathetic to your situation and provides you with a good compromise solution: providing a copy of your prior transcript generat-ed by the existing Transcript Reporting System and a copy of your most recently completed report card. "Together," she says, "both provide equivalent information to an updat-ed transcript." She also provides you with a brief letter explaining why the school could not provide a complete transcript with the most recently completed classes and grades. You thank her for all her help and for a better understanding about what even a small change to a system might entail for an organization.

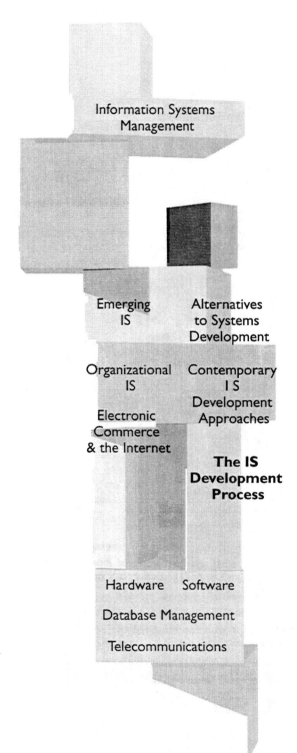

Information Systems
Management

Emerging
IS

Alternatives
to Systems
Development

Organizational
IS

Contemporary
I S
Development
Approaches

Electronic
Commerce
& the Internet

**The IS
Development
Process**

Hardware   Software

Database Management

Telecommunications

Introduction

A fairly common set of systems development methods—such as those used in modifying the Transcript Reporting System—have traditionally been used to construct and modify information systems used in organizations. For example, if you were to develop a new payroll or inventory management system for a firm, you would probably follow a contemporary development approach. With such an approach you would use a set of highly structured techniques and steps. Why use a contemporary development approach in this instance? Information systems such as transaction processing and payroll systems (described in Chapter 7, "Organizational Information Systems") typically have well-defined processes and data. Consequently, there is a natural marriage between a contemporary, structured development approach and a well-defined, structured problem such as a payroll system. Alternatively, decision support and expert systems, whose data and processing requirements are often ill defined, are usually constructed using non-traditional or emerging development methods, which are described in Chapter 10, "Contemporary Information Systems Development Approaches."

This chapter describes the process used by many organizations to design, build, and maintain several types of information systems. As you will read, different approaches have been found to be more appropriate for developing some types of systems and less appropriate for others. Learning all possible ways to develop or acquire a system, and more importantly when to apply the optimal approach, takes years of study and experience. Toward this end, this chapter has several objectives.

After reading this chapter, you will be able to do the following:

1. Understand the process used by organizations to manage the development of information systems.

2. Describe each major phase of the system's development life cycle: systems identification, selection, and planning; system analysis; system design; system implementation; and system maintenance.

FIGURE 9.2

The big picture: focusing on the information systems development process.

3. Explain how organizations identify projects, assess feasibility, identify system benefits and costs, and perform economic analysis of a system project.

This chapter is the first in Part 4, "Information Systems Development." Part 4 focuses on describing how organizations develop and acquire information systems (see Figure 9.2). Given the importance of information and technology to the success of modern organizations, the goal of this chapter is to provide you with a high-level understanding of the information system's development processes.

The Need for Structured Systems Development

The process of designing, building, and maintaining information systems is often referred to as **systems analysis and design**. Likewise, the individual who performs this task is referred to as a systems analyst. (This chapter uses "systems analyst" and "programmer" interchangeably.) Because few organizations can exist without effectively utilizing information and computing technology, the demand for systems analysts far outpaces the supply. Organizations want to hire systems analysts because they possess a unique blend of both managerial and technical expertise—systems analysts are not just "techies." In fact, systems analysts are in hot demand precisely due to their unique blend of technical and managerial expertise. But it wasn't always this way.

The Evolution of Information Systems Development

In the early days of computing, systems development and programming was considered an art that only a few technical "gurus" could master. Unfortunately, the techniques used to construct systems varied greatly from individual to individual. This variation made it difficult to integrate large organizational information systems. Further, many systems were not easily maintainable after the original programmer left the organization. As a result, organizations were often left with systems that were very difficult and expensive to maintain. Many organizations therefore under-utilized these technology investments and failed to realize all possible benefits from their systems.

To address this problem, information systems professionals concluded that system development needed to become an engineering-like discipline (Nunamaker, 1992). Common methods, techniques, and tools had to be developed to create a disciplined approach for constructing information systems. This evolution from an "art" to a "discipline" led to the use of the term **software engineering** to help define what systems analysts and programmers do. Transforming information systems development into a formal discipline would provide numerous benefits. First, it would be much easier to train programmers and analysts if common techniques were widely used. In essence, if all systems analysts had similar training, it would make them more interchangeable and more skilled at working on the systems developed by other analysts. Second, systems built with commonly used techniques would be more maintainable. Both industry and academic researchers have pursued the quest for new and better approaches for building information systems.

Options for Obtaining Information Systems

Organizations can obtain new information systems in many ways. One option, of course, is for the members of the organization to build the information system themselves, which is the approach described in this chapter. However, organizations can also buy a "pre-packaged" system from a software development company or consulting firm. Some information systems that are commonly used in many organizations can be purchased for much less money than what it would cost to build. Purchasing a pre-packaged system is a good option as long as its features meet the needs of the organization. For example, a payroll system is an example of a "pre-packaged" system that is often purchased rather than developed by an organization because tax laws, wage calculations, check printing, and accounting activities are highly standardized. Figure 9.3 outlines several sources for information systems.

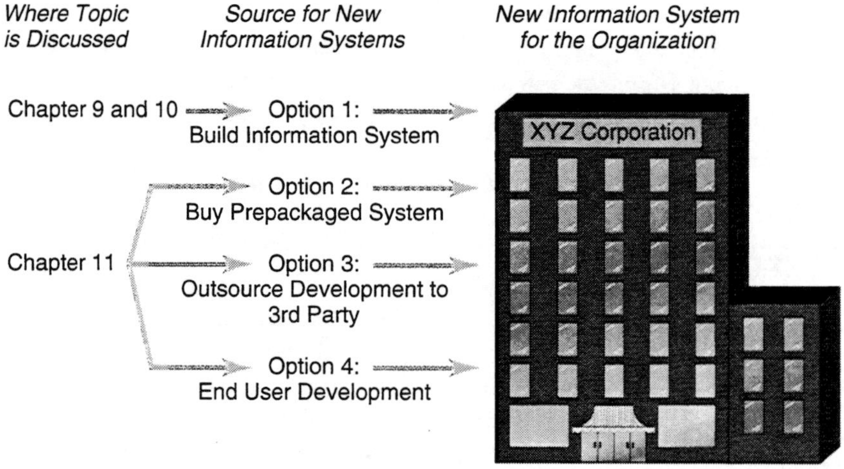

FIGURE 9.3

Sources for information systems.

Where Topic is Discussed	Source for New Information Systems	New Information System for the Organization
Chapter 9 and 10 ➡	Option 1: Build Information System	
	Option 2: Buy Prepackaged System	
Chapter 11	Option 3: Outsource Development to 3rd Party	
	Option 4: End User Development	

(handwritten margin notes: 4 options → ① build is yourself ② buy "prepackaged" is ③ outside source build is ④ end-user development)

A third option is to have an outside organization or consultant custom build a system to an organization's specifications. This is generally referred to as having the development outsourced. This is a good option when the organization does not have adequate systems development resources or expertise. A final option is to let individual users and departments build their own custom systems to support their individual needs. This is referred to as *end-user development*. Most organizations allow end-user development to be used to construct only a limited range of systems. For example, systems that span organizational boundaries or perform complex changes to corporate databases are typically not candidates for end-user development. Alternatively, a common application that might be constructed using end-user development is a data analysis system using a spreadsheet application such as Microsoft Excel. Regardless of the source of the new information system, the primary role of managers and users in the organization is to make sure that any new system will meet the organization's business needs. This means that managers and users must understand the systems development process to ensure that the system will meet their needs.

Information Systems Development in Action

The tools and techniques used to develop information systems are continuously evolving with the rapid changes in information system hardware and software. As you will see, the information systems development approach is a very structured process that moves from step to step. Systems analysts become adept at decomposing large, complex problems into many small, simple problems. Writing a relatively short computer program can then easily solve each simple problem. The goal of the systems analyst is to build the final system by piecing together the many small programs into one comprehensive system. This process of decomposing a problem is outlined in Figure 9.4. An easy way to think about this is to think about using Lego blocks for building a model house. When together, the blocks can create a large and very complex design. Apart, each block is a small, simple piece that is nothing without the others. When systems are built in this manner they are much easier to design, program, and, most important, maintain.

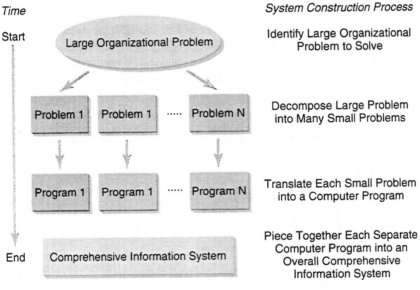

FIGURE 9.4

Problem decomposition process.

The Role of Users in the Systems Development Process

Most organizations have a huge investment in transaction processing and management information systems. These systems are most often designed, constructed, and maintained using structured development methods by systems analysts and programmers within the organization. When building and maintaining information systems, systems analysts rely on information provided by system users, who are involved in all phases of the system's development process. It is important for all members of the organization to understand what is meant by systems development and what activities occur to effectively participate in the process. A close and mutually respectful working relationship between analysts and users is a key to project success.

Now that you understand the history and need for structured systems development, it's time to consider some of the relevant techniques that are used in systems development.

SDLC →
is from
conception +
retirement

Steps in the Systems Development Process

Just as the products that a firm produces and sells follow a life cycle, so do organizational information systems. For example, a new type of tennis shoe follows a life cycle of being introduced to the market, being accepted into the market, maturing, declining in popularity, and ultimately being retired. The term **systems development life cycle (SDLC)** is used to describe the life of an information system from conception to retirement (Hoffer, George, and Valacich, 1999). The SDLC has five primary phases:

1. System identification, selection, and planning

2. System analysis

3. System design

4. System implementation

5. System maintenance

Figure 9.5 is a graphical representation of the SDLC. The SDLC is represented as four boxes connected by arrows. Within the SDLC, arrows flow in both directions from the top box (System Identification, Selection, and Planning) to the bottom box (System Implementation). Arrows flowing down represent the flow of information produced in one phase as being used to seed the activities of the next. Arrows flowing up represent the possibility of returning to a prior phase, if needed. The system maintenance arrow connecting the last phase to the first is what makes the SDLC a cycle.

FIGURE 9.5

Systems development life cycle.

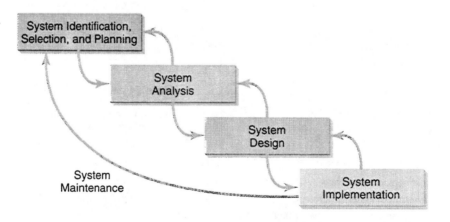

A BRIEF CASE ─────────── **The SDLC at NASA** ───────────

Organizations modify the basic SDLC slightly to fit their specific needs. For example, National Aeronautics and Space Administration (NASA) follows an eight-step approach (NASA, 1998). High-quality software is a key component in the success of NASA. Software is used to control countless earth-based systems such as those used to track, guide, and communicate with the space shuttles and the space-based systems that control the functioning of orbiting satellites. It is easy to imagine that a system failure could have catastrophic results! Consequently, NASA, like many other organizations, has chosen to follow a formal SDLC to help assure software and system quality and, more importantly, to help protect the lives and safety of their astronauts. The value of having standard procedures and steps such as the SDLC when building software not only speeds the development process, but it also ensures the creation of high-quality and reliable systems. As shown in Figure 9.6, the NASA SDLC contains eight phases that are essentially the same as the five-step, generic process described in this chapter. Within every step of the NASA SDLC, guidelines have been developed for accepting and ensuring the quality of work products created within a phase. These guidelines are used to make sure that all work products meet specifications and are error free before developers move to the next phase of the SDLC. The remainder of this section describes each phase in the SDLC.

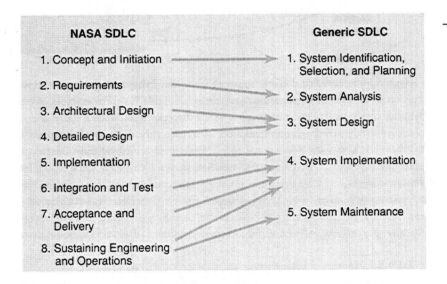

FIGURE 9.6

NASA's systems development life cycle as compared to the generic life cycle.

Phase 1: System Identification, Selection, and Planning

The first phase of the systems development life cycle is **system identification, selection, and planning**, as shown in Figure 9.7. Given that an organization can work on only a limited number of projects at a given time due to limited resources, care must be taken so that only those projects that are critical to enabling the organization's mission, goals, and objectives be undertaken. Consequently, the goal of system identification and selection is simply to identify and select a development project from all possible projects that could be performed. Organiza-tions differ in how they identify and select projects. Some organizations have a formal **information systems planning** process where a senior manager, a business group, an IS manager, or a steering committee identify and assess all possible systems development projects that an organization could undertake. Others follow a more ad hoc process for identifying potential projects. Nonetheless, after all possible projects are identified, those deemed most likely to yield significant organizational benefits, given available resources, are selected for subsequent development activities.

292

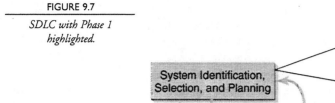

FIGURE 9.7

SDLC with Phase 1 highlighted.

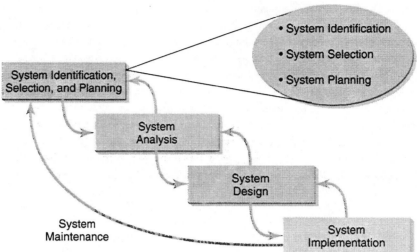

It is important to note that different approaches for identifying and selecting projects are likely to yield different organizational outcomes (see Table 9.1). For example, projects identified by top management more often have a strategic organizational focus, and projects identified by steering committees more often reflect the diversity of the committee and therefore have a cross-functional focus. Projects identified by individual departments or business units most often have a narrow, tactical focus. Finally, the typical focus of projects identified by the development group is the ease with which existing hardware and systems will integrate with the proposed project. Other factors—such as project cost, duration, complexity, and risk—are also influenced by the source of a given project. The source of projects has been found to be a key indicator of project focus and success.

Table 9.1 Sources of systems development projects and their likely focus.

Project Source	Primary Focus
Top management	Broad strategic focus
Steering committee	Cross-functional focus
Individual departments and business units	Narrow, tactical focus
Systems development group	Integration with existing information system focus

Source *Adapted from McKeen, Guimaraes, and Wetherbe. 1994.*

Just as there are often differences in the source of systems projects within organizations, there are often different evaluation criteria used within organizations when classifying and ranking potential projects. During project planning, the analyst works with the customer—the potential users of the system and their managers—to collect a broad range of information to gain an understanding of the project size, potential benefits and costs, and other relevant factors. After this information is collected and analyzed, it can be brought together into a summary planning document that can be reviewed and compared to other possible projects. Table 9.2 provides a sample of the criteria often used by organizations. When reviewing a potential development project, organizations may focus on a single criterion but most often examine multiple criteria to make a decision to accept or reject a project.

Table 9.2 Possible evaluation criteria for classifying and ranking projects.

Evaluation Criteria	Description
Strategic alignment	The extent to which the project is viewed as helping the organization achieve its strategic objectives and long-term goals.
Potential benefits	The extent to which the project is viewed as improving profits, customer service, and so forth, and the duration of these benefits.
Potential costs and resource availability	The number and types of resources the project requires and their availability.
Project size / duration	The number of individuals and the length of time needed to complete the project.
Technical difficulty / risks	The level of technical difficulty involved in successfully completing the project within a given time and resource constraint.

Source Adapted from Hoffer, George, and Valacich. 1999. Modern Systems Analysis and Design. 2d ed. Reading, Massachusetts: Addison Wesley Longman.

Assessing Project Feasibility

Feasibility is another factor to consider when assessing whether or not potential systems should be developed. Feasibility assessment examines the factors influencing the success or failure of a project. Different projects require different types of feasibility assessments, as summarized in Table 9.3.

Table 9.3 Types of feasibility used when assessing an information systems project.

Feasibility Type	Purpose for Assessing
Economic	To identify the financial benefits and costs associated with the development project
Technical	To gain an understanding of the development organization's capability to construct the proposed system
Operational	To gain an understanding of the degree to which and the likelihood that the proposed system solves the business problems or takes advantage of the opportunities outlined in the project request
Schedule	To gain an understanding of the likelihood that all potential timeframe and completion date schedules can be met
Legal and contractual	To gain an understanding of any potential legal ramifications of the construction of the system
Political	To gain an understanding of how key stakeholders within the organization view the proposed system

Source Adapted from Hoffer, George, and Valacich. 1999. Modern Systems Analysis and Design. 2d ed. Reading, Massachusetts: Addison Wesley Longman.

294

Assessing schedule feasibility may uncover that a project's duration will be excessively long. Assessing technical feasibility may show that the internal development group does not possess the expertise to complete a potential project. Performing feasibility analysis is the only way for users or managers to make meaningful comparisons between rival projects.

Organizations focus most of their feasibility assessments on economic feasibility. To perform an economic assessment, an organization must first make an attempt to identify potential system benefits and costs. Analysts work very closely with potential system users and managers to identify these benefits and costs. The next few sections delve deeper into this important aspect of evaluating potential information systems projects: identifying and analyzing system benefits and costs.

Identifying System Benefits

An information system can provide many benefits to an organization. For example, a new or renovated IS can automate monotonous jobs, reduce errors, provide innovative services to customers and suppliers, and improve organizational efficiency, speed, flexibility, and morale. Some benefits can easily be measured in dollars and certainty and are referred to as **tangible benefits.** Examples of tangible benefits include reduced personnel expenses, lower transaction costs, or higher profit margins. **Intangible benefits** refer to items that cannot be easily measured in dollars or certainty. Intangible benefits may have direct organizational benefits such as the improvement of employee morale, or have broader societal implications such as the reduction of waste creation or resource consumption.

Identifying System Costs

Similar to benefits, an information system can have both tangible and intangible costs. **Tangible costs** refer to items that can be easily measured in dollars and certainty such as hardware costs, labor costs, and operational costs such as employee training and building renovations. **Intangible costs** are those items that cannot be easily measured in terms of cost or certainty such as loss of customer goodwill or employee morale. Both tangible and intangible costs can also be distinguished as either one-time or recurring. **One-time costs** refer to those associated with project initiation such as system development, new hardware and software purchases, user training, and site preparation. **Recurring costs** refer to those resulting from the ongoing evolution, use, and maintenance of the system.

Performing an Economic Analysis of a System Project

Most techniques used to determine economic feasibility encompass the concept of the time value of money (TVM). TVM refers to the concept of comparing present cash outlays to future expected returns. Because many projects may be competing for the same investment dollars and may have different useful life expectancies, all costs and benefits must be viewed in relation to their present value when investment options are compared. For example, suppose you want to buy a used personal computer (PC) from an acquaintance and she asks that you make two payments of $1000 over two years, beginning next year, for a total of $2000. If she would agree to a single lump sum payment at the time of sale, what amount do you think she would agree to? Should the single payment be $2000 or should it be less? To answer this question, we must consider the time value of money. Most of us would gladly accept $2000 today rather than two payments of $1000; a dollar today is worth more than a dollar tomorrow because money can be invested and can earn money over time. The rate at which money can be borrowed or invested is called the cost of capital and is referred to as the discount rate for TVM calculations. Suppose that the seller could put the money received for the sale of the PC in the bank and receive a 10% return on her investment. A simple formula can be used when figuring out the present value of the two $1000 payments:

where PV_n is the present value of Y dollars n years from now when i is the discount rate.

From our example, the present value of the two payments of $1000 can be calculated as

$$PV_n = Y \times \frac{1}{(1 + i)^n}$$

where PV_1 and PV_2 reflect the present value of each $1000 payment in year one and two, respectively.

$$PV_1 = 1000 \times \frac{1}{(1 + .10)^1} = 1000 \times .9091 = 909.10$$

$$PV_2 = 1000 \times \frac{1}{(1 + .10)^2} = 1000 \times .8264 = 826.40$$

To calculate the net present value (NPV) of the two $1000 payments, simply add the present values calculated above (NPV = PV_1 + PV_2 = 909.10 + 826.40 = $1735.50). In other words, the seller could accept a lump-sum payment of $1735.50 as equivalent to the two payments of $1000, given a discount rate of 10 percent.

When systems analysts perform an economic analysis of an information system, they typically create a summary worksheet reflecting the present values of all benefits and costs, as well as all pertinent analyses. A summary worksheet is a very powerful tool for comparing alternative projects. For example, Figure 9.8 shows an Excel spreadsheet containing an economic analysis for a systems development project over a five-year project life. In this analysis, benefits, one-time costs, and recurring costs were identified. The systems analyst for this project performed three types of financial analyses: net present value, return on investment, and break-even analysis. (See Table 9.4 for a general description of these techniques.)

FIGURE 9.8

Economic analysis for a systems development project.

	A	B	C	D	E	F	G	H
1	Ascend Systems, Inc. Economic Feasibility Analysis Customer Billing System							
2								
3								
4								
5					Year of Project			
6		Year 0	Year 1	Year 2	Year 3	Year 4	Year 5	TOTALS
7	Net Economic Benefit	$0	$32,000	$32,000	$32,000	$32,000	$32,000	
8	Discount Rate (12%)	1.0000	0.8929	0.7972	0.7118	0.6355	0.5674	
9	PV of Benefits	$0	$28,571	$25,510	$22,777	$20,337	$18,158	
10								
11	NPV of All Benefits	$0	$28,571	$54,082	$76,859	$97,195	$115,353	$115,353
12								
13	One-time COSTS	($22,450)						
14								
15	Recurring Costs	$0	($19,750)	($19,750)	($19,750)	($19,750)	($19,750)	
16	Discount Rate (12%)	1.0000	0.8929	0.7972	0.7118	0.6355	0.5674	
17	PV of Recurring Costs	$0	($17,634)	($15,745)	($14,058)	($12,551)	($11,207)	
18								
19	NPV of All COSTS	($22,450)	($40,084)	($55,829)	($69,886)	($82,438)	($93,644)	($93,644)
20								
21								
22	Overall NPV							$21,709
23								
24								
25	Overall ROI- (Overall NPV/NPV of all COSTS)							0.23
26								
27								
28	Break-even Analysis							
29	Yearly NPV Cash Flow	($22,450)	$10,938	$9,766	$8,719	$7,785	$6,951	
30	Overall NPV Cash Flow	($22,450)	($11,513)	($1,747)	$6,972	$14,758	$21,709	
31								
32	Project Break-even Occurs Between Years 2 and 3							

Table 9.4 Commonly used economic cost-benefit analysis techniques.

Name of Technique	Description of Technique
Net Present Value (NPV)	NPV uses a discount rate determined from the company's cost of capital to establish the present value of a project. The discount rate is used to determine the present value of both cash receipts and outlays.
Return on Investment (ROI)	ROI is the ratio of the net cash receipts of the project divided by the cash outlays of the project. Tradeoff analysis can be made between projects competing for investment by comparing their representative ROI ratios.
Break-Even Analysis	This technique finds the amount of time required for the cumulative cash flow from a project to equal its initial and ongoing investment.

Source Adapted from Hoffer, George, and Valacich. 1999. Modern Systems Analysis and Design. 2d ed. Reading, Massachusetts: Addison Wesley Longman.

As described earlier, other criteria may also be used to evaluate a project (see Table 9.2). For example, suppose that an organization is contemplating the implementation of a new internal communication system (for example, Lotus Notes). It may be relatively easy to identify system costs. It may be very difficult, however, to quantify the potential financial benefits of this new communication environment because the organization does not have experience with this type of technology. If a financial analysis was used to evaluate the merit of a project in which only the tangible project costs could be identified, the organization may miss an important opportunity to improve their organizational communication radically. In such cases, organizations must rely on alternative evaluation criteria such as whether or not the system enables the firm to achieve its strategy.

Regardless of the criteria used to guide the decision, organizations can make a more informed decision regarding project acceptance or rejection after feasibility analysis for a project has been completed. If the project is accepted, system analysis begins.

Phase 2: System Analysis

The second phase of the systems development life cycle is called **system analysis**, as highlighted in Figure 9.9. One purpose of the system analysis phase is for designers to gain a thorough understanding of an organization's current way of doing things in the area for which the new information system will be constructed. The process of conducting an analysis requires that many tasks, or sub-phases, be performed. The first sub-phase focuses on determining system requirements. To determine the requirements, an analyst works closely with users to determine what is needed from the proposed system. Just as they did in the scenario that was used to open this chapter, analysts may interview users, develop questionnaires, or simply watch the day-to-day activities of users to gain an understanding of what the system must do. After the requirements are collected, analysts organize this information using data, process, and logic modeling tools. In short, every information system contains three key elements that must be understood by the systems analyst: data, processing logic, and data flows. These three elements are illustrated in Figure 9.10.

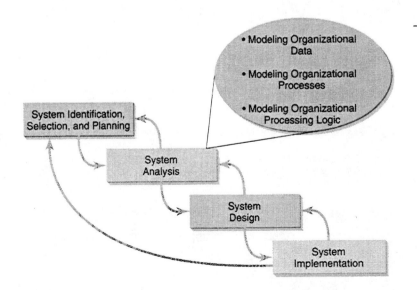

FIGURE 9.9

SDLC with Phase 2 highlighted.

298

FIGURE 9.10

Three key elements to development of a system: Data, Processing Logic, and Data Flows.

Data

Name	Class	GPA
Patty Nicholls	Senior	3.7
Brett Williams	Grad	2.9
Mary Shide	Fresh	3.2

Processing Logic

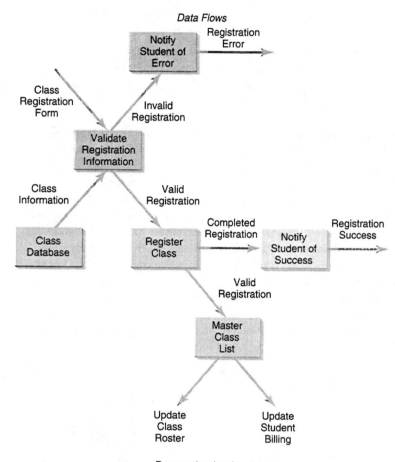

Processing Logic

```
i = read (number_of_classes)
total_hours = 0
total_grade = 0
total_gpa = 0
for j = 1 to i do
        begin
                read (course [ j ], hours [ j ], grade[ j ])
                total_hours = total_hours + hours [ j ]
                total_grade = total_grade + (hours [ j ] * grade [ j ])
        end
current_gpa = total_grade / total hours
```

Modeling Organizational Data

Data are facts that describe people, objects, or events. A lot of different facts can be used to describe a person: name, age, gender, race, and occupation. To construct an information system, systems analysts must understand what data the information system needs to accomplish the intended tasks. To do this, they use data modeling tools to collect and describe the data to users, to confirm that all needed data are known and presented to users as useful information. Figure 9.11 shows an Entity-Relationship Diagram, a type of data model, describing students, classes, majors, and classrooms at a university. Each box in the diagram is referred to as a data entity. Each data entity may have one or more attributes that describe it. For example, a "student" entity may have attributions such as: ID, Name, and Local Address. Additionally, each data entity may be "related" to other data entities. For example, because students take classes, there is a relationship between students and classes: "Student takes Class" and "Class has Student." Relationships are represented on the diagram by lines drawn between related entities. Data modeling tools enable the systems analyst to represent data in a form that is easy for users to understand and critique.

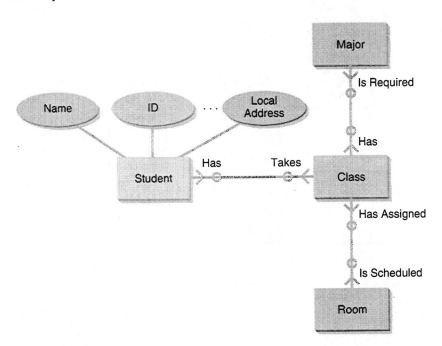

FIGURE 9.11

A sample ERD for students.

Modeling Organizational Processes

As the name implies, **data flows** represent the movement of data through an organization or within an information system. For example, your registration for a class may be captured on a registration form on paper or on a computer terminal. After it is filled out, this form probably flows through several processes to validate and record the class registration as shown as "Data Flows" in Figure 9.10. After all students have been registered, a repository of all registration information can be processed for developing class rosters or for generating student billing information, which is shown as "Data" in Figure 9.10. **Processing logic** represents the way in which data are transformed. For example, processing logic is used to calculate students' grade point averages at the conclusion of a term, as shown in the "Processing Logic" section in Figure 9.10.

After the data, data flow, and processing logic requirements for the proposed system have been identified, analysts develop one or many possible overall approaches—sometimes called "designs"—for the information system. For example, one approach for the system may possess only basic functionality, but have the advantages of being relatively easy and inexpensive to build. A more elaborate approach for the system might also be proposed, but it may be more difficult and more costly to build. Analysts evaluate alternative system approaches with the knowledge that different solutions yield different benefits and different costs. After an alternative system approach is selected, then details of that particular system approach can be defined.

Phase 3: System Design

The third phase of the systems development life cycle is **system design**, as shown in Figure 9.12. As its name implies, it is during this phase that the proposed system is designed; that is, the details of the particular approach chosen are developed. As with analysis, many different activities must occur during system design. The elements that must be designed when building an information system include

- Forms and reports
- Interfaces and dialogues
- Databases and files
- Processing and logic

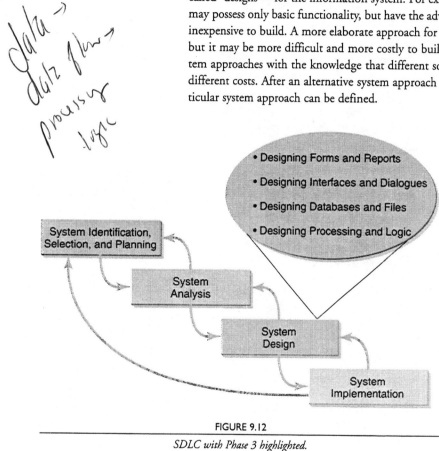

FIGURE 9.12

SDLC with Phase 3 highlighted.

Designing Forms and Reports

Forms and reports represent the typical way in which information is put into or received from an information system. A **form** is a business document containing some predefined data and often including some areas where additional data can be filled in. For example, Figure 9.13 shows an employment application form with predefined information and areas where potential employees provide application information. Forms can be paper-based or computer-based. computer-based forms require that the user enter information via an input device such as a keyboard and view information via a video display device. Figure 9.14 shows a computer-based form taken from the World Wide Web home page of Novell®. Using this form, users can search for a wide variety of product and service information.

Application For Employment	Ascend Systems
Personal Information	
Name:	Date:
Social Security Number:	
Home Address:	
City, State, Zip	
Home Phone:	Business Phone:
U.S. Citizen?	If Not Give Visa No. and Expiration:
Position Applying For	
Title:	Salary Desired:
Referred By:	Data Available:
Education	
High School (Name, City, State):	
Graduation Date:	
Business or Technical School:	
Dates Attended:	Degree, Major:
Undergraduate College:	
Dates Attended:	Degree, Major:
Graduate School:	
Dates Attended:	Degree, Major:
References	

FIGURE 9.13

Employment application.

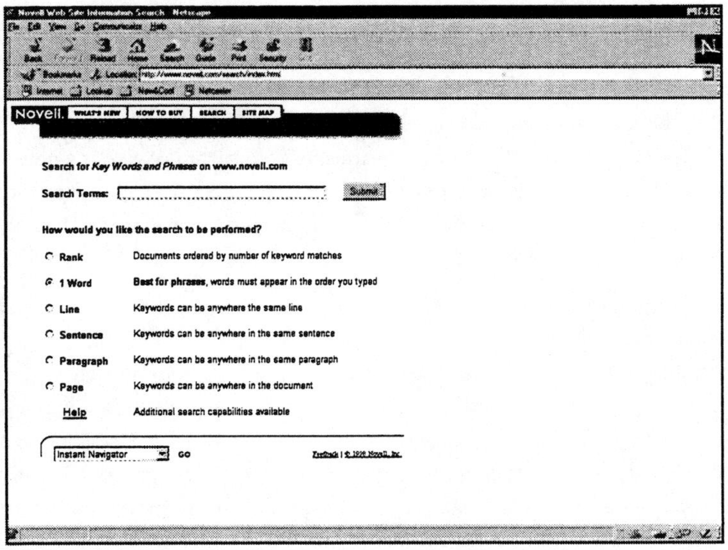

FIGURE 9.14

Novell® Web site search form.

Common business forms include product order forms, employment applications, and class registration sheets. You probably use a computer-based form regularly when you deposit or request currency from an Automated Teller Machine (ATM). On the other hand, a **report** is a business document containing only pre-defined data. In other words, reports are static documents that are used to summarize information for reading or viewing. For example, Figure 9.15 shows a report summarizing regional sales performance for several salespeople. As with forms, reports can be paper-based or computer-based.

FIGURE 9.15

Sales summary report.

Ascend Systems Incorporated
SALESPERSON ANNUAL SUMMARY REPORT 1998

			QUARTERLY ACTUAL SALES			
REGION	SALESPERSON	SSN	FIRST	SECOND	THIRD	FOURTH
Northwest and Mountain						
	Wachter	999-99-9999	16,500	18,600	24,300	18,000
	Mennecke	999-99-9999	22,000	15,500	17,300	19,800
	Wheeler	999-99-9999	19,000	12,500	22,000	28,000
Midwest and Mid-Atlantic						
	Spurrier	999-99-9999	14,000	16,000	19,000	21,000
	Powell	999-99-9999	7,500	16,600	10,000	8,000
	Topi	999-99-9999	12,000	19,800	17,000	19,000
New England						
	Speier	999-99-9999	18,000	18,000	20,000	27,000
	Morris	999-99-9999	28,000	29,000	19,000	31,000

You may be a bit confused by the subtle distinction between forms and reports, because they have many similarities. The biggest difference is that forms provide information and request new information, typically about a single record. In other words, a form would provide or capture information about a single student, a single product, or a single account. Reports, on the other hand, only provide information, and typically for multiple individuals, products, or accounts.

Designing Interfaces and Dialogues

A dialogue is a means of communication. For an information system, the interface and dialogue are the tools that enable users to interact with a system. Think about how you interact with other people. Your interface with others could be friendly and receptive, or it could be unfriendly and closed. You might give lots of non-verbal cues such as nodding your head and gesturing with your arms, or you might not give any non-verbal cues. Similarly, in your dialogue with other people you could ask simple questions that require yes/no answers, or you might describe a list of alternatives to someone else and ask him to choose the right answer.

Just as people have different ways of interacting with other people, information systems can have different ways of interacting with people. A system interface might be text-based, communicating with you through text and forcing you to communicate with it the same way. Alternatively, a system interface could use graphics and color as a way to interact with you, providing you with color-coded windows and special icons. A system dialogue could be developed such that it does nothing and waits for you to type in a command. Or it could ask you questions to which you type in commands, or present to you menus with choices from which you select your desired options. It could even do all these things.

Over the past several years, standards for user interfaces and dialogues have emerged. In the past, most systems had proprietary interfaces and dialogues. Consequently, very few systems looked or acted similarly, which left users frustrated and confused. The evolution of interface and dialogue standards helped to alleviate this problem. The first widely used standard for interacting with computers was proposed by Apple Computer in 1984 for the Macintosh personal computer. Later, Microsoft introduced a similar environment in 1990 called Windows 3.0 (Windows 1.0 was released in 1984, but found no commercial success because it couldn't run effectively on early personal computers); descendants of Windows—Windows 95, NT, and 98—are now the most widely used operating systems for personal computers. Both the Macintosh and Windows environments are generally referred to as being *graphical user interfaces.* (See Chapter 3, "Information Systems Software," for more on GUIs.) As in the Apple operating environment, information systems developed for Windows have a standard look and feel. In GUI environments, the system requests information by placing a standard window (or form) on the computer display. Menu names and the means of accessing operations are also standardized. For example, notice that for almost every Windows program the naming and placement of menus is similar (see Figure 9.16). For most Windows programs, the first menu is File and the last is Help. When systems analysts adopt a standard operating interface for the systems they design, it makes the system easier for users to learn and use. An additional benefit of using interface and dialogue standards is a reduction in the amount of software documentation and training materials needed by users.

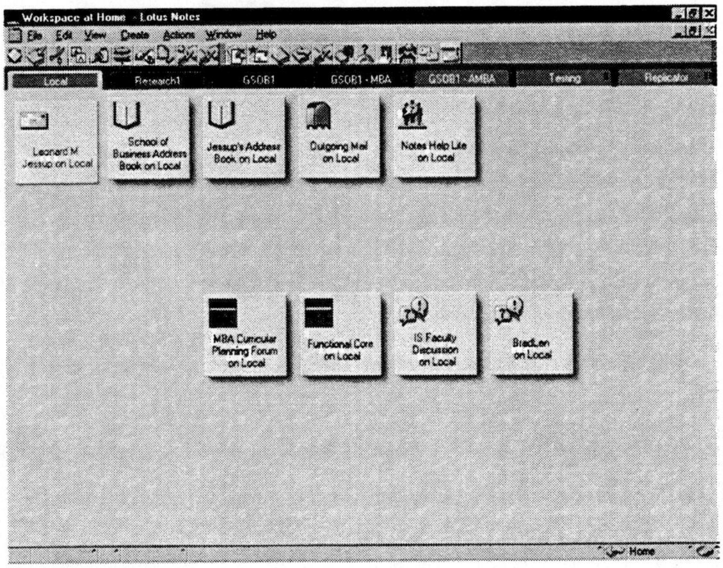

FIGURE 9.16

Most Windows-based programs follow a standard that governs the naming and placement of menus.

Designing Databases and Files

To design databases and files, a systems analyst must have a thorough understanding of the organization's data and informational needs. As described previously, a systems analyst often uses data modeling tools to first gain a comprehensive understanding of all the data used by a proposed system. After the *conceptual* data model has been completed, it can be easily translated into a *physical* data model in a database management system. For example, Figure 9.17 shows a physical data model to keep track of student information in Microsoft Access. The physical data model is more complete (shows more information about the student) and more detailed (shows how the information is formatted) than a conceptual data model. For example, contrast Figure 9.17 with the conceptual model in Figure 9.11 that contains student information.

FIGURE 9.17

An Access database.

C:\MSOFFICCE\ACCESS\STUDENT.MDB   Sunday, June 23, 1998
Table: Students   Page: 1

Properties

Date Created:	6/23/98 10:35:41 PM	Def. Updatable:	Yes
Last Updated:	6/23/98 10:35:43 PM	Record Count:	0

Columns

Name	Type	Size
StudentID	Number (Long)	4
FirstName	Text	50
MiddleName	Text	30
LastName	Text	50
ParentsNames	Text	255
Address	Text	255
City	Text	50
State	Text	50
Region	Text	50
PostalCode	Text	20
PhoneNumber	Text	30
EmailName	Text	50
Major	Text	50
Note	Memo	-

Designing Processing and Logic

The processing and logic operations of an information system are the steps and procedures that transform raw data inputs into new or modified information. For example, in the Transcript Reporting System that opened the chapter, systems people needed to calculate students' grade point averages. Calculating a grade point average would require the following steps to be performed:

1. Obtain the prior grade point average, credit hours earned, and list of prior courses

2. Obtain the list of each current course, final grade, and course credit hours

3. Combine the prior and current credit hours into aggregate sums

4. Calculate new grade point average

The logic and steps needed to make this calculation can be represented many ways. One method, referred to as writing **pseudo code**—a textual notation for describing programming code—enables the systems analyst to describe the processing steps in a manner that is similar to how a programmer might implement the steps in an actual programming language. The "Processing Logic" in Figure 9.10 is an example of pseudo code.

Other tools used by systems analysts during this activity include structure charts and decision trees. **Structure charts** are powerful tools for decomposing large problems into smaller pieces. For example, Figure 9.18 shows a high-level structure chart for a system to support student class registration at a university. **Decision trees** are helpful for designing how the actual logic of a program might be written when there are many different possibilities to consider. For example, Figure 9.19 shows a decision tree for determining undergraduate class standing by considering the number of credit hours earned and degree requirements completed.

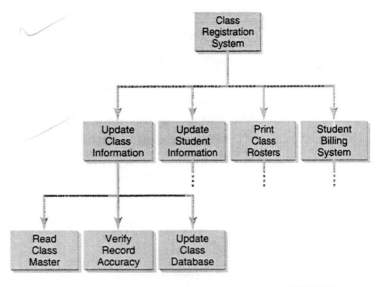

Collectively, pseudo code, structure charts, and decision trees are very powerful but easy-to-use tools for representing complex logic and processing. Converting pseudo code, structure charts, and decision trees into actual program code during system implementation is a very straightforward process.

FIGURE 9.19

A decision tree for a problem.

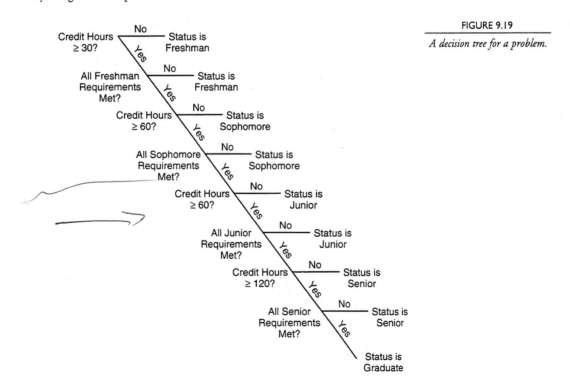

Phase 4: System Implementation

Many separate activities occur during **system implementation**, the fourth phase of the systems development life cycle, as highlighted in Figure 9.20. One group of activities focuses on transforming the system design into a working information system that can be used by the organization. These activities include software programming and testing. A second group of activities focuses on preparing the organization for using the new information systems. These activities include system conversion, documentation, user training, and support. This section briefly describes what occurs during system implementation.

FIGURE 9.20

SDLC with Phase 4 highlighted.

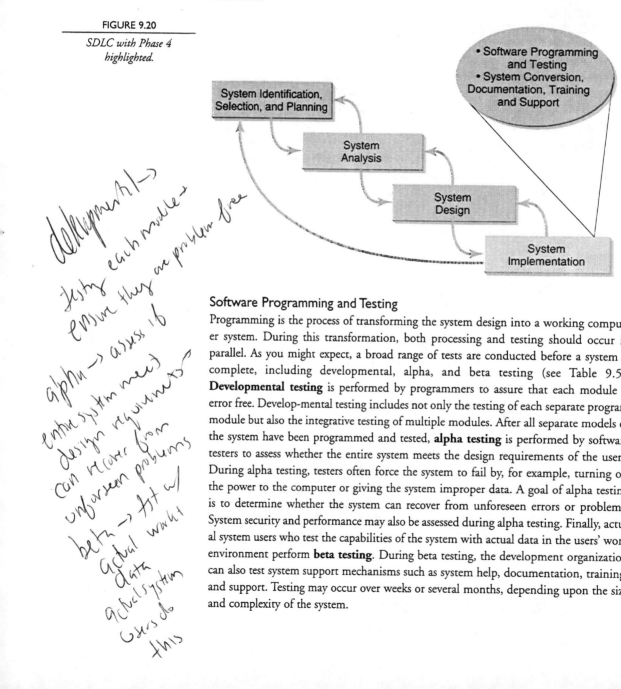

Software Programming and Testing

Programming is the process of transforming the system design into a working computer system. During this transformation, both processing and testing should occur in parallel. As you might expect, a broad range of tests are conducted before a system is complete, including developmental, alpha, and beta testing (see Table 9.5). **Developmental testing** is performed by programmers to assure that each module is error free. Develop-mental testing includes not only the testing of each separate program module but also the integrative testing of multiple modules. After all separate models of the system have been programmed and tested, **alpha testing** is performed by software testers to assess whether the entire system meets the design requirements of the users. During alpha testing, testers often force the system to fail by, for example, turning off the power to the computer or giving the system improper data. A goal of alpha testing is to determine whether the system can recover from unforeseen errors or problems. System security and performance may also be assessed during alpha testing. Finally, actual system users who test the capabilities of the system with actual data in the users' work environment perform **beta testing**. During beta testing, the development organization can also test system support mechanisms such as system help, documentation, training, and support. Testing may occur over weeks or several months, depending upon the size and complexity of the system.

Table 9.5 General testing types, their focus, and by whom they are performed.

Testing Type	Focus	Performed by
Developmental	Testing the correctness of individual modules and the integration of multiple modules	Programmer
Alpha	Testing of overall system to see whether it meets design requirements	Software tester
Beta	Testing of the capabilities of the system in the user environment with actual data	Actual system users

---

Profile of a Software Tester

A software tester spends most of his time trying to break software (see STI, 1998). Breaking software is referred to in the computer industry as "finding bugs." (A bug is a programming error, design flaw, or anything else that results in the computer program not running as intended.) Software testers spend countless hours trying to identify problems, typically long before the software is released to a widespread audience. Most software testers work, as you would guess, for software and computer companies such as Microsoft, IBM, or Netscape Communications. Software testers also work for companies in banking, insurance, and literally any other company devoted to developing high-quality software. In most cases, software testers are not systems developers, but many know how to program. Organizations have discovered that more errors are found if the people testing the software are separate from the development group. Many times, cash bonuses are given to testers for each bug found to give them a strong motivation for finding these pesky errors. Because testers must not only find errors, but also describe them after they are found, software testers must also have good communication skills, and be detail-oriented, patient, self-motivated, and creative. In addition to looking for bugs, software testers are also often assigned to provide customer support and training because of their intricate knowledge of how a new system works. Creating high-quality software requires a cooperative team of system designers, programmers, and testers. Good software testers are in high demand. So, if you like breaking things, and getting paid for it, maybe you would be a good software tester.

System Conversion, Documentation, Training, and Support

System conversion is the process of decommissioning the current system (automated or manual) and installing the new system into the organization. Effective conversion of a system requires not only that the new software be installed, but also that users be effectively trained and supported. System conversion can be performed in at least four ways. **Parallel conversion** is when both the old system and new system are used by the organization at the same time. After the organization is sure the new system is error free, that users are adequately trained, and that support procedures are in place, it can discontinue the old system, as illustrated in Figure 9.21a. Parallel conversion is the safest and least risky conversion strategy. Alternatively, a **direct conversion** is when the old system is discontinued on one day and the new system is used on the next, as illustrated in Figure 9.21b. Direct conversion is the riskiest conversion strategy because if the new system does not work correctly, no backup system is in place. A **phased conversion** is when parts of the system are implemented into the organization over time, as illustrated in Figure 9.21c. As each part is validated as working properly, new modules and features can be added and validated. A **pilot conversion** is when the entire system is used in one location, but not in the entire organization. After the system is validated as operating properly at one location, it can be disseminated throughout the entire organization, as illustrated in Figure 9.21d. Both phased and pilot conversion strategies have moderate levels of risk.

FIGURE 9.21

Software conversion strategies.

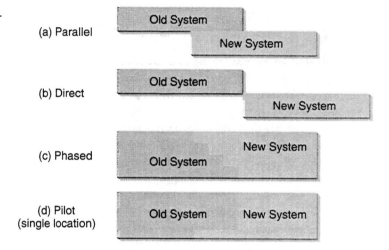

Many types of documentation must be produced for an information system. Programmers develop "system" documentation that details the inner workings of the system to ease future maintenance. Programmers develop system documentation in parallel with programming and testing activities. A second type of documentation is user-related documentation, which is not typically written by programmers or analysts, but by users or professional technical writers. The development of user documentation is a major project in and of itself for most large systems. For example, examine the documentation that accompanies a software system you have recently used or have purchased. It is likely that professional writers spent months developing these support manuals. The range of documents can include the following:

- User and reference guides
- User training and tutorials
- Installation procedures and troubleshooting suggestions

In addition to system documentation, users may also need training and ongoing support to effectively use a new system. Different types of training and support require different levels of investment by the organization. Self-paced training and tutorials are the least expensive options, and one-on-one training is the most expensive. Table 9.6 summarizes various user training options.

Table 9.6 User training options.

Training Option	Description
Tutorial	One person taught at one time by a human or by paper-based exercises
Course	Several people taught at one time
Computer-aided instruction	One person taught at one time by the computer system
Interactive training manuals	Combination of tutorials and computer-aided instruction
Resident expert	Expert on call to assist users as needed
Software help components	Built-in system components designed to train and troubleshoot problems
External sources	Vendors and training providers to provide tutorials, courses, and other training activities

IBM's Global Training Organization — A BRIEF CASE

Given the rapid pace at which software and systems are changing, more organizations are turning to outside vendors to provide user training. This is especially true for popular applications. For example, IBM provides training in more than 100 global locations on most popular PC applications; they provide more than 500 different PC-related courses (IBM, 1998). For one organization, they trained more than 10,000 employees to use Windows 95 and delivered this training in more than 60 different cities around the world. To be successful around the world, IBM offers classes in nine different languages. It is becoming much more cost effective for many organizations to use an outside organization for training employees on popular applications. Yet, for company-specific and custom applications, outside vendors are unlikely sources for training.

In addition to training, providing on-going education and problem-solving assistance for users is also necessary. This is commonly referred to as system support. The range of support activities might include the following:

- Installing the system
- Consulting on basic and advanced features
- Assisting in importing and exporting data from one system to another
- Setting up new users and accounts
- Providing demonstrations for new system uses
- Working with users on new system features and problems

System support is often provided by a special group of people in the organization who make up an information center or help desk. Support personnel must have strong communication skills and be good problem solvers, in addition to being expert users of the system. An alternative option for a system not developed internally is to outsource support activities to a vendor specializing in technical system support and training. Regardless of how support is provided, it is an ongoing issue that must be effectively managed for the company to realize the maximum benefits of a system.

Phase 5: System Maintenance

After an information system is installed, it is essentially in the maintenance phase of the SDLC. In the **maintenance phase**, one person within the systems development group is responsible for collecting maintenance requests from system users. After they are collected, requests are analyzed so that the developer can better understand how the proposed change might alter the system and what business benefits and necessities might result from such a change. If the change request is approved, a system change is designed and then implemented. As with the initial development of the system, implemented changes are formally reviewed and tested before installation into operational systems. The **system maintenance** process parallels the process used to initially develop the information system, as shown in Figure 9.22. Interestingly, it is during system maintenance that the largest part of the system development effort occurs.

FIGURE 9.22

Mapping of maintenance to SDLC.

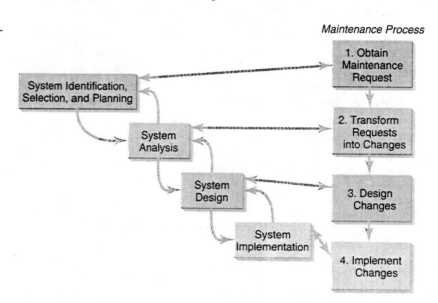

Maintenance Process

⟨ A BRIEF CASE ⟩———— **The Cost of Software and System Maintenance** ——

"When a company budgets $1 million to develop a new software system it is, in fact, committing to spend more than $4 million over the next five years. Each dollar spent on systems development generates, on average, 20 cents for operations and 40 cents for maintenance. Thus, the $1 million expenditure automatically generates a follow-on cost of $600,000 a year to support the initial investment. Development is in many ways the loss leader for maintenance." (Keen, 1991)

The question must be then, why does all this maintenance occur? It is not as if software wears out in the physical manner that cars, buildings, or other physical goods do. Correct? Yes, but software must still be maintained. For example, new features may be added to a system to better support changing business conditions. The Transcript Reporting System that was described at the beginning of the chapter is an example of a system being maintained because of changing business conditions (the University's change from a quarter- to a semester-based academic calendar). Maintenance may also be conducted to overcome internal processing errors not caught during programming and testing. In fact, most information systems development expenditures by organizations are on system maintenance activities. For some organizations, as much as 80 percent of their information systems budget is allocated to maintenance activities (Pressman, 1992). Interestingly, the proportion of systems expenditures on maintenance has also been rising relative to new development because many organizations have accumulated more and more older systems that require more and more maintenance. For example, Figure 9.23 shows that in the 1970s, most information systems expenditures were allocated to new development rather than maintenance. This mix has changed over the years so that the majority of expenditures are now earmarked for maintenance. Given this shift in software expenditures, building maintainable systems is critical to organizational success.

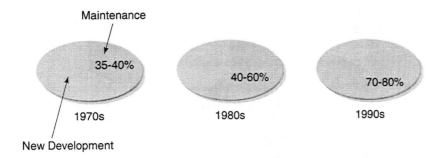

FIGURE 9.23

Pie charts show changing maintenance mix.

All maintenance requests can be classified as being one of four types: corrective, adaptive, perfective, or preventive (see Table 9.7). **Corrective maintenance** refers to making changes to an information system to repair flaws in the design, coding, or implementation. For example, if you recently purchased a used car, corrective maintenance would involve repairing things that are not working correctly. For information systems, most corrective maintenance problems surface soon after installation. When corrective maintenance problems surface, they are typically urgent and need to be resolved to prevent possible interruptions in normal business activities.

Table 9.7 Types of maintenance.

Type	Description
Corrective	Repair design and programming errors
Adaptive	Modify system to environmental changes
Perfective	Evolve system to solve new problems or take advantage of new opportunities
Preventive	Safeguard system from future problems

Source *Adapted from Hoffer, George, and Valacich. 1999. Modern Systems Analysis and Design. 2d ed. Reading, Massachusetts: Addison Wesley Longman.*

Adaptive maintenance refers to making changes to an information system to evolve its functionality to changing business needs or to migrate it to a different operating environment. For a car, adaptive maintenance might be adding snow tires to improve traction and handling during the winter. Adaptive maintenance is usually less urgent than corrective maintenance because business and technical changes typically occur over some period of time.

Perfective maintenance involves making enhancements to improve processing performance or interface usability, or adding desired, but not necessarily required, system features (in other words, "bells and whistles"). In the used car example, perfective maintenance might be the addition of better tires, a better stereo system, or a more efficient carburetor. Many system professionals feel that perfective maintenance is not really maintenance, but new development.

Finally, **preventive maintenance** involves changes made to a system to reduce the chance of future system failure. An example of preventive maintenance might be to increase the number of records that a system can process far beyond what is currently needed or to generalize how a system sends report information to a printer so that the system can easily adapt to changes in printer technology. In the used car example, preventive maintenance would be routine oil changes and tune-ups.

As with adaptive maintenance, both perfective and preventive maintenance are typically a much lower priority than corrective maintenance. Over the life of a system, corrective maintenance is most likely to occur after initial system installation or after major system changes. This means that adaptive, perfective, and preventive maintenance activities can lead to corrective maintenance activities if they are not carefully designed and implemented.

As you can see, there is more to system maintenance than you might think. Lots of time, effort, and money are spent in this final phase of a system's development, and it is important to follow prescribed, structured steps. In fact, the approach to systems development described in this chapter, from the initial phase of identifying, selecting, and planning for systems, to the final phase of system maintenance, is a very structured and systematic process. Each phase is fairly well prescribed and requires active involvement by systems people, users, and managers. It is likely that you will have numerous opportunities to participate in the acquisition or development of a new system for an organization for which you currently work or will work in the future. Now that you have an understanding of the process, you should be better equipped to make a positive contribution to the success of any systems development project. Good luck!

Talking with...

Jared Owens, Analyst at Procter & Gamble

Educational Background

B.A. in Mathematics, Wabash College, Crawfordsville, IN;
M.B.A. in Information Systems and Operations, Indiana University

Job Description

Mr. Owens is a database administrator (DBA) for a midrange Oracle database for Global Research and Development. He is responsible for the overall performance, capacity, and maintenance of six to seven databases on VMS (Digital Alpha machines) and UNIX (HP 9000s) operating platforms. He is also responsible for product and software upgrades and after-hours troubleshooting.

Critical Success Factors

Sell yourself in an interview. An interviewer recognizes if you feel inadequate—leverage the skills you have. A passion for new technology is important. Things are changing daily, even in conservative companies. Be adaptable. Be an effective communicator and take leadership roles on teams. Teamwork is just as important as they say in business schools. Persevere. Don't let snags or shortcomings keep you from achieving the goal you want. If you want to make a career path change, aggressively seek one. In your job, if you want to work with certain products or technologies, keep pushing the buttons until you get there.

Advice to Students

Learn as many technical skills as possible. Most likely, you will not jump straight to technology management—you need to learn it first. Sell the skills that you do have; you can be trained for those you don't. But you need something to get in the door. Learn how all things work; don't just focus on coding or hardware or project management. Try to see the big picture. Find out quickly whether you work well in open environments (consulting or technology) or more structured environments (most industry). If you don't like one or the other, you probably should not seek jobs in that area.

ETHICAL PERSPECTIVE: ACCURACY—WHO IS RESPONSIBLE?

The issue of information accuracy has become highly charged in today's wired world. With all the computerization that has taken place, people have come to expect to receive and retrieve information more easily and quickly than ever before. In addition, because computers "never make mistakes," we have come to expect this information to be accurate. A case in point is at the bank. The combination of Automatic Teller Machines, computerized record systems, and large, electronic client and transaction databases should provide customers with quick and accurate access to their account information. However, we continue to experience and hear about record keeping errors at banks.

An error of a few dollars in your banking records doesn't seem so significant. However, what if it was an error in the bank's favor of hundreds or thousands of dollars? What if the error caused one of your important payments (such as a home mortgage payment) to bounce? Bank errors can be quite important.

There are many now-infamous stories of data accuracy problems with information systems, many of which have involved banks. For example, one such case occurred in Los Angeles, but has surely been repeated many times around this country and others. The basic story is as follows. Louis and Eileen Marches had bought a house in the 1950s with financing through their local bank. Louis dutifully paid the monthly payments in person and made sure that his loan book was stamped "paid" every time, even after the bank's systems had been automated. Several years ago, the Marches were notified that their payments were in arrears. Louis went to the bank with his payment book, but because the account screen showed no payment, the teller, the head teller, and the bank manager refused to honor his stamped book. One month later the same thing happened again, but now two months were in arrears. The bank continued to refuse his proof of payment and based their decisions and actions solely on the computer system. Eventually, the bank foreclosed on the house, causing a near fatal stroke for Eileen. After a long lawsuit, the Marches recovered $268,000 from the bank and the following apology: "Computers make mistakes. Banks make mistakes, too." Similar stories abound about people who have found that mistakes in their credit reports have led to disastrous results.

Now, imagine how significant a data accuracy error might be in other settings. Hospitals use similar automation and computer-intensive record keeping. Imagine what would happen if prescription information appeared incorrectly on a patient's chart and the patient became deathly ill as a result of the medicine that was mistakenly dispensed to him. The significance of such a data accuracy error could be tremendous. Furthermore, it wouldn't be clear who was to blame. Would this be the fault of the doctor, the pharmacist, the programmer, the data entry clerk, or maybe some combination of errors by the system designer, the system analyst, the system programmer, the database administrator, and the vendor? It would be too easy to simply blame the computer; some one person would need to be found to blame.

Computer-based information systems, and the data within those systems, are only as accurate and as useful as they have been made to be. The now infamous quote that "Computers make mistakes. Banks make mistakes, too" would be better restated as, "Computers never make mistakes; only humans make mistakes." This reflects the need for better precautions and greater scrutiny when modern information systems are designed, built, and used. This means that everyone must be concerned with data integrity, from the design of the system, to the building of the system, to the person that actually enters data into the system, and to the people who use and manage the system. Perhaps more importantly, when data errors are found, people shouldn't blame the computer. After all, people designed and built it, and entered data into it in the first place.

Questions for Discussion

1. Who is responsible for the accuracy of data within information systems? Why?

2. When someone is injured, either figuratively or literally, by errors in data from an information system, who should be responsible for making the injured party whole again?

3. Have you encountered data accuracy problems such as these? If so, what was the problem? What were the consequences? How were the problems remedied?

International Perspective: Help Wanted: Monolinguals Need Not Apply

Wanted:

People with advanced degrees in engineering, computer science, or information systems. TCP/IP, HTML, C, and JAVA programming experience a plus. Will provide green card, housing, and outstanding salary. Silicon Valley location.

Wanted:

Managers who are fluently bilingual; experience managing technology projects; experience living abroad and dealing with U.S., European, or Asian clients a must. Locations worldwide.

These job ads represent the kinds of human resource needs that global companies are facing. Currently, businesses all over the world are battling fiercely to attract two sets of employees: those who have high-tech skills and those who can deal effectively in a global marketplace. Companies need people to help them build information systems worldwide using precisely the methodologies described in this chapter.

As many as a third of all Silicon Valley professionals are currently non-native; these engineers, programmers, computer scientists, and information systems specialists from Asia, India, and other countries have been granted work permits (and sometimes permanent residency) by employers, universities, and the U.S. government. There still are not enough workers to fill spots in the booming technology sector, according to Intel, Microsoft, and other technology giants. Business leaders claim that a lack of focus on science, engineering, and technology in U.S. K–12 schools and a lack of interest in the same by American university graduates has caused a major shortage of qualified workers in these areas. Recruiting at U.S. universities has intensified, and the hiring of such a diverse group of workers reflects the growing population of foreign nationals willing to take up the slack. In fact, Silicon Valley companies are lobbying the U.S. government to allow them to hire a greater proportion of foreign nationals.

This same situation is occurring in other countries, where multinational corporations are desperate to hire well-trained workers for excellent salaries. Asian companies are looking for huge numbers of managers and other workers who are able to bridge the gap between Eastern and Western cultures; business owners in Hong Kong, Malaysia, Taiwan, and Japan note that they already have an acute need that will grow as businesses expand. For those contemplating careers with these companies, it may be easier to adapt to their environments than in the past; businesses such as Fujitsu are adopting some of the characteristics of Silicon Valley businesses, such as allowing flex-time, deserting dress codes, and permitting employees to pursue creative projects.

Given that the business world is becoming much more global and electronically connected, there are and will be tremendous opportunities for those individuals who possess technological skills and information systems project management skills, as well as have proficiency in a second language, knowledge of other cultures, and/or skills in dealing with people from other cultures in business contexts. Students who think ahead and acquire these skills during their degree programs will be able to write their own (plane) tickets upon graduation!

Questions for Discussion

1. Would you be willing to work in another country? Why or why not?

2. What are some possible effects if the trend of American businesses hiring foreign nationals continues?

3. What can be done to attract students into the science and technology disciplines?

Summary

1. **Understand the process used by organizations to manage the development of information systems.** The development of information systems follows a process called the systems development life cycle (SDLC). The SDLC is a process that first identifies the need for a system and then defines the processes for designing, developing, and maintaining information systems. The process is very structured and formal and requires the active involvement of managers and users.

2. **Describe each major phase of the systems development life cycle: systems identification, selection, and planning; system analysis; system design; system implementation; and system maintenance.** The SDLC has five phases: system identification, selection, and planning; system analysis; system design; system implementation; and system maintenance. Systems identification, selection, and planning is the first phase of the SDLC, in which potential projects are identified, selected, and planned. System analysis is the second phase of the SDLC, in which the current ways of doing business are studied and alternative replacement systems are proposed. System design is the third phase of the SDLC, in which all features of the proposed system are described. System implementation is the fourth phase of the SDLC, in which the information system is programmed, tested, installed, and supported. System maintenance is the fifth and final phase of the SDLC, in which an information system is systematically repaired and improved.

3. **Explain how organizations identify projects, assess feasibility, identify system benefits and costs, and perform economic analysis of a system project.** When a potential system is identified, organizations must assess the feasibility of the project before proceeding. The types of feasibility that can be assessed are economic, technical, operational, schedule, legal and contractual, and political. A system can provide tangible and intangible benefits, as well as tangible and intangible costs. An economic assessment requires that you identify the project's potential tangible benefits and costs and calculate the net present value, return on investment, or break-even duration. Feasibility analysis helps managers determine the probability of project success and compare alternative projects. Organiza-tions can yield the greatest benefits from their investments in information technology only by following a thorough and systematic feasibility assessment.

Key Terms

Systems analysis and design

Systems analyst

Software engineering

Systems development life cycle

System identification, selection, and planning

Information systems planning

Tangible benefits

Intangible benefits

Tangible costs

Intangible costs

One-time costs

Recurring costs

System analysis

Data flows

Processing logic

System design

Form

Report

Pseudo code

Structure charts

Decision trees

System implementation

Developmental testing

Alpha testing

Beta testing

System conversion

Parallel conversion

Direct conversion

Phased conversion

Pilot conversion

Maintenance phase

System maintenance

Corrective maintenance

Adaptive maintenance

Perfective maintenance

Preventive maintenance

Review Questions

1. According to this chapter, what are the five phases of the systems development life cycle?

2. Describe the four options available to organizations for obtaining information systems.

3. Describe the four major sources of systems development projects within an organization. What is the primary focus of each?

4. What are some of the possible criteria used to evaluate possible systems development projects?

5. Compare and contrast the terms system analysis and design, systems analyst, and system analysis. How are they related?

6. What are the four major components/tasks of the system design phase of the SDLC?

7. Explain the similarities and differences between forms and reports.

8. Describe the major forms of system testing—developmental, alpha, and beta.

9. What are the four processes for system conversion? How do they differ from each other?

10. Compare and contrast the four types of system maintenance.

11. What factors are considered in an economic feasibility study of an information systems project?

Problems and Exercises

◈ **Individual**　　◈ **Group**　　⌒ **Field**　　◖ **Web/Internet**

◈ 1. Match the following terms to the appropriate definitions:

____ Alpha testing

____ System analysis

____ Data flows

____ Structure charts

____ Parallel conversion

____ Adaptive maintenance

____ Tangible benefits

____ One-time costs

a. Data in motion, moving from one place in the system to another

b. Making changes to an information system to evolve its functionality to meet changing business needs or to migrate it to a different operating environment

c. Changing over from the old to a new system by running both at the same time until the organization is sure that the new system is error free, that the users are adequately trained, and that the support procedures are in place

d. Benefits that are easily measured in dollars and with certainty

e. Testing performed by the development organization to assess whether the entire system meets the design requirements of the users

f. Hierarchical diagram that shows how an information system is organized

g. Costs that occur once during the life of a system, typically during project initiation

h. The second phase of the systems development life cycle, in which the current ways of doing business are studied and alternative replacement systems are proposed

 2. A recently hired IS professional in your organization states that following a particular methodology, whether the SDLC from this chapter or any other methodology, causes development projects to take longer than necessary to implement. This person believes that projects should be developed quickly to maximize the benefits to be realized after they are in place. Do you agree? Why or why not? Explain to this person the broad goal of following methodologies for systems development. What about long-term benefits?

 3. Do you agree with the assessment that the use of the systems development steps outlined in the chapter will be around for quite some time? Why or why not? Is this process appropriate when purchasing a system from an outside vendor?

4. Consider the following within a small group: Table 9.1 shows the different sources of systems development projects. Of the four listed, which do you consider the best? Why? What makes it any better than the others? Should companies use only one of these sources for their potential projects? Why or why not?

 5. Explain the differences between data and data flows. How might systems analysts obtain the information they need to generate the data flows of a system? How are these data flows and the accompanying processing logic used in the system design phase of the life cycle? What happens when the data and data flows are modeled incorrectly?

 6. Discuss why interfaces and dialogueues can make or break a new system. What are their key functions? When are they designed? Are there any conventions for producing interfaces and dialogueues? If so, what are they?

 7. When Microsoft posts a new version of Internet Explorer on the Microsoft Web site and states that this is a beta version, what do they mean? Is this a final working version of the software, or is it still being tested? Who is doing the testing? Search the World Wide Web to find other companies that have beta versions of their products available to the public. You might try Corel at http://www. corel.com/. What other companies did you find?

 8. Imagine that you have just finished developing a new system for your company. This new system, unfortunately, cannot operate on the network at the same time as the current/old system. In a small group of classmates, determine what conversion plan you would recommend for this new system. Why? What risks does this plan bring and what advantages does it have over the other options?

 9. Why is the system documentation of a new information system so important? What information does it contain? For whom is this information intended? When will the system documentation most likely be used?

 10. Based on your own experiences with systems and applications, did their user documentation meet your expectations? Were you able to find the information and answers you needed? If you know, who wrote these guides, manuals, and/or procedures? Was it someone from the group that developed the system or someone from the outside?

 11. In a small group, conduct a search on the World Wide Web for "systems development life cycle" using any browser you wish. Check out some of the hits. Compare them to the SDLC outlined in this chapter and the SDLC utilized by NASA. Do all these life cycles follow the same general path? How many phases do the ones you found on the Web contain? Is the terminology the same or different? Prepare a 10-minute presentation of your findings to the class.

 12. Choose an organization with which you are familiar that develops its own information systems. Does this organization follow a systems development life cycle? If not, why not? How many phases does it have? Who developed this life cycle? Was it someone within the company, or was it adopted from somewhere else?

13. Interview an IS manager within an organization with which you are familiar. Determine what methods are used for information systems planning. Is it done entirely within the IS department or is it rooted in upper management? Where do most of the project proposals originate? Has this changed over time?

14. Choose an organization with which you are familiar that utilizes top-down systems planning for determining new projects to be developed. Is there any bottom-up systems planning in this organization? Why or why not? Who within the organization is most involved in this process?

15. Interview an IS manager within an organization with which you are familiar. Determine what techniques the IS department uses for analyzing the economic costs and benefits of a proposed system. Do they use only one technique? If so, why that one? If not, does one technique carry more weight if contradictory results are found? Do IS professionals conduct this analysis, or is it done by someone else? What did your fellow classmates find out from their interviews? Compare and contrast the results.

16. With a group of classmates, describe your experiences with information systems that were undergoing changes or updates (something similar to the scenario in the beginning of the chapter). What kind of conversion procedure was being used? How did this affect your interaction with the system as a user? Who else was affected? If the system was down altogether, for how long was it down? Do you or any of your classmates have "horror" stories, or were the situations not that bad?

Real World Case Problems

1. Software Gains Capital Treatment.

As of December 15, 1998, companies will be required to treat software bought or developed for internal use as an asset on their balance sheets. This rule confirms what IS managers have known for ages: Software can be as valuable as a factory. James Harrington of Coopers & Lybrand states that "Software is equivalent to the bricks and mortar of the information age."

Because the costs of large software projects will now depreciate over several years, like the costs associated with building a new factory, it is much more likely that companies will approve large, long-term IT projects. The IS managers trying to get projects approved may have to go through more red tape, however, such as forecasting a planned system's life span and its return on an investment. This is a difficult call in any environment. One overall benefit of this new rule is that IS managers will probably examine potential applications more closely for long-term solutions.

Company valuation could also change. For any company constantly investing in IT, capitalizing the software costs will increase the earnings and stockholder's equity, thus yielding an increase in the company's stock price, making it easier to borrow or prompt a higher takeover bid from a corporate suitor. Failing to capture the software's value as an asset can reduce the value of a company, especially during an acquisition or sale.

Time will tell whether it is best to record a project's costs as expenses as they are incurred or to capitalize the costs as an asset and depreciate them over the system's useful life. Some costs—such as maintenance, software coding, Year 2000 repairs, and R & D projects—will still be expressed because they do not create new functionality. The initial value of the project is the sum of the developers' salaries and the cost of the packaged software. Expensed means early pain, whereas depreciation delays it.

a. Explain the significant difference between recording an information systems project's costs as expenses as they are incurred versus capitalizing the costs as an asset and then depreciating that asset over the system's useful life. Why is this potentially important to businesses?

b. What effect will this have on the way that managers quantify the costs and benefits of information systems projects?

c. Will this make it easier for some firms to say yes to large, expensive projects? Why or why not?

Source   Hibbard, Justin. 1998. *Software gains capital treatment.* InformationWeek, *January 12, 18–20.*

2. Wright Consulting Services

Wright Consulting Services, Inc. (WCS), of Portland, Oregon, provides information systems (IS) consulting services to clients in the Pacific Northwest, primarily in the Portland/Willamette Valley and Seattle/Puget Sound areas. Services include systems analysis, design, development, and implementation using Oracle Developer/2000. Clients include private sector companies of all sizes, state and local government agencies, schools and universities, and nonprofit organizations.

The purpose of WCS's systems analysis service is to gain an understanding of an organization's existing information systems. Activities include Information Gathering, Physical Process Modeling, Logical Data Modeling, and Logical Process Modeling. In the systems design phase, WCS redesigns clients' systems to more effectively match their requirements. Tasks within the systems design phase include Physical Data Modeling, Physical Process Modeling, Rapid Prototyping, Capacity Planning, and Technology Evaluation and Selection. In the systems development and implementation phase, WCS breaks down a system implementation into smaller steps and builds the system step by step, piece by piece. Activities in this phase include Technology Acquisition and/or Customization, Custom Software Development, System Testing, Data Conversion, Technical Documentation, User Documentation, and User Training.

Among its many successful engagements, WCS developed an application to manage a telecommunications company's stored value (phone/gas/merchandise) cards. Software is used by customer service representatives to view card status and transaction histories and issue manual transactions at customers' requests, by finance analysts to review transactions and issue invoices to retailers, and by merchants to review transactions. Applications were developed using Oracle Developer/2000 Forms 4.5 under Microsoft Windows.

a. How closely do the services of Wright Consulting Services parallel the methodologies described in this chapter?

b. In what ways are WCS's services different from those described in this chapter?

c. Why should companies turn to WCS to perform systems analysis and design rather than doing it themselves in-house?

Source   Wright Consulting Web site: http://www.wriconsult.com/index.html.

References

Hoffer, George, and Valacich. 1999. *Modern systems analysis and design.* 2d ed. Reading, Massachusetts: Addison Wesley Longman.

IBM. 1998. Information from: www.ibm.com. Information verified: March 21, 1998.

Keen, P.G.W. 1991. *Shaping the future: Business design through information technology.* Cambridge, Massachusetts: Harvard Business School Press.

McKeen, Guimaraes, and Wetherbe. 1994. A comparative analysis of MIS project selection mechanisms. *Database* 25: 43–59.

NASA. 1998. Information from: www.ivv.nasa.gov. Information verified: March 21, 1998.

Nunamaker, J.F., Jr. 1992. Build and learn, evaluate and learn. *Informatica* 1(1): 1–6.

Pressman, R.S. 1992. *Software engineering.* New York: McGraw-Hill.

STI. 1998. Information from: www.ondaweb.com/sti/. Information verified: March 21, 1998.

Related Readings

Agarwal, Sinha, and Tanniru. 1996. Cognitive fit in requirements modeling: A study of object and process methodologies. *Journal of Management Information Systems* 13(2): 137–162.

Banker, R.D., and S.A. Slaughter. 1997. A field study of scale economies in software maintenance. *Management Science* 43(12): 1709–1725.

Beath, C.M., and W.J. Orlikowski. 1994. The contradictory structure of systems development methodologies: Deconstructing the IS-user relationship in information engineering. *Information Systems Research* 5(4): 350–377.

Bordoloi, Mykytyn, and Mykytyn. 1996. A framework to limit systems developers' legal liabilities. *Journal of Management Information Systems* 12(4): 161–185.

Cusamano, M.A., and R.W. Selby. 1997. How Microsoft builds software. *Communications of the ACM* 40(6): 53–61.

Fayad, M.E. 1997. Software development process: A necessary evil. *Communications of the ACM* 40(9): 101–103.

Hidding, G.J. 1997. Reinventing methodology: Who reads it and why? *Communications of the ACM* 40(11): 102–109.

McKeen, J.D., and T. Guimaraes. 1997. Successful strategies for user participation in systems development. *Journal of Management Information Systems* 14(2): 133–150.

Newman, M., and R. Sabherwal. 1996. Determinants of commitment to information systems development: A longitudinal investigation. *Management Information Systems Quarterly* 20(1): 23–54.

Rada, R., and J. Moore. 1997. Standardizing reuse. *Communications of the ACM* 40(3): 19–23.

Robey, Smith, and Vijayasarathy. 1993. Perceptions of conflict and success in information systems development projects. *Journal of Management Information Systems* 10(1): 123–139.

Sillince, J.A.A., and S. Mouakket. 1997. Varieties of political process during systems development. *Information Systems Research* 8(4): 368–397.

Vessey, I., and S. Conger. 1993. Learning to specify information requirements: The relationship between application and methodology. *Journal of Management Information Systems* 10(2): 177–201.

Chapter 10: Contemporary Information Systems Development Approaches

Scenario: Information Management at The King of Hearts Ranch

Brett Williams, owner of The King of Hearts Ranch in Great Falls, Montana, raises some of the finest cutting horses in the United States. "Cutting" has its roots in the open-range ranches of the Old West, where individual animals had to be isolated or "cut" from large herds for branding, medical treatment, or sorting. Certain horses showed an uncommon ability for separating cattle from the herd. These were the first cutting horses. Today, cutting horses are specially bred and trained. To identify the best cutting horses, special competitions are held where horse and rider have two and a half minutes to demonstrate their ability to cut a cow and keep it separated from a herd. Top cutting horses are worth more than a hundred thousand dollars. Although it comes from humble roots, cutting is big business!

At The King of Hearts Ranch, dozens of horses are cared for and trained (see Figure 10.1). Some horses are kept for breeding, some are kept for competing in cutting contests, and others—still young and unproved—are kept for training. Those not making "cutting grade" are sold off to riders who are looking for a very high-quality horse that was just not meant for cutting. For each horse, detailed information must be tracked on health, breeding, and competitions. Needless to say, managing information is an important part

of the horse business. Until now, Brett has kept track of his information through the use of several ledgers. He has separate ledgers for tracking health, births and breeding, and competitions. Unfortunately, as his ranch grew, it became more and more difficult to find important information.

One night at a family gathering he talked to his nephew, a senior MIS student at the University of Montana, about his information management problems. After about an hour-long discussion, Brett summarized, "So Greg, I could hire you this summer to build a system to track all my information with a computer. This sounds great, so how would we proceed?"

"Well," replied Greg, "I would need to first interview you for an hour or so to get an idea about what you do. I will also need to get some examples of the kinds of information you use. After we do this, I could create a prototype of the system. Next, you could review this prototype and give me additional information, and suggest changes to make. We would do this until the system looked the way you wanted and provided the information you needed. The best part about building the system this way is that at the end, you have a system that does exactly what you want!"

"How long will it take to do this?" replied Brett.

FIGURE 10.1

Cutting ranch.

324

"It is not uncommon to have more than ten iterations of talking with you, refining the prototype, and then having you review my work," replied Greg. "Each iteration should take about a week to accomplish. Overall, I am confident that I could build your system over the summer, but maybe in less than two months if all goes well. I'll have a better idea of this after our first meeting; after that I'll write you a firm proposal."

Introduction

Chapter 9, "The Information Systems Development Process," talked about the information systems development process and described the systems development life cycle (SDLC). Recall that the SDLC has five phases and is most widely used to guide the development of contemporary organizational information systems such as transaction processing and management information systems. (See Chapter 7 for a review of organizational information systems). As you have read throughout this book and have experienced in your own life, information systems are of many different types, including decision support systems, executive information systems, group support systems, and Internet commerce systems. Each system is radically different from the others and from the typical system built using the SDLC. These differences are analogous to the differences among structures that could be built by a contractor. Some contractors build houses, while others build apartment buildings, warehouses, or skyscrapers.

For the building contractor, the tools and techniques needed to construct each type of structure vary greatly. Building a house is a relatively simple process using wood, nails, saws, and a minimal amount of other equipment. Of course, it is possible to build a skyscraper with the same materials and equipment, but it would probably not be constructed in the most timely and effective way. Steel girders and huge cranes speed the construction and enhance the

structural quality of a skyscraper. These materials are not needed when building a house. Likewise, the tools and techniques that can be used to design and build different types of information systems vary greatly. This does not mean that you can't use the SDLC for all types of systems; you could if you wanted to. But building the best system requires that you use the right tools and techniques for the right job. Consequently, as new and different types of information systems have emerged, so too have new development approaches and tools.

This chapter describes emerging system development approaches. It first focuses on ways to identify and define system requirements—in other words, ways to get information from users on how the system should operate. Getting the system requirements correct at the beginning goes a long way toward building a high-quality system. The next section discusses emerging approaches for managing the entire development process. These approaches represent alternatives to the SDLC. Finally, the chapter describes several tools that have emerged to assist the systems development process. The goal of this chapter is to increase your knowledge of systems development methods. After reading this chapter, you will be able to do the following:

1. Explain contemporary approaches for collecting and structuring the information needed to design and construct an information system.

2. Describe prototyping, rapid application development, object-oriented analysis and design methods of systems development, and each approach's strengths and weaknesses.

3. Understand how and why to use several automated tools for supporting contemporary development, including computer-aided software engineering, group support systems, and advanced programming languages.

326

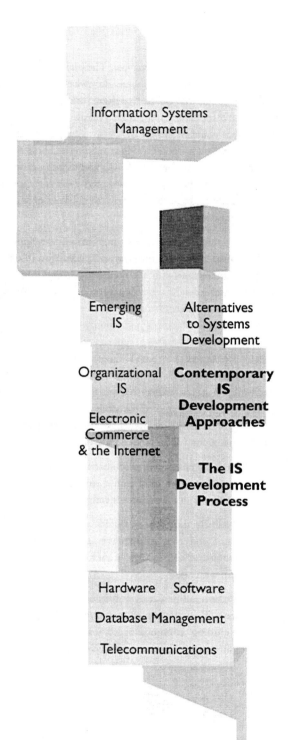

Information Systems
Management

Emerging
IS

Alternatives
to Systems
Development

Organizational
IS

**Contemporary
IS
Development
Approaches**

Electronic
Commerce
& the Internet

**The IS
Development
Process**

Hardware   Software

Database Management

Telecommunications

This chapter is the second in Part 4, "Information Systems Development," and it focuses on describing how organizations develop and acquire information systems (see Figure 10.2). In Chapter 9, we discussed the development process used to design and build most information systems. This chapter describes the various processes used to develop and build most contemporary information systems.

Contemporary Methods for Collecting and Structuring System Requirements

This section examines contemporary approaches for collecting and structuring system requirements, which are the tasks a systems professional performs during the systems analysis phase (the second phase) of the system development life cycle. The collection and structuring of system requirements is arguably the most important activity in the systems development process because all subsequent activities are influenced by how well the information system requirements are defined. The old saying, "garbage in, garbage out," very much applies to the system building process.

As you read in the preceding chapter, one purpose of the systems analysis phase is to gain a thorough understanding of an organization's current way of doing things in an area for which the new information system is to be constructed. System analysts work closely with users to determine what is needed from the proposed system. Analysts have traditionally asked users what information they need to have put into the system and what types of information they need back from the system to do their job well. This chapter describes a method for collecting system requirements that focuses the kinds of questions the analysts ask the users.

FIGURE 10.2

The big picture: focusing on contemporary information systems development approaches.

Critical Success Factors (CSF)

The **Critical Success Factor** (CSF) methodology for collecting system requirements was developed by Jack Rockart of MIT in the late 1970s as a means to help CEOs define their information system needs (Rockart, 1979). It is still quite popular today as a way to obtain a useful set of system requirements from users. A Critical Success Factor, or CSF, is something that must go well to ensure success for a manager, department, division, or organization. It was envisioned by Rockart that if CEOs—and all members of the organization, for that matter—understood and agreed upon a common set of CSFs, it would be a straightforward task to derive the informational needs of the organization.

How the CSF Approach Works

To understand an organization's CSFs, a systems analyst interviews people throughout the organization and asks each person to define her own *personal* CSFs. People asked to participate in the CSF identification process should be from a cross-section of the major functional areas of the organization. After the analyst collects these individual CSFs, he can merge, consolidate, and refine them to identify a broad set of organization-wide CSFs, as shown in Figure 10.3.

Strengths and Weaknesses of the CSF Approach

All approaches for assisting the information systems development process have strengths and weaknesses, and the CSF approach is no exception (see Boynton and Zmud, 1994). The greatest strength of the CSF approach is that senior managers intuitively understand the approach and support its usage. This is in contrast to other systems development approaches that are unintuitive and less strategically focused. A second strength is that the CSF approach provides a way to understand the information needs of the organization in order to make effective decisions. A steering or planning committee for an organization can greatly improve its effectiveness by understanding the organization's CSFs when identifying and selecting projects.

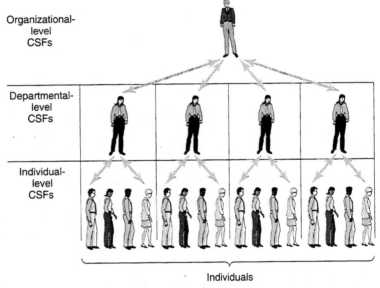

Organizational-level CSFs

Departmental-level CSFs

Individual-level CSFs

Individuals

FIGURE 10.3

Merging individual CSFs to represent organization-wide CSFs.

Weaknesses of the CSF approach are that the method's high-level focus can lead to an oversimplification of a complex situation. For example, people have a limited capacity for dealing with complexity and a limited capacity for keeping track of information. These limits may result in managers recalling only the most recent events, or events that are over-simplified for the complex environment in which the organization operates. As a result, the analyst may be left with a biased or incomplete set of information requirements. Using a broad cross-section of organizational personnel can minimize some of these problems. A second weakness centers on the difficulty of finding analysts trained to perform the CSF process that must both understand information systems and be able to effectively communicate with senior executives. Past research has found that the quality of the analyst is a key factor in the successful application of the process.

A third weakness of the CSF approach is that this method is not user-centered; that is, it relies on an expert systems analyst to glean requirements from users and to organize them appropriately. The next section explores other methods for collecting and organizing system requirements that are more user-centered.

Joint Application Requirements (JAR)/Joint Application Design (JAD)

Joint Application Requirements (JAR) and **Joint Application Design (JAD)** are methods for collecting requirements and creating system designs. Most often, people refer to both JAR and JAD as simply JAD. As with the CSF approach, JAD was introduced in the late 1970s by IBM Canada and is quite popular today as an alternative methodology within the systems analysis phase of the systems development life cycle. The defining aspect of JAD is that "joint" really means group. In other words, the JAD method is a group-based approach for collecting system requirements and for setting system design specifications. JAD was the first method for building information systems that stressed the use of groups. To understand why this is significant, recall the requirements development process within the systems development life cycle (SDLC), first described in Chapter 9.

When collecting system requirements and following the guidelines of the SDLC, a systems analyst interviews potential users of the new information system individually to understand each user's needs. During this process, the analyst may interview a large number of users. In most cases, the analyst will hear a lot of similar requests from most of the users, but will also hear many conflicting requests. The analyst will therefore spend considerable effort consolidating information and following up with users to resolve conflicting requirements and specifications. If many people are being consulted, the process of scheduling and conducting these individual interviews can be quite time consuming.

In contrast to the SDLC approach to determining systems requirements, a JAD is a special type of a group meeting in which all users meet with the analyst at the same time. During this meeting, all users *jointly* define and agree upon system requirements or designs. This process has resulted in dramatic reductions in the length of time needed to collect requirements or specify designs.

How the JAD Approach Works

The JAD meeting can be held in a normal conference room or special-purpose JAD room. Figure 10.4 shows a sample JAD room. JAD meeting rooms are often designed much like a classroom, with facilities for presenting information to the group. Most JAD rooms have overhead projectors, whiteboards, flip charts, and computers to assist in making presentations and to help in recording the ideas and deliberations of the group. Often, JAD meetings are held "off-site" to minimize the potential distractions for participants. Like all good meetings, JAD meetings have a detailed agenda with clear objectives for the session. For example, a JAD session might be used to finalize the format and content of a new report from a system.

A **facilitator** is a JAD expert who organizes the JAD meetings. The

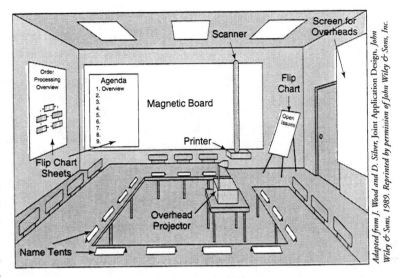

Adapted from J. Wood and D. Silver, Joint Application Design, John Wiley & Sons, 1989. Reprinted by permission of John Wiley & Sons, Inc.

FIGURE 10.4

A JAD room.

facilitator's role is to help the group work effectively during the session. A **scribe** also attends the meeting to record the *jointly* agreed-upon design information. Of course, key ingredients of a JAD meeting are the users—the people who will use the information system and know what it needs to do. Together, the team members work together to quickly identify requirements, resolve disagreements, and finalize design requirements. The objective of this "joint" approach is to involve many users early in the design of their system. Furthermore, JAD is useful across a broad range of organizations and types of information systems. JAD has been used by large organizations, such as the U.S. Army, when designing global logistics systems, and small organizations, such as small electronics companies, when designing a new manufacturing control system.

Strengths and Weaknesses of JAD

The JAD approach to systems development provides several advantages. First, the group-based process enables more people to be involved in the development effort without adversely slowing the process. This results in greater support and acceptance of the new system and can also result in a system of much higher quality. Additionally, because user involvement eases implementation (that is, users were involved in defining what the system would do and how the system would operate), training and support costs for developing the system can be significantly lower. JAD has proven the old adage that more heads are better than one!

JAD also has its weaknesses. First, it is often very difficult to get all relevant users to the same place at the same time to hold a JAD meeting. Large organizations may have users virtually all over the world; getting them all to a meeting (or a series of meetings) would be extremely difficult and expensive. Many believe that JAD requires a high-level executive sponsor pushing the process to ensure that it gets the resources (and the people) necessary to make it successful.

A second weakness of JAD relates to the inherent problems that groups may face, especially large groups. Have you ever worked in a group in which one person dominated? Probably so. Or, have you ever experienced a situation where some people in the group were shy and didn't want to talk? How about working in a group where one or more of the members simply chose not to help and let the other members of the group do the work? Consequently, the possibility of having a "bad" group is a significant potential weakness of JAD. Needless to say, many things can go wrong when groups work together. A skilled facilitator, a clear agenda, and strong management support can go a long way to remedy these problems.

The strengths and weaknesses of the Critical Success Factor (CSF) and the Joint Application Design (JAD) approaches are summarized in Table 10.1. Now that you know the contemporary methods for gathering requirements for an information system, you can consider alternatives for designing and building them.

Table 10.1 Strengths and weaknesses of contemporary methods for collecting and structuring system requirements.

Approach	Strengths	Weaknesses
Critical Success Factors	Easy for senior managers to understand; provides needed structure to the collection process	Broad focus; oversimplification of a complex situation
Joint Application Requirement / Joint Application Design	Enables more people to be involved; broad user involvement eases system implementation	Difficult and expensive to get all people to the same place at the same time; potential to have dysfunctional groups

Contemporary Approaches for Designing and Building Systems

The Systems Development Life Cycle is one approach for managing the development process and is a very good approach to follow when the requirements for the information system are highly structured and straightforward—for example, a payroll or inventory system. Today, organizations need a broad variety of information systems, not just payroll and inventory systems, for which requirements are either very hard to specify in advance or are constantly changing. For example, an organization's Web site is likely to be an information system with constantly changing requirements. How many Web sites have you visited in which the content or layout seemed to change almost every day? For this type of system, the SDLC might work as a development approach, but it wouldn't be optimal. In this section, we describe several approaches needed to develop flexible information systems: prototyping, rapid application development, and object-oriented analysis and design.

Prototyping

Prototyping is a systems development methodology that uses a "trial and error" approach for discovering how a system should operate. You may think that this doesn't sound like a process at all; however, you probably use prototyping all the time in many of your day-to-day activities, but you just don't know it! For example, when you buy new clothes you likely use prototyping—that is, trial and error—by trying on several shirts before making a selection. Likewise, when you buy a new car, computer, shoes, or even when you choose a mate, you use a trial-and-error process. When prototyping is used to design a new system, the systems designer works with users in a trial-and-error process until the system works the way the users want it to work. In our scenario at the beginning of the chapter, Greg was planning to use prototyping to build the new information system for The King of Hearts Ranch.

How Prototyping Works

Figure 10.5 diagrams the prototyping process when applied to identifying/determining system requirements. To begin the process, the system designer interviews one or several users of the system, either individually or as a group using a JAD. After the designer gains a general understanding of what the users want, he develops a prototype of the new system as quickly as possible to share with the users. The users may like what they see or ask for changes. If changes are requested, the designer modifies the prototype and again shares it with the users. This process of sharing and refinement continues until the users approve the functionality of the system.

Strengths and Weaknesses of Prototyping

The greatest strength of prototyping is that the process helps develop a close working relationship between the system designer and users. This relationship helps build trust and acceptance for the new system. A second strength of prototyping is that it is arguably the best systems development method for identifying how a system should operate when the system's specifications are hard to define. For example, when developing an executive information system (EIS) or decision support system (DSS) (see Chapter 7, "Organizational Information Systems," for a review of these two types of systems), prototyping is often used to help the executive or manager "discover" the system requirements through the prototyping process. For many systems that are used to support individual managers and executives like an EIS and DSS, the system must be customized to the individual. In many cases the requirements cannot be defined ahead of time. We have worked with executives on these types of systems, and they literally state, "I can't tell you exactly what I want this system to do, but I'll know it when I see it." In these cases, prototyping is an excellent approach. A key to the successful application of prototyping is that each cycle of the prototyping process proceeds rapidly. In fact, it is through the rapid, iterative process that the benefits of this process are most likely to occur.

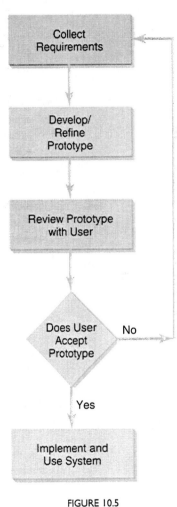

FIGURE 10.5

The prototyping process.

Prototyping also has numerous weaknesses. First and foremost, prototyping is not appropriate for developing every type of information system. For example, prototyping is very problematic in projects with a large number of users that must be consulted during the design process; requiring the systems analyst to consult with more than just a few users not only increases the complexity of the process, but also significantly slows the process. Likewise, systems with more structured requirements (that is, requirements that can be easily identified and defined—such as an inventory management or payroll system) are not good candidates for prototyping. For systems with highly structured requirements, there is little need for prototyping and the systems development life cycle approach to building the system has been found to be much more effective.

Another weakness of prototyping is that the process itself often results in not spending enough effort on important activities within the development process. Consequently, the system development process can be *rushed*, which can result in inadequate analysis and design, poor testing, and little or no documentation. Systems that lack maintainability due to inadequate documentation or some other factor cost the organization significantly more resources to maintain than do systems that are adequately documented. In other words, failing to do the job right the first time can lead to many long-term costs. For example, the quality and completeness of a system's documentation is a key factor influencing how easily a system can be changed and maintained in the future. Given that most of the costs of having a system are incurred during system maintenance, effective management of the systems development process must assure quality documentation.

Rapid Application Development (RAD)

Rapid Application Development (RAD) is a four-phase systems development methodology that combines prototyping, computer-based development tools, special management practices, and close user involvement. In 1991, James Martin conceived RAD as a methodology to develop information systems more quickly and cheaply. Others have developed their own flavors of RAD (see, for example, McConnell, 1996), yet there are some basic principles to most RAD-based methods, which are discussed here.

How Rapid Application Development Works

Martin's version of RAD has four phases: 1) requirements planning, 2) user design, 3) construction, and 4) the move to the new system. Phase 1, requirements planning, is similar to the first two phases of the SDLC, in which the system is planned and requirements are analyzed. To gain intensive user involvement, the RAD methodology encourages the use of JAD sessions to collect requirements. Where RAD becomes *radical* is during Phase 2, where users of the information system become intensively involved in the design process. CASE tools (Computer-Aided Software Engineering, discussed later in this chapter) are used to quickly structure requirements and develop prototypes. As prototypes are developed and refined, they are continually reviewed with users in additional JAD sessions. Like prototyping, RAD is a process in which requirements, designs, and the system itself are developed via iterative refinement, as shown in Figure 10.6. In a sense, with the RAD approach the people building the system and the users of that system keep cycling back and forth between Phase 2 (user design) and Phase 3 (construction) until the system is done. As a result, RAD requires close cooperation between users and designers to be successful. This means that management must actively support the development project and make it a priority for everyone involved.

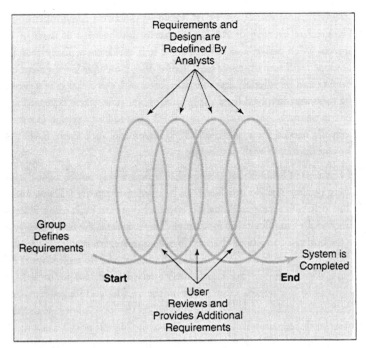

FIGURE 10.6

Iterative refinement is a key to the success of RAD.

— Using RAD at the First National Bank of Chicago — A BRIEF CASE

An example of RAD can be found at First National Bank of Chicago. In 1994, the Internal Revenue Service (IRS) mandated the elimination of paperwork from employers' federal tax withholding payments. In the past, employers submitted a Federal Tax Deposit (FTD) coupon and a check to an authorized bank within three business days of releasing payroll to their employees. In an effort to speed processing and eliminate paperwork, the IRS mandated that employers with a tax liability in excess of $50,000 would have to begin making electronic payments by January 1, 1996. By 1999, employers with a tax liability in excess of $20,000 would also be required to make electronic payments. First National Bank was selected by the IRS to be the clearinghouse for employers in the northern tier of the U.S. Using the RAD approach and the Delphi visual programming environment (Borland, 1998), the bank developed the graphical user interface for their online tax collection system. During the RAD process, they prototyped and tested literally dozens of variations of the interface with customers to make the system very easy to use. In 1997, 1.2 million of the largest employers in the northern tier of the U.S. used the system for processing federal tax payments. By 1999, the number of employers enrolled in the system is expected to be more than 4 million. Because tax records must be maintained for seven years, more than 500 million records will be stored by the year 2000. Using Delphi and the RAD approach, the First National Bank of Chicago was able to meet contract specifications and stringent project deadlines.

Strengths and Weaknesses of Rapid Application Development

The greatest strength of RAD is the active involvement of users in the development process. With active user involvement, it is much more likely that the system being developed will actually meet their needs. Also, close user involvement eases many of the training and installation activities associated with the creation of a new system. Because the users were involved from the beginning, the new system is viewed as "their" new system. In addition, Martin claims that RAD can produce a system in a fraction of the time normally needed for a traditional SDLC approach. As a result, RAD can greatly reduce the cost associated with developing a system.

A weakness of RAD is that some people believe it may not be a good approach for developing systems that do not "need" to be developed rapidly (Gibson and Hughes, 1994). Due to RAD's accelerated analysis approach, systems built using it are often limited in functionality and flexibility for change. This may limit the use of the system in the future as the business conditions change. To develop a system for a longer-term business opportunity, it may be better to stick with the traditional (though slower) SDLC approach. With SDLC, a more thorough, slower analysis would be performed—an analysis that might make the system more robust to the broader and longer-term needs of the organization. In addition, due to the emphasis on the speed of design and development, systems developed using RAD may not be of the highest possible quality. This means that systems builders and users ought to be aware of the potential trade-offs in using the RAD approach. When systems need to be developed in an environment of rapidly changing business conditions, however, RAD is an effective tool.

In short, the RAD approach is intended to improve systems development, and ultimately improve systems quality, by enabling businesses to develop systems more quickly. The following section describes one other alternative approach to building systems—object-oriented analysis and design.

Object-Oriented Analysis and Design

As described in Chapter 3, "Information Systems Software," one key trend in programming languages has been the development of object-oriented languages such as C++. One of the major advantages of using object-oriented languages is the capability they give system designers to easily reuse commonly used modules. Systems are built more quickly and more consistently when they share common building blocks. For example, in Visual C++ it is very easy to design a user interface because the key components for developing the look and feel of the system—such as menus, buttons, and text boxes—are provided by the system, as shown in Figure 10.7. Each of these objects has a standard look and a restricted set of functions. As a result, when a designer decides to use a predefined object, he knows it will behave in the same way from system to system. Numerous object-oriented analysis and design approaches have emerged, both in response to the growth in popularity of object-oriented programming and in an effort to fully utilize object-oriented programming concepts (Booch, 1990; Coad and Yourdon, 1991; Halladay and Wiebel, 1993).

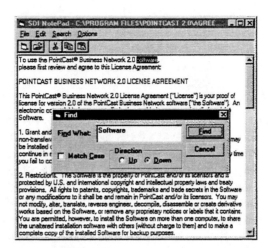

FIGURE 10.7

Building a user interface with reusable objects.

Object-Oriented Analysis and Design (OOA&D) is very similar to other analysis and design approaches. In fact, OOA&D and the traditional SDLC approach have many similarities, such as the ways in which data is modeled. OOA&D is, however, subtly different in the way that system components are thought about and used. OOA&D helps information systems users and managers think in more general terms about the various elements of an information system. The most fundamental element in OOA&D is the *object*. An object represents something tangible, such as a student, course, account, or transaction. As with data modeling (described in Chapter 4, "Database Management"), each tangible thing can have properties. For example, a student can have a name, identification number, and class schedule.

Up to this point, there is little difference between OOA&D and data modeling; however, objects can be used for more than simply defining data. Objects can also contain the operations that can be performed on the tangible thing (for example, an account) so that the data and operations are bundled together within the object. For example, the operations that can be performed with an object within a user interface are tightly coupled with the data that defines the object. Continuing with our user interface example, Figure 10.8 shows how a programmer can set the attributes for a button object on a user interface. The attributes for a button might include its shape, size, and color. When a user clicks on the button, certain pre-programmed events happen. This means that the systems analyst defines both the data describing the button and the operations—or "methods" in OOA&D terminology—that can be performed by clicking on the button. The data and the methods are bundled within the button object. This subtle difference in systems development approach equates to a big difference in how systems are designed.

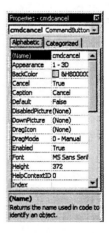

FIGURE 10.8

Setting properties on a button object.

How Object-Oriented Analysis and Design Works

When using the SDLC approach, systems analysts follow primarily a top-down process in which the system requirements are decomposed, or broken down into smaller and smaller pieces until specific programming modules can be defined, programmed, and pieced together to yield a system. Similarly, data and their interrelationships are modeled by the analysts, and these conceptual models are turned over to a programmer who actually implements these data models in a database management system. In most instances, a systems analyst develops a high-level design for the data and the processing and provides this design to programmers, who actually implement the design in programming code and databases. The analyst often never does any coding. This is different with the OOA&D approach due to the tight coupling between the methods and data and between the conceptual model of the system and its actual implementation. OOA&D can turn every programmer into an analyst and every analyst into a programmer. What this means is that the analyst using an OOA&D approach can be thinking simultaneously right from the start about the "what" (the data) *and* the "how" (the operations to be performed) as he defines all the relevant objects that the system entails. Furthermore, the design *and* implementation of the objects can happen quickly and simultaneously if an object-oriented programming language is being used. In sum, OOA&D is a more integrative prototyping process than the SDLC approach, in which data and operations on the data are modeled separately and at a conceptual level and are later implemented and brought together in a subsequent phase of the systems development process.

Strengths and Weaknesses of Object-Oriented Analysis and Design

The strengths of OOA&D are numerous. First, OOA&D forces designers to integrate their thinking to simultaneously consider both operations and data when creating a design. When analysts use SDLC, they separately model system logic, processes, and data. Because OOA&D designers use a broader and more integrated focus, advocates for OOA&D believe that system quality is improved and the duration of the system development process is reduced. Additionally, after objects are defined, they can be reused by other systems. This enables new or improved modules to be easily plugged into new systems or those being maintained.

The OOA&D approach also has some weaknesses. The most notable weakness for many organizations is the requirement that existing analysts and programmers be trained on OOA&D techniques. After they are trained in the SDLC or some other non-object-oriented method, experience has shown that it is often very difficult for people to change the way they approach the systems development process. Many organizations have had to make considerable investments in retraining programmers and analysts to adequately use the OOA&D approach. Also, although it is intuitive to believe that OOA&D will lead to lower development costs and higher-quality systems, little research exists to support this assertion. One problem, for example, is that many programmers and analysts are unwilling to search libraries for reusable code. It is unclear whether this failure to reuse standard modules is due to a lack of adequate training or just plain stubbornness. Nonetheless, one of the key benefits of OOA&D—reusability—may not be adequately utilized, which, of course, greatly limits its benefits.

This section has described some of the more popular information systems development approaches. Although each of the previously described approaches has been discussed separately, the wise organization and skilled analyst often utilize multiple methods when developing a single system. What should be clear to you is that no approach is perfect and that all have strengths and weaknesses (see Table 10.2). To put this another way, a skilled systems developer is much like a skilled craftsman, with many tools at his disposal. The skilled craftsman chooses the most appropriate tool and approach for the task at hand. Using one systems development approach or tool for all systems and problems is akin to using only a hammer to build a house. Building a house with just a hammer might be possible, but it would probably be a strange-looking house!

Table 10.2 Strengths and weaknesses of contemporary development approaches.

Approach	Strengths	Weaknesses
Prototyping	Develops close working relationship between designer and users; works well for messy and hard-to-define problems	Not practical with a large number of users; system may be built too quickly, which could result in lower quality
Rapid Application Development	Active user involvement in design process; easier implementation due to user involvement	Systems are often narrowly focused—limits future evolution; system may be built too quickly, which could result in lower quality
Object-Oriented Analysis and Design	Integration of data and processing during design should lead to higher-quality systems; reuse of common modules makes development and maintenance easier	Very difficult to train analysts and programmers on the object-oriented approach; limited use of common modules

Special types of development tools are often applied to the prototyping approach. For example, CASE (Computer-Aided Software Engineering) is a popular tool that helps to automate many aspects of the systems development process. Fourth-generation languages, object orientation, and visual programming are other tools used to assist in the rapid development of systems. Skilled designers must have a "tool kit" of powerful development tools to gain the benefits from this process. Each of these tools is described in the following section.

Tools for Supporting Contemporary Systems Development

Over the years, the tools for developing information systems have increased in variety and in power. In the early days of systems development, a developer was left to use a pencil and paper to sketch out design ideas and program code. Computers were cumbersome to use and slow to program, and most designers worked out on paper as much of the system design as they could before moving to the computer. Today, system developers have a vast array of powerful computer-based tools at their disposal. These tools have changed forever the ways in which systems are developed.

Computer-Aided Software Engineering

Computer-Aided Software Engineering (CASE) refers to automated software tools used by systems analysts to develop information systems. These tools can be used to automate or support activities throughout the systems development process, with the objective of increasing productivity and improving the overall quality of systems.

Collect America, Ltd. (CA), a company that collects long-overdue customer and commercial debts, uses Oracle Designer/2000 and Developer/2000 CASE tools for developing their information systems (Oracle, 1998). Based in Denver, Colorado, CA tracks and monitors debtors using an Oracle database environment. To make collections, CA has franchise agreements with regional law firms in the U.S., Canada, and Mexico. As their business has grown, so too have their information management needs. As CA has used Oracle's CASE tools to design, construct, and maintain their applications, system quality and speed have improved over their previously non-CASE-developed systems. Systems developed using CASE enable applications to be moved easily from one hardware platform to another. Consequently, as the hardware infrastructure in CA has evolved, their applications have also evolved without major changes. For example, with the rapid growth and easy accessibility of the World Wide Web, CA determined they could save a lot of money if franchise offices around North America could use the Web for accessing CA's database. Using Oracle's CASE tools, system developers reconstructed applications so that they could be accessed using a standard Web browser. Today, because access to this information is through the Web, huge cost savings are being realized by CA; they no longer have to invest in routers, dedicated lines, and all the other technology needed to manage a dedicated network. For CA, CASE has really paid off.

In reference to the SDLC, the tools used to automate the first three phases of the SDLC—system identification, selection, and planning; system analysis; and system design—are generally referred to as **upper CASE** tools. For example, during system analysis activities, it is very useful to represent business processes and information flows using a graphical diagram. CASE helps you draw such diagrams by providing standard symbols to represent business processes, information flows between processes, data storage, and the organizational entities that interact with the business process. Using CASE to diagram this information greatly assists this process. For example, Figure 10.9A shows a high-level business process diagram called a Data Flow Diagram, or DFD, from the CASE system from Visible Systems Corporation called *The Visible Analyst Workbench* (VAW). This view of a business process is the highest level or the most abstract; in DFD terminology, this is called the context-level view. This diagram represents an organization's entities (in this instance, those associated with the Department of Motor Vehicles) and the process of providing licenses to potential drivers. Lower-level processes within this system are shown in Figure 10.9B, where some business processes are likely to be automated while others may not. Using a picture to represent this business process helps facilitate clear communication between the system developers and users.

Likewise, the tools used to automate the system implementation and maintenance phases are generally referred to as **lower CASE** tools. For example, one key activity during implementation is the development of the computer program code for the system. A *code generator* is a feature of lower CASE tools that produces high-level program source code by reading and interpreting the diagrams and screens used to represent the system. Many code generators can produce source code in languages such as COBOL, BASIC, and C. In addition to diagramming tools and code generators, a broad range of other tools assists in the systems development process. The general types of CASE tools used throughout the development process are summarized in Table 10.3.

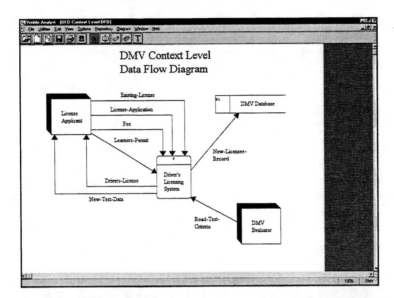

FIGURE 10.9A

High-level data flow diagram from the VAW CASE tool.

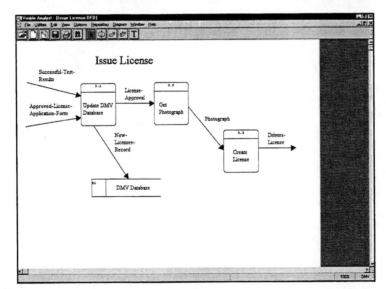

FIGURE 10.9B

Lower-level data flow diagram from the VAW CASE tool.

Table 10.3 General types of CASE tools.

CASE Tool	Description
Diagramming tools	Tools that enable system process, data, and control structures to be represented graphically.
Screen and report generators	Tools that help model how systems look and feel to users. Screen and report generators also make it easier for the systems analyst to identify data requirements and relationships.
Analysis tools	Tools that automatically check for incomplete, inconsistent, or incorrect specifications in diagrams, screens, and reports.
Repository	A tool that enables the integrated storage of specifications, diagrams, reports, and project management information.
Documentation generators	Tools that help produce both technical and user documentation in standard formats.
Code generators	Tools that enable the automatic generation of program and database definition code directly from the design documents, diagrams, screens, and reports.

Source Adapted from Hoffer, George, and Valacich. 1999. *Modern systems analysis and design.* Addison Wesley Longman: Reading, Massachusetts.

CASE can be used to dramatically increase the speed of development and maintenance, not to mention increase the quality of the system. CASE also influences the culture of an organization in many significant ways. In fact, researchers have found that people with different career orientations have different attitudes toward CASE (Orlikowski, 1989). For example, those within the development group with a managerial orientation welcome CASE because they believe it helps reduce the risk and uncertainty in managing development projects. On the other hand, people with a more technical orientation tend to resist the use of CASE because they feel threatened by the technology's capability to replace some skills they have taken years to master. Table 10.4 lists several possible impacts of CASE on the roles of individuals within organizations. CASE is clearly a powerful technology that can have numerous and widespread impacts. Its adoption should be a well-thought-out and highly orchestrated activity.

Table 10.4 Common impacts of CASE on individuals within organizations.

Individuals	Common Impact
Systems analysts	CASE automates many routine tasks of the analyst, making the communication skills (rather than analytical skills) of the analyst most critical.
Programmers	Programmers will piece together objects created by code generators and fourth-generation languages. Their role will become more of maintaining designs than source code.
Users	Users will be much more active in the systems development process through the use of upper CASE tools.
Top managers	Top managers will play a more active role in setting priorities and strategic directions for IS by using CASE-based planning and through user-oriented system development methods.
Functional managers	Functional managers will play a greater role in leading development projects by using CASE to re-engineer their business processes.
IS project managers	IS project managers will have greater control over development projects and resources.

Source Adapted from 1992. Chen and Norman.

Group Support Systems

In Chapter 8, "Emerging Information Systems," we described one type of groupware—*Group Support Systems (GSS)*—that is increasingly being used to help groups communicate, collaborate, and coordinate their activities. A key application of GSS technology is to support the collection of user requirements. In other words, it is more effective to collect user requirements for some types of systems by asking a group to collectively define these requirements through a JAD process. It is also possible to improve the processing and performance of groups by using GSS technology to structure and coordinate the group process. The marriage of GSS and JAD activities is often referred to as an electronic JAD or E-JAD.

—————— Using GSS and JAD in the U.S. Army —————— 〔 A BRIEF CASE 〕

In the early 1990s, the U.S. Army undertook a major initiative to redesign and consolidate many of the major information systems used to manage army installations around the world. At that time the army spent more than $5 billion annually and employed over 250,000 people to operate the many army, National Guard, and Reserve installations in the U.S. and around the world. Each military installation is like a small city: In addition to all the people living there, there are stores, restaurants, police and fire stations, garbage collection services, and so on. Also, at each military installation, the army needs to manage the arrival and departure of personnel (that is, collect medical records, change mailing addresses, and so on) and perform daily landlord functions (for example, rent processing), not to mention the management of military activities and equipment. Unfortunately, most people managing military installations did things their own way when it came to many of the installation support activities. This lack of consistency resulted in poor communication, redundancies, and diverse, incompatible procedures across installations. It was envisioned that if the army could increase the efficiency of installation management, significant resources could be saved and redistributed to activities such as improved personnel training and equipment. For example, a 10 percent cost reduction would yield more than $500 million per year!

To address this problem, the U.S. Congress approved a budget of $172 million to develop an army-wide system to assist in the management of the varied activities that occur at each site (Daniels, Dennis, Hayes, Nunamaker and Valacich, 1991). Because each installation has unique issues to address, any single integrated system had to consider the unique requirements of each site. For example, the procedures for "in-processing" new personnel onto a base are different in the U.S. than in Europe or Asia. To define a system for supporting in-processing that considered the needs of only the U.S. installations would be a failure. As a result, the army worked to define the most appropriate procedures to collect the system requirements correctly the first time, and used JAD as the method to collect system requirements. To make the JAD session work, user representatives of most major installations around the world flew to a central location to work on multi-week JAD sessions to define and structure the requirements for seventeen separate installation support activities. In addition to using JAD, they also combined GSS technology to automate many of the group-based discussions within the JAD sessions. As of today, most of the systems to automate the installation support process have been developed, and the army is gaining significant savings. In fact, this project has been so successful that it is being used as a model for other branches of the U.S. military.

Advanced Programming Languages

One of the greatest bottlenecks in the development and maintenance of information systems is in programming-related activities. It is no surprise that a lot has been changing to make programming faster and easier. This section describes major developments in programming languages that are helping people to effectively use the application development approaches discussed earlier in this chapter. Without these powerful programming tools, systems development (and programming in particular) would remain a slow and tedious process.

Visual Programming

Visual programming, described in Chapter 3, is a new and extremely powerful way to develop systems rapidly. A popular visual programming environment is Visual Basic by Microsoft. This language enables systems developers to quickly build new user interfaces, reports, and other features into existing systems in a fraction of the time previously required and easily links these features to countless database management systems. Rather than build a screen, report, or menu by typing crude commands (see sample commands in Figure 10.10), designers use visual tools to "draw" the design. For example, building a menu system in a visual programming environment is simple. Analysts can quickly list the order of menu commands (see Figure 10.11A) and instantly test the look of their design (see Figure 10.11B). In fact, after they are designed, these systems convert the design into the appropriate computer instructions, but all these details are hidden from the programmer. Visual development programming is also being added to more traditional programming languages, such as C, BASIC, and COBOL, as well as to special-purpose visual programming environments, such as Delphi by Borland and PowerBuilder by Powersoft.

FIGURE 10.10

Sample of programming commands to build a screen.

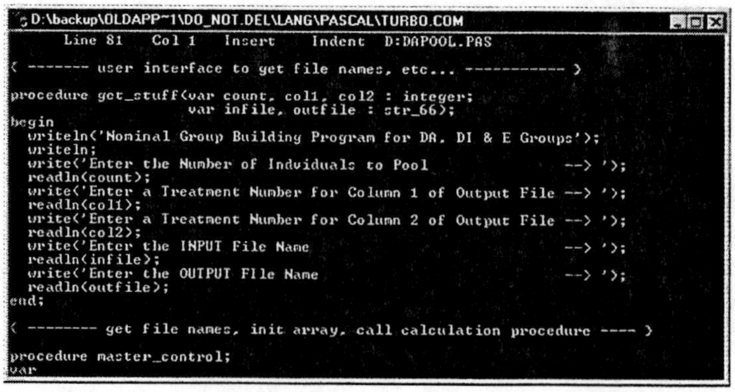

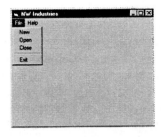

FIGURE 10.11B

*Sample of a screen being drawn
using visual programming tools.*

FIGURE 10.11A

Menu commands.

Maintaining Ad Schedules at Fox Broadcasting ⎯⎯ A BRIEF CASE

The Los Angeles-based Fox Broadcasting Company is the nation's fourth largest television network. The rapidly growing network grew even faster in December 1993, when it beat CBS for the rights to broadcast the weekly National Football Conference games. With this $1.6 billion coup, Fox grew its roster of affiliate stations around the country from 138 to 199 and increased its number of broadcast hours. To accommodate this tremendous growth, Fox is using PowerBuilder to assist in its application development process (Sybase, 1998). One such system is the Sales Traffic and Billing System, which is used to automate many of the complicated tasks involved in selling, scheduling, and tracking advertising air time.

About 70 Fox sales representatives in five regional offices have a fixed pool of commercial airtime to sell. They need immediate access to information about the status of that inventory. They sell about 75 percent of their airtime up to six months before a broadcast season starts. However, deals change frequently. To be effective, reps need to be constantly aware of their colleagues' activities so that they can share the updated schedules of commercials with everyone instantly across the network. The ad programming module of the system feeds directly into Fox's automated broadcast system. The commercial scheduling module of the application automatically slates various ads and program segments into the broadcast system time slots. The application verifies that competing companies' spots don't run back-to-back or that two ads in a row don't have the same theme, such as vacation cruises. As the development process progressed, the benefits of using the visual programming environment became apparent to Fox's executives, who now believe that they could have built such a high-quality system in such a short period of time without PowerBuilder.

Although a programming language may be visual, it may not necessarily be object-oriented. The next section reviews object-oriented programming, another contemporary programming tool that can be used to better develop systems.

Object-Oriented Programming

Many organizations have had a difficult time maintaining their information systems. These systems are often huge, ranging from 100,000 lines of programming code to more than 1,000,000 in a single system. Systems of this size are hard for one person to understand and consequently often very hard to enhance or maintain. Making changes to these large-scale systems is difficult, to say the least. Making matters worse, a large organization can have hundreds of separate application systems to support common business activities such as payroll processing, inventory management, financial analysis, sales, marketing, and countless other activities. Each separate system has the potential for many redundant functions. For example, logging into a system with an approved user account or sending a report to a printer are two common functions that most business applications hold in common. For example, sending a report to a printer is a common function that most business applications hold in common. As a result, the way in which printing works in one system is often different from how it works in another. This has resulted in a system maintenance nightmare for many organizations.

Object-oriented programming (described in Chapter 3) is helping to alleviate maintenance problems plaguing organizations that have multiple systems with redundant functions. Object-oriented languages create objects that are reusable elements in a system. The idea is to make objects that can be infinitely reused and become the building blocks for all systems. Consequently, a well-designed printing object can, for example, be used in all systems. Then, when a modification needs to be made to how the print object works—suppose, for example, that you want to modify the print object to support color printing—*one* module can be changed and *all* systems can use the enhanced color printing functionality. The goal of OOP is to make software easier to create, simpler, more consistent to use, and far more reliable (Verity and Schwartz, 1994). Using object-oriented languages for building information systems is similar to using Lego blocks for building model bridges, planes, and buildings. The Lego block is reusable in an infinite number of structures. Likewise, the well-designed software object is reusable in an infinite number of systems.

Fourth-Generation Languages and Beyond

Two clear trends in the evolution of programming languages and environments used to develop information systems are increased ease and power. As described in Chapter 3, **fourth-generation languages** (4GLs) enable users to "ask" an information system to provide certain information by typing English sentence–like commands into a system. Figure 10.12 shows some sample 4GL commands. In other words, 4GLs enable users to specify what information is wanted from a system in a syntax that is relatively easy to learn and remember. In contrast, with most development environments, programmers must specify each of the minuscule steps needed to obtain this information before it can be displayed. As a result, 4GLs have given nontechnical users the capability to develop their own powerful information system applications and speed the process of obtaining information.

```
SELECT DISTINCTROW STUDENT_ID, GRADE
FROM GRADES
WHERE GRADE = "A"
ORDER BY STUDENT_ID;
```

FIGURE 10.12

Sample of 4GL commands.

A final contemporary approach to programming is to embed artificial intelligence into the development environments. For example, it is envisioned that in the near future, programmers will be able to go well beyond 4GLs and develop large-scale information systems by simply telling their computers what they want them to do. It is envisioned that intelligent agents, created by other programmers, will reside in your computer. When a user or programmer wants something to be done, a request will be made to the agent through a conversational dialogue.

Systems development tools and approaches have evolved rapidly over the past thirty years, and there appears to be no end in sight to this evolution. There is no doubt that many new approaches and tools will be proposed, with some gaining favor, and others not. Organizations and developers will have to be very selective when choosing development approaches and tools. With the selection of any approach or tool will come tremendous costs for employee training and change management. Likewise, systems developers will also find the future to be filled with uncertainty in regard to which skills to master to best equip themselves for the future. On the other hand, this evolution and change will bring a greater capability to build more powerful systems in a shorter period of time.

Talking with...

Jeanne Schaefer, Manager of Strategic Business Support at Weyerhaeuser

Educational Background

B.S. in Business Administration, University of Montana

Job Description

Ms. Schaefer is responsible for managing several project teams that are responsible for acquiring business applications in the corporate area. This includes drafting the project plan, developing the business requirements, writing requests for proposals, selecting vendors, purchasing systems, converting data, and implementing system hardware and software.

Critical Success Factors

Understand the business requirements. Agree on the scope of the project between the customer and the project manager. Complete data conversion, which includes testing the database before production. Work with dedicated people. Have a sense of humor.

Advice to Students

A career in information technology is a wonderful choice for people who enjoy variety and change at a rapid pace. Current technology has a habit of becoming obsolete very quickly in today's environment. Therefore, it is important to continually update your skills. People who are successful in information technology are creative, flexible, and able to adapt to change. IT professionals must also have a strong background in business processes to successfully recommend and implement an appropriate technology. You must develop the ability to translate the business requirements to the technology. Woe to the IT group that implements technology without sound business value.

ETHICAL PERSPECTIVE: THE ETHICS OF IS CONSULTING

Thousands of businesses, large and small, are actively participating in one of the fastest growing industry sectors of the modern world: information systems consulting services. Many large organizations have long been successful in providing IS consulting services, such as IBM, EDS, and Andersen Consulting. New companies enter this industry on a daily basis.

As with other business endeavors, IS consulting services is an area of business that puts people into situations that test their ethics. One potentially problematic area that applies to all consulting—not just IS consulting—is the fundamental conflict between needing to secure consulting contracts to bring revenue into the consulting firm and needing to not over-promise what can be delivered and/or when it can be delivered. The pressure to bring in business to generate revenue is great. New business is, after all, the lifeblood of the consulting firm. There is natural pressure to secure a consulting contract even though it may not be absolutely clear that the firm can deliver exactly what the client wants or needs by the exact deadlines that the client has set. For IS consultants, the pressure is great to promise that the job can be done quickly using "rapid" methodologies, especially given that these methodologies are in vogue. Of course, it is in the consulting firm's long-term interests not to over-promise, but the pressure is there nonetheless.

One other potential ethical dilemma facing IS consultants is the question of whom they work for and where their loyalties lie. With Joint Application Development and the use of systems development teams in which IS consultants work closely with business users, it is sometimes difficult for consultants to determine exactly for whom they work—the client or the consulting firm. On the one hand, they are servicing the client and must satisfy the client's needs. On the other hand, they work for the consulting firm. They may get pulled in two different directions, especially if the relationship between the client and the consulting firm deteriorates. The consulting firm might want the consultant to stick with the letter of the contract, to withhold certain services, or to keep her time with the client to a minimum. On the other hand, the consultant may want to go the extra distance to please the client. After all, with contemporary system development approaches the consultant probably spends more time with the client organization's personnel than with the consulting firm's personnel, and the client organization is likely to be doing the primary evaluation of the consultant's performance. In fact, in some cases the consultants may be housed physically and semi-permanently within the client organization, may be paid directly by the client, and may enjoy other employee benefits provided by the client organization.

With increased use of Joint Application Development and other approaches to partnering with business users, comes one final, fundamental ethical dilemma that all consultants face daily. This dilemma is whether to solve problems for clients in such a way that the client learns how to solve the problems themselves or to solve problems for clients in such a way that the client needs to call the consultant back in again to solve similar problems in the future. There is a natural pressure to do the latter to ensure future business.

A useful analogy for this ethical dilemma is the way that a barber cuts your hair. A barber who wants to ensure that you will have to come back to him again would give you the best possible haircut. In addition, he would have no mirrors in the shop so that you could not see what he was doing, and he would not answer any of your questions about how he was cutting and styling your hair. On the other hand, a barber who wanted you to become self-sustaining and empowered to take care of yourself would not only give you a good haircut, but he would have mirrors all around so that you could see exactly what he was doing. He would explain exactly what he was doing at all times and answer any of your questions. Now, you wouldn't necessarily be able to cut your own hair, but you would know how to do so and could explain this to another person who could then cut your hair. You wouldn't necessarily have to come back to that same barber. Good consultants don't try to generate more business for themselves in this way. They want you to ask them back because you want to have them back, not because you need to have them back.

Questions for Discussion

1. How would you deal with an IS manager who was pushing you to develop a system in a time frame that was too rapid to enable you to do a good job? What if it was the client who was pushing you?

2. To whom should an IS consultant ultimately be loyal, to the client or to the consulting firm? Why?

3. Should IS consultants strive to not only solve clients' problems but help to teach and enable them to solve their own problems in the future? Why or why not?

INTERNATIONAL PERSPECTIVE: MANAGING CROSS-CULTURAL JAD TEAMS

Anne Masters is the leader of a systems development team that is building an inventory control system in Beijing, China, for Quality Products, a mid-sized manufacturing firm based in San Diego, California. This project is in its initial phase, and Anne is currently leading a Joint Application Development (JAD) team in fleshing out the detailed requirements and design elements of the inventory control system. Anne serves as the JAD facilitator, the key person who leads the JAD sessions. Anne has been selected as the JAD facilitator because she is a respected, skillful leader with a good reputation within the organization and excellent group facilitation skills.

The Management Sponsor for this JAD Team is Brad Wheeling, manager of the production area of the firm. He has not actively participated in every one of the JAD sessions, but he did attend the first JAD session to help get things started correctly, and he will likely attend the final session to review the results and make comments. The information specialists in this case are Sulaiman bin Daud and Hasmah binti Johann. Sulaiman and Hasmah were both born in Malaysia, are ethnic Malays, and are Muslim. Both received IS degrees from American universities and were hired right out of school by Quality Products. Their role in the JAD sessions as information specialists is to assist the end users and develop a design according to the end users' needs. Both Sulaiman and Hasmah are experienced systems analysts and good listeners. The scribe for this JAD team is Sue Brownster, who is responsible for documenting the JAD sessions. She has had to learn to accurately capture the important decisions made, who made them, and why.

The three end users participating on this JAD team include Chin Chi Chan and Me Won Huang, two local Chinese women who were hired by Quality Products as inventory control technicians, and Yu Seng Tang, a local Chinese man who was hired as an inventory control supervisor. The IS members of the JAD team know that the end users are essential to the success of the JAD team and to the ultimate success of the inventory control system they are developing. The whole point of JAD is to bring end users and IS people together in a structured environment to build a better system that meets users' needs well and helps the users to feel a sense of involvement and ownership in the system.

Anne has found that it has been much more difficult for her to manage this cross-cultural JAD team than it was for her to manage JAD teams back in the States, where the team members were typically all Americans. In that setting, JAD teams were difficult enough to manage due to conflicting personalities, goals, and expectations, as well as corporate politics thrown in the mix. In this Chinese setting, Anne has found that she must now deal with all the common difficulties of a JAD team plus some interesting new cross-cultural issues.

One such cross-cultural difficulty with this JAD team finds it roots in the historical relationship between Chinese and native Malays in Malaysia. Many argue that control by native Malays in Malaysia has been institutionalized in many ways, causing people of Chinese ancestry in Malaysia to sometimes feel like second-class citizens. Sulaiman and Hasmah certainly don't believe that people in Malaysia who are born of Chinese ancestry are second-class citizens. In any event, the team members from China sometimes feel that the two Malaysian information specialists on the team talk down to the members of the team from China. Anne knows that Sulaiman and Hasmah are not doing this, but given the history between the two ethnic groups in Malaysia, the Chinese team members sometimes perceive Sulaiman and Hasmah to be doing this. Anne has had to work hard to manage this problem by coaching Sulaiman and Hasmah to be careful about how they communicate with the Chinese team members and by continually checking with the Chinese team members to make sure that everything is going smoothly for them.

Questions for Discussion

1. What do you think of the job that Anne Masters appears to be doing thus far? What could she be doing to better manage the difficulties within her cross-cultural JAD team?

2. What other difficulties might cross-cultural JAD teams like this one encounter and how can they best be managed?

3. Would you be interested in working on a JAD team like this one? Why or why not?

Summary

1. **Explain contemporary approaches for collecting and structuring the information needed to design and construct an information system.** Two ways for collecting and structuring systems requirements are the Critical Success Factors (CSF) and Joint Application Design (JAD) approaches. Both are being used to augment other methods used to collect requirements, such as interviewing users and developing questionnaires. The CSF approach is a methodology for collecting system requirements that helps identify those few things that must go well to ensure success for a manager or organization. JAD is a group-based method for collecting requirements and creating system designs.

2. **Describe prototyping, rapid application development, and object-oriented analysis and design methods of systems development and each approach's strengths and weaknesses.** Prototyping is an iterative systems development process in which requirements are converted to a working system that is continually revised through a close working relationship between analysts and users. The strengths of prototyping are that it helps develop a close working relationship between designers and users and that it is a good approach for hard-to-define problems. Its weaknesses are that it is not a practical approach for a large number of users and that it can at times lead to a lower-quality system if the system is built too quickly. Rapid Application Development (RAD) is a systems development methodology that combines prototyping, computer-based development tools, special management practices, and close user involvement. The strength of RAD is that users are actively involved in the design process, which makes system implementation much easier. The weaknesses of RAD are that systems are sometimes narrowly focused—which might limit future evolution—and that quality problems might result if a system is designed and built too quickly (as is the case with prototyping). Object-Oriented Analysis and Design (OOA&D) is a systems development approach that focuses on modeling objects—data and operations bundled together—rather than on modeling these separately. The strengths of OOA&D are the integration of data and processing during the design, which should lead to higher-quality systems, and the reuse of common modules, which should make development and maintenance easier. The weaknesses of OOA&D are that it is very difficult to train analysts and programmers on the object-oriented approach and that analysts often re-create common modules.

3. **Understand how and why to use several automated tools for supporting contemporary development, including Computer-Aided Software Engineering, group support systems, and advanced programming languages.** Computer-Aided Software Engineering (CASE) refers to automated software tools used by systems analysts to develop information systems. These tools can be used to automate or support activities throughout the systems development process with the objective of increasing productivity and improving the overall quality of systems. Group Support Systems (GSSs) are most widely used to help groups communicate, collaborate, and coordinate their activities. In regard to information systems development, a key application of GSS technology is to support the collection of user requirements in electronic JAD sessions. Advanced programming languages, such as visual programming, and object-oriented programming languages are designed to ease programming-related activities. Visual programming enables systems developers to quickly build new user interfaces, reports, and other features into existing systems in a fraction of the time previously required to "draw" the design with visual tools. Object-oriented programming enables reusable objects to be the building blocks for all systems. Using standard objects greatly speeds development and increases system reliability.

Key Terms

Critical Success Factor

Joint Application Requirements and Joint Application Design

Facilitator

Scribe

Prototyping

Rapid Application Development

Object-Oriented Analysis and Design

Computer-Aided Software Engineering

Upper CASE

Lower CASE

Visual programming

Object-oriented programming

Fourth-generation languages

Review Questions

1. What is the major strength of the Critical Success Factor approach?

2. Describe two major weaknesses of the Critical Success Factor approach.

3. Briefly describe the Joint Application Design process of collecting system requirements.

4. What are the possible disadvantages of working in large groups that may arise with JAD?

5. What are the roles of the JAD facilitator and scribe?

6. How does prototyping differ from the traditional SDLC approach to system development?

7. What maintenance issues must be addressed when using prototyping?

8. Describe how intense user involvement strengthens the Rapid Application Development approach to system development.

9. Describe the strengths and weaknesses of the Object-Oriented Analysis and Design approach to system development.

10. How do upper CASE tools differ from lower CASE tools?

11. Describe several tools that have enabled greater programming productivity in system development.

Problems and Exercises

◆ **Individual**   ◆ **Group**   ☞ **Field**   ◖ **Web/Internet**

◆ **1.** Match the following terms to the appropriate definitions:

_____ Joint Application Design

_____ Prototyping

_____ Object-Oriented Analysis and Design

_____ Computer-Aided Software Engineering

_____ Critical Success Factor

_____ Visual programming

_____ Object-oriented programming

_____ Fourth-generation languages

a. A programming technique that utilizes objects or modules to perform common functions within the system

b. A methodology for collecting system requirements that helps to identify those few things that must go well to ensure success for a manager or organization

c. A programming technique in which users "ask" a system for information using English-like commands and syntax

d. Systems development methodologies and techniques based on objects rather than data or processes

e. Software tools that provide automated support for some portion of the systems development process

f. Group-based methods for collecting requirements and creating system designs

g. A programming technique that converts drawn designs into the appropriate computer instructions

h. An iterative systems development process in which requirements are converted to a working system that is continually revised through close work between analysts and users

◆ **2.** Discuss why Rapid Application Development is not always an appropriate development methodology. When is it an appropriate methodology?

◆ **3.** Within a small group of classmates, compare and contrast the Critical Success Factor and Joint Application Design approaches. Is one more effective than the other? Why? Does the group agree? Which approach do you think is utilized more often? Why?

◆ **4.** As part of the traditional SDLC, the development team might show the client a prototype of the proposed system at various stages of development. This is done primarily as a communication tool as well as a progress report. How is this form of prototyping different from the prototyping approach discussed in this chapter?

5. Do you agree with the statement that Object-Oriented Analysis and Design is the future for system development? Why or why not? If so, what time frame do you predict? If not, which methodology will prevail? How do your fellow classmates feel about this? Do they agree with you or do they have different opinions?

6. Describe how you would handle the resistance to implementing CASE tools by those who feel they will be replaced by technology. From whom is this resistance most likely to come? Is this fear legitimate? Why or why not?

7. With the development of advanced programming languages and code-generating CASE tools, will programming in the traditional sense become a lost art? Why or why not? If not, when and where will traditional programming remain as part of the SDLC? Search the World Wide Web for information about advanced programming languages. Be sure to check out Sun Microsystems at http://www.sun.com/. What are others saying about advanced programming languages and how are they being used?

8. Discuss among your classmates whether it is managerially possible (feasible) to employ all the techniques and methodologies discussed in this and the preceding chapter. Is that too much to handle? Why? If it is feasible, under what conditions would you advise it and under what conditions would you recommend employing only some of the methodologies?

9. After reading Chapters 9 and 10, do you have a better understanding of system development? Why or why not? Which methodologies seem the most useful? the least useful? Are there any that you, as a manager, would stay away from altogether? Why?

10. Based on your uses of information systems and applications, which programming languages were used in their creation? Can you discern this at all? Were they visual or object-oriented?

11. Choose an organization with which you are familiar that develops its own information systems. Does this organization or has this organization used CSF or JAD to determine system requirements? In what ways was this advantageous?

12. As a small group, conduct a search on the World Wide Web for "object-oriented analysis and design" using any browser you wish (Hint: Because people write differently, search using both object-oriented and object oriented.). Check out some of the hits. You should have found numerous articles regarding OOA&D's use by IS departments. Are these articles positive or negative regarding OOA&D? Do you agree with the articles? Prepare a 10-minute presentation of your findings to the class.

13. Interview an IS manager within an organization with which you are familiar. Determine whether methodologies such as prototyping, RAD, and/or OOA&D are utilized for system projects. Who makes the choice of methodology? If a methodology has not been used, is it due to choice, or is it due to a lack of need, understanding, or capability to use the methodology?

 14. Choose an organization with which you are familiar that uses Group Support Systems. For what purposes are they used? Electronic JAD or electronic meetings? Do they utilize the terms GSS, JAD, or E-JAD?

 15. Interview an IS manager within an organization with which you are familiar. Determine this person's feelings about the future of system development. What methodologies will be widely used? Why? Are there any emerging technologies that this person feels will make a strong impact?

16. Choose an organization with which you are familiar that uses CASE tools in system development projects. Which types of CASE tools do they use—diagramming, screen and report generators, analysis, repository, documentation generators, or code generators? Why these and not others? Was there any transition problem in the initial stages of their use? If so, how was the problem solved? Compare your findings with those of your classmates. Do CASE tools have a common use, or does everyone do something different? Why do you think this is the case?

 17. Reread the opening scenario to the chapter. It seems that Greg is intending to follow the prototyping method for systems development. Do you agree with this decision? Why or why not? What other methods would work for this situation? What methods would not work?

Real World Case Problems

1. SAS's Rapid Warehousing Methodology

SAS Institute, Inc., is helping people in a variety of organizations implement data warehousing and data mining solutions. Because it needs to generate solutions quickly and efficiently, SAS uses its own Rapid Warehousing Methodology to build data warehouses. Rapid warehousing is the iterative, incremental development of data warehouse projects based on the following development phases: Justification, Requirements Gathering, Design/Prototype, Implementation, and Review. With SAS's new methodology, each iteration of the data warehouse implementation is delivered quickly, with a goal of achieving measurable results within 90 days.

In the Justification phase, the project team is formed and team members evaluate the possible impact a data warehouse can have on the business and whether it is justified to start a data warehouse project right now. In the Requirements Gathering phase, the team finds out what information users need, in what form, and how often, and they examine the site's IT architecture and strategy. A physical model of the warehouse is also defined. In the Design/Prototype phase, sample systems are built and tested and sample queries and other end-user reports are executed. In the Implementation phase, all necessary finished programs and applications are written, the data warehouse is made available to users, and users are trained. Finally, in the Review phase, the system is evaluated immediately after the system has been delivered and again after a certain amount of time has elapsed.

SAS's methodology makes extensive use of Joint Applications Development (JAD) and prototyping. With JAD, the entire data warehouse implementation team is involved in eliciting and validating requirements, reconciling business-user needs with organizational constraints, avoiding costly mistakes and unnecessary iterations, and producing the final model of the data warehouse. In addition, the prototype is shown to all the users of the data warehouse, providing an opportunity for SAS to gather further feedback before moving into final implementation. The prototype can also form the basis on which the project team can continue to build to complete the data warehouse (that is, it doesn't necessarily have to be a throw away demo).

With SAS's use of state-of-the-art development methods—Rapid Warehousing Methodology, Joint Applications Development, prototyping—they can deliver useful data warehousing and data mining solutions quickly and efficiently.

a. How do SAS's development methods differ from traditional, structured development methods?

b. Is the goal of achieving measurable results within 90 days feasible? Why or why not?

c. Why might it be particularly useful to be able to implement data warehousing and data mining solutions quickly?

Source *SAS Institute Inc. 1998. A SAS institute white paper: data warehousing methodology. http://www.ssas.com. April.*

2. Technology Solutions Company Announces Methodology and Support Around Genesys

CTI Software: TSC to include the rapid and reliable deployment of Genesys CTI software.

Technology Solutions Company now offers a dedicated systems development methodology around the implementation and support of Genesys' Computer Telephony Integration (CTI) products. TSC will deploy, implement, and support the Genesys suite of enterprise CTI products as a component of its Enterprise Customer Management (ECM) solutions.

TSC has already successfully implemented the Genesys software within strategic ECM solutions at several of the world's largest financial institutions, pharmaceutical companies, and consumer goods organizations. By extending TSC's ECM framework to include Genesys' CTI software, TSC further enhances its capabilities to deploy and support comprehensive ECM solutions and operate as an end-to-end solutions provider to the marketplace. TSC will extend its ECM framework to include a comprehensive methodology around the rapid and reliable implementation of Genesys' CTI software. TSC will also dedicate resources within its Relationship Architecture

354

Design and Deployment (RADD) Laboratory to execute the implementation of the Genesys methodology, where appropriate. Representing the best practices developed by TSC, the methodology will enable an organization to implement the Genesys technology from concept to pilot in six weeks.

"By using Genesys' CTI objects, and leveraging TSC's knowledge and expertise, Zurich Kemper has been able to meet an aggressive delivery schedule for providing benefit to our customers," said Michael Goodyear, Sales Officer of Zurich Direct Insurance. "TSC's methodologies and best practices have enabled them to implement a pilot of outbound campaign management, softphone functionality, calling identification, and call center statistics within a six week time frame."

"TSC's Enterprise Customer Management framework and methodology have enabled us to quickly drive transformational change throughout organizations that seek to become customer-centric in their operations. This framework provides an end-to-end solution approach to the definition, deployment, and support of these highly complex solutions," added Kelly D. Conway, TSC's Executive

Vice-President of its Worldwide Call Center and Enterprise Customer Management Practice. "We have recognized that a major stumbling block to successful ECM solutions has been the rapid and reliable deployment and support of this complex piece of technology. Our methodology and support capabilities are designed to reduce the time, risk, and cost associated with deploying these solutions. We believe that this represents a major step forward for the call center industry."

a. On which three phases of the traditional systems development life cycle is TSC's new development method focused?

b. TSC has married its alternative development method with which specific type of software and business process? Was this a good move on TSC's part? Why or why not?

c. How does TSC and its customers know that this alternative development method has worked well?

Source 1998. *Technology solutions company announces methodology and support around Genesys CTI software. http://www.techsol.com/news/980121.htm. January 21.*

References

Booch, G. 1990. *Object oriented design with applications.* Redwood City, California: Benjamin/Cummings.

Borland. 1998. Information from: www.borland.com. Information verified: March 22, 1998.

Boynton, A.C., and R.W. Zmud. 1994. An assessment of critical success factors. In *Management of information systems,* ed. Gray, King, McLean, and Watson, 2d ed. 293–299, 368–382. Fort Worth, Texas: The Dryden Press.

Chen M., and R. J. Norman. 1992. Integrated computer-aided software engineering (CASE): Adoption, implementation and impacts. *Proceedings of the Hawaii International Conference on System Sciences,* ed J.F. Nunamaker, Jr. vol. 3, 362–373. Los Alamitos, California: IEEE Computer Society Press.

Coad, P., and E. Yourdon. 1991. *Object-oriented design.* Englewood Cliffs, New Jersey: Prentice Hall.

Daniels, Dennis, Hayes, Nunamaker, Jr., and Valacich. 1991. GroupCASE: Electronic support for group requirements elicitation. *Hawaii International Conference on System Sciences* 3: 43–52. Los Alamitos, California: IEEE Computer Society Press.

Gibson, M.L., and C.T. Hughes. 1994. *Systems analysis and design: A comprehensive methodology with CASE.* Danvers, Massachusetts: boyd & fraser Publishing.

Halladay, S., and M. Wiebel. 1993. *Object oriented software engineering.* Englewood Cliffs, New Jersey: Prentice Hall.

Hoffer, George, and Valacich. 1999. *Modern systems analysis and design.* 2d ed. Reading, Massachusetts: Addison Wesley Longman.

Jessup, L.M., and J.S. Valacich. 1993. *Group support systems: New perspectives.* New York: Macmillian Publishing.

Oracle. 1998. Information from: www.oracle.com. Information verified: March 22, 1998.

Orlikowski, W. J. 1989. Division among the ranks: The social implications of CASE tools for system developers. *Proceedings of the Tenth International Conference on Information Systems,* 199–210.

Martin, J. 1991. *Rapid application development.* New York: Macmillan Publishing.

McConnell, S. 1996. *Rapid development.* Redmond, Washington: Microsoft Press.

Rockart, J.F. 1979. Chief executives define their own information needs. *Harvard Business Review.* (March–April): 81–93.

Sybase. 1998. Information from: www.sybase.com. Information verified: March 22, 1998.

Verity, J.W., and E.I. Schwartz. 1994. Software made simple. In *Management of Information Systems,* ed Gray, King, McLean, and Watson, 2d ed. 293–299. Fort Worth, Texas: The Dryden Press.

Related Readings

Basili, Briand, and Melo. 1996. How to reuse influences productivity in object-oriented systems. *Communications of the ACM* 39(10): 104–116.

Baskerville, R.L., and J. Stage. 1996. Controlling prototype development through risk analysis. *Management Information Systems Quarterly* 20(4): 481–504.

Finlay, P.N., and A.C. Mitchell. 1994. Perceptions of the benefits from the introduction of CASE: An empirical study. *Management Information Systems Quarterly* 18(4): 353–370.

Huh, S.Y. 1993. Modelbase construction with object-oriented constructs. *Decision Sciences* 24(2): 409–434.

Iansiti, M., and A. MacCormack. 1997. Developing products on Internet time. *Harvard Business Review* 75(5): 108–117.

Iivari, J. 1996. Why are CASE tools not used? *Communications of the ACM* 39(10): 94–103.

Orlikowski, W.J. 1993. CASE tools as organizational change: Investigating incremental and radical changes in systems development. *Management Information Systems Quarterly* 17(3): 309–340.

Parsons, J., and Y. Wand. 1997. Using objects for systems analysis. *Communications of the ACM* 40(12): 104–110.

Rai, A. and R. Patnayakuni. 1996. A structural model for CASE adoption behavior. *Journal of Management Information Systems* 13(2): 205–234.

Schmidt, D.C., and M.E. Fayad. 1997. Lessons learned building reusable OO frameworks for distributed software. *Communications of the ACM* 40(10): 85–87.

Sheetz, Irwin, Tegarden, Nelson, and Monarchi. 1997. Exploring the difficulties of learning object-oriented techniques. *Journal of Management Information Systems* 14(2): 103–131.

Subramanian, G.H., and G.E. Zarnich. 1996. An examination of some software development effort and productivity determinants in ICASE tool projects. *Journal of Management Information Systems* 12(4): 143–160.

Wang, S. 1996. Toward formalized object-oriented management information systems analysis. *Journal of Management Information Systems* 12(4): 117–141.

Chapter 11: Alternatives to Systems Development

Scenario: Critical New Application Needed Immediately

Randy is the Manager of Systems Development at a medium-sized manufacturing organization. He has a small but adequate staff of IS professionals who are dedicated to developing new systems, maintaining existing systems, and helping end-users. The organization is implementing new information systems and updating the existing systems at a fairly rapid pace, so Randy's unit has been very busy. His staff is currently working on a new system, an inventory management application and sales lead tracking application, using contemporary and emerging methods for building systems as described in Chapters 9 and 10.

Given how busy Randy's staff has been, these two projects sat in the development "queue" for several months before his team could turn their attention to them. Now, given the complexity of these two new systems, they seem to be taking up all his developers' time—in fact, he often sees his development team working late into the evenings and occasionally on weekends.

Late one afternoon, Randy's boss, Lena, the IS department manager, calls him into her office. She explains to him that one of the organization's senior vice presidents has been pushing hard for a new system that will increase the purchasing departments' efficiency by 50%. This department has had problems in the past meeting its objectives and it seems that a new system could turn the group around. Lena explains that she has reviewed the figures and agrees that a new system should help the department reach its potential. The system would reduce mounting organizational expenses while at the same time enable the department to purchase goods and services faster and at better rates, all of which contribute directly to the organization's bottom line. Lena tells Randy that she understands that existing projects need to be completed, as they are also important; however, it quickly becomes clear to Randy that this new project is a "top priority."

What should Randy do? His development team is already in the middle of two projects that are taxing their time and energy to the limit. Adding another project to their workload does not seem to be an option. Canceling or delaying one of the projects that is currently under development would be costly and might hurt the morale of the users of that system and of those developers who have been "in" on the project from the ground floor. Furthermore, Randy has worked hard to establish some credibility for the IS department as a group that gets things done. In the past, projects were often delayed or canceled, causing managers to lose faith in the IS department's ability to deliver systems they needed. Over the past year, Randy has worked closely with the managers and has started to regain their faith. Canceling one of the existing systems would certainly hurt his and his department's credibility and might leave managers thinking it was back to "business as usual."

Nonetheless, Lena asks Randy to talk with his staff and to come back the next day with some options for getting the new system developed and running as soon as possible. Randy goes back to his office, gathers his people, and begins brainstorming on some options. His team quickly determines that they can pursue one of several options, each with unique advantages and disadvantages. They can simply take on the extra project along with their existing projects. However, without garnering extra resources such as hiring new IS employees, this option is seriously flawed. They could go out and buy one of the "canned" purchasing systems that are available. Unfortunately, these are relatively expensive, they do not provide the specific functionality that is needed, and are written in a development language with which they are not familiar. They could completely outsource the development of the new system to a third party. The downside of this option is that they would lose some degree of control over the development of the system and don't have the time necessary to find a good outsourcing partner.

System Development Options

- **Option 1: In-house development by IS Group**
  - Advantages
    - Control System Quality
    - System Meets User Needs
  - Disadvantages
    - Need to Hire Additional IS Staff
    - Too Busy with Projects Already

- **Option 2: Buy System from Vendor**
  - Advantages
    - Proven System
    - Fast Deployment
  - Disadvantages
    - System Won't Meet All User Needs
    - Expensive
    - System Not Easily Changed and Maintained

- **Option 3: Hire Outside Firm to Develop Custom System**
  - Advantages
    - Little Effort to Gain System
    - System Meets User Needs
  - Disadvantages
    - Expensive
    - Time Needed to Find a Partner

- **Option 4: End-user Development**
  - Advantages
    - User Are Technically Competent
    - System Meets User Needs
    - Inexpensive
  - Disadvantages
    - IS Group Loses Control (Quality Control)
    - IS Group Needs to Support Users

FIGURE 11.1

System development options.

They finally decide to recommend a final option: to help the employees in the purchasing department develop their own system. The purchasing department staff members are among the more technically competent in the firm and have extensive experience with PC-based databases. With some guidance, they could develop their own database application, with the IS staff serving more as consultants than as developers on the project. This option also helps to provide the much-needed "pain relief" to the IS staff and managers. They are a bit leery about relinquishing control of systems development, but they have a good relationship with the people in purchasing and trust them to do a good job.

Randy presents each of the options to Lena along with the respective advantages and disadvantages of each (see Figure 11.1). She asks which option he recommends, and he explains why he thinks that option four, guided end-user development, appears to be the best available given the current circumstances. She likes the arguments and adds that, if managed effectively, this could be exactly the solution that the organization needs for the broader problem of keeping up with the rapid pace of technology-induced change within the firm. She immediately sends an e-mail message calling together the relevant stakeholders to a meeting at which they can decide how to proceed.

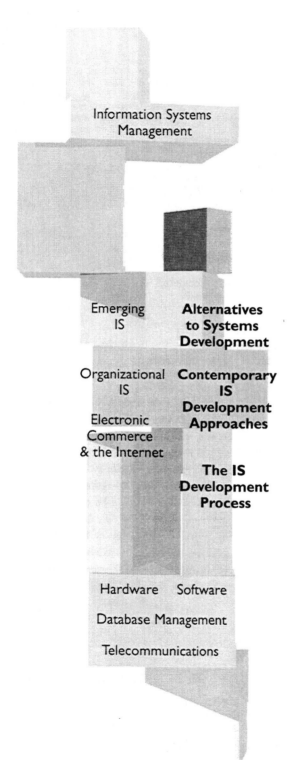

Information Systems Management

Emerging IS

Alternatives to Systems Development

Organizational IS

Contemporary IS Development Approaches

Electronic Commerce & the Internet

The IS Development Process

Hardware   Software

Database Management

Telecommunications

Introduction

This chapter continues the discussion of information systems development. However, the focus here is on alternatives to in-house systems development. If you are a typical business student you might be wondering why we are spending so much time discussing information systems development. The answer is simple: No matter in what area of an organization you are—such as marketing, finance, accounting, human resources, or operations—you *will* be involved in the systems development process. In fact, research indicates that more than 55% of most organizations' IS spending is controlled by specific business functions, with this number expected to jump to more than 80% by 1999 (Kutnick, 1998). What this means is that even if your career interests are something other than IS, it is very likely that you will be involved in the IS development process. Understanding all available options is important to your success.

In the preceding two chapters we discussed different methods for building information systems in-house. Under these options, systems development requests are given to the firm's IS staff, who work with others in the organization to prioritize those requests and allocate resources such as money, people, and equipment to pending projects as time allows. In many situations this option works well; the IS staff is able to deliver high-quality applications relatively quickly and at a reasonable cost. However, there are other situations where building a system in-house is not a feasible option because there may not be an adequate IS staff in-house, the IS staff may not have the required skills, or, as described in the opening scenario, the IS staff may be so overworked that it cannot possibly build a new system. Consequently, it is important to consider other options for creating and implementing new systems besides having the firm's in-house IS staff build it.

FIGURE 11.2

The big picture: focusing on alternatives to systems development.

After reading this chapter, you will be able to:

1. Understand the factors and situations where building a system in-house is not feasible.

2. Explain three alternative systems development options: external acquisition, outsourcing, and end-user development.

This chapter is the last in Part 4, "Information Systems Development." It describes how organizations develop and acquire information systems (see Figure 11.2). It begins by describing why organizations need alternatives to systems development. This is followed by a description of three alternative methods: external acquisition, outsourcing, and end-user development.

The Importance of Finding Alternatives to Building Systems Yourself

Building systems in-house with the IS staff is always an option to consider. Many times, however, this is not a feasible solution. The following are four situations in which you might need to consider alternative development strategies.

Situation 1—Limited IS staff

Often, an organization does not have the capability to build a system itself. Perhaps its IS staff is small or deployed on other activities such as maintaining a small network and helping users with problems on a day-to-day basis. This limited staff may simply not have the capability to take on an in-house development project without hiring several analysts or programmers, which is very expensive in today's labor market.

Outsourcing Helps Xerox Focus ——— A BRIEF CASE

With 1997 sales of approximately $18 billion, Xerox has a relatively small group of IS professionals for its size. Consequently, to allow its 700 IS professionals to focus on moving the copier giant into the flexible network computing company of the 21st century, they signed a long-term contract with Electronic Data Systems (EDS) to manage their mainframe computers and data centers (Verity, 1998). The EDS contract is enabling Xerox managers and IS professionals to focus on developing applications to support new products and services. In other words, Xerox will have its IS staff focus on adding shareholder value by supporting the creation of new products and services; routine and non-strategic activities are being handled by EDS.

Situation 2—IS staff has limited skill set

In other situations, the IS staff may not have the skills needed to develop a particular kind of system. This has been especially true with the explosion of the World Wide Web. Many very large organizations such as ESPN, ABC News, and Walt Disney are having outside organizations manage their Web sites (Starwave, 1998). Although the existing IS staff in these and many other organizations may be highly skilled at producing traditional applications, the sudden rise in demand for new types of systems induces many organizations to seek outside help. It isn't as if the IS director can tell the boss that her department cannot build a new electronic commerce system simply because the IS staff doesn't have the necessary skills to build it! Fortunately, there are alternatives to having the IS staff build the system, which the IS director can turn to when she needs to tap into specialized skills that are not present within the IS staff.

A BRIEF CASE ————— **Citibank Leverages AT&T's Network** ———

In addition to needing human resources to overcome limitations in an organization's capability to develop systems, companies are creating partnerships with other organizations to gain access to infrastructure and proprietary technologies. For example, Citibank signed a five-year, $750 million partnership agreement with AT&T in 1998 to manage Citibank's data network system (Thibodeau, 1998). AT&T's global communication network will provide Citibank with greatly increased Internet bandwidth, which will enable the bank to more rapidly expand and improve its electronic commerce offerings such as home banking (see Figure 11.3). The evaluation process leading to the selection of AT&T took 12 months to complete, and the agreement will affect about 400 Citibank workers, although some of these workers will be hired by AT&T. AT&T had to beat out several other competitors to land the Citibank contract. In addition, this agreement greatly expands AT&T's networking business. In 1997, AT&T Solutions reported $650 million in revenue and is projecting to be a $4 billion company by 2002. To achieve this growth, AT&T Solutions will not only need to be successful in delivering high-quality services, but will also need to hire hundreds of new workers to staff this expansion.

FIGURE 11.3

PC-Banking at Citibank.

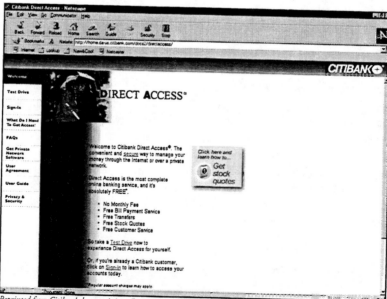

Reprinted from Citibank by permission. One-time use.

Situation 3—IS staff overworked

In some organizations, the IS staff may simply not have the time to work on all the systems that are required or desired by the organization. Obviously, the number of people dedicated to new development is not infinite. Therefore, you must have ways to prioritize development projects. In most cases, systems that are of strategic importance or that affect the whole organization are likely to receive a higher priority than those that offer only minor benefits or affect only one department or a couple of people in a department. Nonetheless, the IS manager must find a way to support all users, even when the IS staff may be tied up with other "higher-priority" projects.

Situation 4—Problems with performance of IS staff

Earlier in this book we discussed how and why systems development projects could sometimes be risky. Often the efforts of IS departments are derailed due to staff turnover, changing requirements, shifts in technology, or budget constraints. Regardless of the reason, the result is the same: another failed (or flawed) system. Given the large expenditures in staff time and training as well as the high risk associated with systems development efforts, the prudent manager tries to limit the risk of any project as much as possible. What if it were possible to see the completed system to know what it looked like before development began? Being able to see into the future would certainly help you learn more about the system and whether it would meet your needs and would help to lower the risk of a project. When building a system in-house, it is obviously not possible to see into the future. However, using some of the alternative methods described in this chapter, you *can*, in fact, see what a completed system might look like. These methods will enable you to know what you are buying, which greatly lowers the risk of a project.

If it is impossible to see the finished system before in-house development starts, how do some alternative systems development strategies enable you to know what you are buying in advance? Read on...

Common Alternatives to In-House Systems Development

Any project has at least four different systems development options. The preceding two chapters presented the first option: building the system in-house with your IS staff. The other options are

■ External Acquisition

■ Outsourcing

■ End-User Development

The following sections examine each of these options in closer detail to see how one or more of them might fit the four situations described earlier.

External Acquisition

Purchasing an existing system from an outside vendor such as IBM, EDS, or Andersen Consulting is referred to as **external acquisition**. How does external acquisition of an information system work? Think about the process that you might use when buying a car. Do you simply walk into the first dealership you see, tell them you need a car, and see what they try to sell you? Hopefully not. Probably you've done some up-front analysis and know how much money you can afford to spend and what your needs are. If you've done your homework, you probably have an idea of what you want and which dealership can provide the type of car you desire (see Figure 11.4).

FIGURE 11.4

A prospective car buyer with a "wish list."

This up-front analysis of your needs can be extremely helpful in narrowing your options and can save you a lot of time. Understanding your needs can also help you sift through the salesmen's hype that you are likely to encounter from one dealer to the next as each tries to sell you on why his model is perfect for you. After getting some information, you may want to take a couple of promising models for a "test drive," where you actually get behind the wheel and see how well the car fits you and your driving habits. You might even talk to other people who have owned this type of car to see how they feel about it. Ultimately, you are the one who has to evaluate all the different cars to see which one is best for you. They may all be good cars; however, one may fit your needs just a little better than the others.

The external acquisition of an information system is very similar to the purchase of a car. When you acquire an IS you should do some analysis of what your specific needs are. For example, how much can you afford to spend, what basic functionality is required, and approximately how many people will use the system? Next, you can begin to "shop" for the new system by asking potential vendors to provide information about the systems that they have to offer. After evaluating this information, it may become clear that several vendors have systems that are worth considering. Those vendors may be asked to come to your organization and set up their systems so that you and your colleagues are able to "test drive" the systems. Seeing how people react to the systems and seeing how each system performs in the organizational environment can help you "see" exactly what you are buying. By seeing the actual system and how it performs with real users, with real or simulated data, you can get a much clearer idea about whether that system fits your needs. Just as you do when you take a car for a "test drive," you learn how the car meets your needs. By seeing how the system meets your needs before you buy, you can greatly reduce the risk associated with acquiring that system.

Steps in External Acquisition

In many cases, your organization will use a competitive bid process for making an external acquisition. In the competitive bid process, vendors are given an opportunity to propose systems that meet the organization's needs. The goal of the competitive process is to help the organization ensure that it gets the best system at the lowest possible price. Most competitive external acquisition processes have at least five general steps:

1. System identification, selection, and planning

2. Systems analysis

3. Development of a Request for Proposal (RFP)

4. Proposal evaluation

5. Vendor selection

You already have learned about the first two because they apply when you build a system yourself *and* when you purchase a system through an external vendor. In the first step, system identification, selection, and planning, you assess whether a proposed system is feasible. During this step, many questions are asked and answered. Can the existing technology be used for such a system? Does the organization have the funds to pay for such a system? Will such a system benefit the organization?

Assuming that the proposed system is feasible and meets your needs, a detailed systems analysis is conducted to determine the requirements of the system. As outlined in Chapter 9, the systems analysis step refines what the needs of the organization are so that a system can be built or purchased that addresses those needs. This step is critical whether building the system yourself or using external acquisition—there is no need to buy a Ferrari when a Chevrolet will do the job just as well or better. Step 3, development of a Request for Proposal, is where the external acquisition process changes significantly from in-house development.

Development of a Request for Proposal (RFP)

A **Request for Proposal**, or RFP, is simply a report that is used to tell vendors what your requirements are and to invite them to provide information about how they might be able to meet those requirements (see Figure 11.5). A RFP is sent to vendors who might potentially be interested in providing hardware and/or software for the system.

Among the areas that may be covered in a RFP are:

■ A summary of existing systems and applications

■ Reliability, backup, and service requirements

■ System performance and required system features

■ The criteria that will be used to evaluate proposals

■ Timetable and budget constraints (how much you can spend)

FIGURE 11.5

Sample RFP document for information systems project.

The RFP is then sent to prospective vendors along with an invitation to present their bids for the project. Eventually, you will likely receive a number of proposals to evaluate. If, on the other hand, you do not receive many proposals, it may be necessary to rethink the requirements—perhaps the requirements are greater than the budget limitations, or the timetable is too short. In some situations, you may need to first send out a preliminary *Request for Information* to simply gather information from prospective vendors. This will help you determine whether, indeed, the desired system is feasible or even possible. If you determine that it is, you can then send out a RFP.

Proposal Evaluation

The fourth step in external acquisition is to evaluate proposals received from vendors. This evaluation may include viewing system demonstrations, evaluating the performance of those systems, and examining criteria important to the organization and how the proposed systems "stack up" to those criteria. Demonstrations are a good way to get a "feel" for the different systems' capabilities. Just as you can go to the showroom to look over a new car and get a feel for whether it meets your needs, it is also possible to screen various systems through a demonstration from the vendor. During a demonstration, a sales team from the vendor presents an oral presentation about their system, its features, and cost, followed by a demonstration of the actual system. In some cases this may take place at your location; other times, it may take place at the vendor's facility or at one of the vendor's clients, particularly when the system is not easily transportable. Although such demonstrations are often useful in helping you understand the features of different systems being proposed, they are rarely adequate enough in and of themselves to warrant purchasing the system without further evaluation.

One of the ways you can better evaluate a proposed system is through **systems benchmarking**. For example, benchmark programs are sample programs or jobs that simulate your computer workload. You can have benchmarks designed to test portions of the system that are most critical to your needs based on the systems analysis. A benchmark might test how long it takes to calculate a set of numbers, or how long it takes to access a set of records in a database, or how long it would take to access certain information given a certain number of concurrent users. Some common system benchmarks include

- Response time given a specified number of users

- Time to sort records

- Time to retrieve a set of records

- Time to produce a given report

- Time to read in a set of data

In addition to benchmarking, workload models can be used to analyze how a given system will perform under the stress of normal daily operations. For example, if you know that you need to process 30,000 records each hour and that you have an average of 5 batch processing jobs and 20 printing requests waiting to be processed at any given time, you can build workload models that include the same mix of activities to help evaluate how a given system will perform.

In addition, vendors may also supply benchmarks that you can use, though you should not rely solely on vendor information. For smaller systems, you may be able to rely on system benchmarks published in computer trade journals such as *PC Magazine* or *PC Week*. However, in most cases, demos and benchmarks alone do not provide the only information you need to make a purchase. The systems analysis phase should have revealed some specific requirements for the new system. These requirements may be listed as criteria that the organization can use to further evaluate vendor proposals. Depending upon what you are purchasing—hardware, software, or both—the criteria you use will change. Table 11.1 provides examples of commonly used evaluation criteria.

Table 11.1 Commonly used evaluation criteria.

Hardware Criteria	Software Criteria	Other Criteria
Clock speed of CPU	Memory requirements	Training and documentation
Memory requirements	Help features	Maintenance and repair
Secondary storage	Usability	Installation
(including capacity,	Learnability	Testing
access time, and so on)	Number of features supported	Price
Video display size		
Printer speed		

Vendor Selection

In most cases, more than one system will meet your needs, just as more than one car will usually meet your needs. However, some probably "fit" better than others. In these cases, you should have a way of prioritizing or ranking competing proposals. One way of doing this is by devising a scoring system for each of the criteria and benchmarking results. For example, look back at the criteria in Table 11.1. Should all these areas be given equal weight or are some more important than others? In most cases, some criteria will be more important than others. For example, it may be very important for a system to do well on the performance benchmarks, moderately important for the system to have a printer speed in excess of 20 pages per minute, and less important for the system to have on-line help.

Some organizations create a scoring system for evaluating different systems, in which scores are assigned to each of the criteria. For example, benchmarking results might be worth 100 total points, while on-line help features are worth only 50 points. All the points for each criterion are then summed to give an overall score for each system. Then, the system with the highest score (or one of the systems among several with the highest scores) is selected. Figure 11.6 shows an example of a form that could be used to evaluate systems and choose a vendor using this method.

Criterion	Max Points (or weight)	Systems Being Evaluated (Score)		
		A	B	C
Disk capacity	20	10	17	12
Compatibility	50	45	30	25
Usability	30	12	30	20
Vendor Support	35	27	16	5
Benchmark Results	50	40	28	30
(add as needed...)				
Total	185	134	121	92

FIGURE 11.6

Sample system evaluation form with subset of criteria.

In the example shown in Figure 11.6, System A looks like the best solution because it scored highest. Using such an evaluation method, it is possible that scoring low on a given criterion might exclude otherwise outstanding systems from being purchased. You can see that Systems B and C fared very poorly on the Vendor Support criterion. It is possible that those systems do not have very good vendor support. However, it is also possible that the vendor did not adequately communicate its commitment to support, perhaps because it did not realize it was such an important issue. Therefore, it is very important for you to communicate with vendors about the evaluation process and what things you value most highly.

Other less formalized approaches to evaluate vendors may also be used. Sometimes simple checklists are used; other times a more subjective process is used. Regardless of the mechanism, eventually the evaluation stage is completed and a vendor is selected, ending the external acquisition process.

The extent to which firms use quantitative analysis such as criteria, weights, and scoring to evaluate vendor proposals varies from organization to organization. In many countries, governmental agencies are often required to perform such an analysis. Furthermore, in some situations, such agencies are required to use specific categories, weights, and scoring methods. For example, many governmental agencies, such as the Internal Revenue Service, have traditionally been required to give significant weight in their evaluation to the criteria of price. Although it is well intended, this has often led to the purchase of systems that, although they were relatively inexpensive, were less than optimal on other dimensions. Governmental agencies in the U.S. have acquired many, many systems that were "cheap" (recall our review of the Denver International Airport in Chapter 1) but in other dimensions did not fare well.

Some organizations also choose to conform to an "in use" requirement, which means that they will accept proposals from only those vendors where the technology proposed has been in actual use by a paying client for some minimum time period, such as six or twelve months. In fact, in some cases vendors are asked to prove that the technology has been in use, usually by showing a dated brochure, a sales order, or some other documentation. The "in use" criteria is meant to ensure the choice of a relatively stable system. Unfortunately, as with the tendency for governmental agencies to weight price so heavily, the "in use" criteria can also sometimes backfire. With hardware, software, and networking technologies changing so quickly, organizations with a strict, long "in use" requirement are doomed to never have new technology.

Outsourcing

A related, but different, alternative to purchasing an existing system is outsourcing. With the external acquisition option discussed above, the organization typically purchases a single system from an outside vendor. **Outsourcing** is the practice of turning over responsibility of some to all of an organization's information systems development and operations to an outside firm. Outsourcing includes a variety of working relationships. The outside firm, or service provider, may develop your information systems applications and house them within their organization, they may run your applications on their computers, or they may develop systems to run on existing computers within your organization. Anything is fair game in an outsourcing arrangement.

In recent years, outsourcing has become a very popular option for organizations. For example, the worldwide IT market for outsourcing services is growing at a rate of 20% per year and will reach a size of nearly $77 billion by the year 2000 (King, 1998). In a recent A.T. Kearney, Inc., study, 90% of the 26 multinational companies it surveyed had outsourced some function in 1995, compared with fewer than 60% in 1992 (Caldwell, 1996). Table 11.2 lists the top 20 IT outsourcing vendors. Outsourcing in the IS arena has become big business!

Table 11.2 Top 20 IT outsourcing vendors.

	Revenue Growth (%)	Revenue by Industry (% of Rev)	Sales, Pricing, & Contracting Model	Number of Regional Operations	Vertical Industry Solutions Expertise	Centers of Expertise	Total Points
1. EDS	10	2	10	10	10	10	52
2. Andersen Consulting	10	2	5	10	10	10	47
3. IBM/ISSC	10	2	5	10	10	10	47
4. CSC	10	10	5	2	10	5	42
5. Hewlett-Packard	10	10	2	5	5	10	42
6. Cap Gemini Sogeti	10	10	5	2	5	5	37
7. Digital	2	10	5	10	5	5	37
8. ICL/CFM	10	10	2	2	5	5	34
9. Sema Group	10	10	2	2	5	5	34
10. MCI/SHL	10	5	2	2	5	10	34
11. CBIS	5	5	5	2	10	5	32
12. Flserv	10	2	2	2	10	5	31
13. M&I Data Services	5	2	5	2	5	10	29
14. AT&T Solutions	5	5	5	2	5	5	27
15. Perot Systems	2	10	2	2	5	5	26
16. Unisys	2	5	2	5	5	5	24
17. Bull	2	10	2	2	2	5	23
18. Alltel IS	5	2	2	2	5	5	21
19. NTT Data	2	5	2	2	5	5	21
20. Debis	2	5	2	2	2	5	18

Source   1996. *Top 20 IT outsourcing vendors.* Information Week, June 24, 56. *Reprinted by permission.*

Why Outsourcing?

Why would a firm outsource any of its information systems services? The main reason is usually cost effectiveness. The service provider may specialize in a particular kind of service such as running payroll. Because it already has the system in place and has many companies that use its services, it is able to spread the cost out across a large number of users. These economies of scale are often not possible in smaller firms or smaller IS groups. In the payroll example, the firm simply provides payroll data such as names, hours worked, and withholding rates to the service provider. For a fee, the service provider takes that data, processes it using its payroll system, and returns paychecks, statements, and designated reports to the company. This may be much cheaper in the long run than developing and operating an in-house payroll system. Furthermore, because other companies already use the service provider for payroll, the service provider has a track record of service that the company can check and rely on. Although it is not foolproof, the fact that the service provider has been providing payroll services successfully for a period of time reduces some of the risk.

In addition to the cost-effectiveness argument, additional reasons why firms often outsource their information systems development are to avoid costs of retraining IS staff and to gain access to specialized capabilities, just as Xerox did with its decision to partner with AT&T described earlier. Avoiding retraining costs is more often used in small or low-technology organizations, where the cost of retraining IS staff to keep them "current" with existing technology is significant. Alternatively, functional business units often require specialized applications to meet unique needs. Rather than rely on in-house development to meet a specialized need, it is often easier to outsource these requirements to service providers who specialize in a particular area.

The Chicago Mercantile Exchange — A BRIEF CASE

The Chicago Mercantile Exchange is the world's leading center for financial risk and asset management (Merc, 1998). The Merc, as it is called, uses open-pit trading floors where buyers and sellers meet to trade futures contracts and options on futures through the process of open outcry (see Figure 11.7). The Merc's diverse product line consists of futures and options on futures within four general categories: agricultural commodities, foreign currencies, interest rates, and stock indexes. All over the world, pension fund and investment advisers, portfolio managers, corporate treasurers and commercial banks trade on the Merc as an integral part of their financial management strategy. In fact, when business, industry and commerce make effective use of futures markets, they help reduce the risks that are part of doing business—which means lower prices for consumers. The Merc is about commerce, but when it came time to develop an electronic commerce Web site, they selected BBN Planet (now called GTE Internetworking after being acquired by GTE Corporation in May 1997), to host their site. Hosting a Web site was not directly related to the core competencies of their IS staff. Yet, Merc officials report that using BBN Planet brought both advantages and disadvantages (Anthes, 1997). BBN offers superb security, network management, and round-the-clock response to operational problems. Additionally, they believe that outsourcing to a large service provider such as BBN Planet is much safer than hosting their own Web site, because global-class companies like BBN Planet have the resources to create huge networks with no single point of failure. A disadvantage is a loss of control. To combat this concern, Merc wrote special monitoring software—running both at BBN and at the Merc's data center—to ensure that real-time data feeds are posted correctly at the Web site.

Reprinted by permission of the Chicago Mercantile Exchange.

Unlike today, outsourcing wasn't a widely used option for most large companies until 1990 when Kodak decided to outsource its *entire* IS operation into three separate contracts with IBM, DEC, and BusinessLand. This was the first large-scale outsourcing agreement from a large international corporation. Before this agreement, outsourcing was relatively small scale, and often limited to IS groups that had suffered performance problems. Since then, the outsourcing trend has become a very important and an increasingly common development alternative. Today, firms have many additional pressures to outsource. Some of these are old reasons, but some are new to today's environment (Applegate, McFarlan, and McKenney, 1996):

■ *Cost and quality concerns:* In many cases it is possible to achieve higher-quality systems at a lower price through economies of scale, better management of hardware, lower labor costs, and better software licenses on the part of a service provider.

■ *Problems in IS performance:* IS departments may have problems meeting acceptable service standards due to cost overruns, delayed systems, underutilized systems, or poorly performing systems. In such cases, organizational management may attempt to increase reliability through outsourcing.

■ *Supplier pressures:* Perhaps not surprisingly, some of the largest service providers are also the largest suppliers of computer equipment: IBM, DEC, and EDS. In some cases, the aggressive sales forces of these suppliers are able to convince senior managers at organizations to outsource their IS functions.

■ *Simplifying, downsizing, and reengineering:* Organizations under competitive pressure often attempt to focus on only their "core competencies." In many cases, organizations simply decide that running information systems is not one of their "core competencies" and decide to outsource this function to companies such as IBM and EDS, whose primary competency *is* developing and maintaining information systems.

- *Financial factors:* When firms turn over their information systems to a service provider, they can sometimes strengthen their balance sheets by liquefying their IT assets. Also, if users perceive they are actually paying for their IT services rather than simply having them provided by an in-house staff, they may use those services more wisely and perceive them to be of greater value.

- *Organizational culture:* Political or organizational problems are often difficult for an IS group to overcome. However, an external service provider often brings enough clout, devoid of any organizational or functional ties, to streamline IS operations as needed.

- *Internal irritants:* Tension between end-users and the IS staff is sometimes difficult to eliminate. At times this tension can intrude on the daily operations of the organization, and the idea of a remote, external, relatively neutral IS group can be appealing. Whether or not the tension between users and the IS staff (or service provider) is really eliminated is open to question; however, simply having the IS group external to the organization can remove a lingering thorn in management's side.

Managing the IS Outsourcing Relationship

McFarlan and Nolan (1995) argue that the ongoing management of an outsourcing alliance is the single most important aspect of the outsourcing project's success. Their recommendations for the best management are

1. A strong, active CIO and staff should continually manage the legal and professional relationship with the outsourcing firm.

2. Clear, realistic performance measurements of the systems *and* of the outsourcing arrangement should be developed, such as tangible and intangible costs and benefits.

3. The interface between the customer and the outsourcer should have multiple levels (for example, links to deal with policy and relationship issues, and links for dealing with operational and tactical issues).

Managing outsourcing alliances in this way has important implications for the success of the relationship. For example, in addition to a strong CIO and staff, McFarlan and Nolan also recommend that firms assign full-time relationship managers and coordinating groups lower in the organization to "manage" the IS outsourcing project. This means that as people within the IS function are pulled away from traditional IS tasks such as systems development, they are moved toward and organized into new roles and groups. The structure and nature of the internal IS activities change from the exclusive builds and manages systems to one that includes managing relationships with outside firms that build and manage systems under legal contract.

Not All Outsourcing Relationships Are the Same

Most organizations no longer enter into a strictly legal contract with an outsourcing vendor, but into a mutually beneficial relationship with a strategic partner. In such a relationship, the firm and the vendor are each concerned with, and perhaps have a direct stake in, the success of the other. Yet, other types of relationships exist, which means that not all outsourcing agreements need to be structured the same way (Fryer, 1998). In fact, at least three different types of outsourcing relationships can be identified:

- Basic relationship

- Preferred relationship

- Strategic relationship

A basic relationship can best be thought of as a "cash and carry" relationship where you buy products and services on the basis of price and convenience. Organizations should try to have a few preferred relationships, where the buyer and supplier set preferences and prices to the benefit of each other. For example, a supplier can provide preferred pricing to customers who do a specified volume of business. Most organizations have just a few strategic relationships, where both sides share risks and rewards.

A BRIEF CASE ▶ ── **A Strategic Outsourcing Relationship for DuPont** ──

An example of a strategic outsourcing relationship where all parties are sharing risks and rewards is among the chemical giant DuPont, Andersen Consulting, and Computer Sciences Corporation (CSC) (Verity, 1997). In this 10-year, $4 billion-plus deal, DuPont is hoping to reduce spending on IS by as much as 10%. In this agreement, CSC and Andersen will develop new products and services that will be used internally and then sold to DuPont's subsidiaries in other countries. Later, these products may be sold to competitors in the chemical and energy industries. CSC will take over 13 of DuPont's data centers and hire 2,600 of their 4,200 data processing employees. Andersen will hire 500. The fees that CSC and Andersen will receive from DuPont will be proportional to the measurable improvements in shareholder value. This relationship shares both the risks and rewards among these strategic partners.

Strategic relationships require partners to work together rather than compete against each other or point fingers at each other. They learn from each other and their pay is based in part on the success of the partners. This is a far cry from the days when outsourcing vendors competed with each other, were secretive, and were quite legalistic, adhering strictly to the letter of the contract and not willing to do or spend any more than they had to. The promise of mutually beneficial outsourcing partnerships appears to be great, both for client organizations and for vendors. It will be interesting to see where this new form for outsourcing takes us, and what the next new form of outsourcing will be. The decision of whether or not to outsource is obviously not an easy one. However, it is one option that you should be aware of and consider, depending on a whole range of different factors including organizational style, access to service providers, geographic area, or scope of operations.

We have now discussed two systems development alternatives that rely on external organizations to either completely or partially alleviate the burden of managing IS development projects in-house. In some cases, however, it may not be possible or convenient to rely on agencies outside the organization for development. In these cases, organizations may rely on another option for systems development projects.

End-User Development

In many organizations, the growing sophistication of users within the organization offers IS managers a fourth alternative for systems development. This fourth alternative is **end-user development**—having users develop their own applications. This means that the people who are actually going to *use* the systems are also those who will *develop* those systems. End-user development, then, is one way IS departments can speed up application development without relying on external entities such as vendors or service providers. However, end-user development also has risks associated with it. This section outlines the benefits of having end-users develop their own applications as well as some of the drawbacks to this approach.

Benefits of End-User Development

To help you to better understand the benefits of end-user development, you should quickly review some of the problems with conventional development that are suggested by the four situations presented earlier in this chapter:

■ *Cost of labor:* Conventional systems development is labor intensive. In Chapter 3, you saw how software costs have increased while hardware costs have declined, as shown in Figure 11.8. As you can see from the figure, it becomes much cheaper for IS managers to substitute hardware for labor. By giving users their own equipment, an IS manager can significantly reduce the cost of application development simply by giving end-users the tools they need and enabling them to develop their own applications. Better yet, the various departments within the organization can purchase their own equipment, and the IS staff can simply provide guidance and other services.

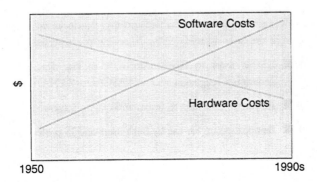

FIGURE 11.8

Rising software costs versus declining hardware costs.

■ *Long development time:* New systems can take months or even years to develop, depending on the scale and scope of the new system and the backlog of systems waiting to be developed. As a result, users' needs may significantly change between when the system was initially proposed and when it is actually implemented. In these cases, the system may be virtually obsolete before it has even been implemented! End-user-developed systems can "skip" the queue of systems waiting to be developed by the IS organization, resulting in more rapidly developed systems.

■ *Slow modification or updates of existing systems:* Related to the time it takes to develop new systems is the problem of maintaining existing systems. Often, updates to existing systems are given a lower priority than developing new systems. Unfortunately, this can result in systems that are unable to keep pace with changing business needs, becoming antiquated and under-used.

When end-users develop their own systems, the users have the responsibility to maintain and update applications as needed. Also, when systems are implemented, they often cause changes to the underlying business processes. These changes may necessitate further change or modification to the application, as highlighted in Figure 11.9. Rather than rely on IS to make these changes, users are able to modify the application in a timely manner to reflect the changed business process.

■ *Work overload:* One reason for long development times and slow modifications is that IS departments are often overloaded with work. When you leverage the talents of end-user developers, you can, in effect, increase the size of the development staff by shifting some of the workload normally handled by IS professionals to end-users, as depicted in Figure 11.10.

End-user development can radically decrease the development workload in the IS department. However, such a shift may cause other areas within IS such as a help desk, for example, to become flooded with requests for assistance. Nonetheless, end-user development can be an excellent option for organizations faced with some of the problems described above.

Encouraging End-User Development

End-user development sounds great, but how can organizations encourage and enable users to develop their own systems? Fortunately, the availability of fourth-generation tools (see Chapter 3) has enabled end-user development to become more practical today than in the early- to mid-1980s. To review, fourth-generation languages should:

■ Enable users to develop software in less time than that required by third-generation languages such as PASCAL or COBOL

■ Be easy to use, easy to learn, and easy to remember

■ Be appropriate for use by both users and IS professionals

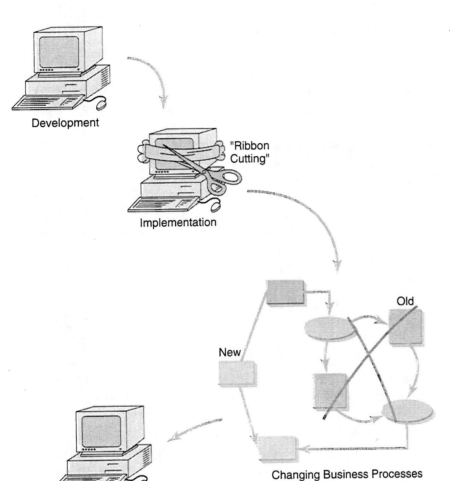

Development

"Ribbon Cutting"

Implementation

New

Old

Changing Business Processes

More Development

FIGURE 11.9

Continuous cycle of development: a system is developed and implemented. However, it eventually becomes inadequate, and new development takes place.

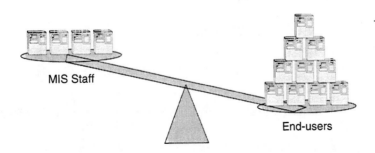

MIS Staff

End-users

FIGURE 11.10

Shifting systems development workload as end-user development has become more prevalent.

There are five categories of fourth-generation tools:

- *Personal computer tools*: Personal computer tools, including spreadsheets, database management systems, and graphics programs, are used by many users throughout an organization. Frequently, these tools enable users to build their own applications using macro languages or embedded tools within the software designed to enable users to customize their own systems.

- *Query languages/report generators*: These tools are usually associated with database systems and enable you to search a database by entering various search criteria. Structured Query Language, or SQL, is the most common query language for this purpose. For example, you may say "Give me the part numbers for any inventory that we have in stock whose quantity exceeds 30." A query language structures that query and presents the results of the query to the user. Report generators are similar to query languages and are designed to easily produce textual and tabular reports. Although query languages are often used by users alone, report generators may require some assistance from IS staff.

- *Graphics generators*: These tools can be used to extract relevant information from databases and convert that data to a graphic such as a pie chart, a line graph, or an area plot. As in report generators, users can specify many different formats.

- *Decision support or modeling tools*: Although spreadsheets can be used as decision support aids, dedicated decision support tools are often available for more complex, multi-dimensional models that may be too complex to easily be handled in a spreadsheet. These tools can enable users to develop decision support systems to aid in making decisions.

- *Application generators*: Application generators are designed to automate much of the relatively tedious programming work associated with systems development. In these tools, you can specify what you want done, then the application generator decides how to accomplish that task and generates the program code. Application generators can be used to get prototypes up and running quickly, get feedback from other potential users, and make necessary changes. Computer Aided Software Engineering (CASE) tools often include an application generator that can be used by end-users or IS professionals.

End-User Development Pitfalls

This chapter has painted a pretty rosy picture of end-user development so far. However, it is important to understand that along with the benefits come some drawbacks, as depicted in Figure 11.11.

The information systems and computer science professions have established software development standards and generally accepted practices that are used throughout different organizations and across different types of systems. Unfortunately, users may not be aware of these standards such as the need for adequate documentation, built-in error checking, and testing procedures. In small, personal applications, not adhering to the standards may not present a problem. However, if the system manages or interconnects to important business data, then lack of adherence to sound principles can quickly become a BIG problem if data becomes corrupted or is not secure.

"OK, TECHNICALLY THIS SHOULD WORK. JUDY, TYPE THE WORD, 'GOODYEAR' ALL CAPS, BOLDFACE, AT 700-POINT TYPE SIZE."

FIGURE 11.11

End-user development can sometimes be problematic.

Another problem for end-user developed systems is a potential lack of continuity. Suppose James develops a new system that meets his needs perfectly. James understands the system and uses it every day. However, one day James is transferred and is replaced by Jordan, a new hire to the company. The system that was so intuitive for James to use may not be so intuitive for Jordan. Jordan may quickly abandon James's system or may be forced to develop her own system. This example shows how end-user development can easily result in a lack of continuity among applications, leading to redundant development efforts and a lot of wasted productivity in the organization. In organizations where turnover is frequent, a lot of time can be lost "reinventing the wheel" simply because systems that are in place are undocumented and cannot be easily used by new employees.

Related to the continuity problem is the question of whether users and managers should be spending their time on IS development. That is, the organization has hired individuals to be financial managers, production managers, marketers, or salespeople. The organization expects these employees to add value to the organization based on the skills that they have to offer. If the time and energy of these individuals are diverted to developing new systems, then the organization loses out on the potential productivity these individuals have to offer in other ways. Also, individual motivation, morale, and performance might suffer if the person is unable to concentrate on her area of expertise and instead spends too much of her time worrying about developing new systems.

Fortunately, organizations that have been successful in moving to end-user development are aware of many of these problems and have established some controls to avoid them. One control mechanism is an Information Center (IC), which is charged with encouraging end users to develop their own applications while at the same time providing some management oversight. The IC staff can assist or train end users on proper development techniques or standards, prevent redundancy in application development, and ensure systems are documented properly. IC staff are often not functional-area experts, but are typically experts in using the fourth-generation tools. Working together, end users and the IC staff can develop useful systems for the organization.

Talking with...

Kraig L. Carrere, Human Resource Representative at SAFECO Insurance Co.

Educational Background

B.A. in Sociology, University of Washington

Job Description

Attract qualified applicants and interview for skills, experience, education, training, and potential to fill existing IT and non-IT openings. Develop action plans to recruit and retain employees, which include working with universities and staff, employment agencies and community-based organizations to attract a potential pool of candidates. Manage employee population to ensure general harmony and a comfortable work environment.

Critical Success Factors

Making contact and following up in a timely manner is very important to the success of hiring a candidate. In a competitive job market such as we have today, we cannot afford to let quality candidates slip by. Networking and homework are also important. Many of the people that are hired are from a referral source. You can also find out critical information on candidates and/or programs via network connections. Also, trying to stay one step ahead of the market and competition are important. Researching new ideas as well as putting a different spin on things that have worked well are important. From a recruiting perspective, the days of "if it's not broke, don't fix it" may be over.

Advice to Students

Make sure that you're looking at the entire picture of the companies with which you'll be interviewing. Focus on things such as the benefits program, opportunity for professional and personal growth, job responsibilities, and whether the people are compatible with your work style. Many students are just looking for the big payday upon graduation. There's nothing wrong with that but don't take a step back just because of the money. In today's market, the opportunities are numerous, so make the correct choice.

ETHICAL PERSPECTIVE: ETHICAL ISSUES IN A CLIENT-VENDOR RELATIONSHIP

As the demands of business grow, so do the demands on information systems. To accommodate this increased emphasis on and demand for technology, managers within many firms have chosen to purchase systems and services from outside vendors or even to completely outsource the development and/or management of entire systems to an external vendor. Just about every large organization, and many smaller ones, have some such form of client-vendor relationship either with a software or hardware vendor, a consultant, or an outsourcing partner. These relationships are typically based on a signed contract. If managed well, these types of relationships do not result in any problems or ethical breaches.

These relationships are primarily legal and contractual in nature. As with any legal, contractual relationships between two parties, problems in a client-vendor relationship can occur when one or both of the parties believe that the contract between them has been broken by the other party. One of the more common contract breaches is when the vendor is late in delivering the product or required services. Another is when the vendor's delivered product or service does meet the expectations or deliver the desired results of the client company. A contract may state that if a vendor is late in delivering computers it will incur a severe penalty, such as having to significantly reduce the price of the computers for the client.

With or without clear contracts, the relationship between vendor and client can quickly and easily deteriorate. Ernest Kallman and John Grillo recently described a case where a client believed that the vendor's software programs were not working properly. When the vendor did not satisfy the client's wishes, the client withheld further payments. However, the vendor had programmed a subroutine in these programs that when activated would stop the software from working at all. The client was unable to operate its business effectively, while the vendor merely stated that the software had been "repossessed" due to a failure to pay.

Perhaps this vendor really was at fault. For example, to provide the software by the agreed-upon date, it may be that they were forced to ship it untested. Perhaps the client was constantly changing requirements and specifications, stretching the letter of the contract and the goodwill of the vendor to the limit.

Other potential ethical issues are also involved in client-vendor relationships. For example, when a vendor creates a system for one client, it may use that same system, or some variant of it, for another similar client. The motivation for the vendor is to benefit from the labor expended and the knowledge gained in building this system and put this to use to generate revenue with other clients. The original client, however, is likely to feel that it expended resources for that system as well and may feel some ownership over it. In addition, the client is not likely to want another firm to be able to use the same system, particularly if the other client is a competitor.

Even with an appropriately worded contract, it is difficult to draw the line between outright duplication of a system and building a different system for another party that builds on knowledge from building and managing the original system. Further, it may be difficult for the original client to ever even find out that ideas or components from its original system have found their way into a different system for another client. Some vendors reserve the right to reuse their technology and systems for other clients as they see fit, while promising not to divulge important business information to competitors.

In cases similar to those described, problems regarding contractual promises made between the vendor and the client have led to requirements that future additions or modifications to the original program are to be contracted back to the vendor. For a variety of reasons the systems people within the client firm may take it upon themselves to access the code within the system and make changes and/or add features. On the one hand, the client has broken the letter of the contract and perhaps done something unethical. On the other hand, the client may have a legitimate reason to take it upon him/herself to alter the software, particularly if the vendor isn't doing its job and/or if the relationship between the client and vendor had already deteriorated. One can see how a client might feel compelled to jump in to fix a system running on its equipment in its business, especially if it feels that the vendor is not responsive or is unnecessarily restrictive. However, one can also see that the vendor might not want anyone else tinkering with its system, particularly if technically the vendor owns the system or if the vendor's head will be on the chopping block even if someone at the client firm damages the system.

Questions for Discussion

1. Do you feel that it is ethical for vendors to program subroutines into their software that can stop the client from using the software when contract disputes arise?

2. Who owns systems that are built for a client in an outsourcing arrangement? The client? The vendor? Both?

3. Should outsourcing vendors have the right to do as they wish with systems that they build for a client? Why or why not? If so, with what constraints?

383

INTERNATIONAL PERSPECTIVE: THE RACE IS ON: GLOBAL OUTSOURCING

International Data Corporation predicts that the global outsourcing market will exceed $121 billion by the year 2000. IDC reports that "Fundamental business events, such as increased competition and the subsequent increasing focus on core competencies are forcing organizations throughout the world to carefully consider what tasks should remain in-house. Other more technical issues are causing agonizing support and maintenance problems for CIOs throughout the world. In many instances, outsourcing is welcomed." U.S. firms offering large-scale and worldwide outsourcing partnerships include Andersen Consulting, AT&T, Computer Sciences, Digital, EDS, Hewlett-Packard, IBM, and Entex.

The Outsourcing Institute agrees that outsourcing has benefits: "By the very nature of their specialization, outsourcing providers can bring extensive worldwide, world-class capabilities to meeting the needs of their customers... Often these vendor capabilities are the results of extensive investments in technology, methodologies, and people—investments made over a considerable period of time. In many cases, the vendor's capabilities include specialized industry expertise gained through working with many clients facing similar challenges. This expertise may be translated in skills, processes, or technologies uniquely capable of meeting these needs."

Outsourcing arrangements can be optimal for businesses around the world that have the capital but do not have the infrastructure or skills to manage, for example, a global telecommunications network or other IT functions. Companies around the world seem to agree: In the international airline industry alone, British Airways, Gulf Air, JAL, and Lufthansa have already taken advantage of outsourcing opportunities, primarily of data and telecommunications.

Experts have argued that the benefits of outsourcing are overestimated, especially as little or no empirical research is available, and companies should not outsource the management of IS. The Outsourcing Institute voices the concerns of many others when it notes that there can be problems associated with outsourcing:

"One of the most important insights gained from working with hundreds of companies looking into and implementing outsourcing is the simple but too-often overlooked fact that for outsourcing to be successful, management must have a clear set of goals and objectives in mind from the start. Outsourcing may entail significant organizational upheaval, transfer of important assets, dislocation of people, and long-term contractual relationships with an outside partner. None of these make sense unless the benefits to be gained and the risks involved are clearly understood and managed from the outset."

They emphasize that businesses must look for long-term results rather than short-term solutions when outsourcing. In the U.S. case, much of the outsourcing specifically for software development is going to Indian and Singaporean firms, taking with it many highly-paid technology jobs.

However, U.S. firms are benefiting from a focus on global outsourcing, with companies around the world partnering with firms such as AT&T to overcome problems in "differing standards, incompatibility of communications equipment and vast up-front investments" and other problems of infrastructure and management. AT&T has targeted the 2,000 largest organizations within specific industry groups such as Utilities and Energy, Health Management, Retail and Wholesale, Transportation, and Hospitality. Its efforts are being rewarded; recently, AT&T was awarded at $1.4 million contract with the Ministry of Railways in the People's Republic of China (funded by the World Bank). One focus of its efforts to attract outsourcing is Europe, where it is expanding its employee base from 26,000. It is offering Internet and other solutions, including leased lines, Web pages and servers, Internet security, and more. Outsourcing has clearly become a worldwide phenomenon: Of the 2,000 companies targeted, 43% are headquartered in the Americas, while 27% are in the Pacific Rim, and 30% are in Europe.

Global outsourcing also means supporting U.S. multinationals. Textron, a multi-industry company, expects to generate over 1/3 of its revenues from outside the U.S. by the year 2000. Textron and AT&T signed a 10-year, $1.1 billion agreement in the fall of 1996; among the goals are assisting Textron in integrating global acquisitions and linking divisions worldwide.

Questions for Discussion

1. Does global outsourcing of information systems and technology make sense as a sound business strategy, or is it too problematic and risky to be viable in the long term?

2. If you were to make a checklist of the critical success factors for a global outsourcing partnership, what would it include? Why?

3. What do you see for the future of global outsourcing? Does it grow or subside? Why?

Summary

1. **Understand the factors and situations where building a system in-house is not feasible.** It is not feasible for an organization to build a system in house in at least four situations. First, some organizations have limited IS staffing and therefore do not have the capability to build a system themselves. Second, the organization may have IS staff with a limited skill set. Existing IS staff may be highly skilled at producing traditional applications, but not have the skills to build new types of systems or systems that require emerging development tools. Third, in many organizations, the IS staff does not have the time to work on all the systems that are desired by the organization. Fourth, some organizations have performance problems with their IS staff, where staff turnover, changing requirements, shifts in technology, or budget constraints have resulted in poor results. In any of these situations, it may be advantageous to an organization to consider an alternative to in-house systems development.

2. **Explain three alternative systems development options: external acquisition, outsourcing, and end-user development.** External acquisition is the process of purchasing an existing information system from an external organization or vendor. External acquisition is a five-step process. Step 1 is system identification, selection, and planning, which focuses on determining whether a proposed system is feasible. Step 2 is systems analysis, which focuses on determining the requirements for the system. Step 3 is the development of a Request for Proposal (RFP). A RFP is a communication tool indicating an organization's requirements for a given system and requesting information from potential vendors on their ability to deliver such a system. Step 4 is proposal evaluation, which focuses on evaluating proposals received from vendors. This evaluation may include viewing system demonstrations, evaluating the performance of those systems, and examining criteria important to the organization and how the proposed systems meet those criteria. Step 5 is vendor selection, which focuses on determining the vendor to provide the system. Outsourcing refers to the turning over of partial or entire responsibility for information systems development and management to an outside organization. End-user development is a systems development method whereby users in the organization develop, test, and maintain their own applications.

Key Terms

External acquisition

Request for Proposal

Systems benchmarking

Outsourcing

End-user development

Review Questions

1. What are the five typical steps of the external acquisition process?

2. How does the external acquisition process differ from the in-house, build-it-yourself method?

3. Describe at least five possible points that may be covered in a Request for Proposal.

4. How are software and hardware vendors able to provide a "test drive" of their system to potential clients?

5. How does systems benchmarking aid in the proposal evaluation process?

6. Describe the basic difference between systems benchmarking and workload modeling.

7. List some of the non-hardware and non-software evaluation criteria used when evaluating systems.

8. What is one of the major drawbacks of the use of a scoring system to evaluate systems?

9. What is the main reason that firms outsource information systems development?

10. What has caused much of the tension between the IS department and many end-user developers?

11. For what scale of systems is end-user development normally successful within organizations?

Problems and Exercises

◆ **Individual**   ◆◆ **Group**   ⌒ **Field**   ◗ **Web/Internet**

◆ 1. Match the following terms to the appropriate definitions:

_____ External acquisition

_____ Request for Proposal

_____ Systems benchmarking

_____ Outsourcing

_____ End-user development

a. A communication tool indicating buyer requirements for a given system and requesting information from potential vendors

b. A systems development method whereby users in the organization develop, test, and maintain their own applications

c. The process of purchasing an existing information system from an external organization or vendor

d. Turning over partial or entire responsibility for information systems development and management to an outside organization

e. A standardized set of performance tests designed to facilitate comparison between systems

◆ ◗ 2. Do you believe that outsourcing will continue to be a prevalent option for systems development? What role does the increasing size of IS departments play in this? Search the World Wide Web for companies that specialize in outsourcing IS needs. You may wish to try Computer Sciences Corporation at http://www.csc.com/. What are they "selling" and how are they marketing their product?

◆ 3. Why is it so important to correctly identify the requirements of a system prior to creating the Request for Proposal? What types of problems may be encountered without this specificity?

◆◆ 4. During the process of external acquisition, what are the advantages and disadvantages of relying on a system that has been "proven" with a good "track record" of performance? Discus your answer with a group of classmates. How do their opinions differ from yours? Is the rapid rate of advancement within the IS field a problem?

5. It would seem that outsourcing the entire IS department is a viable option for many organizations. Pair up with a fellow classmate and decide who will present an argument for and against this notion. Take a few minutes to prepare and then debate this issue. Which parties are most affected in either situation?

6. If an organization is in the business of providing outsourced services to other organizations, what happens when these clients no longer wish to outsource? Who owns the systems? Who owns the data?

7. Discuss the following in a small group: One of the major issues with end-user development is whether users should be spending their time developing systems rather than performing their "regular" responsibilities. What do you feel is the proper balance? Why? Who is responsible for managing this systems development, their normal manager or someone from the IS department?

8. In Chapter 1 of this text, the term benchmarking was introduced as a term relevant to management information systems. Review the definition from Chapter 1, if necessary. How does benchmarking as used in Chapter 11 differ from that in Chapter 1? Are they really two distinct terms with distinct meanings?

9. Argue for or against the following. Support your answer with specific facts from this chapter. "It would be cheaper and easier to manage our information systems if we would just hire more people for our IS department than go through the hassles of outsourcing and end-user development!"

10. In a small group of classmates, use the development alternatives discussed throughout the chapter to develop solutions to each of the four situations presented at the beginning of this chapter. Provide a rationale for each solution, and describe potential drawbacks for each. Prepare a 10-15 minute presentation to the class of your decisions. Conduct this presentation as if your group were presenting your proposals to the Steering Committee in charge of IS Productivity.

11. Consider an organization that is familiar to you. Describe the method(s) of information systems development that are employed. Can you determine the reasons for the adoption of these methods over others? Who made these selections? Who determined the development alternatives?

12. Based on your past work experience, describe the relationship in your organization between end-users and the IS department. Was there substantial end-user development? Were tensions high? Did end-users feel that the IS department was unable to adequately "get things done"? Did other classmates have similar or vastly different situations? Why do you think this is so?

13. Interview an IS manager at an organization with which you are familiar. Determine what balance of systems development methods would be the most beneficial to his/her department (for example, in-house development of 50% of systems, outsource 30%, purchase 10%, and have 10% developed by end-users). What reasons were given for this particular breakdown? Is this something that can be easily quantified?

 14. Interview an IS manager at an organization with which you are familiar. Determine what percentage of a typical day is spent reviewing proposals from vendors, contracting with outsourcing partners, and managing end-user development in comparison with his/her project management responsibilities for in-house projects.

 15. Based on the Ethics Inset discussing some of the ethical issues of client-vendor relationships, discuss your experiences dealing with these issues within a group of classmates. Have you ever had a system delivered that did not meet expectations or pre-set requirements? What action did you and/or your company take? Was the situation resolved equitably? Were there any "horror stories" among the group? Did this system involve proprietary information from your company? Search the World Wide Web for IS vendors that provide their service agreements on their homepage. Who holds the responsibilities in these agreements?

 16. Based on the scenario that opened the chapter, what would you do if you were Linda and had to make the presentation to the meeting of the stakeholders? Would you follow Steve's recommendations? Why or why not? What could you do as the IS department manager to make this project work?

Real World Case Problems

1. Ticona Chooses Andersen Consulting to Develop, Maintain Information Technology System.

Ticona, a member of the Hoechst Group, and Andersen Consulting announced an agreement under which Andersen Consulting will develop and maintain information systems designed to support Ticona's product-line extension and geographic expansion. Ticona, formerly the technical polymers division of Hoechst, is a leading supplier of engineering and high-performance thermoplastics. As part of the recent restructuring of Hoechst AG, Ticona became a stand-alone business but remains part of the Hoechst Group.

Under the contract, Andersen Consulting, combining its consulting and Business Process Management expertise, will upgrade and then maintain Ticona's SAP systems and enable the company to migrate to an information technology model that will provide improved service levels, flexibility, and cost predictability.

"As we become an increasingly independent organization, it is imperative that Ticona have an information technology system that will enable us to keep pace with expected strong growth, both in product offerings and geographic reach," said Russ Bockstedt, Ticona's information technology manager. "Based on its record of success, we are looking to Andersen Consulting to build and maintain an IT system that is in a league with our capability to develop and manufacture world-class, high-performance thermoplastic polymer products and services." Design, Build, Run, developed by Anderson Consulting, is an alternative life-cycle approach to more typical out-sourcing arrangements, encompassing the development and subsequent day-to-day maintenance of information technology systems. Design, Build, Run allows clients to achieve the benefits of new systems more rapidly and affordably while mitigating risk and providing predictability for the system's entire useful life. "We are delighted that Ticona has chosen Andersen Consulting," said Charles Pisciotta, Andersen Consulting's client partner for Ticona. "Through our Design, Build, Run offering, we will help Ticona reap more strategic value from its technology investments. Additionally, this venture clearly bolsters Andersen Consulting's position within the plastics and chemical industries. It fits perfectly with our strategy to focus on our strengths, developing and managing business solutions that help our clients compete more effectively in a dynamic industry environment."

a. What, exactly, is Ticona outsourcing to Andersen Consulting, and why is it useful to Ticona to do this?

b. In what ways is this outsourcing arrangement useful to Andersen Consulting, in addition to its direct profits from the arrangement?

c. In what ways does Andersen Consulting's "Design, Build, Run" approach to building systems parallel with the emerging systems development methodologies discussed in Chapter 10?

Source *Adapted from a press release found at http://www.ac.com/topstories/ ts_frintro_1.html. January 15, 1998.*

2. Visa Expands Outsourcing Deal: Partnership with DMR Helps Company Serve Big Customers.

Quality and on-time delivery, not cost, was the main focus of the outsourcing of Visa's customizable reporting software that is used by large corporate customers worldwide. In 1995 Visa had little choice but to outsource as its 1000 person is group lacked the expertise to develop this reporting software. It selected DMR over nine other systems integrators, but not due to the cost. Focusing on quality and delivery time won the bid. The project came in on time and on budget—something rarely heard of in the software business.

In order to win the bid DMR laid out a full-blown project methodology complete with all of the roles of the participants. Other bidders simply offered one-word answers for project descriptions to Prather, project manager and vice president of information systems at Visa's commercial card division in San Francisco. The answer was always, "Yes," but with no description of how it would be done. DMR used two project managers, Prather and one from their offices. In addition, in an unusual style, they did most of the work off-site by 40 DMR staffers paid less in Canada, in Quebec City saving Prather the money it would have cost for leasing office space.

Prather had intended for many of his staff to work on the project to learn skills that they would need for maintaining the software, but he quickly learned that his staff could not do that and keep up with their jobs. In the end they had no one who knew how to run what was developed. When outsourcing is the entire answer to the project it becomes very risky, as the outsider must understand the entire business and the competition at the same time. Still, Visa was able to maintain control of the project. Feedback from the user was constantly taken into consideration. After pulling together the project, having it delivered on time and on budget credibility gets established and Visa was able to just settle into a relationship upon which fairy tales are based.

a. How did DMR win the outsourcing deal from Visa? Why was this important to Visa?

b. Why was it important for Visa to retain some control in this arrangement? How did this pay off later?

c. Why do you suppose Visa's 1000 person IS group lacked the expertise needed to build the new client/server-based system?

d. Is this common? natural? Why or why not?

Source *King, Julia. 1998. Visa expands outsourcing deal.* ComputerWorld. *January 26, 41–44.*

References

Anthes, G.H. 1997. Outsourcing the 'net. Information from: www.computerworld.com: Information verified: April 6, 1998.

Applegate, McFarlan, and McKenney. 1996. *Corporate information systems management: Text and cases.* Chicago, Illinois: Irwin.

Caldwell, B. 1996. The new outsourcing partnership: Vendors want to provide more than just services. *InformationWeek,* June 24, 50–64.

Fryer, B. 1998. Outsourcing support: Kudos and caveats. Information from: www.computerworld.com. Information verified: April 6, 1998.

King, J. 1998. Outsourcing loses stigma. Information from: www.computerworld.com. Information verified: April 6, 1998.

Kutnick, J. 1998. Shopping smart. Information from: www.computerworld.com. Information verified: April 6, 1998.

Merc, 1998. Information from: www.cme.com. Information verified: April 6, 1998.

Starwave, 1998. Information from: www.starwave.com. Information verified: April 6, 1998.

Thibodeau, P. 1998. AT&T snags $750M Citibank outsourcing job. Information from: www.computerworld.com. Information verified: April 6, 1998.

Verity, J.W. 1997. Megadeals march on. Information from: www.computerworld.com. Information verified: April 6, 1998.

Related Readings

Ang, S., and L.L. Cummings. 1997. Strategic response to institutional influences on information systems outsourcing. *Organization Science* 8(3): 235–256.

Chandhury, Nam, and Rao. 1995. Management of information systems outsourcing: A bidding perspective. *Journal of Management Information Systems* 12(2): 131–159.

Edberg, D.T., and B.J. Bowman. 1996. User-developed applications: An empirical study of application quality and developer productivity. *Journal of Management Information Systems* 13(1): 167–185.

Hu, Sanders, and Gebelt, 1997. Research report: Diffusion of information systems outsourcing: A reevaluation of influence sources. *Information Systems Research* 8(3): 288–301.

Lacity, Willcocks, and Feeny, 1995. IT outsourcing: Maximize flexibility and control. *Harvard Business Review* 73(3): 84–93.

Lawrence, M., and G. Low. 1993. Exploring individual user satisfaction within user-ked development. *Management Information Systems Quarterly* 17(2): 195–208.

Maiden, Ncube, and Moore. 1997. Lessons learned during requirements acquisition for COTS systems. *Communications of the ACM* 40(12): 21–25.

Mirani, R., and W.R. King. 1994. The development of a measure for end-user computing support. *Decision Sciences* 25(4): 481–498.

Montazemi, Cameron, and Gupta. 1996. An empirical study of factors affecting software package selection. *Journal of Management Information Systems* 13(1): 89–105.

Saarinen, T., and A.P.J. Vepsalainen. 1994. Procurement strategies for information systems. *Journal of Management Information Systems* 11(2): 187–208.

Teng, Cheon, and Grover. 1995. Decisions to outsource information systems functions: Testing a strategy-theoretic discrepancy model. *Decision Sciences* 26(1): 75–103.

Wang, Barron, and Seidmann. 1997. Contradicting structures for custom software development: The impacts of informational rents and uncertainty on internal development and outsourcing. *Management Science* 43(12): 1726–1744.

Module 5: Data Networking and Telecommunications

Goal: To be able to demonstrate literacy in the basic technology concepts behind networking, how the Internet works, client-server architectures and information security.

Chapter 12: Basic Concepts and Principles

Glenn Davis sells papayas to wholesalers throughout the United States. His company is Paradise Groceries. A "road warrior," Glenn rarely is far from his notebook computer. Each morning, Glenn dials into the Internet from his hotel room to check his e-mail. He then uses the Internet to connect to his company's webserver to check for current prices and for internal company news. Now he is ready to call on customers.

At the customer site, Glenn can take orders online. While recording orders, he can check on product availability and delivery schedules. By adding the customer's order to the official list of orders, he can even guarantee a delivery date. He also shows the customer a website where he or she can check on the progress of the order.

Although Glenn is happy with the benefits his notebook has brought him, there are still some problems. Most importantly, there often is no telephone around when he wants to check his e-mail and get other information. At the customer's office, he has to ask for permission to use a phone, and this is awkward. Another big problem is that his telephone connections are very slow.

Glenn's company is evaluating a high-speed wireless Internet access service. However, the service is only available in some cities, does not work inside many buildings, and is very expensive. Glenn's private guess is that the company will wait until the technology is beyond the "bleeding edge" and alternatives have become clearer.

In general, Glenn is patient. In the last 10 years he has seen enormous improvements in his network services. He is fairly confident that his company will stay close to the leading edge of network technology without constantly jumping into immature market offerings that turn out to bring more problems than they solve. ∎

Learning Objectives

After studying this chapter, you should be able to describe:

- Basic networking concepts in wide use today: voice and video communication versus data communications, circuit switching versus packet switching, multiplexing, congestion and latency, analog versus digital versus binary, modems, LANs versus WANs, terminal–host processing versus file server program access versus client/server processing, platform independence

- The elements of the Internet and the Internet standards used when you dial into the Internet from home or on the road in order to access a World Wide Web server (webserver)

- The need for quality of service guarantees and improved security

INTRODUCTION

The title of this book is "Business Data Communications and Networking." As Figure 1.1 illustrates, a **network** is an any-to-any communication system. This means that any station can communicate with any other station on the network.

For this to be possible, every station on the network must have a unique **network address**. For example, the telephone network can connect your phone to any other telephone in the world. You only need to know the other party's telephone number.

Data communications, in turn, is communication in which at least one party is a computer. When you use the Internet, therefore, it is data communications. We will discuss many other examples of data communications in this book.

Figure 1.1
Elements of a
Network

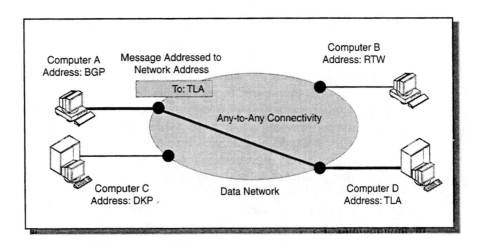

Basic Concepts   In this first chapter, we begin by looking at some core networking concepts we will use throughout this book. Many of these concepts will be familiar to you, but quite a few will be new.

The Internet   The Internet is arguably the most important network today. It is certainly changing the fastest. We will look at the technology of the Internet and the standards you use when you dial into the Internet from home or on the road to access a webserver.

Layered Standards   This chapter will introduce the *hybrid TCP/IP–OSI standards architecture*, which will be the focus of much of this book. This standards architecture governs the Internet and many other networks.

Looking to the Future   We will end this chapter with a discussion of two topics we expect to become increasingly important in the next few years: (1) security and (2) quality of service guarantees for latency (delays) and reliability.

Business Data Communications and Networking   As an **information systems (IS)** professional, you will not build switches or other networking devices. That is what computer scientists and electrical engineers do. Rather, as an IS professional you will be employed by a firm that uses networks to work more effectively and efficiently (or by a company that consults for such firms). Your duties will include everything from needs analysis through implementation and ongoing management. As a business student, it will not be enough to know the technology. You will have to work with users to help them articulate their needs and to help them see how networks can help them better do their work. At the same time, you will have to know the technology very well to do your job.

CORE CONCEPTS

We will begin by looking at some basic concepts in data communications and networking.

Voice and Video Communication

Traditionally, the world of communications has been divided into data communications, in which one or both parties is a computer, on the one hand and voice and video communications on the other hand.

Circuit-Switched Networks   As Figure 1.2 illustrates, the telephone network has traditionally handled both voice and video transmission.

Switches, Trunk Lines, and the Local Loop   Figure 1.2 shows that the telephone network consists of a hierarchy of **switches** connected by high-speed

Figure 1.2
Circuit Switching
for Voice and
Video
Communications

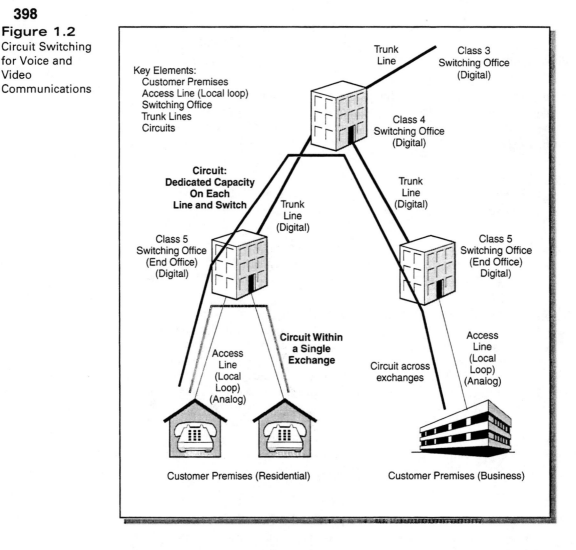

Key Elements:
Customer Premises
Access Line (Local loop)
Switching Office
Trunk Lines
Circuits

Trunk Line

Class 3 Switching Office (Digital)

Class 4 Switching Office (Digital)

Circuit:
Dedicated Capacity
On Each
Line and Switch

Trunk Line (Digital)

Trunk Line (Digital)

Class 5 Switching Office (End Office) (Digital)

Class 5 Switching Office (End Office) Digital

Access Line (Local Loop) (Analog)

Circuit Within a Single Exchange

Circuit across exchanges

Access Line (Local Loop) (Analog)

Customer Premises (Residential)

Customer Premises (Business)

transmission lines called **trunk lines.** Subscribers are connected to the nearest switching office with a transmission line called an **access line,** or, more colorfully, the **local loop.**

Circuits When you dial another party, the telephone system creates a connection called a **circuit** between the two telephones. A circuit may pass through multiple switches and transmission lines, but to the two parties, it seems like a simple point-to-point link.

Guaranteed (Reserved) Capacity The telephone uses **circuit switching,** which **reserves capacity** for your call along each trunk line and within each

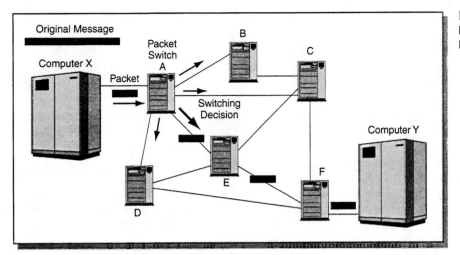

Figure 1.3
Packet-Switched
Network for Data

switch along the circuit's path. No matter how busy the telephone network gets, there will be no delay when you talk.

Wastefulness of Circuit Switching for Bursty Data Traffic On the downside, you must pay for this **dedicated capacity** whether you use it or not. Of course, in a voice call, one of the two parties is talking nearly all the time. In video, in turn, you receive a constant stream of images. Little capacity is wasted.

Data transmission, in contrast, is **bursty,** with short and intense transmissions separated by relatively long silences. Consider what happens when you use the World Wide Web. You download a page in a burst of a few seconds, then stare at the screen for up to several minutes before you start the next download burst. In data communications, you often transmit and receive less than 5% of the time. Yet with circuit switching, you pay for the capacity 100% of the time.

Packet-Switched Data Networks

Because circuit switching is not good for bursty data traffic, **data networks** (i.e., networks designed specifically to carry data) normally use a different type of switching called **packet switching.**

Packets As Figure 1.3 illustrates, large messages are broken into small pieces and sent in shorter messages called **packets.**[1] (We will see later in this chapter that these messages sometimes are called *frames.*) Small packets flow more easily through a switched network than long messages, much like sand flows more smoothly than rocks.

---

[1] A typical packet length is 100 to 1,000 bytes.

Switching Decisions Figure 1.3 shows that when a packet arrives at a packet switch, there may be several ports available for sending the packet on to another router. The packet switch should select the output port best able to move the packet on to its ultimate destination. This **switching decision** may involve consideration of congestion, cost, and other factors.

Multiplexing to Reduce Transmission Costs Figure 1.3 also shows that capacity is not reserved along the trunk lines that connect switches. Packets are **multiplexed** (mixed) on the trunk lines, sharing both the capacity and the cost of these trunk lines.[2] Packets also share the capacity and costs of switches.

On the positive side, packet switching avoids the wasted capacity of circuit switching, reducing costs dramatically. For data transmission, packet switching tends to be much less expensive than circuit switching. Almost all data networks today are packet-switched networks.

Congestion and Latency On the negative side, because there is no capacity reservation, if traffic gets too heavy, there will be **congestion.** When there is congestion, packets may take much longer to get through the network. The length of delay is called the **latency** in the transmission. Users greatly dislike latency. As discussed later in this chapter, and more fully in Chapter 8, efforts are now under way to manage latency in packet-switched networks.

Analog and Digital Communication

Analog Communication Some electrical signals, called **analog** signals, *rise and fall smoothly in intensity among an infinite number of states* (conditions). For instance, when you speak, your voice rises and falls smoothly in volume. The local loop from your home or office to the telephone company is designed to carry analog communication because the electrical signals created when we speak rise and fall smoothly in intensity and therefore are analog. Figure 1.4 illustrates analog communication. Note that we have used voice telephony as an example of an analog signal, but it is only an example. Any signal that rises and falls smoothly in intensity among an infinite number of states is an analog signal.

Digital Communication Computers communicate differently. They use **digital communication.** As Figure 1.4 also shows, a digital signal has three characteristics:

- First, the signal remains at a constant **state** (say a voltage level) during each period of time called a **clock cycle.**
- Second, at the end of each clock cycle, the line can remain in the same state or jump to another state.

---

[2] The telephone network also uses multiplexing on trunk lines between switches. Several voice circuits can share a single high-speed trunk line. However, each circuit is still given dedicated capacity within each trunk line. This limits the economic benefits of circuit-switched multiplexing.

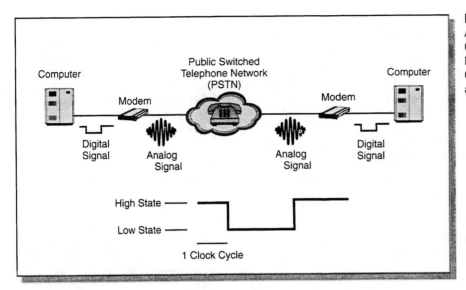

Figure 1.4
Analog **401**
Communication,
Digital
Communication,
and Modems

- Third, there are only a few possible states to jump to at the end of a clock cycle. Sometimes there are as few as two possible states. There are rarely more than 32 possible states.

For example, there are 7 days in a week. On Monday, it is Monday all day, until midnight. Then the day changes immediately to Tuesday. In terms of electrical signaling, there might be two voltages, with one state (voltage) representing a one and the other state (voltage) representing a zero.

Binary Communication   When there are only two possible states, this is a special case of digital communication called **binary** communication. In each time period, we can send a single **bit,** that is, a single zero or one.[3] All binary signals are digital, but not all digital signals are binary. In particular, "digital" does not imply using two states (ones and zeros).

Representing Information Transmission Speeds   Of course, we send many **bits per second (bps)** when we transmit. In increasing multiples of 1,000 (not 1,024 as in computer memory), we have **kilobits per second (kbps),**[4] **megabits per second (Mbps), gigabits per second (Gbps),** and **terabits per second (Tbps).** So 55,300 bps is the same as 55.3 kbps. Twelve million bits per second is 12 Mbps.

---

[3]As Chapter 3 discusses, if there are more than two states, we can send more than one bit per clock cycle.
[4]Note that "kilobits" is abbreviated with a lowercase "k." This is proper metric notation. (Uppercase "K" is reserved for Kelvins, a measure of temperature.)

Modems To send data over a traditional telephone line, you need a device called a **modem.** As Figure 1.4 illustrates, a modem translates outgoing digital computer signals into analog signals that can travel over the access line to the telephone network. When analog signals arrive from the other party, in turn, the modem translates these signals back into digital format and passes the digital signal on to the receiving computer. Chapter 3 looks at modems in considerable detail.

LANs and WANs

In terms of geographical scope, there is a core distinction between local area networks (LANs) and wide area networks (WANs).

LANs As the name suggests, **local area networks (LANs)** cover a small region. Some LANs only serve one or two PCs in a home office. Others serve a dozen PCs in a small office. Still others serve dozens of computers in a single building. The largest LANs serve an entire site, such as a university campus, an industrial park, or a military base.

Figure 1.5 shows a small LAN that connects a few PCs. This LAN consists of a box called a *hub* or a *switch* plus *wiring.* The hub or switch transfers messages from one PC to another. Each computer must have a *network interface card (NIC)* that manages communication with the network.

As shown in Figure 1.5, a LAN often forms the transmission component for a PC network (although a LAN can connect any types of computers). In PC networks, **client PCs** are personal computers that sit on the desks of managers, professionals, and other information workers. The machines that provide services to these client PCs are called **servers.**

Figure 1.5
Small PC Network
Built on a LAN

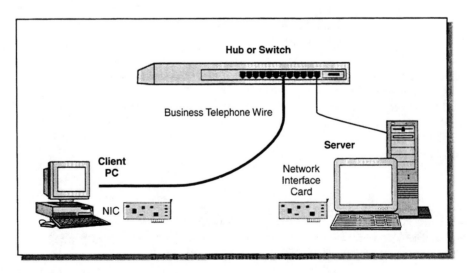

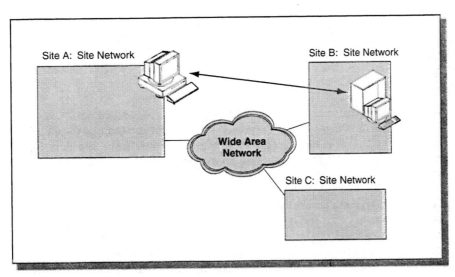

Figure 1.6 **403**
Wide Area
Network (WAN)

Wide Area Networks: Carriers As Figure 1.6 illustrates, many organizations have multiple sites. They need **wide area networks (WANs)** to link the LANs in their various sites together.

Distributed Processing

When you use a stand-alone PC, all of the processing is done in one place. When you have a network, however, new possibilities for *where* to do processing appear. The ability to do processing in different places is called **distributed processing.**

Terminal–Host Systems The first step in distributed processing came in the 1960s, when **terminal–host systems** appeared. As Figure 1.7 illustrates, users work at devices called **terminals.** Terminal–host systems were designed

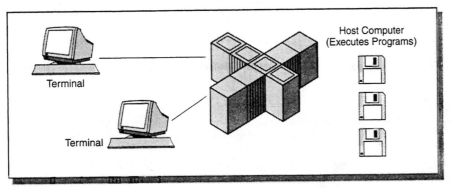

Figure 1.7
Terminal–Host
System

long before microprocessors were invented, so there was no way to put intelligence in these desktop machines. Instead, all intelligence is located in the central **host computer.** When the user types, the keystrokes go to the host for processing. The host then sends characters back to be painted on the terminal screen.

Importance of Mainframe Systems   Although some people think of terminal–host systems as ancient history, terminal–host systems are alive and well. This is especially true for systems that use the largest business host computers, called **mainframes.**[5] Most corporations still have a large amount of their central data stored on terminal–host systems.

Legacy Systems and Downsizing   In information technology, a **legacy system** is one that uses old technology but that would be very expensive to replace. Mainframe systems qualify for this label. While there is a long-term trend to **downsize** mainframe applications to run on smaller and newer processing platforms, mainframe terminal–host systems will be with us for many years to come.

File Server Program Access   Earlier, in Figure 1.5, we saw a small PC network. The most common type of server on PC networks is the **file server.** As its name suggests, it stores program files and data files for client PCs.

Processing on Client PCs   As Figure 1.8 illustrates, when you run a program on a client PC, that program is likely to be stored on a file server.[6] The file server will download a copy of the program to your client PC, which will actually run the program. Associated data files are also downloaded to the client PC.

Figure 1.8
File Server
Program Access

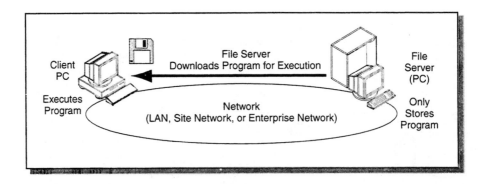

---

[5] Other large hosts include supercomputers, which are optimized for numerical scientific processing. Mainframes and other business hosts are optimized instead for file storage and retrieval, which are characteristic of most business applications.

[6] Of course, you can also store the program on your client PC's hard drive. A client PC can still work entirely locally.

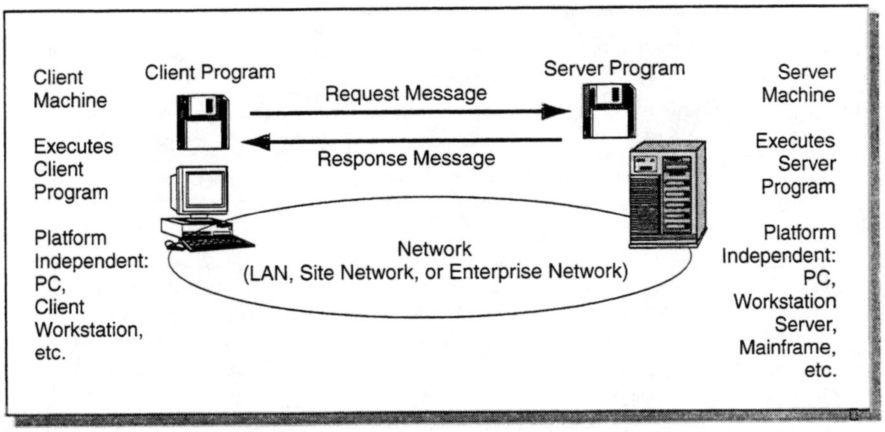

Figure 1.9
Client/Server
Processing

405

No Processing on the File Server Many people are surprised that all processing is done on client PCs, which are often underpowered, instead of on file servers, which usually are much faster machines. However, file servers were only designed to store files, not execute them.

Client/Server Processing Both terminal–host systems and file server program access do processing on a single machine. However, client/server processing does processing on *two* machines, as Figure 1.9 illustrates.

First, there is the **client program** running on the **client computer.** In web-server access, the client program is a browser. The client program sends **request messages** to the **server program** running on the **server computer.** For instance, a World Wide Web request message might ask for a webpage to be downloaded from the webserver to the browser. The webserver application program on the webserver is the server program. It sends a **response message** giving the requested information or explaining why the information cannot be supplied. Many applications other than webservice use client/server processing.

Comparing Forms of Distributed Processing Different distributed processing approaches have different strengths and weaknesses. Figure 1.10 compares the major distributed processing alternatives.

Scalability A crucial factor in any information technology is the degree to which it is **scalable,** that is, can be expanded to meet increasing demand. If demand outgrows a technology, the company will have to install a different technology. This always requires extensive staff retraining. Sometimes, it means the removal of all existing hardware with a forklift and the purchasing of all new equipment. In the worst case, the company cannot serve the demand.

Terminal–host systems are extremely scalable, because the largest mainframes have enormous processing power.

Figure 1.10
Comparing
Distributed
Processing
Alternatives

	File Server Program Access	Client/Server Processing	Terminal–Host Systems
Location of processing	Client PC (not on the file server)	Client computer and server (2 programs)	Host computer (terminals are dumb)
Graphics	Very good because of local processing in client PC	Very good because of local processing in client PC	Poor because rich graphics would require expensive high-speed network traffic.
Response Times	Very good because of local processing in client PC	Very good because of local processing in client PC, although some server delay	Poor because hosts often are overloaded.
Scalability	Low: Client PCs do not get very large.	High: Upgrade the server.	Very high: Mainframes get very large.
Platform independent?	No. For PCs only	Yes. Client and server machines may be of any platform type. The two machines may be of different platform types.	No. For terminals and hosts only

Note: A box shaded blue indicates a platform that is different than the other two along this dimension.

Client/server systems are also extremely scalable. Usually, the heavy processing is done on the server, so growth only requires getting a larger server.

Client/server processing is **platform independent,** meaning that it is not limited to PC servers. If the fastest PC is not fast enough, faster computers can be used. A popular choice is the **workstation server.** As Figure 1.11 illustrates, workstation servers generally use very fast (and very expensive) microprocessors that are faster than those in even the fastest PCs. They also usually run the UNIX operating system, which is more reliable but also more complex than Microsoft Windows.

File server program access has poor scalability, however. All processing must be done on the client PC, and client PCs simply do not get very large. File server program access can only run small programs.

Figure 1.11
Personal
Computers versus
Workstation
Servers

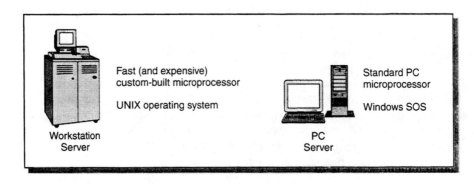

Response Time Another important performance consideration is **response time**, that is, how long the computer takes to respond when the user hits a key. For file server program access and client/server processing, response time usually is instantaneous because much or all of the processing is done on the user's PC. In contrast, terminal–host systems may take several seconds to respond when a user hits a key. This is very frustrating to users.

Graphics Terminal–host systems were designed in the 1960s, when long-distance transmission costs were very high. Graphics screens take many more bits to transmit than text screens. Consequently, many terminal–host systems used no graphics at all—only text, and text in a single color at that. Although some terminal–host systems used color and graphics, they tended to be limited in their use. In contrast, PC-based file server program access and client/server processing offer full graphical user interfaces.

Test Your Understanding

Answer Core Review Questions 1–6, Detailed Review Questions 1–2, and Thought Question 3.

THE INTERNET

Most people would argue that the Internet is the most important network today. Although LANs within corporations handle most of our basic day-to-day processing, the Internet's global reach and vast number of users make it enormously important.

Multiple Networks

Many data networks existed before the Internet. In fact, the existence of many networks was the problem that led to the creation of the Internet. Computers on different networks could not communicate with one another. As Figure 1.12 illustrates, the U.S. **Defense Advanced Research Projects Agency (DARPA)** solved this problem by creating a way for computers on different networks to work together. The collection of networks linked together so that their computers can communicate is called the **Internet**. The Internet, then, really is a network of networks, not a single network.

Routers and Routes

As shown in Figure 1.12, the various networks on the Internet are connected by devices called **routers**, which are capable of forwarding packets from one computer on one network to any other computer on any other network. (The path that a packet takes across the routers is called its **route**.) To users, routers make the Internet look like a single network. Initially, routers were called **gateways**, and they are sometimes still called gateways today, especially by the Microsoft Corporation.

Figure 1.12
The Internet

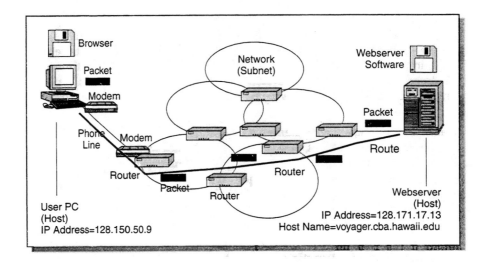

Host Computers

All computers attached to the Internet are called **hosts.** This includes large servers and *also your home PC.*

Note that in *terminal–host computing,* a host is a large machine that serves multiple terminal users. Conversely, in *Internet terminology,* any computer attached to the Internet is a host. In the early days of the Internet, only traditional hosts with terminals were powerful enough to attach to the Internet. Later, when PCs became powerful enough to connect directly, they were lumped into the "host" category on the Internet. You should keep this unfortunate dual use of the term *host* in mind.

IP Addresses

To transmit a message, a **source host** only has to know the Internet address of the **destination host**—just as you only need to know someone's telephone number to call them on the worldwide telephone network.

The Internet actually provides *two* addressing systems. One is the **IP address,** which consists of four numbers separated by dots, for instance, 128.171.17.13. The box, "Dotted Decimal Notation," shows that an IP address really is a string of 32 ones and zeros and that dotted decimal notation is merely a way of representing this string of bits.

The IP address is the host's official address, and every host on the Internet must have an IP address to use the Internet. This includes your home PC when you are on the Internet.[7]

---

[7] In Windows 95 and Windows 98, run the program winipcfg.exe in your Windows directory to see your PC's IP address and other configuration information explained in Chapter 2. Sometimes, winipcfg.exe is not installed by default in Windows 98, and you must load it from the installation disk.

Dotted Decimal Notation

As noted in the body, an IP address really is a string of 32 bits (ones or zeros). However, it is nearly impossible to memorize a long string of ones and zeros. Usually, IP addresses are written in an equivalent but slightly easier-to-remember way. This is dotted decimal notation.

In dotted decimal notation, we begin with a string of 32 bits, as shown in this example:

$$10101010000000001111111111001100$$

Next, we divide the string into four **octets**, which are collections of eight bits. In computer memory, collections of eight bits are called *bytes*. In networking, however, "octet" is more common than "byte."

$$10101010 \ 00000000 \ 11111111 \ 11001100$$

The next step is to convert each octet into a decimal number. The least significant bit—the one farthest right—has the place value 1. Values double with each bit to the left: 2, 4, 8, 16, 32, 64, and 128 for the bit farthest left. This is shown in Figure 1.13.

Figure 1.13   Dotted Decimal Notation Conversion

Octet Bit	7 Farthest Left	6	5	4	3	2	1	0 Farthest Right
IP address Octet	1	0	1	0	1	0	1	0
Place Value*	128	64	32	16	8	4	2	1
Product	128	0	32	0	8	0	2	0
Total of Products	170							

*Place Value = $2^{\text{Octet Bit}}$. For instance, $2^7 = 128$.

Now, for each bit, the place value is multiplied by the value of the IP address bit in that position (either a zero or a one). Consider the example in Figure 1.13. The first octet is 170 in decimal. If you continue the calculations, the second octet is zero. The third is 255. The fourth is 204. So in dotted decimal notation, this IP address is 170.0.255.204.

Figure 1.14
Internet Service
Providers (ISPs)

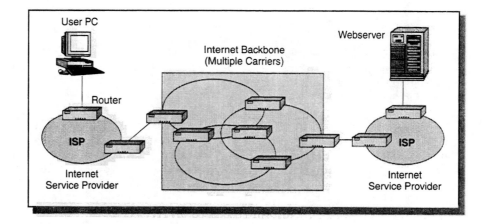

Host Names

While IP addresses are computer-friendly, they are not human-friendly. The other type of address on the Internet is the **host name,** which consists of several text labels separated by dots. For example, the computer with IP address 128.171.17.13 has the host name *voyager.cba.hawaii.edu.*[8] The host name is much easier for people to remember than the official IP address. Although all hosts on the Internet must have IP addresses, host names are optional. Usually, only server hosts have host names.

Internet Service Providers (ISPs)

Initially, commercial activity on the Internet was explicitly forbidden. In time, however, commercial activity began to grow anyway. Rather than fight this trend, the U.S. government privatized its portion of the Internet and turned commercial activity loose in the mid-1990s. As shown in Figure 1.14, all Internet transmission lines and routers in the United States today are owned by commercial organizations.

Technical Role of the ISP To use the Internet from home or from a business, you must connect to an organization called an **internet service provider (ISP).** More specifically, when you connect to the Internet by telephone, you dial into the ISP's router, which connects you to the other routers on the Internet.

Economic Role of the ISP The ISP charges you a fee. Some of this fee pays for its internal operations. To pay for the operations of Internet backbone companies, the ISP passes some of your fee on to them. So ISPs have two roles: (1) providing access and (2) handling the collection of fees.

---

[8] Although there are four labels in this host name, there is no correspondence between them and the four numerical segments in the IP address. Furthermore, many host names do not contain four labels.

Not Universal Although the idea of ISPs and a commercial backbone began in the United States, most countries—although not all—have adopted this approach today. ISP rates vary greatly from country to country.

Test Your Understanding

Answer Core Review Questions 7–9, Detailed Review Questions 3–4, and Thought Question 5.

STANDARDS

Although the Internet has many attractions, one of the most important is a strong body of standards. **Standards** *are rules of operation that most or all vendors follow.* Internet standards are **open standards** (i.e., not under the control of any vendor), so vendors can compete for the Internet hardware and software market. Competition has driven down prices and has led to an explosion of new products.

Layered Standards

As Figure 1.15 illustrates, the Internet uses a **layered standards architecture,** with standards in each of five layers doing specific tasks that together allow applications on different hosts to communicate, even if they are on different individual networks. The specific standards shown in Figure 1.15 are those you would encounter when dialing into the Internet from home or a hotel room to use a webserver.

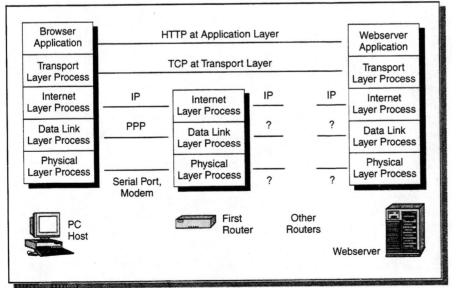

Figure 1.15
Hybrid TCP/IP–OSI Standards Architecture

Application Layer   Standards at the **application layer** *specify how two application programs communicate.* In webservice, these programs are the browser on your client PC and the webserver application program on the webserver.

For webservice, the application layer standard is the **HyperText Transfer Protocol (HTTP).** This is why you type "http://" at the beginnings of uniform resource locators (URLs) for Web information.

Different applications use different application layer standards. For instance, in Chapter 11, we will see that e-mail uses the SMTP and POP application layer standards to send and receive e-mail, respectively.

Transport Layer   Standards at the **transport layer** *specify how two host computers will work together, even if they are of different platform types (e.g., PCs, workstations, mainframes).*

It is the transport layer that gives platform independence. When you use a webserver, it does not matter whether the webserver is a PC, a workstation server, or even a mainframe. Your PC will be able to talk to it using a standardized protocol.

HTTP requires the use of the **Transmission Control Protocol (TCP)** standard at the transport layer. Chapter 3 discusses other transport layer standards.

Internet Layer   Standards at the **internet layer** *specify how hosts and routers will act to route packets end to end, from the source host to the destination host, across many single networks (subnets) connected by routers.* Note that messages at the Internet layer are called **packets.**

The main standard for packet routing on the Internet is the **Internet Protocol (IP).** This is why Internet addresses are called IP addresses.

An internet layer protocol does not say anything about the standards used by subnets. It is only concerned with transmission across single networks. This is the reason for the prefix "inter," which means between, in "Internet."

Data Link Layer   Along the route, each pair of routers is connected by a single network. A single network is called a **subnet.** There is also a subnet between the source host and the first router and another single network between the final router and the destination host.

The bottom two layers govern transmission across a single network. Standards at the **data link layer** *specify how to transmit messages within a single network.* This includes defining the structure of messages and controlling when stations may transmit their messages.

Messages at the data link layer are called **frames.** So in single networks, when we do packet switching (i.e., sending short messages), we are really "frame switching." However, this is still called packet switching.

When you dial in with a telephone line and a modem, the main standard at the data link layer is the **Point-to-Point Protocol (PPP).**

Physical Layer   The physical layer also governs transmission within a single network (subnet). While the data link layer is concerned with the organization and transmission of organized *messages,* standards at the **physical layer** *specify how to transmit **single bits** one at a time.* It leaves the interpretation of these bits as messages to the data link layer.

Physical layer standards govern things you can feel and touch, such as wires, connector plugs, and electrical voltages.

In dial-in access by telephone and modem, physical layer standards govern telephony and modem operation. Most modems today, for instance, follow the **V.90** standard, which governs transmission at 33.6 kbps but reception at 56 kbps.

Hybrid TCP/IP–OSI Standards Architecture

The five layers of standards shown in Figure 1.15 actually are taken from two very different standards architectures, as shown in Figure 1.16.

TCP/IP and the IETF Internet standards at the application, transport, and internet layers are created by the **Internet Engineering Task Force (IETF).** These standards usually are called **TCP/IP** standards after the most important transport and internet layer standards, TCP and IP, respectively. This is confusing, because TCP/IP is a standards architecture, while TCP and IP are individual standards within the TCP/IP architecture.

IETF's TCP/IP standards tend to be very simple, resulting in rapid standards development. In addition, because standards are simple, products are inexpensive and are developed rapidly. "Inexpensive and fast to market" is a good recipe for success in any industry, and TCP/IP standards are becoming dominant above the subnet layers.

TCP/IP Layer	OSI Layer	Hybrid TCP/IP–OSI Layer	Purpose
Application	Application (7)	Application (5)	Allows two application programs to communicate effectively.
	Presentation (6)		
	Session (5)		
Transport	Transport (4)	Transport (4)	Allows two computers to communicate even if they are of different platform types.
Internet	Network (3)	Internet (3)	Governs the transmission of packets across multiple networks, via a mesh of routers. Each pair of routers is connected by a single network (subnet).
Subnet	Data Link (2)	Data Link (2)	Governs the transmission of *frames* within a single network (subnet).
	Physical (1)	Physical (1)	Governs the transmission of *individual bits* wthin a single network (subnet).

Notes: TCP/IP is the standards architecture created and maintained by the IETF.
OSI is the standards architecture created and maintained by ISO and ITU-T.

Figure 1.16
TCP/IP and OSI Standards in the Hybrid TCP/IP–OSI Standards Architecture

OSI, ISO, and ITU-T Despite the dominance of TCP/IP at upper layers, the IETF rarely creates standards for subnets.[9] Instead, standards for single networks at the data link and physical layers usually are set by two other organizations. These are the **International Organization for Standardization (ISO)** and the **International Telecommunications Union–Telecommunications Standards Sector (ITU-T)**.[10] Their joint standards architecture is called **OSI**.[11] Even when ISO and ITU-T do not create standards, they must ratify standards created by others before these standards become official OSI standards.

---

[9] In a rare exception to the general pattern, the IETF did create PPP.

[10] No, the abbreviations do not match the names very well, but these are the official abbreviations.

[11] Reference Model of Open Systems Interconnection. Now you see why everybody uses the abbreviation.

OSI versus TCP/IP Layering

Figure 1.17 compares TCP/IP and OSI layers. Different authors will show different match ups because the two architectures define their layers differently, making comparisons difficult. However, in terms of *actual standards* produced in the two architectures, we argue that they match up very well at the lower four layers.

Figure 1.17   Layering in TCP/IP versus OSI

TCP/IP	OSI	OSI Layer Meaning
Application	Application (7)	Application–application interactions, free of presentation and session concerns.
	Presentation (6)	Allows two sides to negotiate and then use common transfer standards for representing data.
	Session (5)	Used to coordinate application–application interactions, such as setting up rollback points in a series of transactions.
Transport	Transport (4)	Allows two computers to communicate even if they are from different vendors and are of different platform types.
Internet	Network (3)	Now used for internetting.
Subnet: Use OSI Layers	Data Link (2)	Governs the transmission of frames within a single network (subnet).
	Physical (1)	Governs the transmission of individual bits within a single network (subnet).

Physical and Data Link Layers (OSI Layers 1 and 2)
TCP/IP calls for the use of OSI physical and data link layer standards, so by definition, the match-up in these two layers is perfect.

Continued.

Network Layer (OSI Layer 3)
The OSI network layer (layer 3) was created for rather complex single networks of a type that never became popular.[12] However, OSI did create internet standards at the network layer.

Transport Layer (OSI Layer 4)
The OSI transport layer (layer 4) has standards that are functionally similar to those of the TCP/IP transport layer.

Application Layers
The three highest layers of OSI deal with the coordination of applications running on different computers. Together, they serve the function of the single TCP/IP application layer.

Session Layer (OSI Layer 5)
The OSI session layer (layer 5) was created for applications in which several single transactions may be necessary to complete an overall task. The session layer keeps track of the status of the transaction exchanges.

Presentation Layer (OSI Layer 6)
The OSI presentation layer (layer 6) allows the two communicating application processes to negotiate a common syntax for representing various types of information (e.g., text, graphics).

Application Layer (OSI Layer 7)
The OSI application layer (layer 7) deals with the specifics of particular applications, freed from data representation and transaction bookkeeping.

Test Your Understanding
Answer Core Review Questions 10–11 and Detailed Review Question 5.

---

[12]Specifically, networks that have switches connected in a mesh, much like the routers are connected in Figure 1.12. This creates the possibility of many alternative routes between any two end stations. The single network (subnet) standards we will see throughout this book only allow a single possible path between stations. This greatly reduces their complexity and therefore their cost.

Hybrid TCP/IP–OSI Standards Architecture   The five-layer architecture shown in Figure 1.15 that dominates Internet usage today combines standards from these two "pure" architectures, so we call it the **hybrid TCP/IP–OSI standards architecture**.

Standards Architectures   Another name for "standards architecture" is **standards framework**. Just as the architecture of a house is a framework for creating individual rooms within an overall plan, a **standards architecture** is a framework for creating individual standards within an overall layered plan.

OSI versus TCP/IP Layering   The box, "OSI versus TCP/IP Layering," compares OSI and TCP/IP layering in more detail.

Although networking is exciting today, what we now see is only the beginning of the networking era. In 10 years, we will think of today's networks and applications the way we now think of biplanes and Model-T Fords. Although predicting network trends has not had a good track record, there are two sets of issues that most analysts feel will be important in the next few years.

Quality of Service (QoS)

Anyone who has used the Internet extensively knows that it is far from perfect. Often, it is unbearably slow. There are also service quality problems on internal LANs and on commercial WANs. Network standards agencies are beginning to respond with standards for **quality of service (QoS)** in which network service providers can guarantee certain performance limits.

Congestion and Speed   One of the biggest problems facing network users is **congestion,** in which capacity is insufficient for the traffic being sent.

Latency   Congestion creates transmission delays. In networking, delay is called **latency.** We would like to have QoS guarantees for maximum latency. We might like, for example, to be guaranteed a maximum latency of 50 milliseconds (ms).

Throughput   These latency guarantees must be tied to **throughput** guarantees, which would guarantee us a certain transmission rate. For instance, we might require a guaranteed throughput of 1 million bits per second. QoS for latency and throughput are discussed in more detail in Chapter 8.

Reliability   If we pick up a telephone and do not hear a dial tone, we are extremely surprised. The telephone system is enormously reliable. Data networks, in contrast, often have serious reliability problems. We would like QoS guarantees for reliability. In general, we are most concerned with two reliability measures.

Availability   The first is **availability,** which is the percentage of time the network is available for use. We would like our networks to be available over 99.999% of the time.

Error Rate   The second is the **error rate,** which is the percentage of bits or messages that contain errors. Data from 1999 indicate an average loss rate for ISPs of 3% to 6% of all packets.[13] We would like this to be far lower.

---

[13] Greenfield, D., & Williams, M., Top 25 ISPs, *Data Communications,* June 1999, source was online at http://www.data.com/issue/990607/topisps.html.

Security

When network technology was new, security was not a significant concern. Today, however, security is a crucial issue in networks. A great deal of highly sensitive information today is stored in network-accessible databases and flows over the network to get from one location to another. In addition, there is growing evidence that computer crime within corporations and on the Internet has already grown to disturbing levels.

Encryption   One tool for security is **encryption,** in which we encrypt (i.e., scramble) messages before we transmit them. No one intercepting the encrypted messages will be able to read them. However, the receiver will be able to decrypt them back to their original form.

Access Control   Not everyone in an organization should be given access to all resources in the firm. **Access control** tools allow us to specify who should access specific resources and to restrict access to those people (or software processes) who should not have access. Today, access control typically uses **passwords,** most of which are far too easy to guess, thus being ineffective.

Authentication   In **authentication,** the sender proves his or her identity to the receiver. In the non-computer world, for instance, when you wish to cash a check, you often have to show your driver's license to authenticate yourself. Of course, authentication is important in access control. However, it is important in its own right, especially in electronic commerce. You want to be certain that you are dealing with a specific person or company, not with an impostor.

KEY POINTS

Distributed Processing   This chapter looked at three main computer platforms: (1) terminal–host systems, (2) file server program access, and (3) client/server processing. Client/server processing is platform independent, so the server often is a machine faster than a personal computer, for instance, a workstation server. Each platform type has advantages and disadvantages. It is important for you to be able to compare them as alternatives when you create or purchase applications.

Voice and Data Networks   For voice and video communication, the public telephone network uses circuit switching, which guarantees capacity but is wasteful for bursty data communications. In turn, data communications, in which at least one of the communication partners is a computer, normally uses packet-switched networks that send messages in small packets (or frames) and multiplex these packets efficiently along trunk lines between switches. Packet switching reduces costs through multiplexing, but there is a danger that congestion will occur.

The Internet   The Internet is not a single network, but rather thousands of networks connected by devices called routers, which are sometimes called gateways. The Internet routes messages, called packets, from a source host to a destination host across a mesh of routers. Every computer on the Internet is a host computer regardless of size. Every host must have a unique IP address. Some hosts also have host names.

Layered Standards   Multiple standards must be at work for two application programs on different computers on different networks to be able to work together. This chapter introduced the hybrid TCP/IP–OSI standards architecture, which dominates Internet use today and indeed dominates most non-Internet networking. This framework, or architecture, has five layers: (1) application, (2) transport, (3) internet, (4) data link, and (5) physical. When you access a webserver by telephone, the standards at these layers are HTTP, TCP, IP, PPP, and modem standards, respectively.

The Ubiquity of Change   Although the Internet and corporate networks are already exciting, we are only in the early childhood of networking today. The mantra of "anything, anytime, anywhere" will soon become a reality. The last part of the chapter examined two of the many changes we can expect to see in networking in the near future: (1) a growing concern for security and (2) quality of service (QoS) guarantees for speed and reliability. Of course, the most exciting changes will be those we cannot foresee today. The important thing is to avoid thinking of today's networks as the networks we will see in 5 or 10 years.

Fundamental Concepts   Finally, this chapter introduced a number of fundamental concepts that we will see throughout this book, including the following, which you should know thoroughly:

- analog, digital, and binary transmission
- multiplexing
- scalability
- circuit switching versus packet switching
- LANs versus WANs
- congestion and latency
- quality of service guarantees for speed (latency and throughput)
- quality of service guarantees for reliability (availability and error rates)
- encryption, access control, and authentication
- legacy systems
- platform independence
- terminal–host system, file server program access, and client/server processing

The Remainder of the Core Chapters

This book has twelve core chapters that deal with the following topics:

- Chapter 2: Cooperation among standards at different layers
- Chapter 3: Details of the HTTP, TCP, IP, and PPP standards
- Chapter 4: Physical layer concepts
- Chapter 5: Reaching the Internet from home or the road
- Chapter 6: Small PC networks
- Chapter 7: Small Ethernet LANs
- Chapter 8: Site networks using Ethernet, ATM switches, routers, and layer 3 switches
- Chapter 9: Wide area networks
- Chapter 10: Security
- Chapter 11: Standards for networked applications
- Chapter 12: Looking ahead

The Advanced Modules   The advanced modules provide more in-depth information on key topics.

Test Your Understanding

Answer Core Review Questions 12–14.

REVIEW QUESTIONS

For questions with multiple parts, write the answer to each part in a separate line or paragraph.

Core Review Questions

1. **a)** What is a network? **b)** For delivery over a network, what does the sender have to know? **c)** Distinguish between voice and data communications.

2. **a)** Distinguish between circuit switching and packet switching. **b)** What is the switching decision? **c)** Which traditionally has been used for voice? Why? **d)** Which traditionally has been used for data? Why? **e)** What is multiplexing? **f)** Why is it desirable?

3. **a)** Define the following: 1) analog communication, 2) digital communication, and 3) binary communication. **b)** What does a modem do?

4. Distinguish between LANs and WANs.

5. **a)** Distinguish among terminal–host systems, file server program access, and client/server processing in terms of where processing is done. **b)** What is scalability? **c)** Explain the implications of the first part of your

answer (location of processing) for scalability. **d)** What is platform independence, and how does it enhance scalability in client/server processing? **e)** What are the implications of your answer to Part a) for graphics? **f)** What are the implications of your answer to Part a) for response time?

6. **a)** If you wish to increase the size of a client/server processing system, what do you do? **b)** How do PCs and workstations differ?

7. What are the main technical elements of the Internet? Describe each in a separate paragraph.

8. **a)** Distinguish between IP addresses and host names. **b)** Which is the official address of a host? **c)** Does a server host need an IP address? **d)** Does your home PC need an IP address when you are on the Internet? **e)** Does a server host need a host name? **f)** Does your home PC need a host name when you are on the Internet?

9. **a)** Is the Internet free in the United States and most other countries? **b)** What are the two roles of Internet service providers (ISPs)?

10. **a)** Name the five layers in the TCP/IP–OSI hybrid architecture. **b)** What do standards at each layer specify? (Write a separate paragraph for each layer.) **c)** What standard are you likely to use in each layer when you reach the Internet from home to work with a webserver? **d)** What are messages called at the internet layer? **e)** What are messages called at the data link layer?

11. **a)** What standards agency manages TCP/IP standards? **b)** What agencies manage OSI standards? **c)** Which layers in the hybrid TCP/IP–OSI standards architecture use TCP/IP standards? **d)** Which use OSI standards?

12. **a)** What is latency? **b)** What causes latency?

13. **a)** What is Quality of Service (QoS)? **b)** What performance measures does it cover?

14. What are the main elements in security? Briefly describe each.

Detailed Review Questions

1. List and explain the elements of a PC network on a small LAN, one element per paragraph.

2. **a)** Why are terminal–host systems referred to as legacy systems? **b)** Why don't we simply replace them all? **c)** What is replacing them called?

3. What are the two meanings we saw in this chapter for the word "host?"

4. Referring to the box, "Dotted Decimal Notation," convert the following IP address to dotted decimal notation. Show your work. 10101010 11110000 11001100 01010101. (Spaces are included to facilitate reading.)

5. Referring to the box, "OSI versus TCP/IP Layering," **a)** Name the OSI layers and their layer numbers. **b)** Briefly characterize each OSI layer. Write each in a separate paragraph. **c)** Describe how OSI and TCP/IP layers match up.

Thought Questions

1. What was the most surprising thing you learned in this chapter?

2. What was the most difficult part of this chapter for you?

3. **a)** Is the term "legacy system" limited to mainframe terminal–host system? **b)** What would a legacy network be?

4. In the opening vignette, Glenn Davis is a road warrior. **a)** What benefits is he experiencing? **b)** What problems is he experiencing? **c)** Decide whether his company should get the high-speed wireless Internet access service. Justify your decision. **d)** List technical concepts in the chapter that are explicitly illustrated in this vignette.

5. **a)** Why do you think the Internet is so attractive to businesses? **b)** To employees?

Case Studies

For case studies, go to the book's website, **http://www.prenhall.com/panko**, and look at the "Case Studies" page for this chapter.

Projects

1. **Getting Current.** Go to the book's website's "New Information" and "Errors" pages for this chapter to get new information since this book went to press and to correct any errors in the text.

2. **Internet Exercises.** Go to the book's website's "Exercises" page for this chapter and do the Internet Exercises.

3. **Client/Server Computing.** Create two applications in Visual Basic: a client program and a server program. In this programming project, which will continue through later chapters, you will simply create the forms for the two programs in this Chapter 1 portion of the project. Details on the "Internet Exercises" page for this chapter can be found at the book's website, **http://www.prenhall.com/panko**.

Chapter 13: More on Internet Applications

Internet applications have appeared throughout this book, beginning with the World Wide Web in Chapter 1. This module looks at Internet standards for FTP, LISTSERVs, USENET newsgroups, and Telnet. Chapter 11 examines e-mail standards.

Recall that the Internet Engineering Task Force (IETF) creates Internet standards. IETF documents are called **Requests for Comment (RFCs).** Only some RFCs are official standards. Every few months, a new RFC lists official Internet standards currently in force.

FTP

The World Wide Web is a very nice way to **download** information from a server host to a client host. The process is very simple, and webpages can be rich with graphics, animation, and other elements that are attractive to users. However, the Internet also offers a much older way to download files from server to client. This is the **File Transfer Protocol (FTP),** which was one of the earliest application standards on the Internet.

Both Downloading and Uploading

Although the Web is glamorous, FTP offers one important thing that HTTP does not. As Figure G.1 shows, this is the ability to **upload** files in the other direction, from the client host to the FTP server host.[1] So if you work with someone, FTP allows you to send files to that person for his or her use.

---

[1] Although the World Wide Web has a technique for uploading files, it is not widely implemented or used.

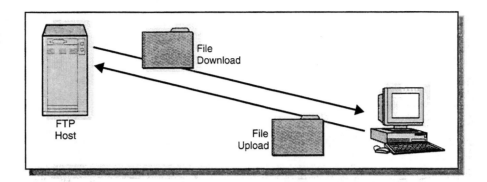

Logging In

If someone can download files from a host computer, this is potentially dangerous. Uploading files is also potentially dangerous. Before you can work with a host computer, FTP requires you to log into that computer.

For this, you need a **username** and a **password**—things you usually do not need on the World Wide Web, with its limited but highly controlled transfer process. In some directories, you will only be allowed to upload files. In other directories, you will only be allowed to download them. In some directories, you will be able to do both. In *most* directories on the computer, you will not be able either to upload or to download files.

The need for the user to obtain a username and password ahead of time and the requirement for the server authority to make certain directories read-only make FTP more cumbersome to use than the World Wide Web.

Anonymous FTP

Some host servers offer **anonymous FTP.** Actually, this is normal FTP, with two exceptions. First, you log in with the user name "anonymous." For the password, in turn, you give your e-mail address.

You then have access to certain directories set aside for public files. You do *not* have access to all files on the computer.

In addition, you usually can *only download* files from these directories. File uploading usually is forbidden in anonymous FTP. Before webservers, anonymous FTP was the most popular way of offering information to the public.

By the way, anonymous FTP is not really anonymous. The host knows your IP address because all IP packets that you send to the server host contain your IP address.

No File Structure Standards in FTP

Application standards usually consist of two types of standards—transfer standards and file structure standards. For instance, the file transfer standard in the World Wide Web is HTTP (see Chapter 3), and the file structure standards are HTML and XML.

FTP, however, is a pure *transfer standard.* It does not have any standards for file structure. The benefit of not defining a file content standard is that there is

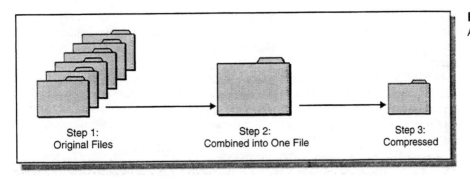

Step 1:
Original Files

Step 2:
Combined into One File

Step 3:
Compressed

no limit to the type of file that FTP can transfer. You can transfer word processing files, spreadsheet files, or any other type of file you need.

On the negative side, the receiver of the file must know how to recognize and handle the transferred file type. This usually requires prior communication between the two parties involved in the transfer, often via e-mail. If the type of file is unknown to the person trying to read it, problems are likely to occur.

Archiving

In addition, files on the FTP server often are archived. As Figure G.2 illustrates, **archiving** first combines several files into a single file. Next, that single file is compressed so that it requires less storage space and can be transmitted faster. At the other end, of course, the file must be dearchived. This decompresses the file and turns it back into multiple files. Of course, you can archive a single file in order to take advantage of compression.

Unfortunately, there are many archiving standards. Although the *zip* archiving standard is the most common, it is far from universal. As a result, the user has to know what archiving process (if any) was used on a file before storage, as well as how to deal with the dearchived file format. FTP dearchiving is not for the faint of heart.

One help in dearchiving is that many archived files are now **self-dearchiving.** These files end with the *.exe* extension. Running the file as a program causes the embedded dearchiving program to decompress the archive and break it into separate files. You do not need separate dearchiving software. You do not even need to know how the archiving was done.

One danger of *.exe* files of any type is that they may contain viruses. So your "self-extracting game program" may actually be a self-extracting malicious virus. You must be very careful with self-extracting files.

LISTSERVs

Suppose you have a project team or wish to participate in a discussion group. You would like to have a shared mailing list that has everyone's e-mail address instead of having to type the addresses individually each time you send a message to the group. In addition, you would like a single person to maintain the mailing list so everyone will be using the same list. (Otherwise, not everyone would get every message.) Maintaining such a list would be difficult because in many project teams, people join and leave the team during the course of the project.

LISTSERV software provides exactly the functionality we would like to have. A program called a **LISTSERV manager** resides on a server. Team members can post messages to the LISTSERV manager when they have something to say to the group. The LISTSERV manager will then send the posting to other members of the group via ordinary Internet e-mail.

Users also can send **supervisory messages** to the LISTSERV manager. Most importantly, they can send *subscribe* and *unsubscribe* messages. These add them to the group mailing list and drop them from the group mailing list, respectively.

Another common supervisory message allows a user to see a list of his or her group's members.

Supervisory functions are also provided for each LISTSERV group's **moderator,** for instance, the ability to drop members from a mailing list if these people cannot send unsubscribe messages themselves.

Subscribing to a LISTSERV Group

Figure G.3 shows the process of subscribing to a LISTSERV group. Here the LISTSERV management program is called *Majordomo*. It manages two LISTSERV groups, *GLOBAL-L* and *CRIME*. The host is *puka.org*.

To: To subscribe, you must first know the name of the LISTSERV manager, which in this case is called *Majordomo*. The names of two other popular LISTSERV program managers are *Maiser* (Mail Server) and LISTSERV. The lat-

Figure G.3
Subscribing to a
LISTSERV group

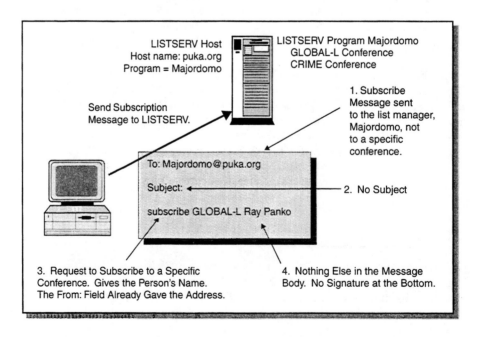

ter program gave LISTSERV conferencing its general name.

You must then know the name of the LISTSERV host computer, which in this case is *puka.org.*

In the *To:* field, you type *Majordomo@puka.org.* Note that the **subscription message** goes to the LISTSERV management program, not to the name of the conference.

Subject: The subject field will be ignored, so you can leave it blank or put in anything you wish.

Body: The body's contents must be entered very precisely. As Figure G.3 shows, the body must have only a single line, and it must have this form exactly:

subscribe conferencename yourname

Note that the line begins with the word *subscribe,* not *subscribe to.*

Note also that there is no period at the end of the line.

Subscribe is the keyword.

GLOBAL-L is the conference to which you wish to subscribe. Many LISTSERV group names end with "-L" to indicate that they are lists. However, this is far from universal.

Finally, *yourname* is your name. You can also give a **handle,** such as "Spidey" or "Ra3y." Using a handle preserves your anonymity to some extent. However, your e-mail address may appear in postings sent on to group members, so you usually do not have real anonymity.

Nothing Else in the Body, Including Signatures Note also that there is nothing else in the body. If you have a signature file that is added automatically at the end of the body in messages you send, you must suspend its use for this message.

Response Message If your subscription message is accepted, the LISTSERV manager sends a **response message** to your e-mail address. This message welcomes you to the conference. It also lays out any conference rules. In particular, it tells you how to unsubscribe from the conference.

Always keep this message in a folder. It is considered rude to send a message to everyone in the conference saying, "Hi, there. I've forgotten how to unsubscribe. Can someone unsubscribe me?"

Posting Messages

Now that you are a member of the group, you can post messages to everyone in the group. Figure G.4 shows how this is done.

To: Supervisory messages are sent to the **LISTSERV manager.** In the previous example, for instance, we sent the supervisory subscribe message to *Majordomo@puka.org.*

Figure G.4
Posting Messages
to a LISTSERV
group

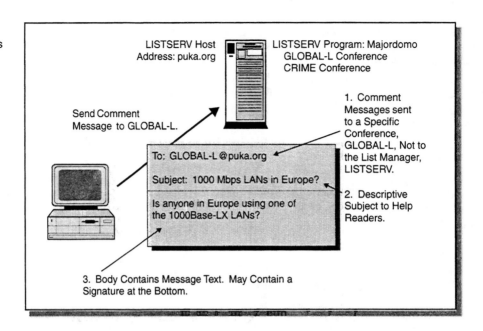

LISTSERV Host
Address: puka.org

LISTSERV Program: Majordomo
GLOBAL-L Conference
CRIME Conference

Send Comment
Message to GLOBAL-L.

1. Comment
Messages sent
to a Specific
Conference,
GLOBAL-L, Not to
the List Manager,
LISTSERV.

To: GLOBAL-L @puka.org

Subject: 1000 Mbps LANs in Europe?

2. Descriptive
Subject to Help
Readers.

Is anyone in Europe using one of
the 1000Base-LX LANs?

3. Body Contains Message Text. May Contain a
Signature at the Bottom.

When you wish to **post** a message to your group, however, you put the *name of the group* in your message's *To:* field, rather than the name of the LISTSERV manager. In this example, you put *GLOBAL-L@puka.org* in the *To:* field.

This is quite confusing. You must keep in mind that when you send a supervisory message, you are communicating with the conference supervisor, the LISTSERV management program. When you send a posting, however, you are communicating within the group.

Other Fields There are no restrictions on other fields in the message, although you should follow the conference rules. For instance, there usually are rules against sending long messages or posting messages with attachments.

Receiving Postings

When other members of your LISTSERV group post messages, the LISTSERV manager forwards the messages to everyone in the group, using ordinary Internet e-mail.

The nice thing about this approach is that postings appear in your e-mail inbox, along with your regular e-mail messages. There is no need to load a special program to read your LISTSERV postings, just as there is no need for a special program to subscribe, to submit postings, or, as we will see next, to unsubscribe.

The bad thing about this approach is that postings appear in your e-mail inbox, along with your regular e-mail postings. If you are in one or more active conferences, you may get a dozen or more postings each day. In the swarm of messages arriving in your mailbox each morning, you may find it difficult to find important regular e-mail messages addressed specifically to you.

Users who receive a large number of LISTSERV postings often set up a filtering rule in their e-mail program. The rule specifies that if the name of a LISTSERV group appears in the *From:* field of the arriving message, then the message should be moved automatically from the in-box to a folder for that conference. This way, when you first read your mail, you will see only messages sent specifically to you. You can go to the folder where you store your incoming LISTSERV messages when you have time.

Leaving a LISTSERV Group

To join the group, you send a *subscribe* message. To leave the group, you send an **unsubscribe** message.

To: Again, you send the message to *Majordomo@puka.org*. This is a supervisory messge, so you send it to the LISTSERV manager, not to your entire group. As noted earlier, it is considered rude to send an unsubscribe message to the entire group.

Subject: The LISTSERV manager ignores the subject field, so you can put anything here that you want, as was the case in your subscribe message.

Body: Again, the body must have a single line. It must be typed exactly, and there must not be a signature file attached to your message. The single line is:

unsubscribe listname

Here, *listname* is the name of the mailing list from which you would like to remove your e-mail address.

USENET NEWSGROUPS

Although LISTSERV works, it is something of a brute force approach. There is a more elegant conferencing system on the Internet. This is **USENET.**[2]

USENET Hosts and Replication

Figure G.5 shows that there are many **USENET hosts** on the Internet. These hosts run the **USENET host program.**

To read or post messages, you need a **newsreader program** on your PC. You can get a special newsreader program designed specifically to read USENET newsgroups. In addition, most browser suites now come with a newsreader module.

To read postings, you can connect to *any* USENET host in the world that will accept your connection. The ability to connect to any USENET host is pos-

---

[2] USENET actually began outside the Internet as a collection of UNIX host computers. However, USENET hosts now usually employ the Internet to communicate with one another and with users.

Figure G.5
USENET Hosts

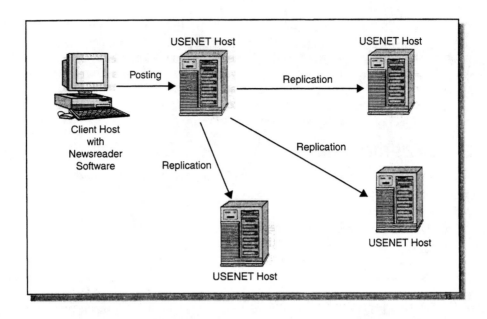

sible because USENET hosts **replicate** (send) their postings to all other USENET hosts, as shown in Figure G.5. When you post a message to one USENET host, your message will go to all other USENET hosts, often within a single day.

Similarly, a posting anywhere in the world will arrive at your selected USENET host within hours or days.

Newsgroups   Each USENET host supports thousands of **newsgroups,** which are discussion groups on particular topics. Figure G.6 shows that news-

Figure G.6
USENET
Newsgroups

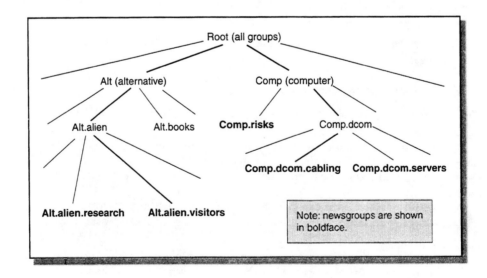

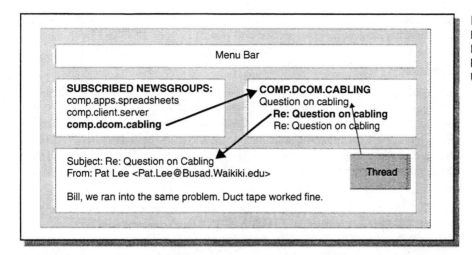

group names are arranged hierarchically. Not all USENET hosts carry all news-groups, especially those in the "Alt" category, in which, generally speaking, "anything goes." The "Comp" family—especially the *Comp.dcom* subfamily—is very popular with networking professionals.

Subscribing to Newsgroups Originally, newsgroups were seen as being like newspapers and magazines. It was envisioned that you would **subscribe** to a few, just as you do newspapers and magazines. You would see only these subscribed newsgroups when you connected to your USENET host, making your life easier.

As a result, dealing with newsgroups is still a two-step process in most USENET newsreader programs. You first look through a list of available news-groups to select ones that interest you. You then subscribe to them. Afterward, you see only subscribed newsgroups unless you specifically ask to see the whole list again.

Reading Postings

When you have finished subscribing, your USENET newsreader program will show your subscribed newsgroups in a window, as shown in Figure G.7. You click on a particular newsgroup to read recent postings. (Your newsreader pro-gram keeps track of messages you have already read.)

Another window shows one-line summaries of recent postings in the selected newsgroup. If you click on a posting, you will see its contents in another window.

Submitting Postings

It is also easy to submit a posting. Your newsgroup reader will have a "post" command or button. If you hit it while in a newsgroup, a window will open that will look very much like the window you use to send e-mail. You will type your posting, and your newsreader will post it to your USENET host.

Threads

Another way to send a posting is to give a "reply" command while reading a particular message. As Figure G.7 shows, replies are not listed in chronological order. Instead, a reply is listed as a subposting under the original posting. This grouping of a message and subsequent replies to it is called a **thread.** Threads are important because we often want to see not only a posting but also subsequent comments on the posting as well.

LISTSERVs Versus USENET Newsgroups

LISTSERVs and USENET newsgroups are both "computer conferencing" systems that support communication within groups. However, they operate differently, and this creates relative advantages.

Delivery: Ordinary E-Mail Versus Newsreader Programs

The most obvious difference between the two is message delivery. In LISTSERV, you use your ordinary e-mail program to subscribe, send and read postings, unsubscribe, and send other supervisory messages.

As we saw earlier, this is both a blessing and a curse. It is a blessing because you do not have to learn how to use a newsreader program and because you do not have to take any special action to receive postings. The postings arrive in your ordinary e-mail in-box.

The curse is that active LISTSERV groups can glut your in-box with messages, making it difficult to find messages sent specifically to you.

USENET is the opposite. You will not get any postings unless you specifically start your newsreader program, connect to the USENET host, and go to a subscribed group.

Finding the Host

One problem with LISTSERV conferences is that you need to know the name of the LISTSERV host. Note in Figure G.3 and Figure G.4 that the name of the host appears in the *To:* field of all messages. There is no central list of LISTSERV hosts on the Internet, much less a list of individual LISTSERV groups.

In contrast, most USENET hosts carry most newsgroups. So to look for interesting newsgroups, all you have to do is connect to *any* USENET host and read through the list of available newsgroups. The newsgroups are even listed hierarchically, to make your searching easy. You can then subscribe to a particular newsgroup and watch the postings for a few days to see if it is a group you wish to continue following.

We saw in Chapter 11 that if you have a POP or IMAP client program, you can download your e-mail from anywhere on the Internet. All you need is a POP or IMAP mail client program on your PC.

Access from Anywhere

Telnet offers another way to read your mail from anywhere, if your mail host supports terminal access. Figure G.8 shows that you first connect to the Internet. You then connect to your mail host using a **Telnet** program. To the host, you look exactly like a terminal user attached directly to the host. To you, your client PC looks like a terminal.

Terminal User Interface

Once connected, you can run any program on the host computer that a directly connected VT100 terminal user can run.[3] Obviously, this includes a mail program. However, Telnet is not limited to e-mail. You can run statistical analysis programs, database programs, or any other programs that are on the host and that will work with Telnet terminals.

Unfortunately, Telnet offers only a very limited terminal. It is limited to simple text, without boldface or other emphasis, without multiple fonts, and without graphics. There is a single color against a contrasting background.

Why Not POP or IMAP?

Chapter 11 noted that there is a more attractive way to read your mail remotely. This is to have a mail client program on your PC. Such mail clients have attractive graphical user interfaces. Like Telnet programs, mail clients can

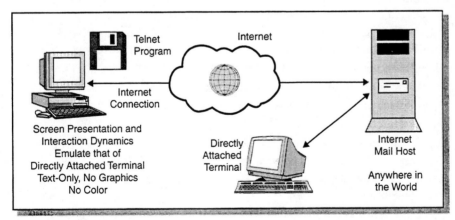

Figure G.8
Telnet

---

[3] Module H discusses VT100 terminals in more detail.

attach to any mail host anywhere in the world. When they download mail, however, they show it to you with an attractive user interface.

However, not all mail hosts support POP and IMAP. In addition, basic POP, which is more common than IMAP, does not give you the ability to manage your messages on the host computer. Telnet does this.

Also, although POP and IMAP deal only with e-mail, as noted above, Telnet can run any terminal-based program, and both UNIX and LINUX work well with terminals.

Of historical note, the original ARPANET, which gave rise to the Internet, was created specifically for Telnet. The idea was to let researchers at different sites use one another's host computers. This way, DARPA money spent to develop software would not be wasted because the software could run on only a single machine, as was common in those days.

This Telnet focus was so strong that when the first e-mail systems appeared, they were bootleg efforts developed without permission by individual ARPANET users, such as Ray Tomlinson.[4] It actually took some time for e-mail traffic to be accepted as legitimate by DARPA. The big breakthrough came when Larry Roberts, who headed the ARPANET effort at DARPA, wrote the first nontrivial program for reading ARPANET mail.

REVIEW QUESTIONS

Core Review Questions

1. **a)** What is FTP? **b)** What can FTP do that HTTP generally does not do?
2. Distinguish between FTP and anonymous FTP **a)** in terms of the need for an account and password and **b)** in terms of what you can do on the host.
3. **a)** In LISTSERVs, to what e-mail address do you send supervisory messages? **b)** To what e-mail address do you send postings to a particular group?
4. **a)** In LISTSERV *subscribe* and *unsubscribe* messages, what must be in the body? **b)** What must NOT be in the body? **c)** Are signatures allowed?
5. Distinguish between USENET and newsgroups.
6. Explain replication in the context of USENET hosts.
7. Explain how you would search for an interesting newsgroup.
8. In USENET newsgroups, what is a *thread*?
9. **a)** Distinguish between LISTSERV and USENET in terms of how postings are received. **b)** What are the relative merits of these approaches?
10. Discuss the relative difficulty of finding interesting LISTSERV groups versus interesting USENET newsgroups.
11. Compare Telnet and POP in terms of ease of use and what they can do.

---

[4] It was Tomlinson who selected the @ sign in e-mail addresses.

Detailed Review Questions

1. Explain the problems of file formats in FTP compared with the problem of file formats in World Wide Web.
2. **a)** What two things does archiving do? **b)** What are self-dearchiving files? **c)** Why are they good? **d)** Why are they dangerous?
3. Give the names of some popular LISTSERV management programs.
4. In LISTSERV conferences, what is a *response message,* and why should you keep the response message when you join a conference?

Thought Questions

1. **a)** How does the LISTSERV program know your e-mail address? **b)** What must you do if you wish to have LISTSERV messages delivered to two or more e-mail addresses?

Projects

1. **Getting Current.** Go to the book's website, **http://www.prenhall.com/ panko,** and see the "New Information" and "Errors" pages for this module to get new information since this book went to press and to correct any errors in the text.
2. **Internet Exercises.** Go to the book's website, **http://www.prenhall.com/ panko,** and see the "Exercises" page for this module. Do the Internet exercises.

Module 6: Technology and Internet Economics

Goal: To be able to critically discuss the basic economic concepts that govern information technology and the Internet.

Chapter 14: Recognizing Lock-In

Visionaries tell us that the Internet will soon deliver us into that most glorious form of capitalism, the "friction-free" economy. How ironic, then, is the event that will usher in the next millennium: the dreaded Year 2000 Problem, a testament to the enormous rigidities that plague the information economy.

We agree that the Internet will make shopping easier than ever, but much of the talk about friction is fiction. You don't have to drive to the store to order a new computer, but your choices for the future will still be hemmed in by the selections you made in the past. Like it or not, in the information age, buyers typically must bear costs when they switch from one information system to another. Understanding these costs of switching technologies, or even brands, is fundamental to success in today's economy.

Compare cars and computers. When the time comes to replace the Ford you've been driving for several years, there is no compelling reason to pick another Ford over a GM or a Toyota. Your garage will hold a Chevy just as well as a Ford, it won't take long to learn the controls of a Toyota, and you can haul the same trailer with either vehicle. In short, you can easily transfer your investments in "automotive infrastructure" to another brand of car. In contrast, when the time comes to upgrade the Macintosh computer you've been using for years, you are going to need a mighty good reason to pick a PC or a Unix machine instead of another Mac. You own a bunch of Mac software, you are familiar with how to use the Mac, your Mac printer may have years of good service left in it, and you probably trade files with other Mac users. You are facing significant costs if you decide to switch from one information technology to another.

With the Mac you have made significant *durable investments in complementary assets* that are specific to that brand of machine. These investments have differing economic lifetimes, so there's no easy time to start using a new, incompatible system. As a result, you face *switching costs*, which can effectively lock you into your current system or brand.

When the costs of switching from one brand of technology to another are substantial, users face *lock-in*. Switching costs and lock-in are ubiquitous in information systems, and managing these costs is very tricky for both buyers and sellers. Simple rules, such as "Don't get locked in" or "Evaluate costs on a life-cycle basis," don't help much. In using or selling information systems, fully anticipating future switching costs, both yours and those of your customers, is critical. Lock-in can be a source of enormous headaches, or substantial profits, depending on whether you are the one stuck in the locked room or the one in possession of the key to the door. The way to win in markets with switching costs is neither to avoid lock-in nor to embrace it. You need to think strategically: look ahead and reason back.

> *To understand lock-in, look ahead and reason back.*

This advice probably seems a bit cryptic, but its implications will become clear in this chapter and the next. Here we describe the common patterns that give rise to switching costs so as to help you properly measure switching costs and recognize situations involving lock-in. In the next chapter we'll show you how to use lock-in to your advantage, or at least to neutralize others who try to use it against you.

But before classifying switching costs and analyzing business strategy in the presence of lock-in, let's look at a few examples of the problems it can cause.

EXAMPLES OF LOCK-IN

The best way to understand the phenomenon of lock-in is to examine lock-in in action. The examples here show how large companies (Bell Atlantic) and individuals (with assigned telephone numbers) alike can fall prey to lock-in.

Bell Atlantic

In the mid- to late-1980s, Bell Atlantic invested $3 billion in AT&T's 5ESS digital switches to run its telephone network. These are large, complex devices that sell for millions of dollars each—essentially, specialized mainframe computers linked to transmission and other equipment. In effect, Bell Atlantic selected AT&T over Northern Telecom and Siemens to bring its telephone system into the digital age. No doubt AT&T's switches were impressive at the time, but did Bell Atlantic look ahead to the mid-1990s and take steps to protect itself from the ensuing lock-in?

The problem? The 5ESS switches employ a proprietary operating system controlled by AT&T. So, every time Bell Atlantic wanted to add a new capability, or connect these switches to a new piece of peripheral hardware, Bell Atlantic found itself reliant on AT&T to provide the necessary upgrades for the operating system and to develop the required interfaces. Since it was extremely expensive for Bell Atlantic to replace the AT&T equipment, Bell Atlantic was locked into the AT&T switches.

This left AT&T in the driver's seat. AT&T was in the powerful position of having monopoly control over a wide range of enhancements and upgrades to its switches. For example, when Bell Atlantic wanted its system to be able to recognize toll-free calls to telephone numbers beginning with "888," Bell Atlantic had to negotiate with AT&T, since AT&T had not provided Bell Atlantic with the computer code necessary for Bell Atlantic to develop this capability itself. Dealing from a position of strength, AT&T charged Bell Atlantic $8 million for the software that recognized 888 numbers. Similarly, when Bell Atlantic wanted to offer "voice dialing," so that customers could speak a name rather than dial a telephone number, Bell Atlantic again had to turn to AT&T, which charged $10 million for the software. In both of these cases, Bell Atlantic believed that it could have obtained the software on better terms had it been able to shop around for the necessary improvements.

From AT&T's position, its installed base of 5ESS switches was an extremely valuable asset, expected to generate a nice stream of revenues. According to Bell Atlantic, AT&T's aftermarket software upgrades account for between 30 percent and 40 percent of its switch-related revenues. Annual upgrades to the operating system from Bell Atlantic alone (one of a number of large switch buyers) were around $100 million per year. In addition, AT&T stood to make lucrative sales of peripheral equipment to Bell Atlantic. AT&T had incentives to provide improvements and upgrades to the switches and the ability to charge dearly for them. AT&T also stood to gain, at least in the short run, by using its control over proprietary interfaces to prevent others from offering compatible equipment that might compete with AT&T's own offerings.

Bell Atlantic was none too happy about AT&T's strong position in the aftermarket for upgrades and plug-ins to AT&T 5ESS switches. In fact, in 1995, Bell Atlantic sued AT&T for monopolization.

Why did Bell Atlantic put up with all this? Because Bell Atlantic would bear substantial costs if it tried to replace the AT&T switches with those of another switch supplier. These switches have a useful lifetime of fifteen years or more, and they are costly to remove and reinstall. Furthermore, the switches Bell Atlantic had paid for and used were worth much less on the used market than they were new, in part because any buyer would also have to deal with AT&T for enhancements and upgrades.

This is a fine example of lock-in. Once Bell Atlantic purchased and installed the AT&T switches, it was locked in to AT&T—that is, dependent on AT&T to use the switches effectively. To put this differently, Bell Atlantic would bear significant switching costs in replacing the AT&T gear with another brand of equipment.

Computer Associates

Another nice example of lock-in is illustrated by the plight of companies that have massive databases on large IBM mainframe computers running highly specialized software. These companies are heavily locked into these computers and their operating systems, making the business of supplying the necessary software quite lucrative, especially for software supplied by only a small number of vendors.

A major beneficiary of this particular lock-in to IBM mainframe computers is Computer Associates. Computer Associates is the leading supplier of a variety of systems management software that works with IBM's MVS (Multiple Virtual Storage) and VSE/ESA (Virtual Storage Extended/Enterprise Systems Architecture) operating systems. Computer Associates' products include tape management software, disk management software, job scheduling software, and security software for the VSE operating environment, and tape management software and job scheduling software for the MVS operating environment.

Computer Associates earned $3.5 billion in revenues in its fiscal year ending March 1996, making it the third largest independent software company, behind Microsoft and Oracle. Computer Associates enjoyed revenues of $432,000 per employee, versus Microsoft's $422,000 and Oracle's $180,000.

Lock-in occurs in this market on two separate levels: the system level and the vendor level. Customers are certainly loathe to switch computers or operating systems; they are locked into an IBM system. But they are also wary of switching vendors for their systems management software; they are locked into their software suppliers, too. Since this software is mission critical, the risks in using a new vendor, especially an unproven one, are substantial. Switching costs for customers include the risk of a substantial disruption in operations. And for critical pieces of information technology, the danger of disruption can dwarf out-of-pocket switching costs. The fact that Computer Associates software is known to work allows it to command a hefty premium for its software.

Of course, a customer strongly locked into an IBM VSE or MVS operating system is not as firmly locked into Computer Associates for its systems management software. Much of this software is available from alternative sources. However, in 1995 Computer Associates moved to reduce those choices and gain greater control of these customers by acquiring Legent Corporation, the second largest independent supplier of software for IBM-compatible mainframe computer systems, for $1.8 billion. Recognizing that this acquisition would restrict the choices of these locked-in consumers, the U.S. Department of Justice required

Computer Associates to spin off certain software products as a condition of completing the acquisition of Legent.

In this situation, locked-in customers were partially protected from exploitation by the oversight of the Justice Department's Antitrust Division. You can ill afford to be passive if you seek this protection, however. If a proposed merger or acquisition narrows your choices materially, you can improve your chances of blocking the deal, or extracting concessions from the merging parties, by alerting the Federal Trade Commission (FTC) and the Justice Department of your concerns. These agencies have strong powers to prevent deals that are adverse to the interests of consumers. But beware: to really help yourself, you must be ready to testify to your own vulnerability in open court.

Mass Market Lock-In

Our examples so far have involved huge switching costs, like those to Bell Atlantic of replacing switches worth billions of dollars. Do not be misled: even when switching costs appear low, they can be critical for strategy. A million customers, each of whom has switching costs of $100, are just as valuable, collectively, as a single customer whose switching costs are $100 million. The point is that you must compare any switching costs to revenues on a *per-customer basis* and add up these costs across your entire installed base to value that base. These principles apply equally to customers who are businesses or households.

Compare switching costs to revenue on a per-customer basis.

To illustrate how "small" switching costs can have a profound impact on strategies and market outcomes, one need only follow the current contentious debate in telecommunications regarding "number portability," namely, your ability to keep your local telephone number when (and if) you choose a new local telephone company. The issue: do you have the right to keep your telephone number when you select MCI as your local carrier, or does your local Bell company have the right to hang onto your phone number, forcing you to change numbers if you want to use MCI? AT&T, MCI, and Sprint are pushing for number portability; the local Bell companies are dragging their feet. Everyone recognizes that number portability is critical if local telephone competition is to become a reality. The cost per person of changing phone numbers may not be huge, but when you add up these costs across millions of telephone subscribers, the stakes grow large.

Regulatory obligations are forcing the incumbent local telephone companies to offer number portability as soon as possible. Debate is currently raging over whether these local monopolists are in fact complying with those duties by offering "interim number portability," which typically involves remote call forwarding. Would-be competitive local exchange carriers are pushing hard for incumbent carriers to develop "true" number portability. This is reminiscent of the debate over "equal access" long-distance dialing in the mid-1980s. Back then, MCI and Sprint were handicapped in the long-distance telephone market when customers had to dial extra digits to use their services. The lesson is that small consumer switching costs can constitute large barriers to entry, especially for mass-market products.

The market for on-line services provides another example of how "small" switching costs can have a large market impact. Changing from America Online to another Internet service provider (ISP) requires changing one's e-mail address. In comparison with buying a new mainframe computer, it is cheap to switch e-mail addresses. However, in comparison with the monthly fees for on-line services, the cost of changing e-mail addresses is not negligible. Furthermore, the incumbent Internet service provider may raise these switching costs by refusing to forward mail sent to an old address. For example, e-mail sent to AOL users who have discontinued their service is bounced back to the sender.

One Internet business that has exploited this e-mail address lock-in is Hotmail. Hotmail offers *free* e-mail service via a Web browser that can be used from any Internet service provider. So how does Hotmail make money? Hotmail places ads on the border surrounding the e-mail workspace. Hotmail also asks each new user to fill out a form indicating his or her interests, and the ads are then targeted to each user's special interests. This is an example of the kind of personalized advertising we discussed earlier in the book. Hotmail's 9.5 million subscribers made its Web site the fourteenth most visited site on the Web and caught the attention of both Microsoft and Netscape. Microsoft recently acquired

Hotmail for an estimated $300 million–$400 million: not bad for a company that has yet to turn a profit.

Some professional organizations, such as the Association for Computing Machinery, offer e-mail forwarding as a way to avoid address lock-in. CalTech and other universities offer this service to alumni, which, not incidentally, helps them keep in touch with potential donors.

Address lock-in may be a "small" problem for individual users, but it is a major headache for large organizations. One of the reasons that the recent debates about how to manage Internet domain names have been so heated is the potential lock-in problems. Imagine starting a Web site, building a customer following, and then being told that your Web address was being taken away from you by the central authority, or that your annual fees for using "your" Web address were being raised sharply. Fears such as these have prompted intense interest in the management of the Domain Name System and other aspects of Internet governance.

A final example of why small lock-in matters involves user behavior on the Web. Several user studies have documented that people don't read Web content the way they read paper content. Web readers are very fickle; if you lose their interest, you quickly lose their presence. Web years move seven times as rapidly as ordinary years, but Web attention spans are seven times shorter as well.

Part of the explanation for this behavior is ergonomic—it's just unpleasant reading text on a computer monitor. But part of the explanation is switching costs. When you pick up a magazine or a book and sit in your favorite chair, you have to exert effort, however small, to switch to a different magazine or book. When you are looking at one Web page, other pages are just a mouseclick away.

This means that writing for the Web is different from writing for paper. You have to get your message across quickly and concisely. Requiring readers to change the screen, by either scrolling or clicking, gives them a good excuse to go to a different site. A Web surfer in motion tends to stay in motion—and a Web reader standing still has probably just gone for a snack.

Switching Costs Are Ubiquitous

Switching costs are the norm, not the exception, in the information economy. As you consider your own business, we suspect that you, too, will recognize lock-in and switching costs as factors that you must deal with on a regular basis. Perhaps your customers will become locked into your products and services; certainly you are susceptible to lock-in yourself in your own use of information systems.

You compete at your own peril if you do not recognize lock-in, protect yourself from its adverse effects, and use it to your advantage when possible. In many markets involving the storage, manipulation, or transmission of information, hard-core, tangible lock-in is substantial, and fortunes can be made or lost by anticipating or neglecting its role. If you are a supplier seeking new customers, you have to overcome customer inertia and lock-in to rivals. If you are a locked-in customer, you may find yourself in a weak bargaining position that could have been avoided by negotiating protections for yourself at the outset. Alternatively, you might seek an initial "sweetener" to compensate you for anticipated lock-in, if you can see it coming.

This chapter will help you learn to recognize switching costs and lock-in and to assess their significance. Remember, lock-in is a two-edged sword; you may loathe it as a customer yet embrace it as a supplier. Either way, you must understand switching costs and be able to anticipate and measure them. In the next chapter, we'll see how to craft strategy based on that understanding.

VALUING AN INSTALLED BASE OF CUSTOMERS

To understand lock-in and deal with it effectively, the first step is to recognize what constitutes true switching costs. Switching costs measure the extent of a customer's lock-in to a given supplier. When America Online (AOL) decides how aggressively to seek new customers, and how to price to its existing customers, it must be able to measure customers' switching costs. Put differently, AOL must value what is perhaps its most important asset, namely, its installed base of customers. Like credit-card companies, long-distance telephone companies, and cable-television companies, Internet service providers need to estimate their revenue stream from a new customer to figure out how much to spend to acquire that customer. A similar exercise is necessary when buying customers wholesale, as when banks buy credit-card portfolios or when IBM acquired Lotus. This is harder than you might think.

We've emphasized the customer's switching costs so far, but the

448

supplier also bears some costs when it acquires a new customer. These may be small, such as creating a new entry in a database, or they may be quite large, such as assembling a team of support personnel. Both the customer's and the supplier's costs are important. Adding them up gives the *total switching costs* associated with a single customer; these costs are the key to valuing an installed base.

The total cost of switching = costs the customer bears + costs the new supplier bears.

The total cost associated with Customer C switching from Supplier A to Supplier B is the cost that must be borne collectively by Customer C *and by Supplier B* to place the customer in a position with Supplier B that is comparable to the one that Customer C currently has with Supplier A.

Look at how this concept plays out in the long-distance telephone business. When you switch your long-distance service from AT&T to MCI, the total switching costs include your time and trouble in making the move, plus the marketing and setup costs incurred by MCI. There's not a lot that MCI can do to reduce these costs. If MCI offers you $25 to change carriers, this tactic has no impact on total switching costs: the switching costs borne by you fall by $25, and those borne by MCI rise by $25. What if MCI offers you 100 free minutes of calling as a sweetener? If you value these minutes at 15 cents per minute, or $15 in total, they reduce your switching costs by $15. If the cost to MCI of offering these minutes is 5 cents per minute (for access charges, say), or $5 in total, the costs borne by MCI rise by only $5. The free-minutes offer has reduced total switching costs by $10. Whenever the seller enjoys a nice margin (price minus marginal cost) on its products or services, there is scope for in-kind sweeteners of this sort to lower total switching costs.

You might find it odd to look at extra costs borne not just by the customer but also by the new supplier, but this is essential for a sound analysis of whether it is worthwhile to acquire a new customer. Whether you or MCI spends the time or bears the cost of shifting your long-distance account from AT&T does not alter the fact that the time and money spent is a cost of switching brands. Indeed, very often new suppliers will help subsidize customers who are switching brands; for example, the Apollo computerized reservation system compensated travel agents for payments owed by the travel agent to the rival Sabre system if the agent stopped using Sabre. Nowadays, long-distance telephone companies are offering signing bonuses in the form of free minutes to attract customers from rival carriers.

How much should you spend to attract a new customer? The answer depends on the costs that you and your new customer both bear. Suppose, for example, that you are an ISP trying to build your customer base. Imagine that switching Internet providers involves $50 worth of hassle for the customer, and it costs you $25 to set up a new account, so the total switching costs are $75. You should encourage a customer to switch only if you expect the discounted flow of profit from this customer to be greater than $75. If you anticipate a discounted flow of profit of $100, you can afford to offer the consumer a couple of free months of service (valued at $25 per month) to overcome the $50 switching costs, pay the $25 account setup costs, and still be left with $25 of profit. Alternatively, you could invest $50 in advertising (rather than the free months) to convince the customer that switching to your service from his or her current ISP is worth the hassle. But if you anticipate a present value of only $70 of profit from the new customer, it just isn't worth trying to attract him, since the total switching costs of $75 exceed the benefits of $70.

In many cases, the disruption in service associated with changing suppliers is a major consideration, as we saw in the Computer Associates case. For mission-critical information and communications, these disruption costs can make up the bulk of the switching costs. Worse yet for customers, these costs are potentially subject to strategic manipulation by the vendor. For example, would-be competitors in local telephone service are finding in trials that customers tend to lose telephone service for a period of time when switching service to them from the incumbent local exchange carriers. Needless to say, this disruption is a huge barrier to switching local telephone companies, especially for business customers, and the subject of repeated complaints to regulators.

Measuring customer switching costs is a big piece of valuing an installed base of customers. As a rule of thumb, the profits a supplier can expect to earn from a customer are equal to the total switching costs, as just defined, *plus* the value of other competitive advantages the supplier enjoys by virtue of having a superior product or lower costs than its rivals. Customer perceptions are paramount: a brand premium based on superior reputation or advertising is just as valuable as an equal premium based on truly superior quality. As a general principle, if your rivals have cost and quality similar to yours, so that your market is highly competitive, the profits that you can earn from a customer—on a going-forward, present-value basis—*exactly equal the total switching costs.*

> **Profit from current customer = total switching costs + quality/cost advantage.**

Life is more complicated if you cannot easily measure these switching costs, especially if customers differ widely in their switching costs, but the same principle still applies.

To illustrate this principle, consider the value of your patronage to your local telephone company. Under current FCC rules, local phone companies are required to make their facilities available at cost to would-be competitors seeking to provide basic telephone service. Under these conditions, the local phone company can expect to earn a profit on basic service only if it can command a premium based on its brand name, or if consumers bear switching costs in using other carriers. Take a customer for whom the hassle of switching phone numbers has a monetary cost of $100. Our valuation principle says that the incumbent telephone company can earn precisely $100 in extra profits from this customer, in present-value terms. This might come in the form of a $1 per month premium over the rates charged by competitors (since $1 per month in perpetuity has a present value of roughly $100 at conventional interest rates).

The day the regulators mandate full number portability, and ensure that switching phone companies is easy and involves no disruption in service, consumer switching costs will tumble close to zero—essentially, to the transaction costs of changing carriers. When that day comes, the value of the incumbent phone company's installed base will decline. The prospect of that day arriving reduces the per-customer value of the incumbent carrier's installed base from a perpetuity to a shorter and shorter annuity. You can see why incumbent carriers are resisting the move to full number portability. Likewise, entrants are fighting hard to force the Bell companies to reconfigure their operational support systems to enable customers to switch smoothly to their services. Once full number portability is in place, the Bell companies will lose one (of several) advantages that they currently enjoy based on their incumbency position in local telephone markets. Anticipating the arrival of competition, local companies are seeking to enter long-distance markets, to become ISPs, and generally to bolster their customer relationships and customer loyalty to withstand the eventual reduction in customer switching costs.

This same valuation principle applies when switching costs are based on the ownership of durable capital equipment or long-term contractual commitments. For example, Ticketmaster enters into multi-year contracts to provide stadiums and other venues with ticketing services. A would-be competitor of Ticketmaster (there are a few, encouraged by Pearl Jam's very public dispute with Ticketmaster) must either wait for these contracts to expire (by which time the contract-based switching costs will be absent) or buy the venue out of its contract. If the venue purchases a ticketing system dedicated to Ticketmaster, trains its employees to use the Ticketmaster system, or publicizes that its customers can obtain tickets at Ticketmaster outlets, the switching costs will outlive the contract, however. As we'll see, one of the distinctive features of information-based lock-in is that it tends to be so durable: equipment wears out, reducing switching costs, but specialized databases live on and grow, enhancing lock-in over time.

Our valuation principle can be used for several purposes:

- First, by anticipating the value of tomorrow's installed base of customers, you can determine how much to invest today—in the form of price discounting, advertising, or R&D, for example—to attract more customers and build that installed base.

- Second, you can use these methods to evaluate a target company whose installed-base of customers constitutes a major asset. Rather than figure out the revenue and cost streams associated with the target company's customers, you may be able to take a shortcut and calculate these customers' switching costs.

- Third, valuation information will help inform decisions affecting your customers' switching costs—for example, your product design and compatibility decisions.

452

CLASSIFICATION OF LOCK-IN

So far we've said the following about lock-in:

- Customer lock-in is the norm in the information economy, because information is stored, manipulated, and communicated using a "system" consisting of multiple pieces of hardware and software and because specialized training is required to use specific systems.

- Switching costs must be evaluated relative to revenues on a per-customer basis. Even "small" switching costs can be critical in mass markets such as the telephone industry or consumer electronics.

- Total switching costs include those borne by the consumer to switch suppliers and those borne by the new supplier to serve the new consumer.

- As a rule of thumb, the present discounted value to a supplier of a locked-in customer is equal to that customer's total switching costs, plus the value of all other advantages enjoyed by the incumbent supplier based on lower costs or superior product quality, real or perceived.

We are now ready to look more closely at the underlying *sources* of switching costs, with an eye to their strategic implications. There are a handful of types of switching costs that arise in one industry after another. Table 5.1 summarizes our classification of lock-in. Knowing these patterns will help you identify and anticipate lock-in, estimate your switching costs or those of your customers, and plan accordingly. We will examine each entry of the table in detail.

Contractual Commitments

Our first category of lock-in is the most explicit: a contractual commitment to buy from a specific supplier. Common sense dictates that you should not commit yourself to a single supplier unless the price is specified. Nonetheless, many contracts give the seller the discretion to make annual adjustments in rates, subject to certain limits, or even to

Table 5.1. Types of Lock-In and Associated Switching Costs

Type of Lock-In	Switching Costs
Contractual commitments	Compensatory or liquidated damages
Durable purchases	Replacement of equipment; tends to decline as the durable ages
Brand-specific training	Learning a new system, both direct costs and lost productivity; tends to rise over time
Information and databases	Converting data to new format; tends to rise over time as collection grows
Specialized suppliers	Funding of new supplier; may rise over time if capabilities are hard to find/maintain
Search costs	Combined buyer and seller search costs; includes learning about quality of alternatives
Loyalty programs	Any lost benefits from incumbent supplier, plus possible need to rebuild cumulative use

charge so-called "reasonable" rates. Beware of these vague protections when you are buying. Even with ironclad price protection, there is inevitably some room for the vendor to control nonprice variables, such as the quality of service provided. Buyers are well advised to consider such "noncontractible" aspects of the product or service in advance.

Beware of contracts that guarantee price but not quality.

Indeed, price commitments sought by customers from vendors can be positively harmful if they merely induce the vendor to exploit lock-in by reducing quality and other nonprice dimensions of service.

The extent of lock-in depends on the nature of the contract. One contractual form, a *requirements contract*, commits the buyer to purchase all of its requirements exclusively from a specific seller for an extended period of time. In another form, a *minimum order-size commitment*, the buyer promises to make a certain quantity of purchases, potentially leaving open the option of turning elsewhere for additional supplies as needed if the original vendor is not performing well.

With explicit contractual commitments, the damages for breach of the contract can loom large and may constitute the bulk of the switching costs. Of course, a new supplier may be willing to buy you out of your current contract (probably to lock you in anew). Alternatively, you can compensate your existing supplier under your contract and still come out ahead if your new supplier offers a sufficient discount. If the liquidated damages in your existing contract are large enough, you really will be locked in. Also, be careful about *evergreen contracts*, which automatically renew sixty or ninety days before the initial ending date.

When negotiating such contracts, think beyond the terms, conditions, and duration of the contract itself. Anticipate your switching costs and options *after* the contract terminates. For example, if you purchase a specialized piece of equipment with a ten-year lifetime, and if you arrange for a three-year service contract at the time of purchase, consider what your service options will be for the remaining seven years after the initial contract expires. If you enter into a five-year contract with a vendor to manage your customer databases, think carefully about the switching costs you will face in five years time if you seek to change vendors. Design the contract to minimize those costs, perhaps by reserving for yourself nonexclusive rights to some of the computer code developed to manage or exploit your data.

Durable Purchases

In looking at Bell Atlantic and Computer Associates, we examined examples of lock-in involving the purchase of expensive, durable equipment (telephone switches and mainframe computers and operating systems, respectively) at one point in time, followed by purchases of complementary products at a later time (transmission equipment or voice messaging equipment, and systems management software, respectively). This is one of the most common and important patterns of lock-in: after the initial purchase is made, the customer must buy follow-on products that work with the durable equipment. As a result, many suppliers of durable equipment—be it medical equipment sold by Siemens to hospitals, large copiers sold by Xerox to corporations, or Zip drives sold by Iomega to individuals and businesses—derive the bulk of their profits, if not their revenues, from "aftermarket" sales.

In these situations, the economic lifetime of the durable equipment is critical. If the equipment quickly depreciates in economic value, perhaps because of rapid technological progress, then expenditures on that equipment do not lock customers in for very long, or very strongly. If there is a market for used equipment, so the customer can recover some of the initial outlay for the equipment upon replacing it, switching costs are again reduced. Indeed, rival vendors seeking to make their own new-equipment sales often reduce customers' switching costs by accepting used equipment for trade-in at above-market prices. Active used-equipment markets facilitate this tactic.

With durable hardware, switching costs tend to fall over time as the hardware depreciates. Thus, lock-in tends to be self-limiting. The switching costs, which here are the cost of replacing the existing hardware with equally capable hardware (or the cost of replacing the existing hardware with superior, state-of-the-art hardware, less the extra benefits of that hardware) fall as the user's machine ages. Rapid technological advance reduces hardware lock-in.

With durable equipment, switching costs fall over time because of depreciation.

There is an exception to the principle that hardware lock-in declines with time: when a customer has multiple pieces of similar equipment and enjoys efficiencies from having all or most of its equipment come from the same vendor. In this case, even when one machine is fully depreciated, the customer still bears large switching costs because of the other complementary equipment. The customer is least attached to the incumbent supplier when most of its equipment is nearing the end of its useful lifetime. The supplier is most vulnerable to being replaced at just such a point of *minimal* lock-in, just as the weakest link governs the strength of a chain. Recognizing this, the supplier may aim for its customers to have staggered equipment vintages or may offer inducements to replace older equipment before the end of its lifetime to maximize the minimal lock-in.

One effective way for customers to reduce or eliminate switching costs based on durable equipment is to rent or lease the equipment rather than buying it. By pushing more transactions into the "foremarket" and out of the "aftermarket," the buyer takes advantage of the flexibility to be enjoyed prior to becoming locked-in. For example, if you contract for complements such as repair parts and maintenance service when you initially rent or lease a copier, you need not worry that service prices will rise during the lifetime of the lease. Extended warranties serve the same function. In contrast, if you buy the copier, even with an initial service contract, you may still be subject to a steep price increase to renew when the original service contract expires.

Another key issue with this type of lock-in is the extent of choice available to the locked-in consumer: *technology lock-in is not the same as vendor lock-in.* Customer lock-in is far less important if there remain many alternative suppliers of the complementary products purchased later. Bell Atlantic is not reliant on AT&T if there are alternative suppliers of transmission equipment (or other software and hardware) that attaches to the AT&T switch. In other words, the aftermarket choices are an important part of understanding the entire pattern of equipment purchase and lock-in, an observation that will be important in our discussion of interfaces and compatibility in Chapter 7.

The fact is, most durable equipment requires follow-on purchases, making this pattern of lock-in extremely common. Obviously, a great deal of equipment is durable. Beyond that, however, there are all manner of complementary products that customers need in the future. Upgrades and product improvements are common, both for durable equipment and for other durable investments including computer software. Very often only the original vendor offers these upgrades, perhaps owing to patent or copyright protection that the vendor enjoys. Aftermarket service and spare parts are a necessity for most equipment, and they may also be supplied exclusively or largely by the equipment manufacturer. Notable examples include computer hardware, high-speed printers and copiers, telecommunications equipment, aircraft, weapons systems, and medical equipment. In fact, aftermarket policies constitute a key strategic choice for manufacturers of high-tech, durable equipment.

The limits of these strategies are now being tested in the courts. Indeed, a whole cottage industry has sprung up in which customers are suing manufacturers under the antitrust laws via class actions, alleging that the manufacturers have impeded their ability to obtain aftermarket service from independent service organizations (ISOs). These ISOs also are suing manufacturers directly, emboldened by a key 1992 Supreme Court decision (*Image Technical Services v. Eastman Kodak*) ruling that manufacturers may be found to have monopoly power in their own brand-specific aftermarkets and are not immune from antitrust challenges by competition with other equipment manufacturers.

Brand-Specific Training

A pattern of lock-in similar to that associated with the purchase of durable products results when personnel are trained to use them. This training is often brand-specific, in that considerable additional time and effort would be required to learn to work with a new brand of product with equal proficiency. In this case, the complementary products are the durable product itself and the training that is specific to it. General training (as opposed to brand-specific training) does not give rise to lock-in. As we will discuss in Chapter 8 in regard to strategic standard setting, a key question for buyers and sellers is whether training can be effectively transferred to other brands of software, perhaps through the use of standardized user interfaces or protocols.

With brand-specific training, switching costs tend to *rise* with time, as personnel become more and more familiar with the existing system. The opposite is true for durable hardware, which becomes less costly to replace as it ages and as new models with superior performance are introduced.

The obvious example for many of us is computer software. We all know how time consuming it can be to learn to use a new piece of software, much less to become adept at it. And the training costs associated with replicating one's proficiency with a familiar piece of software tend to grow the more experience one has with the familiar program. Moreover, the software vendor can maintain high switching costs by introducing a series of upgrades that offer enhanced capabilities in return for the investment of additional time learning the new features.

> **With brand-specific training, switching costs rise over time.**

Of course, a new brand can emerge that is easy to learn, thus reducing switching costs. Indeed, one strategy for breaking into a market with significant brand-specific customer training is to imitate existing brands or otherwise develop a product that is easy to learn. Borland tried this with Quattro Pro, aimed at Lotus 1-2-3 users, and Microsoft Word has built-in, specially designed help for (former!) WordPerfect users.

With brand-specific training, lock-in can easily outlive an individual piece of equipment. This is most evident when customers desire to standardize all of their equipment by using a single vendor. For example, commercial airlines now place great value on "fleet commonality"—that is, on having most if not all of the aircraft in their fleet come from a single airframe manufacturer, and even with a similar cockpit configuration. Airlines have found that a uniform fleet can result in substantial savings on maintenance and training costs and can improve flight safety. This is one of the reasons why American, Delta, and Continental recently agreed to buy all of their new aircraft from Boeing over the next twenty years. Indeed, the demand for fleet commonality hastened the demise of McDonnell-Douglas: lacking a full family of aircraft, and lacking loyal customers with an all-Douglas fleet, McDonnell-Douglas threw in the towel in 1996, concluding that it could no longer survive in the commercial aircraft industry, and agreed to be acquired by Boeing.

Information and Databases

In our third type of switching cost, the complementary products giving rise to lock-in are the hardware and software used to store and manage information, on the one hand, and the information or database itself, on the other. Users with massive information encoded in a specialized format are vulnerable if and when they require new hardware or improved software to work with the data. In these situations, a key question is whether the information can easily be ported over to another system. You must ask yourself what are the costs of transferring the information and what aspects of the information would be lost in a transfer.

Many of the examples in this book fit into this category. For example, consumers purchase a CD player and then build up a library of CDs. When the CD player starts skipping (a seemingly inevitable event), or when new and better audio technologies appear on the scene, the consumer is locked into the CD format. In this case, the information cannot be transferred, making it important for anyone selling equipment that reads new formats, such as DVD, to make that equipment backward-compatible—that is, capable of reading CDs as well. Videotape players, laser disks, DVDs, and phonographs in an earlier day all conform to this pattern of hardware/software switching costs.

Computer software programs and data files are another critical category of format-specific information. In these cases, like the library of CDs, the library of information grows over time, causing lock-in to grow stronger with time. Any system in which information is collected over time in special formats raises these issues. Tax preparation software that incorporates tax information from prior years, accountant software that relies on historical data, and graphics software that uses designs developed over time are all examples of this type of lock-in. For years, Ashton-Tate's dBase language was enormously valuable because so many users had written programs in the dBase language. It's typically far easier to transfer raw data from one format to another than to port over code. In all of these cases, vendors' strategies revolve around methods designed to raise or lower consumers' switching costs and capitalize on the crucial distinction between proprietary and standardized formats.

Keep control of information and databases by using standardized formats and interfaces.

With information and databases, switching costs tend to rise with time as more and more information comes to reside in the historical database. One way for users to limit these switching costs is to insist on employing standardized formats and interfaces, if possible, or to insist that the vendor publish its interface specifications so as to permit competition from fully or largely compatible products. We discuss such "open" interfaces further in Chapter 8.

Specialized Suppliers

Another important pattern arises when buyers purchase specialized equipment gradually over time. As a buyer, remember that your choices today will dictate your needs tomorrow. By picking a single supplier of that equipment, you will become dependent on that source in the future. Your initial purchases of the equipment are complementary to later purchases because of the advantages of sticking with a single brand for all of your purchases.

Worse yet from the customer's point of view, comparable alternative suppliers may no longer exist after the initial bid is awarded to a single winner. Remember, with specialized equipment, the switching costs depend on the ability of new suppliers to offer comparable equipment when needed in the future. If the durable equipment or software is highly specialized, it will be relatively difficult to find alternative suppliers in the future, giving the incumbent vendor the advantage of substantial lock-in for the next round of purchases.

More and more companies in the information economy are facing lock-in to specialized suppliers. Yet this pattern is hardly unique to information industries. In fact, a large sector of our economy has been dealing with this problem for decades at least: the defense sector. The Department of Defense takes flack now and again for its procurement practices, but we believe that today's information sector can learn much from the Pentagon's methods of dealing with specialized suppliers, especially in the 1990s, during which time the defense contractor base has been sharply downsized.

Very often the Pentagon finds that the losers in the bidding to produce a complex weapons system cannot maintain the necessary specialized capabilities without ongoing business. Furthermore, the winner surely gains from its experience and comes to know the customer's needs better as part of fulfilling its contract. This problem plagues all buyers of state-of-the-art technology: now that NASA has picked Lockheed Martin's "Venturestar" design for its next-generation, single-stage-to-orbit space shuttle, it won't be easy for NASA to turn to others in the future should Lockheed's performance prove lacking. To a lesser extent, relationships between advertising firms, accounting firms, and law firms and their corporate clients also exhibit lock-in to specialized suppliers.

The upshot is that large buyers with specialized needs commonly find their options limited after they initially pick a supplier to serve them. The Pentagon often handles this by carefully structuring the competition for a single, huge, long-term procurement contract. For example, in 1996 the Pentagon "down-selected" from three to two the number of possible suppliers for the Joint Strike Fighter, funding additional development by Boeing and Lockheed Martin but dropping McDonnell Douglas. Over the next five years, Lockheed Martin and Boeing will develop prototypes for this new combat aircraft, with funding of some $2.2 billion by the Department of Defense. Then, around 2002, the Pentagon will pick a single supplier after a fly-off between the competing prototypes. The winner stands to earn revenues of some $200 billion over the lifetime of the Joint Strike Fighter program.

If the Pentagon could fully anticipate its needs and obtain contractual commitments from the winner as part of the process of selecting the ultimate winner, lock-in would not be an issue. But the world is not so simple. Even if the Pentagon obtains the option to buy a large number of planes at a specified cost, there will inevitably be issues down the line—such as the cost of making improvements to the plane in 2006 that were not envisioned in 2002—in which the winner will have some bargaining leverage by virtue of the Pentagon's lock-in. True, the Pentagon is a powerful buyer, with strong auditing rights to monitor costs and limit payments, and the contractor has a strong incentive not to be seen as exploiting its position as the sole supplier so as not to lose future competitions. Nevertheless, a significant degree of lock-in is inevitable.

We discuss procurement strategies below, but note here two important ones from the Pentagon's perspective: (1) get a variety of commitments and options as part of selecting the winner for a big contract and/or (2) keep alive an alternative source of supply, a strategy commonly known as *dual sourcing*. For example, in 1997 the Air Force decided to fund development of new low-cost rockets known as Evolved Expendable Launch Vehicles by both Lockheed Martin and Boeing rather than choosing just one of the companies. The Pentagon realized that two companies could be supported in part because of the growing commercial demand for rockets. Even when true dual sourcing is not possible because of specialized needs and large fixed costs, a large buyer can make efforts to nurture capabilities at more than one supplier to spur future rivalry. The Pentagon does this by providing its contractors with funds to maintain their capabilities to develop new designs and to bid on the next major contract.

Many high-tech firms are familiar with dual sourcing from the now-famous story of IBM and Intel. IBM attempted to keep its options open via dual sourcing when it selected a supplier of the microprocessors for its personal computers back in the early 1980s. In choosing Intel, IBM insisted on having a second source as an alternative to Intel. This created an opening for Advanced Micro Designs (AMD). To us, the Intel story illustrates the limitations of dual sourcing from the buyer's (IBM's) point of view: disagreements between Intel and AMD over the scope and duration of AMD's rights under its dual-sourcing agreement led to protracted litigation between Intel and AMD, and Intel has captured a commanding share of the market during the 1990s. The lesson: dual sourcing is most likely to be successful in the long run with two strong sources rather than one strong and one weak source. In rapidly moving markets, the buyer is best protected if each source has the independent ability to develop and improve its own technology over time.

Dual sourcing is clearly in the interest of purchasers who want to keep their options open. Less obvious is the fact that dual sourcing can also be in the interest of suppliers. If you are trying to get your technology established, the comfort of two or more sources can help convince potential customers to put their trust in you. We'll discuss this tactic further in Chapter 8 when we examine the logic of open systems and standards.

> **Dual sourcing is usually in the interest of buyers and sometimes in the interest of sellers.**

Search Costs

Our next category includes switching costs that are more mundane, but not to be ignored, especially in mass markets: the search costs incurred by buyers and sellers to find each other and establish a business relationship. These costs may seem small, but ask yourself how often you shop around for a new travel agent, insurance agent, or bank. Do you really know you are getting the best deal possible? Will your search behavior or loyalty change as more vendors become available on-line?

As we stressed above in defining switching costs, what matters in evaluating the extent of lock-in caused by search costs are the "two-sided" search costs, as borne by both customers and would-be suppliers. Search costs borne by consumers when switching brands include the psychological costs of changing ingrained habits, the time and effort involved in identifying a new supplier, and the risks associated with picking an unknown supplier. Search costs borne by would-be suppliers in reaching and acquiring new customers include promotional costs, the costs of actually closing the deal, the cost of setting up a new account, and the risks involved in dealing with an unknown customer, such as credit risk.

The credit card industry displays many of these search costs: customers tend not to move their credit card balances from one bank to another, and card-issuing banks spend considerable amounts on direct mail and other promotional activities in search of new customers. Likewise, banks find it costly to attract new accounts because of the danger of adverse selection—that is, ending up with customers who will ultimately default on their balances or, oddly enough, customers who will *not* incur finance charges at all and thus who are less profitable to the bank. Banks recoup these expenses in the form of high interest rates on consumer credit. Indeed, a bank portfolio with $100 million in credit card receivables would typically be worth around $120 million when sold to another issuer or when securitized. This is one nice example in which the market explicitly values a bank's installed base of "loyal" credit card customers.

Search costs depend on the time and expense involved in locating an attractive new supplier and the costs incurred by vendors in locating customers. If you are a customer who tends to be loyal, switching vendors only rarely, this can work to your advantage: if you can communicate this to potential suppliers, they will value your account all the more if your "churn" rate is likely to be low.

In the information economy, various search costs are likely to be reduced. This claim of the proponents of the "friction-free economy" is certainly correct. Distribution on the Internet is going to be far cheaper than it has ever been in the past, both for information products and for traditional items. Based on our principles for valuing an installed base of customers, reductions in search costs can represent a grave threat to the value of established mass-market companies lacking truly superior products. Advances in distribution will have an especially important effect on consumers who are currently the most costly to reach.

Even if search costs fall, however, there will always be some degree of pure consumer inertia and loyalty to incumbent vendors. This inertia and loyalty are due in part to our human limitations: no matter how inexpensive it becomes for suppliers to send messages to prospective customers, it will remain costly for customers (even with the help of their computer agents) to review and evaluate these proposals. So, even if banks can broadcast messages to prospective customers via the Internet, saving on direct mail costs, consumers will still need to take the time to sort through the proposals and run the risk of rejection, or loss of privacy, if they apply for a new credit card.

Loyalty Programs

Our next category of lock-in might be called "artificial lock-in" because it is entirely a construct of firms' strategies. We are referring to the increasingly popular programs in which customers are rewarded for their repeat purchases. These loyalty programs involve explicit inducements to customers to buy largely or exclusively from a single vendor.

The most popular and well-known of these are the airlines' frequent flier programs. Recently, hotels have followed suit with frequent guest programs. Even local retailers use this tactic, giving one unit for free after ten purchases. For example, our local film store will develop one roll of film for free after you have paid for ten rolls. The nearby Mexican restaurant does the same with burritos, if you remember to bring along your card and have it punched.

Loyalty programs create switching costs in two ways. First, you may forfeit certain credits if you stop buying from your regular supplier. If you have 15,000 miles in your airline account, and it takes 25,000 miles to get a free ticket, the 15,000 miles will be lost if you fail to fly another 10,000 miles before they expire. These switching costs can be minimized by changing carriers after cashing in the bulk of your credits. Second, and more important, are benefits based on cumulative usage, such as double miles or preferential service for members who fly more than 50,000 miles a year. These benefits become part of the total switching costs: either the customer loses them (a customer switching cost) or the new carrier matches them (a supplier switching cost). As on-line commerce explodes, more and more companies will adopt loyalty programs giving preferential treatment to customers based on their historical purchases precisely to create such switching costs.

Loyalty programs will become far easier to administer as companies keep more and more information about their customers' purchasing patterns, as we saw in the discussion of personalized pricing in Chapter 2. Already, many retailers collect detailed information on individual customers' buying patterns; with these databases at their disposal, these suppliers are well placed to target their promotional efforts based on customers' historical buying patterns or to offer discounts based on cumulative purchases. We predict an enormous informational tug-of-war: companies will increasingly use customer-specific information both to identify and contact attractive new prospects and to implement loyalty programs to retain existing customers.

In the information economy, the traditional sources of friction such as search costs and distribution costs will be eroded. But the same computational power that reduces these frictions allows for the creation of new "synthetic frictions" such as loyalty programs. Frictions don't disappear—they just mutate into new forms.

The variations on these discount programs are virtually endless. You can offer your customers a discount for buying exclusively from you or for committing to a certain minimum order size. You can offer discounts for customers who buy more than they did last year. You can utilize volume discounts to encourage customers to keep

Loyalty programs will proliferate.

buying from you rather than sampling other suppliers. Or, to attract new customers, you can offer introductory discounts as a way of helping defray their costs of switching to you from a rival. Perhaps the ultimate weapon here is to base the offer you make to a prospective new customer on information about that customer's status in your rival's loyalty program.

We anticipate that more and more businesses will use loyalty programs as customer information becomes more detailed and more widely available. In addition, complementary suppliers will coordinate their programs, much as hotels and airlines now cooperate in their repeat-buyer programs. With on-line trading, the possibilities will explode. And keeping track of historical sales of different products will be a lot easier than licking Green Stamps or having your card punched every time you buy a burrito.

With loyalty-inducing programs, customers can with relative ease calculate the costs they bear when switching vendors, both in terms of lost awards and of reduced marginal returns to additional business. Some vendors will buy credits from their competitors, much like competitive upgrades in the software industry. For example, an airline will often offer "gold status" to someone who holds gold status on a competing airline in hopes of inducing them to switch carriers.

The on-line book store Amazon.com has a very nice twist on a loyalty program. In the "Associates Program," anyone who recommends a book on his or her Web site can add a link to Amazon that can be used by those who wish to purchase the book through Amazon. In exchange, the site that created the link to Amazon gets a "referral fee" of $5\frac{1}{8}$ percent of the purchase price of the book. As of March 1998, there were more than 35,000 Amazon associates.

This base of associates gives Amazon a potent weapon in its battle with Barnes & Noble. Barnes & Noble has struck back with its Affiliates Program, which offers on-line bookstores order processing, payment, and shipping services and up to 7 percent of the revenue from book sales. Amazon responded with a special deal for the top 500 Web sites, giving them a bonus 50 percent larger than the standard payment.

We think Amazon could make an even better response: they should base the royalty rate on *cumulative* referrals, giving a payoff only after the consumer passes certain milestones. If Amazon structures the rates correctly, their associates will want to stick with only one on-line book provider, who will most likely be Amazon. Just as it is costly to switch to another frequent flyer program, it will be costly for associates to switch to another on-line book service.

SUPPLIERS AND PARTNERS FACE LOCK-IN, TOO

We've spoken so far as if buyers are uniquely susceptible to switching costs. Not so. Although we will continue to focus on buyers' switching costs, suppliers are hardly immune to lock-in. The fact is, anyone who makes investments that are specific to a particular supplier, customer, or partner is subject to lock-in for the economic lifetime of those investments. The key point is that the investments will have to be written down if the customer or partner walks, balks, or simply fails.

In fact, it is not uncommon for suppliers and customers to be locked in to each other at the same time. Such bilateral, or two-sided, lock-in can lead to a certain balance of terror, not to mention some high-stakes negotiations. The classic case was that of a railroad that built a spur line to serve an individual customer, such as a coal mine or a coal-fired power plant. Once the line was built, it had little or no value apart from serving the one customer, so the railroad was locked into that customer. At the same time, the customer would find it very expensive to finance a new spur line, so the customer was locked into the railroad, leading to what economists call a bilateral monopoly. The same relationship exists in the information economy when a software vendor writes a specialized piece of software for an individual client.

Nor is lock-in restricted to customers and suppliers; partners are susceptible as well. For example, Pratt & Whitney, as the manufacturer of certain aircraft engines designed specifically for Douglas aircraft, was long locked into McDonnell Douglas, even though it had no intention of selling the engines directly to McDonnell Douglas.

We see seller lock-in, bilateral lock-in, and partner lock-in frequently in information industries. Software houses that initially specialized in writing software for Apple computers learned all too soon that they needed to retool and thus bear very real switching costs: they had to become adept at writing programs to run on DOS or Windows. Likewise for companies specializing in writing games for Sony's PlayStation or the Nintendo 64 platform.

The same economic principles that give rise to buyer lock-in also describe seller lock-in and partner lock-in. Even when you're not the buyer, you need to be alert when making investments that will leave you in a weak bargaining position in the future. If you're a supplier, you can protect your downside by getting your customer(s) to commit to buying enough from you to cover most, if not all, of your costs. One nice way to do this is to have a large customer defray some or all of the costs of designing a product tailored to that customer, while reserving the rights to make distinct versions of the product for other customers. If you're a partner, think like a customer: get commitments from your partner on rollout dates, product specs, and prices. There's no point in developing software for a machine that is late to market or so expensive that few end users buy one.

THE LOCK-IN CYCLE

Lock-in is inherently a dynamic concept, growing out of investments made, and needs realized, at different points in time. Switching costs can grow or shrink with time, but they do not stand still.

We have developed a diagram to help you think dynamically about lock-in. The diagram applies to all of the flavors of lock-in we have just discussed. We call this the lock-in cycle, as shown in Figure 5.1.

The easiest place to hop onto the lock-in cycle is at the *brand selection point*—that is, when the customer chooses a new brand. Brand choice could mean purchasing a new multimillion dollar switch, buying a videodisk player, purchasing a new software program, or signing up for a new frequent-flier program. The first time a specific customer picks a brand, that customer will have no preference for any one brand based

Figure 5.1. *The Lock-In Cycle*

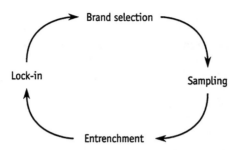

on lock-in. You are not born "locked in"; you only get locked in by virtue of choices you make. The next time around the cycle, the playing field will not be so level, however.

Brand selection is followed by the *sampling phase,* during which the customer actively uses the new brand and takes advantage of whatever inducements were made to give it a try. One of the dangers of offering powerful sweeteners to attract new customers is that they will take the free sample but never turn into revenue-paying customers. Some book clubs take this risk in offering eight books for a dollar; others require new members to buy a minimum number of books at regular prices. As we discussed in Chapter 2 on pricing, extending introductory offers to new customers is especially tempting for information providers because of the low marginal cost of information. This is all the more so with a CD that costs less than a dollar to produce, in comparison with printed material that could cost five dollars or more to produce.

Customers who do more than sample move into the *entrenchment phase.* This is when the consumer really gets used to the new brand, develops a preference for that brand over others, and perhaps becomes locked in to that brand by making complementary investments. Usually, the supplier tries to drag out this phase and delay active consideration of other brands, hoping that the customers' switching costs will go up. The entrenchment phase culminates in *lock-in* when the switching costs become prohibitively expensive.

We return to the brand selection point when the customer either switches brands or actively considers alternative brands without selecting them. Of course, circumstances will have changed in comparison with their last time around the cycle. Certainly the customer's switching costs are higher than the first time around. For specialized products, as in our Pentagon examples, some alternative suppliers may have dropped out in the interim or lost capabilities. On the other hand, new technologies can emerge.

The most basic principle in understanding and dealing with lock-in is to anticipate the entire cycle from the beginning. In fact, you need to go beyond any one trip around the circle and anticipate multiple cycles into the future in forming your strategy from the outset. Valuing your installed base is part of looking ahead: by figuring out how much customers will be worth to you in the future (next time around the cycle), you can decide how much to invest in them now (by inducing them to take the next step and enter the sample phase, for example). This is especially true if switching costs are rising over time (as with information storage and brand-specific training) rather than falling over time (as with durable equipment that depreciates and will be replaced by new and superior models).

The next chapter looks more closely at each point in this cycle, both from the perspective of buyers and suppliers, drawing out lessons and suggesting winning strategies.

LESSONS

- **Switching costs are the norm in information industries.** They can be huge—as when Bell Atlantic invested billions of dollars in telephone switches with a proprietary AT&T operating system—or small—as when consumers must obtain credit approval to get a new credit card. Either way, fortunes can be made or lost based on lock-in and switching costs. You just cannot compete effectively in the information economy unless you know how to identify, measure, and understand switching costs and map strategy accordingly.

- **As a customer, failure to understand switching costs will leave you vulnerable to opportunistic behavior by your suppliers.** Even if you cannot avoid some lock-in, you may miss out on the up-front sweetener that would help the bitter lock-in pill go down better.

- **As a supplier, switching costs are the key to valuing your installed base.** You will be unlikely to successfully build an installed base of customers—one of the most potent assets in the information economy—unless you can overcome the initial costs of switching customers from rival firms. To help defray these costs, you must anticipate customers' lock-in cycle, including the costs your would-be customers will incur if they ever leave *you*.

- **Fortunately, lock-in arises in one industry after another according to certain identifiable patterns.** All of these patterns conform to the lock-in cycle, from brand selection point, through the sampling and entrenchment phases, and back to the next brand selection point. To map strategy for one part of the lock-in cycle, you must understand and anticipate the entire cycle.

- **The essence of lock-in is that your choices in the future will be limited by your investments today. These linkages differ from one technology to another, but are predictable.** We have identified seven primary economic patterns leading to lock-in: contractual commitments, durable equipment and aftermarkets, brand-specific training, information and databases, specialized suppliers, search costs, and loyalty programs. By taking stock of your own expenditures over time in these areas, and those of your customers (and suppliers), you can systematically identify how lock-in affects your business.

In the next chapter, we build on these principles to help you shape your strategies to make lock-in work for you, not against you.

Chapter 15: Networks and Positive Feedback

The industrial economy was populated with oligopolies: industries in which a few large firms dominated their markets. This was a comfortable world, in which market shares rose and fell only gradually. This stability in the marketplace was mirrored by lifetime employment of managers. In the United States, the automobile industry, the steel industry, the aluminum industry, the petroleum industry, various chemicals markets, and many others followed this pattern through much of the twentieth century.

In contrast, the information economy is populated by temporary monopolies. Hardware and software firms vie for dominance, knowing that today's leading technology or architecture will, more likely than not, be toppled in short order by an upstart with superior technology.

What has changed? There is a central difference between the old and new economies: the old industrial economy was driven by *economies of scale;* the new information economy is driven by the *economics of networks.* In this chapter we describe in detail the basic principles of network economics and map out their implications for market dynamics and competitive strategy. The key concept is *positive feedback.*

The familiar if sad tale of Apple Computer illustrates this crucial concept. Apple has suffered of late because positive feedback has fueled the competing system offered by Microsoft and Intel. As Wintel's share of the personal computer market grew, users found the Wintel system more and more attractive. Success begat more success, which is the essence of positive feedback. With Apple's share continuing to decline, many computer users now worry that the Apple Macintosh will shortly become the Sony Beta of computers, orphaned and doomed to a slow death as support from software producers gradually fades away. This worry is cutting into Apple's sales, making it a potentially self-fulfilling forecast. Failure breeds failure: this, too, is the essence of positive feedback.

> *Positive feedback makes the strong grow stronger . . . and the weak grow weaker.*

Why is positive feedback so important in high-technology industries? Our answer to this question is organized around the concept of a *network*. We are all familiar with physical networks such as telephone networks, railroad networks, and airline networks. Some high-tech networks are much like these "real" networks: networks of compatible fax machines, networks of compatible modems, networks of e-mail users, networks of ATM machines, and the Internet itself. But many other high-tech products reside in "virtual" networks: the network of Macintosh users, the network of CD machines, or the network of Nintendo 64 users.

In "real" networks, the linkages between nodes are physical connections, such as railroad tracks or telephone wires. In virtual networks, the linkages between the nodes are invisible, but no less critical for market dynamics and competitive strategy. We are in the same computer network if we can use the same software and share the same files. Just as a spur railroad is in peril if it cannot connect to the main line, woe to those whose hardware or software is incompatible with the majority of other users. In the case of Apple, there is effectively a network of Macintosh users, which is in danger of falling below critical mass.

Whether real or virtual, networks have a fundamental economic characteristic: the value of connecting to a network depends on the number of *other* people already connected to it.

This fundamental value proposition goes under many names: network effects, network externalities, and demand-side economies of scale. They all refer to essentially the same point: other things being equal, it's better to be connected to a bigger network than a smaller one. As we will see below, it is this "bigger is better" aspect of networks that gives rise to the positive feedback observed so commonly in today's economy.

Throughout this book we have stressed the idea that many aspects of the new economy can be found in the old economy if you look in the right places. Positive feedback and network externalities are not a creation of the 1990s. To the contrary, network externalities have long been recognized as critical in the transportation and communications industries, where companies compete by expanding the reach of their networks and where one network can dramatically increase its value by interconnecting with other networks. Anyone trying to navigate the network economy has much to learn from the history of the postal service, railroads, airlines, and telephones.

In this chapter we introduce and illustrate the key economic concepts that underlie market dynamics and competitive strategy in both real and virtual networks. Based on these concepts, we identify four generic strategies that are effective in network markets. We then show how these concepts and strategies work in practice through a series of historical case studies.

In the two chapters that follow this one, we build on the economic framework developed here, constructing a step-by-step strategic guide to the key issues facing so many players in markets for information technology. In Chapter 8 we discuss how to work with allies to successfully establish a new technology—that is, to launch a new network. As you might expect, negotiations over interconnection and standardization are critical. In Chapter 9, we examine what happens if these negotiations break down: how to fight a standards war, how to get positive feedback working in favor of your technology in a battle against an incompatible rival technology.

POSITIVE FEEDBACK

The notion of *positive feedback* is crucial to understanding the economics of information technology. Positive feedback makes the strong get stronger and the weak get weaker, leading to extreme outcomes. If you have ever experienced feedback talking into a microphone, where a loud noise becomes deafening through repeated amplification, you have witnessed positive feedback in action. Just as an audio signal can feed on itself until the limits of the system (or the human ear) are reached, positive feedback in the marketplace leads to extremes: dominance of the market by a single firm or technology.

The backward cousin of positive feedback is *negative feedback*. In a negative-feedback system, the strong get weaker and the weak get stronger, pushing both toward a happy medium. The industrial oligopolies listed in the beginning of this chapter exhibited negative feedback, at least in their mature phase. Attempts by the industry leader to capture share from smaller players would often trigger vigorous responses as smaller players sought to keep capacity utilization from falling. Such competitive responses prevent the leading firm from obtaining a dominant position. Furthermore, past a certain size, companies found growth difficult owing to the sheer complexity of managing a large enterprise. And as the larger firms became burdened with high costs, smaller, more nimble firms found profitable niches. All of these ebbs and flows represent negative feedback in action: the market found a balanced equilibrium rather than heading toward the extreme of a single winner. Sometimes sales fell below a critical mass, and companies like Studebaker went out of business or were acquired by more efficient rivals. But by and large, dramatic changes in market share were uncommon and oligopoly rather than monopoly was the norm.

Positive feedback should not be confused with growth as such. Yes, if a technology is on a roll, as is the Internet today, positive feedback translates into rapid growth: success feeds on itself. This is a *virtuous cycle*. But there is a dark side of this force. If your product is seen as failing, those very perceptions can spell doom. The Apple Macintosh is now in this danger zone, where "positive" feedback does not feel very positive. The virtuous cycle of growth can easily change to a *vicious cycle* of collapse. A death spiral represents positive feedback in action; "the weak get weaker" is the inevitable flip side of "the strong get stronger."

When two or more firms compete for a market where there is strong positive feedback, only one may emerge as the winner. Economists say that such a market is *tippy*, meaning that it can tip in favor of one player or another. It is unlikely that all will survive. It was clear to all parties in the battle over 56Kbps modem standards that multiple, incompatible modems could not coexist for long; the only question was which protocol would triumph or if a single, compromise standard could be negotiated.

Other examples of tippy markets were the video recorder market in the 1980s (VHS v. Beta) and the personal computer operating systems market of the 1990s (Wintel v. Apple). In its most extreme form, positive feedback can lead to a *winner-take-all market* in which a single firm or technology vanquishes all others, as has happened in several of these cases.

> **Positive feedback is a more potent force in the network economy than ever before.**

Figure 7.1 shows how a winner-take-all market evolves over time. The technology starting with an initial lead, perhaps 60 percent of the market, grows to near 100 percent, while the technology starting with 40 percent of the market declines to 10 percent. These dynamics are driven by the strong desire of users to select the technology that ultimately will prevail—that is, to choose the network that has (or will have) the most users. As a result, the strong get stronger and the weak get weaker; both effects represent the positive feedback so common in markets for information infrastructure.

The biggest winners in the information economy, apart from consumers generally, are companies that have launched technologies that have been propelled forward by positive feedback. This requires patience and foresight, not to mention a healthy dose of luck. Successful strategies in a positive-feedback industry are inherently dynamic. Our primary goal in this part of the book is to identify the elements of winning strategies in network industries and to help you craft the strategy most likely to succeed in your setting.

Figure 7.1. *Positive Feedback*

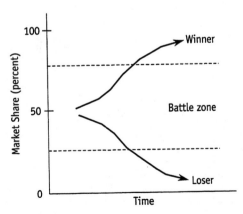

Nintendo is a fine example of a company that created enormous value by harnessing positive feedback. When Nintendo entered the U.S. market for home video games in 1985, the market was considered saturated, and Atari, the dominant firm in the previous generation, had shown little interest in rejuvenating the market. Yet by Christmas 1986, the Nintendo Entertainment System (NES) was the hottest toy on the market. The very popularity of the NES fueled more demand and enticed more game developers to write games to the Nintendo system, making the system yet more attractive. Nintendo managed that most difficult of high-tech tricks: to hop on the positive-feedback curve while retaining strong control over its technology. Every independent game developer paid royalties to Nintendo. They even promised not to make their games available on rival systems for two years following their release!

Our focus in this chapter is on markets with significant positive feedback resulting from demand-side or supply-side economies of scale. These scale economies apply most directly to the market leaders in an industry. But smaller players, too, must understand these same principles, whether they are planning to offer their own smaller differentiated networks or to hook into a larger network sponsored by an industry leader.

Positive-feedback systems follow a predictable pattern. Again and again, we see adoption of new technologies following an S-shaped curve with three phases: (1) flat during launch, then (2) a steep rise during takeoff as positive feedback kicks in, followed by (3) leveling off as saturation is reached. The typical pattern is illustrated in Figure 7.2.

Figure 7.2. *Adoption Dynamics*

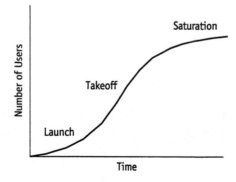

This S-shaped, or "logistic," pattern of growth is also common in the biological world; for example, the spread of viruses tends to follow this pattern. In the information technology arena, the S-shaped pattern can be seen in the adoption of the fax machine, the CD, color TV, video game machines, e-mail, and the Internet (we can assure you that current growth rates will slow down; it is just a matter of when).

DEMAND-SIDE ECONOMIES OF SCALE

Positive feedback is not entirely new; virtually every industry goes through a positive feedback phase early in its evolution. General Motors was more efficient than the smaller car companies in large part because of its scale. This efficiency fueled further growth by General Motors. This source of positive feedback is known as *economies of scale* in production: larger firms tend to have lower unit costs (at least up to a point). From today's perspective, we can refer to these traditional economies of scale as *supply-side economies of scale.*

Despite its supply-side economies of scale, General Motors never grew to take over the entire automobile market. Why was this market, like many industrial markets of the twentieth century, an oligopoly rather than a monopoly? Because traditional economies of scale based on manufacturing have generally been exhausted at scales well below total market dominance, at least in the large U.S. market. In other words, positive feedback based on supply-side economies of scale ran into natural limits, at which point negative feedback took over. These limits often arose out of the difficulties of managing enormous organizations. Owing to the managerial genius of Alfred Sloan, General Motors was able to push back these limits, but even Sloan could not eliminate negative feedback entirely.

In the information economy, positive feedback has appeared in a new, more virulent form based on the *demand* side of the market, not just the supply side. Consider Microsoft. As of May 1998, Microsoft had a market capitalization of about $210 billion. This enormous value is *not* based on the economies of scale in developing software. Oh, sure, there are scale economies, in designing software, as for any other information product. But there are several other available operating systems that offer comparable (or superior) performance to Windows 95 and

Windows NT, and the cost of developing rival operating systems is tiny in comparison with Microsoft's market capitalization. The same is true of Microsoft's key application software. No, Microsoft's dominance is based on *demand-side economies of scale*. Microsoft's customers value its operating systems *because* they are widely used, the de facto industry standard. Rival operating systems just don't have the critical mass to pose much of a threat. Unlike the supply-side economies of scale, demand-side economies of scale don't dissipate when the market gets large enough: if everybody else uses Microsoft Word, that's even more reason for you to use it too.

The positive relationship between popularity and value is illustrated in Figure 7.3. The arrow in the upper-right portion of the curve depicts a *virtuous cycle:* the popular product with many compatible users becomes more and more valuable to each user as it attracts ever more users. The arrow in the lower-left portion of the curve represents a *vicious cycle:* a death spiral in which the product loses value as it is abandoned by users, eventually stranding those diehards who hang on the longest, because of their unique preference for the product or their high switching costs.

Lotus 1-2-3 took great advantage of demand-side scale economies during the 1980s. Based on superior performance, Lotus 1-2-3 enjoyed the largest installed base of users among spreadsheet programs by the early 1980s. As personal computers became faster and more companies appreciated the power of spreadsheets, new users voted overwhelmingly for Lotus 1-2-3, in part so they could share files with other users and in

Figure 7.3. *Popularity Adds Value in a Network Industry*

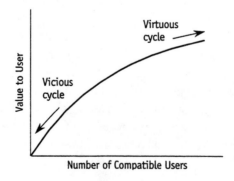

part because many users were skilled in preparing sophisticated Lotus macros. This process fed on itself in a virtuous cycle. Lotus 1-2-3 had the most users, and so attracted yet more devotees. The result was an explosion in the size of the spreadsheet market. At the same time, VisiCalc, the pioneer spreadsheet program for personal computers, was stuck in a vicious cycle of decline, suffering from the dark side of positive feedback. Unable to respond quickly by introducing a superior product, VisiCalc quickly succumbed.

Suppose your product is poised in the middle of the curve in Figure 7.3. Which way will it evolve? If consumers expect your product to become popular, a bandwagon will form, the virtuous cycle will begin, and consumers' expectations will prove correct. But if consumers expect your product to flop, your product will lack momentum, the vicious cycle will take over, and again consumers' expectations will prove correct. The beautiful if frightening implication: success and failure are driven as much by consumer expectations and luck as by the underlying value of the product. A nudge in the right direction, at the right time, can make all the difference. Marketing strategy designed to influence consumer expectations is critical in network markets. The aura of inevitability is a powerful weapon when demand-side economies of scale are strong.

> *The aura of inevitability is a powerful weapon when demand-side economies of scale are strong.*

Demand-side economies of scale are the norm in information industries. In consumer electronics, buyers are wary of products that are not yet popular, fearing they will pick a loser and be left stranded with marginally valuable equipment. Edsel buyers at least had a car they could drive, but PicturePhone customers found little use for their equipment when this technology flopped in the 1970s. As a result, many information technologies and formats get off to a slow start, then either reach critical mass and take off or fail to do so and simply flop.

We do not mean to suggest that positive feedback works so quickly, or so predictably, that winners emerge instantly and losers give up before trying. Far from it. There is no shortage of examples in which two (or more) technologies have gone head-to-head, with the outcome very much in the balance for years. Winner-take-all does not mean give-up-if-you-are-behind. Being first to market usually helps, but there are dozens of examples showing that a head start isn't necessarily decisive: think of WordStar, VisiCalc, and DR-DOS.

Nor are demand-side economies of scale so strong that the loser necessarily departs from the field of battle: WordPerfect lost the lion's share of the word processor market to Microsoft Word, but is still a player. More so than in the past, however, in the information economy the lion's share of the *rewards* will go to the winner, not the number two player who just manages to survive.

Positive feedback based on demand-side economies of scale, while far more important now than in the past, is not entirely novel. Any communications network has this feature: the more people using the network, the more valuable it is to each one of them. The early history of telephones in the United States, which we discuss in detail later in the chapter, shows how strong demand-side scale economies, along with some clever maneuvering, can lead to dominance by a single firm. In the case of telephony, AT&T emerged as the dominant telephone network in the United States during the early years of this century, fending off significant competition and establishing a monopoly over long-distance service.

Transportation networks share similar properties: the more destina-

Supply-side and demand-side economies of scale combine to make positive feedback in the network economy especially strong.

tions it can reach, the more valuable a network becomes. Hence, the more developed network tends to grow at the expense of smaller networks, especially if the smaller networks are not able to exchange traffic with the larger network, a practice generally known as *interlining* in the railroad and airline industries.

Both demand-side economies of scale and supply-side economies of scale have been around for a long time. But the combination of the two that has arisen in many information technology industries is new. The result is a "double whammy" in which growth on the demand side both reduces cost on the supply side and makes the product more attractive to other users—accelerating the growth in demand even more. The result is especially strong positive feedback, causing entire industries to be created or destroyed far more rapidly than during the industrial age.

NETWORK EXTERNALITIES

We said earlier that large networks are more attractive to users than small ones. The term that economists use to describe this effect, *network externalities,* usefully highlights two aspects of information systems that are crucial for competitive strategy.

First, focus on the word *network*. As we have suggested, it is enlightening to view information technologies in terms of *virtual networks,* which share many properties with *real networks* such as communications and transportation networks. We think of all users of Macintosh users as belonging to the "Mac network." Apple is the *sponsor* of this network. The sponsor of a network creates and manages that network, hoping to profit by building its size. Apple established the Mac network in the first place by introducing the Macintosh. Apple controls the interfaces that govern access to the network—for example, through its pricing of the Mac, by setting the licensing terms on which clones can be built, and by bringing infringement actions against unauthorized hardware vendors. And Apple is primarily responsible for making architectural improvements to the Mac.

Apple also exerts a powerful influence on the supply of products that are complementary to the Mac machine, notably software and peripheral devices, through its control over interfaces. Computer buyers are picking a network, not simply a product, when they buy a Mac, and Apple must design its strategy accordingly. Building a network involves more than just building a product: finding partners, building strategic alliances, and knowing how to get the bandwagon rolling can be every bit as important as engineering design skills.

Second, focus on one of economists' favorite words: *externalities.* Externalities arise when one market participant affects others without compensation being paid. Like feedback, externalities come in two flavors: negative and positive. The classic example of a negative externality is pollution: my sewage ruins your swimming or drinking water. Happily, *network externalities* are normally positive, not negative: when I join your network, the network is bigger and better, to your benefit.

Positive network externalities give rise to positive feedback: when I buy a fax machine, the value of your fax machine is enhanced since you can now send faxes to me and receive faxes from me. Even if you don't have a fax machine yet, you are more tempted to get one yourself since you can now use it to communicate with me.

Network externalities are what lie behind *Metcalfe's law,* named after Bob Metcalfe, the inventor of Ethernet. (Metcalfe tells us it was George Gilder who attributed this law to him, but he's willing to take credit for it.)

> **Metcalfe's law: The value of a network goes up as the square of the number of users.**

Metcalfe's law is more a rule of thumb than a law, but it does arise in a relatively natural way. If there are n people in a network, and the value of the network to each of them is proportional to the number of *other* users, then the total value of the network (to all the users) is proportional to $n \times (n - 1) = n^2 - n$. If the value of a network to a single user is $1 for each other user on the network, then a network of size 10 has a total value of roughly $100. In contrast, a network of size 100 has a total value of roughly $10,000. A tenfold increase in the size of the network leads to a hundredfold increase in its value.

COLLECTIVE SWITCHING COSTS

Network externalities make it virtually impossible for a small network to thrive. But every new network has to start from scratch. The challenge to companies seeking to introduce new but incompatible technology into the market is to build network size by overcoming the *collective switching costs*—that is, the combined switching costs of all users.

As we emphasized in Chapter 5, switching costs often stem from durable complementary assets, such as LPs and phonographs, hardware and software, or information systems and the training to use them. With network effects, one person's investment in a network is complementary to another person's similar investments, vastly expanding the number of complementary assets. When I invest by learning to write programs for the Access database language, then Access software, and investments in that language, become more valuable for you.

In many information industries, collective switching costs are the biggest single force working in favor of incumbents. Worse yet for would-be entrants and innovators, switching costs work in a nonlinear way: convincing ten people connected in a network to switch to your incompatible network is *more* than ten times as hard as getting one customer to switch. But you need all ten, or most of them: no one will want to be the first to give up the network externalities and risk being stranded. Precisely because various users find it so difficult to *coordinate* to switch to an incompatible technology, control over a large installed base of users can be the greatest asset you can have.

The layout of the typewriter keyboard offers a fascinating example of collective switching costs and the difficulties of coordinating a move to superior technology. The now-standard keyboard configuration is known as the QWERTY keyboard, since the top row starts with letters QWERTY. According to many reports, early promoters of the Type Writer brand of machine in the 1870s intentionally picked this awkward configuration to *slow down* typists and thus reduce the incidence of jamming, to which their machines were prone. This was a sensible solution to the commercial problem faced by these pioneers: to develop a machine that would reliably be faster than a copyist could write. QWERTY also allowed salesmen to impress customers by typing their brand name, Type Writer, rapidly, using keys only from the top row.

Very soon after QWERTY was introduced, however, the problem of jamming was greatly reduced through advances in typewriter design. Certainly, today, the jamming of computer keyboards is rare indeed! And sure enough, alternative keyboards developed early in the twentieth century were reputed to be superior. The Dvorak layout, patented in 1932 with a home row of AOEUIDHTNS that includes all five vowels, has long been used by speed typists. All this would suggest that QWERTY should by now have given way to more efficient keyboard layouts.

Why, then, are we all still using QWERTY keyboards? One answer is straightforward: the costs we all would bear to learn a new keyboard are simply too high to make the transition worthwhile. Some scholars assert that there is nothing more than this to the QWERTY story. Under this story, Dvorak is just not good enough to overcome the individual switching costs of learning it. Other scholars claim, however, that we would *collectively* be better off switching to the Dvorak layout (this calculation should include our children, who have yet to be trained on QWERTY), but no one is willing to lead the move to Dvorak. Under this interpretation, the collective switching costs are far higher than all of our individual switching costs, because coordination is so difficult.

Coordination costs were indeed significant in the age of the type-writer. Ask yourself this question: in buying a typewriter for your office, why pick the leading layout, QWERTY, if other layouts are more efficient? Two reasons stand out. Both are based on the fact that the typewriter keyboard *system* has two elements: the keyboard layout and the *human* component of the system, namely, the typist. First, trained typists you plan to hire already know QWERTY. Second, untrained typists you plan to hire will prefer to train on a QWERTY keyboard so as to acquire marketable skills. Human capital (training) is specific to the keyboard layout, giving rise to network effects. In a flat market consist-ing mostly of replacement sales, buyers will have a strong preference to replace old QWERTY typewriters with new ones. And in a growing market, new sales will be tilted toward the layout with the larger in-stalled base. Either way, positive feedback rules. We find these coordi-nation costs less compelling now, however. Typists who develop proficiency on the Dvorak layout can use those skills in a new job simply by reprogramming their computer keyboard. Thus, we find the ongoing persistence of the QWERTY keyboard in today's computer society at odds with the strongest claims of superiority of the Dvorak layout.

IS YOUR INDUSTRY SUBJECT TO POSITIVE FEEDBACK?

We do not want to leave the impression that *all* information infrastruc-ture markets are dominated by the forces of positive feedback. Many companies can compete by adhering to widely accepted standards. For example, many companies compete to sell telephone handsets and PBXs; they need only interconnect properly with the public switched telephone network. Likewise, while there are strong network effects in the personal computer industry, there are no significant demand-side economies of scale *within* the market for IBM-compatible personal computers. If one person has a Dell and his coworker has a Compaq, they can still exchange files, e-mail, and advice. The customer-level equipment in telephony and PC hardware has been effectively stan-dardized, so that interoperability and its accompanying network effects are no longer the problem they once were.

Another example of a high-tech industry that currently does not experience large network effects is that of Internet service providers. At one time, America Online, CompuServe, and Delphi attempted to provide proprietary systems of menus, e-mail, and discussion groups. It was clumsy, if not impossible, to send e-mail from one provider to another. In those days there were network externalities, and consumers gravitated toward those networks that offered the best connections to other consumers.

The commercialization of the Internet changed all that. The availability of standardized protocols for menus/browsers, e-mail, and chat removed the advantage of being a larger ISP and led to the creation of thousands of smaller providers. If you are on AOL, you can still exchange e-mail with your sister in Boston who is an IBM network customer.

This situation may well change in the future as new Internet technology allows providers to offer differential quality of service for applications such as video conferencing. A large ISP may gain an advantage based on the technological fact that it is easier to control quality of service for traffic that stays on a single network. Video conferencing with your sister in Boston could be a lot easier if you are both on the same network—creating a significant network externality that could well alter the structure of the ISP industry and lead to greater consolidation and concentration. A number of observers have expressed concern that the proposed acquisition of MCI by Worldcom will permit Worldcom to gain dominance by providing superior service to customers whose traffic stays entirely on Worldcom's network.

Our point is that you need to think carefully about the magnitude and significance of network externalities in your industry. Ford used to offer costly rebates and sell thousands of Tauruses to Hertz (which it owns) to gain the title of best-selling car. But was

Not every market tips.

it really worth it? Who buys a car just because other people buy it? Don't let the idea of positive feedback carry you away: not every market tips.

Will *your* market tip toward a single dominant technology or vendor? This is a critical question to ask before forging ahead with any of the basic strategies we have just described. If your market is a true winner-take-all market subject to such tipping, standardization may be critical for the market to take off at all. Plus, these same positive feedback conditions make it very risky to compete because of the dark side

Table 7.1. Likelihood of Market Tipping to a Single Technology

	Low Economies of Scale	High Economies of Scale
Low demand for variety	Unlikely	High
High demand for variety	Low	Depends

of positive feedback: a necessary implication of "winner-take-all" is "loser-gets-nothing." On the other hand, if there is room for several players in your industry, competition takes on a different tone than if there will be only one survivor in a standards war.

Whether a market tips or not depends on the balance between two fundamental forces: economies of scale and variety. See Table 7.1 for a classification.

Strong scale economies, on either the demand or the supply side of the market, will make a market tippy. But standardization typically entails a loss of variety, even if the leading technology can be implemented with a broad product line. If different users have highly distinct needs, the market is less likely to tip. In high-definition television (HDTV), different countries use different systems, both because of the legacy of earlier incompatible systems and because of the tendency to favor domestic firms over foreign ones. As a result, the worldwide market has not tipped, although each individual country has. The fact is, most network externalities in television do not cross national or regional borders: not very many people want to take a TV from the United States to Japan, so little is lost when different regions use incompatible transmission standards.

We've emphasized demand-side scale economies, but tippiness depends on the sum total of all scale economies. True, the strongest positive feedback in information industries comes on the demand side, but you should not ignore the supply side in assessing tipping. Traditional economies of scale that are specific to each technology will amplify demand-side economies of scale. So, too, will dynamic scale economies that arise based on learning-by-doing and the experience curve.

Even though we started this section by saying that there are no significant demand-side economies of scale for IBM-compatible personal computers, it doesn't follow that this market is immune from positive feedback since there may well be significant economies of scale on the *production* side of the market. Four companies, Compaq, Dell,

HP, and IBM, now control 24 percent of the market for personal computers, and some analysts expect this fraction to grow, claiming that these companies can produce desktop boxes at a smaller unit cost than their smaller competitors. This may be so, but it is important to recognize that this is just old-fashioned supply-side economies of scale; these different brands of personal computers interoperate well enough that demand-side economies of scale are not particularly important.

Information goods and information infrastructure often exhibit *both* demand-side and supply-side economies of scale. One reason Digital Equipment Corporation has had difficulty making its Alpha chip fly as an alternative to Intel chips, despite its impressive performance, is that Digital lacks the scale to drive manufacturing costs down. Digital is now hoping to overcome that obstacle by sourcing its chips from Intel and Samsung, which can operate chip fabrication facilities at far greater scale than Digital has achieved. Still, whether Digital can attract enough partners to generate positive feedback for the Alpha chip remains to be seen. The United States and Europe are currently competing to convince countries around the world to adopt their HDTV formats. Tipping may occur for HDTV not based on network effects but because of good old-fashioned economies of scale in making television sets.

We have emphasized the network nature of information technology, with many of our examples coming from the hardware side. The same effects occur on the software side. It is hard for a new virtual reality product to gain market share without people having access to a viewer for that product . . . but no one wants to buy a viewer if there is no content to view.

However, the Internet has made this chicken-and-egg problem a lot more manageable. Now you can download the viewer prior to, or even concurrently with, downloading the content. Want to read a PDF file? No problem—click over to Adobe's site and download the latest version of Acrobat. New technologies like Marimba even allow your system to upgrade its viewers over the Internet automatically. If your viewer is written in Java, you can download the viewer *along with* the content. It's like using your computer to download the fax machine along with the fax!

The Internet distribution of new applications and standards is very convenient and reduces *some* of the network externalities for software by reducing switching costs. Variety can be supported more easily if an entire system can be offered on demand. But the Internet certainly doesn't *eliminate* network externalities in software. Interoperability is still a big issue on the production side: even if users can download the appropriate virtual reality viewer, producers won't want to produce to half-a-dozen different standards. In fact, it's because of this producer resistance that Microsoft and Netscape agreed on a Virtual Reality Markup Language standard, as we discuss in Chapter 8.

IGNITING POSITIVE FEEDBACK: PERFORMANCE VERSUS COMPATIBILITY

What does it take for a new technology to succeed in the market? How can a new technology get into a virtuous cycle rather than a vicious one? Philips and Sony certainly managed it when they introduced compact disks in the early 1980s. Fifteen years later, phonographs and long-playing records (LPs) are scarce indeed; our children hardly know what they are.

How can you make network externalities work for you to launch a new product or technology? How can you overcome collective switching costs and build a new network of users? Let there be no doubt: building your own base of users for a new technology in the face of an established network can be daunting. There are plenty of failures in consumer electronics alone, not to mention more arcane areas. Indeed, Sony and Philips have had more than a little trouble duplicating their CD feat. They teamed up to introduce digital audio tape (DAT) in 1987, which offered the sound quality of CD along with the ability to record music. But DAT bombed, in part because of the delays based on concerns about copy protection.

Philips tried on its own with the digital compact cassette (DCC) in 1992. These cassettes had the advantage that DCC machines (unlike DAT machines) could play conventional cassettes, making the new technology *backward compatible*. But the sound quality of the DCC offered no big improvement over conventional CDs. Without a compelling reason to switch, consumers refused to adopt the new technology. Sony, too, had its own offering around this time, the minidisk. While minidisks are still around (especially in Japan), this product never really got on the positive feedback curve, either.

There are two basic approaches for dealing with the problem of consumer inertia: the *evolution* strategy of compatibility and the *revolu-*

Figure 7.4. *Performance versus Compatibility*

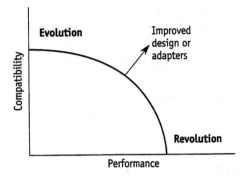

tion strategy of compelling performance. Combinations are possible, but the key is to understand these two fundamental approaches. These strategies reflect an underlying tension when the forces of innovation meet up with network externalities: is it better to wipe the slate clean and come up with the best product possible (revolution) or to give up some performance to ensure compatibility and thus ease consumer adoption (evolution)?

> *The evolution strategy offers consumers a smooth migration path. The revolution strategy offers compelling performance.*

Figure 7.4 illustrates the trade-off. You can improve performance at the cost of increasing customer switching costs, or vice-versa. An outcome of high compatibility with limited performance improvement, in the upper-left corner of the figure, characterizes the evolution approach. An outcome of little or no compatibility but sharply superior performance, in the lower-right corner of the figure, characterizes the revolution approach. Ideally, you would like to have an improved product that is also compatible with the installed base, but technology is usually not so forgiving, and adapters and emulators are notoriously buggy. You will inevitably face the trade-off in Figure 7.4.

EVOLUTION: OFFER A MIGRATION PATH

The history of color television in the United States, discussed later in the chapter, teaches us that compatibility with the installed base of equipment is often critical to the launch of a new generation of technology. The CBS color system, incompatible with existing black-and-white sets, failed despite FCC endorsement as the official standard. When compatibility is critical, consumers must be offered a smooth migration path to a new information technology. Taking little baby steps toward a new technology is a lot easier than making a gigantic leap of faith.

The evolution strategy, which offers consumers an easy migration path, centers on reducing switching costs so that consumers can gradually try your new technology. This is what Borland tried to do in copying certain commands from Lotus 1-2-3. This is what Microsoft did by including in Word extensive, specialized help for WordPerfect users, as well as making it easy to convert WordPerfect files into Word format. Offering a migration path is evolutionary in nature. This strategy can be employed on a modest scale, even by a relatively small player in the industry.

In virtual networks, the evolution strategy of offering consumers a migration path requires an ability to achieve compatibility with existing products. In real networks, the evolution strategy requires physical interconnection to existing networks. In either case, interfaces are critical. The key to the evolution strategy is to build a new network by linking it first to the old one.

One of the risks of following the evolution approach is that one of your competitors may try a revolution strategy for its product. Compromising performance to ensure backward compatibility may leave an opening for a competitor to come in with a technologically superior market. This is precisely what happened to the dBase program in 1990 when it was challenged by Paradox, FoxPro, and Access in the market for relational database software.

Intel is facing this dilemma with its Merced chip. The 32-bit architecture of Intel's recent chips has been hugely successful for Intel, but to move to a 64-bit architecture the company will have to introduce some incompatibilities—or will it? Intel claims that its forthcoming Merced chip will offer the best of both worlds, running both 32-bit and 64-bit applications. There is a lot of speculation about the Merced architecture, but Intel is keeping quiet about strategy, since it recognizes that it will be especially vulnerable during this transition.

Can you offer your customers an attractive migration path to a new technology? To lure customers, the migration path must be smooth, and it must lead somewhere. You will need to overcome two obstacles to execute this strategy: technical and legal.

Technical Obstacles

The technical obstacles you'll face have to do with the need to develop a technology that is at the same time compatible with, and yet superior to, existing products. Only in this way can you keep customers' switching costs low, by offering backward compatibility, and still offer improved performance. We'll see in our example of high-definition television how this strategy can go awry: to avoid stranding existing TV sets in the early 1990s, the Europeans promoted a standard for the transmission of high-definition signals that conventional TV sets could decipher. But they paid a high price: the signal was not as sharp as true HDTV, and the technology bombed despite strong government pressure on the satellite industry to adopt it.

Technical obstacles to the thorny compatibility/performance trade-off are not unique to upstart firms trying to supplant market leaders. Those same market leaders face these obstacles as well. Microsoft held back the performance of Windows 95 so that users could run old DOS applications. Microsoft has clearly stated that Windows 95 is a transition operating system and that its eventual goal is to move everyone to Windows NT.

One way to deal with the compatibility/performance trade-off is to offer *one-way* compatibility. When Microsoft offered Office 97 as an upgrade to Office 95, it designed the file formats used by Office 97 to be incompatible with the Office 95 formats. Word 97 could read files from Word 95, but not the other way around. With this tactic, Microsoft could introduce product improvements while making it easy for Word 97 users to import the files they had created using older versions.

This one-way compatibility created an interesting dynamic: influential early adopters had a hard time sharing files with their slower-to-adopt colleagues. Something had to give. Microsoft surely was hoping that organizations would shift *everyone* over to Office 97 to ensure full interoperability. However, Microsoft may have gone too far. When this problem became widely recognized, and potential users saw the costs of a heterogeneous environment, they began to delay deployment of Office 97. Microsoft's response was to release two free applications:

Word Viewer, for viewing Word 97 files and Word Converter, for converting Word 97 to Word 95.

Remember, your strategy with respect to selling upgrades should be to give the users a reason to upgrade and then to make the process of upgrading as easy as possible. The reason to upgrade can be a "pull" (such as desirable new features) or a "push" (such as a desire to be compatible with others). The difficulty with the push strategy is that users may decide not to upgrade at all, which is why Microsoft eventually softened its "incompatibility" strategy.

In some cases, the desire to maintain compatibility with previous generations has been the undoing of market leaders. The dBase programming language was hobbled because each new version of dBase had to be able to run programs written for all earlier versions. Over time, layers of dBase programming code accumulated on top of each other. Ashton-Tate, the maker of dBase, recognized that this resulted in awkward "bloatware," which degraded the performance of dBase. Unable to improve dBase in a timely fashion, and facing competition from Borland's more elegant, object-oriented, relational database program, Paradox, dBase's fortunes fell sharply. Ashton-Tate was slain by the dark side of positive feedback. Ultimately, Borland acquired Ashton-Tate with the idea of migrating the dBase installed base to Paradox.

We offer three strategies for helping to smooth user migration paths to new technologies:

Use creative design. Good engineering and product design can greatly ease the compatibility/performance trade-off. As shown in Figure 7.4, improved designs shift the entire trade-off between compatibility and performance favorably. Intensive effort in the early 1950s by engineers at NBC enabled them to offer a method of transmitting color television signals so that black-and-white sets could successfully receive these same signals. The breakthrough was the use of complex electronic methods that converted the three color signals (red, green, and blue) into two signals (luminance and color).

Think in terms of the system. Remember, you may be making only one component, but the user cares about the whole system. To ease the transition to digital television, the FCC is loaning broadcasters extra spectrum space so they can broadcast both conventional and HDTV digital signals, which will ease the burden of switching costs.

Consider converters and bridge technologies. HDTV is again a good example: once broadcasters cease transmitting conventional TV signals, anyone with an analog television will have to buy a converter to receive digital over-the-air broadcasts. This isn't ideal, but it still offers a migration path to the installed base of analog TV viewers.

Legal Obstacles

The second kind of obstacle you'll find as you build a migration path is legal and contractual: you need to have or obtain the legal right to sell products that are compatible with the established installed base of products. Sometimes this is not an issue: there are no legal barriers to building TV sets that can receive today's broadcast television signals. But sometimes this kind of barrier can be insurmountable. Incumbents with intellectual property rights over an older generation of technology may have the ability to unilaterally blockade a migration path. Whether they use this ability to stop rivals in their tracks, or simply to extract licensing revenues, is a basic strategy choice for these rights holders. For example, no one can sell an audio machine in the United States that will play CDs without a license from Philips and Sony, at least until their patents expire. Sony and Philips used their power over CD technology in negotiating with Time Warner, Toshiba, and others over the DVD standard. As a result, the new DVD machines will be able to read regular audio CDs; they will also incorporate technology from Sony and Philips.

REVOLUTION: OFFER COMPELLING PERFORMANCE

The revolution strategy involves brute force: offer a product so much better than what people are using that enough users will bear the pain of switching to it. Usually, this strategy works by first attracting customers who care the most about performance and working down from there to the mass market. Sony and Philips appealed first to the audiophiles, who then brought in the more casual music listeners when prices of machines and disks fell. Fax machines first made inroads in the United

States for exchanging documents with Japan, where the time and language differences made faxes especially attractive; from this base, the fax population exploded. HDTV set manufacturers are hoping to first sell to the so-called vidiots, those who simply must have the very best quality video and the largest TV sets available. The trick is to offer compelling performance to first attract pioneering and influential users, then to use this base to start up a bandwagon propelled by self-fulfilling consumer beliefs in the inevitable success of your product.

How big a performance advance must you offer to succeed? Andy Grove speaks of the "10X" rule of thumb: you need to offer performance "ten times better" than the established technology to start a revolution. We like the idea, and certainly agree that substantial improvements in performance are necessary to make the revolution strategy work. But in most applications performance cannot easily be reduced to a single measure, as implied by the 10X rule. Also, as economists, we must point out that the magnitude of switching costs enters into the calculation, too. Sega's ability to make inroads against Nintendo in the video game business in the early 1990s was aided by the presence of lots of customers with low switching costs: there is a new crop of ten-year-old boys every year who are skilled at convincing Mom and Dad that they just *have* to get the system with the coolest new games or graphics.

Likewise, a growing market offers more opportunities to establish a beachhead against an established player. New customers alone can provide critical mass. More generally, a rapidly growing market tends to enhance the attractiveness of the revolution strategy. If the market is growing rapidly, or if consumer lock-in is relatively mild, performance looms larger relative to backward compatibility.

The revolution strategy is inherently risky. It cannot work on a small scale and usually requires powerful allies. Worse yet, it is devilishly difficult to tell early on whether your technology will take off or crash and burn. Even the successful technologies start off slowly and accelerate from there, following the logistic, or S-shaped, growth pattern we noted earlier.

IGNITING POSITIVE FEEDBACK: OPENNESS VERSUS CONTROL

Anyone launching a new technology must also face a second fundamental trade-off, in addition to the performance/compatibility trade-off. Do you choose an "open" approach by offering to make the necessary interfaces and specifications available to others, or do you attempt to maintain control by keeping your system proprietary? This trade-off is closely related to our discussion of lock-in in Chapters 5 and 6.

Proprietary control will be exceedingly valuable if your product or system takes off. As we discussed in Chapter 6, an installed base is more valuable if you do not face rivals who can offer products to locked-in customers. Likewise, your network is far more valuable if you can control the ability of others to interconnect with you. Intel's market capitalization today would be far less if Intel had previously agreed to license all the intellectual property embodied in its Pentium chips to many rival chip makers.

However, failure to open up a technology can spell its demise, if consumers fear lock-in or if you face a strong rival whose system offers comparable performance but is nonproprietary. Sony faced precisely this problem with its Beta video cassette recorder system and lost out to the more open VHS system, which is now the standard. Openness will bolster your chances of success by attracting allies and assuring would-be customers that they will be able to turn to multiple suppliers down the road.

Which route is best, openness or control? The answer depends on whether you are strong enough to ignite positive feedback on your own. Strength in network markets is measured along three primary dimensions: existing market position, technical capabilities, and control of intellectual property such as patents and copyrights. In Chapter 9 we will explore more fully the key assets that determine companies' strengths in network markets.

Existing market position, technical capabilities, and control of intellectual property are critical strengths.

Of course, there is no one right choice between control and openness. Indeed, a single company might well choose control for some products and openness for others. Intel has maintained considerable control over the MMX multimedia specification for its Pentium chips. At the same time, Intel recently promoted new, open interface specifications for graphics controllers, its accelerated graphics port (AGP), so as to hasten improvements in visual computing and thus fuel demand for Intel's microprocessors. Intel picked control over MMX, but openness for AGP.

In choosing between openness and control, remember that your ultimate goal is to maximize the *value* of your technology, not your *control* over it. This is the same point we discussed in the case of intellectual property rights in Chapter 4. Ultimately, your profits will flow from the competitive advantages you can retain while assembling enough support to get your technology off the ground.

Think of your reward using this formula:

Your reward = Total value added to industry
× your share of industry value

The total value added to the industry depends first on the inherent value of the technology—what improvement it offers over existing alternatives. But when network effects are strong, total value also depends on how widely the technology is adopted—that is, the network size. Your share of the value added depends on your ultimate market share, your profit margin, any royalty payments you make or receive, and the effects the new technology has on your sales of other products. Does it cannibalize or stimulate them?

Roughly speaking, strategies to achieve openness emphasize the first term in this formula, the *total value added to the industry*. Strategies to achieve control emphasize the second term, *your share of industry value*. We will focus on openness strategies in Chapter 8 and on control strategies in Chapter 9.

The fundamental trade-off between openness and control is shown in Figure 7.5: you can have a large share of a small market (the upper-left portion of the diagram), or a small share of a large market (the

Figure 7.5. *Openness versus Control*

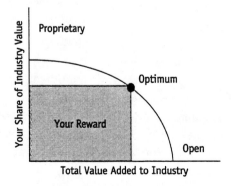

lower-right portion of the diagram). Unless you have made a real technical breakthrough or are extremely lucky, it is almost impossible to have it both ways. At the optimum, you choose the approach that maximizes your reward—that is, the total value you receive.

This trade-off is fundamental in network markets. To maximize the value of your new technology, you will likely need to share that value with other players in the industry. This comes back to the point we have made repeatedly: information technology is comprised of *systems*, and an increase in the value of one component necessarily spills over to other components. Capturing the value from improvements to one component typically requires the cooperation of those providing other components. Count on the best of those suppliers to insist on getting a share of the rewards as a condition for their cooperation.

Unless you are in a truly dominant position at the outset, trying to control the technology yourself can leave you a large share of a tiny pie. Opening up the technology freely can fuel positive feedback and maximize the total value added of the technology. But what share of the benefits will you be able to preserve for yourself? Sometimes even leading firms conclude that they would rather grow the market quickly, through openness, than maintain control. Adobe did this with its Post-Script language, and Sun followed its example with Java.

The boundary between openness and control is not sharp; intermediate approaches are frequently used. For example, a company pursuing an openness strategy can still retain exclusive control over *changes* to the technology, as Sun is attempting to do with Java. Likewise, a company pursuing a control strategy can still offer access to its network for a price, as Nintendo did by charging royalties to game developers who were writing games for its Nintendo Entertainment System.

Openness

The openness strategy is critical when no one firm is strong enough to dictate technology standards. Openness also arises naturally when multiple products must work together, making coordination in product design essential.

Openness is a more cautious strategy than control. The underlying idea is to forsake control over the technology to get the bandwagon rolling. If the new technology draws on contributions from several different companies, each agrees to cede control over its piece in order to create an attractive package: the whole is greater than the sum of the parts.

The term *openness* means many things to many people. The Unix X/Open consortium defines *open systems* as "systems and software environments based on standards which are vendor independent and commonly available."

As we emphasized in our discussion of lock-in, beware vague promises of openness. Openness may be in the eye of the beholder. Netscape insists that it is congenitally open, but some observers detect efforts by Netscape to keep control. Cisco is often lauded for using open Internet standards for its routers and switches, but, again, some see a deep proprietary streak there, too.

Openness involves more than technical specifications; timing is also important. Microsoft has been accused of keeping secret certain application programming interfaces (APIs), in violation of its earlier promises that Windows would be open. Even harder to assess, independent software vendors (ISVs) have at times been very concerned that Microsoft provides APIs for new versions of Windows to its in-house development team before giving them to the ISVs. To some extent this seems inevitable as part of improving the operating system and making sure it will work smoothly with new applications. On the other hand, ISVs are justifiably unhappy when placed at a competitive disadvantage relative to Microsoft's own programmers, especially since they already face the threat of having their program's functionality subsumed into the operating system itself.

Within the openness category, we can fruitfully distinguish between a *full openness* strategy and an *alliance* strategy for establishing new product standards. We study full openness and alliance strategies in Chapter 8 in the context of standards negotiations.

Under full openness, anybody has the right to make products complying with the standard, whether they contributed to its development or not. Under an alliance approach, each member of the alliance contributes something toward the standard, and, in exchange, each is allowed to make products complying with the standard. Nonmembers can be blocked from offering such products or charged for the right to do so. In other words, the alliance members all have guaranteed (usually free) access to the network they have created, but outsiders may be blocked from accessing it or required to pay a special fee for such access.

In some industries with strong network characteristics, full openness is the only feasible approach. For years, basic telecommunications standards have been hammered out by official standard-setting bodies, either domestically or internationally. The standard-setting process at the International Telecommunications Union (ITU), for example, has led to hundreds of standards, including those for fax machines and modems. The ITU, like other formal standard-setting bodies, insists, as a quid pro quo for endorsement of a standard, that no single firm or group of firms maintains proprietary control over the standard. We will discuss tactics in formal standard setting in detail in Chapter 8.

The full openness strategy is not confined to formal standard setting, however. Whatever the institutional setting, full openness is a natural way of overcoming a stalemate in which no single firm is in a position to drive home its preferred standard without widespread support.

One way to pursue a full openness strategy is to place the technology in the hands of a neutral third party. Even this approach can be plagued with difficulties, however. Is the third party really neutral, or just a cover operation for the company contributing the technology? Doubts have arisen, for example, over whether Microsoft has *really* ceded control of ActiveX. We'll address ActiveX more fully in the next chapter.

In the end, it's worth asking who really wants openness and how everyone's interests are likely to evolve as the installed base grows or competition shifts. Usually, the upstart wants openness to neutralize installed-base disadvantages or to help assemble allies. In the Internet arena, where Microsoft was a latecomer, it initially pushed for open standards. Open Internet standards, at least initially, shift competition to marketing, brand name, and distribution, where Microsoft is strong. In desktop applications, where Microsoft is the dominant player, the company has not pushed for open standards and, it is claimed, has actively resisted them.

Build alliances to ignite positive feedback in the network economy.

Alliances are increasingly commonplace in the information economy. We do not mean those so-called strategic alliances involving widespread cooperation between a pair of companies. Rather, we mean an alliance formed by a group of companies for the express purpose of promoting a specific technology or standard. Alliances typically involve extensive wheeling and dealing, as multiple players negotiate based on the three key assets: control of the existing installed base, technical superiority, and intellectual property rights.

The widely heralded convergence between the computer and telecommunications industry offers many opportunities for alliances. Recently, for example, Compaq, Intel, and Microsoft announced a consortium for setting standards for digital subscriber line (DSL) technology, which promises to offer high-speed access to the Internet over residential phone lines. These three superstars of the information industry have partnered with seven of the eight regional Bell operating companies to promote unified hardware and software interfaces

Alliances come in many forms, depending on the assets that the different players bring to the table. Some of them operate as "special interest groups" (SIGs) or "task forces," groups of independent companies that meet to coordinate product standards, interfaces, protocols, and specifications. Cross-licensing of critical patents is common in this context, as is sharing of confidential design information under nondisclosure agreements. Some players hope to achieve royalty income and negotiate royalty arrangements that will attract critical allies. Others hope to gain from manufacturing skills or time-to-market prowess, so long as they are not blocked by patents or excessive royalty payments.

Alliances span the distance between full openness and control. At one end of the spectrum is an alliance that makes the technology freely available to all participants, but not (necessarily) to outsiders. Automatic teller machine networks and credit card networks work this way. For example, Visa and MasterCard both require merchant banks to make payments to card-issuing banks in the form of "interchange fees" as a means of covering the costs and risks borne by card-issuing banks, but the Visa and MasterCard associations themselves impose only modest fees on transactions to cover their own costs. And membership in Visa and MasterCard is generally open to any bank, so long as that bank does not issue rival cards, such as the Discover card.

At the other end of the spectrum is an alliance built like a web around a sponsor, a central actor that collects royalties from others, preserves proprietary rights over a key component of the network, and/or maintains control over the evolution of the technology. We described how Apple is the sponsor of the Macintosh network. Likewise, Sun is the sponsor of Java. If the sponsor charges significant royalties or retains exclusive rights to control the evolution of the technology, we would classify that situation as one of control, not openness. Sun is walking a thin line, wanting to retain its partners in the battle with Microsoft but also wanting to generate revenues from its substantial investment in Java.

Control

Only those in the strongest position can hope to exert strong control over newly introduced information technologies. Usually these are market leaders: AT&T was a prime example in its day; Microsoft, Intel, TCI, and Visa are examples today. In rare cases, strength flows from sheer technical superiority: at one time or another, Apple, Nintendo, Sony, Philips, and Qualcomm have all been in this privileged position.

Companies strong enough to unilaterally control product standards and interfaces have power. Even if they are not being challenged for supremacy, however, they have much to lose by promoting poorly conceived standards. For example, Microsoft is not about to lose its leadership position in desktop operating systems, even if it slips up when designing new APIs between its operating system and applications or makes some design errors in its next release of Windows. But this is not to say that Microsoft can be reckless or careless in this design process: Microsoft still needs to attract independent software developers to its platform, it still has powerful incentives to improve Windows to drive upgrade sales and reach new users, and it wants the overall Windows "system" to improve to make further inroads against Unix-based workstations.

GENERIC STRATEGIES IN NETWORK MARKETS

We are now ready to introduce the four generic strategies for companies seeking to introduce new information technology into the marketplace. These four strategies for igniting positive feedback follow logically from the two basic trade-offs discussed in the previous sections: (1) the trade-off between performance and compatibility as reflected in the choice between revolution and evolution and (2) the trade-off between openness and control. The combination of each of these two trade-offs yields the four generic strategies shown in Table 7.2.

The first row in Table 7.2 represents the choice of compatibility, the

Table 7.2. Generic Network Strategies

	Control	Openness
Compatibility	Controlled migration	Open migration
Performance	Performance play	Discontinuity

evolution strategy. The second row represents the choice to accept incompatibility in order to maximize performance, the revolution strategy. Either of these approaches can be combined with openness or control. The left-hand column in Table 7.2 represents the decision to retain proprietary control, the right-hand column the decision to open up the technology to others.

The four generic network strategies that emerge from this analysis can be found in Table 7.2: performance play, controlled migration, open migration, and discontinuity. In the next few pages, we describe the four strategies, say a bit about their pros and cons, and give examples of companies that have pursued them. We offer a more in-depth discussion of how the generic strategies work and when to use them in Chapters 8 and 9.

These four generic strategies arise again and again. The players and the context change, but not these four strategies. Incumbents may find it easier to achieve backward compatibility, but entrants and incumbents alike must choose one of our generic strategies. In some markets, a single firm or coalition is pursuing one of the generic strategies. In other cases, two incompatible technologies are engaged in a battle to build their own new networks. In these standards wars, which we explore in Chapter 9, the very nature of the battle depends on the pair of generic strategies employed by the combatants.

Performance Play

Performance play is the boldest and riskiest of the four generic strategies. A performance play involves the introduction of a new, incompatible technology over which the vendor retains strong proprietary control. Nintendo followed this approach when it introduced its Nintendo Entertainment System in the mid-1980s. More recently, U.S. Robotics used the performance play with its Palm Pilot device. Iomega did likewise in launching its Zip drive.

Performance play makes the most sense if your advantage is primarily based on the development of a striking new technology that offers users substantial advantages over existing technology. Performance play is especially attractive to firms that are outsiders, with no installed base to worry about. Entrants and upstarts with compelling new technology can more easily afford to ignore backward compatibility and push for an entirely new technology than could an established player who would have to worry about cannibalizing sales of existing products or stranding loyal customers.

Even if you are a new entrant to the market with "way cool" technology, you may need to consider sacrificing some performance so as to design your system to reduce consumer switching costs; this is the controlled migration strategy. You also need to assess your strength and assemble allies as needed. For example, you might agree to license your key patents for small or nominal royalties to help ignite positive feedback. The more allies you need, the more open you make your system, the closer you are to the discontinuity strategy than the performance play.

Controlled Migration

In controlled migration, consumers are offered a new and improved technology that is compatible with their existing technology, but is proprietary. Windows 98 and the Intel Pentium II chip are examples of this strategy. Upgrades and updates of software programs, like the annual release of TurboTax by Intuit, tend to fit into this category as well. Such upgrades are offered by a single vendor, they can read data files and programming created for earlier versions, and they rely on many of the same skills that users developed for earlier versions.

If you have secure domination in your market, you can introduce the new technology as a premium version of the old technology, selling it first to those who find the improvements most valuable. Thus, controlled migration often is a dynamic form of the versioning strategy described in Chapter 3. Controlled migration has the further advantage of making it harder for an upstart to leapfrog ahead of you with a performance play.

504

Open Migration

Open migration is very friendly to consumers: the new product is supplied by many vendors and requires little by way of switching costs. Multiple generations of modems and fax machines have followed the open migration model. Each new generation conforms to an agreed-upon standard and communicates smoothly with earlier generations of machines.

Open migration makes the most sense if your advantage is primarily based on manufacturing capabilities. In that case, you will benefit from a larger total market and an agreed-upon set of specifications, which will allow your manufacturing skills and scale economies to shine. Owing to its fine engineering and skill in manufacturing, Hewlett-Packard has commonly adopted this strategy.

Discontinuity

Discontinuity refers to the situation in which a new product or technology is incompatible with existing technology but is available from multiple suppliers. The introduction of the CD audio system and the 3½″ floppy disk are examples of discontinuity. Like open migration, discontinuity favors suppliers that are efficient manufacturers (in the case of hardware) or that are best placed to provide value-added services or software enhancements (in the case of software).

HISTORICAL EXAMPLES OF POSITIVE FEEDBACK

The best way to get a feel for these strategies is to see them in action. In practice, the revolution versus evolution choice emerges in the design of new product standards and negotiation over those standards. The openness versus control choice arises when industry leaders set the terms on which their networks interconnect.

Fortunately, positive feedback and network externalities have been around for a while, so history can be our guide. As we have stressed, while information technology is hurtling forward at breathtaking speeds, the underlying economic principles are not all that novel. Even in this consummately high-tech area of standards, networks, interfaces, and compatibility, there is much to learn from history.

The case studies that follow illustrate the generic strategies and foreshadow some of the key strategic points we will develop in the next two chapters. All of our examples illustrate positive feedback in action: the triumph of one technology over others, in some cases by virtue of a modest head start or a fleeting performance advantage. One of the great attractions of historical examples is that we can see what happened after the dust finally settles, giving us some needed perspective in analyzing current battles.

When you stop to think about it, compatibility and standards have been an issue for as long as human beings have used spoken language or, more to the point, multiple languages. The Tower of Babel reminds us that standardization is hard. You don't hear Esperanto spoken very much (though its promoters do have a site on the Web). English has done remarkably well as an international language for scientific and technical purposes and is being given an extra boost by the Internet, but language barriers have hardly been eliminated.

Turning from biblical to merely historical times, Eli Whitney amazed President John Adams in 1798 by disassembling a dozen muskets, scrambling the parts, and then reassembling them in working order. As a result, Whitney received a government contract for $134,000 to produce 10,000 army muskets using his "uniformity system." This standardization of parts allowed for mass production and ushered in the American industrial revolution.

A humorous standards battle of sorts was triggered by the invention of the telephone. The early telephone links involved a continuously open line between two parties. Since the phone did not ring, how was the calling party to get the attention of those on the other end of the line? Thomas Edison consciously invented a brand-new word designed to capture the attention of those on the other end: "Hello!" This was a variant of the English "Hallow!" but reengineered by Edison to make it more effective. Edison, who was hard of hearing, estimated that a spoken "Hello!" could be heard ten to twenty feet away.

Soon thereafter, when telephones were equipped with bells to announce incoming calls, the more pressing issue was how to *answer* the telephone. This was a touchy issue; in the 1870s it was considered impolite to speak to anyone else unless you had been introduced! In 1878, when Edison opened the first public telephone exchange (in New Haven, Connecticut, on January 28, 1878), his operating manuals promoted "Hello!" as the proper way to answer the phone. ("What is wanted?" was noted as a more cautious alternative.) At the same time, Alexander Graham Bell, the inventor of the telephone, proclaimed that "Ahoy!" was the correct way to answer the telephone. By 1880, "Hello" had won this standards battle. This is an early example of how control over distribution channels, which Edison had through his manuals, can lead to control over interface standards.

Railroad Gauges

A more instructive example of standards battles involves the history of railroad gauges in the United States during the nineteenth century.

As railroads began to be built in the early nineteenth century, tracks of varying widths (gauges) were employed. Somewhat arbitrary early choices had major, lasting impacts. One of the first railroads in the South, for example, the South Carolina, picked 5-foot gauge tracks. Over time, other railroads all over the South followed suit. In the North, by contrast, the "standard" gauge of 4'8½", popular in England for mining, was common. Evidently, this was about the width of cart track in Roman times, being the most efficient width of a loaded vehicle that could be pulled by a flesh-and-blood (not iron) horse. The persistence of the 4'8½" gauge, which now is standard in the United States, is a good reminder that inertia is a powerful and durable force when standards are involved and that seemingly insignificant historical events can lead to lasting technological lock-in.

By 1860, seven different gauges were in use in America. Just over half of the total mileage was of the 4'8½" standard. The next most popular was the 5-foot gauge concentrated in the South. As things turned out, having different gauges was advantageous to the South, since the North could not easily use railroads to move its troops to battle in southern territory during the Civil War. Noting this example, the Finns were careful to ensure that their railroads used a gauge different from the Russian railroads! The rest of Europe adopted a standard gauge, which made things easy for Hitler during World War II: a significant fraction of German troop movements in Europe were accomplished by rail.

Despite these examples, standards are generally socially beneficial, since they allow for easy "interconnection" and thus larger networks.

But private interests can diverge from social interests. Battles over which standard to set, or whether there should be a standard at all, are common. Such battles can be severe, if not bloody, when there are entrenched users on both sides with high switching costs, when it is difficult for the various users to coordinate, and when some industry participants have much to lose from standardization. Railroad gauge standardization faced three major obstacles: (1) it was costly to change the width of existing tracks, (2) each group wanted the others to make the move, and (3) workers whose livelihoods depended on the incompatibilities resisted the proposed changes. In 1853 in Erie, Pennsylvania, where three different widths of railroad track met, there were riots over plans to standardize: workers were fearful of losing their jobs associated with loading and unloading cargo and jacking up cars to change their wheels.

Nonetheless, standardization was gradually achieved between 1860 and 1890. How? The westward expansion provided part of the answer. The big eastern railroads wanted to move western grain to the East and pushed for new lines to the West to be at standard gauge. Since the majority of the eastbound traffic terminated on their lines, they got their way. The Civil War played a role, too. The Union had pressing needs for efficient east-west transportation, giving further impetus for new western lines to be built at standard gauge. The Civil War and westward expansion interacted as well. In 1862, Congress specified the standard gauge for the transcontinental railroads. By this date, the southern states had seceded, leaving no one to push for the 5-foot gauge. After the war, the southern railroads found themselves increasingly in the minority. For the next twenty years, they relied on various imperfect means of interconnection with the North and West: cars with a sliding wheel base, hoists to lift cars from one wheel base to another, and, most commonly, a third rail.

Southern railroad interests finally met and adopted the standard gauge in 1886. On two days during the spring of 1886, the gauges were changed, converting the 5-foot gauge into the now-standard 4'8½" gauge on more than 11,000 miles of track in the South to match the northern standard. A belated victory for the North!

Many of the lessons from this experience remain relevant today.

- Incompatibilities can arise almost by accident, yet persist for many years.

- Network markets tend to tip toward the leading player, unless the other players coordinate to act quickly and decisively.

- Seceding from the standard-setting process can leave you in a weak market position in the future.

- A large buyer (such as the U.S. government) can have more influence than suppliers in tipping the balance.

- Those left with the less popular technology will find a way to cut their losses, either by employing adapters or by writing off existing assets and joining the bandwagon.

We will see these themes over and over again in current-day standards battles.

Battle of the Systems: AC versus DC Power

Another classic nineteenth-century standards battle concerned the distribution of electricity. Thomas Edison promoted a direct current (DC) system of electrical power generation and distribution. Edison was the pioneer in building power systems, beginning in New York City in 1882. Edison's direct current system was challenged by the alternating current (AC) technology developed and deployed in the United States by George Westinghouse. The key to the commercialization of AC was the development of the transformer, which permitted power to be transmitted efficiently at high voltages and then stepped down to lower voltages for local distribution and use. The AC technology permitted the distribution of electricity over far greater distances than did DC.

Thus was joined the "Battle of the Systems." Each technology had pros and cons. Direct current had, for practical purposes relating to voltage drop, a one-mile limit between the generating station and the user, but it was more efficient at generating power. Direct current also had two significant commercial advantages: a head start and Edison's imprimatur.

Unlike railroads, however, electricity was not in great need of standardization. Indeed, the two technologies initially did not compete directly but were deployed in regions suited to their relative strengths. DC was most attractive in densely populated urban areas, while AC made inroads in small towns.

Nonetheless, a battle royal ensued in the 1887–1892 period, a struggle that was by no means confined to competition in the marketplace but rather to the courtroom, the political arena, public relations, and academia. We can learn much today from the tactics followed by the rival camps.

The Edison group moved first with infringement actions against the Westinghouse forces, which forced Westinghouse to invent around Edison patents, including patents involving the Edison lamp. Edison also went to great lengths to convince the public that the AC system was unsafe, going so far as to patent the electric chair. Edison first demonstrated the electric chair using alternating current to electrocute a large dog, and then persuaded the State of New York to execute condemned criminals "by administration of an alternating current." The Edison group even used the term "to Westinghouse" to refer to electrocution by alternating current. But electrocution was not the "killer app" of the power industry: lighting was what people wanted.

Ultimately, three factors ended the Battle of the Systems. First and foremost, advances in polyphase AC made it increasingly clear that AC was the superior alternative. Second, the rotary converter introduced in 1892 allowed existing DC stations to be integrated into AC systems, facilitating a graceful retreat for DC. Third, by 1890 Edison had sold his interests, leading to the formation of the General Electric Company in 1892, which was no longer a DC-only manufacturing entity. In this context, Edison's efforts can be seen as an attempt to prevent or delay tipping toward AC, perhaps to obtain the most money in selling his DC interests. By 1893, both General Electric and Westinghouse were offering AC systems and the battle was over.

All of the tactics found in this historical episode are regularly used today. True, few high-tech companies rely on death row to gain competitive advantage, but they frequently attempt to influence consumer expectations. In network markets, expectations are crucial and can easily be self-fulfilling: the product or technology expected to prevail *does* prevail. Keep this in mind when we discuss the recent standards battle over 56k modems in Chapter 9.

The battle between Edison and Westinghouse illustrates other important points:

- Technologies can seek well-suited niches if the forces toward standardization are not overwhelming.

- Ongoing innovation (here, polyphase AC) can lead to victory in a standards war.

- A first-mover advantage (of DC) can be overcome by a superior technology (of AC) if the performance advantage is sufficient and users are not overly entrenched.

- Adapters can be the salvation of the losing technology and can help to ultimately defuse a standards war.

Telephone Networks and Interconnection

The story of how "Hello!" triumphed over "Ahoy!" is amusing but not very important. However, many quite serious compatibility and inter-connection issues arose in the early days of our telephone system. With the Internet emerging as a new form of network, and with the Telecom-munications Act of 1996 mandating that telephone companies open up their networks to competition, we have much to learn from the early days of telephone competition and interconnection.

The story begins in the mid-1890s, when several key Bell patents expired and the country emerged from a depression, causing inde-pendent (non-Bell) companies to proliferate. By 1903, Bell companies controlled less than half of the phones in America. Independents and rural cooperatives had the majority. In fact, more than half of incorpo-rated towns and cities had more than one service. Perhaps by 2003 we can achieve this level of competition again!

There was no obvious reason at that time why these many inde-pendent phone companies could not thrive in the twentieth century. Sure, head-to-head competition in a given locale might be ruinous, given the high fixed costs and low marginal costs associated with the telephone network. Traditional economies of scale would thus suggest consolidation at the local level. But what forces and strategies led to the emergence of a dominant *national* telephone company, the Bell Sys-tem?

Oddly enough, the key was long-distance telephone service. We say "oddly" because long-distance service did not appear to be a decisive competitive advantage at the turn of the century. In 1900, a mere 3 percent of all calls were long distance. Evidently, most people did not care much about long-distance service, and many telephone companies did not even offer long-distance service; they made their money on short-distance toll service. Furthermore, long-distance capability was a technical problem of some magnitude.

But the handwriting was on the wall. Local phone companies were finding it very profitable to combine adjacent towns and extend their reach. And some businesses, especially in urban areas, were willing to pay a great deal for long-distance service.

The Bell System, with by far the most extensive long-distance network, thus faced a fundamental strategic issue: would it be better to restrict long-distance access to its affiliates or to open up its network to independents? At first, Bell allowed only its affiliates to have access to its long-distance network. After 1900, with the proliferation of independents, Bell hit upon the winning strategy: open up to *nonaffiliated* companies that met Bell's technical and operating standards and that were not direct local competitors. This strategy stimulated traffic throughout the Bell network, enhanced the value of Bell service by increasing the number of parties that could be reached, and made Bell stronger versus the independents where Bell faced local competition.

Soon, the Bell System's advantage based on its long-distance network reversed the tide of competition. The peak percentage of total telephones controlled by nonconnecting independent telephone companies, some 41 percent, was achieved in the year Bell implemented the loading coil in the system, which greatly enhanced its long-distance capabilities. Bell was able to charge more than rival independents for its local service but also remain attractive because of its ability to connect long-distance calls. The independents tried but failed to establish a national alternative to the Bell System, in part because Bell controlled key cities.

Over time, these advantages allowed the Bell System to grow into the dominant local and long-distance carrier that it remained, under the corporate name of AT&T, until its breakup in 1984. AT&T denied local rivals access to its long-distance network, arguing that interconnection with independents with inferior standards (driven by competition) could compromise the integrity of its entire network. More generally, AT&T pushed for a natural monopoly model for the telephone system. After 1907, AT&T bought out many of its local competitors, which presumably had been weakened by these tactics. AT&T's acquisitions were accepted to support universal service, at the expense of competition.

Many of today's companies face interconnection issues not unlike those facing AT&T a hundred years ago. Just as independent telephone companies complained then about their inability to offer long-distance service, independent software vendors today fear that Microsoft will provide its own programmers interface information that is superior (in quality or timing) to what they are provided. The economic lesson is timeless: if you control a key interface or bottleneck, you should open it up, but on your own terms and conditions. These include technical conditions necessary to preserve the integrity of your product and economic terms that compensate you for any foregone business. The early Bell System story also illustrates how control of certain key customers (for example, New York and Chicago) can be parlayed into a dominant market position in the presence of network effects.

Color Television

Our next historical example is considerably more recent: the adoption of color television in the United States. Television is perhaps the biggest bandwagon of them all. Some 99 percent of American homes have at least one television, making TV sets more ubiquitous than telephones or flush toilets.

The color television technology used in the United States is known as the National Television Systems Committee (NTSC) system. (Critics insist that NTSC really means "Never Twice the Same Color.") This system was formally adopted by the Federal Communications Commission in 1953. The story of this adoption is a sobering example of formal standard setting gone awry.

We begin our story with the inauguration of commercial black-and-white television transmission in the United States on July 1, 1941. At that time, RCA, the owner of NBC and a leading manufacturer of black-and-white sets, was a powerful force in the radio and television world. But the future of television was clearly to be color, which had first been demonstrated in America by Bell Labs in 1929.

Throughout the 1940s, CBS, the leading television network, was pushing for the adoption of the mechanical color television system it was developing. During this time RCA was busy selling black-and-white sets, improving its technology, and, under the legendary leadership of David Sarnoff, working on its own all-electronic color television system. As the CBS system took the lead in performance, RCA urged the FCC to wait for an electronic system. A major obstacle for the CBS system was that it was not backward-compatible: color sets of the CBS type would not be able to receive existing black-and-white broadcasts without a special attachment.

Despite this drawback, the FCC adopted the CBS system in October 1950, after a test between the two color systems. The RCA system was just not ready. As David Sarnoff himself said: "The monkeys were green, the bananas were blue, and everyone had a good laugh." This was a political triumph of major proportions for CBS.

The market outcome was another story. RCA and Sarnoff refused to throw in the towel. To the contrary, they redoubled their efforts, on three fronts. First, RCA continued to criticize the CBS system. Second, RCA intensified its efforts to place black-and-white sets and thus build up an installed base of users whose equipment would be incompatible with the CBS technology. "Every set we get out there makes it that much tougher on CBS," said Sarnoff at the time. Third, Sarnoff intensified RCA's research and development on its color television system, with around-the-clock teams working in the lab. The resulting technology literally was done with mirrors.

CBS was poorly placed to take advantage of its political victory. To begin with, CBS had no manufacturing capability at the time and had not readied a manufacturing ally to move promptly into production. Following the FCC decision, CBS did purchase a TV set maker, Air King, but it would be a few years before Air King could economically manufacture color sets in commercial quantities. As a result, the official premier of CBS color broadcasting, on June 25, 1951, featuring Ed Sullivan, among others, was largely invisible, seen only at special studio parties. There were about 12 million TV sets in America at the time, but only a few dozen could receive CBS color.

Luck, of a sort, entered into the picture, too. With the onset of the Korean War, the U.S. government said that the materials needed for production of color sets were critical instead for the war effort and ordered a suspension of the manufacture of color sets. Both CBS and RCA were secretly pleased. CBS was unable to make sets anyhow. RCA was happy to delay the sales of color sets that would compete with its own black-and-white sets, welcomed the time to further advance its own technology, and was delighted to have time to further build an installed base of black-and-white sets incompatible with the CBS color system.

By the time the ban was modified in June 1952, the RCA system was ready for prime time. A consensus in support of the RCA system had formed at the NTSC. This became known as the NTSC system, despite the fact that RCA owned most of the hundreds of patents controlling it. This relabeling was a face-saving device for the FCC, which could be seen to be following the industry consortium rather than RCA. In March 1953, Frank Stanton, the president of CBS, raised the white flag, noting that with 23 million black-and-white sets in place in American homes, compatibility was rather important. In December 1953, the FCC officially reversed its 1950 decision.

But, yet again, political victory did not lead so easily to success in the market. In 1954, Sarnoff predicted that RCA would sell 75,000 sets. In fact, only 5,000 sets were purchased, perhaps because few customers were willing to pay $1,000 for the 12½″ color set rather than $300 for a 21-inch black-and-white set. With hindsight, this does not seem surprising, especially since color sets would offer little added value until broadcasters invested in color capability and color programming became widespread. All this takes time. The chicken-and-egg problem had to be settled before the NBC peacock could prevail.

As it turned out, NBC and CBS affiliates invested in color transmission equipment quite quickly: 106 of 158 stations in the top forty cities had the ability to transmit color programs by 1957. But this was of little import to viewers, since the networks were far slower in offering color programming. By 1965, NBC offered 4,000 hours of color, but CBS still showed only 800 color hours, and ABC 600. The upshot: by 1963, only about 3 percent of TV households had color sets, which remained three to five times as expensive as black-and-white sets.

As brilliant as Sarnoff and RCA had been in getting their technology established as the standard, they, like CBS, were unable to put into place all the necessary components of the system to obtain profitability during the 1950s. As a result, by 1959, RCA had spent $130 million to develop color TV with no profit to show for it. The missing pieces were the creation and distribution of the programming itself: content. Then, as now, a killer app was needed to get households to invest in color television sets. The killer app of 1960 was *Walt Disney's Wonderful World of Color,* which Sarnoff obtained from ABC in 1960. RCA's first operating profit from color television sales came in 1960, and RCA started selling picture tubes to Zenith and others. The rest is history: color sets got better and cheaper, and the NBC peacock became famous.

We can all learn a great deal from this episode, ancient though it is by Internet time. First and foremost, adoption of a new technology can be painfully slow if the price/performance ratio is unattractive and if it requires adoption by a number of different players. For color TV to truly offer value to viewers, it was not enough to get set manufacturers and networks to agree on a standard; they had to produce sets that performed well at reasonable cost, they had to create compelling content, and they had to induce broadcasters to invest in transmission gear. The technology was just not ready for the mass market in 1953, much less 1950. Interestingly, the Europeans, by waiting another decade before the adoption of PAL and SECAM, ended up with a better system. The same leapfrogging is now taking place in reverse: the digital HDTV system being adopted in the United States is superior to the system selected years before by the Japanese, as we explain in the next section.

Second, the collapse of the CBS standard shows that first-mover advantages need not be decisive, even in markets strongly subject to tipping. Since the CBS technology circa 1950 was not backward-compatible, market tested, or ready for commercialization, it never really got started. In the presence of a committed rival that would just not quit, the game was far from over after the 1950 FCC vote.

Third, the color television experience highlights the importance of building alliances. CBS had the political allies necessary to obtain FCC approval for its system in 1950, but this was a phyrric victory since CBS lacked the manufacturing capability, or a suitable ally, to start to pump out sets in commercial volumes. Then as now, winners must take greater risks, building the manufacturing capacity and even the hardware before a formal standard is set. Indeed, as we discuss later, flooding the market with equipment built to your own specs can be a way of tipping the standard-setting process in your favor. But this is not a strategy for the timid.

Fourth, the color TV example shows the dangers of sitting back and assuming that you can maintain market dominance just because you control the current generation of technology or have a large installed base. Sarnoff, visionary though he was, was naturally tempted to milk the cash cow of RCA's black-and-white business rather than rush forward with the introduction of color television. The FCC's adoption of the CBS color technology in 1950 was a wake-up call. Sarnoff was then able to snatch victory from the jaws of defeat only by taking risks and redoubling his efforts. In the end, CBS played a vital role in spurring RCA forward with the development of its color system.

High-Definition Television

Our last extended example is high-definition television, now sometimes referred to as digital television. The HDTV story is of course far more recent than our other examples. Still, plans to adopt HDTV in the United States have been unfolding for more than a decade, HDTV is the successor to the NTSC color television standard just discussed, and the HDTV experience bolsters our theme: the technology changes, as does the cast of characters, but not the underlying economics.

HDTV—when it finally arrives—will be a major improvement over today's broadcast television. HDTV proponents claim it offers picture quality equivalent to 35 millimeter film, with roughly twice the resolution of the NTSC standard, not to mention six-channel digital surround-sound. You may wonder then why a decade after the FCC established the Advisory Committee on Advanced Television Service to study HDTV standards, HDTV has yet to be launched in the United States.

Not only has HDTV been touted as the future of television. HDTV has also been held out as critical to the health of America's consumer electronics industry. Back in the late 1980s and early 1990s, one observer after another proclaimed that American industrial strength would be in peril if we were to "lose" the HDTV battle against the Japanese and the Europeans. These pundits noted, accurately, that the United States imports the vast majority of its TV sets and that it has been the slowest of the three regions to put into place a set of standards for HDTV.

In this context, calls for the federal government to take an active role in promoting HDTV grew sharper and more urgent. How, it was asked, could the "market" be relied on to coordinate the introduction of HDTV production equipment, HDTV programming, HDTV transmission systems, and HDTV receivers? Stay tuned.

Back in the 1970s, the Japanese government coordinated and subsidized the development of the various technologies needed to make HDTV work. The Japanese public broadcasting company, NHK, began experimental transmissions using its analog "Muse" system back in 1979. Japanese firms and the government spent as much as $1.3 billion to develop their HDTV technology. In 1986, the United States backed the

Japanese system as a global standard, an outcome that was only thwarted by European protectionism. By 1991, NHK was broadcasting eight hours per day. But sets remained extremely expensive, and the advantages of HDTV were evident only on the largest sets (36 inches and up).

An interesting episode in February 1994 shows how fragile standards bandwagons can be. A senior official in the Ministry of Posts and Telecommunications (MPT) stated that the Japanese government was considering abandoning the (analog) Muse system because "the world trend is digital." In a stunning demonstration of the importance of expectations and consumer confidence in standards battles, this statement alone threw the market into a turmoil. An executive at Matsushita remarked, "This is like pouring water in a sleeping person's ear." The very next day, the presidents of Matsushita, NEC, and Sony, along with top executives of eight other television manufacturers, held a news conference to defend the Muse technology, and the MPT official was forced to retract his statement. But the damage had been done: how could the retraction be credible?

In fact, sales of HDTV sets in Japan have remained sluggish for years. Given the Japanese penchant for gadgets, this may be more a matter of simple high prices than fear of being stranded with an incompatible piece of electronics. By 1994, the cheapest HDTV sets still cost $6,000, and only about 20,000 HDTV sets had been sold in Japan. Sales did accelerate in 1995, when 81,000 sets were sold; sales more than doubled in 1996, to 198,000 sets. Still, as of early 1997, cumulative sales came to only 330,000 sets, a drop in the bucket in the world of television, that most mass-market of products.

Today, the Japanese are banking on an all-digital, satellite-based system scheduled to go into service around the year 2000 (accelerated from 2007 to reflect the poor reception of the Muse system). The Japanese will not use the transmission system employed in the United States, somewhat reducing the scale economies available to set manufacturers. But, in a victory for the United States, the Japanese have adopted the same standard for producing and displaying digital video signals. Thus, the same cameras, monitors, and related equipment can be used in TV studios worldwide, and videotapes made in the United States will be able to play in VCRs around the world. The European, Japanese, and American digital television systems will all use the same MPEG-2 standard to compress images for transmission.

The Europeans were second in the "race" and fared no better. They formed an HDTV joint venture called Eureka 95 in 1986. Eureka 95 enjoyed European Commission funding of $180 million, along with the participation of Philips, Thomson, Bosch, and others. This project developed an analog system "HD-MAC" designed to facilitate the transition from Europe's existing PAL and SECAM systems. However, since HD-MAC signals could not be interpreted by existing sets, the EC pushed satellite broadcasters to use transitional systems (D-MAC and D2-MAC) in the early 1990s. Backward compatibility could be achieved only at a stiff price: broadcasters complained that the image quality of D-MAC and D2-MAC was little better than PAL's. By 1993, the Europeans had abandoned HD-MAC. Now the Europeans are planning to adopt an all-digital system similar, but not identical, to the Japanese system.

Meanwhile, the United States was far behind, in no small part because of the political power of broadcasters, who had little to gain from the arrival of HDTV. A technical standard was nowhere in sight in 1989, when NHK began regular HDTV broadcasting.

The United States chose a unique way to manage the transition from analog to digital television. Still burned by the debacle of the incompatible CBS color standard of 1950, and beholden as usual to broadcasting interests, the FCC decided to give away billions of dollars of valuable spectrum space to broadcasters to enable "simulcasting." Each broadcaster was allocated a second 6-MHz channel to simultaneously broadcast HDTV and NTSC signals for roughly a decade. After that, the broadcasters are supposed to return the extra spectrum, and owners of analog sets will need to purchase converters to receive HDTV broadcasts. This arrangement arose out of a clever lobbying ploy by broadcasters back in the 1980s: by scaring Congress with the prospect of the Japanese beating out the United States in HDTV, broadcasters were able to preserve for themselves vacant channel space in the UHF portion of the spectrum that was in danger of being reassigned to uses other than television. Remember this key point as the HDTV story unfolds: the broadcasters have long lusted after more (free) spectrum space but have never had much appetite for HDTV itself.

In 1988, the FCC helped establish an industry body to actually pick the HDTV transmission standard, based on performance tests. Twenty-three proposals were floated in 1988, but only six remained when the testing was to begin in the fall of 1991. The six systems were sponsored by four teams: (1) NHK, (2) Zenith and AT&T, (3) General Instrument and MIT (two proposals), (4) Philips, Sarnoff Research Labs, NBC, and Thomson (two proposals). In May 1993, after NHK had dropped out, the three remaining teams formed a "Grand Alliance," merging their technologies and agreeing to engage in cross-licensing. This effectively ended their rivalry in the standards battle. Finally, in February 1994, parts of the original Zenith system were picked over those of the General Instrument system. Despite the presence of the cross-licensing agreements, Zenith's stock soared on the news.

Ironically, the United States has now leaped into the lead precisely *because* it entered the fray belatedly. The U.S. system is all-digital, whereas the NHK and MAC systems were analog. This turn of events not only shows the perils of rushing ahead prematurely. It also illustrates the advantages of using competition, rather than central authority, to select technology. The reason the United States has an all-digital HDTV system is because, on the very last day for entries into the HDTV sweepstakes in May 1991, General Instrument entered an all-digital system. The other teams had previously questioned the feasibility of fitting an all-digital system into the 6-MHz bandwidth available. Stunned by General Instrument's example, all but NHK developed all-digital systems within a year.

In 1996, when the FCC was finally ready to issue the new HDTV standard, a group of computer companies and Hollywood honchos sought to change the specifications, arguing that they would impede convergence and competition between the TV and PC industries, disadvantaging them in the "war for viewers." When the broadcasters agreed to drop the objectionable specs in late 1996, a broad agreement on the digital TV standard was reached by the broadcasting, consumer electronics, and computer industries. On the day before Christmas, at long last, the FCC officially adopted an HDTV standard. In a victory for the computer industry, "the standard does not include requirements with respect to scanning formats, aspect ratios and lines of resolution."

The selection of the HDTV technical standard was hardly the end of the story, however. It was more like the crack of the starting gun in a bicycle race in which no rider desires to take the lead and fight the wind. Remember how the broadcasters were dragging their feet on HDTV early on, far more keen on spectrum space than HDTV as such? Well, sure enough, they fought hard for the right to use the new spectrum as they please, to take their time initiating digital transmissions, and to keep the extra spectrum for as long as possible.

Some of these issues were resolved in April 1997 when the FCC issued rules for the adoption of digital television. In what could be another blow for speedy introduction of HDTV, the FCC "will not require broadcasters to air 'high definition' programming or initially to simulcast their analog programming on the digital channel." And the "build-out" schedule agreed to by broadcasters as a quid pro quo for obtaining their new "digital channels" is hardly breathtaking. FCC rules require the affiliates of the top four networks and the top ten markets to be on the air with a digital signal by May 1, 1999. Affiliates of the top four networks in markets eleven to thirty must be on the air by November 1, 1999. So, about half of American households will be able to receive over-the-air digital signals by January 1, 2000. (The FCC has tentatively set a date of 2006 by which time broadcasters must return their second channel.)

What all this will mean for the sales of HDTV sets is far from clear, however. About 65 percent of U.S. households have cable TV, and so far none of the major cable operators has made plans to provide high-definition programming. Quite the contrary, many are trying to expand the number of programs they can offer by *reducing* the quality of each channel. TCI, for example, is implementing half-resolution images, known as VHS-quality pictures, since VHS recording leaves a picture only about half as clear as the original. This is a sobering development for HDTV. The satellite broadcast industry has announced no plans to offer high-definition programming, either. Digital TV is more likely to mean extra channels than high definition, at least for now, especially since HDTV sets are likely to sell for as much as $10,000.

Inevitably, then, a major fight is brewing between those who distribute video programming, notably the broadcasters, and those who sell television sets. The finger pointing is hot and heavy. No one wants to go first. But no one wants to appear to be holding back HDTV, either. The networks say they cannot put into place specific plans for the use of their new digital channels until television manufacturers make their intentions known. But the manufacturers made the same criticism of the broadcasters, resulting in a high-stakes game of chicken. Moreover,

Congress is feeling snookered by broadcasters, who got free spectrum with a promise of HDTV and now seek to use that spectrum for other purposes. We predict the fairly rapid emergence of *digital* television, with set-top boxes receiving digital signals and translating and relaying them to TV sets. But the prospects for significant sales of *high-definition* television sets remain bleak.

At times, HDTV just seems jinxed. In February 1998, when WFAA-TV in Dallas became one of the nation's first regular digital broadcasters, yet another obstacle to HDTV was discovered: the HDTV broadcasts interfered with heart monitors at two nearby hospitals. The hospitals were using a frequency that the FCC has now assigned to TV stations for HDTV broadcasts. No heart patients were harmed, but the incident was yet another reminder of the many costs of switching to a new television standard.

The HDTV story certainly shows how difficult and time consuming it can be to establish a new technology standard when so many pieces of the puzzle have to fit together for the picture to come into view. The tortured HDTV history highlights several other economic principles as well, which we will develop in the next chapter:

- Early leaders (Japan) can easily fall behind if they standardize on technology that is not a sufficient advance on previous generations to obtain critical mass.

- A powerful group (the computer industry) can upset the apple cart late in the day.

- It is often possible to make a truce in a standards war (the Grand Alliance) by merging technologies and agreeing to cross-license essential patents.

- It can be hard to hold a coalition together if some members (broadcasters) would rather delay or sabotage the new standard.

Just as a chain is only as strong as its weakest link, the pace of adoption can be set by the component supplier that is least interested in the new standard. This is a reminder that you must give your alliance partners incentives to push the technology forward if you are keener than they are to push for rapid adoption.

LESSONS

The information age is built on the economics of networks, not the economics of factories. Positive feedback is central to the network economy. Happily enough, some guiding principles are available to help us understand network economics. Better yet, many of the economic forces so powerful today in the network economy are not entirely new. They have been faced by several industries in the past, and we can learn much from their experience.

Following are the main lessons to take away from the economics of networks and positive feedback, from our analysis of the basic trade-offs and generic strategies in network markets, and from our historical case studies of the emergence of new technologies:

- **Positive feedback is the dynamic process by which the strong get stronger.** But there is a dark side to the force: positive feedback also makes the weak get weaker.

- **Adoption dynamics in the presence of positive feedback tend to follow a predictable pattern.** The typical pattern involves an S-shaped, or "logistic," growth path: a slow start, followed by explosive growth, then saturation.

- **Consumers value information technologies that are widely used, just as they value communications networks with broad reach.** The resulting demand-side economies of scale, or network externalities, are a major cause of positive feedback in the information economy.

- **Positive feedback works to the advantage of large networks and against small networks.** This principle applies to real networks, such as the telephone network or a network of compatible modems, and to virtual networks, such as the network of users of the Lotus 1-2-3 spreadsheet program.

- **Consumer expectations are vital to obtaining the critical mass necessary to fuel growth.** During the early stages of product introduction, expectations management is critical.

- **Firms introducing new products and technologies face a fundamental trade-off between performance and compati-**

bility. The evolution strategy involves a high degree of backward compatibility but limited performance improvement. The revolution strategy involves little or no compatibility with existing products but compelling performance.

- **Firms introducing new products and technologies also face a fundamental trade-off between openness and control.** Technologies that are made open are more likely to gain popularity, but the rewards from such success are far greater for an innovator that can retain control over the use and design of its technology.

- **There are four generic strategies for innovators in network markets: performance play, controlled migration, open migration, and discontinuity.** These strategies differ along the performance/compatibility and openness/control dimensions.

- **Many of the tactics for dealing with positive feedback and network externalities have been tried in the past.** We all have much to learn from historical examples, ranging from the early days of the telephone industry to the introduction of color television.

Module 7: Electronic Commerce and Web Business Models

Goal: To be able to describe how information technology and the Internet are
changing firms, markets and business models.

Chapter 16: Strategy and the New Economics of Information

by Philip B. Evans and Thomas S. Wurster

A fundamental shift in the economics of information is under way – a shift that is less about any specific new technology than about the fact that a new behavior is reaching critical mass. Millions of people at home and at work are communicating electronically using universal, open standards. This explosion in connectivity is the latest – and, for business strategists, the most important – wave in the information revolution.

Over the past decade, managers have focused on adapting their operating processes to new information technologies. Dramatic as those *operating* changes have been, a more profound transformation of the business landscape lies ahead. Executives – and not just those in high-tech or information companies – will be forced to rethink the *strategic* fundamentals of their businesses. Over the next decade, the new economics of information will precipitate changes in the structure of entire industries and in the ways companies compete.

Early signs of this change are not hard to find. Consider the recent near-demise of Encyclopædia Britannica, one of the strongest and best-known brand names in the world. Since 1990, sales of Britannica's multivolume sets have plummeted by more than 50%. CD-ROMs came from nowhere and devastated the printed encyclopedia business as we traditionally understand it.

How was that possible? The *Encyclopædia Britannica* sells for somewhere in the region of $1,500 to $2,200. An encyclopedia on CD-ROM, such as Microsoft Encarta, sells for around $50. And many people get Encarta for free because it comes with their per-

Philip B. Evans is a senior vice president of the Boston Consulting Group in Boston, Massachusetts. Thomas S. Wurster is a vice president of the Boston Consulting Group in its Los Angeles office. They are the global coleaders of BCG's Media & Convergence Practice, which provides consulting services to media companies and to a wide variety of other clients focused on the convergence of media, information, telecommunications, and computing.

sonal computers or CD-ROM drives. The cost of producing a set of encyclopedias – printing, binding, and physical distribution – is about $200 to $300. The cost of producing a CD-ROM is about $1.50. This is a spectacular, if small, example of the way information technologies and new competition can disrupt the conventional value proposition of an established business.

Imagine what the people at Britannica thought was happening. The editors probably viewed CD-ROMs as nothing more than electronic versions of inferior products. Encarta's content is licensed from the Funk & Wagnalls encyclopedia, which was historically sold in supermarkets. Microsoft merely spruced up that content with public-domain illustrations and movie clips. The way *Britannica's* editors must have seen it, Encarta was not an encyclopedia at all. It was a toy.

Judging from their initial inaction, *Britannica's* executives failed to understand what their customers were really buying. Parents had been buying *Britannica* less for its intellectual content than out of a desire to do the right thing for their children. Today when parents want to "do the right thing," they buy their kids a computer.

The computer, then, is *Britannica's* real competitor. And along with the computer come a dozen CD-ROMs, one of which happens to be – as far as the customer is concerned – a more-or-less perfect substitute for the *Britannica*.

When the threat became obvious, Britannica did create a CD-ROM version – but to avoid undercutting the sales force, the company included it free with the printed version and charged $1,000 to anyone buying the CD-ROM by itself. Revenues continued to decline. The best salespeople left. And

The way *Britannica's* editors must have seen it, Encarta wasn't an encyclopedia, it was a toy.

Britannica's owner, a trust controlled by the University of Chicago, finally sold out. Under new management, the company is now trying to rebuild the business around the Internet.

Britannica's downfall is more than a parable about the dangers of complacency. It demonstrates how quickly and drastically the new economics of information can change the rules of competition, allowing new players and substitute products to render obsolete such traditional sources of compet-

itive advantage as a sales force, a supreme brand, and even the world's best content.

When managers hear this story, many respond, "Interesting, but it has nothing to do with *my* business. Britannica is in an information business. Thank goodness I'm not." They feel less secure, however, when they learn that the largest chunk of Britannica's cost structure was not the editorial content – which constituted only about 5% of costs – but the direct sales force. Britannica's vulnerability was due mainly to its dependence on the economics of a different kind of information: the economics of intensive personal selling. Many businesses fit that description, among them automobiles, insurance, real estate, and travel.

Every Business Is an Information Business

In many industries not widely considered information businesses, information actually represents a large percentage of the cost structure. About one-third of the cost of health care in the United States – some $300 billion – is the cost of capturing, storing, and processing such information as patients' records, physicians' notes, test results, and insurance claims.

More fundamentally, information is the glue that holds together the structure of all businesses. A company's value chain consists of all the activities it performs to design, produce, market, deliver, and support its product. The value chains of companies that supply and buy from one another collectively make up an industry's value chain, its particular configuration of competitors, suppliers, distribution channels, and customers.[1]

When we think about a value chain, we tend to visualize a linear flow of physical activities. But the value chain also includes all the information that flows within a company and between a company and its suppliers, its distributors, and its existing or potential customers. Supplier relationships, brand identity, process coordination, customer loyalty, employee loyalty, and switching costs all depend on various kinds of information.

When managers talk about the value of customer relationships, for example, what they really mean is the proprietary information that they have about their customers and that their customers have about the company and its products. Brands, after all, are nothing but the information – real or imagined, intellectual or emotional – that consumers have in their heads about a product. And the tools used to build brands – advertising, promotion, and even shelf space – are themselves information or ways of delivering information.

Similarly, information defines supplier relationships. Having a relationship means that two companies have established certain channels of communication built around personal acquaintance, mutual understanding, shared standards, electronic data interchange (EDI) systems, or synchronized production systems.

In any buyer-seller relationship, information can determine the relative bargaining power of the players. Auto dealers, for example, know the best local prices for a given model. Customers – unless they invest a lot of time shopping around – generally do not. Much of the dealer's margin depends on that *asymmetry* of information.

Not only does information define and constrain the relationship among the various players in a value chain, but in many businesses it also forms the basis for competitive advantage – even when the cost of that information is trivial and the product or service is thoroughly physical. To cite some of the best-known examples, American Airlines for a long time used its control of the SABRE reservation system to achieve higher levels of capacity utilization than its competitors. Wal-Mart has exploited its EDI links with suppliers to increase its inventory turns dramatically. And Nike has masterfully employed advertising, endorsements, and the microsegmentation of its market to transform sneakers into high-priced fashion goods. All three companies compete as much on information as they do on their physical product.

In many ways, then, information and the mechanisms for delivering it stabilize corporate and industry structures and underlie competitive advantage. But the informational components of value are so deeply embedded in the physical value chain that, in some cases, we are just beginning to acknowledge their separate existence.

When information is carried by things – by a salesperson or by a piece of direct mail, for example – it goes where the things go and no further. It is constrained to follow the linear flow of the physical value chain. But once everyone is connected electronically, information can travel by itself. The traditional link between the flow of product-related information and the flow of the product itself, between the economics of information and the economics of things, can be broken. What is truly revolutionary about the explosion in connectivity is the possibility it offers to unbundle information from its physical carrier.

The Trade-Off Between Richness and Reach

Let's back up for a minute to consider why this is such a revolutionary proposition. To the extent that information is embedded in physical modes of delivery, its economics are governed by a basic law: the trade-off between richness and reach. *Reach* simply means the number of people, at home or at work, exchanging information. *Richness* is defined by three aspects of the information itself. The first is *bandwidth*, or the amount of information that can be moved from sender to receiver in a given time. Stock quotes are narrowband; a film is broadband. The second aspect is the degree to which the information can be *customized*. For example, an advertisement on television is far less customized than a personal sales pitch but reaches far more people. The third aspect is *interactivity*. Dialogue is possible for a small group, but to reach millions of people the message must be a monologue.

In general, the communication of rich information has required proximity and dedicated channels whose costs or physical constraints have limited

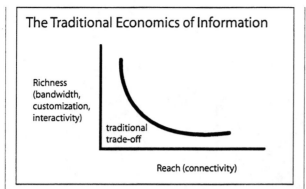

The Traditional Economics of Information

Richness (bandwidth, customization, interactivity)

traditional trade-off

Reach (connectivity)

the size of the audience to which the information could be sent. Conversely, the communication of information to a large audience has required compromises in bandwidth, customization, and interactivity. (See the graph "The Traditional Economics of Information.") This pervasive trade-off has shaped how companies communicate, collaborate, and conduct transactions internally and with customers, suppliers, and distributors.

A company's marketing mix, for example, is determined by apportioning resources according to this trade-off. A company can embed its message in an advertisement, a piece of customized direct mail, or a personal sales pitch –alternatives increasing in richness but diminishing in reach.

When companies conduct business with one another, the number of parties they deal with is inversely proportional to the richness of the information they need to exchange: Citibank can trade currencies with hundreds of other banks each minute because the data exchange requires little richness; conversely, Wal-Mart has narrowed its reach by moving to fewer and larger long-term supplier contracts to allow a richer coordination of marketing and logistical systems.

Within a corporation, traditional concepts of span of control and hierarchical reporting are predicated on the belief that communication cannot be rich and broad simultaneously. Jobs are structured to channel rich communication among a few people standing in a hierarchical relationship to one another (upward or downward), and broader communication is effected through the indirect routes of the organizational pyramid. Indeed, there is an entire economic theory (pioneered by Ronald H. Coase and Oliver E. Williamson[2]) suggesting that the boundaries of the corporation are set by the economics of exchanging information: organizations enable the exchange of rich information among a narrow, internal group; markets enable the exchange of thinner information among a larger, external group. The point at which one mode becomes less cost-effective than the other determines the boundaries of the corporation.

The trade-off between richness and reach, then, not only governs the old economics of information but also is fundamental to a whole set of premises about how the business world works. And it is precisely this trade-off that is now being blown up.

The rapid emergence of universal technical standards for communication, allowing everybody to communicate with everybody else at essentially zero cost, is a sea change. And it is as much the agreement on standards as the technology itself that is making this change possible. It's easy to get lost in the technical jargon, but the important principle here is that the *same* technical standards underlie all the so-called Net technologies: the *Internet*, which connects everyone; *extranets*, which connect companies to one another; and *intranets*, which connect individuals within companies.

Those emerging open standards and the explosion in the number of people and organizations connected by networks are freeing information from the channels that have been required to exchange it, making those channels unnecessary or uneconomical. Although the standards may not be ideal for any individual application, users are finding that they are good enough for most purposes today. And they are improving exponentially. Over time, organizations and individuals will be able to extend their reach by many orders of magnitude, often with a negligible sacrifice of richness.

Where once a sales force, a system of branches, a printing press, a chain of stores, or a delivery fleet served as formidable barriers to entry because they took years and heavy investment to build, in this new world, they could suddenly become expensive liabilities. New competitors on the Internet will be able to come from nowhere to steal customers. Similarly, the replacement of expensive, proprietary, legacy systems with inexpensive, open extranets will make it easier and cheaper for companies to, for example, bid for supply contracts, join a virtual factory, or form a competing supply chain.

Inside large corporations, the emergence of universal, open standards for exchanging information over intranets fosters cross-functional teams and accelerates the demise of hierarchical structures and their proprietary information systems. (See the insert "The End of Channels and Hierarchies.")

The Deconstruction of the Value Chain

The changing economics of information threaten to undermine established value chains in many sectors of the economy, requiring virtually every com-

The End of Channels and Hierarchies

In today's world, rich content passes through media, which we call *channels*, that can reach only a limited audience. The existence of channels creates *hierarchy*, both of choice (people have to gather rich information in an order dictated by the structure of the channels) and of power (some people have better access to rich information than others do). Hierarchy of choice is illustrated by the decision tree along which consumers are compelled to do their shopping in the physical world: they must choose a street, then a shop, then a department, then a shelf, then a product. They cannot select in any other sequence. They can return to the street and search along a different path, of course, but only by expending time and effort.

Hierarchical Decision Tree

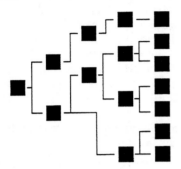

Hierarchy of power is illustrated by the traditional organization chart, in which senior executives have a wider span of knowledge than do their subordinates.

Hierarchical Organization

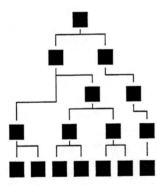

Hierarchy enables richness but constrains choice and creates asymmetries in information. The alternative to hierarchy is *markets*, which are symmetrical and open to the extent that they are *perfect*. But traditional markets trade only in less rich information.

When the trade-off between richness and reach is eliminated, channels are no longer necessary: everyone communicates richly with everyone else on the basis of shared standards. This might be termed *hyperarchy* after the hyperlinks of the World Wide Web.

Hyperarchy

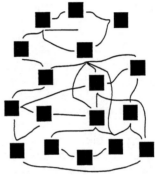

The World Wide Web is a hyperarchy. So are a deconstructed value chain within a business and a deconstructed supply chain within an industry. So are intranets. So are structures allowing fluid, team-based collaboration at work. So, too, is the pattern of amorphous and permeable corporate boundaries characteristic of the companies in Silicon Valley. (So, too, incidentally, are the architectures of object-oriented programming in software and of packet switching in telecommunications.)

Hyperarchy challenges *all* hierarchies, whether of logic or of power, with the possibility (or the threat) of random access and information symmetry. It challenges all markets with the possibility that far richer information can be exchanged than that involved in trading products and certificates of ownership. When the principles of hyperarchy are thoroughly understood, they will provide a way to understand not only positioning strategies within businesses and industries but also more fundamental questions of corporate organization and identity.

---

pany to rethink its strategy – not incrementally, but fundamentally. What will happen, for instance, to category killers such as Toys "R" Us and Home Depot when a search engine on the Internet gives consumers more choice than any store? What will be the point of having a supplier relationship with General Electric when it posts its purchasing requirements on an Internet bulletin board and enter-

tains bids from anybody inclined to respond? What will happen to health care providers and insurers if a uniform electronic format for patient records eliminates a major barrier that today discourages patients from switching hospitals or doctors?

Consider the future of newspapers, which like most businesses are built on a vertically integrated value chain. Journalists and advertisers supply

532

copy, editors lay it out, presses create the physical product, and an elaborate distribution system delivers it to readers each morning.

Newspaper companies exist as intermediaries between the journalist and the reader because there are enormous economies of scale in printing and distribution. But when high-resolution electronic tablets advance to the point where readers consider them a viable alternative to newsprint, those traditional economies of scale will become irrelevant. Editors – or even journalists – will be able to E-mail content directly to readers.

Freed from the necessity of subscribing to entire physical newspapers, readers will be able to mix and match content from a virtually unlimited number of sources. News could be downloaded daily from different electronic-news services. Movie reviews, recipes, and travel features could come just as easily from magazine or book publishers. Star columnists, cartoonists, or the U.S. Weather Service could send their work directly to subscribers. Intermediaries – search engines, alert services, formatting software, or editorial teams – could format and package the content to meet readers' individual interests. It does not follow that all readers will choose to unbundle all the current content of the physical newspaper, but the principal logic for that bundle – the economics of printing – will be gone.

This transformation is probably inevitable but distant. As newspaper executives correctly point out, the broadsheet is still an extraordinarily cheap and user-friendly way to distribute information. Little electronic tablets are not going to replace it very soon.

However, the timing of total deconstruction is not really the issue. *Pieces* of the newspaper can be

Retail banks will not become obsolete, but their current business definition will.

unbundled today. Classified advertising is a natural on-line product. Think how much easier it would be to submit, pay for, update, search through, and respond to classified ads electronically. Stripping away classifieds, however, would remove 25% of the typical newspaper's revenues but less than 10% of its costs.

Newspaper companies have moved aggressively into the electronic-classifieds business. They have exploited their advantage as makers of the original

print marketplace to provide an integrated print and electronic offering that reaches the widest population of buyers and sellers. This electronic offering preserves the margins of 60% to 80% that newspapers need from the classifieds to cover their fixed printing costs.

But as more and more people use the electronic medium, companies focused on targeted segments of the electronic-classifieds market (operating on, say, 15% margins) will gain share. The greater their share, by definition, the more attractive they will become to buyers and sellers. Eventually, the newspapers will either lose business or (more likely) retain it by settling for much lower margins.

Either way, the subsidy that supports the fixed costs of the print product will be gone. So newspapers will cut content or raise prices for readers and advertisers, accelerating their defection. That, in turn, will create opportunities for another focused competitor to pick off a different part of the value chain. Thus the greatest vulnerability for newspapers is not the total substitution of a new business model but a steady erosion through a sequence of partial substitutions that will make the current business model unsustainable.

Retail banking is ripe for a similar upheaval. The current business model depends on a vertically integrated value chain through which multiple products are originated, packaged, sold, and cross-sold through proprietary distribution channels. The high costs of distribution drive economies of utilization and scale and thus govern strategy in retail banking as it works today.

Home electronic banking looks at first glance like another, but cheaper, distribution channel. Many banks see it that way, hoping that its widespread adoption might enable them to scale down their higher-cost physical channels. Some banks are even offering proprietary software and electronic transactions for free. But something much deeper has happened than the emergence of a new distribution channel. Customers now can access information and make transactions in a variety of new ways.

Some 10 million people in the United States regularly use personal-financial-management software such as Intuit's Quicken or Microsoft Money to manage their checkbooks and integrate their personal financial affairs. Current versions of these programs can use modems to access electronic switches operated by CheckFree or VISA Interactive, which in turn route instructions or queries to the customers' banks. Such a system lets customers pay bills, make transfers, receive electronic statements, and seamlessly integrate account data into their personal financial plans. In addition, almost all financial institutions supply information at their Web sites, which anybody on-line can access using a browser.

No single software program can achieve both richness and reach, yet. Quicken, Money, and proprietary bank software permit *rich* exchanges but only with the customer's own bank. Web browsers do much less but *reach* the entire universe of financial institutions. However, the software vendors and switch providers have the resources, and ultimately will be motivated, to form alliances with financial institutions to eliminate this artificial trade-off. Bridges between financial management software and the Web, combined with advances in reliability, security, digital signatures, and legally binding electronic contracts, will enable financial Web sites to provide the full range of banking services.

If that happens, the trade-off between richness and reach will be broken. Customers will be able to contact any financial institution for any kind of service or information. They will be able to maintain a balance sheet on their desktop, drawing on data from multiple institutions. They will be able to compare alternative product offerings and to sweep funds automatically between accounts at different institutions. Bulletin boards or auctioning software will allow customers to announce their product requirements and accept bids. Chat rooms will permit customers to share information with each other or get advice from experts.

The sheer breadth of choice available to potential customers will create the need for third parties to play the role of navigator or facilitating agent. For example, some companies will have an incentive to create (or simply make available) databases on interest rates, risk ratings, and service histories. Others will create insurance and mortgage calculators or intelligent-agent software that can search for and evaluate products. Still other companies will authenticate the identity of counterparties or serve as guarantors of performance, confidentiality, or creditworthiness. (See the diagram "The Transformation of Retail Banking.")

As it becomes easier for customers to switch from one supplier to another, the competitive value of one-stop shopping and established relationships will drop. Cross-selling will become more difficult. Information about customers' needs or behavior will be harder for companies to obtain. Competitive advantage will be determined product by product, and therefore providers with broad product lines will lose ground to focused specialists.

In this new world, distribution will be done by the phone company, statements by financial management software, facilitation by different kinds of agent software, and origination by any number of different kinds of product specialists. The integrated value chain of retail banking will have been deconstructed.

Deconstructed but not destroyed. All the old functions will still be performed, as well as some new ones. Banks will not become obsolete, but their current business definition will – specifically, the concept that a bank is an integrated business where multiple products are originated, packaged, sold, and cross-sold through proprietary distribution channels.

Many bankers – like encyclopedia executives – deny all this. They argue that most customers do not have personal computers and that many who do are not choosing to use them for banking. They point out that people worry about the security of on-line transactions and that consumers trust banks more than they trust software companies. All true. However, on-line technology is advancing inexorably. And because they generate a dispropor-

The Transformation of Retail Banking

In today's integrated business model, the retail bank stands between the customer and the full range of financial services. But soon, through Internet technologies, customers will have direct access to product providers. As choices proliferate, totally new businesses will arise to help customers navigate through the expanded range of banking options.

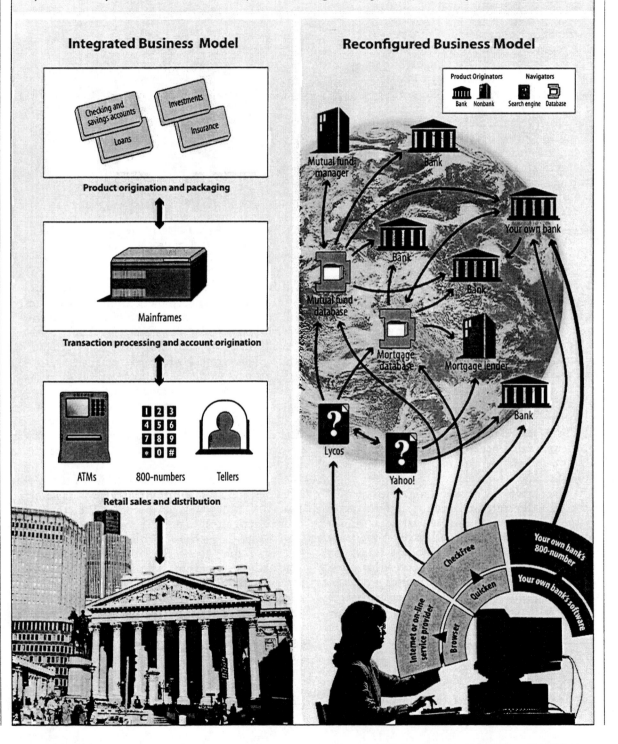

Integrated Business Model

Checking and savings accounts
Investments
Loans
Insurance

Product origination and packaging

Mainframes

Transaction processing and account origination

ATMs   800-numbers   Tellers

Retail sales and distribution

Reconfigured Business Model

Product Originators   Navigators
Bank   Nonbank   Search engine   Database

Mutual fund manager
Bank
Bank
Your own bank
Bank
Mutual fund database
Mortgage database
Mortgage lender
Bank
Lycos
Yahoo!

Your own bank's 800-number
Your own bank's software
CheckFree
Quicken
Internet or on-line service provider
Browser

tionate share of deposits and fees, the 10% of the population that currently use personal-financial-management software probably account for 75% of the profits of the banking system.

Market research suggests that Quicken users are more likely to be loyal to their software than to their banks. In one study, half of them said that if they were changing banks *anyway*, they would require their new bank to support the software – that is, allow them to transact their business on-line using Quicken. Now, bank accounts churn at the rate of about 10% per year. If a bank that doesn't support Quicken loses half of the new Quicken-using customers it might otherwise attract every year, and if such customers churn at the average rate, then it follows that the bank will lose 3% to 5% of its retail-customer margin per year. Refusal to support Quicken (or provide an acceptable alternative) could undermine the entire value of a franchise within just a few years.

The deconstruction of the value chain in banking is not unprecedented. Fifteen years ago, *corporate banking* was a spread business – that is, banks made money by charging a higher interest rate for loans than they paid for deposits. Their business model required them to form deep relationships with their corporate customers so that they could pump their own products through that distribution system. But then, thanks to technology, corporate customers gained access to the same financial markets that the banks used. Today, corporate banking consists of small businesses that largely stand alone (even when they function under the umbrella of a big bank) and compete product by product. Credit flows directly from the ultimate lender to the ultimate borrower, facilitated by bankers who rate the risk, give advice, make markets, and serve as custodians. The bankers make money through the fees they charge for those individual services. Clients no longer bundle their purchases, and relationships are more volatile. Once critical, an advantage in distribution today counts for little.

Newspapers and banking are not special cases. The value chains of scores of other industries will become ripe for unbundling. The logic is most compelling – and therefore likely to strike soonest – in information businesses where the cost of physical distribution is high: newspapers, ticket sales, insurance, financial information, scientific publishing, software, and of course encyclopedias. But in any business whose physical value chain has been compromised for the sake of delivering information, there is an opportunity to unbundle the two, creating a separate information business and allowing (or compelling) the physical one to be streamlined.

All it will take to deconstruct a business is a competitor that focuses on the vulnerable sliver of information in its value chain. (See the insert "What Will Happen to Your Business?")

Implications for Competitive Advantage

Deconstructing a vertically integrated value chain does more than transform the structure of a business or an industry – it alters the sources of competitive advantage. The new economics of information therefore not only present threats to established businesses but also represent a new set of opportunities. Every industry will shift according to its own dynamics, and those shifts will occur at different speeds and with varying intensity. No single set of predictions can be applied across the board, but some fundamental strategic implications of the changing economics of information can be drawn:

Existing value chains will fragment into multiple businesses, each of which will have its own sources of competitive advantage. When individual functions having different economies of scale or scope are bundled together, the result is a compromise of each – an averaging of the effects. When the bundles of functions are free to re-form as separate businesses, however, each can exploit its own sources of competitive advantage to the fullest.

What Will Happen to Your Business?

All businesses will eventually be affected by the shifting economics of information, but not all at the same rate or in the same way. Answers to the following questions are a first step in determining how a business could be restructured:

1. How and where in the current value chain of this business is information a component of value?
2. Where are trade-offs currently being made between richness and reach in this business?
3. In what situations will these trade-offs be eliminated?
4. Which critical activities – especially informational activities – could be peeled off as stand-alone businesses?
5. Could the underlying physical business be run more efficiently if the information functions were stripped away?
6. What new activities – especially facilitating-agent roles – might be required?
7. Among the successor businesses, how would risks and rewards be distributed?
8. How would losing control over key activities affect the profitability of the current business model?
9. Which current strategic assets could become liabilities?
10. What new capabilities are needed to dominate the new businesses that will emerge?

536

Take, for example, car retailing in the United States. Dealerships provide information about products in showrooms and through test-drives. They hold inventory and distribute cars. They broker financing. They make a market in secondhand cars. They operate maintenance and repair services. Although most of these activities are physical, the bundle of functions is held together by the classic *informational* logic of one-stop shopping. A dealer's competitive advantage is therefore based on a mixture of location, scale, cost, sales force management, quality of service, and affiliations with car manufacturers and banks.

Bundling these functions creates compromises. Each step in the value chain has different economies of scale. If the functions were unbundled, specialty companies that offer test-drives could take cars to prospective buyers' homes. Distributors of new cars could have fewer and larger sites in order to minimize inventory and transportation costs. Providers of after-sales service would be free to operate more and smaller local facilities to furnish better service. Auto manufacturers could deliver product information over the Internet. And car purchasers could obtain financing by putting their business out for bid via an electronic broker. Eliminate the informational glue that combines all these functions in a single, compromised business model, and the multiple businesses that emerge will evolve in radically different directions.

Some new businesses will benefit from network economies of scale, which can give rise to monopolies. In a networked market, the greater the number of people connected, the greater the value of being connected, thus creating *network economies of scale.* There is no point, for example, in being the only person in the world who owns a telephone. As the number of people who own telephones rises, the value to any one individual of hooking up increases progressively.

This self-reinforcing dynamic builds powerful monopolies. Businesses that broker information, make markets, or set standards are all taking advantage of this dynamic. The implication: the first company to achieve critical mass will often take all, or nearly all – although the continuing battle between first-mover Netscape and Microsoft in the market for network browsers illustrates that the lead of the first mover is not always definitive.

Reaching critical mass can be an enormous challenge. General Electric may have solved the problem by using its own huge purchasing power. GE has opened its internal electronic-procurement system to other buyers of industrial goods, turning its own sourcing system into a market-making business.

As value chains fragment and reconfigure, new opportunities will arise for purely physical businesses. In many businesses today, the efficiency of the physical value chain is compromised for the purpose of delivering information. Shops, for example, try to be efficient warehouses and effective merchandisers simultaneously and are often really neither. The new economics of information will create opportunities to rationalize the physical value chain, often leading to businesses whose physically based sources of competitive advantage will be more sustainable.

Consider the current battle in bookselling. Amazon.com, an electronic retailer on the Web, has no physical stores and very little inventory. It offers an electronic list of 2.5 million books, ten times larger than that of the largest chain store, and customers can search through that list by just about any criterion. Amazon orders most of its books from two industry wholesalers in response to customers' requests. It then repacks and mails them from a central facility.

Amazon cannot offer instant delivery; nor can customers physically browse the shelves the way they can in a traditional bookstore. Its advantages are based on superior information and lower physical costs. Customers can, for example, access book reviews. They have greater choice and better searching capabilities. And Amazon saves money on inventory and retail space.

But Amazon's success is not a given. The discount chains are aggressively launching their own Web businesses. There is nothing defensible about Amazon's wide selection since it really comes from publishers' and wholesalers' databases. By double-handling the books, Amazon still incurs unnecessary costs.

In fact, the wholesalers in the book industry could probably create the lowest-cost distribution system by filling customers' orders directly. If competition pushes the industry in that direction, electronic retailers would become mere search engines connected to somebody else's database – and that would not add much value or confer on them much of a competitive advantage. The wholesalers could be the big winners.

When a company focuses on different activities, the value proposition underlying its brand identity will change. Because a brand reflects its company's value chain, deconstruction will require new brand strategies. For instance, the importance of branches and automated teller machines today leads many banks to emphasize *ubiquity* in their brand image (Citibank, for example). However, the reconfiguration of financial services might lead a company to focus on being a product provider. For such a strategy, *performance* becomes the key message, as it is for Fidelity. Another brand strategy might focus on helping customers navigate the universe of third-party products. The key message would be *trust,* as it is for Charles Schwab.

New branding opportunities will emerge for third parties that neither produce a product nor deliver a primary service. Navigator or agent brands have been around for a long time. The Zagat guide to restaurants and *Consumer Reports* are two obvious examples. It's Zagat's own brand – its credibility in restaurant reviewing – that steers its readers toward

Where the New Businesses Will Emerge

In a world of limited connectivity, choices at each point in the value chain are, by definition, finite. In contrast, broadband connectivity means infinite choice. But infinite choice also means infinite bewilderment. This navigation problem can be solved in all sorts of ways, and each solution is a potential business.

The navigator could be a database. The navigator could be a search engine. The navigator could be intelligent-agent software. The navigator could be somebody giving advice. The navigator could be a brand providing recommendations or endorsements.

The logic of navigation can be observed in a number of businesses in which choice has proliferated. People often react to clutter by going back to the tried and true. Customer research indicates that people faced with complex choices either gravitate toward dominant brands or confine their search to narrow formats, each offering a presorted set of alternatives. In the grocery store, for example, where the number of products has quadrupled over the last 15 years, hundreds of segmented specialty brands have gained market share in almost every category. But so have the one or two leading brands. The proliferation of choice has led to the fragmentation of the small brands and the simultaneous concentration of the large ones. The losers are the brands in the middle.

Similarly, television viewers seem to flock to the hit shows without caring which network those shows are on. But they select specialty programming, such as nature documentaries or music videos, by tuning in to a cable channel offering that format. In essence, the viewer selects the channel, and the channel selects the content. In the first case, the product's brand pulls volume through the channel; in the second, the channel's brand pushes content toward receptive viewers.

Those two approaches by the consumer yield different patterns of competitive advantage and profitability. Networks need hit shows more than the hit shows need any network: the producers have the bargaining power and therefore receive the higher return. Conversely, producers of low-budget nature documentaries need a distributor more than the distributor needs any program, and the profit pattern is, therefore, the reverse. In one year, the popular comedian Bill Cosby earned more than the entire CBS network; the Discovery Channel probably earns more than all of its content providers put together. Despite the fact that CBS's 1996 revenues were about six times those of the Discovery Channel, Discovery's 52% profit margin dwarfed CBS's 4%.

The economics playing out in the television industry are a model for what will likely emerge in the world of universal connectivity. Think of it as two different value propositions: one is a focus on popular content; the other, a focus on navigation.

Navigation might have been the right strategy for Encyclopædia Britannica in responding to the threat from CD-ROMs. Its greatest competitive asset, after all, was a brand that certified high-quality, objective information. Given the clutter of cyberspace, what could be more compelling than a Britannica-branded guide to valuable information on the Internet?

If Britannica's executives had written off their sales force, if they had built alliances with libraries and scientific journals, if they had built a Web site that had hot links directly to original sources, if they had created a universal navigator to valuable and definitive information validated by the Encyclopædia Britannica brand, they would have been heroes. They might have established a monopoly, following the example of Bill Gates. In fact, he might have been forced to acquire them.

a particular establishment. A more recent example is the Platform for Internet Content Selection (PICS), a programming standard that allows browsers to interpret third-party rating labels on Web sites. With it a parent might search for sites that have been labeled "safe for children" by Evalu-Web. PICS enables anybody to rate anything, and it makes those ratings ubiquitous, searchable, sortable, and costless. The dramatic proliferation of networked markets increases the need for such navigators and other facilitating agents, those that guarantee a product's performance or assume risk, for example. Thus there will be many new opportunities to develop brands. (See the insert "Where the New Businesses Will Emerge.")

Bargaining power will shift as a result of a radical reduction in the ability to monopolize the control of information. Market power often comes from controlling a choke point in an information channel and extracting tolls from those dependent on the flow of information through it. For example, sellers to retail customers today use their control over the information available to those customers to minimize comparison shopping and maximize cross-selling. But when richness and reach extend to the point where such channels are unnecessary, that game will stop. Any choke point could then be circumvented. Buyers will know their alternatives as well as the seller does. Some new intermediaries – organizers of virtual markets – may even evolve into aggregators of buying power, playing suppliers off against one another for the benefit of the purchasers they represent.

Customers' switching costs will drop, and companies will have to develop new ways of generating customer loyalty. Common standards for exchanging and processing information and the growing numbers of individuals accessing networks will drastically reduce switching costs.

Proprietary EDI systems, for example, lock companies into supply relationships. But extranets linking companies with their suppliers using the Internet's standard protocols make switching almost costless. The U.S. auto industry is creating such an extranet called the Automotive Network eXchange (ANX). Linking together auto manufacturers with several thousand automotive suppliers, the system is expected to save its participants around a billion dollars a year, dramatically reduce

ordering and billing errors, and speed the flow of information to second- and third-tier suppliers. By reducing switching costs and creating greater symmetry of information, ANX will intensify competition at every level of the supply chain.

Incumbents could easily become victims of their obsolete physical infrastructures and their own psychology. Assets that traditionally offered competitive advantages and served as barriers to entry will become liabilities. The most vulnerable companies are those currently providing information that could be delivered more effectively and inexpensively electronically – for example, the physical parts of sales and distribution systems, such as branches, shops, and sales forces. As with newspapers, the loss of even a small portion of customers to new distribution channels or the migration of a high-margin product to the electronic domain can throw a business with high fixed costs into a downward spiral.

It may be easy to grasp this point intellectually, but it is much harder for managers to act on its implications. In many businesses, the assets in question are integral to a company's core competence. It is not easy psychologically to withdraw from assets so central to a company's identity. It is not easy strategically to downsize assets that have high fixed costs when so many customers still prefer the current business model. It is not easy financially to cannibalize current profits. And it is certainly not easy to squeeze the profits of distributors to whom one is tied by long-standing customer relationships or by franchise laws.

Newcomers suffer from none of these inhibitions. They are unconstrained by management traditions, organizational structures, customer relationships, or fixed assets. Recall the cautionary tale of Encyclopædia Britannica. Executives must mentally deconstruct their own businesses. If they don't, someone else will.

---

1. For a complete discussion of the value chain concept, see Michael Porter's Competitive Advantage *(New York: The Free Press, 1985). Differences in value chains – that is, differences in how competitors perform strategic activities or differences in which activities they choose to perform – are the basis for competitive advantage.*

2. Ronald H. Coase, "The Nature of the Firm," Economica, vol. 4, no. 4, 1937, p. 386; Oliver E. Williamson, Markets and Hierarchies: Analysis and Antitrust Implications (New York: Free Press, 1975).

Reprint 97504   To place an order, call 800-988-0886.

Chapter 17: Value Innovation through Business Webs

THE MP3 STORY

"We record anything—anywhere—anytime," proclaimed Sam Phillips on his business card. Phillips was a white man who wanted black musicians to feel comfortable at Sun Records, his two-person recording studio in segregation-era Memphis, Tennessee. In July 1953, a shy-looking eighteen-year-old named Elvis Presley came by the studio and paid Phillips $3.98 to record his version of "My Happiness." The young man took home the sole copy of his vinyl disk. Although Elvis hung around the studio persistently after that, Phillips only twigged his potential a year later, when he launched the future star's career with a haunting cover of "That's All Right." Then, after 1½ years of working his way up the hillbilly circuit, Elvis finally cut his first RCA hits.[1]

If Elvis were trying to break into the music business today, then he would not need to wait 2½ years to get national distribution. Instead, like thousands of others, he could use MP3, which fulfills the bold claim on Sam Phillips's business card. MP3 really does record—and distribute—any music, anywhere, anytime. It does so free and unmediated by agents and record companies.

Through Elvis's career and beyond, an oligopoly of industrial-age record companies and broadcast networks like RCA and CBS controlled the music distribution business. Today, their dominion is in tatters. While partisans quibble about its profitability, convenience, sound quality, or long-term prospects, the MP3 phenomenon has rent forever the rule book of this $38 billion industry.

The Fraunhofer Institute, a German industrial electronics research company, released MP3 in 1991 as a freely available technical standard for the compression and transmission of digital audio. The user "business case" for MP3 is simple: Buy a CD burner for three hundred dollars, and you can download and save an entire pirated Beatles collection on two CDs. At this point, you've made back your hardware investment, and now you can build the rest of your music library for the cost of the blank CDs.

Viscerally appealing to youngsters in the Net Generation demographic, MP3 attained critical mass in 1998, when it whirled through the Internet almost overnight. Millions of technology-literate kids and teenagers, high on music, low on cash, and sold on the mantra that "information wants to be free," used the Net to freely create and share MP3 software tools and music content. MP3 shows how internetworking and critical market mass can drive change with breathtaking speed. Piracy cost the music industry $10 billion in 1998; at any one time, more than half a million music files were available on the Internet for illegal downloading.[2] While the recording industry scrambled to deal with this hurricane of music piracy, most people were not even aware that all this was going on!

MP3's success is the product of an Internet-based alliance—a business web—of consumers, businesses (content and software distribution sites like MP3.com, and technology manufacturers like Diamond, maker of the Rio MP3 player), and content providers (musicians). It exemplifies how business webs have risen to challenge the industrial-age corporation as the basis for competitive strategy.

MP3 meets our definition of a business web (b-web): a distinct system of suppliers, distributors, commerce services providers, infrastructure providers, and customers that use the Internet for their primary business communications and transactions. Without such an Internet-enabled system, MP3 would almost certainly never have succeeded—and certainly not as fast as it did.

Though the MP3 b-web is an informal, grassroots phenomenon, it has shaken the foundations of an entire industry. Most other b-webs emanate from businesses, rather than college and high school students. They have identifiable leaders who formally orchestrate their strategies and processes. But no matter where they come from, b-webs provide challenge and opportunity to every business. They are the only means for accessing and increasing what we call digital capital, the mother lode of digital networks.

Simply put, digital capital results from the internetworking of three types of knowledge assets: human capital (what people know), customer capital (who you know, and who knows and values you), and structural capital (how what you know is built into your business systems). With internetworking, you can gain human capital without owning it; customer capital from complex mutual relationships; and structural capital that builds wealth through new business models.

This book shows business leaders how to form and build reserves of such digital capital by harnessing the power of business webs.

DRIVING FORCES OF THE DIGITAL ECONOMY

The question facing leaders and managers is not just "What is driving change in the economy today?" It is "What should I *do* to respond to all these changes?" This book is intended to help answer the second question. But before doing so, we will quickly describe the forces that drive the new economy, forces that are leading to the inevitable rise of the b-web.

The industrial economy depended on physical goods and services. Mass production addressed the problems of scarcity and the high costs of mobilizing raw materials, fabricating and assembling goods, and delivering them to their destinations. In the new economy, many offerings (like software and electronic entertainment) are nonphysical and knowledge-based, whereas the value of "physical" items (like pharmaceuticals and cars) depends on the knowledge embedded in their design and production.

Consequently, the economy shifts from scarcity to abundance. We can reproduce and distribute knowledge products like software and electronic entertainment for near zero marginal cost. Knowledge-intensive physical goods also become cheaper. Self-evident in the case of computer chips, this principle even applies to natural resources. Satellite imaging quickens the hunt for mineral resources. Ocean fisheries collapse, but the applied science of aquaculture fills markets with fish. Everywhere, knowledge yields new abundance.

Network economics drive the interlinked phenomena of increasing returns and network effects: Many (but by no means all) knowledge-based goods obey a law of increasing returns: once you have absorbed the cost of making the first digital "copy" (e.g., of a piece of software or an electronic publication), the marginal reproduction cost approaches zero—resulting in huge potential profits. Certain goods also display network effects: The more widely they are used, the greater their value. The more people who buy videodisc players, the more manufacturers are motivated to publish titles; this in turn makes the players more valuable to the people who own them. In such situations, those who control the standards can make a lot of money. Other examples include PC operating systems, the Web, and word processing software.

As MP3 illustrates, hurricanes of change can hit hard, and without warning. To prepare for such events, managers in every industry must learn to lead and change in "Internet time."

Space and time have become elastic media that expand or contract at will. Global financial markets respond to news in an instant. Nonstop software projects "follow the sun" around the world each day. Online auctioneers host millions of sessions simultaneously, with worldwide bidding stretched over a week instead of the moments available in a traditional auction gallery.

The new economics of knowledge, abundance, and increasing returns precipitate long-term deflationary trends. Networked computing cuts the cost of doing business in every industry, which inevitably means better deals on just about everything. There is a lot of room for growth well into the twenty-first century, in both rich and poor countries. And growth with little or no inflation is the best kind.

In this world of abundance, attention becomes a scarce commodity because of three factors. First, no person can produce more than twenty-four hours of attention per day. Second, the human capacity to pay attention is limited. Third (a result of the first two and exacerbated by the Internet), people are inundated with so much information that they don't know what to pay attention *to*.[3] To capture and retain customer attention, a business must provide a pertinent, attractive, and convenient total experience.

Industrial-age production, communications, commerce, and distribution were each the basis of entirely different sets of industries. Now, these activities implode on the Net. Industry walls tumble as companies rethink their value propositions. Car manufacturers reinvent their offering as a service-enhanced computer-communications package on wheels. Publishers confront today's Net-based periodical and tomorrow's digital paper; with the Web, all businesses must become publishers. Who will move in on your markets—and whose markets should you move in on?

To win in such an economy, you must deliver much better value at a much lower price. But no single company can be a world-class, lowest-cost provider of everything it needs. Another key transformation comes to the rescue: the driving forces of the digital economy slash transaction costs—the economic underpinnings of the integrated industrial-age enterprise. The twentieth-century enterprise is giving way to the b-web, driven by the disaggregation and reaggregation of the firm.

DISAGGREGATION AND REAGGREGATION OF THE FIRM

Why do firms exist? If, as Economics 101 suggests, the invisible hand of market pricing is so darned efficient, why doesn't it regulate *all* economic activity? Why isn't each person, at every step of production and delivery, an independent profit center? Why, instead of working for music publishers like Sony and PolyGram, doesn't a music producer auction recordings to marketers, who in turn sell CDs to the street-level rack jobbers who tender the highest bids?

Nobel laureate Ronald Coase asked these provocative questions in 1937. Some sixty years later, several thinkers, seeking to understand how the Net is changing the firm, returned to Coase's work.[4]

Coase blames transaction costs (or what he calls the cost of the price mechanism) for the contradiction between the theoretical agility of the market and the stubborn durability of the firm. Firms incur transaction costs when, instead of using their own internal resources, they go out to the market for products or services. Transaction costs have three parts, which together—and even individually—can be prohibitive:

- *Search costs.* Finding what you need consumes time, resources, and out-of-pocket costs (such as travel). Determining whether to trust a supplier adds more costs. Intermediaries who catalog products and product information could historically reduce, but not eliminate, such search costs. Music distributor Sony, through its Epic Records label, hires a stable of producers and marketers, cuts long-term deals with artists, and operates its own marketing programs—all in the name of minimizing search costs for itself and consumers.

- *Contracting costs.* If every exchange requires a unique price negotiation and contract, then the costs can be totally out of whack with the value of the deal. Since Sony owns Epic Records, it does not need to negotiate a distribution deal when Epic signs a new artist like Fiona Apple.

- *Coordination costs.* This is the cost of coordinating resources and processes. Coase points out that with "changes like the telephone and the telegraph," it becomes easier for geographically dispersed firms to coordinate their activities. Industrial-age communications enable big companies to exist. Sony's internal supply chain includes finding and managing talent, and producing, marketing, and distributing recorded music.

Coase says that firms form to lighten the burden of transaction costs. He then asks another good question. If firm organization cuts transaction costs, why isn't everything in one big firm? He answers that the law of diminishing returns applies to firm size: Big firms are complicated and find it hard to manage resources efficiently. Small companies often do things more cheaply than big ones.

All this leads to what we call Coase's law: *A firm will tend to expand until the costs of organizing an extra transaction within the firm become equal to the costs of carrying out the same transaction on the open market.*[5] As long as it is cheaper to perform a transaction inside your firm, says Coase's law, keep it there. But if it's cheaper to go to the marketplace, don't try to do it internally. When consumers and artists use the Net as a low-cost marketplace to find one another and "contract" for tunes, the Sonys of the world must face the music.

Thanks to internetworking, the costs of many kinds of transactions have been dramatically reduced and sometimes approach zero. Large and diverse groups of people can now, easily and cheaply, gain near real-time access to the information they need to make safe decisions and coordinate complex activities. We can increase wealth by adding knowledge value to a product or service—through innovation, enhancement, cost reduction, or customization—at each step in its life cycle. Often, specialists do a better value-adding job than do vertically integrated firms. In the digital economy, the notion of a separate, electronically negotiated deal at each step of the value cycle becomes a reasonable, often compelling, proposition.

This proposition is now possible because the Net is attaining ubiquity (increasingly mobile through wireless technologies), bandwidth, robustness, and new functionality. The Net is becoming a digital infrastructure of collaboration, rich with tools for search transactions, knowledge management, and delivery of application software ("apps on tap").

Call it hot and cold running functionality and knowledge. This explosion, still in its early days, is spawning new ways to create wealth. A new division of labor that transcends the traditional firm changes the way we design, manufacture, distribute, market, and support products and services. Several examples illustrate the success enjoyed by companies that employ this new division of labor.

- MP3.com is a Web-based music distributor that uses, but does not control, the MP3 standard and that offers legal, non-pirated music. In September 1999, it listed 180,000 songs from 31,000 artists, ranging from pop to classical to spoken word. Music downloads are free and nearly instantaneous. Fans also purchased 16,000 CDs online for a typical price of $5.99.

- Global Sources is a b-web that provides manufacturers, wholesalers, and distributors with access to products from 42,000 Asian makers of computers and electronics, components, fashion items, general merchandise, and hardware.

- The GE Trading Process Network (GETPN) enables companies to issue fully documented requests for quotations to participating suppliers around the world via the Net, and then to negotiate and close the contract. Through a partnership with Thomas Publishing Company, a publisher of buying guides, GETPN provides an even bigger transactional database for manufacturing procurement.

Consider James Richardson, owner of a two-person industrial-design firm in Weston, Connecticut. In 1998, he received a contract to design and build a running-in-place exercise machine. He set out to find manufacturers of membrane switches, essentially pressure-sensitive circuits printed on Mylar polyester film. Richardson first went to the Thomas Register Web site. Then he explored other sites on the Internet. He found dozens that listed products and described the companies that made them, their delivery schedules, and whether the products met international quality standards. Then he hunted up assemblers, who described their quality levels. Richardson produced a set of engineering drawings on his computer and e-mailed them to a list of prospective suppliers. A few weeks later, his chosen suppliers were mass-producing the exercise machine. Richardson had set up a virtual factory without leaving his office or investing any of his own money.[6] *He created a new business model by using internetworking to cut transaction costs.*

Adrian Slywotzky defines a business model as "the totality of how a company selects its customers, defines and differentiates its offerings (or response), defines the tasks it will perform itself and those it will outsource, configures its resources, goes to market, creates utility for customers, and captures profits. It is the entire system for delivering utility to customers and earning a profit from that activity."[7] He points out that companies may offer products or they may offer technology, but these offerings are embedded in a comprehensive system of activities and relationships that represent the company's business design. Slywotzky emphasizes activities and relationships, both of which are changing dramatically.

In this ever-changing tapestry, which thread should you grab first? Our research and experience suggest that you should begin with disaggregation—and its natural complement, reaggregation. Richardson's story shows that because the Net cuts transaction costs, a company can create value through a disaggregated business architecture. The challenge facing today's manager is to turn disaggregation from threat to opportunity.

Webster's defines the verb *disaggregate* as "to separate into component parts," and *reaggregate* as "to cause to re-form into an aggregate or a whole." These themes apply both to the transformation of the value proposition and to the design of new organizational structures for enhanced value creation. In the digital economy, Coase's law goes into overdrive. On the one hand, the discrete value-creating activities of firms, even entire industries, become easier and cheaper to disaggregate out to the open market. On the other, the coordination tools of the digital infrastructure enable firms to expand massively in highly focused areas of competency. In this book, we describe how companies like eBay and Cisco Systems provide models for doing both these things simultaneously.

Disaggregation enables entirely new kinds of value, from entirely new kinds of competitors. As a result, relegating digital technologies to nifty Web-site designs or superficial cost-saving initiatives are potentially fatal errors of an industrial-age mind-set. Disaggregation should begin with the end-customer's experience—the value proposition. It breaks out that experience—as well as the goods, services, resources, business processes, and organizational structures that make it possible—into a set of logical components. Effective strategists honestly face the many weaknesses inherent in industrial-age ways of doing things. They redesign, build upon, and reconfigure the components to radically transform the value proposition for the benefit of the end-customer. Planners must imagine how networked digital technologies enable them to add new forms of value every step of the way, to each component part. Then, they creatively reaggregate a new set of value offerings, goods, and services, as well as the enabling resources, structures, and processes.

The *Wall Street Journal*, founded in 1889, spent its first century as an aggregated collection of content (news, listings, advertising), context (the physical newspaper), and infrastructure (printing, physical distribution), bundled into a single tightly integrated offering. With the arrival of the Internet, the *Journal*, working with partner companies and even readers, disaggregated these elements into separate component parts, and then reaggregated them into an entirely new value proposition. The old value proposition was a physical package of yesterday's news, delivered to your doorstep or newsstand. The new one is a twenty-four-hour customizable information service, increasingly available anywhere—at the point of need. Subscribers can use the online *Wall Street Journal Interactive (WSJI)* to track their personal stock portfolios, set up the "newspaper" to present the stories they care about the most, join online discussions, and access the Dow Jones Publications Library to research just about any business topic. For Internet time, the *WSJI* value proposition may not be quite up to snuff: Avid readers note that some "current" news stories are as much as twenty-four hours old (and more on weekends)!

Disaggregated from its physical wrapper, the content is now available through a variety of electronic contexts, including the publication's own *WSJI*, and a variety of third parties like a Microsoft Web channel, the PalmPilot wireless network, and mobile phones. These services share an underlying delivery infrastructure—the Internet—but each enables a different shade of customer value. The *Journal's* own Web site posts the entire contents of the printed newspaper and much more, which the serious reader can customize. Microsoft and PalmPilot provide quick, though sometimes perforce superficial, news updates for desktop and mobile users, respectively. The *Journal* redefines and enhances its value proposition to meet a particular set of customer needs. A specific cast of players—not only Microsoft and Palm Computing, but also network companies like BellSouth—participates in the b-web that supports a specific distribution context. All collaborate and compete in the creation of value, with an eye to the changing needs and expectations of the dig-ital end-customer.

In the digital economy, the essence of the value proposition itself is destabilized. But so is the structure that enables the creation of value—the vertically integrated firm. The *Wall Street Journal* can no longer rely on its own printing presses and delivery trucks to mass-produce its daily information feed. To get the new, customized message out, it must now form partnerships with Microsoft, Palm Computing, and many others.

The reaggregation of the value proposition leads companies to change in other important ways. The *Journal* adds content to the Web site that readers of the print edition never get to see. It learns how to present and customize this content for Internet users. Microsoft and Palm extend their mandates from technology to information services. While intensifying its focus on its core competencies, each company uses partners to broaden its range of customer attractions. This is the payoff of reaggregation for the digital economy.

POPULAR APPROACHES TO
BUSINESS-MODEL INNOVATION

We present here a brief tangent to our main focus: popular approaches to business-model innovation that turned out to be forerunners of the b-web phenomenon.

The first stage of innovation was the vertically integrated industrial-age corporation, with supply-driven command-control hierarchies, division of labor for mass production, lengthy planning cycles, and stable industry pecking orders. Henry Ford's company—the first archetypal industrial-age firm—didn't just build cars. It owned rubber plantations to produce raw materials for tires and marine fleets for shipping materials on the Great Lakes. Hearst didn't just print newspapers; it owned millions of acres of pulpwood forest. IBM's most profitable products during the Great Depression were cardboard punch cards, and the company built and sold clocks until well into the 1970s.[8] Mania for diversification reached an absurd peak in the conglomerate craze of the 1970s, when companies like ITT Industries poured billions into building Rube Goldberg-like corporate contraptions that simply did not hang together.

It took sixty years for the global business environment to converge with the potential implicit in Ronald Coase's insights. As the twentieth century unfolded, the accelerating progress of computer and communications technologies peeled back transaction costs at an ever-increasing rate. In the late 1970s, the vertically integrated mass-production manufacturing company went into crisis. North American companies had become dozy, fat, hierarchical, and bureaucratic in the twenty-five years after World War II. They gradually awoke to a U.S. defeat in Vietnam, an oil price shock instigated by a Middle Eastern cartel, and frightening competition from Japan and other Asian countries. Japanese manufacturers shook the ramparts of the industrial heartland—steel and automotive. Customers flocked to their innovative, reliable, and cheaper products. In 1955, American-owned companies built 100 percent of the cars sold in the United States. Thirty years later, their share had dropped below 70 percent.[9] And other industries, from textiles to computers, felt the same heat.

Managers responded with innovation in two business dimensions: process and structure. *Process* innovations included concepts like agile manufacturing, total quality, supply-chain management, and business process reengineering (BPR). These techniques helped fend off the challenges of offshore competition, cost, and customer dissatisfaction. They remain vitally important in their updated forms of today. But the techniques did not attack the core issues of value innovation and strategic flexibility. BPR's single-minded focus on cost cutting often led to forms of corporate anorexia that did more harm than good.[10]

Structural (business model) innovations were important forerunners of the b-web. Popular approaches to business model innovation included the virtual corporation, outsourcing, the concept of the business ecosystem, and the Japanese *keiretsu*.

At the height of their crisis of self-confidence, North American managers and strategists stumbled across the *keiretsu*. It struck terror in their hearts. *Keiretsu* members in automotive, electronics, banking, and many other industries had suddenly emerged as global samurai. Rooted in centuries-old fighting clans, a *keiretsu* is a semipermanent phalanx of companies bound by interlocking ownership and directorates. *Keiretsu* battled aggressively with one another and on the international front, drawing strength from a strong us-versus-them mind-set. *Keiretsu*, along with cartels, were not just a strategic option for Japanese companies. They defined the business environment: The Japanese Fair Trade Commission estimated that over 90 percent of all domestic business transactions were "among parties involved in a long-standing relationship of some sort."[11] The strength of *keiretsu* also proved to be their downfall. Their tight, permanent linkages—the very opposite of an agile business structure—help to explain Japan's economic difficulties during the latter half of the 1990s.

Ironically, now that the *keiretsu* have been increasingly discredited in Japan, they have become fashionable in Silicon Valley as companies in all sectors discover the power of strategic partnering via the Internet. Proponents like the industry analyst Howard Anderson have not developed a new view of the *keiretsu*. Rather, they use the term as a pop epithet to describe partnerships ranging from loose associations to corporate conglomerates like AOL/Time Warner.[12] In our view this application of the term is not helpful and obfuscates the much more important underlying dynamics of the business web.

Though in part a response to the *keiretsu*, the North American virtual corporation was a fundamentally different idea. Proponents mystically described it as "almost edgeless, with permeable and constantly changing interfaces between company, supplier, and customers. Job responsibilities will regularly shift, as will lines of authority—even the very definition of employee will change as some customers and suppliers begin to spend more time in the company than will some of the firm's own workers."[13] Other proponents depicted the virtual corporation as good, but elective, business medicine. But in Japan, *keiretsu* are like oxygen: Breathe them or die. Also, a virtual corporation is a temporary, opportunistic partnership: "Complementary resources existing in a number of cooperating companies are left in place, but are integrated to support a particular product effort *for as long as it is economically justifiable to do so.*"[14] *Keiretsu* relationships, on the other hand, are institutional and permanent. As we describe in this book, b-webs are, in one sense, more like *keiretsu* than virtual corporations. They are not merely good medicine, but part of the "air" of the digital economy. And a b-web—like the now twenty-year-old Microsoft software alliance—can go on for a very long time. However, unlike a *keiretsu,* a b-web is not necessarily a permanent arrangement, nor does it need to use ownership to integrate its participants.

Outsourcing was a less ambitious idea than the virtual corporation: Pick a non-core activity and contract it out to a supplier who can do it more cheaply or better than you. Outsourcing is often a way to unload a problem function—like transportation or information technology. But outsourcing relationships can be tough. Outsourcer and outsourcee often perceive that they are in a zero-sum financial game, and they lack openness or trust. Such a mind-set characterized supply-chain relationships in the automotive industry for years.

More fundamentally, in a world of b-webs, outsourcing is dead, not because big firms will take over all business functions, but rather the opposite. Managers will no longer view the integrated corporation as the starting point for assigning tasks and functions. Rather, they will begin with a customer value proposition and a blank slate for the production and delivery infrastructure. Through analysis, they will parcel out the elements of value creation and delivery to an optimal collection of b-web partners. The lead firm in a b-web will want to control core elements of its digital capital—like customer relationships, the choreography of value creation and management processes, and intellectual property. Depending on the particulars, partners can take care of everything else.

None of these models—*keiretsu,* virtual corporation, or outsourcing—fully reflected how the world was changing by the mid-1990s. Then, with blazing insight, James Moore announced the business ecosystem, "an economic community supported by a foundation of interacting organizations and individuals—the organisms of the business world."[15] The ecosystem includes customers, suppliers, lead producers, competitors, and other stakeholders, who "coevolve their capabilities and roles, and tend to align themselves with the directions set by one or more central companies."

Moore's ecosystem metaphor illuminated the workings of the personal computer industry and others like it, in which many companies and individuals innovate, cooperate, and compete around a set of standards. Bill Gates, the Henry Ford of the information age, pioneered and popularized ecosystem management techniques that have become common principles for b-web leadership: *Context is king. Ensure voluntary compliance with your rules. Facilitate independent innovation. Harness end-customers for value creation. Go for critical mass fast.* Moore's ecosystem metaphor, though powerful, has limitations. It evokes a natural world in which biology and animal instinct rule, instead of human thought, judgment, and intentional actions. Animal instinct may be a big part of business life, but it does not explain everything.

By the mid-1990s, only a handful of corporations had made genuine progress toward any of these popular approaches to business model innovation. Two factors stood in their way. For industrial-era firms, all these approaches required too much of a break from established management cultures. And even the most advanced information technologies of the time—client server computing and electronic data interchange (EDI)—reinforced a centralist, hub-and-spoke business architecture. These technological systems had to be custom built, and at great expense. The Internet's universal-knowledge utility did not yet exist.

At this point in the mid-1990s, the sense of anticipation was nearly palpable. The worlds of business and communications were on the eve of revolutionary changes. It was as if the air had gradually become saturated with a combustible mix of gases; the tiniest spark would set off a vast explosion. The explosion came with the creation and discovery of the World Wide Web—a revolutionary new medium of human communications based on a few simple lines of software code. By the end of the decade, the Net was driving over $160 billion in transactions per year, most performed in and by b-webs.[16]

WHAT IS A B-WEB?

If the corporation embodied capital in the industrial age, then the b-web does the same for the digital economy. In b-webs, internetworked, fluid—sometimes highly structured, sometimes amorphous—sets of contributors come together to create value for customers and wealth for their shareholders. In the most elegant of b-webs, each participant focuses on a limited set of core competencies, the things that it does best.

Business webs are inventing new value propositions, transforming the rules of competition, and mobilizing people and resources to unprecedented levels of performance. Managers must master a new agenda for b-web strategy if they intend to win in the new economy.

As stated earlier, a b-web is a distinct system of suppliers, distributors, commerce services providers, infrastructure providers, and customers that use the Internet for their primary business communications and transactions. Several b-webs may compete with one another for market share within an industry; for example, the MP3 b-web competes with the SDMI (Secure Digital Music Initiative) b-web launched by the Recording Industry Association of America (RIAA) in December 1998.

Three primary structures of the b-web universe are internetworked enterprises, teams, and individuals; b-webs themselves; and the industry environment (figure 1-1). Internetworked enterprises, teams, and individuals are the fundamental components of b-web collaboration and competition. Typically, any single entity participates in several—sometimes competing—b-webs. Microsoft leads its own b-web and also participates, for better or worse, as a licensed developer in the competing Java b-web. Meanwhile, its fierce competitors, IBM and Oracle, contribute applications to Microsoft's b-web and (in IBM's case) sell Windows-compatible personal computers. An industry environment (e.g., the software industry) is a distinct space where several b-webs compete.

How do you tell a b-web when you see one? Look for nine features, which are also key design dimensions for an effective and competitive b-web (table 1-1).

1. *Internet infrastructure.* The participants in a b-web capitalize on the Internet's ability to slash transaction costs, using it as their primary infrastructure for interpersonal communications and business transactions. If you scratch a business exchange on the Net, then you will likely find a b-web. Spot ways that the Net can cut transaction costs, and you'll find b-web opportunities.

2. *Value proposition innovation.* A b-web delivers a unique, new value proposition that renders obsolete the old way of doing things. MP3 doesn't just let fans play cheap tracks. It infinitely expands the music community, making tunes almost as easy to share as the printed word. B-webs deliver wildly diverse forms of value, ranging from liquidity in financial markets to restaurant supplies, computer operating

FIGURE 1-1   Three Phases to B-Webs

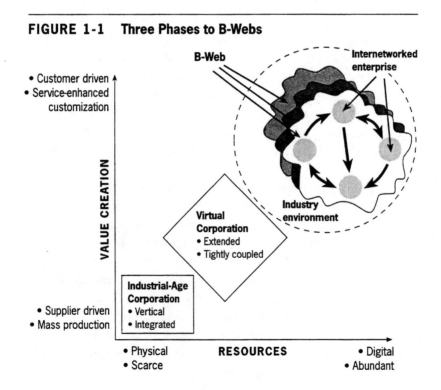

systems, and *X-Files* fan clubs. End-customers don't always pay for these outputs. Often, third parties such as governments, advertisers, and volunteers subsidize the creation and delivery of customer value.

3. *Multienterprise capability machine.* Leaders of b-webs increasingly prefer a market model of partnership to the "internal monopoly" of a build-or-acquire model. Relying on b-web partners helps maximize

---

TABLE 1-1   Nine Features of a B-Web

Feature	Description
Internet infrastructure	B-webs use the Internet as their primary infrastructure for business communications and transactions.
Value proposition innovation	A b-web delivers a unique, new value proposition that renders the old way of doing things obsolete.
Multienterprise capability machine	A b-web marshals the contributions of many participating enterprises. B-web leaders rely on partners to maximize return on invested capital.
Five classes of participants	A typical b-web structure includes five types—or "classes"—of value contributors:
	Customers, who not only receive but also contribute value to the b-web.
	Context providers, the interface between the customer and the b-web. A context provider leads the choreography, value realization, and rule-making activities of the system.
	Content providers design, make, and deliver the "intrinsic" forms of value—goods, services, or information—that satisfy customer needs.
	Commerce services providers enable the flow of business, including transactions and financial management, security and privacy, information and knowledge management, logistics and delivery, and regulatory services.
	Infrastructure providers deliver communications and computing, electronic and physical records, roads, buildings, offices, and the like.
Coopetition	B-web participants cooperate *and* compete with one another.
Customer-centricity	Rather than making, then selling, b-webs focus on customer value. They build mutual relationships and respond to individual customers at the point of need.
Context reigns	The context provider manages customer relationships and choreographs the value-creating activities of the entire system. Such b-web leaders get the captain's share of the spoils.
Rules and standards	Key participants know and adhere to the b-web's rules of engagement.
Bathed in knowledge	B-web participants exchange a variety of data, information, and knowledge.

return on invested capital. For example, in 1999 eBay facilitated $3 billion in auction sales via a $200 million technology and marketing system, with profit margins that exceeded Wal-Mart's. Traditional distributors like Sony sign artists to exclusive long-term deals; MP3.com's agreements are nonexclusive, and artists can end them at any time. While a traditional corporation defines its capabilities as its employees and the assets that it owns, a b-web marshals the contributions of many participating enterprises. The advantages—cost, speed, innovation, quality, and selection—typically outweigh the risks of partner opportunism. And it's much easier to switch from a non-performing partner than it is to drop a weak internal business unit.

4. *Five classes of participants.* A typical b-web's structure includes five types, or classes, of value contributors:

- *Customers,* who not only receive but also contribute value to the b-web (e.g., MP3.com's music consumers).

- *Context providers* facilitate the interface between the customer and the b-web. A context provider leads the choreography, value realization, and rule-making activities of the system (e.g., the company MP3.com).

- *Content providers* design, make, and deliver the intrinsic forms of value—goods, services, or information—that satisfy customer needs (e.g., musicians who distribute through MP3.com).

- *Commerce services providers* enable the flow of business, including transactions and financial management, security and privacy, information and knowledge management, logistics and delivery, and regulatory services (e.g., Cinram International, which burns CDs for MP3.com on a just-in-time basis).

- *Infrastructure providers* deliver communications and computing, electronic and physical records, roads, buildings, offices, and the like (e.g., CERFnet and Exodus Communications host MP3.com's Web servers).

5. *"Coopetition."*[17] Since participants cooperate and compete with one another, b-webs demand coopetition. Issuers of stocks, mutual

funds, and other financial instruments have always cooperated by sharing press releases and other information, while competing for investor dollars. As financial markets shift to the Internet infrastructure, these processes accelerate and gain millions of new participants. Sometimes, as in the Wintel b-web, coopetition can be nasty. Its b-web participants, including the U.S. government, won a court case accusing Microsoft of using its control over the operating system context to deal itself unfair advantages in the applications content arena.

6. *"Customer-centricity."* Effective b-webs function as highly responsive customer-fulfillment networks. Instead of building goods and services to sit in warehouses in accordance with an inventory plan, they closely monitor and respond to individual customers—at the point of need. MP3.com has a tool that reviews customers' past selections and, based on their preferences, suggests other music that they might like. Members of a traditional supply chain, such as in the auto industry, tend to focus only on the next link to which they ship their products. Well-choreographed b-webs encourage all participants to focus on the *end*-customer: Cisco product assemblers Solectron and Celestica increasingly ship goods directly to consumers' homes. And, recognizing their own self-interest, these customers often willingly contribute knowledge value to such b-webs. Amazon devotees write book reviews and get virtual recommendations from other readers who share their reading preferences.

7. *Context reigns.* The context provider typically manages customer relationships and choreographs the value-creating activities of the entire system. By defining, piloting, and managing the context, a b-web leader gets the captain's share of the spoils. The company MP3.com, having branded itself with the name of the popular MP3 standard, has levered this advantage into a market leadership position. Within its own b-web, MP3.com defines the core value proposition and is lead manager of the customer relationship, the competitive strategy, the admission of participants, the rules of engagement, and the value exchanges. Other sources provide content and other services; MP3.com plays a limited role in defining the specific day-to-day details of the content that its customers see.

8. *Rules and standards.* Participants must know and adhere to the b-web's rules of engagement. Voluntary adherence to open standards and technologies minimizes dependence on the proprietary methods of individual b-web participants; the MP3 standard has attracted dozens of companies, including Amazon.com, Yahoo!, and America Online (AOL). Some rules can't just be voluntary. Stock markets have tough rules about disclosure and compliance; if you break some of these rules, the government might put you in jail. The context provider often originates rules and monitors compliance. But rules—and enforcement—can come from anywhere, including government, key customers, and suppliers.

9. *Bathed in knowledge.* Participants in a b-web use the Internet to exchange operational data, information, and knowledge instantaneously among all participants who "need to know"—sometimes in depth, other times to a limited degree. In addition to music, MP3.com offers personal playlist management, musician biographies and tour schedules (as well as links to *their* Web sites), industry news, message boards, online forums, and the preference-based selection tools mentioned above. Knowledge sharing is also important in a negative sense. In the baseline definition of a b-web, participants evidently share operational data, such as product information. But they do not necessarily share strategic or competitive information with one another.

B-WEB COROLLARIES

Everyone seems to agree that the new world of Internet commerce works differently. New modes of operation mean new rules, and several authors have offered up lists. Instead of rules, we would like to suggest corollaries of the b-web phenomenon: some obvious propositions, logical deductions and inferences, and natural consequences to consider as you ponder the implications of this new corporate form.

We are in uncharted territory. Unlike the traditional industrial corporation, b-web structures and processes are highly malleable. Creative business-model architects like the leaders of MP3, Priceline, Linux, and Cisco have already seized on the b-web to create arrestingly new and competitive value propositions and organizational designs. In 1999, the MP3 phenomenon took another leap into the unknown when a company called Napster.com (quickly sued by the RIAA) launched a free service to let users seek and share tunes directly from one personal computer to another. Who knows where all this will end up? The first twenty years of the new century will be a golden age of business model innovation, which will set the course for decades to come.

Exceptionally high returns on invested capital (the capital resources at a firm's disposal) can occur. A b-web requires less physical capital (stores, warehouses, and inventory) than do traditional firms, meaning lower fixed costs and higher operating margins. The b-web's leaders can leverage the capital assets of partners, but need to carry none of the associated liabilities. For such reasons, by our calculation, for several years Cisco's return on invested capital was about twice Nortel's. Moreover, firms in b-webs can exhibit exponential returns to scale where revenue growth is exponential, while costs grow at a modest linear rate. Amazon.com expects to increase revenues in new markets like toys and auctions by leveraging the relationship (brand, customers) capital and structural (business processes, technology) capital it amassed as an online bookseller. The company's high market capitalization of its early years assumed both high returns on invested capital and exponential returns to scale.

Industrial-age businesses (like supermarkets) often put customers to work doing physical labor (like picking and delivering their own groceries). In b-webs, where customers mainly contribute information and knowledge, *customers have more power than ever before.* They have the power of choice, because a move to a new supplier is only a click away. They have the power of customization, as new technologies increase their expectations that vendor offerings will match their unique needs and tastes. They have power coming from near perfect information: If Tide stops washing whiter than white, everyone will find out faster than fast. And customers have collective power. MP3 illustrates how customers can go "out of control" and change the course of an industry. Customers gain both tangible (cost, quality) and intangible (information, control, relationships) benefits while themselves contributing ever more value to the b-webs in which they participate. All of this means that to attract and retain customers, sellers must build trustworthy, two-way relationships that deliver real value.

Disaggregation leads to "disintermediation" and "reintermediation"—
the elimination and replacement of physical-world agents and other
intermediaries between producers and customers. New, low-cost,
knowledge-value-enhanced intermediaries like MP3.com have placed
music distributors under siege. But, for the time being at least, the
old intermediaries will not simply fold up their tents and disappear.
Rather than a single "killer app" intermediary in each space, we see a
growing variety of intermediation models, each offering a distinct
form of value added. To acquire music, you can go directly to the Sony
site, an alternative like MP3.com, an online distributor like Amazon.
com, or any of the traditional physical-world options. For a music
publisher or musician, each of these intermediaries is an element of
the b-web distribution channel mix. Each has a place, depending on
the customer's situation and needs of the moment. So, although some
individual intermediaries may be gasping for air, as a species, intermediaries are alive and well—in fact, busily mutating and multiplying.
We (apologetically!) propose a neologism to describe this phenomenon: *polymediation.*

The b-web poses a challenge to asset-based models of market control. As
the world shifts from physical to digital distribution models, it is obvious that assets like music stores become less relevant to controlling markets. But big, capital-heavy assets are also losing clout in other, less obvious places. Sometimes, as in telecommunications, the pace of mergers
and acquisitions camouflages this deeper industry challenge. The value
and performance of a telecom company have traditionally depended
on physical capital (wires and rights-of-way) and physical capital metrics (return on assets). With the emergence of wireless networking, such
physical assets decline in relative value. A wireless network—whether for
voice or data—can be cheaper to set up and run, and more flexible, than
a wire-based one. Such networks will empower both customers and content providers with new kinds of flexibility and choice. Customers will
be able to choose among a variety of competing service providers. Meanwhile, a galaxy of services, comparable to those on the Internet itself, will
emerge for the new wireless communications infrastructure. Constella-
tions of converging customer and content provider power will squeeze
the economics of telecom even more. The result will be a competitive

commodity market for mobile communications, in which network assets become less relevant than customer choice and value-added services. As we describe in chapter 6, this type of analysis applies to several other asset-oriented industries.

Proponents of b-webs tout big ideas of business excellence as good medicine. Take a dose of the virtual corporation, process redesign, or knowledge management, and your company will feel better in the morning. Whether b-webs seem attractive or not, ignoring them is perilous. *Unlike other big ideas, b-webs are inevitable.* The MP3 b-web arose spontaneously, not because a manager read an illuminating book on business strategy. *The b-web is emerging as the generic, universal platform for creating value and wealth.* Like the corporation itself, the b-web concept is descriptive, not prescriptive; it will come in many different flavors, shapes, and sizes. Management practices—and everyday life—in a b-web will take many forms. Some b-webs will be wonderful places to work and do business, while others will be nasty and brutish. Some will succeed, others will fail. There is no single path to b-web success. Approaches that seem vitally important in most situations will be irrelevant, even counterproductive, in others.

To paraphrase Mao Tse-tung, *the b-web revolution is not a tea party!* A b-web is a market space in which organizations both collaborate and compete with one another. The competition is often aggressive, sometimes wicked, and even unfair. Consider how Microsoft's treatment of its b-web partners landed it in court. At the same time, collaboration and partnerships are critical to the performance of most b-webs. Cooperation with competition—*coopetition*—is a b-web theme song.

B-webs breed internetwork effects, a form of digital fusion among business entities. Physics describes how the fusion of hydrogen atoms releases energy. Under conditions of critical mass, a chain reaction occurs, with explosive results. Internetwork effects can display similar critical mass. MP3 experiments on the Net began in 1995–1996 and required vast amounts of energy just to keep moving. At a certain point in 1998, MP3 achieved critical mass of users and market momentum, took a quantum leap, and began to grow exponentially. In physics, fusion has a dark side—the release of terrible, destructive forces. Similarly in business, the internetwork effect blasts the bastions of the old economy.

DIGITAL CAPITAL

Former Citibank chairman Walter Wriston observed that information about money has become almost as important as money itself. Since this prophetic statement, new business models that deploy digital capital have wreaked havoc in the financial services industry, challenging the very existence of traditional banks, stockbrokers, and insurance companies. When intellectual capital moves to digital networks, it transforms entire industries and creates wealth in entirely new ways.

Digital capital adds new dimensions to the three kinds of intellectual capital described by knowledge-management thinkers Leif Edvinsson and Hubert Saint-Onge: human, structural, and customer.[18] One explanation for the high valuations of Internet stocks is the market's growing recognition of digital capital.

Knowledge-management theory describes *human capital* as the sum of the capabilities of individuals in the enterprise. It consists of skills, knowledge, intellect, creativity, and know-how. It is the capability of individuals to create value for customers. The IBM stock of human capital includes the knowledge and experience of technology developers and consultants and the creativity and moxie they apply to innovation; the expertise of its sales people in closing deals; and the brain and determination of its CEO Lou Gerstner. A problem with human capital, as the saying goes, is that "it rides down the elevator every night." More than one IBM brain has made off to Hewlett-Packard, Sun, or a Silicon Valley start-up.

The key shift in the digital economy is that the enterprise's human capital now extends to people across the b-webs in which it participates. MP3.com's human capital is internetworked. It includes the Net awareness and creativity of the 31,000 musicians who use it as a distribution channel; customers' willingness to set up their own "My MP3" home pages; and their involvement in personal playlist management, message boards, online forums, and preference-based selection tools. Sometimes, customers even participate in the design and creation of products. Users created the entire Linux operating system. The Java b-web depends on the design contributions of many different business partners and customers. When human capital becomes internetworked, participants share knowledge and commitments, dwarfing what was possible in the old economy. We describe the challenges and opportunities of choreographing internetworked human capital in chapter 7.

Customer capital is the wealth contained in an organization's relationships with its customers and, according to most thinkers, its suppliers. It is IBM's brand equity, its depth (penetration) and breadth (coverage) in customer accounts, the trust of its customers, its deals with universities to seed IBM technology in the experience of future decision makers, the willingness of CIOs to share their plans with its sales force, and its customers' reluctance to switch suppliers. It also refers to relationships with Intel (which manufactures microprocessors for IBM personal computers), contract manufacturers that assemble its products, and software developers.

When internetworked in your b-web, customer capital becomes relationship capital. In the digital world, customer capital intensifies into profoundly reciprocal linkages. It is also multidirectional, involving all b-web participants—customers and providers of context, content, commerce services, and infrastructure. Dynamic two-way relationships replace the concept of the brand as a one-way image that a vendor defines through print and broadcast media. Old marketing mind-sets become obsolete, as we describe in chapter 8.

Structural capital consists of the codified knowledge and business processes that enable an enterprise to meet market requirements. Because structural capital does not reside in the minds of individual people, it helps mitigate the human capital brain drain. IBM's structural capital includes software development methodologies, project management tools, and development platforms for designers, analysts, and programmers. It includes sales management systems, product descriptions, training courses, and marketing databases. And it includes business processes for manufacturing, customer support, and myriad other functions.

The digital extension of structural capital consists of, first, networked knowledge, processes, and tools available at the point of need and, second, new b-web business models that change the rules of market leadership. "MP3 shock," which combined networked knowledge, processes, and tools with new business models, quaked the industrial-age music business. Similarly, the Linux b-web ambushed Sun and Microsoft, mobilizing a volunteer army to create a new computer operating system that anyone can get for free. A major focus of this book is the transformation of structural capital that occurs in the digital economy.

B-WEB TAXONOMY

Not all b-webs are equal. We have investigated many hundreds and have written more than two hundred case studies. A number of distinct patterns emerged, with direct bearing on competitive strategy. Central to our analysis is a new typology of business models (figure 1-2).

The typology applies to the physical business world almost as well as to the digital world. However, its digital application has some key differences.

First, organizations often shift the basis of competition from one type to another as they move from the physical world to a b-web approach. A traditional full-service broker works (at least in theory) as a Value Chain, expertly tailoring advice to each individual investor. An online broker like Charles Schwab or E*Trade shifts the model to an Aggregation of advisory information and investment services, available to their customers for picking and choosing.

Second, business model innovation becomes the basis of competitive advantage. Innovators like eBay, Cisco, and Priceline develop new ways to create and deliver value. In the process, they dramatically change the playing field and the rules of the game.

Finally, in the physical world, one of the types of business models—the Alliance—is rare and primitive. In the world of b-webs, however, Alliances, including innovation collaboratives like Linux, become highly visible as powerful and dynamic drivers of change.

FIGURE 1-2   The B-Web Typology

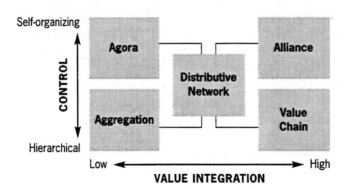

Dimensions of Differentiation: Control and Value Integration

Business webs differentiate along two primary dimensions: control (self-organizing or hierarchical) and value integration (low or high).

Economic control. In our analysis, control is about economics. Some b-webs are *hierarchical*; they have a leader who controls the content of the value proposition, the pricing, and the flow of transactions. General Motors designs and leads the integrated supply networks to produce preconceived products (e.g., the Cadillac Catera). Retailers like Amazon.com and Wal-Mart function hierarchically, taking responsibility for product selection, pricing, and customer satisfaction. Other b-webs *self-organize*. The market and its dynamics define the value and price of goods and services. Open-source software follows no management-imposed blueprint, because the product evolves through an organic development process open to all programmers. In stock exchanges and other types of auctions, the participants, not a single leader, drive content and price. Anyone can sell anything on an eBay auction (with the exception of prohibited items like weapons, animal parts, and other contraband!). Trading activity in the stock market continually responds to internal and external forces, whether a crisis of confidence in Asia, a speech by the chairman of the U.S. Federal Reserve, or a stampeding herd of institutional investors.

Value integration. Some b-webs focus on high value integration, that is, facilitating the production of specific product or service offerings (like cars, computers, consulting services) by integrating value contributions from multiple sources. We define *value* as the benefit that a user gains from a good or service. IBM achieves high value integration by taking contributions from many suppliers and turning them into a computer. Other b-webs focus on selection (low value integration); that is, providing a basket of choices rather than a single integrated solution. Ingram Micro, a leading wholesaler of computer hardware and software, does not alter the product offering. It focuses on distributing high-tech products, not making them. It currently offers products from more than 1,500 manufacturers. In between high and low value integration lie services like Instill, a restaurant industry supplier, which

566

aggregates online catalogs from food producers, but also manages part of the restaurant supply chain, reducing inventory and minimizing stock outs.

Five Types of B-Webs

These two parameters—economic control and value integration—define the fundamental characteristics of five basic types of b-web: Agora, Aggregation, Value Chain, Alliance, and Distributive Network (table 1-2). As we describe later, each type also has subtypes. Agoras, for example, include open markets, sell-side auctions, buy-side auctions, and exchanges.

TABLE 1-2   Key Features of B-Web Types

	Agora	Aggregation	Value Chain	Alliance	Distributive Network
Main theme	• Dynamic pricing	• Selection and convenience	• Process integration	• Creativity	• Allocation/ distribution
Value proposition	• Liquidity— converting goods into a desirable price	• Optimization of selection, organization, price, convenience, matching, and fulfillment	• Design and delivery of an integrated product or service that meets a specific set of customer needs	• Creative collaboration in aid of a goal shared across a community of contributors	• Facilitate the exchange and delivery of information, goods, and services
Customer role	• Market player	• Buyer	• Value driver	• Contributor	• Sender/ recipient
Knowledge focus	• Timing • Market intelligence	• Market segmentation • Supplier offerings • Fulfillment	• Innovation • Supply-chain management	• Community • Creativity • Standards and roles	• Network optimization • Visibility and transparency
Key process	• Price discovery	• Needs matching	• Product design • Supply-chain management	• Innovation	• Distribution
Examples	• Yahoo! classifieds • eBay • Priceline • AdAuction • NASDAQ • MetalSite • FreeMarkets	• Amazon.com • Chemdex • HomeAdvisor • Webvan • E*Trade • Travelocity • WSJI	• Cisco Systems • Dell Computer • General Motors • Celestica • Bidcom	• America Online • NetNoir • Linux • MP3 • Wintel	• Enron • UPS • AT&T • Wells Fargo • Internet

Typically, a b-web is recognizable as a single, specific type. At the same time, as with most such models, every real-world b-web blends features of several types. Business design entails crafting a competitive b-web mix that draws on the many shades of this typology.

Agora. The agora of ancient Greece was originally the assembly of the people, convoked by the king or one of his nobles. The word then came to mean the place where assemblies gathered, and this place then evolved to become the city's center for public and especially commercial intercourse.[19] We apply the term to markets where buyers and sellers meet to freely negotiate and assign value to goods (figure 1-3).[20]

An Agora facilitates exchange between buyers and sellers, who jointly "discover" a price through on-the-spot negotiations. Price discovery mechanisms in Agoras include one-to-one haggling, multiparty auctions, and exchanges. Examples include eBay, an Internet-based consumer auction, and Freemarkets, an innovative online business procurement site.

Typically in an Agora, many participants can bring goods to market, or decide what the price should be. Because sellers may offer a wide and often unpredictable variety or quantity of goods, value integration is

FIGURE 1-3   Agora

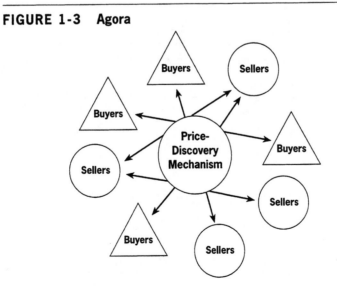

low. Internet Agoras offer significant benefits: many more sellers with a wider variety of products (benefiting buyers) and many more buyers to push prices up (benefiting sellers); convenience, low distribution and marketing costs, lots of information about all aspects of the deal; and entertainment—the thrill of the chase.

Aggregation. In an Aggregation b-web, one company—like Wal-Mart—leads in hierarchical fashion, positioning itself as a value-adding intermediary between producers and customers (figure 1-4). The lead aggregator takes responsibility for selecting products and services, targeting market segments, setting prices, and ensuring fulfillment. The aggregator typically sets prices and discount schedules in advance. An Aggregation offers a diverse variety of products and services, with zero to limited value integration. Retailers and wholesalers are prime examples of Aggregations.

HomeAdvisor, Microsoft's Web context for home buying, not only offers half a million listings, but also provides real-time mortgage calculators, crime and school statistics, maps covering every U.S. metropolitan area, live e-mail updates, and loan qualification—all made possible through partnerships with b-web content providers. HomeAdvisor offers a total solution—from searching to financing—under one virtual roof. By bundling real estate information and services around a mortgage offering, it captures this profitable portion of the financial services industry away from banks and other lending institutions.

E*Trade has aggregated many companies to create a virtual brokerage

---

FIGURE 1-4   Aggregation

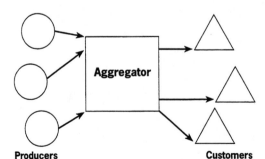

firm, charging one-tenth the fees of a traditional broker. Its dozens of content and service providers include stock quote services (Reuters, Quote.com), news (Reuters, PR Newswire, Businesswire), proprietary issuers (Robertson, Stephens), research (Briefing.com, InvesTools), market trends and projections (Baseline Financial Services), and personal financial tools (Quicken)—to name but a few. Internet delivery reduces customer costs; more important, customers gain intelligence that was formerly only visible to the high priests of the investment industry.

Value Chain. In a Value Chain, the context provider structures and directs a b-web network to produce a highly integrated value proposition (figure 1-5). The output meets a customer order or market opportunity—from an individual's buying of a Jeep with custom trim or Procter & Gamble's manufacturing of 20,000 case lots of Crest, to EDS's implementation of an electronic commerce infrastructure for one of its clients. The seller has the final say in pricing. It may be fixed (a tube of toothpaste), somewhat negotiable (the Jeep), or highly negotiable (the EDS deal).

Cisco Systems makes networking products—such as routers—that shuffle data from one computer to another over the Internet or corporate computer networks. The company sits at the top of a $12 billion Web-enabled Value Chain. It reserves for itself the tasks of designing

FIGURE 1-5   Value Chain

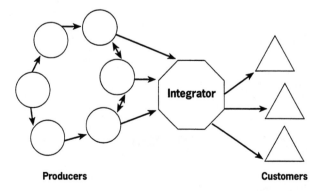

Producers   Customers

core technologies, coordinating processes across the b-web, marketing, and managing relationships. Other b-web participants do just about everything else, including most manufacturing, fulfillment, and on-site customer service.

Alliance. An Alliance, the most "ethereal" of b-webs, strives for high value integration without hierarchical control (figure 1-6). Its participants design goods or services, create knowledge, or simply produce dynamic, shared experiences. Alliances include online communities, research initiatives, games, and development communities like the PalmPilot and Open Source innovation initiatives. The MP3 phenomenon is an Alliance.

FIGURE 1-6   Alliance

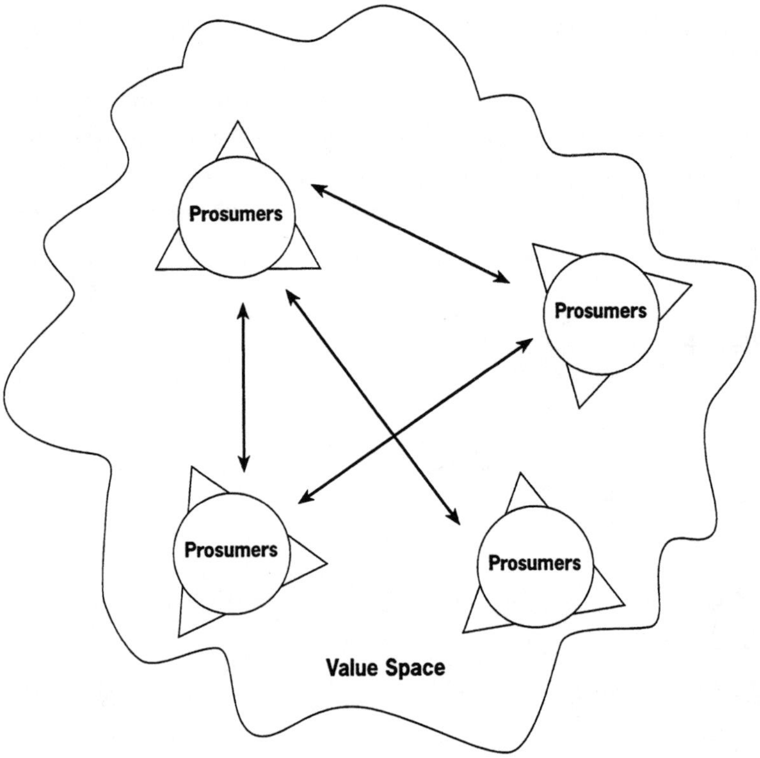

Alliances typically depend on rules and standards that govern interaction, acceptable participant behavior, and the determination of value. Often, end-customers or users play a prominent role in value creation, as contributors to an online forum or as designers (e.g., of PalmPilot software or of the next piece of encoding in the Human Genome Project). Where products come from an Alliance, the end-customer often handles customizing and integrating the solution.

Alliance b-webs often enjoy network effects. The more customers who buy PalmPilots, the more developers who decide to create applications. The value cycle is continuous and accelerating: As the value increases, usage mushrooms, and the applications market grows.

Smart managers appreciate the power of Alliance b-webs. They willingly sacrifice some control over product evolution for the extra momentum that hundreds or even thousands of contributors can provide.

Distributive Network. The fifth type of b-web to have emerged from our research thus far is the Distributive Network (figure 1-7). These are the b-webs that keep the economy alive and mobile.

In addition to the roads, postal services, telephone companies, and electrical power grid of the industrial economy, Distributive Networks include data network operators, the new logistics companies, and banks. These networks play a vital role in ensuring the healthy balance of the

FIGURE 1-7   Distributive Network

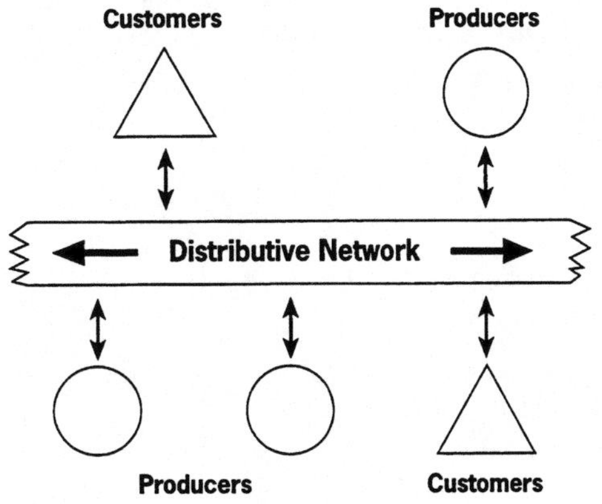

systems that they support. Like the human blood system, Distributive Networks neither create nor consume their essential cargo. But when these services fail, their host systems can die. And when a Distributive Network clots, its host can turn severely ill.

Distributive Networks, in their purest forms (which is not always how you find them), service the other types of b-webs by allocating and delivering goods—whether information, objects, money, or resources—from providers to users. Along with Alliances, Distributive Networks often evince network effects: The more customers who use a Distributive Network (e.g., a telephone network), the more value it provides to all its customers.

In relation to our two axes of b-web analysis—value integration and nature of control—Distributive Networks are "pure" hybrids. Their value integration is both high and low. It is high, because Distributive Networks must vouchsafe the integrity of their delivery systems, often a critical performance metric, for example, in a bank or a courier company. The value integration of Distributive Networks is also low, because their outputs can be diverse and unpredictable; from one day to the next, you can't foresee with certainty the pattern flow of cash through the banking system, or the flow of packages through UPS. Control of a Distributive Network's value is both hierarchical (tight network management is critical) and self-organizing (the continuous fluctuation of supply and demand determines value and price, as in electrical power and financial capital systems).

In the following chapters, we present business model innovation strategies for the five types of b-webs: Agoras, Aggregations, Value Chains, Alliances, and Distributive Networks.

Chapter 18: How do you Weave a B-Web

Disaggregation and reaggregation may be powerful concepts, but how do you bring them to life? This chapter provides the answers. Step by step, we show you how to take apart the old value proposition, envision and structure a new one, and turn an industrial-age business into a digital economy b-web.

The first step of b-web strategy is to disaggregate the value proposition that the end-customer experiences. Focus on the *end*-customer, the person who really pays the bills and whose needs and appetites your b-web must meet. Think about the genuine customer needs that your product or service addresses, not just the "thing you (or the market incumbents) do" to get the business. And avoid preoccupation with the production or distribution channels that today stand between you and the real customer.

As we said in chapter 1, disaggregation frees you to generate entirely new kinds of value. It also encourages entirely new kinds of competitors. If you relegate digital technologies to flashy Web sites or short-term cost savings, you will likely fail. Begin disaggregation with the end-customer's experience. Dissect that experience in terms of your value proposition, as well as the enabling goods, services, resources, business processes, and organizational structures, into individual components. Honestly face the many weaknesses inherent in the industrial-age mind-set and tool-set. Challenge what you know, then redesign; build upon, and reconfigure the components to radically transform the value proposition for the end-customer's benefit. Imagine how networked, digital technologies liberate contributors to add new forms of value every step of the way—to each component. Then, creatively reaggregate a new set of value offerings, goods, and services, as well as the supporting resources, structures, and processes.

A business's value proposition differs from its products and services. The value that a customer needs—and that an effective business delivers—endures, regardless of the particulars. When a traveler needs to get from point A to point B, how he or she gets there matters much less than actually getting there.

A clear and precisely defined value space for your strategy initiative is vitally important. An inquiry on privately owned personal transportation, for example, may lead to very different conclusions from one on personal transportation as a service.

Identify opportunities to build human, relationship, and structural capital. Where do these capital reserves reside in the old business model? What are the gaps and vulnerabilities? What new forms of digital capital can we create to enhance customer and shareholder value? For example, consider how to convert human capital (wisdom in the minds of employees across the b-web) into structural capital (knowledge management systems and software-encoded business processes).

To describe, disaggregate, and reaggregate the core value proposition, the strategist should ask the following fundamental questions about the business system in question: Why does it exist at all, and should it continue to exist? Who benefits from it? What are its strengths and weaknesses from the customer perspective? How could we improve it? Who can help us, or who could improve it and kill us?

We have identified six steps for b-web strategy design:

1. Describe the current value proposition from the customer's viewpoint, that is, why this system exists.

2. Disaggregate: Consider the contributors and their contributions, strengths, and weaknesses. Compare the parts and capabilities of your business to those in other systems.

3. Envision b-web-enabled value through brainstorming and other creative design techniques. Decide what the new value proposition will be.

4. Reaggregate: Define what it will take to deliver the new value proposition, including processes, contributors, contributions, applications and technologies, and other success factors.

5. Prepare a value map: Design a visual map that depicts value exchanges in the b-web.

6. Do the b-web mix: Define a b-web typing strategy that will improve your competitive advantages.

STEP 1: DESCRIBE THE CURRENT VALUE PROPOSITION

Before envisioning a new future, assess the current state of things. For the marketspace in question, what value is offered, delivered, and consumed that justifies a business's right to exist? Three guidelines are useful in this assessment. First, focus on the essence, rather than a small, fascinating, or rarefied aspect of it. If looking at publishing, then describe the underlying value to the readers of the publication rather than the printed page or the table of contents. Second, begin with the end in mind, as in how to improve radically the value that the "real" end-customer receives from your business system. Nothing less will ensure your survival as a winner in the twenty-first century. Last, prepare and inform all steps of this process with an assessment of: customer, market, and channel trends; supply-side trends; competition; current and expected product and service innovations; industry use of human, relationship, and structural capital; business events (e.g., consolidation); environmental issues; and regulation.

We ask the following four questions to drive a "customer-down" approach to the current value proposition:

1. Who are your end-customers, as opposed to the intermediary customers such as the buyers and channels, of your products and services? Define the customer categories in today's market system and who else is serving them, regardless of value proposition.

2. What product and service offerings does the current business system provide its customers?

3. From the customer's standpoint, what value propositions can you attribute to these product and service offerings? List only the top ones that come to mind. Once you have listed several dimensions of the value proposition, construct a concise catch-all statement that accommodates all of them. This summary should nail your current business—its raison d'être.

4. From the end-customer's perspective, what are the main strengths and weaknesses of the value proposition and the enabling products and services? Who else delivers more value, and in what ways?

Consider the brokerage business transformation led by companies like Charles Schwab & Co., E*Trade, and TD Waterhouse Securities. Some might have described the purported value proposition of the traditional full-service brokerage industry in the mid-1990s as guiding customers in managing their investments through personal, knowledgeable advice and proactive customer service. In theory, an investment adviser at a firm like Merrill Lynch or Goldman Sachs develops an intimate knowledge of the goals and preferences of each individual client. Following a Value-Chain service model, the adviser integrates his or her firm's unique proprietary research with the client's personal strategy to provide customized service, particularly buy/sell advice at the critical moment.

Reality, of course, is different. Have you ever used a broker? If yes, then were you 100 percent happy with the relationship and service? If no, then join the club. Although many factors contribute to such disappointment, most traditional brokers make their money from maximizing the number of orders they process, rather than faithfully representing client interests. Many customers perceive that the quality of advice and service they receive does not warrant the fee structure. Table 9-1 illustrates how a full-service retail brokerage might have answered the above four questions during the mid- to late 1990s.

STEP 2: DISAGGREGATE

Disaggregation identifies the entities that contribute to the total value-creation system. We include customers in the model since they often perform work that contributes to the overall system value. Once identified, this work can be automated, eliminated, transferred to others, or left with the customer.

Where are the opportunities to capture digital capital? The grocery industry, as mentioned in chapter 3, calculates that customer effort represents 13 percent of the system's total value. Industrial-age grocers might argue that this labor is relationship capital (shoppers like to squeeze tomatoes); online grocers say that this labor is an obsolete form of structural capital (underpaid work), which online convenience turns to relationship capital ripe for the picking.

In conducting this analysis, look at the total value system—again, from the perspective of the end-customer. In securities markets, the broker is not the sole source of value. The broker acts as gatekeeper to the real "content" value of the system, which consists of access to financial markets, individual securities, and other investment instruments. The

TABLE 9-1 Current Value Definition for Traditional Full-Service Brokerage Firm

Customers	Product/Service Offerings	Value Proposition	Strengths	Weaknesses
• Retail investors	• Use of personal broker • Investment strategy advice • Proprietary research • Buy/sell advice • Transaction services • Portfolio/records management • Educational materials	• Counseling • Matching investment choices to customer needs and preferences • Quality and utility of research and analysis • Personal service	• Personalized advice and attention • Hand-holding • Quality of research • Professional management	• Costs • Restricted hours • Inconsistent quality of service and advice • Limited, often unpredictable access to research materials • Customers not in control • Some conflict of interest (broker income depends on transaction churn)

customer cares about asset growth, not the broker relationship. A useful disaggregation analysis of this value proposition, one with transformational potential, must look at the whole picture (figure 9-1).

Consider the five categories of value contributors that we introduced in chapter 1: end-customers, context providers, content providers, commerce services providers, and infrastructure providers. Each category typically includes several classes of participants; also, a single participant may play different roles in various categories. Cisco is the prime context provider for its b-web, but when KPMG and EDS integrate Cisco's

FIGURE 9-1　Five Layers of Value Contributors

Customers

Receive and contribute value to the b-web.

Context

The interface between the customer and the b-web. A context provider leads the choreography, value realization, and rule-making activities of the system.

Content

The core value—goods, services, or information that satisfy customer needs. Content providers design, make, and deliver value.

Commerce

Enables the flow of business, including transactions and financial management, security and privacy, information and knowledge management, logistics and delivery, and regulatory services.

Infrastructure

Communications and computing, paper and physical records, roads, buildings, offices, and the like.

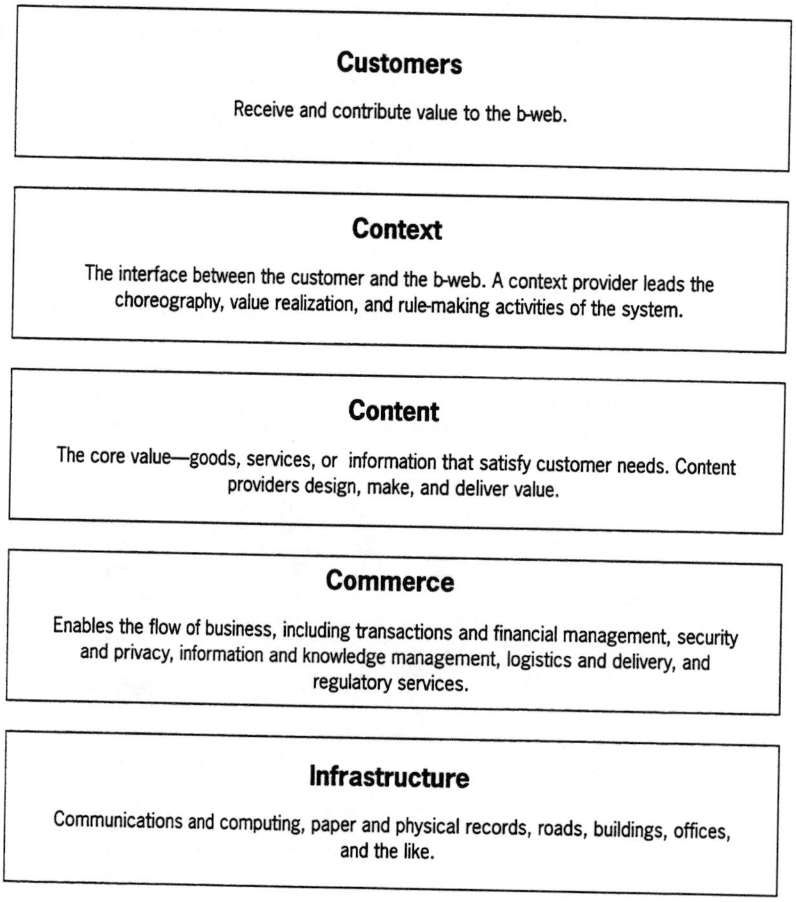

solutions for customers, they become context providers. Cisco also adopts a content-provider role when it creates networking software for its products.

The economics of the system often depend on customer contributions. Some observers point to customer labor as a breakthrough innovation unique to electronic commerce. In fact, as the grocery industry illustrates, customers have been pitching in since the beginning of time. In the shift to b-webs, customers sometimes do less work, sometimes more. Web grocers like Peapod and Streamline reduce consumer labor. At eBay, customers do nearly all the work and shoulder most of the risks and costs.

The context provider is the interface between the customer and the system that creates the value. Because of this privileged position, the context provider dominates the b-web, orchestrating its choreography, value realization, and rule-making. The context provider manages, accumulates, and allocates (to b-web partners) digital capital assets. In the online world, context assumes even greater importance than before, since millions of customers can frequent a site in a day or an hour. Business-to-business aggregators like MetalSite and Chemdex derive disproportionate influence and rewards for providing industry contexts. And as portals like Yahoo! and Excite draw more visitors daily than do television channels, their influence and business value increase. Depending on b-web type, the primary context provider performs one or another typical role: Agora (auction or exchange system operator), Aggregation (storefront or portal), Value Chain (product/service designer and production manager), Alliance (setter of rules and standards), and Distributive Network (network services provider).

Content providers design, make, and deliver the core value—the goods and services—that ultimately satisfy customer needs. Content can be information (e.g., a TV show, an online publication, a personal health care record), physical goods (e.g., potato chips and computer chips), or services (air travel, heart surgery, etc.).

Commerce services providers facilitate transactions, exchanges, and the transfer of value. Their services include informational and financial transaction management, security and privacy, information and knowledge management, logistics and delivery, and regulation.

Infrastructure services include communications and computing, paper and other physical records, roads and transportation systems, buildings, offices, and the like. Commerce and infrastructure services often involve Distributive Networks (chapter 6).

As the preceding descriptions show, a business system usually comprises several layers of value creation. Disaggregation entails (1) identifying the key participants in each layer; (2) describing what each participant contributes to the system, and how they do so; and (3) pinpointing the weaknesses and opportunities for improvement in the current arrangement.

Wind back the clock, and imagine that you are a strategy adviser at Schwab in 1996 or 1997. At this time, full-service brokers act like Value Chains, integrating solutions for their customers—retail investors. What value do they give, and what do they get in return?

In days gone by, brokerage firms owned a monopoly of access to markets, few consumers engaged in personal investing, and many were naive and inexperienced. Back then, the traditional retail-broker model was a fair exchange. The customer gave the broker a personal profile, commission fees, and a set of investment objectives, and, in exchange, got tailored advice and the ability to trade.

But this model has a fundamental flaw. Retail investors do not and cannot yet receive the value commensurate with their contributions to the system. Retail investors are not mere customers; instead, they fuel the system from both directions, providing both financial liquidity (as buyers) and the "goods" (sellable securities and information) that make the whole system work. Other players, such as institutional investors and mutual-fund companies, may do the same thing—and have more clout due to their higher trading volumes. But the collective clout of retail investors—who in the United States represent close to 40 percent of trading value—is unrealized.[1] The deep weakness of this system is that the true contributors of value (retail investors) find themselves subordinate to self-serving intermediaries (full-service brokers) (table 9-2).

Couple this fundamental flaw with other weaknesses in the five categories of our value contributor model, and it becomes clear why online brokers seemed likely to succeed:

- Retail investors became knowledgeable and confident as the Internet provided them with real-time access to market information and transactions. The interested investor gained access to the industry's structural capital, acquiring knowledge tools comparable to those available to professional brokers.

TABLE 9-2   Current Value Disaggregation of Full-Service Brokerage Firms

Who	What Do They Contribute?	How?	Weaknesses
End-Customers			
• Retail investors (as buyers)	• Investment goals • Demand/liquidity • Fees	• Self-evaluation • Research • Analysis • Orders	• Disempowered by brokers and self-dealers despite providing both liquidity and content to the system • Increasingly knowledgeable and confident but disempowered
Context Providers			
• Full-service brokers	• Access to trading markets • Tailored personal service	• Personal contact, mostly via phone	• Untenable monopoly of access • Cost • Conflict of interest due to commission structures • Service quality uneven • Eroding credibility • Restricted hours
Content Providers			
• Full-service brokers	• Research reports • Advice • Trades	• Paper • Personal contact • Market access	• Advice and service often inadequate
• Media	• News • Opinion	• Print • TV • Internet	• Growing quality, timeliness, diversity of investment news educating investors and increasing self-sufficiency
• Retail investors (as sellers) • Institutional investors • Issuers	• Tradable securities and instruments	• Offers via broker channels	• Retail investor control not commensurate with contribution • Issuers bypassing brokers to communicate to investors
• Market makers and traders	• Price setting through bid/asks	• Floor trading • Electronic markets	• Insider self-dealing • Excessive transaction costs
Commerce Services Providers			
• Exchanges	• Exchange mechanisms	• Regulations • Facilities	• Pervasiveness of electronic trading • Emergence of alternative trading mechanisms (ECNs) • Feasibility of global 24×7 markets
• SEC and other authorities	• Regulation	• Regulations • Monitoring • Enforcement	• Monopoly regulatory models losing credibility
Infrastructure Providers			
• Exchanges	• Trading environments	• Physical trading floors • Electronic trading	• Obsolescent proprietary boundaries
• Technology providers	• Information and communications applications	• Computer/ communications systems	• Extending common infrastructure to all at low marginal cost

- Full-service brokers owed their privileged position as monopoly context providers who controlled access to financial markets to accidents of history in the securities industry. Their fee-per-transaction business model meant that many brokers were torn between maximizing turnover and ensuring the portfolio performance of their customers. Thus the industry's deployment of its human capital was flawed.

- As content providers (of advice and research), brokers failed to keep up their quality standards with the exploding market. Meanwhile, other media stepped in.

- The commerce services environment changed, with the shift to global markets and a growing trend toward continuous trading, twenty-four hours a day, seven days a week. Why should investors only trade during business hours? Why not any time of day or night? Why can't markets, too, be "live" all the time?

- As the infrastructure shifted from physical trading floors to cheap, ubiquitous networked computing, the transaction costs assessed by low-value-adding human brokers became unsupportable.

STEP 3: ENVISION B-WEB-ENABLED VALUE

Planners must step outside their day-to-day mental models to develop creative, discontinuous pictures of what they desire and can achieve. This activity draws on educated feelings, aspirations, intuitions, and hunches. Imagine a reinvented, hugely successful, and highly value-adding future three to five years hence. Suspend disbelief and consider several forward-looking questions: How will your value proposition change when the customer gains full control? What would you want if you were the customer? What might your customers' world be like five years from now? What could you achieve if there were no technological or organizational obstacles? What new business models—ways of creating, setting, and delivering value and of facilitating relationships with customers, suppliers, and partners—could you envisage? What could your competition do? What about new market entrants? What can you learn from innovators in other industries and other places? What is the state of the art in management thinking in the domains that affect your customers and you?

Revisit the original statement of your value proposition (like the full-service broker's "guiding customers in managing their investments through personal, knowledgeable advice and proactive customer service"). Modify it to reflect the new vision. This restated value proposition should inspire an original, competitive b-web strategy.

Consider the retail investment world that has begun to hatch. This, a different kind of full-service world, is cost effective and timely; the individual investor controls the inputs (information) and outputs (orders) of portfolio management.

Markets for all securities are live and directly accessible to individual investors worldwide, twenty-four hours a day, seven days a week. Investors can choose any media for conducting business—in person, online, wireless, or telephone. Technology has reduced the transaction costs that financial market intermediaries collect to below 5 percent of their former levels. Individual investors can participate directly in markets with a time delay approaching zero, so the price of the moment is the price they pay or receive for a security.

In a b-web-enabled investment situation, investors obtain advice from a variety of sources:

- Human advisers, motivated by asset value and growth rather than number of trades

- Automated alerts, triggered by investors' programmed threshold preferences

- Holistic financial planning tools that incorporate online research and analysis (as good as any available through full-service brokerages) and provide cradle-to-grave life-cycle planning

- Anytime, anywhere easy linkages to the consumer (wireless, intelligent agents, etc.) and his or her other financial activities (pay processing, mortgage, taxes, etc.)

- Investor communities, including online forums, chat groups, Web sites, and games

- Virtual advisers (software agents that provide real-time advice based on the investor's personal profile and portfolio management pattern)

- Analysis and simulation tools (to help investors understand why particular stratagems might work—or not)

- Aggregated real-time tracking of the most successful investor segments—what have the top 1 percent bought and sold today?

The investment industry builds relationship capital by designing its structural capital to suit the needs of the end-customer. This world is not here yet, but its outlines have begun to emerge. The restated value proposition for this new world could be Schwab's 2000 Statement: "Demystify investing and empower individual investors, providing them with the tools, access, and objective information they need to become better investors."

One technique that we have used to brainstorm and draw scenarios for the future is the e-business opportunity matrix (figure 9-2). The Biz.com quadrant in the figure includes opportunities to sell or deliver physical products and/or services using the Internet. The quadrant addresses the question, How can we provide value to the customer by moving our physical products and/or services to the Internet?

FIGURE 9-2   The B-Web Opportunity Matrix

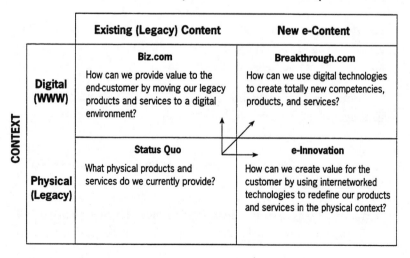

CONTENT (PRODUCTS AND SERVICES)

		Existing (Legacy) Content	New e-Content
CONTEXT	**Digital (WWW)**	**Biz.com** How can we provide value to the end-customer by moving our legacy products and services to a digital environment?	**Breakthrough.com** How can we use digital technologies to create totally new competencies, products, and services?
	Physical (Legacy)	**Status Quo** What physical products and services do we currently provide?	**e-Innovation** How can we create value for the customer by using internetworked technologies to redefine our products and services in the physical context?

The e-Innovation quadrant is for out-of-the-box strategies that contribute additional value to the customer for physical (often mature and commoditized) offerings. In other words, How can we use digital technologies to redefine, extend, or complement our physical products and/or services to create value for the customer in our current physical context?

Breakthrough.com represents the most spectacular opportunities: How can the Internet and other digital technologies help us create totally new competencies, products, and/or services?

The status-quo quadrant is no less important than the others. It sets the baseline from which further e-business opportunity springs forth.

Some examples further explain this matrix. Schwab.com moved the physical-world brokerage model online (i.e., a "Biz.com" step in the opportunity matrix). E-innovation opportunities include initiatives like delivering stock quotes and trade through wireless handheld devices. A Breakthrough.com opportunity might be anytime, anyplace decision support (tailored, real-time scenario and risk-return analysis).

STEP 4: REAGGREGATE

We have disaggregated the old value proposition, identified its weaknesses, and envisioned a transformed value proposition for the digital economy. Now we fashion a new b-web model for the reinvented value proposition.

This step entails repopulating the categories of value contributors and assigning contributions to the various classes of participants. The analysis defines the human, relationship, and structural capital on the supply side of the b-web.

Return to the earlier disaggregation analysis (step 2 above) and reassess the value contributions. Decide whether each relates to the new value proposition. If so, decide how to improve the value dramatically, who—in and outside your enterprise—should deliver it, and by what means they should do so. Think creatively about shifting responsibilities from one type of contributor to another.

For example, the full-service broker's value proposition typically includes tracking and researching the market. Schwab has disaggregated this task into a number of components and parceled them to three classes of b-web participants. A variety of content providers such as Big Charts, Quote.com, and First Boston provide market data, research, and analysis. End-customers identify and track relevant information and synthesize appropriate conclusions. Schwab itself aggregates and digests this content into an easy-to-navigate online package. Also, unlike many of its online competitors, Schwab also provides advisers, who, on request, help its customers decide what information best meets their needs.

Another task is to identify new value contributions that will enhance the customer experience and/or business performance. Assign these contributions to existing (or potential) b-web participants. Schwab's "live" telephone investment forums let customers interact directly with industry experts.

Expect and encourage polymediation (see chapter 3). Schwab uses portals like Excite and iVillage to drive traffic to its Web site. In addition, its AdvisorSource program reaches customers through some five thousand independent investment advisers.

Consider how a pervasive, application-rich, Web-enabled, internetworked infrastructure will support real-time, customer-responsive, integrated b-web communications and transactions. Assume that technology innovation will foster creative opportunities for improvement.

Think about the context provider as focusing on service or product strategy, relationship management, and b-web leadership, rather than on actual creation of "content." Assign "content"-oriented value-creating functions to the context provider when it makes sense for competitive advantage or cost effectiveness. In addition to organizing content from a variety of external suppliers (like Dow Jones), Schwab offers its own online training for new investors. Other b-web participants—including customers—will also provide content. Often, where the context provider delivers content, it invites competition from other content providers. Schwab offers customers its own mutual funds, but provides equal access to those of the competition.

Identify and engage a variety of best-of-breed participants to deliver other b-web value elements. Schwab has cultivated partnerships with leading information, product, and service providers, as well as community stars like AOL, Excite, and iVillage and site designer Razorfish.

Recognize and amply reward all participants, including customers, for their value contributions. Particularly diligent on this point, Schwab coddles its partners with great care. "I'm nervous of any deal where one of our partners doesn't seem to be making enough money," says Schwab's chief strategy officer Dan Leeman.

Remember that participants will both cooperate and compete within the b-web, itself a competitive marketspace. In Schwab's OneSource mutual-fund marketplace, companies collaborate to attract customers to the site while competing fiercely for customer business.

Anticipate public and government responses to your innovations, and consider how to maximize their support. Schwab and other online brokers led a successful public relations campaign for "booting your broker," including messages on prudently minimizing risk and protecting retirement nest eggs.

Table 9-3 is our depiction of Schwab as a b-web. Note the shifts in partners and roles from the current state analysis in table 9-2 to the one described here.

STEP 5: PREPARE A VALUE MAP

A value map is a graphical depiction of how a b-web operates, or will operate in the future (this technique is based on the work of our collaborator, Verna Allee).[2] We identify all the key classes of participants, including strategic partners, suppliers, and customers. In mapping, we view b-webs as complex systems in which the players exchange three qualitatively different, yet equally vital kinds of value:

1. Tangible benefits: goods, services, and money, including direct exchanges for paid services; the delivery of goods, services, contracts, and invoices; and the receipt of orders, requests for proposals, confirmations, and payment. Treat knowledge as a tangible good when it is part of a product or service for customers.

2. Knowledge: strategic information, planning, process, and technical knowledge that flows around value-creation processes.

3. Intangible benefits: other value and benefits, such as brand, community, customer loyalty, and image enhancement.

To visualize the new value-creating system, construct a value map. Include all key classes of participants and the most important value

TABLE 9-3 Schwab Reaggregation as a B-Web

Who?	What Value Will They Contribute?	How?	Key Success Factors
End Customers			
• Retail investors (as buyers)	• Investment goals • Research • Proactive portfolio management • Demand/liquidity • Fees	• Self-evaluation • Online research • Online portfolio management and analysis tools • Orders	• Trust • Market literacy • Technology literacy and access • Agility, risk tolerance
Context Providers			
• Schwab	• User interface, integrated environment • Content selection and management • Access to trading • Real-time portfolio management	• Online environment • Personal contact (phone/office)	• Seamless, consistent, easy-to-use interface • System reliability • Partnering capability • Willingness to share rewards • Quality of tools and research
• Investment advisers	• Access to trading bundled with advice	• Schwab resources and channels	• Paid for overall service and results, not for trades • Special services for advisers
• Portals and other Web destinations	• Alternative access points and channels	• Schwab information and click-through	• Customer-appropriate interface and content
Content Providers			
• Third-party data and research companies	• Research and analysis	• Electronic • Paper • Personal contact	• Timeliness • Depth, quality, quantity • Ease of use
• Media	• News and views	• Real-time Net • Print • TV	• Selection • Brand • Quality
• Investment advisers (Schwab, third party)	• Personal advice	• Web phone/video • Telephone • In person	• Objective • Proactive • Tailored to customer objectives, interests, preferences • Congenial
• Other investors	• Shared perspectives • Advice • Community	• Online forums • Affinity group meetings	• Self-regulating dialogue • Segmented by interests • Forums for quality • Facilitation and monitoring

exchanges among them. Schwab's value map (figure 9-3) depicts the company's key relationships and value exchanges.

STEP 6: DO THE B-WEB MIX

In the digital marketplace, companies employ business models as competitive weapons. Business model agility can be the determining factor separating success from failure. David Ellington, president of NetNoir, says the company's business model has changed five times since he cofounded it in 1995: "Each model was absolutely right for its time and wrong for the next round of competition."

Every business has a core organizing principle that corresponds to one of the five b-web types: Agora, Aggregation, Value Chain, Alliance,

Content Providers (continued)			
• Portfolio tool developers, Schwab	• Portfolio self-management	• Integrated into Schwab site	• Seamless integration • Compatibility with desktop applications • Quality/functionality
• Retail investors (as sellers) • Institutional investors • Issuers	• Tradable securities, mutual funds, and other instruments	• Offers via online and broker channels	• Breadth of offering (mutual funds, IPOs, special offers) • Timeliness of deal closing
• Market makers and traders	• Price setting through bid/asks	• Floor trading • Electronic markets	• Less insider dealing
Commerce Services Providers			
• Exchanges	• Exchange mechanisms	• Regulations • Facilities	• Extended trading hours • Quicker and more direct access for retail customers
• SEC and other authorities	• Regulation	• Regulations • Monitoring • Enforcement	• Continuing, paced deregulation • Protections for individual investors
Infrastructure Providers			
• Exchanges	• Trading environments	• All-electronic trading	• Internetworking among major and parallel exchanges
• Technology providers	• Information and communications applications	• Internet/Web applications infrastructure	• Price performance • Ubiquity • New wireless/handheld appliances

FIGURE 9-3   Schwab Value Map

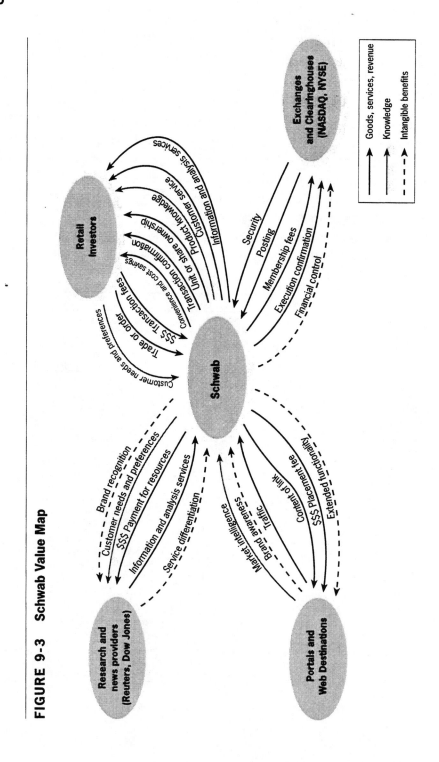

or Distributive Network. Each type has further subtypes, which provide for a more precise business model definition: Agora eBay is a supply-side auction, whereas NASDAQ is an exchange. Beyond its core organizing principle, a specific b-web will incorporate aspects of other types in its b-web mix. eBay's online forums add the dimension of an Alliance discussion community to its value proposition.

In designing the b-web mix, consider how each type and subtype might apply to a creative package that enhances customer value, provides competitive differentiation and advantage, and reduces costs for all participants. Does the new business essentially create value, as in an Alliance and a Value Chain? Or does it distribute value, more like an Aggregation, an Agora, or a Distributive Network? This answer profoundly affects work design, competitive positioning, the definition of competency, and sources of profit.

As mentioned, a full-service retail broker is a Value Chain that provides a focused process of client interaction, market tracking, research, and analysis. Drawing on various resources, within the firm and outside it, the adviser comes up with just the right buy or sell recommendation at the moment of truth: the client conversation. To succeed, the broker must excel at customer intimacy and relationship development and know how to integrate information resources to reach conclusions and make recommendations tailored to the customer's interests and priorities. Brokerage firms face the challenge of attracting, motivating, and retaining professionals who genuinely possess these capabilities.

Schwab and other online brokers shifted the business model from Value Chain to Aggregation. Schwab customers expend the time and effort to determine their own investment objectives. They track the market and conduct their own research. On its Web site, Schwab assists the customer by aggregating and delivering current market data, news, and analysis. Such informational content aggregation is a revolutionary business-model innovation for brokerage firms—even (especially) for discount brokers like Schwab. The company's advertising makes much of this resource, seeking to boost investors' self-confidence and reduce their sense of dependence on traditional brokers.

(Arguably, Schwab also aggregates access to a menu of securities in which investors invest. In fact, the stock exchanges themselves aggregate securities directly. Schwab, in its discount-broker days, was the first investment firm to aggregate hundreds, then thousands, of mutual funds from dozens of different issuers—adopting an Amazon-like strategy long before the Web.)

Despite exponential market success, Schwab concluded early in 1999 that an Aggregation model—no matter how well executed—no longer sufficed. Through its retail branches and the telephone, Schwab had always offered some personal service to large account holders and others who wanted it. Now the company needed to extend a higher quality of personal service to a much greater proportion of its customer base. Schwab embarked on becoming the world's first full-service Internet broker, in effect, adding a Value-Chain dimension to its b-web.

E*Trade, the online discount broker pioneer, adopted a very different strategy. Rather than become an electronic full-service broker, the company broadened its Aggregation model to become a mid-market financial services portal with a variety of offerings, including a stock trading game, online community facilities, and a shopping mall. E*Trade also acquired ClearStation, a community of online financial forums. Rather than turn itself into a proactive "expert" online broker as Schwab did, E*Trade added a customer discussion and help community (an Alliance) to its b-web mix.

Schwab, positioning itself up-market from the E*Trades of the world, focused on its core business-model transition strategy. At the same time, it collaborated with mass-market portal Excite, a general-purpose Aggregation, which distributed Schwab financial content. Schwab sought to benefit from an E*Trade-like portal strategy while building professional and electronic advice into its online offering—a unique hybrid of Aggregation and Value Chain.

MAIN MESSAGES

The strategy for weaving a b-web can be summarized by the following points:

- Begin by disaggregating and reaggregating your core value proposition from a customer perspective, and be guided by your core corporate values. What are the vulnerabilities in the industrial-age deployment of human, relationship, and structural capital?

- Disaggregate in three main steps: (1) identify the key contributors in each of five b-web participant layers (customer, context, content, commerce services, and infrastructure); (2) describe what each participant contributes to the system, and how they do so; and (3) pinpoint the weaknesses and opportunities for improvement in the current arrangement.

- Answer these questions: How would the value proposition change if the customer were at the center and in full control? What "impossible" things could you do if technology-enabled capabilities were limitless, and there were no organizational barriers to change? What new business models—ways of creating, defining, and delivering value, and facilitating relationships with customers, suppliers, and partners—could you envisage?

- Define how the context provider will lead and add value by changing the rules, orchestrating the b-web, and facilitating the accumulation of digital capital.

- Creatively design your b-web, using the five categories of value contributors, value maps, and the b-web mix.